A Place to Be

A Place to Be

Brazilian, Guatemalan, and Mexican Immigrants in Florida's New Destinations

EDITED BY

PHILIP J. WILLIAMS

TIMOTHY J. STEIGENGA, AND

MANUEL A. VÁSQUEZ

RUTGERS UNIVERSITY PRESS

NEW BRUNSWICK, NEW JERSEY, AND LONDON

LIBRARY OF CONGRESS CATALOGING-IN-PUBLICATION DATA

A place to be : Brazilian, Guatemalan, and Mexican immigrants in Florida's new
destinations / edited by Philip J. Williams . . . [et al.].

    p. cm.

    "This book is the product of a collaborative transnational research project that
grew out of a workshop held at the University of Florida in 2001."
Includes bibliographical references and index.
ISBN 978-0-8135-4492-2 (hardcover : alk. paper)
ISBN 978-0-8135-4493-9 (pbk : alk. paper)

    1. Latin Americans—Florida—Social conditions—Congresses. 2. Latin
Americans—Florida—Religion—Congresses. 3. Transnationalism—Congresses.
4. Florida—Emigration and immigration—Social aspects—Congresses. I. Williams,
Philip J., 1959–

F320.S75P53 2009
304.8'75908—dc22   2008026185

A British Cataloging-in-Publication record for this book is available
from the British Library.

CONTENTS

ACKNOWLEDGMENTS

This book is the product of a collaborative transnational research project that grew out of a workshop held at the University of Florida in 2001. A planning grant from the Ford Foundation enabled us to hold of a series of workshops throughout 2002 and 2003 to discuss the project's goals, theoretical issues, and research design and methodologies. In addition to our core team members, we are grateful to a number of scholars who participated in these workshops, including members of our advisory board (Roberto Goizueta, Lois Lorentzen, Otto Maduro, Verónica Melander, Robert Orsi, Omar McRoberts, and Kathryn Tanner) and scholars at the University of Florida and elsewhere (Allan Burns, Sheila Croucher, Caetana Maria Damasceno, Jorge Estuardo, Susan Gillespie, Luis León, Milagros Peña, David Smilde, and Alex Stepick). A generous grant from the Ford Foundation supported the research for this project and a series of outreach activities to benefit the immigrant communities that we studied. At the Ford Foundation, we are especially grateful to Constance Buchanan for all her guidance, encouragement, and support.

At a December 2005 conference in Antigua, Guatemala, our team members had the opportunity to present and discuss our findings with scholars and activists from immigrant communities. We thank especially the Instituto Centroamericano de Estudios de Desarrollo Económico y Social (INCEDES) for co-sponsoring the conference and those scholars and activists who participated on panels: Manuel Ángel Castillo, Jerónimo Camposeco, Alejandro Frigerio, Heloisa Maria Galvão, Peggy Levitt, Joel Magallán, Robert Orsi, Brian Payne, Teresa Sales, and Richard Wood. We also thank the anonymous readers and Alex Stepick for their invaluable comments and suggestions on the manuscript.

The Center for Latin American Studies and the departments of Political Science and Religion at the University of Florida supported graduate assistants who deserve mention for their contributions to the project: Julia Albarracín, Neda Bezerra, Martín Maldonado, Gayle Lasater, Anna Pagano, Ani de la Quintana, Rosana Resende, Iran Rodrigues, and Anouk St. Arnaud. We are also grateful for the hard work of many other people at the University of Florida, particularly, John Corr, our project manager; the late Myrna Sulsona, Margarita Gandía, Charles Wood, and Carmen Diana Deere at the Center for Latin American Studies; Michael Martinez and Debbie Wallen in the Department of Political Science; and David Hackett and Anna Peterson in the Department of Religion.

At Florida Atlantic University (FAU), we would like to thank Sandra Ogden for her assistance in facilitating the details of our outreach workshops. A number of undergraduates at the Wilkes Honors College of FAU also deserve recognition for the many hours they spent working alongside our researchers both in the field and through their own honors thesis research. We extend a special thanks to Anya Canache, Karla Domínguez, Ariana Magdeleno, Jocelyn Sabbagh, and Sandra Lazo de la Vega. We are also grateful to Johanna Sharp for her extensive tri-lingual translation, coding, and data entry work on the survey portion of this project.

The Brazilian team (Lúcia Ribeiro, José Claúdio Souza Alves, Keyla Thamsten, Anna Pagano, and Manuel Vásquez) would like to thank many people who kindly gave us access to their lives, homes, and congregations. Among Protestants, the team is particularly grateful to pastors Silair de Almeida, Francisco Pires, Riva, Ulisses, and Abraão, as well as to Etelmo. Among Catholics, the team extends its gratitude to fathers Vilmar, Carlos, Marcelo, and Sergio and lay leaders Beth, Sandra, Glória, Brasil Patinho, and Suely. At the Spiritist center, Maurício and Luide offered warm hospitality, while Marcello French and Pai Cornélio provided invaluable insights into African-based religions among Brazilian immigrants. Fausto Mendes da Rocha of the Brazilian Immigrant Center and Ilma Paixão of BRAMAS shared their knowledge of the Brazilian community in Boston to help the team understand comparatively the experiences in South Florida. Finally, Serginho and Renata of Brasliced and Luis Carlos of the Curso de Inglês assisted with new contacts.

The Guatemalan team (Carol Girón Solórzano, Silvia Irene Palma, and Timothy Steigenga) owe a special debt of gratitude to the members and friends of Corn-Maya Inc. and the Jacaltec Association who welcomed us into their communities both in Jupiter and Jacaltenango. In Jupiter the team would like to express their deepest gratitude to Jerónimo Camposeco, Juan Patricio Silvestre, Marcos Cota Diaz, Auricio Camposeco, Antonio Gelacio Delgado, Mario Gervacio and Antonio Quiñones, Galindo Diaz, Pablo Hernández, Julia Guillermina Diaz, Darvi López, and Prudencio Camposeco. We also extend a special thanks to our friends and contacts in Indiantown: Andres Cruz and Antonio Silvestre. In Guatemala, we would like to acknowledge the support of the Latin American Social Science Faculty (FLACSO) in the early stages of the project and INCEDES for seeing it through to completion. Jacobo Dardón and Edit Gonzáles were especially supportive both logistically and academically, providing critical local knowledge in Guatemala. Mayor Moisés Pérez and the other political authorities in Jacaltenango facilitated our many visits to the region. We are particularly indebted to people of Jacaltenango and the surrounding areas for welcoming us into their homes and communities over the course of this study.

The Mexican team (Patricia Fortuny Loret de Mola, Mirian Solís Lizama, and Philip Williams) would like to thank a number of people who were instrumental during the field research stage of the project in Immokalee and Mexico. We are especially grateful to Damara Luce and Brian Payne for their hospitality and insight during our first visits to Immokalee and Elizabeth Juárez Cerdi for her participation in the research during the first year of the project. We extend our gratitude to María Márquez and Father Ettore Rubin of the Our Lady of Guadalupe Catholic Church and Pastor Josué Rincón of the Bethel Assemblies of God Church. We also thank Lupita Rodríguez and Cristina Vázquez, who welcomed us into their homes and provided us with contacts in Chamácuaro, and Romeo Ramírez and Gerardo Reyes, who helped us to better understand the work of the Coalition of Immokalee Workers. And finally, we are especially grateful to Hannoy Segura for her unending friendship and support during our research in Immokalee.

A Place to Be

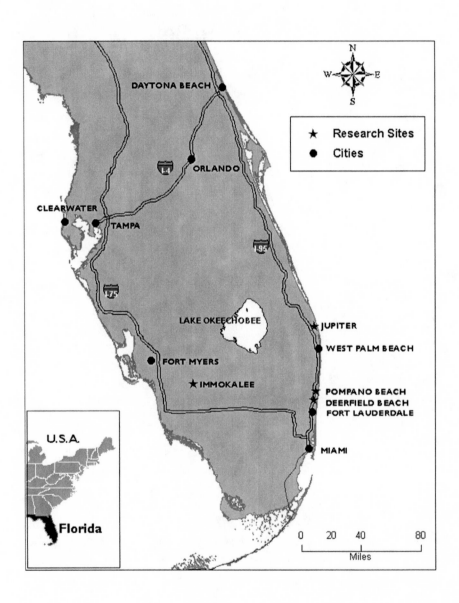

DAYTONA BEACH ●

N
W · E
S

★ Research Sites
● Cities

⬡I₄ ● ORLANDO

CLEARWATER
●   ● TAMPA

⬡I₉₅

⬡I₇₅

LAKE OKEECHOBEE

★ JUPITER

● WEST PALM BEACH

● FORT MYERS

★ IMMOKALEE

★ POMPANO BEACH
● DEERFIELD BEACH
FORT LAUDERDALE

● MIAMI

U.S.A.

Florida

0   20   40   80
Miles

1

Introduction

Understanding Transnationalism, Collective Mobilization, and Lived Religion in New Immigrant Destinations

PHILIP J. WILLIAMS, MANUEL A. VÁSQUEZ, AND TIMOTHY J. STEIGENGA

This book explores processes of identity and community formation among Mexican, Guatemalan, and Brazilian immigrants in the "non-conventional destinations" of Immokalee, Jupiter, Pompano Beach, and Deerfield Beach in South Florida. The volume brings together the contributions of scholars from Latin America and the United States who, for the last four years, have engaged in an integrated, transnational research project to analyze systematically the challenges that these immigrant groups face, the resources they bring, and the collective strategies they deploy as they settle in places that have only recently been affected by large-scale immigration and/or that have received scant scholarly attention, since most of the research has concentrated on large gateway cities like New York, Los Angeles, Houston, and Miami. Our collaborative project has been driven by three interconnected clusters of questions, relating to transnationalism, collective mobilization, and lived religion.

Our previous work has shown that Latin American immigrants participate in economic, political, and religio-cultural networks that link societies of origin and settlement as a strategy to deal with the daunting challenges of globalization.[1] In this project, we wanted to see if transnationalism is also affected by the dynamics of new destinations. To what extent is it possible and/or necessary for Latin American immigrants in new destinations to engage in transnational relations with their countries of origin while struggling to carve out new spaces of livelihood in the United States? In other words, does the need to establish themselves in hostile new destinations take precedence for new immigrants over the desire and demand to create transnational linkages? Is the precarious process of settlement facilitated or hindered by transnationalism? If transnationalism does exist among Latin American immigrants in new destinations, what forms does it assume and how is it played out differently among different national (and even sub-national) groups?

Second, in light of the current anti-immigrant national mood and the frequently hostile local environments Latin American immigrants face as they
move into new destinations, we were interested in the dynamics of community
formation and collective political mobilization. What obstacles do immigrants
confront and what resources are available to them to build collective solidarity
and engage in collective action? Can immigrants afford to be visible in places
that are unaccustomed to immigration? What are the conflicts and opportunities generated by this visibility?

Finally, our research teams set out to document the multiple and complex
roles that religion plays in the process of incorporation. Because religion has
only recently begun to receive sustained attention in migration studies, we
sought to explore the connections in new destinations between religious
beliefs, practices, and organization and processes of immigrant community formation, collective political mobilization, and transnationalism.

The focus on the interplay among transnationalism, collective mobilization, and religion in new destinations responds to emerging dynamics of Latino
migration that are having a powerful impact not only in Florida, but throughout
the United States, at a time when immigration is a controversial issue. Thus, we
feel that our empirical case studies have national relevance. We now turn to
these new patterns of Latino migration to frame our case studies.

The Larger Context: Latin American
Immigrants in New Destinations

Latinos have become the largest minority in the United States. According to the U.S.
census, in 2005 there were 42.7 million Hispanics,[2] constituting 14 percent of the
country's total population. Fueled by internal growth—Latinos are a fairly young
population, with a median age of 27.2 compared to 36.2 for Euro-Americans—and
by ongoing migration from Latin America, Hispanics are projected to become 24
percent of the U.S. population by the year 2050.[3] Naturally, this rapid growth is
bound to have a profound impact on American society, politics, and culture.
However, the potential transformative power of Latinos is not just about sheer
numbers. It is also about emerging patterns of settlement. Historically, Latinos have
settled in traditional gateway states such as California, New York, and Texas and
within those states in large cities like Los Angeles, San Francisco, New York, Dallas,
and Houston. Increasingly, however, Latinos are settling in new destinations,
including many in the so-called New South. For example, between 1980 and 2000,
new Latino destinations like Atlanta (995 percent) and Orlando (859 percent)
experienced much faster growth rates than established Latino metro areas like
Miami (123 percent), New York (60 percent), and Los Angeles (105 percent).[4]

The shift in new destinations is also evident at the regional and state level.
Between 1990 and 2000, the proportion of Latinos living in the South and

However, the widespread intensification of migratory flows across national borders which has accompanied systemic changes during the last half century has foregrounded new forms of transnationalism, "transnationalisms from below" or "grassroots globalizations."[18] In an attempt to negotiate the demands of rapidly changing and globally integrated labor markets, immigrants have not only moved across national borders in increasing numbers, but now use technological advances ranging from the Internet and cellular phones to inexpensive air travel in order to tap strategically into the resources and networks available to them in their countries of origin. Yet, even as they manage to keep in close contact with their societies of origin, immigrants become integrated into their countries of settlement. This "bifocality" allows immigrants to draw from grassroots resources in multiple settings to cope with the new cartography ushered in by flexible production as well as with diverse phenomena such as civil wars, disorderly transitions to democracy, the decline of subsistence agriculture, rapid urbanization, and natural disasters.[19]

The rapid expansion of grassroots transnationalism has given impetus to an ethnographic turn in the study of this phenomenon. Beginning in the early 1990s with Linda Basch, Nina Glick Schiller, and Cristina Szanton Blanc's groundbreaking *Nations Unbound: Transnational Migration, Postcolonial Predicaments, and the Deterritorialized Nation-State*, a growing body of literature has explored how immigrants build relations across national borders, constructing realms of activity, thought, and feeling that bridge localities in two or more nation-states.[20] According to the classic definition in *Nations Unbound*, transnationalism denotes "the processes by which immigrants forge and sustain multi-stranded social relations that link together their societies of origin and settlement. We call these processes transnationalism to emphasize that many immigrants today build social fields that cross geographic, cultural, and political borders."[21] Basch, Glick Schiller, and Szanton Blanc call those immigrants engaged in multiple social relations spanning national borders "transmigrants." They argue that "transmigrants take actions, make decisions, and develop subjectivities and identities embedded in networks of relationships that connect them simultaneously to two or more nation-states."[22]

This classic definition has been refined and challenged in a proliferating literature, which has sought, among other things, to operationalize the concept, measure its intensity, durability, and overall incidence, as well as characterize the types of actors and practices and levels of institutionalization involved.[23] At the theoretical level, three conceptual innovations stand out in the efforts to refine transnationalism as an analytical framework. The first one is the concept of a transnational social field, which Glick Schiller defines as "an unbounded terrain of interlocking egocentric networks,"[24] a "network of networks that stretch across the borders of nation-states."[25] As immigrants attempt to sustain transnational livelihoods, they produce and reproduce networks, chains of social relations through which practices and material and symbolic goods flow, often unevenly, producing hierarchies and power asymmetries.[26] Depending on factors such as their "thickness," extensiveness, intensity, and level of institutionalization, these networks, in turn, carve out landscapes of experience, relationality, and power, spaces marked by a mixture of interdependence, altruism, mimesis, and exploitation, where immigrants lead their daily lives. In other words, although they are deterritorializing in the sense that they may be shaped by the nation-state but not coterminous with its boundaries, transnational social fields have a strong spatial dimension predicated on the power to build meaningful places to dwell and to articulate individual and collective identities across the networks. As we shall see in several chapters in this volume, particularly at a time of widespread nativism, the struggle to construct physical community and coherent selfhood is one of the great challenges of settlement in new destinations. Transnational networks play instrumental albeit differential roles in this construction.

The second important theoretical innovation behind the concept of transnationalism is the notion of "social remittances," which Peggy Levitt defines as "the ideas, behaviors, and social capital that flow from receiving to sending communities. They are the tools with which ordinary individuals create global culture at the local context."[27] The notion of social remittances allows us to move beyond purely economistic understandings of immigrant behavior. This notion enables scholars not only to examine monetary and non-monetary (i.e., services and consumer and durable goods) exchanges and their impact on local and national economies, but also to explore the sociocultural dimensions of living transnationally. In particular, the phenomenological and hermeneutic dimensions of existence across national borders, the questions of meaning, belonging, attachment to place, memory, nostalgia, imagination, psychological trauma, embodied experience, and expressive performance, which have traditionally been central to the study of religion, are brought to the fore. Several chapters in this volume point very poignantly to these dimensions of transnationalism, particularly to the work of religious and familial resources in dealing or failing to deal with dislocation and relocation in areas that are, if not outright hostile to immigrants, at least radically different from the communities of origin.

The third and final theoretical innovation is the notion of "simultaneity," or multiple embeddedness, which compels scholars to abandon the idea that it is fruitful to study the individual immigrant without making explicit reference to multiple contexts in which he or she is embedded, without taking into account his or her trajectory in the transnational social field.[28] Manuel Vásquez and Marie Marquardt have argued that because religion usually seeks to link individual and community renewal with global transformation in the name of universal values, it is one of the institutions best suited to navigate multiple embeddedness.[29] Most religions have a long tradition of operating transnationally, a fact that is reflected not only in their beliefs and symbols, but in their practices and forms of organization.[30]

Levitt has identified at least three types of transnational religious organizations. First, "extended transnational religious organizations" basically "broaden and deepen a global religious system that is already powerful and legitimate."[31] The prime example here is the Catholic Church, which is sustained by the complex interaction among the Vatican, the global religious order, the regional and national episcopal bodies, and the parish, all buttressed by a universalizing doctrine. The second type is "negotiated transnational religious organizations" that present a more flexible and decentralized form of organization. In these organizations, "relations between sending and receiving country churches evolve without a strong federated institutional structure or rules. Instead, individuals and organizations enter into informal agreements with one another that have weaker connections to political circles but are more flexible constituted."[32] The example here would be many small Pentecostal churches that have set up churches in the receiving country to minister to immigrants transnationally. Finally, there are "recreated transnational religious organizations" formed by "groups with guidance from home-country leaders" which seek to replicate local practices, beliefs, and modes of organization abroad; "these are franchise-like groups [that] are run by migrants who receive periodic resources, financing, and guidance from sending-country leadership while chapters are supported and supervised regularly by those who remain behind."[33] Examples of this last category would be the Igreja Universal do Reino de Deus, which emerged in Rio de Janeiro, Brazil, and the Iglesia La Luz del Mundo, established in Guadalajara, Mexico, both of which have temples throughout Latin America and in the major cities in the United States.[34]

Contributors to this volume build on Levitt's insights but go beyond them, examining the roles that religion plays in the process of multiple embeddedness when the new destinations in the migration trajectory are not used to the kind of forced cosmopolitanism entailed in transnational ways of being and belonging. For example, what does it mean to be Maya, to affirm one's local traditions and language, surrounded by Ladinos and considered as Hispanic by the native Euro-American population? And how can this affirmation of Mayanness take place in a region like Palm Beach County, where migration from Latin America is only a recent phenomenon? What ideational and organizational precedents are there to negotiate simultaneity?

At the methodological level, scholars of transnationalism have been accused of making "overextended claims" by sampling on the dependent variable, "focusing on instances where the phenomenon of interest is present, but not on those where it is absent. In this particular instance, qualitative studies were able to document the existence of immigrant transnationalism, but not its numerical incidence. Yet the very impetus generated by the early empirical findings led to their generalization to the entire immigrant population."[35] Responding to this critique, Levitt,[36] Itzigsohn et al.,[37] and others have proposed ways to gauge the scope and intensity of transnationalism. They define as "core transnationalism" those activities that "(a) form an integral part of the individual's habitual life; (b) are undertaken on a regular basis; and (c) are patterned and therefore somewhat predictable. 'Expanded' [or 'broad'] transnationalism, in contrast, includes migrants who engage in occasional transnational practices, such as responses to political crises and natural disasters."[38]

In other words, the task of measuring the frequencies and types of transnationalism involved in a particular case study is an empirical question. As Portes argues, "not all immigrants are 'transmigrants' and claims to the contrary needlessly weaken the validity of empirical findings on the topic. It is more useful to conceptualize transnationalism as one form of economic, political, and cultural adaptation that co-exists with other, more traditional forms."[39] However, this does not mean, as Portes suggests, that we have to delimit transnationalism only to "occupations and activities that require regular and sustained social contacts over time across national borders for their implementation." He continues: "What constitutes truly original phenomena and, hence, a justifiable new topic of investigation, are the high intensity of exchanges, the new modes of transaction, and the multiplication of activities that require cross-border travel and contacts on a sustained basis."[40] For one thing, individuals are likely to be involved in core transnational activities in some realms of social life, while in others they might only engage in occasional transnational contacts. Still, when making daily decisions, they may think transnationally. Moreover, the balance of core and expanded transnational practices may change over time, in response to the demands of life cycle and to transformations in the societies of origin and settlement. Finally, since, as a social field, transnationalism touches the lives of not only immigrants but those in their kinship and community networks, including those who stay behind, it is not fruitful to delimit the concept too narrowly. Rather, we develop a flexible concept that allows us to study empirically the multiple forms of transnationalism without it becoming a catch-all category.

Our contribution to this discussion is in assessing the scope, intensity, and morphology of transnationalism in nontraditional immigrant destinations. Does the fact that there are not solidified immigrant pathways that facilitate settlement and integration encourage reliance on transnational networks? If so, what kind of transnational linkages tend to be favored—kinship linkages or transnational circuits? Can we speak of what Thomas Faist calls transnational communities in new destinations?[41] Does an inhospitable context of reception compel the immigrants to concentrate on survival in the society of settlement rather than to spend their resources cultivating transnational relations? Is the immigrant group's level of social and cultural capital, particularly as manifested in ethnic solidarity and membership in a religious community, more crucial in building transnational linkages in the contexts of nontraditional destinations? And finally, how does transnationalism assist or hinder attempts by immigrant groups to mobilize around their collective interests? This final question leads us to another of our primary themes; the issue of immigrant mobilization in new destinations.

Immigrant Mobilization

As the new geography of Latino immigration continues to expand in the United States, questions about how and when immigrants can successfully organize to promote their local interests have become increasingly urgent. The rapid growth of the immigrant population in new destinations has fuelled increasing hostility toward immigrants, as evidenced by the highly polarized debates about immigration at the national level and the increasing number of state laws and local ordinances directed against undocumented immigrants.[42] In response to these initiatives, Latino immigrants have begun to mobilize in unprecedented numbers, dramatized by the massive mobilizations that took place in April and May 2006. Even more astonishing than the size of the protests was the large number of protests organized in new destinations in the Midwest and South.

It is beyond the scope of this chapter to provide a comprehensive review of the literature on social movements and identity politics.[43] Our goal is more modest: we would like to offer enough elements to highlight the larger implications of our case studies for immigrant collective action. The first element we need to factor in is the macro-context in which immigrants seek to mobilize. This structural and systemic context is defined by the deepening and expansion of neoliberal capitalism in the Americas. Following Arjun Appadurai, we conceptualize immigrant mobilizations as local responses to the disjunctures and dislocations related to globalization.[44] Within the context of deepening economic globalization, "the rise of technocratic policy-making, the decline of trade unions, the growing disillusionment with political parties and elections, and the dismantling of the welfare state" have led to a growing gap between government and citizens in both Latin America and the United States.[45] Appadurai refers to the new forms of resistance that have emerged to challenge and reverse these developments as examples of "grassroots globalization" or "globalization from below" that are concerned with "mobilizing specific local, national, and regional groups on matters of equity, access, justice, and redistribution" in the face of "increased inequalities within and across societies."[46] These emergent forms of resistance are often locally oriented, as in the case of the labor center initiative in Jupiter (as outlined in chapter 5) or efforts to organize against city ordinances targeting undocumented immigrants. However, they can also develop self-consciously global strategies, as with the Coalition of Immokalee Workers, that link together people and organizations across borders "by shared values, a common discourse, and dense exchanges of information and services."[47]

Roger Rouse, from a neo-Marxist perspective, warns of the limitations to transnational activism rooted in identity politics. He argues that the shift from a national toward a "transnational regime of accumulation" has produced significant changes in the structure of class relations and a marked increase in social inequalities.[48] Immigrants, women, and people of color, while gaining some representation in the expanding professional-managerial class, disproportionately populate the ranks of the "secondary sector proletariat and the reserve army."[49] According to Rouse, for the state and bourgeoisie to maintain a transnational system of accumulation, they have adopted political and cultural strategies that encourage people to express dissent through identity-based forms of organizing instead of more radical class-based movements. The resulting growth in idioms of identity has "intensified the processes by which people have been discouraged from bringing issues of exploitation to the fore alongside questions of prejudice and discrimination."[50]

The idioms of racial and ethnic difference that infuse the discourse in support of anti-immigrant initiatives like California's Proposition 187 or the more recent Sensenbrenner bill (H.R. 4437) are an important source of "defensive" identities,[51] or what Alejandro Portes and Rubén Rumbaut refer to as "reactive ethnicity." According to Portes and Rumbaut, "reactive ethnicity is the product of confrontation with an adverse native mainstream and the rise of defensive identities and solidarities to counter it."[52] In turn, reactive ethnicity can provide the basis for collective solidarity and mobilization in opposition to attempts to crack down on undocumented immigration. As we will see in chapter 5, whereas in Jupiter a hostile context of reception combined with greater ethnic homogeneity fosters mobilization based in reactive ethnicity, in Immokalee, ethnic heterogeneity and economic deprivation combined with a less hostile community can produce multi-ethnic, class-based mobilization. Moreover, for first-generation rural immigrants from Mexico and Guatemala, reactive ethnicity can also foster transnational organizations that are aimed "at improving material and political conditions in their places of origin."[53] The question is whether these reactive movements can move beyond "defensive identities" to produce "project identities" that lead to more far-reaching structural transformation.[54]

Traditional concepts of mobilization may not be as appropriate for studying immigrants in new destinations, especially undocumented immigrants. In discussing the case of Mexican immigrants in northern California, Rouse writes that in response to the state's "politics of identification" most immigrants simply try to "elude the machinery of identification or to neutralize its impact."[55] They do their best "to avoid the reach of agencies seeking to identity them and [give] elusive answers to anyone who seemed official."[56] Many have to obtain false documents, living under other people's identities for varying periods of time. Rather than participating in organized collective action to further their interests, undocumented immigrants are more likely to develop and maintain personal, family, religious, and labor networks to address their everyday problems. Given the purposeful invisibility of many undocumented immigrants and their social networks, focusing only on the most visible markers of collective mobilization may provide an incomplete picture.

Alberto Melucci provides an alternative two-pole model of mobilization: latency and visibility. According to this model, most immigrants are involved in "submerged networks," which constitute a system of exchange within which persons and information circulate.[57] These networks are usually latent but can burst into the open over specific issues, as in the case of the April and May 2006 massive mobilizations in opposition to the Sensenbrenner bill. As we will see in chapters 2 and 6, a focus on submerged networks provides a useful corrective to the normative assumptions underlying the contested and problematic concept of "community." The notion of community assumes that associational life must have visible and institutionalized expressions such as ethnic, civic, or neighborhood organizations. The absence of these manifestations is understood as a social pathology, a condition of anomie with low levels of social interdependence and solidarity. Given the assumptions behind the notion of community, relying on this concept to understand social life in new destinations may result in erroneous conclusions. In new destinations, where Latin American immigrants cannot tap into pre-established networks built by previous migrant waves and where they often confront hostile environments, the lack of visible and institutionalized expressions of community life should not be automatically taken to be mean that there is no sociality among immigrants or that they are not interested in building connections with their compatriots and co-ethnics. In fact, not building visible forms of political organization might be a defensive strategy by recent immigrants to remain invisible, to continue to work, study, play, and pray without calling the attention of a native population that, at best, feels deeply ambivalent toward them. For example, among Brazilian immigrants in Pompano Beach and Deerfield Beach, although there are few visible markers of community organization and mobilization, we found a vibrant and diverse array of interpersonal networks among which Brazilians feel protected and "at home." To the extent that these networks extend beyond the household or the intimate circle of friends, they do so only by connecting with churches and small businesses, almost never venturing into the political arena, which is perceived as time-consuming, baffling, and dangerous. The existence of a thick social infrastructure leads Manuel Vásquez, in chapter 2, to challenge the traditional readings of Brazilians abroad as uniquely anomic.

Whether latent and submerged networks may provide the resources necessary to stage public mobilizations is an open question. Most scholars of social movements recognize that social networks "are the most common sources of recruitment into social movements."[58] However, the challenge is to build the "connective structures" between interpersonal and local networks and sources of power at more macro levels.[59]

In the face of these obstacles to mobilization, what resources can immigrants draw upon to mount successful collective challenges? Various chapters in this volume explore the role of social capital in immigrant mobilization. Pierre Bourdieu and Loic Wacquant define social capital as "the sum of resources, actual or virtual, that accrue to an individual or a group by virtue of possessing a durable network of more or less institutionalized relationships of mutual acquaintance and recognition."[60] The accumulation of social capital can enable some immigrants and their families to increase and diversify their social networks and to enjoy socioeconomic advancement. However, for many immigrants, limited social capital, combined with their undocumented status and weak social networks, undermines their opportunities for social mobility. Some scholars have found that social capital grounded in tightly knit ethnic communities can provide important resources in confronting obstacles to socioeconomic advancement.[61] This is especially true for immigrants of limited means. However, as Cecilia Menjívar argues in her study of Salvadoran immigrants in San Francisco, social networks will not automatically result in social capital: "social capital cannot be generated automatically when immigrants do not have access to desirable resources, because reciprocal obligations are undermined under these conditions."[62] With average annual earnings of approximately $7,500, migrant farmworkers have few possibilities to accumulate the kind of economic, social, or symbolic capital available to other types of immigrants.

Although much of the literature on social capital emphasizes the benefits of cooperation, Portes points to studies that identify several negative consequences, including the exclusion of outsiders, excess claims on group members, constraints on individual freedom, and downward leveling norms.[63] Social capital generated by bounded solidarity among more established immigrants is sometimes used to exclude newer immigrants from the economic advantages of group membership.[64] For example, the Cuban immigrant community in Miami is often cited as an example of a successful ethnic enclave, where co-ethnic solidarity has facilitated the economic and political ascendance of Cuban immigrants. According to Portes and Stepick, "the common circumstance of exile and a common experience of successive political defeats . . . cemented a strong sense of 'we-ness' " and the consolidation of a "moral community."[65] Similarly, in chapter 4 we will see how a group of Otomí immigrants from Hidalgo, Mexico, has constructed a "transnational moral community" that rests upon a system of shared meanings, norms, and practices rooted in a strong ethnic identity that links them to their place of origin. However, while membership in these moral communities defines to a large extent who receives access to jobs and business loans, other immigrant groups are largely excluded from the benefits of membership, thus creating potential barriers to the emergence of more inclusive Pan-Latino organizations.[66]

Recent literature on religion and social capital also tends to emphasize the more positive consequences of social capital. Robert Putnam, in his widely cited book *Bowling Alone*, argues that religious organizations "are arguably the single most important repository of social capital in America" and religiosity is a powerful correlate of civic engagement.[67] Similarly, in his study of faith-based community organizing in the United States, Richard Wood argues that churches often provide a reservoir of social capital developed over the years through face-to-face interactions during worship, prayer, and Bible study groups.[68] The networks that churches make available to members can "enhance feelings of social solidarity, provide formal and informal help in times of need, and give participants access to whatever resources those links come with."[69]

Following Putnam and others,[70] we distinguish between "bonding" social capital and "bridging" social capital. Bonding social capital is inward oriented and tends to reinforce group identity, as in the case of the bounded solidarity of Miami Cubans or Otomíes from Hidalgo. Strong social bonds within communities can provide the foundation on which immigrants "can develop the capacity to address the problems of poverty" and "to achieve a measure of control over their lives."[71] In contrast, bridging social capital can facilitate "links among communities that frequently coexist in relative isolation from one another."[72] Because churches are embedded in broader networks—denominational ties, links to other churches and community organizations, relations with government agencies—they often serve as an important source of these bridging ties. However, churches will vary in the degree to which they emphasize within-group networks (bonding social capital) as opposed to networks outside the congregation (bridging social capital).[73]

Despite the important role that religion can play in fostering social capital, it is important not to exaggerate its transformative potential. In an essay on religious change and social capital in Peru and Guatemala, Daniel Levine and David Stoll acknowledge that the gap between empowerment and power can be a long-term process.[74] Building on Putnam's use of the concept of social capital, Levine and Stoll argue that religious activism must first concentrate on accumulating social capital before engaging in political activism. If the move from religious to political activism occurs before the establishment of bonds of solidarity and trust, then grassroots movements are unlikely to accomplish their goals. Similarly, Michael Foley and Dean Hoge, in their study of religion and new immigrants in Washington, D.C., point out that churches can "vary both in the civic skills cultivated and in the degree to which these might transfer to actual participation in the political system."[75]

For religious activism to have political significance, it needs to go beyond social capital and "foster attitudes and behaviors that actually influence regimes in some way."[76] Whereas social capital "is useful in understanding the role of religious organizations dedicated to individual redemption or community self-help activism, it is less helpful in studying social movements committed to social justice and political transformation."[77] Following John Booth and Patricia Richards, it is important to distinguish between social capital and "political capital" that refers to attitudes and behavior that influence government or public policy in some way.[78] The concept of political capital is more appropriate to understanding the civic skills and political competences developed within social movements and deployed for political ends. As we will see in chapter 5, unlike churches, the Coalition of Immokalee Workers creates social capital not only for the personal empowerment of its members, but for the purpose of enhancing the organization's political influence and power.

As we engaged in our research in Florida's new destinations, we hoped to uncover and analyze the contextual elements that make immigrant mobilization more or less successful, the factors that motivate immigrants to mobilize to pursue their collective interests, the tools they have at their disposal to achieve their goals, and the implications of various forms of immigrant mobilization. In particular, we wanted to know how religious institutions, practices, and beliefs promote or hinder immigrant mobilization and community formation. In the process of exploring these questions, we found ourselves drawn directly into the study of "lived religion," the study of how immigrants from Latin America practice their religion in everyday life and the sociopolitical implications of these practices.

Lived Religion and Immigration

Understanding what is meant by "lived religion" requires a brief historical overview of the evolution of this concept in the fields of religious studies and sociology of religion. Until recently, the study of religion and social change has been dominated by the secularization paradigm. While this paradigm takes many forms, its core claim is that there is a close correlation between the process of modernization and religion's retreat from the public sphere.[79] In the face of the structural changes brought about by modernization (urbanization, industrialization, differentiation, and individualism), religion becomes fragmented, privatized, and rationalized. Thus, modern societies characteristically do not have an overarching "sacred canopy" that frames all aspects of social life.[80] Rather, they present a plethora of religions, all making competing and ultimately unsuccessful claims to universality. Eventually, such an approach predicts the correlation between the advance of modernization and declining rates of church affiliation and participation, as is evident in western Europe.[81]

The secularization paradigm has yielded valuable insights into the relation between religion and immigration. For example, Renato Poblete and Thomas O'Dea draw from this paradigm to explain the rapid rate of conversion to evangelical Protestantism among Puerto Rican Catholics who arrived in large cities in the Northeast, such as New York and Philadelphia, as part of the "great migration" (1940–1965).[82] A recent survey conducted by the Pew Forum on Religion and Public Life and the Pew Hispanic Center also seems to validate some of the predictions of the secularization paradigm.[83] On the one hand, the accentuated trend toward a charismatic Christianity among Latinos, which Poblete and O'Dea observed in the 1950s and '60s, continues. On the other hand, there are growing numbers of Latinos who are not affiliated with or do not participate in any churches. Thus, the raw numbers might be interpreted as a validation of the secularization hypotheses.[84]

But this is not the only interpretation. Since many Latinos are interested in achieving a piece of the American dream, they often work long hours, frequently at two or even more jobs. The heavy work schedule leaves precious little time and energy to become involved in a religious organization. Latinos may, instead, choose to spend their free time at the park, playing soccer or baseball, or at home watching television.[85] The lack of participation in established religious organizations does not mean that Latinos have rejected religion altogether. Rather, they may be developing their own forms of "spirituality" that take place in different contexts.[86]

Before we flesh out the notion of lived religion, we need to introduce the "New Paradigm" (NP), which emerged in the early 1990s, following the publication of Stephen Warner's landmark essay.[87] For, in challenging the core assumptions of the secularization paradigm, the NP paved the way for a renewed focus on religious vitality, creativity, and innovation. To demonstrate that secularization is not an irreversible structural process that is pushing religion out of the public arena, NP theorists point to the strength of religion throughout the world, from the rapid growth of evangelical Christianity in Latin America and Africa to the spread of Islamic "fundamentalism" in the Middle East, in Asia, and among immigrants in Europe and to the rise of Hindutva in India and the Hindu diaspora. In particular, NP theorists hold up the United States, a country that is simultaneously hypermodern and highly religious, as a fatal anomaly that the secularization model cannot explain.[88] Taking the United States as its point of departure, the NP holds that there is no contradiction between religious pluralism and religious vitality. In fact, religion is at its most vibrant in a pluralistic setting that encourages the religious producers to innovate and improve their products in order to maintain their edge vis-à-vis competitors. Thus, in contrast to the claims of the secularization paradigm, which assumes that religion is at its strongest in a monopolistic situation, when there is a single sacred canopy, the NP states that religious monopolies are highly susceptible to decay because there is no incentive for innovation and entrepreneurship.[89]

As part of its effort to show empirically how religion thrives in a pluralistic setting, the NP has focused on congregations, arguably the most visible form of religious organization made possible by the separation of church and state in the United States. Whereas the secularization paradigm has tended to favor quantitative methods to measure church attendance and religious affiliation, the focus on congregations has led the NP to adopt a more ethnographic method. The best work done under the general rubric of the NP, in fact, includes rich descriptions of the local practices of believers as they build and maintain community.[90] These practices often blend religious and civic dimensions, thus contributing not only to a vibrant religious pluralism but to democracy. In its stress on the practitioner's agency and creativity and on the public impact of religious life, New Paradigm is, thus, a precursor to the lived religion school.

Through its focus on congregations, the NP has also offered useful tools to study how immigrants transform established institutions and/or construct their own as they settle in the United States.[91] It is clear that the concepts of social capital, moral community, ethnic enclave, and networks, which we highlighted above in the section on collective mobilization, dovetail nicely with the focus on congregations. As we shall see in the chapters that follow, Latino immigrants rely heavily on congregations as they move to a new destination. Unlike traditional gateway cities that often have an array of civic and advocacy organizations developed over the years to service and incorporate new immigrant groups, new destinations generally lack the institutional infrastructure designed to serve immigrant populations.[92] In such a context, congregations can provide important material and moral support for immigrants and serve as an important source of social norms and values in a sometimes hostile environment.

Some of the findings in the Pew survey confirm the wisdom of the New Paradigm's focus on congregations to understand how religion works for Latino immigrants. For example, it found that Latino religion is "distinctively ethnic. Two thirds of Latino worshipers attend churches with Latino clergy, services in Spanish and heavily Latino congregations. While most predominant among foreign born and Spanish speakers, Hispanic-oriented worship is prevalent also among native born and English-speaking Latinos. That strongly suggests that the phenomenon is not simply a product of immigration or language but that it involves a broader and more lasting form of ethnic identification."[93]

For all the New Paradigm's strengths, it suffers from significant weaknesses. First, theorists working within this paradigm tend to understand congregations as coherent subcultures with clear, even if porous, boundaries. Our research will show that congregations are not only embedded in "local ecologies" or "religious districts."[94] In addition to being located in particular socioeconomic contexts and religious fields, congregations are also crisscrossed by transnational networks linking multiple nodes. For example, religious lay leaders may create hometown associations as one aspect of their congregational work, to collect funds to rebuild the church in their village of origin or to send bodies for burial in the homeland or to sponsor and organize transnational celebrations of the patron saint, as we describe in chapters 7 and 8. Consequently, "congregations" do not fit within a single template nor do they necessarily take on the "congregational form" often associated with American Protestant churches.[95]

A transnational prism, thus, offers a fruitful way to contextualize congregational ethnographies. Transnationalism allows us to explore the production, circulation, and consumption of religious practices and worldviews across spatiotemporal arrangements that include but are not reducible to bounded congregations. To map out the multi-scalar practice of religion, several of our contributors use the trope of networks or a transnational social field, conceptualizing congregations as important territorialized nodes.[96]

The second weakness of the focus of the NP has to do with the fact that not all public and material expressions of religion are congregational.[97] The vast majority of the immigrants we studied in South Florida are not reached by or intensely involved in congregations. Rather, because of geographical dispersal, busy work schedules, the demands to be mobile, and the fear to be visible in an increasingly anti-immigrant climate, Latin American immigrants are more likely to "do religion" at home, school, workplace, and other settings where they carry out their daily routines, very often among other immigrants. In many cases, these spaces of everyday life are linked to congregations. Yet, these links tend to be tenuous, ephemeral, and sporadic, depending on the changing needs of the life cycle or the challenges of their immigrant trajectories.

In order to go beyond the New Paradigm's narrow focus on congregations and the creativity of religious entrepreneurs, our teams draw from the lived religion approach, which seeks "to study how particular people, in particular places and times, live in, with, through, and against the religious idioms available to them in culture."[98] The lived religion approach builds on and goes beyond previous studies on "popular" religion. The concept of popular religion has tended to emphasize the tension between orthodoxy and heresy, between institutional domination and lay, grassroots resistance. Particularly, in Latin America, the concept was traditionally read through a class-based prism that understood the religious beliefs and practices of the common people as either reproducing or contesting the hegemony of religious and secular elites.[99] The lived religion approach takes up some of these concerns but shifts the stress to the phenomenological description of everyday practices. The lived religion approach is primarily interested in exploring how practitioners (both clergy and laity) materialize, embody, and emplace religion as they engage each other in daily life.[100]

Since lived religion scholars see religion as ways of being in the world, they argue that "religion cannot be understood apart from its place in everyday lives, preoccupations, and commonsense orientations of men and women."[101] "Crafted and recrafted by many hands, in many different places, and in contradictory circumstances, religious media constitute the way living people experience and construe events in their social world (war, economic distress, the organization and experience of work, to cite three examples) and perennial human problems (always encountered within specific historical frames, although never completely and securely so)."[102]

Thus, the lived religion approach seeks to develop textured, reflexive ethnographic accounts of "the experiences and beliefs of people in the midst of their lives, to encounter religion in its place in actual men and women's lived experience, in the places where they live and work."[103] As part of the qualitative focus on everyday existence, lived religion scholars have paid particular attention to the practices of women, who among immigrants often deal most directly with the needs of their children and the struggles to preserve family and cultural traditions. Robert Orsi, for example, found that, amid the turmoil caused by the Great Depression in the 1930s and the Second World War, women turned to Jude, the saint of the hopeless causes, "in socially defined roles, identifying themselves in their petitions as daughters, mothers, and wives praying for husbands, parents, and children."[104] Here, in its focus on family and its embeddedness in sociopolitical realities, the lived religion approach dovetails with the growing literature on religion and gender in Latin America. This literature documents how women draw from their religious traditions to curb destructive behaviors and social forces that threaten to dismantle the family and, in the process, empower themselves without directly challenging male dominance.[105] In chapter 9, Patricia Fortuny Loret de Mola, Lúcia Ribeiro, and Mirian Solís Lizama build on this literature to show how religion helps Brazilian and Mexican women to deal with the dislocations produced by migration and settlement in new destinations, allowing them to articulate "intermediate spaces" between the public and private spheres.

In approaching religion, all the contributors to this volume have taken to heart the lived religion school's call to focus on everyday practices and narratives. However, we have sought to locate these practices and narratives within the larger institutional context, showing their interplay with national and transnational sociopolitical and religious dynamics. This embedding shows the fragility of lived religion. For many Latino immigrants, especially for those who come to a hostile new destination where they are subject to exploitative labor arrangements, it is not just generating congregational life that is nearly impossible. Even engaging in quotidian religious practices is extremely difficult. The question then arises: Given the structural and existential constraints to religious life that Latinos face in many new destinations, to what extent is religion an important variable in the process of migration and settlement? We will return to this question in the conclusion, once we have discussed different ways in which religion interacts with transnationalism, collective mobilization, and integration.

Having laid out the key questions that drive this volume as well as the larger context and the theoretical framework that orient the collaborative project, we would like now to characterize the communities that served as our case studies and the methodologies we used to explore them.

New Faces, New Places, and Transnational Methodology

From 2001 to 2005, our interdisciplinary research teams undertook fieldwork in Florida and in selected communities of origin in Brazil, Mexico, and Guatemala. We believed that a research strategy combining ethnographic methods with survey research would provide a more solid basis for our comparative study.[106] In each of these locations, we utilized a range of qualitative methods including participant observation, in-depth interviews, oral histories, and focus groups with men, women, and youths, as well as with church and civic activists. Based upon our first rounds of qualitative work and community mapping, we then designed a survey instrument and collected survey data across the Florida communities under study. Because Guatemalans and Mexicans are highly concentrated in Jupiter and Immokalee, we were able to conduct random surveys based on census tracks. However, because Brazilians are widely dispersed within the significantly larger populations of Deerfield and Pompano, we utilized a snowball technique for the Brazilian sample. Thus, while our survey data for Brazilians yields useful comparisons with the other groups, the data cannot be assumed to be broadly representative of the over-all Brazilian population.

Several factors justify our choices of immigrant groups and sites to study. In terms of our target groups, we wanted first to compare and contrast the dynamics of settlement in new destinations for relatively recent immigrants from Latin America, such as Brazilians and Guatemalans,[107] and the older, more established immigrants from Mexico. Second, we sought to break new ground by examining comparatively the experiences of Brazilians with those of other immigrants from Latin America. Except on the issue of race, Brazilian immigrants have thus far been studied in isolation from other groups in the hemisphere. By studying Brazilians, who tend to include both men and women and show more diversity in socioeconomic status and level of formal education, side by side with Guatemalan and Mexican immigrants, who are predominantly single men with few years of formal education, we are able to highlight the impact of the variables of gender and class in the migration and incorporation process. Third, including Guatemalans in our study allows us to focus on the specific contributions of ethnicity, particularly indigenous identities, in the articulation of political, religious, and transnational practices. And since Guatemalans and Mexicans overlap in their settlement patterns, we can study variations and similarities between these two groups in the same localities.

In terms of the choice of research sites, our selection of Jupiter, Immokalee, Deerfield Beach, and Pompano Beach allowed us to examine community formation in a variety of spatial scales and geographic logics. In particular, we were interested in exploring the differential impact of a rural setting like Immokalee (dominated by Mexican migrant farm workers) versus suburban and exurban spaces (like Jupiter for Guatemalans and Pompano Beach and Deerfield Beach for Brazilians) on the process of settlement. We believed that a mix of new-destination contexts would make the findings of our project more useful for the ongoing national debate on immigration. Throughout the United States, Latino populations are experiencing the fastest rates of growth not in the large traditional gateway cities but in rural, suburban, and exurban regions that have much in common with our three communities in Florida. A brief description of the three communities and the primary immigrant groups we studied in each helps to draw out the commonalities with other new destinations for Latino immigration.

Guatemalans and Mexicans in Jupiter

Jupiter, Florida, is a relatively small (with a population of approximately forty thousand) coastal city on the northern edge of Palm Beach County, less than ten miles north of West Palm Beach. A popular winter vacation destination for "snowbirds" from the Northeast, Jupiter was in the midst of a sustained housing and construction boom during the course of our fieldwork. The construction industry, lawn-and-garden industry, and the golf course industry rely heavily on immigrant (primarily Guatemalan and Mexican Mayan) labor. Each day, hundreds of day-laborers crowded the sidewalk and parking lots in front of apartments on a local throughway (Center Street), waiting for contractors and private individuals to arrive and offer work. As in other small communities from New York State to Georgia, these gatherings became the focus of increasing tensions in the primarily Anglo community, forcing town authorities to initiate a series of meetings and policy changes to address the tensions surrounding the growing immigrant community.

The majority of Jupiter's immigrants come from rural areas in northern Guatemala (primarily Huehuetenango, with 42 percent of those we sampled in our survey research) and southern Mexico (Chiapas, with nearly 15 percent). Based on interviews with key informants, we estimate that approximately 1,500 of Jupiter's 2,500 Guatemalan immigrants come from the town of Jacaltenango and its surrounding *aldeas* in northwestern Guatemala. We thus traced the transnational connections back from Jupiter and conducted field research in the primary communities of origin as well.

The first Jacaltecos arrived in Jupiter after a long and intense displacement between countries (Guatemala, Mexico, and the United States) and between various locations within the United States.[108] They arrived in Florida for diverse reasons: from the need to safeguard their lives in the context of Guatemala's intense armed conflict of the 1980s, to more recent waves of immigrants who have come primarily as international migrant workers, to fill the demand for laborers in

Jupiter's burgeoning landscaping and construction industries. Since 1995, the Guatemalan immigrant population in Jupiter has grown rapidly as economic conditions in Guatemala and southern Mexico have deteriorated, the demand for immigrant labor has continued to grow, and transnational family and labor networks have become institutionalized between Jupiter and Jacaltenango.

Mexicans and Guatemalans in Immokalee

Immokalee (population 19,763) is located in Collier County in southwest Florida, very close to the Everglades. Beginning in the 1950s and '60s, Immokalee and surrounding areas came to play a major role in Florida's agricultural expansion. Today southwest Florida accounts for more than 25 percent of the state's citrus production and more than 30 percent of its tomato production. During the harvest season (November through April), the population can swell to 30,000, while during the off-season it decreases by about a half. Although up until the 1970s the permanent labor force in Immokalee was primarily Euro-American and the migrant labor force predominantly African American, today Immokalee's population is overwhelmingly Latino. Immokalee has become a major gateway for migrant workers entering the East Coast agricultural labor stream and an important crossroads for Mexican immigrants to Florida. According to the 2000 census, the population is 71 percent Hispanic (almost 90 percent of whom are of Mexican origin and 9 percent Guatemalan), 6 percent Caucasian, 9 percent Haitian, 9 percent African American, and 0.7 percent Native American.

Our survey of Mexican and Guatemalan immigrants in Immokalee highlights the geographic diversity and mobility of the immigrant population, with large concentrations from Oaxaca (13.1 percent) and Chiapas (13.1 percent), Mexico, the next largest from Guanajuato, Mexico (11.0 percent), and Huehuetenango, Guatemala (10.3 percent), and the remainder primarily spread throughout the other Mexican states. Moreover, 60 percent of respondents said that they had lived elsewhere in the United States, and 32 percent reported frequently traveling to other states. The arrival of increasing numbers of immigrants from indigenous communities in southern Mexico is representative of the new geography of Mexican immigration. In this sense, Immokalee is both an old and new destination—an old destination for immigrants from traditional sending states in central and western Mexico and a new destination for immigrants from nontraditional sending states from southern Mexico.

Brazilians in Pompano Beach and Deerfield Beach

Pompano Beach (population 78,191) and Deerfield Beach (population 64,583) are two cities at the northern edge of Broward County. The area is heavily populated by a combination of Euro-American and Canadian "snowbirds," who come during the winter to enjoy the warm weather and the beaches, and middle-class families that have moved north to find affordable housing, while still being relatively close to Miami (separated by between thirty-five and forty miles). As in many of the new destinations for Latino immigration throughout the United States, Brazilians are a largely "hidden" community, dispersed throughout the area and intermingled with other Hispanic groups.

It is impossible to state with certainty the number of Brazilians in these two cities. According to the 2000 census, Pompano Beach and Deerfield Beach have a total of approximately 6,300 residents of Latino/Hispanic descent who are not of Mexican, Puerto Rican, or Cuban origin. However, most local leaders estimate the Brazilian population to fall between 25,000 and 30,000. Our non-randomized survey found that Brazilian migration to the area is fairly recent: 91 percent of our respondents indicated that they came to the region only after 1990 (with close to half of those stating that they arrived after 2000). While we met immigrants from virtually all states of Brazil, our sample included a heavy presence of Mineiros (28 percent) and Cariocas (from Rio de Janeiro at 23 percent), and Paulistas (11 percent). This breakdown mirrors the patterns found in older migration flows to New York and Boston.[109] Our survey respondents were also relatively young (55 percent in the twenty- to thirty-nine-year-old range) and educated (85 percent have completed at least eight years of schooling and nearly half of those affirmed to have finished high school), and close to 70 percent self-identified as white when asked to list their race. About 40 percent told us that their occupations in Brazil required a significant level of qualification. Among those surveyed, we found lawyers, doctors, teachers, dentists, business administrators, and entrepreneurs.

In terms of occupation in Pompano Beach and Deerfield Beach, Brazilians are all well represented in the service and construction sectors of the local economy. For men, the most common jobs are roofing, dry-walling, landscaping, and working at restaurants either as dishwashers, busboys, or delivery drivers. For women, it is cleaning, both of private homes and of the many condominiums and hotels in the region, as well as waitressing. Some Brazilian women also take care of retired, elderly people, helping with transportation, shopping, and other domestic chores. While 42 percent of respondents in our survey indicated that they earn monthly salaries between $1,400 and $2,000, 17 percent stated that they earn over $3,000 per month.

The Structure of the Book

As the discussion of our criteria for selecting groups and sites to study demonstrates, this volume, while focusing on communities with their own specificities, touches upon dynamics in Latin American migration that are evident beyond Florida, in the New South and throughout the United States. To draw the larger empirical and theoretical implications of our case studies, we have divided them into three parts, addressing the key clusters of question that have driven our research: transnationalism, collective mobilization, and lived religion. For each part, we have tried to include chapters about the three groups we studied, in order to facilitate comparisons and contrasts. In the conclusion, we will offer an assessment of what our findings at the local level mean for debates on immigration around these three overarching topics.

NOTES

1. See Anna Peterson, Manuel A. Vásquez, Philip Williams, eds., *Christianity, Social Change, and Globalization in the Americas* (New Brunswick, NJ: Rutgers University Press, 2001); Edward L. Cleary and Timothy J. Steigenga, eds., *Resurgent Voices in Latin America: Indigenous Peoples, Political Mobilization, and Religious Change* (New Brunswick, NJ: Rutgers University Press, 2004); and Manuel A. Vásquez, Chad E. Seales, and Marie Friedmann Marquardt, "New Latino Destinations," in *Latinos/as in the United States: Changing the Face of America*, ed. Havidán Rodríguez, Rogelio Sáenz, and Cecilia Menjívar, 19–35 (New York: Springer, 2007).

2. This estimate does not include the 3.9 million residents from Puerto Rico.

3. While we are acutely aware of the specific inaccuracies (particularly in the case of indigenous Mayan immigrants) and the socially constructed nature of the terms "Latino" and "Hispanic," we utilize the terms interchangeably throughout this volume following their usage in the U.S. Census. For the 2000 U.S. Census definition see http://quickfacts.census.gov/qfd/meta/long_68188.htm. For a more complete discussion of the debate see Linda Martín Alcoff, "Latino vs. Hispanic: The Politics of Ethnic Names," *Philosophy and Social Criticism* 31 (2005): 395–407.

4. Roberto Suro, "Latino Growth in Metropolitan America: Changing Patterns, New Locations," published report, Brookings Institution, Washington, D.C., July 2002.

5. Betsy Guzmán and Eileen Diaz McConnell, "The Hispanic Population: 1990–2000 Growth and Change," *Population Research and Policy Review* 21 (2002): 109–128.

6. Stanley K. Smith and June M. Nogle, "An Evaluation of Hispanic Population Estimates," *Social Science Quarterly* 85, no. 3 (2004): 731–745.

7. Pew Hispanic Center, "The New Latino South: The Context and Consequences of Rapid Population Growth," published report, Washington, D.C., July 26, 2005.

8. Alejandro Portes and Alex Stepick, *City on the Edge: The Transformation of Miami* (Berkeley: University of California Press, 1993).

9. Stanley K. Smith, "Florida Population Growth: Past, Present and Future," Bureau of Economic and Business Research, published report, University of Florida, June 2005.

10. Net migration into the state accounted for 85.3 percent of the growth. Foreign immigrants now account for 26 percent of all persons moving to Florida. Contrary to popular belief, between 1995 and 2000 only 15.4 percent of immigrants to Florida were age sixty-five or older (Smith, "Florida Population Growth").

11. See Jorge Durand and Douglas Massey, *Clandestinos, Migración México-Estados Unidos en los Albores del Siglo XXI* (Zacatecas, Mexico: Universidad Autónoma de Zacatecas y Porrua, 2003); Victor Zúñiga and Rubén Hernández-León, eds., *New Destinations: Mexican Immigration in the United States* (New York: Russell Sage Foundation, 2005); H. Smith and Owen Furuseth, *Latinos in the New South: Transformation of Place* (Hampshire, UK: Ashgate, 2006).

12. Zúñiga and Hernández-León, *New Destinations*; William Kandel and Emilio Parrado, "Industrial Transformation and Hispanic Migration to the American South: The Case of the Poultry Industry," in *Hispanic Spaces, Latino Places: A Geography of Regional and*

Cultural Diversity, ed. Daniel D. Arreola, 255–276 (Austin: University of Texas Press, 2004).

13. Ann Millard and Jorge Chapa, *Apple Pie and Enchiladas: Latino Newcomers in the Rural Midwest* (Austin: University of Texas Press, 2004).

14. Mary Waters and Tomás Jiménez, "Assessing Immigrant Assimilation: New Empirical and Theoretical Challenges," *Annual Review of Sociology* 31 (2005): 117.

15. Randolph Bourne, "Trans-National America," *Atlantic Monthly* 118 (July 1916): 86–97.

16. Manuel Castells, *The Rise of the Network Society* (Oxford: Blackwell, 1996); David Harvey, *The Condition of Postmodernity* (Oxford: Basil Blackwell, 1989), Anthony Giddens, *Runaway World: How Globalization Is Reshaping Our Lives* (Oxford: Blackwell, 2000).

17. Leslie Sklair, *The Transnational Capitalist Class* (Malden, MA: Blackwell, 2001).

18. Arjun Appadurai, "Grassroots Globalization and the Research Imagination," *Public Culture* 12, no. 1 (2000): 1–19; Luis Eduardo Guarnizo and Michael P. Smith, "The Locations of Transnationalism," in *Transnationalism from Below: Comparative Urban and Community Research*, ed. M. P. Smith and Luis Guarnizo, 3–34(New Brunswick, NJ, and London: Transaction Publishers, 1998).

19. Roger Rouse, "Mexican Migration and the Social Space of Postmodernism," *Diaspora* 1 (spring 1991): 8–23.

20. Linda Basch, Nina Glick Schiller, and Cristina Szanton Blanc, *Nations Unbound: Transnational Migration, Postcolonial Predicaments, and the Deterritorialized Nation-State* (Langhorne, PA: Gordon and Breach, 1994).

21. Ibid., 7.

22. Ibid.

23. Alejandro Portes, Eduardo Guarnizo, and Patricia Landolt, "The Study of Transationalism: Pitfalls and Promise of an Emergent Research Field," *Ethnic and Racial Studies* 22 (March 1999): 217–237.

24. Nina Glick Schiller, "Transmigrants and Nation-States: Something Old and Something New in the U.S. Immigrant Experience," in *The Handbook of International Migration*, ed. Charles Hirschmann, Philip Kasinitz, and Josh DeWind in (New York: The Russell Sage Foundation, 1999), 97.

25. Nina Glick Schiller, "Transnational Social Fields and Imperialism: Bringing a Theory to Transnational Studies," *Anthropological Theory* 5, no. 4 (2005): 442.

26. Nina Glick Schiller and Georges Fouron, "Terrains of Blood and Nation: Haitian Transnational Social Fields," *Ethnic and Racial Studies* 22 (1991): 340–366.

27. Peggy Levitt, *The Transnational Villagers* (Berkeley: University of California Press, 2001), 11.

28. Peggy Levitt and Nina Glick Schiller, "Conceptualizing Simultaneity: A Transnational Social Field Perspective on Society," *International Migration Review* 38 (2004):1002–1039.

29. Manuel Vásquez and Marie Marquardt, *Globalizing the Sacred: Religion across the Americas* (New Brunswick, NJ: Rutgers University Press, 2003).

30. Susanne H. Rudolph and James Piscatori, eds., *Transnational Religion and Fading States* (Boulder, CO: Westview Press, 1997).

31. Peggy Levitt, "Redefining the Boundaries of Belonging: The Institutional Character of Transnational Religious Life," *Sociology of Religion* 65 (2004): 6.

32. Ibid., 8.

33. Ibid., 11–12.

34. Eric Kramer, "Spectacle and the Staging of Power in Brazilian Neo-Pentecostalism," *Latin American Perspectives* 32 (January 2005): 95–120; Patricia Fortuny, "The Santa Cena of el Luz Del Mundo Church: A Case of Contemporary Transnationalism," in *Religion across Borders: Transnational Immigrant Networks*, ed. Helen Rose Ebaugh and Janet Saltzman Chafetz, 15–50 (Walnut Creek, CA: Altamira Press, 2002).

35. Alejandro Portes, "The Debates and Significance of Immigrant Transnationalism," *Global Networks* 1 (July 2001): 182–183.

36. Levitt, *Transnational Villagers.*

37. José Itzigsohn, C. D. Cabral, E. H. Medina, and O. Vazquez, "Mapping Dominican Transnationalism: Narrow and Broad Transnational Practices," *Ethnic and Racial Studies* 22 (1999): 316–339.

38. Levitt, *Transnational Villagers,* 198. Along the same lines, Thomas Faist argues that transnational linkages may take at least three forms. First, there are "transnational kinship groups" built on one-on-one reciprocity, such as when immigrants send remittances to family members in their country of origin. Second, there are "transnational circuits" constructed around instrumental exchanges, as in the business transactions among migrant entrepreneurs. Finally, Faist refers to "transnational communities" that encompass shared meanings and beliefs expressed in the form of collective identity. Thomas Faist, "Transnationalization in International Migration: Implications for the Study of Citizenship and Culture," *Ethnic and Racial Studies* 23, no. 2 (2000): 89–222.

39. Portes, "The Debates and Significance," 183.

40. Portes, Guarnizo, and Landolt, "The Study of Transnationalism," 219.

41. Faist, "Transnationalization."

42. Cities and towns as diverse as Avon Park, Florida; Escondido, California; Farmers Branch, Texas; Hazleton, Pennsylvania; Riverside, New Jersey; and Valley Park, Missouri, have passed local ordinances that prohibit businesses from hiring undocumented immigrants or renting/leasing to them. At the state level, a number of states have passed legislation to prohibit undocumented immigrants from obtaining driver's licenses. In Georgia, the state legislature passed Immigration Law 529 in 2006, which denies state benefits to undocumented workers, requires employers to withhold 6 percent of wages from workers who cannot prove their legal status, and authorizes state and local police to enforce federal immigration laws.

43. For an example of such an overview in the context of Latin American social movements, see Charles Hale, "Cultural Politics of Identity in Latin America," *Annual Review of Anthropology* 26, no. 6 (1997): 567–590.

44. Appadurai, "Grassroots Globalization."

45. Anna Peterson, Manuel Vásquez, and Philip Williams, "Christianity and Social Change in the Shadow of Globalization," in *Christianity, Social Change, and Globalization in the Americas,* ed. Anna L. Peterson, Manuel A. Vásquez, Philip J. Williams (New Brunswick, NJ: Rutgers University Press, 2001), 12.

46. Appadurai, "Grassroots Globalization," 15–16.

47. Keck and Sikkink refer to these examples of transnational activism as "transnational advocacy networks." Margaret Keck and Kathryn Sikkink, *Activists beyond Borders* (Ithaca, NY: Cornell University Press, 1998), 2. Despite Appadurai's cautious optimism that transnational advocacy networks "might offset the most volatile effects of runaway capital," he acknowledges that the social imagination of these movements is often disciplined by and controlled by states, markets, and other powerful global interests. Appadurai, "Grassroots Globalization," 16.

48. Roger Rouse, "Thinking through Transnationalism: Notes on the Cultural Politics of Class Relations in Contemporary United States," *Public Culture* 7 (1995): 368–371.

49. Ibid., 370.

50. Ibid., 385.

51. According to Manuel Castells, while the rise of societies crisscrossed by global networks encourages new forms of identity construction, the search for meaning is more

likely to take the form of "defensive" identities, "trenches of resistance and survival on the basis of principles different from, or opposed to, those permeating the institutions of society." Manuel Castells, *The Power of Identity* (Oxford: Blackwell, 1997), 8.

52. Alejandro Portes and Rubén Rumbaut, *Legacies: The Story of the Immigrant Second Generation* (Berkeley: University of California Press, 2001), 284.

53. Alejandro Portes, Cristina Escobar, and Alexandria Walton Radford, "Immigrant Transnational Organizations and Development: A Comparative Study, *International Migration Review* 41 (spring 2004): 247.

54. Castells distinguishes between "defensive identities" and "project identities." Project identity refers to political projects that seek to "build a new identity that redefines their position in society and, by so doing, seek the transformation of overall social structure." Castells, *Power in Movement*, 8.

55. Rouse, "Thinking through Transnationalism," 372.

56. Ibid.

57. Alberto Melucci, "A Strange Kind of Newness: What's 'New' in New Social Movements," in *New Social Movements*, ed. Enrique Laraña, Hank Johnston, and Joseph Gusfield (Philadelphia: Temple University Press, 1994), 127.

58. Sidney Tarrow, *Power in Movement* (Cambridge: Cambridge University Press, 1998), 124.

59. According to Tarrow, connective structures "link leaders and followers, center and periphery, and different parts of a movement sector, permitting coordination and aggregation between movement organizations and allowing movements to persist even when formal organization is lacking." Ibid.

60. Pierre Bourdieu and Loic Wacquant, *An Invitation to Reflexive Sociology* (Chicago: University of Chicago Press, 1992), 119.

61. Portes and Rumbaut, *Legacies*, 64–65.

62. Cecilia Menjívar, *Fragmented Ties: Salvadoran Immigrant Networks in America* (Berkley: University of California Press, 2000), 234.

63. Alejandro Portes, "Social Capital: Its Origins and Applications in Modern Sociology," *Annual Review of Sociology* 24 (1998): 1–24.

64. Roger Waldinger, "The 'Other Side' of Embeddedness: A Case Study of the Interplay between Economy and Ethnicity," *Ethnic and Racial Studies* 18 (1995): 555–580.

65. Alejandro Portes and Alex Stepick, *City on the Edge: The Transformation of Miami* (Berkeley: University of California Press, 1993), 135.

66. Portes and Stepick discuss how upper-class Nicaraguan exiles who arrived in Miami during the 1980s were able to tap into the resources of the Cuban "moral community" because of their common history of exile from a left-wing regime and their staunchly anti-communist political ideology. However, other immigrant groups, like Haitians, were excluded from membership in the moral community.

67. Robert Putnam, *Bowling Alone* (New York: Simon and Schuster, 2000), 66.

68. Richard Wood, *Faith in Action* (Chicago: University of Chicago Press, 2002).

69. Michael Foley, "Religious Institutions as Agents for Civic Incorporation: A Preliminary Report on Research on Religion and New Immigrants," 9. Paper presented at the 97th Annual Meeting of the American Political Science Association, San Francisco, CA, August 30–September 2, 2001.

70. Putnam, *Bowling Alone*; Mark R. Warren, J. Phillip Thompson, and Susan Saegert, "The Role of Social Capital in Combating Poverty," in *Social Capital and Poor Communities*, ed. Saegert, Thompson, and Warren, 1–28 (New York: Russell Sage Foundation, 2001).

71. Ibid., 8.

72. Wood, *Faith in Action*, 144.

73. Foley, "Religious Institutions."

74. Daniel Levine and David Stoll, "Bridging the Gap between Empowerment and Power in Latin America," in *Transnational Religion and Fading States*, ed. Susanne Rudolph and James Piscatori, 63–103 (Boulder, CO: Westview Press, 1997).

75. Foley and Hoge found that whereas Protestant evangelical churches "rarely encouraged their members to exercise these skills outside the worship community," Catholic parishes "promoted widespread participation among parishioners, volunteering outside the community, and civic activism." Michael Foley and Dean Hoge, *Religion and the New Immigrants: How Faith Communities Form Our Newest Citizens* (New York: Oxford University Press, 2007), 233.

76. John Booth and Patricia Richards, "Civil Society, Political Capital, and Democratization in Central America," *Journal of Politics* 60, no. 3 (1998): 782.

77. Patricia Fortuny and Philip Williams, "Religion and Social Capital among Mexican Immigrants in Southwest Florida," *Latino Studies* 5, no. 2 (2007): 233–253.

78. Booth and Richards, "Civil Society," 782.

79. The literature on secularization is vast. For a sampling, see Steve Bruce, *God Is Dead: Secularization in the West* (Oxford: Blackwell, 2002); José Casanova, *Public Religions in the Modern World* (Chicago: University of Chicago Press, 1994); Marcel Gauchet, *The Disenchantment of the World: A Political History of Religion* (Princeton: Princeton University Press, 1997); David Martin, *General Theory of Secularization* (Aldershot, U.K.: Ashgate Publishing, 1993); Pippa Norris and Ronald Inglehart, *Sacred and Secular: Religion and Politics Worldwide* (Cambridge: Cambridge University Press, 2004).

80. Peter Berger, *The Sacred Canopy: Elements of a Sociological Theory of Religion* (Garden City, NY: Doubleday, 1967).

81. Norris and Inglehart, *Sacred and Secular*.

82. Poblete and O'Dea argue that, particularly in the United States, Puerto Ricans encounter a complex and fast-paced society in tension with their rural worldview and values. This tension, added to the economic exclusion and racial discrimination they face, opens Puerto Rican immigrants to alienation and anomie, to a loss of sense of self and communal connection, ultimately leading them to explore other religious options or eventually turn toward secularization. Renato Poblete and Thomas O'Dea, "Anomie and the 'Quest for Community': The Formation of Sects among the Puerto Ricans of New York," *American Catholic Sociological Review* 21 (spring 1960): 18–36.

83. See the Pew Forum on Religion and Public Life and the Pew Hispanic Center, *Changing Faiths: Latinos and the Transformation of American Religion* (Washington, DC: Pew Research Center, 2007).

84. The Pew survey also found that, compared to Catholic Latinos, "secular" Latinos tended to show the traditional signs of "assimilation": English dominance or bilingualism (63 percent), higher levels of formal education (66 percent are high school graduates), and higher household incomes (59 percent with incomes above $30,000). In other words, integration into modern U.S. society seems to correlate with a more secular outlook among Latinos. Pew Forum, *Changing Faiths*.

85. Pew Forum, *Changing Faiths*.

86. Stephen Warner, "Immigration and Religious Communities in the United States," in *Gatherings in Diaspora: Religious Communities and the New Immigration*, ed. Stephen Warner and Judith Wittner (Philadelphia: Temple University Press, 1998), 17.

87. See R. Stephen Warner, "A Work in Progress toward a New Paradigm for the Sociological Study of Religion in the United States," *American Journal of Sociology* 98 (March 1993): 1044–1093. For examples of the New Paradigm at work, see Rodney Stark

and Roger Finke, *Acts of Faith: Explaining the Human Side of Religion* (Berkeley: University of California Press, 2000); and Christian Smith et. al., *American Evangelicalism: Embattled and Thriving* (Chicago: University of Chicago Press, 1998).

88. Some secularization theorists have all but repudiated the secularization model. For a dramatic example, see Peter Berger, ed., *The Desecularization of the World: Resurgent Religion and World Politics* (Grand Rapids: Wm. B. Eerdmans Publishing, 1999); Peter Berger, "Reflections on the Sociology of Religion Today," *Sociology of Religion* 62 (winter 2001): 443–454.

89. Stark and Finke, *Acts of Faith*; Roger Finke and Rodney Stark, *The Churching of America, 1776–1990: Winners and Losers in Our Religious Economy* (New Brunswick, NJ: Rutgers University Press, 1992).

90. Nancy Ammerman, *Congregation and Community* (New Brunswick, NJ: Rutgers University Press, 1997); Mark Chaves, *Congregations in America* (Cambridge, MA: Harvard University Press, 2004).

91. Stephen Warner and Judith Wittner, eds., *Gatherings in Diaspora: Religious Communities and the New Immigration* (Philadelphia: Temple University Press, 1998); Helen Rose Ebaugh and Janet Saltzman Chafetz, *Religion and the New Immigrants: Continuities and Adaptations* (Walnut Creek, CA: AltaMira Press, 2000).

92. Mary Waters and Tomás Jiménez, "Assessing Immigrant Assimilation: New Empirical and Theoretical Challenges," *Annual Review of Sociology* 31 (2005): 105–125.

93. Pew Forum, *Changing Faiths*, 4.

94. For an attempt to emplace congregations within the larger local context, see Nancy Eiesland, *A Particular Place: Urban Restructuring and Religious Ecology in a Southern Exurb* (New Brunswick, NJ: Rutgers University Press, 2000); and Omar McRoberts, *Streets of Glory: Church and Community in a Black Urban Neighborhood* (Chicago: University of Chicago Press, 2003).

95. In their recent study of religion and new immigrants in Washington, D.C., Foley and Hoge reject the term "congregation" in favor of "local worship communities." They argue that the use of the term "congregation" implies a congregational template characteristic of American Protestant churches that "obscures important differences" between worship communities. Foley and Hoge, *Religion and the New Immigrants*, 218–219.

96. Vásquez and Marquardt, *Globalizing the Sacred*.

97. Karen Leonard, Alex Stepick, Manuel Vásquez, and Jennifer Holdaway, *Immigrant Faiths: Transforming Religious Life in America* (New York: AltaMira, 2005).

98. Robert Orsi, "Everyday Miracles: The Study of Lived Religion," in *Lived Religion in America*, ed. David Hall (Princeton: Princeton University Press, 1997), 7.

99. Daniel Levine, ed., *Religion and Political Conflict in Latin America* (Chapel Hill: University of North Carolina Press, 1986).

100. Thus, Hall writes, "Where lived religion goes its own way is in breaking with the distinction between high and low that seems inevitably to recur in studies of popular religion. That is, [case studies operating under this approach] are not built around a structure of opposition. Nor do they displace the institutional or normative perspectives on practice, as historians of popular religion so commonly do." David Hall, ed., *Lived Religion in America: Toward a History of Practice* (Princeton: Princeton University Press, 1997), ix.

101. Robert Orsi, *Between Heaven and Earth: The Religious Worlds People Make and the Scholars Who Study Them* (Princeton: Princeton University Press, 2005), 167.

102. Ibid., 168.

103. Ibid., 147.

104. Robert Orsi, *Thank You, St. Jude: Women's Devotion to the Patron Saint of Hopeless Causes* (New Haven: Yale University Press, 1996), 43.

105. For example, see Elizabeth Brusco, *The Reformation of Machismo: Evangelical Conversion and Gender in Colombia* (Austin: University of Texas Press, 1995).

106. See Russell Bernard, *Research Methods in Anthropology: Qualitative and Quantitative Approaches* (Thousand Oaks, CA: Sage, 1994); and Charles Ragin, *Constructing Social Research* (Thousand Oaks, CA: Pine Forge Press, 1994).

107. With the exception of a handful of significant works, these two immigrant groups have not received detailed scholarly treatment. For the major studies of Guatemalan immigrants, see Leon Finke, *The Maya of Morganton: Work and Community in the Nuevo New South* (Chapel Hill: University of North Carolina Press, 2003); Allan Burns, *Maya in Exile: Guatemalans in Florida* (Philadelphia: Temple University Press, 1993); and Jacqueline María Hagan, *Deciding to Be Legal: A Maya Community in Houston* (Philadelphia: Temple University Press, 1994). For studies on Brazilians, see Maxine Margolis, *Little Brazil: An Ethnography of Brazilian Immigrants in New York City* (Princeton, NJ: Princeton University Press, 1994); Ana Cristina Braga Martes, *Brasileiros nos Estados Unidos. Um estudo sobre imigrantes em Massachusetts* (São Paulo: Paz e Terra, 1999); and Teresa Sales, *Brasileiros Longe de Casa* (São Paulo: Cortez, 1999).

108. See Burns, *Maya in Exile*, for the history of Mayan settlement in Florida.

109. Margolis, *Little Brazil*; and Martes, *Brasileiros nos Estados Unidos*.

PART ONE

Transnational Lives

Networks, Families, and Solidarities across Borders

2

꽃꽃꽃꽃꽃꽃꽃꽃꽃꽃꽃꽃꽃꽃꽃꽃꽃꽃꽃꽃꽃꽃꽃꽃꽃꽃꽃

Beyond *Homo Anomicus*

Interpersonal Networks, Space, and Religion among Brazilians in Broward County

MANUEL A. VÁSQUEZ

Scholars of immigration, such as Maxine Margolis, Teresa Sales, and Ana Cristina Martes, have long documented the fact that Brazilians abroad consistently complain about the lack of community and collective solidarity among themselves.[1] Margolis, for instance, found a pervasive "ideology of disunity" among Brazilians in New York. She writes:

> Brazilians often talk about the absence of an esprit de corps in their community and compare themselves unfavorably in this regard to New York's other new immigrant groups. All the Brazilians present at a gathering in Queens insisted that they alone among ethnic groups in the city lack a sense of community. Lamented one, "We have no club, no school, no union, no support from other Brazilians." "Everyone in New York has a community association except us," said another. Over and over, I was told that there are no Brazilian ethnic, social, or professional associations, no Brazilian occupational specialties akin to those of Korean greengrocers and Indian newsstand dealers—only commercial enterprises, such as those on West 46th Street.[2]

Margolis did the bulk of her fieldwork in the late 1980s and early 1990s, and much has changed since then, including the virtual disappearance of the business enclave known as Little Brazil and the rapid concentration of Brazilians in Queens neighborhoods, such as Astoria. However, more recent studies show that this concern with a lack of community life persists. In her study of Brazilian immigrants in Massachusetts, Martes states that one of her most unexpected findings was "the way in which Brazilians referred to each other. Throughout the interviews and participant observation, the complaints about the lack of solidarity, the hunger for [personal] gain, and the low community participation characterized a discursive field full of ambivalence, since the complaints also

33

came with repeated strong expression of love for Brazil and for its people."[3] Given the deep internal divisions among Brazilians, Martes found that "churches are the institutions that offer the most support to Brazilians. Yet, the ways in which this support is organized institutionally lead to significant differentials."[4] The centrality of churches amid a weak communitarian base is confirmed by Margolis's later work.[5]

Our research in Pompano Beach and Deerfield Beach also revealed a generalized critical attitude among Brazilians for the failure to organize and build a sense of community. The following statements by Brazilians in Broward County illustrate this self-critical attitude:

> We see other [immigrant] communities more organized, like Hispanics. They have a whole organization, unions ... but here we are missing Brazilian [public] faces. I see many Hispanics leading [*na frente*] ... but Brazilians helping each other? What they do more here is complain. If it were to get Brazilians together: "Let's organize our community and such," then people here would not respond. (Focus Group with Evangelical Church Fonte de Vida)
>
> First of all, a Brazilian when he comes from Brazil does not trust other Brazilians because they will trip you [*passar a perna*] and that is generalized. And another thing, a Brazilian only thinks about saving himself and the rest be dammed [*que se dane*]. That mentality continues. There are very few who help and those who would like to help end up being hurt [*lesados*]. (Focus Group with Baptist Church)
>
> Here everybody is very concerned [*preocupado*] with him/herself, with trying to make it, to gather some money, to build a patrimony there [in Brazil] or here, and then I believe that the concern for the other person does not exist much, as we have in Brazil. The guy is just worried about what is his/hers. Unfortunately, it is like that. (Catholic man)

Close to one-fifth of our survey respondents indicated that the single most important "community" need is group solidarity.[6] This is all the more striking considering that the second most selected community need was legalization of immigrant status, chosen by 16.5 percent of respondents.[7]

Nevertheless, we also found strong indications that Brazilians do help each other. One Catholic man told us, for example, "We help a lot of people whom we don't know, people whom we heard about. Here in the church especially. One gives messages: 'Ah! So and so needs a house or a job, or suffered an accident, or maybe is having financial difficulties. And so, everybody helps everybody." How, then, do we make sense of the contrasting perceptions of community life among Brazilian immigrants and the scholars who study them?

The contrast might be partly the result of the notion of community itself, which is highly complex and contested, containing "objective" referents, such as the presence of visible voluntary associations and/or shared, bounded living and working spaces, as well as "subjective" components like the widespread feeling of group belonging and identity.[8] Since "the word *community* itself is a Rorschach blot upon which myriad hopes and fears are projected,"[9] the use of this concept to assess the nature and degree of sociability of a particular group is highly problematic. Moreover, in recent years, scholars of migration and globalization have challenged the functionalism and static nature of the notion of community: community is traditionally construed as a territorially bounded social organism with identifiable parts harmoniously integrated by a unified and shared culture.[10] As anthropologist Roger Rouse puts it, in the modern social sciences, community has become "the abstract expression of an idealized nation-state."[11] This romanticized and abstract expression, in turn, does not correspond to the increasing interconnectivity and fluidity generated by globalization and transnationalism.

Due to its problematic assumptions and uses, the concept of community is not very helpful to explore the disjunctive flows and processes that characterize globalization today. As we saw in chapter 1, some migration scholars, including Nina Glick Schiller and Peggy Levitt, have used "transnational social fields" as an alternative analytical tool to understand how individuals and groups manage multiple time-space scales. We saw how transnational social fields are generated out of the evolving intersection of a myriad of personal networks. This chapter follows the lead of these scholars, focusing on interpersonal networks as a way to understand sociability among Brazilians in Broward County, without falling prey to the functionalist weaknesses behind the concept of community, which has been the mainstay of research on Brazilian immigration.

Network analysis has a long and distinguished trajectory in the social sciences,[12] particularly in the sociology of migration.[13] In the study of immigrant religions, the concept of networks is emerging as tool to enrich and critique work on territorially bounded congregations, which has been the dominant paradigm in the field.[14] In this chapter, I do not use the concept of network in its more abstract, mathematical version, nor do I see networks in a functionalist manner, as wholes that automatically bring the social group together. Networks are "open" and "highly dynamic" structures of relationality. They mark relatively stable but always tensile differentials of power, of inclusion and exclusion, of cooperation and conflict, of boundary-crossing and boundary-making. As sociopolitically, culturally, and ecologically embedded relational processes, networks are not only constraining but enabling.[15] Thus, as Barry Wellman and S. D. Berkowitz put it, network analysis allows us to study "processes in terms of patterned interrelationships rather than on the basis of individual essences."[16] Finally, networks are negotiated "phenomenological realities."[17] In other words, meaning and intentionality are not just commodities that circulate alongside social and symbolic capital but are constitutive of the networks themselves.[18]

Using network analysis and drawing from surveys, focus groups and interviews, I argue that, despite the lack of civic organizations, Brazilians in Pompano
Beach and Deerfield Beach sustain a rich sociability. In chapter 6, José Cláudio
Souza Alves describes the more institutionalized expressions of this sociability:
the interacting local, national, and transnational networks anchored on church
and business nodes. Here, I will focus on infrastructural sociability, on the
wealth of mostly informal interpersonal networks that keep Brazilians in
Broward County connected to each other in everyday life. Connections at the
infra-level are not restricted to locality. They stretch transnationally, linking
households, families, and villages in the society of settlement and origin. In fact,
infra-level networks among Brazilians in Broward County constitute an incipient transnational social field.

Given the richness of infrastructural sociability, the lack of visible markers
of community life has to do, at least in the case of Brazilians in Pompano Beach
and Deerfield Beach, with the paucity of bridging spaces and ties between the
more established institutional networks, described by Souza Alves in chapter 6,
and interpersonal networks. In other words, the ideology of disunity, while certainly present in ways that reproduce cultural and social hierarchies brought
from Brazil and thus generate new internal divisions, is strongly conditioned by
the new destination's structural and spatiotemporal dynamics that make it difficult to translate interpersonal relations into collective mobilization.

Before proceeding, a word of caution is in order here. Since the survey was
conducted using the snowball technique, following networks of acquaintances,
the results may have produced a significant bias in the number of friends
reported, showing higher levels of interconnection among Brazilians.[19] This bias
notwithstanding, the fact that there are many vital networks to follow is in itself
an important sign that there is a sociability among Brazilians that has hitherto
been below scholars' radars.

Personal Networks: Sociability at the Crevices

Despite the lack of voluntary associations and the widespread discourse of mistrust and contempt for compatriots, Brazilians in Pompano Beach and Deerfield
Beach sustain a relatively strong sociability, built on relations not just with passing acquaintances but also with (elective) best friends and affinitive relations
(family).[20] When asked, "How many good friends do you have in this city?" more
than half of the respondents (53 percent) indicated that they had at least three
close friends in the city and the average number of close friends was slightly more
than five.[21] In contrast, recent studies have found that over 50 percent of
Americans have no more than two close friends.[22] Brazilians are, then, not particularly isolated. Further, 70 percent of all respondents stated that they did not have
any friends who were not from Brazil. In other words, the Brazilians surveyed build

the majority of their strong friendships with compatriots. Moreover, 67.5 percent of respondents affirmed that they knew none of these friends before coming to the United States. This shows the preponderance of new intra-national ties forged during the immigrant experience.

Household data in the survey shed further light on the personal networks among Brazilians in Broward. In our sample, Brazilians live in households with an average of two and a half rooms. The average number of Brazilians per household was 3.4. That average can be compared with the mean of those living in the same household from the respondent's hometown: 2.0, and with the number of relatives living in the same household: 2.3. In other words, in terms of housing arrangements and the articulation of private space, which we will argue later is central to Brazilians in Broward County, those surveyed strongly tend to live with individuals from the same village or with relatives. This might be an indirect indication of the strength of local-level and family networks.

What are we to make of this data in light of the generalized impression that Brazilians lack a strong sense of community? In a study of East York, a fairly homogeneous working-class and lower-middle-class residential area in Toronto, Canada, Barry Wellman, Peter Carrington, and Alan Hall initially

> expected to see visible, almost palpable communities: neighbors chatting on front porches, friends relaxing on street corners, cousins gathering for Sunday dinners, and storekeepers retailing local gossip. But wherever we looked, we found few signs of active neighborhood life. We eventually realized that we were only seeing part of the picture. We had only been looking for the obvious physical signs of local community—on front porches and street corners—without noticing the more subtle reality of community ties. Although the streets of East York were usually empty, the residents were heavily involved in community networks. They had persons with whom they could visit, commune, share information, and exchange help. Community, like love, is where you find it. East Yorkers were finding it in ties, not in public places.[23]

To get to the nuances of community life that they missed initially, Wellman, Carrington, and Hall posited the notion of "personal communities." They write: "We look for the social essence of community in neither locality nor solidarity, but in the ways in which networks of informal relations fit persons and households into social structures. Our approach focuses attention on the characteristics of 'community ties'—informal links of companionship and aid between individuals—and on the patterns formed by these links."[24]

Could the idea of personal communities explain what we found among Brazilians in Pompano Beach and Deerfield Beach? Are Brazilians engaged in small-scale yet intensive community-building ties that observers like Margolis and Martes may have missed because they are focused primarily on visible and formal associational manifestations? A focus on interpersonal networks rather than on an abstract concept of community does indeed reveal interesting and hitherto unseen dynamics among Brazilians in Broward County. Nevertheless, Wellman, Carrington, and Hall's approach is also flawed. Working under a functionalist, quasi-Durkhemian framework, they assume that interpersonal ties, because they are more intimate (like love), are necessarily cooperative and that, as a result, they automatically build solidarity and community. As Cecilia Menjívar rightly argues, there has been a general tendency in immigration scholarship to concentrate "on depicting a one-dimensional view of immigrant informal networks that focuses exclusively on their positive aspects. Largely absent from portrayals of immigrant social networks is the potential for tension or even dissolution in these ties, which reinforces images of immigrant social ties as excessively cohesive and 'organic.' "[25] According to Menjívar, "the same networks that are supportive at one point can be riddled with conflict at others,"[26] and some of the most exploitative relations occur among close friend or even relatives.[27]

Therefore, the fact that Brazilians in our survey sample are heavily interpersonally linked should not necessarily lead us to conclude that there is a dormant or invisible community in the making. Nevertheless, we should be careful not to "pathologize" the Brazilian immigrant as uniquely anti-communitarian. Internal divisions and relations of exploitation among Brazilians bear strong similarities with Latino groups, such as Salvadorans, Colombians, Dominicans, and Puerto Ricans,[28] despite perceptions among Brazilians that Hispanics are different. In chapter 5, our colleagues working in Immokalee have also found deep inequalities and severe internal exploitation among Mexicans on the basis of time of arrival and legal status. Moreover, similar patterns of co-ethnic or co-national exploitation have been documented among other non-Latino immigrants.[29]

Thus, we should not replace "the romantic, almost idyllic vision of immigrants and their communities"[30] with another type of essentialism: the Brazilian immigrant as *Homo anomicus*.[31] Rather we need to "downplay the assumption of altruism and universal consensus within . . . immigrant institutions in favor of an approach that emphasizes their contingent, shifting nature."[32] In our case, the question is not whether the Brazilian immigrant is overly self-interested and elitist, but under which constellation of cultural, socio-structural, and ecological conditions interpersonal and institutional ties fail to lead to collective action, generate a sense of solidarity, or become exploitative. We will address this question in the next section and conclusion. Now, I would like to touch briefly on the transnational dimension of the interpersonal ties we found.

From the Personal to the Transnational

Like the notion of community, the concept of transnationalism is polyvocal and contested. According to the classic definition in Linda Basch, Nina Glick

Schiller, and Cristina Szanton Blanc's *Nations Unbound*, transnationalism denotes "the processes by which immigrants forge and sustain multi-stranded social relations that link together their societies of origin and settlement. We call these processes transnationalism to emphasize that many immigrants today build social fields that cross geographic, cultural, and political borders."[33] Basch, Glick Schiller, and Szanton Blanc call those immigrants engaged in multiple social relations spanning national borders "transmigrants." They argue that "transmigrants take actions, make decisions, and develop subjectivities and identities embedded in networks of relationships that connect them simultaneously to two or more nation-states."[34]

Chapter 1 offers a more systematic treatment of debates around the concept of transnationalism. For my intents and purposes here, it suffices to say that I agree with Alejandro Portes's cautionary claim that "not all immigrants are 'transmigrants' and claims to the contrary needlessly weaken the validity of empirical findings on the topic. It is more useful to conceptualize transnationalism as one form of economic, political, and cultural adaptation that co-exists with other, more traditional forms."[35] Yet, even with this caveat, we find that the concept of transnationalism is very helpful in highlighting the worldviews and practices of a growing number of immigrants who are bifocal,[36] that is, who keep their feet in their homelands and host societies. Particularly valuable are the concepts of transnational social field, as "an unbounded terrain of interlocking egocentric networks,"[37] and of "social remittances," which Peggy Levitt defines as "the ideas, behaviors, and social capital that flow from receiving to sending communities. They are the tools with which ordinary individuals create global culture at the local context."[38]

Even limiting our definition of transnationalism to cross-national social fields constituted by clusters of interpersonal networks and by flows of remittances, social and otherwise, Brazilians in Broward are significantly engaged in transnational activities. Close to half of those surveyed (49.7 percent) have not traveled to Brazil since they came to the United States, while only 11.0 percent stated that they have visited their home country more than ten times since arriving in the United States. These numbers seem to indicate that, in contrast to what might be expected of wealthy Brazilians in Miami, only a small, relatively cosmopolitan elite of Brazilians in Pompano Beach and Deerfield Beach has the facility to move across national borders. Transnationalism, however, is not just about physical movement from country of origin to that of settlement.

Indeed, the great majority of the Brazilian population in Broward maintains close connections with Brazil through other means. Seventy-one percent of our respondents phone Brazil at least once a week, taking advantage of inexpensive calling cards widely available in various Brazilian commercial establishments. Further, 46 percent stated that they send e-mails to Brazil at least once a week. Here, Brazilians in Pompano and Deerfield appear to evince a digital gap similar to that in mainstream United States. More significantly, 60 percent of our respondents send remittances at least once a month. Fifty-seven percent sent between \$1 and \$250 per month. Slightly more than 86 percent send their remittances through Brazilian agencies, while 85 percent of those remittances go to families back home, once again indicating that Brazilians draw from their own networks to circulate goods and capital from household to household, across national borders. Other important indexes of simultaneous embeddedness in our sample include the following:

43.4 percent receive news about Brazil from Brazilian friends frequently or very frequently;

38.0 percent read Brazilian newspapers frequently or very frequently;

35.1 percent read news about Brazil from the Internet frequently or very frequently;

31.3 percent watch Brazilian TV frequently or very frequently;

27.8 percent receive news about Brazil from their churches; and

21.6 percent attend events organized by people coming from Brazil specifically for the event

The following exchange during an in-depth interview with an evangelical pastor gives a qualitative flavor to these indexes:

INT: Do you always stay in touch with Brazil?

RES: Yes, at the end of the week . . . I sometimes, when there is a need, but there is always a need, so I call. . . . I have family in Brazil, my cousins, other relatives.

INT: Brothers and Sisters?

RES: Yes, recently I had to get in touch for a bad reason. I lost a nephew, so, one of the advantages is that I could help, help my nephew's family.

INT: Did you send financial aid?

RES: I sent financial aid to take care of the wake and to pay all related things.

INT: Do you send financial aid to your family?

RES: Yes, I usually do, because we know how things are in Brazil . . .

INT: And do you stay in touch through the phone?

RES: Yes.

INT: And the Internet?

RES: Internet is more to stay in touch with my friends. I send them faxes, e-mail . . .

INT: E-mail? You know a bit about that world? It is cheaper . . .

RES: Yes, it is and it is very fast. You send a message and it is there right away.

INT: Telephone calls are more expensive . . .

RES: Yes, but here phone calls are also cheap. With $5 you can talk two hours with folks in Brazil.

Thus, the respondents in our sample are actively involved with their country of origin, preferring ego-centric networks of friends to keep in touch.[39] In the forging of a transnational social field at the everyday level, institutions such as churches do not seem to play the most significant roles.[40] Also, public events organized to host visiting Brazilians do not appear to be as central in the transnational flows. These observations point once again to the gap between a rich sociability at the level of everyday life and the existence of visible organizational forms. The question is, What sociocultural and ecological conditions have conditioned this gap?

Space and the Limits to Associational Life

In her study of social relations in African American enclaves, Patricia Fernandez-Kelly found that the relative viability and effectiveness of networks are affected by the socioeconomical and spatiotemporal contexts in which they are embedded. According to her, "the form and effect of cultural and social capital are defined [among other things] by physical vectors, such as the characteristics of urban space." She continues: "Because people derive their knowledge from the physical spaces where they live, they also anticipate that which is probable in their nearby environment, and they recognize as reality that which is defined as such by members of their interpersonal network occupying proximate spheres of intimacy. For that reason, social and cultural capital are *toponomical*, that is dependent on physical and social location."[41] Fernandez-Kelly's insight is, of course, not entirely new. As Mustafa Emirbayer and Jeff Goodwin note, it builds on the Chicago school's pioneering work, which construed all social facts as "*ecologically embedded* within specific contexts of time and space— that is to say, within particular *interactional fields* composed of concrete, historically specific 'natural areas' and 'natural histories.' "[42]

Space and time matter greatly for Brazilians in Broward County. They are generally not concentrated in particular neighborhoods or even in a territorially bounded locality. Rather, they are spread out over an approximately forty-mile-long corridor that extends from Boca Raton to Hollywood. This is essentially a sprawling exurban cartography built around the logic of the car, with long and busy thoroughfares linking scattered large shopping malls and gated communities. Such a landscape stands in sharp contrast to hometown geographies in Brazil, which are usually built around heavily populated neighborhoods that mix residences, stores, restaurants, and public space. In fact, these neighborhoods are normally anchored around public spaces like plazas, parks, and beaches. In South Florida, even beaches which could serve as shared spaces are deeply segregated, many of them in private hands. Broward County's wide avenues more often than not have no sidewalks, forcing people to drive for even short distances. Moreover, public transportation is generally inadequate and inconvenient, compelling most Brazilians to own cars, despite the difficulty of obtaining and renewing driver's licenses for undocumented immigrants.

The landscape in Broward is also radically different from that faced by other Brazilians in the United States. For example, in Newark, New Jersey, Brazilians are heavily concentrated in Ironbound, an area previously mapped out by Portuguese immigrants. Newark is a traditional industrial city divided into organic neighborhoods of row houses with a well-defined town center. This town center is full of businesses, restaurants, and churches owned by Brazilians. It is not surprising, thus, to hear Portuguese in the streets, as people gather around to chat about the neighborhood or Brazil. In New York City, although the Brazilian population is fairly dispersed, there is at least access to an extensive system of public transportation that allows people to keep in touch with each other. Also, there are well-established ethnic and immigrant neighborhoods, like Astoria and Long Island City in Queens, where there are concentrated pockets of Brazilians serving as anchors for newcomers. Finally, in the Boston area, Brazilians have concentrated in relatively small towns at the periphery of the city, such as Somerville and Framingham, where they have gradually built dense networks around not only churches and businesses but also civic and cultural organizations. Here we have to keep in mind that migration to the Boston area is at least a decade older than that to the Broward County region. As we know, social networks are strongly affected by the length of residency.[43]

Thus, in comparison to other destinations, Broward's topography makes it particularly difficult for Brazilians to build connectivity across distances and public spaces, contributing to the lack of traditional markers of community life. As one of our informants put it:

> The way of life of Brazilians up there [in Boston and New York] is very different to what we have here in Florida. And one of the reasons is the ease which one has up there to make connections, your own network, to find your people and easy work. Today it is a little more difficult because jobs are becoming scarce, but it is easier there for someone coming from Brazil with a go-get it mentality [*mentalidade de fazer o pe de meia e ir embora*]. The north is much more attractive than Florida. And another thing is the means of transportation in Boston or Massachusetts. I worked in Boston for almost four years without needing a car because I lived close to a train station. I walked to the station and caught the bus that took me to the airport where I worked. So, in about five minutes I was

at the airport. In Boston, you can go any place by train or bus, and here if you don't have a car, you go nowhere.

Social interaction is also affected by work schedules. Survey respondents told us that they work an average of 43.3 hours per week. However, 48 percent of our respondents indicated that they work more than 40 hours per week, and 17 percent work more than 60 hours.[44] With Brazilians often working multiple jobs six days a week, the only opportunity to visit public spaces where they can relax and interact affectively with other compatriots comes during lunch or on Saturdays and Sundays. In fact, close to 40 percent of our respondents stated that the main places where they go to "have fun" are private establishments like bars, restaurants, discos, and small shopping malls, most of which are owned by Brazilians. In other words, in comparison to interpersonal networks, reciprocal exchanges in Brazilian public spaces, including churches, tend to be of low frequency and duration, even though these spaces are built in the immigrant's life world. The low frequency and duration of the exchanges, in turn, may explain why Brazilians seek spaces highly charged with affective energy, such as Pentecostal and charismatic churches. In these churches, exchanges might be restricted to weekends, but they are charged with great emotional intensity, an intensity that may serve as a break from or a catharsis for the routine and pressures of everyday life.

Religion and the Management of Lived Spaces

Brazilians try to cope with Broward's de-centered geography, the lack of established immigrant networks, their busy schedules, and the newness of their immigration through a variety of ways. I have already hinted at one: they draw from their religious resources to come together and carve out meaningful lived spaces and cogent individual and collective identities. More specifically, for a recently arrived population in an alien, even hostile environment, churches and, more generally, congregations of various types serve as social spaces for recreation and emotional support. Two of our informants articulate this function well:

> Here in our center, we eat together, we play [*a gente brinca*], socialize [*confraterniza*], and get involved with other Brazilians. It is where I can practice [the charity and philosophy of life] what I'm learning. (Spiritist man, 2003)
>
> The Brazilian church has been a channel; it is as if through it people enjoy [*sentir mais prazer*] being here more. Because before [coming to church] it was as if one was isolated, as if one was in a foreign land. Now, no, everybody feels at ease [*mais à vontade*]. And then one begins to feel good. (Catholic woman, 2003)

Churches also provide a space for the collective affirmation of national identity, making it possible for Brazilians to relate to the sacred through their mother tongue and autochthonous rituals. As a Brazilian Catholic bishop in Newark, New Jersey, told us, "There are things that can only be done in one's mother tongue, for example praying. Brazilians have the right to be able to pray in Portuguese." More generally, religion provides interpretive frameworks in the form of narratives, tropes, or symbols, to make sense of the process of migration and build the self in close relation with the power of the sacred.

> I did not have anyone to rely on: my childhood friends, my family, or the certainty [*segurança*] of being in my own country. Well, I thought, now I can only rely on God. I have to hold on to Him to be able to keep going. And so once I saw myself alone in an ocean, shipwrecked, and He was my only life raft. (Catholic man, 2004)
>
> Logically, religion helps. This is particularly true when people participate in Spiritism. . . . People understand ideas, achieve a high morality and become more balanced, more motivated. One then contributes not just for the other [*o próximo*] through charity but even in one's own professional work. (Spiritist man, 2002)

These two quotes show the different ways in which Brazilians draw from their religious traditions to understand their immigration experiences. The Catholic man uses metaphors common to charismatics, who place a strong emphasis on the emotive aspects of religion. He uses tropes that portray the migration process as a tempest and stress the importance of an intense personal relationship with God. Amidst all the chaos, human agency is frail; only God is powerful, stable, and reliable enough. In contrast, the Spiritist man conceives of the migration process as a stage in the process of individual intellectual and moral development, a process that gives him the chance to be charitable to others and thus to benefit from the positive karma of good works. Very much in sync with Spiritism's emphasis on a rational approach to the world, our informant knows that, with the right attitude, he can control his fate.

Taken together, these testimonies demonstrate that networks and the flows that accompany them are phenomenological realities, that they are closely intertwined with what historian Amy DeRogatis calls "maps of piety" and moral behavior, which chart meaning, volition, emotion, and practice onto the socioecological spaces.[45] If "every story is a travel story—a spatial practice," as Michel de Certeau claims, then, religion, with its compelling tales of spiritual and moral quest—narratives of salvation, redemption, conversion, pilgrimage, healing, and fate—is a particularly crucial repository of resources for immigrants to create and manage lived spaces.[46]

Further, the testimonies resonate with Martes's findings among Brazilians in south Boston. There she found that churches are a "safe space of sociability" (*espaço seguro de sociabilidade*). According to Martes, "the main motivation for Brazilians to attend churches of any [denomination] is that they believe that they can find in them a space characterized by solidarity, trust, and mutual help. Put in other words, Brazilian immigrants seek churches in Massachusetts primarily because they want to socialize."[47] She elaborates, "The welcoming environment of churches stands in contrast to the situation experience 'out there,' which is perceived as competitive and with low solidarity and community spirit."[48] In Broward County's sprawling and hostile environment, the role of churches as safe spaces of sociability is even more crucial. This fact may help explain the built religious geography of the area. Brazilian congregations are distributed as "pearls in a string," as nodes strung along the main thoroughfares, such as Federal Highway, Atlantic Boulevard, and Sample Road, where people can access them with relative ease and where they mark a sharp (spiritual if not architectural) break with the undifferentiated exurban ecology.

However, we should be careful not to romanticize the role of churches, for they also respond in contradictory ways to the spatiotemporal context. Particularly in the case of some evangelical Protestant churches, the strategy to deal with demographic dispersion and busy work schedules is, paradoxically, to raise admission and affiliation standards sharply, demanding more commitment, sacrifice, and loyalty from practitioners in exchange for a more affectively charged and doctrinally certain social experience. Such a strategy raises the issue of internal "social control" and "a polarization between solidarity (within) and competition (without)," which is not necessarily conducive to the formation of community across religious affiliation.[49] Furthermore, as Souza Alves's discussion of the intersection of business and religious networks shows in chapter 6, as part of the immigrant mode of production, churches are also susceptible to the commodification of social relations and economic exploitation. Pastors may minister to their storefront congregations on Saturday night, while during the week they may oversee some of the faithful in the roofing companies or car dealerships they own. Often this blurring of the sacred-profane distinction is accompanied by a gospel of health and wealth that finds no contradiction between faith and success in attaining a piece of the American dream. In a particularly striking example of this ethos, we observed a pastor preach to the congregation about his green card, his new car in the parking lot, and his big beautiful house, all of which he affirmed he achieved through his faith and hard work. He asked the congregation to follow his example and contribute to his church to gain all of God's blessing. Such a case may be extreme. However, it points to the need not to separate automatically business and religious networks. Religious networks often act not only to provide moral sanction to certain types of economic activities, as Max Weber would argue, but also to serve as business relays themselves.

Churches and congregations are, however, not the only or even the main strategy that Brazilians use to negotiate their reality in Broward County. Despite the significant public role of churches, our informants' primary response to the spatiotemporal setting which they face is to retreat to the private space of the home. Eighty-four percent of the respondents to our survey indicated that the place in which they feel most comfortable in the city is their homes. Churches came a distant second with only 9 percent of the respondents selecting them as the place in which they feel most comfortable (the third option was a generic "public places" category with only 4 percent). The percentages are almost the same for men and women. Brazilians revealed some of the reasons for preferring their homes in the focus groups:

> Life here is very tumultuous. There are times when one has to do a thousand things during the day and [then] one returns home, takes off one's shoes, takes a bath, and goes to heaven [esta no ceu]. For me my home is that; it is a place of peace, where the running ceases. Despite the fact that with all the household chores, one does not stop, I know I'm in my place and I disconnect myself. I try to disconnect myself from the world because it is my time to rest. My home is the only place where I can sleep and I love to sleep. (Catholic woman, 2004)

> First, I like to stay at home more because I believe that here people stay out too much, too many hours outside of home. Everyone works and people spend too little time with the family. Then, my second place is the church, because it is home-church and church-home. And this ends up stressing people a bit because we also need to go to other environments [ambientes], to go to a park, or the beach, to go to a place where you have different people, because we stay a lot at home. On Sunday we go to church and that would be the day we would also stay at home, because on the other days, we work the whole day, from Monday to Saturday. My husband works until Saturday also and then usually we go to church on Sunday and then return home. (Catholic woman, 2003)

> The thing about home, that is a thing about fear. It is more comfortable to be in one's own ghetto, where you know all things, every reality. There you have control over the situation, but if you go out, you are going into the unknown, right? Just imagine those who don't have any knowledge, those who are undocumented, those who don't have any future [perspectiva] and fear anything that may happen to them; for them the move is to enclose themselves [se fechar] and to exaggerate what you hear. Like once in a while we hear [immigration] is having a dragnet [uma batida] there in Pompano. (Protestant woman, 2003)

In the hostile exurban ecology of Broward County, affective life among Brazilian immigrants is strongly concentrated in the proximate sphere of intimacy. Against the centripetal forces they confront, Brazilians counterpose the most powerful trope of intimacy they can draw from their cultural tool kit: the idea of home (*o lar*).[50] Some of our informants build stable spaces of safety, intimacy, and meaning by mapping the homeland into their homes in Florida. A member of a Brazilian Baptist church told us in no uncertain terms: "Here inside my house is a piece of Brazil. When you come in you see the Brazilian flag." Others effectively fuse domestic and religious spaces into one, turning the home into a sacred space against the dangerous and profane outside world. They also elevate and extend the meaning of family to include the tight interpersonal networks they have built in South Florida. As a Brazilian evangelical Protestant stated in a focus group, "Those who don't have families here have the church, which is our family. Our friends here are our relatives here. They are the ones on whom we can rely." This emotive extension of the domestic space and family relations into the church is also evident among Catholics. Angela, a member of Nossa Senhora Aparecida Mission, told us, "Church is like my mother's house, a safe port, a place where you go to get support [*onde você vai para se apoiar*]." To the extent that churches function effectively, then, it may be as extensions of the relations and experiences anchored at home.

In one of the classics of Brazilian anthropology, *O que faz o Brasil, Brasil*, Roberto DaMatta writes about the tension between home and street (*a casa e a rua*). According to him, "there is a clear division between two fundamental spaces in Brazilian social life." On the one hand, there is the street, a "place of work, movement, surprise, and temptation," an often unforgiving space of "struggle [*luta*]" characterized by the constant flux of "undifferentiated and unknown individuals." On the other hand, there is home, the realm of "peace and tranquility." "At home we are members of a family and of a self-contained group with clearly defined borders and limits."[51] DaMatta takes an essentialist view of Brazilian culture, seeing it as a self-contained totality that can be decoded once and for all and then compared and contrasted with the cultures of the United States or India. Nevertheless, we do not have to subscribe to this cultural holism or to his methodological nationalism to recognize that he has identified an enduring organizing trope for Brazilians.[52]

Confronting the harsh reality of Broward County, Brazilians deploy the duality of home and street as a key interpretive framework. This hermeneutic device allows them to carve spaces of meaning and self-centering in response to the profound dispersion and dislocation they encounter in South Florida. Faced with invisibility and marginality in Broward, Brazilians sacralize home.[53] Angela, a Catholic, describes how she and her family looked for a house when they were settling down in Broward. She prayed to God to help her find the right place. When they finally found and bought the house, a miracle took place:

> Before going in we prayed a Holy Father and Hail Mary, asking Mary to bless and protect us. And you know that when I went in the house, it was completely empty but there were two statues of Mary and a cross which

had the following message: "I and my household always serve the Lord."
I didn't ask Him specifically to give me something like, "I chose this
house for you." "You came because I need you here; you came to serve
me." Today one [statue] of Our Lady is in the same place, in the bathroom
that the children use, and the cross is in the garage with the other statue,
where my husband works, in the same spot where they were. Didn't I ask
for a sign [uma prova]?

DaMatta has argued that for Brazilians home "is not just a physical space,
but a moral one: a sphere where we fulfill ourselves as human beings with a
physical body but also with a moral and social dimension. At home we are
unique and irreplaceable [insubstituíveis]."[54] As Angela's case shows, in diaspora,
this physical-moral space becomes super-charged with religious symbolism,
nostalgia, memory, longing for recognition, and lost intimacy. The collective
energy behind the super-charged notion of home then spills into churches,
domesticating them as it were, transforming them into a distended and protective domestic space across a hostile landscape.

Still, as it is the case with the social role of churches and with the notion of
communities, we need to be careful not to adopt an idealized vision of home.
Brazilians themselves know that their domestic life in Broward stands in tension
with their "real" and imagined homes in Brazil. For example, very often Brazilians
in Broward County are forced to live in crowded apartments, where no one
knows each other and everybody works all the time. As in the case of Mexican
and Guatemalan immigrants discussed in chapter 8, in situations like these, the
"home" in Florida becomes a space of alienation and mistrust, the antithesis of
the remembered home in Brazil. According to an informant: "Many immigrants
live on their own and often share an apartment with other Brazilians. Sometimes,
five or six live in a two-bedroom apartment, all adults who are here just to work,
and then they become totally alienated." Yet another told us: "In Brazil my home
space was literally different from the one here, because there I had my family. . . .
Here I felt very strange when I fell into a house in which everyone was different.
In Brazil, I loved to be with my family on those days I stayed home, since we are
very close to each other. So, it felt weird here."

Further, the construction of home in the country of origin, as well as in the
country of settlement, is gender specific. Brazilian women feel particularly
ambivalent about the multiple homes they imagine and inhabit. Lara, a Spiritist
who came to the United States in 1984, has images of Brazil, and particularly of
her city in Minas Gerais, as "violent and disorganized." She also has negative
memories of domestic life in Brazil.

I saw that my husband thought that he had the right to do everything he
wanted and I didn't have that right. I had to stay at home, being pretty,
taking care of the children. I worked the entire week. I helped with

household expenses and at the end of the week I wasn't part of his plans, to be able to go out and have fun with the children. So, there was discrimination and he started to go out only with his friends to drink, to parties, plus he began to plan trips alone. So, I experienced it firsthand [*o senti na pele*]. Only he had the rights and the responsibilities were mine.

In contrast, having become a U.S. citizen, she feels "much freer" in Florida, since "a woman of any age can take her car and go visit her friends, have breakfast or lunch together. She can go play golf, or tennis, or cards. Women have activities, so the lifestyle here is very different from Brazil." Besides, in Florida she feels safe: "I don't have to worry about my purse. How many times I forgot my wallet inside my car, left there overnight, and the next morning it was still there. I never had a problem with violence. It is true that it exists, but I never was a victim." Still, she "dreams" to be able one day to spend half a year in Brazil and the other half in the United States.

Home, therefore, is a conflictive space. However, even with this caveat, the point remains that for Brazilians in South Florida home is a powerful organizing trope, charged with familiarity and emotion. Brazilians in Broward County pull back into proximate spaces of intimacy and build networks outwards, connecting families and households to their places of origin, to relatives and friends left behind, and only tentatively to local networks like churches, which resonate with the affective charge that is part and parcel of their ideals of home. This defensive modus operandi is a creative attempt to make "virtue out of necessity," to invent within limits, as Pierre Bourdieu puts it.[55] However, homemaking may also have the unintended consequence of widening the gap between rich inter-personal networks and more formal networks like those built around business and labor.

Conclusion: Beyond *Homo Anomicus*

In this chapter, I drew from fieldwork among Brazilians in Broward County to offer a new angle in the ongoing debate of whether Brazilians do and can form collective identity and community. I identified some of the same structural constraints uncovered by Margolis in her pioneering work on Brazilians in New York City: namely, the lack of distinctive physical areas inhabited by Brazilians, the scarcity of economic capital to form a large business class, and the busy work schedules that allow the flow of remittances back to Brazil but discourage local involvement beyond the private sphere. However, through the use of the analytical tool of networks, I tried to avoid some of the pitfalls of the concept of community as it has been applied to the Brazilian immigrant experience in the United States. Although "community" is an emic term, one that is used by the migrants themselves to express their frustrations and longings, it obscures the complexity and diversity of the forms of sociability sustained by Brazilian immigrants in Pompano Beach and Deerfield Beach. Precisely because it is emic, the category of community carries a whole set of unreflected normative assumptions of what a real community should be: community as characterized teleologically, as a set of visible goals that if not present indicate a social pathology that is almost impossible to remedy.

The focus on networks, in contrast, tries to meet immigrants where they are, understanding sociability as processual, non-teleological, and contextual (at times expressing simultaneously cooperation and conflict). The study of networks allows us to see interaction and everyday practice in their own right, not subsumed under the functionalism and methodological holism that the notions of community and collective identity entail. In other words, although many times social interaction and collective identity go hand in hand, they are not automatically synonymous, such that the lack of visible markers of communal life necessarily implies that there is no social intercourse. To paraphrase Wellman, Carrington, and Hall, social connectivity, like love, is where you find it, warts and all.

The one-sided attention to community or lack thereof has often been accompanied by culturalist explanations of the perceived lack of community cohesion among Brazilians. Margolis, for example, highlights a pervasive ideology of disunity among Brazilians, as well as the denial by Brazilians of their immigrant status and their class-based or region-based contempt for each other, among her key explanatory variables. To deny that these ideological patterns are significant would be plainly wrong, for we found some of the same prejudicial attitudes among many Brazilians in Broward County. However, without a rigorous contextualization, culturalist explanations run the risk of essentializing Brazilian immigrants.[56] At their best, explanations that focus on the contradictory cultural patterns that Brazilians bring to their societies of settlement serve to demythologize overly romanticized understandings of the immigrant identities and experiences. At worst, these kinds of culturalist explanations end up creating another kind of stereotype: that among immigrants, particularly vis-à-vis Latinos, Brazilians are uniquely *Homo anomicus*. Because it resonates with some of the experiences of the immigrants themselves, this stereotype then becomes part of their discursive universe. In this sense, scholars of Brazilian migration and Brazilian immigrants have engaged in an exercise of self-fulfilling prophecy.[57] They are mutually implicated in the creation of a certain view of the Brazilians in diaspora, which, while containing some elements of truth, has become a conceptual and political straightjacket. By focusing on networks, we can break this straightjacket and gain a fine-grained understanding of the structural, ecological, and relational contexts in which ideologies of exclusion and hierarchical order operate.

To the extent that we can generalize from a small snowball survey and in-depth qualitative research, the problem of solidarity among Brazilians in

Pompano Beach and Deerfield Beach is primarily a case of social network truncation generated by the toponomical constraints of a new destination. Borrowing from Robert Putnam's recent research on the impact of immigration on social solidarity, the failure to produce bridging civic institutions may have to do with the newness of Brazilian migration to Broward County. According to Putnam, in the short term, immigration and cultural diversity tend to produce social fragmentation, as all groups involved "hunker down" and form enclaves. Only through long-term cross-cutting interactions in common public spaces can a more "capacious we" that encompasses both immigrants and natives emerge.[58] For Brazilians in Pompano Beach and Deerfield Beach, as for the other groups we have studied, the long-term process of integration will very likely be affected by the increasing anti-immigrant climate at the national and local levels, which is compelling immigrants to retreat to their protective private spaces of livelihood and to rely more than ever on their personal networks.

If the lack of a tangible sense of community among Brazilians in Pompano and Deerfield is powerfully shaped by structural factors, which are mediated by ideational elements, the question then is how to resolve the problem. How can we encourage collective solidarity and mobilization among Brazilian immigrants? I have tried to show that religious resources play a significant role for new immigrants in nontraditional contexts of settlement. Particularly in the climate of resurgent nativism following September 11, 2001, religion may be crucial for recently arrived immigrants to carve out meaningful lived spaces and identities in the crevices of a society that is increasingly criminalizing them, representing them as "illegal aliens" and "lawbreakers." Religion might be helping immigrants negotiate the tension between visibility and invisibility, making them visible to each other in protective interpersonal spaces at a time when their survival and well-being is more and more predicated on their invisibility to the larger society. Whether the protective affective spaces of religion will remain inward-looking or will eventually become spaces of collective empowerment—whether they will become "heavens," not just "havens," as Manuel Castells puts it in relation to social movements in the "network society"—is an open question.[59]

We saw that, among Brazilians in South Florida, churches and congregations do indeed tap into the affective, axiological, and relational resources concentrated in the protected private sphere. Despite clear contradictions, churches have a good potential for strengthening bridging social action. According to Robert Putman, "faith communities in which people worship together are arguably the single most important repository of social capital in America." They are "an important incubator for civic skills, civic norms, community interests, and civic recruitment."[60] Sociologist David Smilde argues that in Latin America religious movements such as evangelical Christianity can function as transnational "popular publics," "intentionally organized relational context[s] in which a specific network of people from popular classes seek to bridge to other networks, form coalitions, and expand the influence of its discourses."[61]

Whether religion among Brazilians in Broward County can contribute to the rise of popular publics will depend on the theologies and pastoral approaches developed by immigrant churches, particularly on how they explain and address the situation of immigrants in religious terms. Trends in the religious field in Brazil (and in Latin America, for that matter) do not give reason for optimism. In the 1970s and 1980s the Brazilian Catholic Church adopted a strong liberationist approach that stressed social justice and grassroots empowerment. Such an approach would dovetail nicely with efforts to build popular publics among immigrants in South Florida. However, today, this liberationist perspective shares the stage with the growing Charismatic Renewal Movement, which tends to take a more emotive, personalistic, and otherworldly pastoral style. Whether liberationist and charismatic modalities of Catholicism stand in tension with each other or cross-fertilize and, thus, strengthen each other depends ultimately on the priests' leadership. We found both currents very much alive among Brazilians in Broward, operating more or less independently of each other.

Dynamics within the Catholic Church intersect with the increasing influence of neo-Pentecostalism among Protestant circles. This Pentecostalism works with a gospel of health and wealth that, while strongly this-worldly, may discourage a holistic approach to self and society because it stresses the power of faith to achieve personal success and well-being.

Despite trends in the religious field that may not be conducive to strengthening social action among immigrants, there are hopeful signs of the positive role that churches can play for Brazilians in Broward County. For example, as Souza Alves demonstrates in chapter 6, Nossa Senhora Aparecida Catholic Mission has a strong social outreach program, which is linked with the Scalabrinis and the transnational "pastoral do imigrante," supported by the Brazilian Conference of Catholic Bishops (CNBB). The Brazilian Baptist Church has also been at the forefront of the Associação de Pastores, working to collect signatures in opposition to draconian immigration reform proposals in Congress. As researchers concerned with the dire plight of immigrants post-9/11, it behooves us not to reproduce unreflectively discourses about the lack of community. Instead, we must generate rigorous analytical work on the complexity and ambivalence of social action in multiple spatiotemporal scales. Hopefully, this work will spur new kinds of social outreach and network formation.

NOTES

1. Ana Cristina Martes, *Brasileiros nos Estados Unidos: Um estudo sobre imigrantes em Massachusetts* (São Paulo: Paz e Terra, 2000); Maxine Margolis, *Little Brazil: An Ethnography of Brazilian Immigrants in New York City* (Princeton: Princeton University Press, 1994); Teresa Sales, *Brasileiros longe de casa* (São Paulo: Editora Cortês, 1999).

2. Margolis, *Little Brazil*, 196.

3. Martes, *Brasileiros nos Estados Unidos*, 24–25.

4. Ibid., 27.

5. Maxine Margolis, "Na virada do milênio: A emigração brasileira para os Estados Unidos," in *Fronteiras cruzadas: Etnicidade, gênero e redes sociais*, ed. Ana Cristina Martes and Sorava Fleischer, 51–72 (São Paulo: Paz e Terra, 2003).

6. As stated in chapter 1, it was not possible to conduct a random survey of Brazilians in Broward County. Instead, we relied on the snowball technique. Thus, survey results should not be seen as representative of the entire universe. However, they identify certain significant patterns, which we cross-checked with other data derived from qualitative methods such as participant observation, interviewing, and focus groups.

7. Identification of community needs varied by gender: 22.5 percent of male respondents chose group solidarity as the most important need, the same percentage that selected legalization of immigrant status. For women, in contrast, group solidarity came in third place (with 14.9 percent), behind 16.1 percent for family and psychological counseling, and 21.8 percent who indicated that the most important need is adequate health care and medical assistance. During the interviewing process women consistently affirmed that, despite the hectic schedules and long distances, they did not lack meaningful friendships. However, they felt that pressure to ensure the well-being of their families fell disproportionately on them. This may explain why a higher percentage of them selected family and psychological counseling and health care as the most important community need.

8. Anthony Cohen, *The Symbolic Construction of Community* (New York: Routledge, 1995).

9. David Kirp, *Almost Home: America's Love-Hate Relationship with Community* (Princeton: Princeton University Press, 2000), 6.

10. See Ferdinand Tonnies, *Community and Society* (Edison, NJ: Transaction Publishers, 1988). He writes that community (*Gemeinschaft*) is characterized by a "reciprocal, binding sentiment as a peculiar will," an "understanding (consensus). It represents the special social force and sympathy which keeps human beings together as members of a totality" (47). In contrast, in society (*Gesellschaft*), "everybody is by himself and isolated, and there exists a condition of tension against all others. Their spheres of activity and power are sharply separated, so that everybody refuses to everyone else contact with and admittance to his sphere" (65).

11. Roger Rouse, "Mexican Migration and the Space of Postmodernism," *Diaspora* 1, no. 1 (1991): 8–23.

12. Barry Wellman and S. D. Berkowitz, eds., *Social Structures: A Network Approach* (Cambridge: Cambridge University Press, 1988); J. Clyde Mitchell, *Social Networks in Urban Situations* (Manchester: Manchester University Press, 1969); Mark Granovetter, "The Strength of Weak Ties," *American Journal of Sociology* 78, no. 6 (1973): 1360–1380.

13. Alejandro Portes, ed., *The Economic Sociology of Immigration* (New York: Russell Sage Foundation, 1995); Caroline Bretell and James Hollifield, *Migration Theory: Talking across Disciplines* (London: Rutledge, 2000); Cecilia Menjívar, *Fragmented Ties: Salvadoran Immigrant Networks in America* (Berkeley: University of California Press, 2000); Jacqueline Hagan, "Social Networks, Gender and Immigrant Incorporation: Resources and Constraints," *American Sociological Review* 63 (1998): 55–67; Monica Boyd, "Family and Personal Networks in International Migration: Recent Developments and New Agendas," *International Migration Review* 23, no. 3 (1989): 638–670; Steven Vertovec, "Migration and Other Modes of Transnationalism: Towards Conceptual Cross-Fertilization." *International Migration Review* 37, no. 3 (2003): 641–665.

14. Helen Rose Ebaugh and Janet Chafetz, *Religion across Borders: Transnational Immigrant Networks* (Walnut Creek, CA: AltaMira Press, 2002); Manuel A. Vásquez and Marie Friedmann Marquardt, *Globalizing the Sacred: Religion across the Americas* (New Brunswick, NJ: Rutgers University Press, 2003).

15. Peter Dicken et al, "Chains and Networks, Territories and Scales: Towards a Relational Framework for Analyzing the Global Economy," *Global Networks* 1, no. 2 (2001): 89–112.

16. Wellman and Berkowitz, *Social Structures*, 4.

17. Harrison White, *Identity and Control* (Princeton: Princeton University Press, 1992).

18. Mustafa Emirbayer and Jeff Goodwin, "Network Analysis, Culture, and the Problems of Agency," *American Journal of Sociology* 99, no. 6 (1994): 1411–1454; Robert Fishman, *Democracy's Voices: Social Ties and the Quality of Public Life in Spain* (Ithaca, NY: Cornell University Press, 2004).

19. As we saw in the introduction, Portes has criticized the transnationalism literature for a similar "sampling on the dependent variable." This criticism certainly helps us avoid making the faulty claim that transnationalism is the new paradigmatic mode of livelihood among immigrants. Nevertheless, foregrounding a phenomenon that has been ignored by dominant approaches can open new epistemological spaces. Alejandro Portes, "The Debates and Significance of Immigrant Transnationalism," *Global Networks* 1 (July 2001): 182–183.

20. Alain Degenne and Michel Forse, *Introducing Social Networks* (London: Sage, 1999).

21. The average number of good friends in the city for men was six, whereas for women it was slightly less than five. Normally, we would expect women to have more dense interpersonal networks, but perhaps the process of migration transforms men's sociability.

22. See Miller McGherson, Lynn Smith-Lovin, and Matthew E. Brashears, "Social Isolation in America: Changes in Core Discussion Networks over Two Decades," *American Sociological Review* 71 (2006): 353–375.

23. Barry Wellman, Peter Carrington, and Alan Hall, "Networks as Personal Communities," in *Social Structures*, ed. Wellman and Berkowitz, 130–131.

24. Ibid., 131.

25. Menjívar, *Fragmented Ties*, 33.

26. Ibid., 234.

27. Eduardo Guarnizo, Ignacio Sanchez, and E. M. Roach, "Mistrust, Fragmented Solidarity, and Transnational Migration: Colombians in New York City and Los Angeles," *Ethnic and Racial Studies* 22 (1999): 367–395; Sarah Mahler, *American Dreaming: Immigrant Life on the Margins* (Berkeley: University of California Press, 1995).

28. David Kyle, *Transnational Peasants: Migration, Networks, and Ethnicity in Andean Ecuador* (Baltimore: Johns Hopkins University Press, 2000); Mahler, *American Dreaming*; Patricia Pessar, "Sweatshop Workers and Domestic Ideologies: Dominican Women in New York's Apparel Industry," *International Journal of Urban and Regional Research* 18, no. 1 (1994): 127–142.

29. Howard Aldrich and Roger Waldinger, "Ethnicity and Entrepreneurship," *Annual Review of Sociology* 16 (1990): 111–135; Peter Li, "Occupational Achievement and Kinship Achievement among Chinese Immigrants in Chicago," *Sociological Quarterly* 18 (1977): 478–489.

30. Martes, *Brasilieros nos Estados Unidos*, 26.

31. *Homo anomicus*—the term "anomie" was first used by Emile Durkheim to characterize the breakdown of social norms connected with increasing social differentiation and specialization. More specifically, anomie refers to modern society's failure to integrate

the individual into its binding collective representations. The anomic individual is thus bereft of strong social ties and lacks a sense of belonging and collective identity.

32. Menjívar, *Fragmented Ties*, 116.

33. Linda Basch, Nina Glick Schiller, and Cristina Szanton-Blanc, *Nations Unbound: Transnational Projects, Postcolonial Predicaments, and Deterritorialized Nation-States* (New York: Gordon and Breach, 1994), 7.

34. Ibid.

35. Alejandro Portes, "Introduction: The Debates and Significance of Immigrant Transnationalism," *Global Networks* I, no. 3 (2001): 181–193.

36. Rouse, "Mexican Migration and the Space of Postmodernism."

37. Nina Glick Schiller, "Transmigrants and Nation-States: Something Old and Something New in the U.S. Experience," in *Handbook of International Migration*, ed. Charles Hirshman et al. (New York: Russell Sage Foundation, 1999), 97.

38. Peggy Levitt, "Transnational Migration: Taking Stock and Future Directions." *Global Networks* I, no. 3 (2001): 181–193.

39. The activities described above stand in the middle of a continuum between what Levitt calls "core transnationalism"—regular and well-institutionalized practices that are "an integral part of the individual's life"—and "expanded transnationalism," which refers to occasional activities in response to crises. Ibid.

40. Peterson and Vásquez found a similarly vibrant "grassroots transnationalism" among Salvadoran charismatic Catholics in Washington, D.C., which is not matched in terms of frequency and extensiveness by the institutional church. Anna L. Peterson and Manuel A. Vásquez, " 'Upwards, Never Down': The Catholic Charismatic Renewal in Transnational Perspective," in *Christianity, Social Change, and Globalization in the Americas*, ed. Anna Peterson, Manuel Vásquez, and Philip Williams, 188–209 (New Brunswick, NJ: Rutgers University Press, 2001).

41. Patricia Fernandez-Kelly, "Social and Cultural Capital in the Urban Ghetto: Implications for the Economic Sociology of Immigration," in *The Economic Sociology of Immigration*, ed. Alejandro Portes, (New York: Russell Sage Foundation, 1995), 215.

42. Mustafa Emirbayer and Jeff Goodwin, "Network Analysis, Culture, and the Problems of Agency," *American Journal of Sociology* 99, no. 6 (1994): 1416.

43. Monica Boyd, "Family and Personal Networks in International Migration: Recent Developments and New Agendas." *International Migration Review* 23, no. 3 (1989): 638–670.

44. There is a significant gender variation, only 8.4 percent of women surveyed stated that they work more than sixty hours, while 27.0 percent of men do. This variation may explain why a higher percentage of men consider group solidarity the single most important community need. They simply have less time to build powerfully affective bonds outside work.

45. Amy DeRogatis, *Moral Geography: Maps, Missionaries, and the American Frontier* (New York: Columbia University Press, 2003).

46. Michel de Certeau, *The Practice of Everyday Life* (Berkeley: University of California Press, 1984), 115.

47. Martes, *Brasileiros nos Estados Unidos*, 146.

48. Ibid., 147.

49. Ibid., 148.

50. On the notion of cultural tool kit, see Anne Swidler, "Culture in Action: Symbols and Strategies," *American Sociological Review* 51 (1986): 273–286.

51. Roberto DaMatta, *O que faz o Brasil, Brasil* (Rio de Janeiro: Rocco, 1989), 23–33.

52. For an interesting comparison, see Orsi's treatment of the centrality of the *domus*, a notion that brings together the home and the extended family in a religio-moral unit, among Italian immigrants in Harlem. Robert Orsi, *The Madonna of 115th Street: Faith and Community in Italian Harlem, 1880–1950* (New Haven: Yale University Press, 1985).

53. This finding resonates with the recent spatial turn in religious studies. Thomas Tweed, for example, writes that religion is about "constructing, adorning, and inhabiting domestic space. Religion, in this sense, is housework. It is homemaking." Thomas Tweed, *Crossing and Dwelling: A Theory of Religion* (Cambridge, MA: Harvard University Press, 2006), 103.

54. DaMatta, *O que faz o Brasil, Brasil*, 29.

55. Pierre Bourdieu, *Outline of Theory of Practice* (Cambridge: Cambridge University Press, 1977), 72–158.

56. This is the classic problem in anthropology of taking emic categories for etic concepts. I thank David Smilde for this insight and his helpful comments.

57. I thank Teresa Sales for this insight.

58. Robert Putnam, "E Pluribus Unum: Diversity and Community in the Twenty-first Century. The 2006 Johan Skytte Prize Lecture," *Scandinavian Political Studies* 30, no. 2 (2007): 137–174.

59. Manuel Castells, *The Rise of the Network Society* (Oxford: Blackwell, 1996).

60. Robert Putnam, *Bowling Alone: The Collapse and Revival of American Community* (New York: Touchstone, 2000), 66.

61. David Smilde, "Popular Publics: Street Protest and Plaza Preachers in Caracas," *International Review of Social History*, 49, no. supplement 12 (2004): 181. His notion of popular publics is an elaboration of philosopher Nancy Fraser's concept of "subaltern counter-publics," which she sees as "parallel discursive arena(s) where members of subordinated social groups invent and circulate counter-discourse, which in turn permit them to formulate oppositional interpretations of their identities, interests, and needs." Nancy Fraser, *Justice Interruptus: Critical Reflections on the Post-Socialist Condition* (New York: Routledge, 1997), 81.

3

𓃭𓃭𓃭𓃭𓃭𓃭𓃭𓃭𓃭𓃭𓃭𓃭𓃭𓃭𓃭𓃭𓃭𓃭𓃭𓃭𓃭𓃭𓃭𓃭𓃭𓃭

From Jacaltenango to Jupiter

Negotiating the Concept of "Family" through
Transnational Space and Time

SILVIA IRENE PALMA, CAROL GIRÓN SOLÓRZANO,
AND TIMOTHY J. STEIGENGA

This chapter argues that "family" is a key concept for understanding the life of the Guatemalan immigrant community living in Jupiter, Florida. Family-related necessities serve as the primary motor of emigration. Preoccupation with the family is the principle axis in the hearts, minds, and daily lives of Jupiter's immigrants. The strength of family ties are such that they allow immigrants to accept and tolerate the many sacrifices associated with daily living in a foreign and often hostile community. At the same time, the process of conducting multiple life histories, in-depth interviews, and focus groups with Jupiter's immigrants illuminated the heavy burden created by the distance between the immigrants, their families, and their communities of origin. As sociologist Pierrette Hondagneu-Sotelo has argued, these burdens underlie the fundamentally ambiguous (and increasingly common) construction of transnational families.[1] In this chapter, we argue that Jupiter's immigrants negotiate these tensions and transnational spaces with the assistance of local organizations and through the construction and reproduction of images associated with the passage of time: images of their home communities in the past, their present realities in Jupiter, and the conceptualization of a future which for the vast majority of the recent immigrants includes a return to their community of origin.

According to the 2000 census, approximately 28,650 Guatemalans live in the state of Florida, with approximately 6,576 located in Palm Beach County. These figures, however, drastically undercount the actual number of Guatemalan immigrants in Florida.[2] In the case of Jupiter alone, our survey research and qualitative interviews suggest that the population of Guatemalans is closer to 2,500, the majority from Jacaltenango, a municipality located in the department of Huehuetenango in northwest Guatemala. As outlined in chapter 1, the first Jacaltecos arrived in Jupiter after a long and intense displacement between countries (Guatemala, Mexico, and the United States) and between various locations within the United States.[3] They arrived in Florida for diverse reasons: from the need to safeguard their lives in the context of Guatemala's intense armed conflict of the 1980s to more recent waves of immigrants who come as international migrant workers to fill the demand for laborers in Jupiter's burgeoning landscaping and construction industries.

In this chapter we show how Guatemalan immigrants in Jupiter fulfill their commitments to their families in their communities of origin through working to produce remittances, frequent telephone communications, and other transnational connections.[4] We demonstrate that the immigrants experience a daily tension: the need to take on the new values of the community in which they live in the United States (modernization, personal autonomy, self-control, and institutionalized norms) while also maintaining the values they bring with them from their community of origin (community values and traditional forms of family authority). These pressures induce difficult changes in the lives of immigrants. The communal and family authorities who would normally provide behavioral limits and norms in the community of origin are absent in Jupiter. In the absence of these family and group authorities, churches and other civic organizations take on, at least in a compensatory form, the roles of family members or other local authorities in providing a framework of self-control and an understanding of "proper" behavior. In short, these institutions assist migrants in meeting their family commitments, in spite of the difficulties of space and time that create distance between families. They also provide one of the scarce sources of "bridging" social capital for Jupiter's Guatemalan immigrants.[5] With regard to these dynamics, we observed important differences between distinct immigrant groups such as asylum seekers/refugees and recently arrived (and more likely to be undocumented) international migrant workers, between men and women, as well as among immigrants at different stages in life.

On one hand, Jupiter may be understood as a community in which Guatemalan symbols and meanings of social and cultural order are recreated.[6] At the same time, Jupiter is a disputed space, an environment of cultural appropriation and reproduction in which immigrants insert themselves while attempting to learn a new and different set of life skills appropriate to survival in an upscale Florida community. This tension requires a sharp learning curve and produces significant psychological and emotional stress among recent immigrants. Civic and religious organizations play a key role in mediating these tensions, reinforcing family ties, and connecting immigrants to organizational resources that might otherwise remain elusive.

Methodological Considerations

The dynamics of daily life of the Jupiter Jacaltec community is complex and multifaceted. Thus it was necessary to design a methodology that began with an analysis of this reality and at the same time allowed the protagonists of the individual and collective stories to participate in the construction of their narratives in a self-reflective manner. As a consequence, our respondents were able to actively participate in the delineation of proactive survival strategies in their new environment.[7] Our data collection focused on obtaining qualitative information through the use of field observation, life histories, focus groups, in-depth interviews, and the development of communal timelines. The principal contribution of these procedures was the gradual and progressive generation of information that allowed new layers and complimentary themes to emerge as respondents described and discussed their daily community life. This methodological design favored a natural cognitive construction among respondents, whose narratives combined notions of time (past/present/future), circumstances and place (community of origin and receiving community), and multiple levels of community (personal, family, community, and nation). This process of self-reflection in respondent's personal and collective stories confirmed the relative nature of their conceptions of space and time.

We discovered that for immigrants in Jupiter, the community of origin appears in the past, but at the same time it exists in daily life in an imagined form and through the constant desire to fulfill responsibilities to family members at home. Probing this generally invisible dual sense of time and place uncovered real tensions between there and here, then and now. Jupiter represents the present, with a daily life of working, paying rent, and seeking shelter. At the same time, it is difficult to imagine a clear present or future in the home community, particularly because the very presence of the significant numbers of Jacaltecos in Jupiter provokes irrevocable changes in the places and the people they have left behind.

The Family as Motive for Immigration:
Past, Present, and Future Images

The family clearly constitutes the principal motor of recent Guatemalan immigration to Jupiter. Nevertheless, the centrality of the role of family varies between different migrant groups, especially between refugees and the more recent international migrant workers. For the more recent immigrants, thoughts of the family at home serve as the basis for tolerating the adversity of daily life and the difficulties of finding and keeping steady work in Jupiter. The family is associated with the realization of hopes and dreams structurally integrated with the following elements: sustaining a basic well-being and a better standard of living, strengthening the capacity (generally through education) of family members, and creating a basis for a better life for the next generation. In the words of one respondent, "I came here for my young children. . . . [M]y wife was always telling me that we simply did not have enough money, and I was desperate, so we decided that it would be better if I left, because otherwise we were not going to make it." These sentiments were common among the majority of our male respondents. As another Jacaltec father explained, "I had to come, work was scarce, and I have three children who are growing and who need everything. My wife didn't really say much but I knew she was worried about us. When I told her that I was going to come here, the first thing she said to me was, what would she do by herself, and then she asked what money I was going to use to pay for the trip. . . . Now what makes me feel better is that they're better, and my wife tells me how she feels."

When we examine immigrants' images of family life in the sending community, at one level we find an almost idealized version of the family. In other words, when Jupiter's immigrants think of their families, they think of unity, happiness, communication, shared celebrations, and shared spaces. These positive thoughts are, however, a photographic negative of another set of grave concerns that immigrants simultaneously entertain about their families, the very concerns that drive them to make the dangerous trek from Jacaltenango to Jupiter in the first place: poverty, a lack of economic opportunity, and worries about the future of their families and communities of origin. When asked to describe family life in the home community, one of our Jacaltec respondents exhorted, "Yes! Jacal is really beautiful. There you can live peacefully and happy, although you have to eat beans with tortillas you at least eat all together. . . . [T]he boys can play in the street; the women go to the market, and at least you have some time to rest."

These positive elements are maintained as an image of the past. But the present brings other concerns and troubles. In the present, the distance between immigrants and their families brings concerns about family disintegration, insecurity, the potential for infidelity, and profound concern for their children. In particular, the young male immigrants worry about the management of their households, their potential loss of authority, and the rapid social changes taking place among their children, accelerated by new modes of technology available in Jacaltenango, such as cell phones and the Internet. In the words of one young man, "You're asking me about here [Jupiter] and not Jacal? Look, here life is hard because I don't have anyone to cook for me or wash my clothes. There my kids behave well; when I talk to my oldest son I tell him to listen to his mother because he's the man of the house now and it's his job to take care of them. I give my kids permission to go out only if my wife tells me they've been good; if not, they can't." As another Jacalteco explained, "Nothing's the same anymore. . . . [I]t's harder because you're not with them; you have to be clear when you tell them what you want. When I send money my wife already knows what it's for and what she has to spend it on, and I'm clear about how long it has to last, so she knows that it's hard here too. But there's no problem with her because she's good and she never asks me for anything. To the contrary, I'm always asking her if she needs anything. The other day I helped her buy medicine for her mother who had gotten sick."

Those who remained behind in Jacaltenango expressed a reciprocal set of issues and concerns for the present. During our interviews in Jacaltenango on Father's Day in 2004, we asked the children present if they would like us to carry messages back to Jupiter with us for their fathers. The vast majority of the children exhorted their fathers to be safe, to come home soon, and, most frequently, to *no chupar* (not drink). Wives and mothers expressed similar worries, including concerns about infidelity.

As Jocelyn Sabbagh has recently argued, the issue of transnational gossip plays a key role in framing the tension between images of the present and the future for transnational families in both the sending and receiving communities. As one of her Jacaltec respondents explained, "When men leave, we are afraid of gossip. Because when men are over there [in the United States], people tell them that we are doing bad things. That is my fear. What if my husband hears a rumor about me? What if he leaves me because of it? What will happen to me and my children?"[8] Back in Jupiter, another respondent described the other side of the scenario: "For example, there are a lot of guys here that have another woman and some even forget about their family that they left in Jacaltenango, and they leave the poor wife alone with the kids and they're here unhappy, drinking, and with another woman."

While these ambivalent and problematic images of the present may appear self-evident, they serve as a necessary corrective to descriptions of transnationalism that may otherwise verge on the celebratory. Returning to Pierrette Hondagneu-Sotelo's warning, it is worth recognizing the construction of transnational families "as an achievement, but one that is accompanied by numerous costs and attained in a context of extremely scarce options."[9] The role of transnational gossip in the complex web of social remittances surely merits further research and attention.

Turning to an imagined future, most of our respondents associated families with great hope and enthusiasm, in spite of the fact that the actual date of return remained uncertain. As one Jacalteco put it, "I don't have an exact return date, but what I do know is that I'm going back soon. I just have to save some cash so when I get back to Jacal I can do something. Right now, I've been here three years and I'm still not used to it because I miss my town; there you can relax and have a conversation! When I get back I'm going to start some kind of business. I don't know what yet."

The temporal uncertainty of family reunification was a common theme among our interviews in Jupiter. One respondent said, "The only thing we could do for our children was to come to the United States. My wife was crying and she didn't want me to go, but I had to do it for the kids. . . . [H]ere I'm going to work for about three years, I think, and then return to Guatemala because my children need me." The words of another Jacaltec father capture the common sentiments we discovered in our interviews and focus groups: "I just spoke on the phone to Guatemala. . . . I was desperate here [almost crying] because everything is different here; life is harder; people are different; what is most difficult is to be far from my wife and kids. The worst thing is that finding work is hard and it doesn't pay well. If only I could be there now, but I can't."

In sum, for the vast majority of our respondents, family is the principal motive for migration. The effort and risks undertaken can only be explained by the search for better living conditions for family members. The image of the family is frozen somewhere between an idealized past and the difficult reality of the present. The reestablishment of a unified family life lies in an undetermined future.

Gender and Migratory Flow: Key Variables for Understanding Family Relations

Gender and temporal location within migration flows are two key variables that frame the images of family held among immigrants in Jupiter. Table 3.1 provides a succinct outline of the key differences in family dynamics between men and women and different times and status of migration. Here we see some of the differences in family relations among different groups of immigrants from the same location. Asylees and the family members who came to join them frequently suffer difficulties with cultural adjustment and cultural differences, particularly with children who are born in Jupiter. The mothers of these children suffer the greatest amount of isolation, sometimes even within their own family. As one young mother explained, "What you see now is that our kids have already learned English in school, and some don't want to speak Spanish, not even at home, and so their parents are having problems with them. But other kids, now that they know English, help their parents when they go out to places like the hospital or they need to communicate."

These tensions are not limited to those with children born in the United States. In some cases, the tensions are even greater between parents who have papers and their grown children who followed them. As one young man put it,

Me, when I came to Jupiter [two years ago] I came here to live in a rental with my dad [he already lived in the United States] but after a little while I moved out because we had a lot of problems; he complained to my mother [by phone] all the time and we fought almost every day because he didn't like the friends that I hang out with. Now I live somewhere else and I've bought my own car to go to work in and to go out with my buddies on weekends to dance since my dad doesn't hassle me anymore,

TABLE 3.1

Images of the Family Held by Guatemalans in Jupiter

Migratory flow	Men			Women		
	Asylees	Reunited	Migrant workers	Asylees	Reunited	Migrant workers
Family relations	Relationship with the family continues but is less strong

A family support system has been put into place for the arrival of Mayan international migrant workers

Many are adults, alone, without family commitments in the community of origin | Family ties have facilitated migration of other groups

Inter-generational difficulties especially between children born in the U.S. and their parents

Communication problems are apparent in the new context due to the tendency to reproduce inappropriate systems of control | Men who are alone but with commitments in Guatemala

Preoccupation for children/spouse/ mother/father

Constant communication with family | Maintenance of the family unit in the new context

Cultural discrimination because of language and social isolation, even within the family unit

Difficulty in the relationship with children who arrived young or were born in the U.S.

Possible loss of contact with family members in Guatemala | Interfamily violence

Difficulty in the relationship with children who arrived young or were born in the U.S.

Maintenance of the family unit in the new context | Relatively greater liberty due to obtaining work that provides independent income and due to the distance from family/community in Guatemala

Preoccupation for mothers in Guatemala |

even though when I call my mom she always tells me to behave; why don't I send enough money, and here sometimes there's enough work and sometimes there isn't.

A relatively common element among the distinct groups of Guatemalan immigrants in Jupiter is the attempt to reproduce social and cultural gender roles and expectations from the communities of origin. In other words, there is an implicit (and sometimes explicit) expectation that women should behave in the same manner that they behave in the community of origin. Not surprisingly, this provokes serious tension and causes many women to suffer social isolation and/or physical and emotional violence in the home. In the words of one young Jacaltec man, "Here women aren't the same as the ones in Jacaltenango; when they come here they want to behave differently since here they work. . . . [O]thers are worse! They want to go to the dances and some actually drink! Here if they have a bad friend they become bad too. But there are others who, when they get to Jupiter, they find their husband right away and stay at home; they only work if they have permission and they watch the kids."

For some of the immigrant women, the new context allows opportunities to question their traditional roles and provides opportunities for outside assistance in the event of interfamilial violence. Local churches, social service organizations, and county programs offer the opportunity for women to escape situations of domestic abuse and to augment their self-esteem through participation in local programs for immigrant women. Although the problems of isolation and abuse remain grave, our research uncovered cases of women who had effectively used local support networks to extract themselves from situations of domestic violence and, in the process, adopt a new and different set of values that allowed them greater freedom and autonomy. The story of one young Mexican mother, though harrowing, illustrates this process of transformation:

My husband changed a lot. Two years ago my husband hit me hard, we always fought, and he took whatever I earned. One day, since I worked, he came home and asked me for money and hit me in the face, then gave me a kick and I fainted and could hardly see my two boys. The police came and an ambulance to bring me to the hospital. . . . My husband was in jail for a month, and during that month I had a lot of work and I even went to Disney and spent like $1,500 with my kids. . . . [A]fter a year he had a car and rent money so I went back to him. I didn't go back because I wanted a husband, rather because my boys needed their dad and were bad psychologically, and one of them was pulling his hair out and a psychologist told me it was because he missed him. Now we're okay; now I don't ask him permission for anything. Now I participate in an association and I go out when I want.

Work as the Path to Facilitating Jacaltec Dreams

According to studies conducted by the program DECOPAZ/PNUD-UNOPS in the year 2000, Jacaltenango suffered from severe problems of unemployment and poverty. The unemployment rate among the population between fifteen and twenty-nine years old was 58.3 percent, for those between thirty and thirty-four it is 50.4 percent, and over forty-five it was 54.0 percent. In a separate report on poverty rates in Guatemala conducted by SEGEPLAN in 2001, 74 percent of Jacaltenango's population was reported as living in poverty, with 22 percent rated as living in extreme poverty.[10] With prospects for work scarce to non-existent in Jacaltenango, it is no surprise that many Jacaltec families choose a survival strategy which includes sending a family member to seek employment through the well-established route from Jacaltenango to Jupiter. According to the most recent census, 388 households (7 percent of the total households in the municipality) report at least one family member living in the United States.[11]

Clearly, finding and keeping a job in Jupiter is a critical element of the survival strategy of many Jacaltecos and the key to their dream of a better life for their family. As one young mother explained, "I work cleaning houses. When I arrived in Jupiter I had really bad experiences with work; now I'm better because I learned. I don't care about how hard the work is; the important thing is to send money back to my girls, who are with my mother." The income differential between Jacaltenango and Jupiter is sufficiently great that immigrants are willing to take the risks associated with the long and difficult passage and to suffer the difficulties of working in the Jupiter environment. As one lawn-care worker put it, "Here you earn well; the only thing is that it's really hard because you have to spend all day in the hot sun cutting the grass. But here what you earn in two weeks you don't earn in two months there. When I got here it took a while to learn to use the machinery."

This worker's financial estimation was borne out in our survey results. We found that pay rates for immigrant labor in Jupiter oscillate between $8.00 and $15.00 per hour, depending upon level of experience and type of work. In Guatemala, the going rate for agricultural work is 38 *Quetzales* per day ($5.00) with a working day that frequently runs as long as ten hours. According to our survey results, the average weekly income among immigrants in Jupiter is $339, more than double a month's pay for an agricultural worker in Guatemala.

The majority of Jupiter's Guatemalan immigrants arrive with little formal education and almost no English-speaking ability.[12] Thus they are employed primarily in jobs that require little education or technical skills, such as landscaping, gardening, golf course maintenance, and construction.[13] While there is consensus that learning English is the key to better pay and more stable employment, the daily demands of work combined with the notion of imminent return to the sending community keep many immigrants from improving their

English-speaking abilities. As one young worker explained, "I began to go to English classes, but then I stopped going because I got back late from work. . . . [S]ome Jacaltecos speak English because they're really smart, but others like me aren't interested. You can't just not go to work two hours a day to go to school, because what's your family supposed to do if you don't send money?"

Jupiter's Guatemalan immigrants take great pride in their work and the fact that they are considered excellent workers by their employers. Indeed, among both the employers and the employees we interviewed, there was unanimous agreement about the quality of Guatemalan workers. In the words of another Jacaltec worker, "Americans say that the Guatemalans are great workers because we'll do whatever they ask. It's true, because I was doing the garden in my boss's house, and he asked if I could fix some floors in his kitchen and, even though I don't understand English that well, I told him that I would. He was really happy with my work and now calls me for any job." As another explained, "I work with a gringo from Boca Raton—I go with him to paint houses, to do repairs and all kinds of things, and then he drops me off at my place. I've worked with him for a while and he likes the way I work; he says that even though I'm only twenty-three I'm strong because I help him carry all the material with no problem."

Despite their reputation as excellent workers, there are many obstacles that stand between the new Guatemalan arrivals and their ultimate dreams of returning home with enough money to support their families. Although their jobs are primarily in manual labor, they require immigrants to quickly learn how to use the proper machinery, how to engage in systems of work contracting, and a minimal understanding of English so that they can follow directions at work. As one recently arrived Guatemalan put it, "When I arrived, my very first night here they already told me how life really was here, and they told me that the next day I had to start working with them, that I would have to learn to use the machinery if I wanted to earn more. They told me what Guatemalans do here." Another respondent echoed these sentiments, "When I got here it was like two in the morning, but the next evening they told me I had work, that I'd have to learn to use the lawn equipment if I wanted to earn better. . . . [T]he first thing I remember them telling me is that the food is different here and that it's not as easy as everyone thought. . . . [T]hat made me think."

Once the preliminary necessities of finding work and a place to stay have been completed, the third major obstacle blocking the immigrant's long-term dream of sending funds home to their families is debt. The majority of Jupiter's most recent Guatemalan immigrants contract the services of "coyotes" to assist them in the difficult process of traversing Mexico, crossing the border, and making the trek from the border to Jupiter. During our research in 2004, we found that the average cost for such services was $5,500 per person. Respondents reported, however, that the cost increases annually and has jumped significantly since the mid 1990s with the institution of various programs to tighten the border. According to one respondent, "Look, here most come with a coyote. The only thing is that they charge a lot, but they're good because in the end they get you here. My brother-in-law helped me because he was the one who asked the coyote to help me, and we only paid a part there and he paid the other half here when I arrived. What happened on the way here isn't important anymore—what matters is that I'm here."

Living conditions for immigrants are particularly difficult, as rental space in Jupiter is scarce and the cost of living is high. For those who come to work in Jupiter, there are many hardships and sacrifices before the dream of building capital begins to come true. In the words of one Jacaltec respondent, "To me it's not important that I have a lot of money here, only that I have enough. The most important is rent, and the rest I send to Guatemala because my wife has to pay the debt that I have there that's for the coyote, she has to take some for household expenses, and the most important is to buy things for my kids' school." As another explained, "I think that the most difficult thing for me here was to pay the debt, because I sent and sent money to my village and almost all of it was to pay the coyote and hardly anything was left over for my family. I've paid off the debt there, I only owe a little here, but they're more patient here, so now my wife receives a few more pennies. Yeah, I always send for the Fiesta de Candelaria to buy something special."

For Guatemalan immigrants in Jupiter, work also provides a space for socialization and exchange with other immigrants, including Mexicans, Colombians, Haitians, and others. This exchange assists Guatemalans in learning the rules and expectations of contract labor, negotiation of wages, and other survival strategies. For example, the employers who used to contract the day-laborers congregated each day on Center Street were aware that the workers would not contract with them for less than a certain minimum of hours and/or daily wage.[14] These wage and hourly parameters were set informally in the street and communicated to the new arrivals so that they would not upset the balance and pay scale. As one day-laborer explained, "We on Center Street already have an agreement that we won't go with a boss who pays less than we want. . . . Sometimes people are desperate that no one will hire them because it's already noon and then a boss arrives who wants to pay $6.00 an hour and they go because they want to have work and we yell at them, 'Don't go, man! It's better to lose a day's work than giving your labor away!' If we permit this, they won't want to pay anything."

As we might expect, the newest arrivals generally occupied the lowest rung on the ladder of day-labor opportunities on the street corner market. Because the process of day labor is informal, those with the most work experience, the most English-speaking ability, more established networks, and their own mode of transportation are more likely to find work. The newest arrivals have also been the most likely to be taken advantage of by employers. Workers report frequent cases of employers who promise a weekly check but disappear at the end of the week after the work has been completed. Because many of the workers are undocumented, they fear local authorities and frequently do not report these abuses.[15] As one day-laborer explained, "We've had some bad experiences. I mean, almost every day something happens with one of our countrymen; sometimes there are people getting workers and they contract them for two weeks but only pay them one. It can happen because then the boss doesn't show up on the last day of the second week when it's time to pay. . . . [and] even though the people know where the American lives, they don't say anything because they're scared they'll call immigration. What can they do for us? There are lots of cases like this, all the time, who don't pay us!"[16]

The struggle to find work is only the beginning. Because contractors pick up laborers starting at 5:00 a.m. in the morning, workdays frequently run from 5:00 a.m. until 6:00 or 7:00 p.m. Work in construction and landscaping is physically demanding and requires attention to detail. Thus, for many workers, the hours, days, weeks, months, and years pass as they concentrate on the immediate demands of their labor. Most return to their crowded apartments exhausted, with little time to address daily necessities (shopping for food, washing clothing, and medical issues), let alone time for recreation or interaction with friends. Many respondents described their experience of the passage of time in Jupiter as a near dream state, a rhythm of work and sleep that is only rarely interspersed with the opportunity for recreation or social gatherings.

Nonetheless, these sacrifices are made in the name of complying with their primary responsibilities as fathers, providers, and moral leaders of their families back home. The money earned is regularly channeled to the community of origin to provide for the family. In some cases these remittances come at the expense of basic necessities for the workers themselves. According to one day-laborer we interviewed while he was waiting to find work, "I always have to send the money to my family. What I earn is for them, and I keep rent money, money for calling cards since I call once a week, sometimes every three days, depending on my mood. . . . I can stop eating, but not stop calling Guatemala."

Remittances: The Key Transnational Connection with Home

Our collective and individual interviews suggest that there are four primary motivations that drive the process of sending economic remittances to the home community. First and foremost, the money is sent to satisfy family needs, from daily necessities such as food and clothing to long-term costs such as healthcare and education. Second, the funds are transferred to pay debts to coyotes and other debts incurred by the family. Third, the money is intended to facilitate the dreams of a better life for family members in the future, through education and through the hope of establishing a long-term survival strategy through initiating a business transaction or purchasing land. Finally, some immigrants remit for community projects, generally through transnational religious connections.

The sending of remittances is fairly regularized among Guatemalans in Jupiter, with a little more than half sending funds monthly. In our survey, we found that 11.2 percent send between $1 and $100 monthly; 21.7 percent send between $101 and $250; 28.0 percent remit between $251 and $500; 25.9 percent remit between $501 and $1,000; and 8.4 percent remit between $1,001 and $2,000.[17] In terms of frequency, we found that only 2.0 percent send remittances once a year and 6.6 percent send bi-annually. As a regularized process, 59.2 percent of our respondents reported that they remit monthly, with 15.8 percent reporting bi-monthly remittances. It is important to point out, however, that these transfers do not necessarily translate into community development in the sending community. Furthermore, the longer an immigrant stays in the United States, the trend is that the amount and frequency of remittances diminishes.[18] After living for thirteen years in Florida, one Jacalteco explained, "When I came I always sent more money to my mother; on the other hand, now I can't anymore because I have other commitments."

In one sense, remittance sending serves as a partial antidote to the feelings of guilt and nostalgia immigrants feel as they live and work so far away from their families. Remittances allow fathers to fulfill both the role of provider and the traditional role of decision-maker in the family, as the economic force of their remittances serves as a replacement for their physical presence in the home. As one father pointed out, "I can't be with them; at least I can send money, you know? If not, why am I their father? They know if I'm far away it's because the situation is difficult and I want them to be well."

The final mode of remittance sending relates to community projects. These forms of remitting are sporadic and generally require a formal or informal transnational connection between Jupiter and Jacaltenango. In this case, institutions and groups connected with the Catholic Church have played a key role. For example, the Tepeyac Project, connected with a local Catholic Church near Jupiter, has channeled immigrant remittances and sought external funding to assist the Nutritional Center Hospital in Jacaltenango. Informal collection of funds to return the dead to be buried in Jacaltenango represents another such transnational connection.

As with conceptions of the family, the role and process of remittance sending varies with gender and location within the migration stream. Table 3.2, provides a brief summary of the key differences between these groups.

While the economic aspects of remittances are critical, as Peggy Levitt and others have argued, remittances are much more than simple economic transactions.[19] As discussed in chapter 1, social remittances include ideas, social capital, cultural practices, technology, and other factors that flow between the sending

TABLE 3.2

The Role of Remittances

Migratory flow	Men			Women		
	Asylees	*Reunited*	*Migrant workers*	*Asylees*	*Reunited*	*Migrant workers*
Work	Improved opportunities/ conditions Better income May be owners	Better work conditions/family support networks	Low income Heavy labor	Probable improved working conditions	Young people in competition with others of different nationalities (Mexicans, Haitians, others)	Labor diversification Socialization with men of diverse nationalities
Remittances	Not for family survival in the community of origin Eventual sending to the community	Scarce sending of remittances	Constant sending of remittances for family survival/ debt payment	No sending of remittances	Interest in sending diminishes	Constant sending of remittances to children/debt Contribution to family survival

and receiving communities. These transnational connections affect lifestyle, aesthetic notions of beauty, clothing styles, uses of technology, communication, and value changes. While financial remittances are the primary vehicle connecting family members, immigrants send home much more than just their money. As one respondent explained, "I've already sent clothes and shoes to my kids. It was a very small box because postage is really expensive. I took advantage and sent some toys and gifts for my wife and some things for my mother. They were really happy, and when I talked to them they told me they liked them a lot."

Thus, remittances include more than funds, but also articles for the home, computer equipment, cellular phones, videos and DVDs, clothing, and other items. These forms of exchange allow the family in the community of origin to become more familiar with the social environment in which the immigrant is located. They become a transnational cultural and material bridge, which, in turn, frequently serves as the motivation for new waves of migration, particularly among the younger generation. As one migrant explained, "When I call I tell them it's nice here, that it's really different. I tell them about my work, and I also tell them that there are a lot of modern things here . . . but I also tell them that here life is hard, that it's really difficult to earn money." In the words of another young Jacaltec worker, "Ah! Yes, I tell my buddies that they should study and get their teaching degrees and then come. Yes, I do think that Jacaltecs are going to keep coming here; we all know each other and help each other, and anyway it's hard there to get a teaching degree and it doesn't pay well."

Transnational Communication:
Reach Out and Touch Jacaltenango

Communication via telephone forms a critical part of immigrant's strategies for surviving the daily hardships imposed by time and space. In the process, families in the rural and isolated communities of origin have become rapidly socialized into the use of telecommunication tools, including cell phones, text messaging, and the Internet. As one of our Jacaltec respondents explained, "Here there are phone cards for calling Jacaltenango. You can get ones for different prices, depending on how long you want to talk. Here almost everyone buys a card; when we speak during the week we buy one for $2.00, but for the weekend we buy one for $5.00 or $10.00 because we have more time." The use of the phone cards establishes regularized and critical communication between transmigrants and their family members. Another respondent emphasized the centrality of this communication in his case: "Me, the last time my mother got sick, I called every day to see how she was; thank God there's a phone! That's why the first thing I bought my mother in Guatemala was a telephone; she just told me how much it cost and I sent her the money, because before we had to go with the man at the store and it was more expensive, but he let us use it."

The sending of audio cassettes, videos of celebrations and events, and video recorders so that videos from the home community can be returned also forms part of this transnational network of communication. For the most part, these forms of remittances demonstrate emotional ties of love, loyalty, and mutual celebration to be shared by family members separated by time and space. Once again, however, these transnational lines of communication are a double-edged sword. As the young spouse of one of Jupiter's migrants explained when she was interviewed in Jacaltenango, "There is a problem here; when there is a party or festival, the first thing people do is film it. They film it and later send the video to our husbands in Jupiter. This sometimes creates conflicts; say sometimes you are just dancing and they start saying things that are not true just because you were dancing. So I am a little bit afraid of that. I am not doing anything wrong, but people always comment on everything, so you have to always be careful." Again, the potential for transnational gossip foments divisions and inhibits the behavior of spouses who remain in Jacaltenango.

Furthermore, the cost of all of these forms of communication demands a significant portion of the earnings for transmigrants. By our estimates, the costs of calling home take up nearly 15 percent of the average monthly income of Jupiter's transmigrants.[20] During the past few years, the number of companies offering various phone cards in Jupiter has multiplied significantly. Our preliminary estimates suggest that the average immigrant in Jupiter spends between $50 and $100 per month purchasing international calling cards. Considering the 2000 census figure of 28,650 Guatemalans living in Florida (a figure which, we have already noted, drastically undercounts Guatemalans), we can conservatively estimate that Guatemalan immigrants in Florida spend between $1 and $2 million a month communicating with friends and family in Guatemala.

A 2000 study of phone calls between the United States and Guatemala counted 31,497,001 calls adding up to 33,090,127 minutes of airtime.[21] The companies benefiting most from these conversations include Americatell, Sprint, AT&T, MCI, and BellSouth. Preliminary calculations, based on a cost of $10 per 45 minutes of airtime (2003 figures), suggest that these firms likely brought in close to $52 million in calls to Guatemala alone.[22] The magnitude of these economic interactions remains relatively invisible and has yet to enter into any official discourse on migration with governmental authorities either in the United States or in Guatemala.

From another perspective, we can see that the use of these new modes of communication have created new notions of time and space among Guatemalan immigrants and their families. Unlike in Mexico, where this process unfolded over a long history of migration, in Guatemala the changes have been abrupt and drastic. These frequent communications have allowed immigrants to continue with their roles and functions within family life in the present in a manner that differs from past waves of migration. Thus, migrant fathers frequently continue in their role as moral guide, authority, and decision maker for the family at home in the community of origin. As one young father explained,

> We talk about everything by phone; she tells me how the family is, if everything is okay. We also talk about stuff that's going on, about my kids' school. . . . [F]or example, I spoke with her two days ago and she told me that my in-laws had gone to Huehuetenango and she also told me that everyone is getting ready for the fiesta in Jacaltenango; we talked about all that. She asks permission to go see her parents; she tells me if they call from school or if she needs to buy something. That's right, she *cannot* leave town. I don't give her permission to do that and she knows it; that's why she never says anything about it, because there she has everything.

To a large degree, these new and frequent forms of communication are contributing to a redefinition and reconfiguration of family relations in the communities of origin. Studies in Guatemala have concluded that these mediums of communication have introduced new and foreign values that are rapidly altering family and community relations.[23] Foremost among these changes is the desire for "modern" conveniences and styles that have been transmitted through social remittances. While ideas, styles, and demands have changed, the material economic basis of life in the home community has not. One consequence of this process is an increase in the motivation for further migration, as individuals and families come to the realization that their material resources and opportunities in Guatemala will never match the new expectations and values generated through contact with their family members in the United States.

The Role of Religious and Civic Organizations

The role of religious and civic institutions among the immigrant population in Jupiter also has much to do with time and location of arrival within the immigrant stream. Guatemalans who arrived in Florida during Guatemala's civil war were more likely to have the opportunity to apply for asylum and to eventually gain legal status. Thus, these initial war refugees and their families have been able to establish deep roots in the Jupiter area. They have more connections to local institutions, greater opportunities for education, and often serve as leaders and resources for newer arrivals.

This is not the case with the postwar flows of Guatemalan immigrants. For these later arrivals, their primarily non-authorized status and lower levels of education and economic status have limited their process of integration into the local community. Thus, local civil and religious organizations have taken on the role of cultural reproduction while simultaneously serving as a bridge between the immigrants and local authorities.

The role of religious and civic organizations in Jupiter is complex and constantly changing. For the most part, these organizations evolve as they assist immigrants with the adjustments necessary for living in a very new and different environment. Initially, some of these organizations (such as the Mayan Jacaltec Association) tended to replicate schemes and models of organization that originated in the community of origin. Over time, however, they have evolved and adjusted to meet the social and political requirements of the new community, establishing more formalized ties, creating institutional status, and promoting linkages with local and state authorities. The evolution of the organization Corn-Maya provides one such example.

Beginning with the informal planning of the Jacaltec Maya Association for the first Fiesta Maya in Jupiter, the evolution of Corn-Maya as a political and social organization was initiated. Thus, an organization with an informal nature has evolved into an official nonprofit organization which has successfully brought resources to Jupiter's immigrant community (ESL classes, health and human services, counseling, mobile consulates, and other services), served as a key link between immigrants and town authorities, and worked to secure stable working conditions for immigrant laborers through the creation of a neighborhood resource center. At the same time, Corn-Maya serves as a vehicle for cultural reproduction, sponsoring soccer leagues and organizing the annual Fiesta Maya.

The principal actions or motivations among the institutional and informal groups in Jupiter include public policy issues (such as lobbying for changes in immigration policy), cultural reproduction (such as soccer games and the Fiesta Maya), actions designed to project civic participation (such as participation in community cleanups or working to promote the neighborhood resource/labor center), solidarity and reinforcement of relations with the community of origin (such as sending back the dead and communal remittances), and the exercise of spiritual life (including official religious affiliation and participation as well as prayer groups and participation in traditional Mayan rituals and practices). The tangible results of these actions are further outlined in chapters 5 and 7.

The level of cohesion between diverse groups and organizations in Jupiter is flexible and dynamic. While certain events and services bring large numbers of Guatemalans (and other immigrants) together, there are also points of controversy and division. As noted in chapter 7, ethnic and religious divisions frequently limit broad-based cooperation among immigrant groups. Nonetheless, certain events, such as the 2003 visit of Guatemalan vice president Eduardo Stein and the 2007 visit by President Oscar Berger (organized by Corn-Maya), bring together diverse groups who might otherwise not communicate on a regular basis.[24]

On one level, some of the tensions that exist between immigrant groups in Palm Beach County reflect historic tensions between ethnic groups in Guatemala. Interviews with key informants suggest that some of the difficulties of cooperation between Jacaltecos and Q'anjob'ales can be traced to conflicts between these groups that date back to the colonial period in Guatemala. Some of the indigenous leaders we interviewed referenced the fact that Jacaltenango was the center of an *encomienda* during the colonial period, which led to conflicts with the Q'anjob'al population living in the periphery of the region. According to some of our informants, historical animosities continue to complicate relations between these two ethnic groups, with immigrants geographically concentrated in the two cities of Jupiter (Jacaltecos) and Lake Worth (Q'anjob'ales).

The case of Jupiter suggests that local institutions can serve as a bridge to local and intergovernmental authorities. The sister city initiative (see chapters 5 and 7) between Jacaltenango and Jupiter can serve as a model for other immigrant communities. This accord was possible due to a combination of factors, including connections between the local university (Florida Atlantic University), Jupiter's new planned urban community (Abacoa), and institutional actors in Guatemala (such as INCEDES, the Central American Institute for Social Research and Development). It is precisely these kinds of transnational cooperative networks and their attendant bridging social capital that make local immigrant-serving organizations most effective.

Concluding Thoughts

The factors that drive the process of migration from Jupiter to Jacaltenango have not changed sufficiently to slow the flow of migrants. Furthermore, the exchange of resources, information, experiences, values, and knowledge acquired by the immigrants and their families, rather than diminishing migration, are more likely to increase the motivations for those left behind in Jacaltenango to consider migrating as well.[25]

In Jupiter, the primary factor affecting the lives of migrants is their status as documented or undocumented. Relations between Jacaltenango and Jupiter, between families, and between institutions are all affected by this key variable. Family life in Jupiter, relations with families in Jacaltenango, the fulfillment of responsibilities to the home community, and participation in civic and religious organizations are all conditioned by migratory status. Those who came as refugees can participate with some degree of ease in multiple organizations that reproduce their culture. On the other hand, when these same individuals are members of evangelical churches, or if they become charismatic Catholics who participate intensively in their churches, they tend to have the resources to cognitively construct an image of their future that includes remaining in the United States. In these cases, reflection upon the past can be painful, and there is a tendency to disconnect with families and friends in the community of origin.

The establishment of support networks in Jupiter favors the insertion of newcomers into the labor market and assists in their daily survival. But these processes also come with high costs for the new immigrants as they struggle to negotiate the tensions between the rules of life in Jupiter and the values and authority that come from the community of origin. Religious institutions serve as sources of both bonding and bridging social capital. They promote religious doctrines that serve, to some degree, to reproduce and strengthen ties with the home community (ties to the past, in the case of the Catholic Church) and/or new relations with the new community of origin (ties to the future in the case of the evangelicals and charismatic Catholics).

For immigrant women in search of a better life in Jupiter, the option of the "stable husband" emerges as a key variable. Men who work hard, fulfill their role as provider, and do not waste family resources on drinking are in high demand. To some degree, this translates into a certain form of pressure for the young men who seek to live up to this image of the potentially "good husband." The pressure is increased because the same demands are translated across borders from mothers, fathers, and other family members. Among the young immigrants, these pressures lead to varying patterns of behavior (from bouts of drinking to sudden religious conversions), but with the constant risk of being devalued by the community for improper behavior. For this reason, the concerns of this group of young immigrants are particularly acute, as is the necessity to constantly remember the old patterns of conduct from the community of origin. As a consequence of these pressures, we noted the tendency of many of these young immigrants to participate in civic or religious organizations that offer a certain degree of institutional control (such as charismatic prayer groups or evangelical churches). However, the daily pressures of seeking work and living far from home frequently lead to backsliding and a pattern of passages in and out of different religious communities.

The role of Jupiter's immigrant organizations and the reach of their influence have been developed in a context that has slowly and fitfully created greater receptivity on the part of the receiving community. In the future, it will be critical to fortify these organizations through the active inclusion and attention to the needs of two previously underrepresented groups: immigrant women and the children of immigrants reunified with their families or those born in the United States.

The transnational initiatives undertaken in Jupiter (such as the sister city agreement) have been important for the immigrant community because they have facilitated communication, diminished feelings of distance, and favored better conditions for groups who are frequently excluded from political and economic initiatives in their communities of origin. In the future, Jupiter's immigrants face the challenge of promoting development in the home community, combined with the opportunity for mutual cultural exchange. This will require the reframing of the manner through which immigration has been understood in both the sending and the receiving community, both by the immigrants themselves and by their families at home.

It remains to be seen how the values and cultural practices of the community of origin will continue to interact and evolve with the values of the receiving community. These processes of transition must be understood by taking into account the life cycle of the migrants, with particular attention to the case of the young migrants who have yet to develop the emotional maturity to face the pressures generated by this clash of values.

Nevertheless, the older migrants also face difficulties in dealing with the new realities of Jupiter without losing their sense of who they are and their ties to their community of origin. The values of individual autonomy and the formation of a personal set of goals, which takes place outside of the traditional norms and controls of the community of origin, generate a significant degree of tension that is likely to alter many an individual's capacity to construct notions of the future that include multiple values from each community.

The most likely path to creating an ordered and stable cognitive map for Jupiter's immigrants lies in their participation in religious and civic organizations. But even this participation can be insufficient for many immigrants. The theme that dominated the discourse of our respondents throughout our four years of research in Jupiter and Jacaltenango is that there is a permanent tension in the interpretation and reinterpretation among immigrants of the following key concepts: their community of origin and their destination community in Jupiter; their commitments to their family in Jacaltenango and their individual needs in Jupiter; their idealized past and their ambivalent present; and, finally, their sense of autonomy based in the individual acceptance of collective norms and their struggle to negotiate the normative control that comes from outside sources such as religious institutions and the family. The transnational community that exists between Jacaltenango and Jupiter brings both opportunities and liabilities for immigrants and their families. Without major structural changes in Guatemala and/or regularization of undocumented workers in the United States, the dynamics of negotiating families across transnational time and space, with all of the attendant ambiguities and tensions, is likely to continue well into the future of both Jupiter and Jacaltenango.

NOTES

1. See Pierrette Hondagneu-Sotelo, "I'm Here, but I'm There: The Meanings of Latina Transnational Motherhood," in *Gender and U.S. Immigration: Contemporary Trends*, ed. Hondagneu-Sotelo (Berkeley: University of California Press, 2003), 336. Also see Norma Ojeda, "Familias transfronterizas y familias transnacionales: Algunas reflexiones," *Migraciones Internacionales* 3 (2005): 167–174.

2. The census undercounts Guatemalans because many Guatemalans self-identify under other categories, including Native American, white, Mayan, or other. See Michael E. Fix and Jeffrey S. Passel, "U.S. Immigration at the Beginning of the 21st Century: Testimony before the Subcommittee on Immigration and Claims Hearing on 'The U.S.

Population and Immigration' Committee on the Judiciary U.S. House of Representatives," Urban Institute, 2001 (http://www.urban.org/url.cfm?ID=900417).

3. California and Arizona are among the most important other destinations for Jacaltecos.

4. For a more complete overview of the emerging field of transnationalism in immigration studies see Peggy Levitt, *The Transnational Villagers* (Berkeley: University of California Press, 2001); Luis Guarnizo Portes and Patricia Landolt, "Introduction: Pitfalls and Promise of an Emergent Research Field," *Ethnic and Racial Studies* 22 (1999): 217–238; Anna L. Peterson, Manuel A Vasquez, and Philip J. Williams, eds., *Christianity, Social Change, and Globalization in the Americas* (New Brunswick, NJ, and London: Rutgers University Press, 2001).

5. See Robert Putnam, *Bowling Alone* (New York: Simon and Schuster, 2000), 66; Richard Wood, *Faith in Action* (Chicago: University of Chicago Press, 2002), 144; Mark R. Warren, J. Phillip Thompson, and Susan Saegert, "The Role of Social Capital in Combating Poverty," in *Social Capital and Poor Communities*, ed. Saegert, Thompson, and Warren, 1–28 (New York: Russell Sage Foundation, 2001).

6. See chapter 7 for a more complete description of this process. Also see Nadje Al-Ali and Khalid Koser, eds., *New Approaches to Migration? Transnational Communities and the Transformation of Home* (London and New York: Routledge University Press, 2002).

7. This concerns the procedure by which researchers and interviewers simultaneously produce the systemization of information gathered and form conclusions in a like manner.

8. Jocelyn Sabbagh, "What Remittances Can't Buy: The Social Cost of Migration and Transnational Gossip on Women in Jacaltenango" (honors thesis, directed by Dr. Timothy J. Steigenga, Wilkes Honors College of Florida Atlantic University, May 2007), 29.

9. Hondagneu-Sotelo, "I'm Here, but I'm There," 336.

10. Programa DECOPAZ/PNUD-UNOPS, "Informe sobre la Pobreza en Guatemala," (Guatemala: SEGEPLAN, 2001).

11. X Censo Nacional de Población y V de Habitación (Guatemala, 1994).

12. Levels of education of those interviewed during this research were the following: 28.4 percent with a primary education; 27.7 percent without primary education; 16.8 percent with secondary education; 12.2 percent with secondary incomplete; 1.9 percent with a technical degree; 1.9 percent with some university; 0.6 percent with a completed university degree; 10.5 percent with no response.

13. According to the Jupiter survey, 40 percent of the sample (which includes both Mexicans and Guatemalans) is employed in the service sector (gardener, landscaping, domestic service); 20 percent, in construction, 2 percent, in agriculture; and 38 percent, in other activities (electricians, machine and equipment operators, cashiers, waiters, clerks).

14. The situation for day-laborers has improved significantly since this research was originally conducted. The opening of the El Sol Neighborhood Resource Center in September of 2006 has provided a more orderly and sanitary locale for day-labor transactions as well as a significant resource for immigration, health, education, and other social services for the immigrant community.

15. Since the opening of the El Sol Resource Center, this sort of abuse has been significantly curbed as wage claims have been negotiated or referred to an attorney.

16. Beginning in September of 2007, the Town of Jupiter put into place a non-solicitation ordinance which effectively eliminated the Center Street labor market. At the same time, Catholic Charities, Corn-Maya, and the Friends of El Sol opened a labor center

on town property. The center now provides an orderly location for the labor market and negotiates wage claims for workers who have not been paid (along with providing ESL classes and multiple other social services).

17. Only 0.7 percent send more than $2,000, and only 2.8 percent did not respond to this question.

18. Taken from Dardón Sosa, "La migración internacional en el municipio Jacaltenango, Huehuetenango: Un acercamiento desde las comunidades. Estudio de Caso. Aplicación de Encuesta de Hogar" (Guatemala: Programa de Migración/ FLACSO Guatemala, 2003). Part of the conclusion states: "A strong communal impact exists from migration in social, cultural, and economic terms; growth without development. The real amount of the remittances that are received can be underestimated and without doubt taken in financial speculation. The longer they stay in the United States, the lower the transfer of remittances."

19. Levitt, *The Transnational Villagers.*

20. We arrived at this calculation using $339 as the average weekly income of Guatemalans in Jupiter.

21. "International Telecommunications Data" (Federal Communications Commission, December 2001).

22. Conservative estimates of the benefit generated by this income indicate that these businesses could obtain close to $26 million with only the communications between the United States and Guatemala. These numbers could be expected to rise when one considers, for example, the communications that could have happened between the United States and Mexico (http://168.234.170.2/docsit/E4022003.PDF).

23. See Irene Palma C. Silvia and Antonio Vásquez Bianchi, "Cuando las ilusiones se dirigen al norte: Aproximación al análisis de la migración a Estados Unidos y las implicaciones de ese proceso en comunidades del altiplano occidental de Guatemala" (Guatemala: FLACSO Guatemala and University of Southern California, July 2002); and Antonio Vásquez Bianchi, "Factores condicionantes de la migración a Estados Unidos en comunidades rurales," in *Después de Nuestro Señor, Estados Unidos. Perspectivas de análisis del comportamiento e implicaciones de la migración en Guatemala*, coordinated by Irene Palma C. Silvia et al. (Guatemala: Flacso Guatemala, 2005), 91–105.

24. This is the case of the visit of electoral candidate Eduardo Stein to Jupiter in August 2003. As a result of this first approach, the vice president, true to his word, returned to Jupiter after the elections. Although he was unable to attend, he sent Guatemalan foreign minister Jorge Bríz to sign the sister city agreement between Jupiter and Jacaltenango, which became effective in June 2005. Two years later, Guatemalan president Oscar Berger visited the newly inaugurated El Sol Center and gave a speech in which he promised to utilize Jupiter as an example in his discussion with President Bush about immigration reform.

25. Indeed, the role of family networks is well established in the study of migration. See Monica Boyd, "Family and Personal Networks in International Migration: Recent Developments and New Agendas," *International Migration Review* 23 (1989): 638–670.

4

Solidarities among Mexican Immigrants in Immokalee

PATRICIA FORTUNY LORET DE MOLA, MIRIAN SOLÍS LIZAMA,
AND PHILIP J. WILLIAMS

In this chapter we analyze the varied forms of solidarity[1] that are constructed among mobile populations of peasant, *mestizo*, and indigenous Mexican immigrants in Immokalee, Florida.[2] Our intention is to elucidate the spontaneous, informal, and more formal elements that these diverse groups utilize to form bonds of solidarity across national, cultural, and religious borders.[3] We refer to the phenomena analyzed in this chapter as "solidarities" because the groups that we studied are characterized by a certain degree of cohesion that leads individuals to act in the pursuit of collective benefits and goals. As we will see, mobile populations contain many heterogeneous actors that often do not belong to the same nationality, ethnic group, or social class: therefore, such collectivities do not constitute unified groups per se, despite the importance of their internal links. We use the concept of solidarity, then, in the sense of mutual support and union among different groups whose own nature determines the specific elements they may include as well as the mutable social conditions in which they emerge and as a result of which they develop their spontaneity, fragility, permanence, and structure.

In the first case, we describe mutual support networks that form spontaneously, or out of contingent circumstances, between members of two different national groups that find themselves in a social space that is alien to them. Although this case does not rely on transnational linkages in the traditional sense, it may be seen as an example of "horizontal linkages,"[4] where immigrants from different national groups transgress political, economic, and cultural boundaries that would normally separate them. The second case concerns a mestizo sector of Immokalee's immigrant population, made up of families from Chamácuaro, Guanajuato, who exemplify the traditional model of transnationalism that unites established immigrants to their place of origin through *fiestas patronales*. Finally, the third case reveals the density of social ties in a "transnational moral community" constructed by members of the Otomí ethnic group, from the state of Hidalgo, Mexico. Despite their relatively recent arrival to Immokalee, the Otomíes exhibit a higher degree of bonded social capital and solidarity than the rest of Immokalee's Mexican immigrant community.

Close observation of these three distinct cases, involving peasants, mestizos, and an indigenous group, respectively, allows us to highlight the variety of elements that come into play in the building of solidarities in a "transnational social field,"[5] in which social subjects cross national, cultural, and religious borders. As they navigate these different cultural spaces, immigrants reconfigure and transform their social identities. On the one hand, they are victims of economic globalization because they are mobilized, together with commodities and money, at the service of capitalism. On the other, they are social actors who respond to globalization by exploiting the resources that this process itself provides, as a means of extending and reproducing their lifestyles wherever they may find themselves. Although Arjun Appadurai goes much further in affirming that "a series of social forms have emerged to contest, interrogate, and *reverse*" globalization (emphasis added),[6] we do agree that mobile populations are capable of constructing and transferring knowledge and that they can move and act in ways that are independent of the actions of global capitalism and nation-states. Appadurai uses the terms "globalization from below" and "grassroots globalization" to refer to such phenomena.[7]

How, and Among Whom Do Solidarities Emerge?

Unlike the cases of Jupiter and Pompano Beach and Deerfield Beach, Immokalee is both an old and new destination for Mexican immigrants. One of the cases presented here—immigrants from Chamácuaro, Guanajuato—is representative of established immigrants from traditional sending communities of Mexico. The other two cases—peasants from Chiapas and indigenous Otomíes from Hidalgo—reflect the new geography of Mexican immigration to Florida and elsewhere in the United States. Immokalee is a relatively new destination for these groups of immigrants from newly emerging migratory states in Mexico. Moreover, these newer arrivals from nontraditional sending states often face the regional prejudices of more established immigrants who view them as coming from less developed, even backward regions of Mexico.

Given the exceptionally diverse ethnic, class, and regional origins of its immigrant population, Immokalee is a place rife with contradictions. The atmosphere that reigns on the streets around the center of town and to the north of the main road is filled with perils, real or imagined, that haunt those who live there. The dispersion, the diversity, and the fear of being assaulted or knifed make the residents of certain neighborhoods uneasy, especially after nightfall. As we will discuss in chapter 5, compared to Jupiter, immigrants in Immokalee generally have lower levels of social capital and are less likely to see their co-nationals as sources of support or assistance. However, such a one-dimensional view would only allow us to perceive the dark side of this reality and would lead us to conceive of all immigrants as isolated, anomic individuals. In the case of Brazilian immigrants discussed in chapter 2, we saw that despite the absence of visible markers of community organization, Brazilians sustain a rich sociability and engage in a diverse array of interpersonal networks. Even in a place like Immokalee, loyalties emerge, festivals are celebrated, people go to church, go shopping, play soccer, struggle for their rights, communicate with their loved ones back home, fall in love, have children, send money to their families, and sometimes carry out successful collective projects (see the discussion of the Coalition of Immokalee Workers in chapter 5).

"Spontaneous Solidarities" between Dominicans and Chiapanecos

In a place where dispersion and diversity predominate, we had to search for social spaces where we could observe the actions of immigrants who remain at the margin of churches and other organizations that constitute the most visible spaces of encounter in Immokalee.[8] One such meeting place turned out to be Helena's money transfer agency, as the constant flow of immigrants through her office endows it with a certain "sense" and "meaning" that go far beyond the relatively simple, utilitarian services it provides which consist of sending monetary remittances to Mexico and Guatemala and offering long-distance telephone service. This office comes to resemble a "space of sociability,"[9] where recent immigrants who first approach it for practical reasons find that through frequent visits and social interaction their social relations become transformed into what we call "spontaneous solidarities."

In the specific case alluded to here, it is important to note the charismatic personality of the person who manages the money transfer agency: Helena is around thirty years old and arrived to Immokalee in 2003. She was born in the province of Azua (northern Dominican Republic), in a very poor rural town called Los Indios, in the municipality of Padre Las Casas, where most people work cultivating coffee and bananas. Today, this young Dominican woman's parents depend almost totally on the remittances their daughter sends home. She managed to finish high school in Santo Domingo before migrating to the United States for economic reasons, where she soon obtained residency. During our fieldwork in Immokalee, her agency became an extension of our project, as it was there that many of our interviews took place. Moreover, it was the place where we were able to learn about events, conflicts, and celebrations in town. We succeeded in establishing a climate of trust with immigrants there, largely due to their fondness for this young woman, many of whose clients confided their worries, concerns, and loneliness to her. A sympathetic listener, she offered them encouragement and a helping hand whenever she could.

Helena rents a house in Immokalee, where she lives with her husband, their three-year-old son, a sister-in-law, and a cousin. In this chapter, we limit our discussion to the relations that developed among this young Dominican woman, her cousin Roger and a family clan[10] made up of five brothers and sisters from Chiapas, examining how loyalties emerged among them. There are approximately twenty Dominicans living in the area, most of whom arrived about four years ago. Almost all of these immigrants are related and come from the same town in the Dominican Republic. Two of them own most of the local money transfer offices, where their relatives are often employed. Those who cannot find work in the agencies take jobs in other businesses around town, such as in Laundromats or in a nearby casino that is run by Seminole Indians. Most of the Dominicans have legal residence or citizenship status and none has ever worked in the agricultural fields that surround Immokalee.

With respect to the immigrants from Chiapas (Chiapanecos), the first to arrive were the eldest brothers of the Rodríguez family, Octavio and Eleuterio, in late 1990. They subsequently sent money home so that their brothers, Roberto and Dionisio, and, later, their only immigrant sister, Rosaura, could also make it to the United States. Just a year and a half ago Lidia, Roberto's eldest daughter, a young girl of eighteen, also arrived. Rosaura lives with her husband in Immokalee, though their children are back home in Chiapas, where they live with their grandparents. Meanwhile, Eleuterio and his wife, a Guatemalan, live with their twelve-year-old twins who were born in Immokalee and speak only English. All of these immigrants, except Lidia, work picking tomatoes in the harvest season, before moving further north in the summer months to harvest fruits. Back in Chiapas they all worked as small-scale peasant farmers.

The youngest brother, José, was the only male sibling who stayed behind in Chiapas. Thanks to the remittances sent by his older brothers, José was able to study to become a clinical nurse. Shortly after graduating he found a job at a health center in San Cristóbal de Las Casas. His brothers spoke with him and the rest of the family regularly by telephone. Then, for several weeks these telephone calls home became more and more frequent, as it turned out that José had begun to suffer from a mysterious ailment. Telephone calls and remittances intensified as José's siblings in Immokalee made decisions about their brother based on the information they received about his state of health. They came to believe that José's illness was due to witchcraft (*mal de puesto*), brought on by someone who envied his job as a nurse. Then, while still in Florida, they decided that José should be taken to the neighboring state of Oaxaca to be examined by a *brujo* (traditional healer) who was believed to have the ability to cure that particular spell or curse. They proceeded to contract the brujo's services by phone and he soon informed them that he had performed the cure: according to his report, their younger brother had "expelled stones and sand from his head" and would soon be well. To pay the hospital bills and a series of treatments for José, his siblings in Florida sent more than five thousand dollars to Mexico, but that was insufficient to save the young man's life, as he died in March 2004. Rosaura and Octavio traveled to Mexico to attend the funeral. The hastily made arrangements for the trip involved the money transfer agency, because getting them to the airport in Miami entailed coordinating several movements. First, Rosaura's husband drove them to the Okeechobee highway. There, Helena's cousin Roger was awaiting them. It turned out that in that moment he was living temporarily in Miami and offered to drive them from their rendezvous point on the highway to the Miami airport, where they would then catch their flight to Mexico City.

Despite the fact that there were disagreements and tensions among the Rodríguez siblings—one of them actually avoided all contact with the others, and vice-versa—they all shared the same pain of separation from the rest of their clan back home in Chiapas. During the crisis caused by José's illness they all congregated at the money transfer office to speak with their relatives at home, to discuss the next steps they should take, to send money, and to hammer out agreements. Similar to the transnational Jacaltec families discussed in chapter 3, the Rodríguez family took advantage of transnational communications to overcome the constraints of time and space in making collective decisions about the fate of their loved one back in Chiapas.

Because of her close relationship to the members of the family in both the United States and Mexico, Helena received messages from Chiapas that she would transmit to José's brothers and sisters when they came to her office. Moreover, if because of some technical problem they were unable to communicate with Chiapas, she would make sure that messages got through to their relatives as soon as communication was restored. This situation allowed her to play the role of intermediary, and she was often the first to receive the latest news from both sides of the border. Despite this somewhat advantageous position, out of respect for the family Helena never voiced her skepticism concerning their evaluation of José's illness as the result of witchcraft. Nor did she express her disagreement with their decision to hire the services of a brujo to cure the malady they called *mal de puesto*, even though her involvement with the aggrieved family from Chiapas led her to attend meetings outside her agency where the siblings discussed this painful matter.

Months later, relations between Helena and the Chiapanecos became even closer when one of the immigrants suffered a traffic accident. She actually closed her business in order to go and help him. Similarly, the Rodríguez family offers her support when circumstances require it, either with her business or with her son or husband. Although there are numerous other money transfer agencies available where they could send money to Mexico, it goes without saying that the Rodríguez's would never visit any other agency: they simply prefer to wait until their friend opens hers. In addition to their daily interactions at the office, Helena and the Chiapanecos see each other with a certain frequency in the evenings to chat or have dinner together. The women of the Rodríguez clan spend more time with Helena, as they accompany one another to go shopping, do their banking, tend to school affairs, or simply get together to chat. The friendship that unites Helena and these young women is stronger than her ties to other women from her own country that also live in Immokalee. The social networks that come to be woven in multicultural, multiethnic settings among groups with no natural links, such as those that characterize co-nationals or people who share class identities or common beliefs, are achieved precisely because individuals cross boundaries of nation, class, belief, and even gender when necessary.

This case illustrates some of the conditions that allow simple interpersonal relationships to be transformed into spontaneous solidarities among immigrants from different national groups. Participation in collectivities of this nature opens the possibility of creating social capital that benefits the people involved by giving them access to collective resources such as useful information and/or knowledge that can be converted into economic capital, power, or social prestige. In the case examined above, Helena provides news of job opportunities because she interacts with such a large number of people on a daily basis. In exchange, those people bring new clients to her agency to send their remittances, purchase prepaid telephone cards, or buy some other product from among the diverse wares that she sells there. In this way, both parties benefit from their social relationship, not only by resolving problems of everyday life, but also by generating more tangible forms of capital.

In the episode narrated here, one aspect that stands out is the absence of other Dominicans, except for Roger, who played only a collateral role. Much of the support that Helena receives in the town does not come from her co-nationals, but mainly from Mexican immigrants (like the Rodríguez family from Chiapas) who can be seen as dispersed or *solos*,[11] and who accompany her and help her in difficult times. Such spontaneous solidarities first arise due to contingent circumstances and at critical junctures, but then become solidified in the midst of the precarious conditions in which immigrants so often find themselves. We call these relations "spontaneous solidarities" because they evolve at the margins of more formal, institutionalized networks, unlike those discussed in the two cases that follow. This case does not rely on the typical vertical linkages associated with transnationalism that link sending and receiving communities. Moreover, the solidarity between this Dominican woman and the Chiapanecos is not rooted in a common territory or shared past, reflecting the transitory nature of the alliance and the people involved.

The nexus established between these immigrants from two different national groups transgresses the boundaries that at first glance would seem to separate them, making them tenuous or, perhaps in some cases, erasing them completely. They are brought together by the shared aspects of their lives—the social, economic, and political disadvantages of not speaking the official language. They are forced to survive on the meager wages they obtain through their daily labor, which is often insecure and exhausting. In addition, they are united by their involuntary exile that separates them from their relatives, who often end up becoming their dependents. These forms of solidarity, though temporary, enable mobile populations to confront everyday problems of survival as they respond to the conditions of the global capitalist system.[12] On an imaginary continuum of solidarity, this case would represent the most fragile form, one that emerges in specific junctures but lacks continuity and that, therefore, contrasts strongly to the other two cases we discuss below.

The Transnational Fiesta of Santa Cruz among Mestizos from Chamácuaro

Chamácuaro is located in the municipality of Acámbaro in the state of Guanajuato and has a population of some fifty-five hundred inhabitants. Since the turn of the twentieth century, this town has had one of the highest rates of migration to the United States in all of Mexico. The long history of out-migration together with the discovery of new labor markets has produced a kind of diaspora among its people throughout the United States, such that today immigrants from Chamácuaro can be found in Cicero and Chicago, Illinois; Santa Rosa, Windsor, and Hillsborough, California; Immokalee, Palm Beach, and Lehigh, Florida; Dalton, Georgia; and in other cities and towns scattered around the states of Nebraska, Ohio, Texas, and Oregon.

Immigrants from Chamácuaro (Chamacuarenses) began to arrive in Immokalee in the 1970s, constituting the first flows of Latino immigrants to the area, and are considered the "founders" of the town. Among the first to arrive were members of several interrelated extended families who had first settled in Texas but later moved to Florida, where they found work as agricultural laborers. The networks that these "pioneer" families created allowed and encouraged the migration of other townspeople and eventually led to the formation of social networks in this area of Florida. As Douglas Massey and Jorge Durand write, "Each act of migration creates social capital among people to whom the migrant is related, thereby raising the odds of their migration."[13]

Over the years many Chamacuarenses became permanently established in Immokalee, though most continued to work in agricultural tasks (la labor). Others, however, favored by their migratory status as residents and/or U.S. citizens, obtained new employment opportunities, and some even managed to set up their own small businesses. The second generation, those born in Florida and better educated than the first, has a wider array of employment alternatives available to them than their parents did, and this has allowed them to take jobs in the service sector. The salient point here is that some Chamacuarenses have been able to escape, definitively, from the grueling work characteristic of the agricultural sector.

Of the three immigrant groups analyzed in this chapter, it is those from Chamácuaro who have accumulated the most social capital, as they have relationships with people located across a wide social and economic spectrum. By virtue of their condition as established immigrants, they have been able to adapt, conquer, and appropriate new social spaces that emerged in the milieu which they inhabit. They also face fewer hardships than other immigrants. It is perhaps due to these historical circumstances that their need to associate among themselves has diminished markedly in comparison to the situation that more recent arrivals face.[14] In reality, they succeeded in widening and diversifying their social networks through the inclusion of local or regional actors, such as Texans, Chicanos, Mexican Americans, and Euro-Americans, and this allowed them to escape from the exclusive bonds that united them at the beginning; though by the same token it also isolated them from the rest of the society. By interacting on a daily basis in social arenas that go beyond traditional spheres of employment, the Chamacuarenses, like other established immigrants, build close and, at times, long-lasting relationships with the local schoolteachers who teach their children or grandchildren, employees of hospitals and government agencies, professional people,[15] and authorities of the Catholic Church. In fact, they have now attained a certain level of social status in all of these contexts.

The commitment of Chamacuarenses to the local Catholic Church is an excellent illustration of their adaptation to this social milieu, because, as pointed out in chapter 8, it is precisely the more established immigrants who have the closest relationship to this institution, as evidenced not only by their constant attendance at Sunday mass and other rituals—like the Vía Crucis at Easter—but also by their active participation in annual events such as the pre-*carnaval* and *carnaval*. They contribute time and personal resources to these two church-related activities and, in 2003, collected funds that totaled almost seventy thousand dollars.[16] Though these Chamacuarenses have succeeded in overcoming the precarious conditions and hostile environment that they encountered initially in Immokalee, this does not mean that they have been "assimilated"[17] into mainstream American life; rather, they conserve their traditions, language, and Mexican roots and reject some of the cultural elements of the receiving society.[18]

The informal and unstructured character of Chamacuarense community life in Immokalee is reflected in the annual collection drive they have organized for more than twenty years as a means of underwriting the costs of the celebration of the Fiesta de Santa Cruz (Feast of Holy Cross). In 2004, Chamacuarenses in Immokalee collected a little over one thousand dollars to send home as a contribution to support the costs of their *fiesta patronal*. But this is a precarious union that rests upon the simplest and most informal level of organization: the individual entrusted with the responsibility for fund-raising simply visits the homes of *paisanos* from Chamácuaro, asking them to make voluntary donations to the fund that will be sent back to their hometown. There is no need to hold meetings to reach an agreement on a fixed, per-person donation, as each individual decides how much he or she can, or wishes to, contribute. This group shows a greater willingness to establish permanent solidarities in order to carry out joint activities related to organizing the fiesta patronal.[19] However, the unstructured nature of immigrant participation in the fiesta resembles the kind of decentralized, flexible transnational religious ties that Peggy Levitt refers to as "negotiated transnational religious organization."[20]

Most Chamacuarenses maintain close ties to their town of origin. Though some may have been living in Florida for thirty years or more, many of the members of the first and second generations still travel to Chamácuaro every year for the commemoration of their patron saint. As scholars of religion and migration have demonstrated for other Mexican localities,[21] fiestas patronales operate as one of the social mechanisms par excellence that serve to reunite those who have departed and those who remain behind, bringing them closer together and thus reaffirming their sense of belonging.

If we were to travel back in time to Chamácuaro some twenty years ago, we would witness a celebration that lasted just three days and included only one dance, but no live music. As collective remittances began to arrive, however, the fiesta was extended to nine days with dances every night accompanied by the music of several live bands. The fiesta now gets underway on April 24 and continues through May 3. It involves both religious and profane elements. Among the former we find processions, *novenas*, and masses, while the latter includes dances, cockfights, and bull-riding events that mark the end of the festivities.

During the fiesta, the townspeople recognize and legitimize the efforts of "the absent ones" through their economic contributions, as was expressed to us by one of the organizers: "What we want is for the people to have a good time. They come from far away, so they should enjoy themselves. Attending the fiesta is really nice; it makes you feel good. Some families don't spend money up there so that they can come; they don't make payments and sacrifice all year long. Up there, they're like slaves. . . . You can't walk in the street with a beer like here, so they come here to rest, to the Santa Cruz to feel good." For the *norteños* (those who live in the United States), the celebration is an opportunity to get together with friends and relatives. During the fiesta, immigrants participate in activities for collective benefit that reinforce their belonging to—and identity with—their place of origin. A local official offered the following example: "The day before yesterday we received a very good response because some childhood friends just arrived from California and they told me, 'Are you selling tickets? Well, we'll help you.' And because they know a lot of people who come from the U.S., this is the meeting point, they say hello and we made really good sales. Today I saw them and told them 'I need you' and they were the first ones to buy."

The fiesta constitutes a transnational social space because it reinforces bonds and keeps immigrants coming back. It entails a multiplicity of symbols that bring the Chamacuarenses closer together, both among themselves and with their town. The intense emotive, affective, and religious experiences that appear in the narratives recounted by participants during the "extraordinary time" of the fiesta contribute, on the one hand, to the symbolic reconstruction of their territory beyond political borders and, on the other, to the desire and dream of returning.[22]

Catholicism is the central element that agglutinates and gives continuity to this encounter. Everyone participates in a kind of "popular religiosity"[23] manifested by participating in processions, novenas, dawn serenades, rosaries, masses, and the adoration of the Holy Cross. The local priest told us that in reality his involvement in the organization of some of the events was quite limited. On the day set aside for their procession (May 2), immigrants are given a space and time that the priest uses to reintegrate them into the religious community, in order to reaffirm their faith and keep them from abandoning the ranks of Catholicism in a Protestant country. For most immigrants, the fiesta is their only opportunity to keep in touch with their paisanos, as telephone calls and remittances tend to become more and more infrequent and may even lapse entirely as people establish long-term residence in *el norte*. Thus, the mestizos from Chamácuaro, mediated by the symbolic efficacy of their beliefs that bring them back for the fiesta patronal, reflect a more stable and enduring form of solidarity that dates back several decades and has several common elements that resemble an emergent transnational community: a shared origin, a shared history, and a shared physical/symbolic territory.[24] These elements lead us to place them on a second level of our imaginary "continuum of solidarity."

A "Transnational Moral Community" of Otomíes

Through a young woman from Chiapas named Lorena, we met a group of Otomíes made up of her husband, Lázaro, and his brother, Miguel, both from Santa Teresa Davoxtha; another pair of brothers, Alfonso and Ambrosio, from El Mandhó, Ixmiquilpan; and Lucio from Pozuelos, who had only recently arrived from Atlanta with his wife and two small children, all of whom were living in a trailer. Lázaro was serving for a year (January 2004–January 2005) as the leader of an association of *hñahñus* (Otomíes, in the indigenous language) that brought together some fifteen fellow hñahñus living in Immokalee, five more in Clearwater, Florida, and another thirty in Las Vegas, Nevada. This group of

Otomíes had direct links to a small community called Santa Teresa Davoxtha, located in Cardonal, Hidalgo, Mexico, a town that, according to the 2000 census, had only 486 inhabitants. This group emerged just two years ago on the initiative of the immigrants themselves, who solicited approval and recognition from the authorities in their hometown as a means of establishing their legitimacy. The local *delegado* (delegate) sent Lázaro Palma an official appointment that named him the "leader of the immigrants of Santa Teresa Davoxtha." This same model of transnational organization has been reproduced in immigrant destinations of other Otomí immigrants from several localities in the state of Hidalgo, including Pozuelos, El Mandhó, and La Florida. In Las Vegas, Nevada, there is another group of immigrants from Santa Teresa Davoxtha that has its own leader, also legitimized by the "delegation" back home in Hidalgo.

The principal objective of these hometown associations[25] is to raise funds among immigrants in the United States to undertake public works projects in their towns of origin. To give one example, immigrants from Pozuelos (Ixmiquilpan, state of Hidalgo) first restored their church building and then went on build a kiosk in the central square, a track for horse races, and a bull-riding ring. The funds collected are also used to underwrite fiestas patronales.

The first activities carried out in Santa Teresa Davoxtha consisted of repairing the paving stones in the church atrium, constructing a building to house the delegation, and erecting stands at the local bull-riding ring. In the year 2004, immigrants organized two fund-raising drives: in the first, each person donated $100 dollars, while in the second the contribution was $150 dollars. Likewise, the association supports the celebrations to honor Santa Teresita de Jesús, the town's patron saint, which are held every year, from October 15 to 20. Remittances are used to purchase flowers, pay the *charros* (Mexican cowboys) for the bull-riding events, and buy the *castillos* (elaborate towers with fireworks). In Immokalee, Lázaro and other immigrants from Santa Teresa Davoxtha—just like their paisanos back home—celebrated their patron saint on Saturday, October 16. For this event, the group (*teresitos*) collected a total of some $1,300 dollars; funds that were used, among other things, to buy young goats and beer.

In his role as leader, Lázaro is in charge of collecting money from his fellow paisanos and assuring that it is sent back home.[26] Every time we observed him making or receiving phone calls on his cellular telephone to or from Clearwater, Las Vegas, or to his associates in Immokalee, he invariably spoke in Otomí. From time to time, Otomíes in Clearwater travel to Immokalee for meetings held by the organization. In 2004, immigrants from Santa Teresa Davoxtha also "reinvented" the fiesta of the Virgin of Guadalupe in their hometown, celebrated on December 12. This was the first time that this particular festival was held there, and it was made possible by the funds sent by immigrants. This celebration is an example of the important function that social remittances—remittances that go beyond simple economic transactions—fulfill in the process of reactivating traditions in the contemporary era.[27]

Otomí migration to Florida began in the 1980s and was concentrated in Clearwater, a tourist city on the west coast of the peninsula, already populated by some twenty thousand immigrants from the state of Hidalgo who worked mostly in the service sector, though a few had managed to set up some fifty small businesses.[28] The hñahñus in Clearwater have created a plethora of civic, social, and political organizations to unite forces and undertake a range of projects, both in Clearwater and back home in Ixmiquilpan, Hidalgo.

Like many other Otomíes, Lázaro first migrated to the Federal District (Mexico City), where he worked in construction. There, the Otomíes organized themselves and returned home to attend annual fiestas, so that leaving their communities did not constitute a cultural rupture but, rather, a redefinition of ethnic belonging and identity upheld by continuous returns and remittances. The forms of cooperation and communalism in which Otomíes are socialized include "cargo" systems that continue to function even though the *mayordomos* (those named to positions in the system) may live outside the locality or even in the United States. For example, Miguel held such a post for two consecutive years from afar while living in *el norte*, though he was obliged to buy the supplies needed to feed the musicians during the days of the fiesta back in his community of origin.

Although recognizing the limitations related to the concept of "community" discussed in chapter 2, we argue that the Otomíes in Immokalee constitute an emergent "transnational moral community" whose boundaries transcend physical or territorial space. As Regina Martínez Casas and Guillermo de la Peña put it, what is important is "not the place, but belonging, and this is defined by a set of meaningful elements manifested as symbolic borders."[29] The Otomíes share millenarian cultural traditions and values that maintain their unity and, at the same time, their links with their place of origin. Similar to Miami Cubans discussed in chapter 1, they function as a "moral community."[30] Moreover, the Otomí community is organized on different levels. On one level we find the transnational organization that links them to Santa Teresa Davoxtha through an official appointment that defines their responsibilities to the town. On another level, however, there is a complex support network that sustains them as an ethnic group in a much broader sense.

This group's ethnic identity and bounded solidarity was even more marked in Immokalee, where, despite the immigrants' distinct places of origin in Hidalgo (Santa Teresa Davoxtha, El Mandhó, Pozuelos, La Heredad, San Nicolás, and La Florida, among others), they all knew and supported each other and celebrated shared times and spaces in which they re-created their customs and lifestyles. Rites of passage, such as baptisms or fifteenth birthday celebrations for young girls (*quinceañeras*) or the commemoration of Santa Teresa, were all occasions to get together and celebrate in style. Most hñahñus attended such events, whether alone or with their families. There they speak their maternal language, though many—especially men—can also speak Spanish, and some even understand a few words of English.[31] Almost all of these immigrants work as housepainters, carpenters, or in other occupations related to the construction sector. As new immigrants arrive from Mexico or from other places in the United States, they are placed in jobs by their better-connected paisanos, normally outside the agricultural sector (*la labor*). If for some reason one of them has to work in the fields, the group "tries to pull him" into better job markets—like construction—as soon as possible.

Despite their relatively recent arrival in Immokalee—in the early 1990s—the Otomíes have already conquered several employment niches, including housepainters, carpenters, gardeners, sub-contractors, agricultural workers, and also *pinteros*[32] and small business men. Their economic advancement can be seen in the frequency with which they celebrate cultural rituals in Immokalee. On one Saturday, for example, we attended the baptism of two children where there were over one hundred guests. Though most (perhaps eighty) of them were young men of Otomí origin, there were also entire families, married women, and young unmarried girls from the same ethnic group. Macondo, the "light and sound" company hired for the event, was also owned by Otomíes. The young people who promised to serve the meal were not allowed to imbibe alcoholic drinks. The abundance displayed on this occasion showed the Otomíes' capacity to turn social capital into economic capital and then to spend it copiously in symbolic-religious social rites that are culturally important and that contribute to strengthening mutual ties.

The transnational moral community made up of Otomíes constitutes a form of solidarity rooted in "bonding" social capital, with higher density and stronger ties than that exemplified in the two previous cases. This is related to the Otomíes' long history of confrontation with state authority, dating back to pre-Hispanic times and continuing with the colonial and postcolonial state. The Otomíes oppose and sometimes reject the Mexican state, claiming that their communities' economic development has been achieved without the state's help, in part thanks to remittances from paisanos in the United States. On the one hand, while their history of exploitation and subordination produces a defensive, reactive ethnicity,[33] it also reinforces their cohesion and autonomy as an ethnic group. However, in contrast to the Jacaltecos in Jupiter (see chapter 3) who look to churches and other civic organizations to replace communal and family sources of social control, the Otomíes continue to maintain a close, perhaps even rigid, relationship with their community of origin, exemplified by their continuing loyalty to the normative system of authority in Santa Teresa Davoxtha.[34]

The confrontations with authorities that occasionally occur, far from sowing disunity, strengthen Otomí ethnicity, which is expressed in the continuity of such cultural values as language, the *cargo* system and its *mayordomos*, social normativity (family values, uses, and customs), traditions, worldview, and links to their territory (both physical and symbolic) that serve to identify and unite them. This group cohesion contributes to converting the social capital they generate through their networks into concrete benefits. Despite their position of social, economic, political, and cultural disadvantage due to their status as undocumented, indigenous immigrants with comparatively little migratory experience, these Otomíes have already succeeded in escaping from the lowest rung on the economic ladder of the "dependent empire" of agricultural labor. Paradoxically, it is also their ethnicity that has given them the means to overcome this situation of socioeconomic disadvantage.[35] In comparison to the two cases discussed above, the Otomíes' accelerated success in transforming their scarce social capital into economic resources can be explained by the greater density and intensity of their ties, including transnational ties, rooted in a positive ethnic identity.

Conclusions

In the examples described above, we can perceive varying degrees of solidarity among different groups of immigrants, a phenomenon that arises from a series of factors, including legal status, ethnic origin, common beliefs, and the precarious conditions in which immigrant populations live. In this study, we have presented analyses of three cases along a continuum of solidarity: from looser, less formal groups like the peasants from Chiapas to the case of the Otomíes, characterized by denser, stronger ties of solidarity. We would now like to highlight elements that are common to all three cases, and those that serve to distinguish among them.

All three examples of solidarity simultaneously take advantage of and benefit from the technological advances that foster transnational linkages. Thanks to long-distance telephone services, the fax machine, computer-mediated communication, instant monetary remittances through wire transfers, and frequent trips by legal immigrants, all three groups are able to communicate more quickly and efficiently among themselves, reinforce their transnational ties, stay informed, and exercise control, despite the fact that they are living on the other side of the U.S. border. The use of these technologies directly influences the functionality of these solidarities. The information and knowledge that flow through these circuits (*auditorios*) also constitute part of the social capital to which these groups have access and which can be transformed into economic or symbolic resources, such as prestige and power.

The first and third cases include more recent immigrants from emerging migratory states like Chiapas and Hidalgo. The second case is different, as it centers on well-established immigrants from Guanajuato, a state with a long-standing migratory tradition. It is precisely the long history of such mobile populations that seems to affect the creation of networks of solidarity. Those immigrants who have been established in their destinations for more than thirty years require less support from their paisanos than more recently arrived immigrants who are still carving out spaces in their new destinations. The Chamacuarenses who arrived earlier soon attained legal status as residents or citizens, and this endowed them with greater stability and the prospect of better job opportunities. However, the case of the Otomíes shows that, though they lack the legal status of immigrants from Guanajuato, their stronger ties and networks have allowed them to escape from the kind of agricultural work in which some Chamacuarenses are still trapped. As with the case of Jacaltecos in Jupiter discussed in chapter 3, the ethnic identity of the Otomíes has played a fundamental role in this process by allowing them to move into labor markets and then advance through them with a certain ease and in a relatively short time, an element that is absent among the mestizos from Guanajuato.

Mark Granovetter argues that the "pervasive use of strong ties by the poor and insecure is a response to economic pressures."[36] Instead of relying on weak ties with acquaintances, the most vulnerable immigrants are more likely to rely on strong ties with kin and close friends, or, in this case, co-ethnics, for survival. However, despite the advantages of strong ties, "the heavy concentration of social energy in strong ties has the impact of fragmenting communities of the poor into encapsulated networks with poor connections between these units."[37] In other words, the strong ties developed in this model of solidarity can undermine the formation of "bridging" ties that can link different groups together in broader community organizations.

The Otomíes and Chamacuarenses share the common practice of popular Catholicism, characterized by fiestas patronales, that informs the transnationalism that exists within both groups; though due to their status as undocumented immigrants the former are unable to attend the celebrations in their places of origin. However, in contrast to the close relationship that exists between the Chamacuarenses and the Catholic Church in Immokalee, the Otomí community lacks formal or informal links with any religious organization. Most of the Otomíes we interviewed did not know the priests and had never entered the Catholic Church, and only a few had attended a religious baptism. Though the Chiapanecos admitted to being "nominal" Catholics, they live on the margins of their faith, as do many other immigrants who share that creed (see the discussion of the congregational life of immigrants in chapter 8). Nonetheless, in their places of origin they attend mass on occasions of symbolic rituals such as baptisms, weddings, and quinceañeras.

The cases analyzed here also share a strong orientation toward magical-religious activities and practices by virtue of the fact that all three groups (peasants, mestizos, and indigenous) invest a significant proportion of their income in sumptuary or ritual activities. The Chiapanecos financed treatment for their brother José, spending over five thousand dollars to pay a traditional healer associated with *brujería* (witchcraft) rather than trusting Western medicine. The mestizos from Guanajuato, though they apparently send small quantities of money to their place of origin once a year, also make extraordinary expenditures, not only in the consumption of (ceremonial) alcoholic beverages during the fiesta, but also in the form of individual donations to the church during the ritual. If we were to add up all the donations made by the Chamacuarenses dispersed across the United States, the total amount would come to several hundred thousand Mexican pesos, sums that are used to underwrite the costs of the festival. We could say the same about the Otomíes, who, though still in the first phase of economic accumulation, not only send thousands of dollars back to Hidalgo for various religious celebrations, but also make substantial economic outlays in their communities of arrival, where they reproduce their fiestas patronales and celebrate the rites of passage of their lifecycles, as exemplified by the case of the double baptism.

The cases of immigrants from Chamácuaro and Otomíes from Hidalgo both resemble emerging transnational communities that encompass shared meanings and beliefs expressed in the form of collective identity.[38] However, one important difference between the Otomíes and the Chamacuarenses has to do with the wide social networks that are established among hñahñus living in different cities in the United States (Immokalee, Clearwater, Las Vegas). In contrast, though we can find Chamacuarenses living in more than ten cities in at least eight different U.S. states, they have no links or organizations that might unite them beyond their shared place of origin. This diaspora of Chamacuarenses finds its primary nexus precisely in the fiesta patronal, and it is there that they contribute their collective remittances to investments in projects designed to improve the town's infrastructure or in the consumption of sacred goods.

It may be that because Immokalee is a new destination for Otomíes, the absence of immigrant pathways that facilitate settlement and integration encourages Otomíes to develop transnational networks that link them with paisanos in other cities in the United States and with their communities of origin. In other words, cultivating transnational relations is part of a survival strategy for Otomíes, whereas for Chamacuarenses their participation in transnational networks in support of the fiesta is unrelated to questions of survival in the community of settlement. These findings suggest that the emergence of transnational communities has less to do with the time of arrival of immigrants than with the group's level of social and cultural capital as manifested in ethnic solidarity.

Social processes such as those analyzed in this chapter represent only some of the new combinations of old forms of solidarity that are created and re-created as responses to economic globalization, which first displaces the poor from countries in the south,[39] where unemployment and misery prevail, and then pushes them toward the rich countries, where demand for cheap labor is high. These economic immigrants are forced to occupy the lowest level of the labor market, which is at once indispensable for, but disdained by, people in the United States. These spontaneous, permanent, and/or dense solidarities are thus expressions of the agency of Mexican immigrants in the face of global capitalism.

NOTES

1. The sociology of solidarity refers to linkages among individuals in a group or collectivity. Solidarity becomes a quality that emerges from groups and facilitates social coordination and is a precondition of all collective, non-spontaneous action. Neil Smelser and Paul B. Baltes, eds., *International Encyclopedia of the Social and Behavioral Sciences*, vol. 26 (New York: Elsevier Ltd., 2001), 14,588.

2. We use the terms "peasant," "mestizo," and "indigenous" to signal the differences in the social and cultural origins of these groups. Except for the Otomíes, who define themselves as such, these social subjects identify themselves in relation to their place of origin (locality, state, nation).

3. In Immokalee, there are other, more institutionalized forms of solidarity, including some forty Christian churches and two civic organizations that defend the rights and working conditions of agricultural laborers. These latter two organizations, the Coalition of Immokalee Workers (see chapter 5) and the Asociación Campesina (Peasant Association), have relatively large memberships and maintain a clear presence in the town. Both the Coalition of Immokalee Workers and the Asociación Campesina have links to external organizations that support them with economic, political, and logistical resources. See Patricia Fortuny, "Jornaleros agrícolas, víctimas de agricultores y de Taco Bell. La lucha por un centavo más," *La Jornada* (March 23, 2003): 8–9; Patricia Fortuny and Philip Williams, "Religion and Social Capital among Mexican Immigrants in Southwest Florida," *Latino Studies* 5, no. 2 (2007): 233–253.

4. Unlike the traditional vertical linkages associated with transnationalism that link immigrants with their communities of origin, "horizontal linkages" refer to "linkages that immigrants of various nationalities and social conditions sustain among each other and with nonimmigrants in increasingly multicultural host societies." Larissa Ruíz-Baía, "Rethinking Transnationalism: National Identities among Peruvian Catholics in New Jersey," in *Christianity, Social Change, and Globalization in the Americas*, ed. Anna Peterson, Manuel Vasquez, and Philip Williams (New Brunswick, NJ: Rutgers University Press, 2001), 152.

5. As discussed in chapter 1, "transnational social field" refers to a "network of networks that stretch[es] across the borders of nation-states." Nina Glick Schiller, "Transnational Social Fields and Imperialism: Bringing a Theory to Transnational Studies," *Anthropological Theory* 5, no. 4 (2005): 442.

6. Arjun Appadurai, "Grassroots Globalization and the Research Imagination," *Public Culture* 12, no. 1 (2000): 1–19.

7. In his article, Appadurai explains that the idea of an international civil society depends on the success of these efforts at globalization from below. Appadurai, "Grassroots Globalization," 3.

8. Here, we refer to institutionalized associations such as the churches or worker organizations mentioned at the outset. In chapters 5 and 8 there is more detailed discussion of these organizations' objectives, forms of operation, and relations with different migrants.

9. Nancy Ammerman, *Congregation and Community* (New Brunswick, NJ: Rutgers University Press, 1997).

10. The term "clan" is used as a synonym of "group" (a figure of speech), to avoid repetition.

11. Alarcón and Miles suggest that "since 1994 there has been a growing predominance of men who travel without family in the flow of persons who go 'north' to work in agriculture. In many rural towns in the U.S., they are commonly known as *solos*." Rafael Alarcón and Rick Mines, "El retorno de los '*solos*.' Migrantes mexicanos en la agricultura de los Estados Unidos," in *Migración internacional e identidades cambiantes*, ed. María Eugenia Anguiano Téllez and Miguel J. Hernández Madrid, (Zamora, México: El Colegio de Michoacán-El Colegio de la Frontera Norte, 2003), 43–44.

12. Appadurai, "Grassroots Globalization."

13. Douglas Massey and Jorge Durand, *Beyond Smoke and Mirrors* (New York: Russell Sage Foundation, 2002), 19.

14. The legal status attained by the Chamacuarenses over the years establishes a marked class differentiation between them and more recent migrants; one expressed when they refer to their "high" social position in contrast to the precarious situation of "other" migrants.

15. Some members of the second generation have joined the army, while others have gone on to study at university.

16. During the pre-*carnaval*, the faithful (mostly established immigrants like the Chamacuarenses) prepare and serve lunch. They donate the ingredients and their time and the meal is sold at a per-plate price. The money they collect is used to set up food stands and mechanical rides during the three nights of carnaval. Immigrants in Immokalee use the word "carnaval" to refer to the fair that is set up around the Catholic Church and includes food stands and rides.

17. Assimilation is one pattern of adaptation characteristic of immigrants, but by no means the only one. See Richard Alba and Victor Nee, *Remaking the American Mainstream: Assimilation and Contemporary Immigration* (Cambridge: Harvard University Press, 2003).

18. As one established migrant put it to his son who was born in the United States: "you've got a *nopal* on your forehead but you're speaking English."

19. In April 2004, some forty Chamacuarenses who live in Immokalee traveled together from Mexico City to Chamácuaro.

20. Peggy Levitt, "You Know, Abraham Was Really the First Immigrant: Religion and Transnational Migration," *International Immigration Review* 37 (2003): 847–873.

21. According to a 1996 survey of the Mexican Migration Project, of thirty Mexican towns, migrants from twenty-six had strong links with the place of origin, marked by their massive return for annual fiestas. Jorge Durand and Douglas S. Massey, *Clandestinos. Migración México-Estados Unidos en los albores del siglo XXI* (México: Universidad Autónoma de Zacatecas-Miguel Ángel Porrúa, 2003). See also Víctor Espinosa, "El día del emigrante y el retorno del purgatorio: Iglesia, migración a los Estados Unidos y cambio sociocultural en un pueblo de los Altos de Jalisco," *Estudios Sociológicos* 17 (1999): 375–418; Mónica Gendreau and Gilberto Giménez, "La migración internacional desde una perspectiva sociocultural: Estudio en comunidades tradicionales del centro de México," *Migraciones Internacionales* 1 (2002): 147–178; Luis Rodolfo Morán, "Representaciones religiosas de los mexicanos exiliados," *Estudios Jaliscienses* 39 (2000): 5–16; Olga Odgers, "La práctica religiosa entre los mexicanos residentes en el condado de San Diego," in *Migración Internacional e identidades cambiante*, ed. Maria Eugenia Anguiano and Miguel J. Hernández Madrid, 205–228 (Zamora, México: El

Colegio de Michoacán-El Colegio de la Frontera Norte, 2003); and Javier Serrano, "La dimensión cultural de las remesas: Los tapalpenses y su comunidad transnacional" (MA thesis in Social Anthropology, Centro de Investigaciones y Estudios Superiores en Antropología Social-Occidente, 2002).

22. For example, see Patricia Fortuny, "The Santa Cena of el Luz Del Mundo Church: A Case of Contemporary Transnationalism," in *Religion across Borders: Transnational Immigrant Networks*, ed. Helen Rose Ebaugh and Janet Saltzman Chafetz, 15–50 (Walnut Creek, CA: Altamira Press, 2002); Nina Glick Schiller, "Transmigrants and Nation-States: Something Old and Something New in the U.S. Immigrant Experience," in *The Handbook of International Migration: The American Experience*, ed. C. Hirschman, P. Kasinitz, and J. De Wind, 94–119 (New York: Russell Sage Foundation, 1999); Peggy Levitt, *The Transnational Villagers* (Berkeley: University of California Press, 2001); and Bryan R Roberts, Reanne Frank, and Fernando Lozano-Ascencio, "Transnational Migrant Communities and Mexican Migration to the U.S.," *Ethnic and Racial Studies* 22, no. 2 (1999): 238–266.

23. This refers to those religious experiences that believers make their own, characterized by a certain separation from, and independence of, the faithful in relation to the formal hierarchy and institutional theology. Thomas A. Kselman, "Ambivalence and Assumption in the Concept of Popular Religion," in *Religion and Political Conflict in Latin America*, ed. Daniel H. Levine, 24–41 (Chapel Hill: University of North Caroline Press, 1986).

24. Thomas Faist, "Transnationalization in International Migration: Implications for the Study of Citizenship and Culture," *Ethnic and Racial Studies* 23, no. 2 (2000): 89–222.

25. For background on Mexican hometown associations, see Víctor Espinoza, *El dilema del retorno: Migración, género y pertenencia en un contexto transnacional* (Zamora, México: El Colegio de Michoacán, 1998); Luin Goldring, "The Mexican State and Transmigrant Organizations: Negotiating the Boundaries of Membership and Participation," *Latin American Research Review* 37, no. 3 (2000): 55–99; Robert Smith, "Transnational Localities: Community, Technology, and Politics of Membership within the Context of Mexico and U.S. Migration," in *Transnationalism from Below*, ed. Michael P. Smith and Luis Eduardo Guarnizo, 196–238 (New Brunswick, NJ: Transaction Publishers, 1998); and Carol Zabin and Luis Escala Rabadan, *Mexican Hometown Associations and Mexican Political Empowerment in Los Angeles* (Washington, DC: Aspen Institute, 1998).

26. One person in Hidalgo is in charge of receiving and administering these funds. Lázaro sends a list with the names of those who made donations. In 2003, the townsfolk sent a video of the Santa Teresa festival.

27. Peggy Levitt, *Transnational Villagers*.

28. Ella Schmidt and María Crummett, "Heritage Re-created: *Hidalguenses* in the United States and Mexico," in *Indigenous Mexican Migrants in the United States*, ed. Jonathan Fox and Gaspar Rivera-Salgado, 401–415 (La Jolla, CA: Center for U.S.-Mexican Studies/Center for Comparative Immigration Studies, 2004).

29. Regina Martínez Casas and Guillermo de la Peña, "Migrantes y comunidades morales: Resignificación, etnicidad y redes sociales en Guadalajara," in *Ciudad, pueblos indígenas y etnicidad*, ed. Pablo Yanes et al. (México, D.F.: Universidad de la Ciudad de México, 2004), 91.

30. For a discussion of the moral community among Miami Cubans, see Alejandro Portes and Alex Stepick, *City on the Edge: The Transformation of Miami* (Berkeley: University of California Press, 1993).

31. Ambrosio and Miguel studied English for three months. Their main purpose was to try to improve their wages.

32. *Pinteros* are individuals who own some means of transportation (truck, or *troca*) in which they carry agricultural laborers to pick tomatoes, called *pinto*, so named because they have begun to ripen and must be picked for sale in local markets.

33. According to Portes and Rumbaut, "reactive ethnicity is the product of confrontation with an adverse native mainstream and the rise of defensive identities and solidarities to counter it." Alejandro Portes and Rubén Rumbaut, *Legacies: The Story of the Immigrant Second Generation* (Berkeley: University of California Press, 2001), 284.

34. In November 2004, the traditional authorities in Hidalgo ordered that Cirilo return home for a year to work as a policeman. In Immokalee, his paisanos were in a quandary, as they felt it was inconvenient for him to return at that time. Upon learning of Cirilo's refusal to occupy the post, the town's authorities imposed a 20,000 peso fine that would be used to pay someone to take his place. The association began to collect funds so that Cirilo would not have to return or lose certain rights back home.

35. Portes and Rumbaut, *Legacies.*

36. Mark Granovetter, "The Strength of Weak Ties: A Network Theory Revisited," *Sociological Theory* 1 (1983): 213.

37. Ibid.

38. Faist, "Transnationalization," 195.

39. Estimates indicate that there are currently some 150 to 200 million people in the world who are classified as economic immigrants, that is, individuals who move from nations in the south to northern countries in search of employment opportunities and better wages.

PART TWO

Collective Mobilization and Empowerment

5

Transnationalism and Collective
Action among Guatemalan
and Mexican Immigrants in
Two Florida Communities

TIMOTHY J. STEIGENGA AND PHILIP J. WILLIAMS

We all came together in 1993 in the struggle to improve our immigration
situation. We organized first in Florida and later at the national level. We
managed to halt the massive detentions and deportations that were taking place. The United States finally understood that there are
Guatemalans here in the country. It was a large movement. . . . The
Mayans are calm people, but they take action when they have to.

–Guatemalan Mayan community leader interviewed in South Florida

In his examination of the labor struggle waged by Mayan immigrants in a
Morganton, North Carolina, poultry plant, historian Leon Fink describes both a
juxtaposition and a collision between the forces of globalization and community. As Fink explains, "In ways that recall their nineteenth century immigrant
predecessors, the émigré Mayan workers 'use' community to at once defend
themselves against employer exploitation and to advance the interests of their
friends and families across international borders."[1] A similar struggle is currently playing out across the United States in non-conventional sites of immigrant settlement, stirring public debate in many local areas and sending waves
of repercussions back across borders to communities of origin. When do immigrants mobilize to pursue their collective interests and what tools do they have
at their disposal to achieve their goals? Which contextual factors are likely to
make immigrant mobilization more or less successful? What are the implications of various forms of mobilization? These are some of the most important
questions facing social scientists studying migration and advocates working to
promote immigrant rights.

In this chapter we attempt to provide a partial answer to these questions by comparing the very different cases of Mexican and Guatemalan immigrant community organization, transnationalism, and collective action in Jupiter and Immokalee, Florida. We explore the hypothesis that in Jupiter higher levels of social capital and cultural/ethic homogeneity among transmigrants, combined with low levels of social/cultural acceptance, facilitate greater reactive ethnicity.[2] Reactive ethnicity, in turn, provides the basis for greater collective solidarity and political mobilization in defense of ethnic group interests. Alejandro Portes has argued that reactive ethnicity also provides a strong foundation for extensive and intensive transnational activities.[3] As Portes explains, "there is no recourse but to draw a protective boundary around the group, identifying it with traditions and interests rooted in the home country and separating it symbolically and, at times, physically from the host society."[4] Ethnographic data from the two communities clearly suggests that Jupiter's immigrant population has more institutionalized group-level transnational connections than does Immokalee's.

Unlike the case of Jupiter, our research in Immokalee suggests that Mexican and Guatemalan immigrants experience lower levels of social capital and cultural/ethnic heterogeneity and extreme economic deprivation. We hypothesize that this context provides little grounds for reactive ethnicity and thus presents obstacles to ethnic-based collective solidarity and mobilization. When mobilization does occur in the context of Immokalee, it is more likely to be multi-ethnic and class based and focused on economic issues. Given the lower levels of reactive ethnicity in Immokalee, we also expect fewer and less formalized group transnational activities than in the Jupiter case.

We begin with a discussion of the findings from our survey on social capital, transnationalism, and collective action.[5] The next section presents comparative insights on transnationalism and collective action gleaned from our ethnographic research and qualitative interviews in Jupiter and Immokalee. We conclude with a discussion of the role of reactive ethnicity in immigrant communities, outlining the advantages and disadvantages in terms of collective action.

Comparing Jupiter and Immokalee

As noted in the introduction to the volume, Jupiter and Immokalee present us with a study in contrasts. Jupiter is a relatively small and extremely wealthy coastal community of approximately fifty thousand on the northern edge of Palm Beach County. The Latin American immigrant community makes up a bit more than 7 percent of the total population of Jupiter and is primarily made up of Mayans from southern Mexico and Guatemala. Immokalee, by contrast, is a majority Latino agricultural community in southwestern Florida's agricultural belt, located near the everglades in Collier County. Immokalee's population is more than 70 percent Hispanic, with a total population that rises to nearly thirty thousand during harvest season and then falls again to nearly half that figure as farmworkers move north along with the harvest. Immokalee's immigrants are primarily from rural communities and, above all, indigenous Mexican communities in Oaxaca, Chiapas, Hidalgo, Guerrero, and Veracruz.

Between January and March of 2004, we conducted survey research in both Jupiter and Immokalee to generate comparative data and gain further insights into the themes and hypotheses outlined above.[6] In this section, we provide a brief introduction to our findings, highlighting the background variables that distinguish the immigrant population in each community, migration trajectories, social capital and discrimination (as preconditions for reactive ethnicity), collective action, and measures of transnationalism.

Demographic and Background Information

When comparing socioeconomic variables between Jupiter and Immokalee, the biggest difference is in income. The mean score for weekly income in Jupiter is $339 per week while the mean for Immokalee was only $271. This is not surprising, as the biggest employment category for Immokalee was "agricultural worker," with over 50 percent of all respondents in this group. In contrast, less than 2 percent of the Jupiter sample works in agriculture. The largest employment category in Jupiter was domestic and other personal services (including gardening and landscaping) with nearly 40 percent of the sample. Nearly 20 percent of the Jupiter sample reported working either as skilled or unskilled labor for construction. Thus the wage differences in the two communities are clearly attributable to the very different employment opportunities in the two areas, with migrant farmworkers primarily concentrated in Immokalee.

The different labor and employment contexts in Jupiter and Immokalee also contribute to differences in terms of the permanency of the population. When asked if they had lived in other U.S. states, 60.0 percent of Immokalee respondents said that they had, while only 34.4 percent of Jupiter respondents have lived elsewhere in the United States. In Immokalee, 32.0 percent reported frequently traveling to other states while only 9.0 percent of the Jupiter sample reported frequent traveling.

The major finding in terms of educational level is that 64 percent of the entire sample has an elementary education or less, with no significant differences between the Immokalee and Jupiter samples.

As we knew from our interviews and community mapping, a large portion of the Jupiter population is from the same geographic area. In Jupiter, 42.4 percent of the sample is from the Guatemalan department of Huehuetenango. The second largest concentration is from Chiapas, Mexico, with 14.6 percent. The remainder of the Jupiter sample is spread between Guatemalan departments and Mexican states, with the next largest concentration from the Mexican state of Michoacán, with 8.6 percent. Immokalee's population is significantly more geographically diverse, with the largest concentrations from Oaxaca (13.1 percent) and Chiapas (13.1 percent), Mexico. The next largest concentrations come from Guanajuato, Mexico (11 percent), and Huehuetenango, Guatemala (10.3 percent), with the remainder primarily spread throughout the other Mexican states.

Migration Trajectories and Helping Co-nationals

Data on how and why respondents came to the United States illustrate some of the key differences between the immigrant populations in Jupiter and Immokalee. In the Jupiter sample, 60.5 percent reported that they had paid someone to bring them to their present location. In Immokalee, the figure was only 41.2 percent. Here we see what appears to be a more institutionalized network in the case of Jupiter. Since links to *coyotes* generally begin in the community of origin, we would expect that a population that comes from a more concentrated geographical area would report a higher use of these services than those from more geographically disperse sending communities. Data on why residents come to Jupiter provide further evidence for these more institutionalized transnational connections. In table 5.1, we see that significantly more Jupiter residents came to that city for family reunification reasons (50.7 percent) than did residents of Immokalee (only 33.1 percent). Nearly 15 percent of Jupiter respondents reported that they came due to contacts or friends, while less than 5 percent reported this reason in Immokalee (see table 5.1).

When asked to provide yes or no answers to a series of reasons why they might have come to the United States, Jupiter respondents continued to report family reunification, study, work, and a better life for their children at higher levels than Immokalee respondents (see table 5.2). Many of the earliest immigrants

TABLE 5.1
Reasons for Coming to Jupiter/Immokalee

Why did you come to this city?	Jupiter %	n	Immokalee %	n
Job, work, salary, study	19.4	26	52.0	77
Coyote brought me here	6.0	8	4.7	7
Family reunification	50.7	68	33.1	49
Contacts, friends	14.9	20	4.7	7
Weather, quality of life, personal choice	5.2	7	3.4	5
Guatemalan or Mexican community	2.2	3	1.4	2
Other	1.5	2	0.7	1

to arrive in Jupiter came during Guatemala's civil war, leading to a higher affirmative response on political repression in the Jupiter sample as well.

We also asked respondents to rate how often people in their city helped their co-nationals. As is clear from table 5.3, nearly twice as many Jupiter residents believed that residents helped their co-nationals a lot. In Immokalee, nearly 20 percent of those interviewed believed that residents helped their co-nationals "not at all."

These figures begin to fill in the key contrasts between Jupiter and Immokalee. Jupiter has a more geographically and ethnically homogenous immigrant population, with higher incomes, less mobility, more institutionalized immigration networks, and greater family connections. Jupiter residents are also more likely to believe that mutual assistance is available from their co-nationals.

TABLE 5.2

Reasons for Coming to the United States

	Jupiter		Immokalee	
Why did you come to the United States?	*% yes*	*n*	*% yes*	*n*
Family reunification	41.9	65	24.3	36
Study	30.3	47	8.8	13
Work	82.6	128	68.9	102
Better life for children	65.8	102	51.4	76
Political repression	12.9	20	4.1	6

TABLE 5.3

Co-national Solidarity

	Jupiter		Immokalee	
Do you think that people here help their co-nationals (paisanos)?	*%*	*n*	*%*	*n*
Not at all	11.6	18	19.7	29
A little	27.7	43	34.7	51
Some	26.5	41	29.3	43
A lot	26.5	41	13.6	20
No response	7.7	12	2.7	4

In Immokalee, by contrast, the immigrant population is more geographically and ethnically diverse, with lower incomes, more mobility, and less family reunification. Immokalee residents are less likely to see their co-nationals as sources of support or assistance.

Social Capital and Perceived Discrimination

So how do these differences translate into social capital and the other catalysts for reactive ethnicity? In order to get a more direct measure of social capital, we asked respondents about their number of friends before and after arriving in their current location. The disparity in terms of this measure of social capital was striking. The mean score for number of friends (living in the same city) in Immokalee was only 2.22, while the mean score in Jupiter was 7.01. When asked how many of these friends they knew prior to coming to the United States, the mean scores were 1.07 for Immokalee and 4.08 for Jupiter. Clearly, the Jupiter residents have a larger existing circle of friends as well as a greater transnational network of friends.[7]

The higher levels of social capital evident among the Jupiter Maya are accompanied by some more negative aspects of living among an affluent, largely Anglo population. When asked, "What is the worst part of living in this city," 29.8 percent of Jupiter residents cited culture and communication barriers, while only 12.4 percent of Immokalee residents cited these problems. In Immokalee, 52.4 percent cited material issues such as jobs, bills, and housing as the worst part of living in that city.

The data on perceived discrimination are even more revealing. When asked how often they felt discriminated against, 62.3 percent of Immokalee respondents said never or almost never. Only 51.0 percent of Jupiter residents gave those responses (see table 5.4).[8]

TABLE 5.4
Perceptions of Discrimination

Have you ever felt discriminated against in the United States?	Jupiter %	Jupiter n	Immokalee %	Immokalee n
Never/almost never	51.0	79	62.3	91
Once in a while	36.8	57	28.1	41
Frequently	11.6	18	9.6	14
No response	0.6	1	0	0

When asked who discriminates against them the most, 67.1 percent of Jupiter respondents specified Anglo-Americans, while only 37.3 percent of Immokalee residents did so. In Immokalee, respondents perceived that they were discriminated against by blacks (12.0 percent), Chicanos (6.0 percent), and other Hispanics (16.9 percent) at a much higher rate than in Jupiter (3.5 percent, 0 percent, and 9.4 percent, respectively). As Mexican and Guatemalan migrants constitute an overwhelming majority of Immokalee's population, societal reception of migrants tends to be more neutral than in Jupiter, in the sense that the minority Anglo population accepts the presence of migrant farmworkers as a necessary feature of the community and its principal economic activities. In Jupiter, by contrast, the majority Anglo population has reacted to the presence of Mayan immigrants with some alarm. In 2004, a group of Jupiter residents formed a nonprofit called Jupiter Neighbors against Illegal Labor (JNAIL) with the help of the Federation for American Immigration Reform (FAIR). The group staged a series of protests against the town's planned labor center. Since the center began operations in 2006, it has been targeted by two further protest groups (from outside of the town) and a local candidate for town council.[9]

Associational Participation and Collective Action

Given our findings on discrimination and social capital, we would expect that associational participation and activities would be greater in the context of Jupiter than in Immokalee. To some degree, the data substantiate this expectation. Jupiter residents do tend to participate in religious organizations more frequently than Immokalee residents (see table 5.5). While 71.3 percent of Immokalee respondents said that they never or almost never participated in a religious organization, only 52.5 percent of Jupiter residents reported such infrequent participation. More than twice as many Jupiter residents reported very frequent participation in religious organizations (see table 5.5). Given that

TABLE 5.5

Participation in Religious Organizations

How often do you participate in a religious organization?	Jupiter		Immokalee	
	%	n	%	n
Never/almost never	52.5	81	71.3	102
Once in a while	24.0	37	18.2	26
Frequently/very frequently	23.3	36	10.5	15

churches are the primary type of voluntary organization open and available to recent immigrants, religious participation provides a good proxy for associational participation in general.

When asked how often they teamed up with neighbors to improve something in their community, Jupiter residents also answered that they did so more frequently than Immokalee residents. On a scale from never to very frequently, only 21.1 percent of Immokalee respondents reported that they teamed up with neighbors once in a while, frequently, or very frequently. In Jupiter, however, participation was much higher, with 35.0 percent reporting that they teamed up once in a while, frequently, or very frequently.[10] Not surprisingly, we found that rates of religious participation were also significantly correlated with teaming up with neighbors. While religious affiliation had no effect on such participation, the frequency of participation in a religious organization is significantly correlated with the frequency of teaming up with neighbors to improve the community.[11]

In sum, the populations of Mexican and Guatemalan immigrants in Jupiter experience the social and economic conditions necessary to produce reactive ethnicity at higher rates than the Mexican and Guatemalan populations in Immokalee. The survey results confirm higher levels of social capital and perceived discrimination in the Jupiter case. Higher associational participation, collective action, more institutionalized family and friend networks, and greater stability and income also characterize the Jupiter case, confirming the links between reactive ethnicity and collective action. We now turn to a brief comparison of transnational processes and connections in the two communities.

Comparing Measures of Transnationalism

As Alejandro Portes, Peggy Levitt, and Sarah Mahler have argued, the concept of "transnational social fields" spanning host and receiving countries provides a useful tool for understanding elements of transnationalism among immigrant communities.[12] Individuals within these communities actively move between sending and receiving countries or use other means to maintain active lives in their new home and their country of origin. Many of these connections relate to religious and cultural institutions and practices.

For the most part, the standard measures of individual transnationalism in our surveys did not vary greatly between Immokalee and Jupiter. In other words, individual respondents in Jupiter were no more likely than those in Immokalee to call home or send money home to their families. However, immigrants living in Jupiter were more likely to attend events related to their country of origin (see table 5.6). This finding is important because it further demonstrates the greater institutionalization of transnational linkages in Jupiter. While the number of individual financial and communication transactions is just as high in Immokalee, organized group participation in transnational events (fiestas or other events) is greater in Jupiter.

TABLE 5.6

Participation in Guatemalan/Mexican Events

How often do you attend Guatemalan/ Mexican events organized by people who came specifically for that?	Jupiter		Immokalee	
	%	n	%	n
Never/almost never	63.8	99	77.6	114
Once in a while	23.2	36	15.0	22
Frequently/very frequently	11.6	18	7.5	11
No response	1.3	2	0	0

TABLE 5.7

Receive News from Guatemala/Mexico

How often do you get news from Guatemala/Mexico from friends?	Jupiter		Immokalee	
	%	n	%	n
Never/almost never	24.6	38	38.7	57
Once in a while	51.3	79	46.9	69
Frequently/very frequently	22.7	35	14.3	21
No response	1.3	2	0	0

In table 5.7 we see that Jupiter residents get their news from home more frequently from friends than do Immokalee residents. Given the higher numbers of friends found in the Jupiter sample, this finding is expected. Again, we find evidence for a stronger network of transnational ties in the Jupiter case, this time through the transnational "grapevine."

Tables 5.8, 5.9, and 5.10 present data on transnational media. Here the findings suggest that Immokalee has a greater presence of Mexican and Guatemalan media. This finding can be explained by the fact that the larger Guatemalan and Mexican community in Immokalee provides a larger target for Spanish-based media, leading to greater readership and viewing. Multiple generations of immigrants in Immokalee provide a long-standing audience for newspapers, radio transmissions, and television channels from the home country. In Jupiter,

TABLE 5.8
Read Newspapers from Guatemala/Mexico

How often do you read newspapers from your home country?	Jupiter		Immokalee	
	%	n	%	n
Never/almost never	87.1	135	70.3	104
Once in a while	10.3	16	23.0	34
Frequently/very frequently	1.9	3	6.1	9
No response	0.6	1	0.7	1

TABLE 5.9
Watch Guatemalan/Mexican Television

How often do you watch Guatemalan/Mexican television?	Jupiter		Immokalee	
	%	n	%	n
Never/almost never	59.4	92	25.1	37
Once in a while	15.5	24	19.7	29
Frequently/very frequently	24.5	38	55.1	81
No response	0.6	1	0	0

TABLE 5.10
Receive Home Country Information from Radio

How often do you hear information from Guatemala/Mexico on the radio?	Jupiter		Immokalee	
	%	n	%	n
Never/almost never	77.3	119	54.7	81
Once in a while	13.6	21	29.1	43
Frequently/very frequently	7.1	11	16.2	24
No response	1.9	3	0	0

by contrast, there are fewer Spanish-language media outlets, and interactive radio transmissions from Guatemala only began in 2006.

The survey results suggest that differences in transnationalism are primarily evident at the level of organized group participation in transnational events, while the degree of individual transnational transactions does not differ greatly between communities. The overall picture that emerges fits closely with our analysis of the conditions for reactive ethnicity in the Jupiter case. As Alejandro Portes and Eric Popkin have elaborated in the cases of Salvadorans and Kanjobal Mayans in Los Angeles, discrimination combined with strong ethnic networks can give rise to greater transnational organization.[13] The interaction between these variables is mutually reinforcing, as transnational networks, in turn, serve as resources for mobilization and collective action. Our three years of in-depth ethnographic research in the two communities provides ample evidence to fill in the snapshot of the relationship between transnationalism and collective action that emerges from the survey results.

Transnationalism and Collective Action in Jupiter

In the case of Jupiter, our qualitative research revealed important connections between transnationalism, identity, and collective action in the immigrant community. The celebration of fiestas, organization of soccer tournaments, collection of funds to return the dead to Jacaltenango, presence of the marimba at community gatherings, and transmission of information (community news, videos of celebrations, and fireworks for celebrations) all serve to reinforce the connections between the hometown and the present location. In the process, the foundation, networks, and institutions necessary for collective action among the predominantly Jacaltec Maya community in Jupiter have emerged. A brief description of the events and organization surrounding the annual Fiesta Maya in Jupiter serve to illustrate this process.

The fiesta was first celebrated in 2002, in the recently constructed town center of Jupiter's largest planned community, Abacoa. Initially conceived as a parallel celebration of *La Fiesta de la Virgen de Candelaria*, the most important fiesta of the year in Jacaltenango, the fiesta has grown in size and importance since its inception. Each year, members of the Jacaltec community form sets of commissions, each responsible for different elements of the festival. The groups meet weekly in the months leading up to the festival to prepare for the Mass, procession, food, publicity, and other aspects of the celebration. Students and faculty from Florida Atlantic University's Wilkes Honors College also attend these organizational meetings and participate in planning for the festival.

The first year, the festival drew more than seven hundred community residents, primarily Guatemalan Mayans, to the new planned community of Abacoa for a day of cultural exchange, celebration, music, sports, and food. In the following years, the festival has grown in size (drawing nearly fifteen hundred participants each year) and has expanded to include participating music and dance groups from Mexico, Venezuela, Colombia, and Chile. The results of the festival continue to reverberate within the Guatemalan community and in the larger Jupiter community.

The initial organizers of the fiesta continued to meet and eventually filed for nonprofit status under the name of a previously active group, Corn-Maya Inc. The nonprofit has grown significantly since 2002, garnering grant support from the United Way, the Community Foundation, and multiple private donors. Representatives of Corn-Maya successfully lobbied on behalf of Jupiter's immigrant community, built a strong coalition with local grassroots political and religious groups, and now collaborate with town authorities, Catholic Charities, and the Friends of El Sol to operate the El Sol Neighborhood Resource Center, a multi-service center that has addressed day-labor issues in the town while also providing key educational and other resources to the immigrant community.

Since 2002, Corn-Maya's office has served as an unofficial employment office, a hurricane relief center, a community care closet, and a clearinghouse for immigration, legal, counseling, health, and other services to the immigrant community. In August 2005, Corn-Maya collaborated with the local Catholic church (St. Peter's) to sponsor a sister city agreement between Jupiter and Jacaltenango. The agreement was signed by the mayors of the two cities and the Guatemalan foreign minister, Jorge Briz. In February 2007, Corn-Maya hosted a visit by Guatemalan president Oscar Berger to the El Sol Center in Jupiter. Berger praised the center's work and promised to raise it as an example in his subsequent meetings with President George W. Bush.[14]

Corn-Maya has also played a key role in sponsoring soccer tournaments for Guatemalan and Mexican teams on Sundays. Teams are organized around the sending communities, each with its own *reina*, who gives a speech prior to the beginning of the tournament. Soccer plays a crucial role for the Mayan community as it is the primary social event of the week and serves as the location for the dissemination of community information. The finals of each tournament are broadcast live via cell phone to a radio station in Jacaltenango.

The planning, organizing, and celebration of the fiesta provide Jupiter's immigrant community with both a sense of collective identity and an organizational basis for further mobilization. The frequent experience of discrimination and social exclusion is superseded, at least for a day; as the community comes together to proudly display their traditions in the newly minted Abacoa development. The process of organizing, though frequently stressful, leads to a sense of mutual accomplishment and solidarity among the participants once all of the complicated details required to make the fiesta work are completed.

As outlined in chapter 7, this solidarity among Jacaltecos is rooted not just in the fiesta, but also in shared images of home, shared practices, shared language, and a shared sending community. When any Jacalteco dies in the United States, an informal group raises funds to return the body to be buried in Jacaltenango. When a new immigrant arrives from Jacaltenango he/she may be offered a low-interest (or no-interest) loan to pay off the higher-interest charges associated with the journey from Guatemala. When the soccer tournaments are organized, the teams represent the various physical locations surrounding Jacaltenango. When the fiesta is celebrated in Abacoa, it is organized, as much as possible, in direct parallel with the fiesta in Guatemala.

The elements of solidarity and self-help that have emerged among the Jupiter Maya have also translated into public action. Organizing for the festival morphed into organizing to reinvigorate the nonprofit Corn-Maya. Representatives of Corn-Maya have met frequently with Jupiter's political authorities, sought funding for community services, participated in community events, sponsored the sister city agreement and visits from Guatemalan dignitaries, and worked to coordinate the various civic and religious groups related to the immigrant community.

The members of Corn-Maya also played a leading role in demanding that the Catholic Diocese address the fact that the church located closest to the Guatemalan community in Jupiter did not have any mission to the immigrant community. A 2002 letter addressed to the new bishop reads in part: "As a community of faith with very traditional and strong Catholic values, we wanted to worship, practice, and share them in a congregation that can receive us as equals. Nevertheless, you did not include us in the convocation 15 years ago and you have excluded us to this very day. . . . [Y]ou are one of us, our brother in Christ who doesn't know it, and we love our wayward brother. As you go to your powerful position the prayer meetings will ask that God be with you. Don't be mad at us for reminding you that there is no Holy Communion when people are excluded."[15] In 2003, the diocese instituted Spanish services at the Catholic Church in Jupiter. Since that time, St. Peter's has played a key role in advocating for the immigrant community in Jupiter.

The most notable achievement that has emerged from the growth of Corn-Maya is the El Sol Neighborhood Resource Center. In 2004, after two years of intense lobbying, the Jupiter Town Council placed two hundred thousand dollars in the five-year Community Investment Program (CIP) to fund a labor center in the town. In 2005, the town council voted to allow Corn-Maya and Catholic Charities to use a town building to establish a neighborhood resource center. Corn-Maya, the Friends of El Sol, and Catholic Charities opened the center in September 2006. The center is now run exclusively by El Sol and Corn-Maya.

In short, it appears as though the organizing and collective action necessary to carry out the public celebration of the fiesta has acted both as a unifying force and an impetus to public action for the Jacaltec community and their fellow immigrants in Jupiter. The many transnational elements of the celebration of the fiesta, along with other imagined and real conceptions of home (such as sending back the dead and organizing the soccer leagues), are linked with increased activism and civic engagement among the Jacaltec community in Jupiter. At the same time, the celebration of the fiesta helped to forge links between the immigrant community, the university, and representatives of the town. These connections began to bring institutional support for the immigrants as well as opportunities for internships and service learning for students and volunteer opportunities at El Sol for interested community members. A process that began with what Robert Putnam has called "bonding" social capital—celebrating a local town's festival—transformed into a process of "bridging" social capital: bringing multiple groups and individuals together for the common purpose of creating a resource center that addresses local community needs related to the growing immigrant community.[16]

Transnationalism and Collective Action in Immokalee

In the case of Immokalee, low levels of social capital and cultural/ethnic heterogeneity and extreme economic deprivation present significant obstacles to constituting and reproducing transnational ties. Following Luis Guarnizo and Michael Smith, "the image of transnational migrants as deterritorialized, free-floating people represented by the now popular adage 'neither here nor there' deserves closer scrutiny."[17] In Immokalee, both our survey research and qualitative interviews provide plenty of evidence of "migrant-led transnationalism"[18] or "transnationalism from below,"[19] such as sending remittances, videos, and letters, maintaining kinship networks across borders, and participating in return migration. However, with the exception of a group of Otomíes from Hidalgo (see below), more institutionalized forms of transnationalism (hometown associations and collective community projects) are largely absent in the Immokalee case.

This is also true for religious institutions in Immokalee; although some maintain translocal relations with churches in nearby communities, we uncovered few examples of more institutionalized networks with churches in migrants' communities of origin. More typical were informal, decentralized cross-border initiatives, such as the pastor of the local Assembly of God church who maintains close ties with sister congregations in Mexico. The pastor regularly visits and supports a church in Hidalgo founded by a former member of the Bethel Assembly of God church, and individual church members have participated in evangelistic campaigns in Veracruz. The church in Immokalee also hosts frequent visits by preachers from Mexico and elsewhere in Latin America. Levitt refers to these examples of decentralized, flexible transnational religious ties as "negotiated transnational religious organization."[20]

Another example of flexible, decentralized transnational ties is the case of migrants from Chamácuaro, Guanajuato, who return each year in May for the Fiesta de Santa Cruz.[21] As described in chapter 4, migrants from Chamácuaro first began arriving in Immokalee during the 1970s and count themselves as among the "pioneers" of the Mexican presence in town. Despite lacking a formal organizational structure, each year migrants from Chamácuaro throughout the United States collect money to support the fiesta back home. In May 2004, migrants in Immokalee contributed approximately one thousand dollars to the fiesta, and about forty people traveled together to Mexico to participate in the annual festivities. They were joined in Chamácuaro by a few thousand migrants from all over the United States. The establishment of translocal networks between Chamácuaro and diverse localities in the United States, the systematic return of migrants, and the economic contributions from migrants in the United States have transformed the celebration into a transnational fiesta.

The Otomíes as the Exception

As demonstrated in the Jupiter case, for immigrants of limited means, social capital rooted in ethnic networks can provide key resources in confronting obstacles to socioeconomic advancement.[22] In Immokalee, a small group of Otomíes from the state of Hidalgo appear to be on a similar trajectory as the Jacaltec Maya in Jupiter.[23] As discussed in chapter 4, after less than a year, the Otomíes were able to multiply their social networks and use them to their economic advantage. Most moved out of agricultural labor and found employment in the construction industry in nearby Naples. New Otomí migrants arriving from Hidalgo are steered into construction work, unlike most Mexican migrant workers.[24] Why is it that indigenous Otomíes, lacking economic means, appear to be more successful in accumulating social capital than other recent migrant workers in Immokalee? The density of ties, including transnational ties, grounded in a reactive ethnic identity seems to be crucial. Although Mexican and Guatemala migrants face a less hostile reception in Immokalee, as compared to Jupiter, there is some hostility on the part of more established immigrants (mostly from traditional migrant sending states in western Mexico) toward recent migrants from southern Mexico and Guatemala. The denser ties among Otomí migrants have given rise to cooperative efforts such as the formation of a hometown association, bringing together Otomíes in Immokalee, Clearwater, and Las Vegas. The association raises money to support the annual fiesta and for small community development projects.

This group of Otomí migrants appears to be the exception, however, as the Mexican immigrant population in Immokalee is highly stratified in terms of class, ethnic, and regional origin, and there is generally limited interaction between Mexican immigrants and other immigrant groups (Guatemalans and Haitians). The structural obstacles that undermine the accumulation of social capital for most migrant workers also limit the possibilities for collective solidarity and mobilization in Immokalee. Not surprisingly, the overwhelming majority of immigrants in Immokalee do not participate in civic, religious, or political organizations. Moreover, the mobile livelihoods of migrant farmworkers make it difficult for organizations to sustain collective action.

The Coalition of Immokalee Workers as a Second Exception

The Coalition of Immokalee Workers presents a second exception to the rule of low levels of participation in Immokalee. Founded in the late 1980s, the Coalition emerged to challenge the oppressive working conditions of migrant farmworkers in Immokalee. In contrast to most religious organizations in Immokalee, the Coalition has been able to generate bridging social capital in its efforts to forge a multi-ethnic social movement. Its members are Mexican, Guatemalan, Haitian, and Euro-American. They construct their individual and collective identity as exploited farmworkers in opposition to the growers, crew leaders, and transnational businesses, such as Taco Bell. The organization has links with many labor and student organizations around the country as well as with interfaith movements from all over the United States. It is precisely through liberal Christian denominations that the Coalition is able to survive economically, the paradox being that most of its members are not active in any churches in Immokalee.[25]

The actions of the Coalition gradually evolved from a strategy based on "organizing farmworkers by emphasizing solidarity and commitment to *la causa*"[26] to one that combines community-based organizing with mobilizing external support through a direct attack on the "public identity"[27] of both farmworkers and the agricultural industry. After hunger strikes and marches organized by the Coalition failed to convince growers to negotiate with the farmworkers, in spring 2001 Coalition leaders turned their attention to organizing a nationwide boycott of Taco Bell. Taco Bell is the major client of Six L's Packing Company, the largest single-company tomato grower, packer, and shipper in Florida. Given Six L's repeated refusals to initiate talks with the Coalition, the aim of the boycott was to pressure Taco Bell to use its leverage with Six L's to improve wages and working conditions for tomato pickers.

The Coalition hoped to build off the success of consumer boycotts sponsored by farmworker organizations in other parts of the country. Moreover, it reframed its struggle to appeal to a broader audience. Appropriating the discourse of the "global justice" movement, Coalition leaders constantly referred to the sweatshop-like conditions in the fields of southwest Florida as a consequence of global capitalism. In addition, they depicted Taco Bell and its parent company, YUM Brands, as global fast-food giants who refused to accept corporate responsibility for their food supply chain. In adopting the global justice "master frame,"[28] Coalition leaders hoped to amplify and extend their boycott to include new constituencies.

This "scale shift"[29] from localized actions to a national boycott of Taco Bell garnered extensive national media attention, most of it sympathetic to the farmworkers' plight. As part of the boycott, the Coalition of Immokalee Workers and the Student Farmworker Alliance (SFA)[30] mobilized external support from a wide array of religious organizations, labor unions, and student groups throughout the country. After the first national caravan in spring 2002, Taco Bell representatives agreed to meet with Coalition leaders. Despite their grudging consent to sit down with farmworkers, company representatives were unwilling to get involved in what they considered an internal labor dispute between farmworkers and growers in southwest Florida. Nevertheless, in May 2003 the negative publicity generated by the boycott encouraged a substantial number of YUM Brands shareholders (35 percent) to support a resolution calling for a review of company policies related to corporate responsibility.[31] In March 2005, the Coalition ended its boycott when Taco Bell acceded to all of its demands, including a penny-per-pound "pass through" with its tomato suppliers in Florida that will go directly to tomato pickers.[32]

At the March 8 press conference announcing the agreement, Lucas Benitez spoke on behalf of the Coalition:

> Human rights are universal, and if we as farmworkers are to one day indeed enjoy equal rights, the same rights all other workers in this country are guaranteed, this agreement must only be a beginning. To make those rights truly universal, other leaders of the fast-food industry and the supermarket industry must join us on this path toward social responsibility. With a broad coalition of industry leaders committed to these principles, we can finally dream of a day when Florida's farmworkers will enjoy the kind of wages and working conditions we deserve. And when that day comes, the restaurants and markets of this country will truly be able to stand behind their food, from the fields to America's tables.[33]

Opportunities and Constraints

Particular localities provide differing opportunities and constraints for transnationalism and collective action.[34] Both our quantitative and qualitative data suggest that higher levels of social capital, greater cultural/ethnic homogeneity, and lower levels of social/cultural acceptance help foster and sustain more institutionalized forms of transnationalism in Jupiter, as compared to Immokalee. Not surprisingly, it is the more established immigrants in Immokalee that are most able to participate in transnational ties that require travel back to Mexico. In addition, social capital rooted in ethnic solidarity in the case of the Jacaltec Maya in Jupiter and the Otomíes in Immokalee provides a stronger foundation for more extensive and intensive transnational activities as well as bonding social capital. Finally, in Jupiter collective solidarity and mobilization that began with a form of reactive ethnicity and focused on gaining acceptance and visibility in the community became transformed, over time, into a broader coalition that crossed institutional boundaries. In Immokalee, mobilization has been multi-ethnic, class based, and focused on overcoming economic exploitation through the work of the Coalition.

Evaluating Reactive Ethnicity and Collective Action in Two Florida Communities

As Portes and others have argued, reactive ethnicity can provide a solid foundation for collective identity and political mobilization.[35] The mobilization of Latinos in California in response to Proposition 187 is a good example. Similarly, Popkin has documented the rise of reactive ethnicity on the part of Guatemalan Kanjobal migrants in Los Angeles in response to extensive discrimination.[36] In addition to reinforcing old forms of ethnicity, Kanjobals have linked with the growing Pan-Mayan movement in Guatemala.

In the case of Otomí migrants in Immokalee, dense social networks rooted in reactive ethnicity provide greater opportunities for social and economic advancement; however, the benefits of these dense ties do not extend beyond the Otomí community. In contrast, the Coalition of Immokalee Workers is a multi-ethnic movement that plays down ethnicity and focuses on the root causes of economic deprivation among migrant farmworkers. The Coalition has been successful in projecting its struggle beyond the local level, leading a nationwide boycott of fast-food giant Taco Bell. The agreement with Taco Bell in March 2005 provides real benefits to farmworkers and serves as a model for other farmworkers' organizations that have achieved minimal success in pressuring agricultural producers to negotiate farmworkers' demands. Soon after the agreement with Taco Bell, the Coalition organized a similar campaign targeting McDonald's. After two years of mobilizing, on April 7, 2007, the Coalition reached an agreement with McDonald's and its suppliers, modeled after the Taco Bell settlement.[37]

The disadvantage of such a "scale shift" from localized action to broader national contention is that the Coalition has tended to neglect some issues of more local concern to the migrant community in Immokalee in favor of projecting itself on a national stage. Local issues that receive less attention from the Coalition include wages for farmworkers outside the tomato industry, inadequate housing, pesticide use, and immigration reform. A farmworker from Guanajuato, Mexico, who was a member of the Coalition for three years, complained: "Sometimes they do good things and sometimes they turn things around. What they do is go *hacer un escándalo* [make trouble] in different states in the U.S. and not achieve anything. Many members ask, 'Why don't we do the marches here? Why do they have to go to California to hacer un escándalo.' A big group of people go to some office and shout slogans; then it's over and everyone returns to Immokalee."

The challenge for social movements like the Coalition is to remain rooted in local communities even as they adopt global frames and opportunities for scale shift. As Sidney Tarrow writes, "Global framing can dignify and generalize claims that might otherwise remain narrow and parochial. . . . But by turning attention to distant targets, it holds the danger of detaching activism from the real-life needs of the people they want to represent."[38]

In our case study in Jupiter, we found that Jacaltec Mayans face significant cultural and communication barriers and sometimes outright hostility to their presence. Not surprisingly, the early mobilization of immigrant groups in Jupiter tended to be inward-oriented, focused on reaffirming a Jacaltec identity and sense of belonging through transnational religious and cultural activities. Since then, the organizing efforts growing out of the Fiesta Maya have been aimed at achieving a more positive public image for the Mayan community and recognition for its contributions to the local economy.

While receiving some support from prominent town officials and civic and religious leaders, Corn-Maya's struggle to create a neighborhood resource center also met with significant opposition from some corners. As noted earlier, local neighborhood complaints about day-laborers and overcrowded houses were quickly transformed into an anti-immigrant lobbying group when representatives of the Federation for American Immigration Reform (FAIR) began organizing in town. Although small in number, the members of the JNAIL organization received extensive press coverage from the local paper (the *Jupiter Courier*) and other local media as the town council debated the opening of a center. At the same time, public acts of intolerance toward the immigrant community increased, including public insults and derogatory statements at town council meetings, targeted acts of vandalism, and a sign that reads "Slow—Illegal Immigrant Children at Play" placed near the local elementary school. As Jupiter's immigrants took to a more public stage to address concerns within their community, they also became the target of greater hostility on the part of some residents and found themselves in the sights of national groups such as FAIR.

Another potential drawback to mobilization through reactive ethnicity is that it can contribute to defensive and even exclusionary politics. This may militate against the formation of broader collective solidarities. For example, during the planning for the second Fiesta Maya in Jupiter, a group of Mayan dancers from Totonicapán were invited to perform during the festivities. After much discussion among the members of the Jacaltec Association, it was decided that the invitation should be withdrawn because people back in Jacaltenango who viewed videos of the event might be upset by the intrusion. Despite the previous year's decision that the event was to be open to various groups, the Jacaltec leaders were more concerned with their own particular connections with home than with building a sense of community with other groups. In other words, the very factors that facilitated unity and collective action among the Jacaltecos produced the opposite effect when applied to the larger Mayan community, the Hispanic community, and the immigrant community in general.

Alejandro Portes and Rubén Rumbaut also argue that reactive ethnicity may have a less positive impact at the individual level: "Youthful solidarity based on opposition to the dominant society yields an adversarial stance toward mainstream institutions, including education."[39] The result, according to Portes and Rumbaut, may be a form of downward assimilation. In Jupiter, we found little evidence of downward assimilation among the second generation. Rather, the children of immigrants in Jupiter appear to gain as much (in terms of spiritual and psychological resources) from the celebration of the fiesta as their parents. While they do face discrimination and even outright intimidation in some cases, the celebration of fiestas and other activities sponsored by Corn-Maya and St. Peter's Catholic Church allow the children of Jupiter's immigrants to experience and take pride in their Mayan culture. As Portes explains, "participation in transnational political activities can empower immigrants and invest them with a sense of purpose and self-worth that otherwise would be absent."[40] In regards to the second generation, Portes adds that transnationalism "offers a valuable counterweight to a relentless process of acculturation" that "carries the price of learning and interjecting one's inferior place in the social hierarchy."[41] In Jupiter, the transnational connections elaborated through the fiesta and other events appear to serve as something of an antidote to the process of downward assimilation among the second generation.

On the other hand, young male migrants who arrive in Jupiter and Immokalee without family connections or extensive networks of friends are more susceptible to downward assimilation. Through interviews with both adults and youths, it quickly became clear that levels of participation in both religious and civic organizations are much lower among the youths than adults. Informal youth groups promote entertainment, distraction, and social activities including consumption of drugs and alcohol. In Jupiter, many of the youth travel to West Palm Beach to visit pay-per-dance clubs on the weekend, spending much of the money they have made for the week. For the most part, this cohort includes boys who leave Guatemala at age fourteen or fifteen to make the trip to Jupiter. In Immokalee, young immigrants who do not find work in the fields loiter along the main streets, while others whittle away the hours drinking alcohol on curbsides and in empty parking lots. At night, the drinking often gives way to street fights. These youths are truly in cultural limbo, arriving with hopes of making enough money to return, only to be quickly socialized by their peers into a very different culture. It is these youths who are most at risk of adopting the "adversarial stance" described by Portes. Far apart from their families and sending communities and unwelcome in the host community, young first-generation immigrants are highly susceptible to problems with substance abuse and a cycle of economic deprivation.

Conclusions

Across the United States, groups of Mexican, Guatemalan, and other immigrants continue to arrive in new destinations, following employment opportunities and struggling to build their lives under difficult and even hostile conditions. Although limited to the very different cases of Jupiter and Immokalee, our study does shed light on how immigrants may organize themselves in variant contexts, and what the advantages and drawbacks of various forms of immigrant mobilization may be.

First, our analysis supports many of the findings from earlier studies of Portes, Rumbaut, and others regarding the relationship between social capital, discrimination, and reactive ethnicity in traditional gateway cities. In contexts such as Jupiter, where high levels of discrimination from the primarily Anglo receiving community combine with greater ethnic homogeneity, we can expect mobilization based in reactive ethnicity, more institutionalized transnational linkages, greater mutual assistance, and higher levels of social capital. In contexts such as Immokalee, where ethnic heterogeneity and a less hostile community combine with economic deprivation, we will find less institutionalized transnationalism, less mutual assistance, and lower levels of social capital, but greater potential for the formation of an identity politics based on employment.

Second, we confirm that specific locations provide particular opportunities and constraints for immigrant mobilization, each with its own advantages and disadvantages. In Immokalee, immigrants have mobilized across ethnic and other divides as farmworkers, successfully gaining concessions from major transnational corporations. In the context of the many struggles of immigrant laborers in the United States, this is truly a historic accomplishment. At the same time, the quality of life for agricultural workers in Immokalee remains deplorably low, there is little sense of community and mutual support, and the members of the Coalition of Immokalee Workers, in adopting a strategy of global framing of local issues, risk the danger of becoming "rootless cosmopolitans,"[42] no longer connected to the real-life needs of the migrant farmworkers they claim to represent.

In Jupiter, on the other hand, a greater diversity of employment opportunities makes employment-based mobilization less likely. While the day-laborers who gather to find work each day clearly have some common interests, their employers shift from week to week and even day to day, creating a moving target that makes organization more difficult.[43] Ethnically based mobilization (reactive ethnicity) among the Jaceltec community has provided much needed leadership and institutional support for immigrant laborers in Jupiter. Furthermore, the quality of life, sense of community, and connections with sending community are much more institutionalized and stronger in Jupiter than in Immokalee. As outlined above, however, the potential downsides to this form of mobilization include ethnic cleavages, downward assimilation, and possible counter-mobilization from nativist and other groups.

Finally, the trajectory of both cases hints at the critical role of bridging social capital for successful mobilization. As discussed in chapter 1, bridging social capital is distinct from more inward oriented "bonding" social capital in that it provides links between groups and organizations that live in relative isolation and aids in bridging racial, ethnic, and other social dividing lines.[44] In Jupiter, connections with the university provided student workers, grant-writing resources, and links to local politicians that were otherwise not accessible to immigrant organizers. These links proved invaluable in terms of both providing a space for the fiesta and building the institutional capacity of Corn-Maya. In Immokalee, the links forged through churches and interfaith organizations and the widespread student support for the boycott of Taco Bell were central to the unprecedented victory for tomato pickers in their negotiations with YUM Brands.

As the new geography of Latino immigration continues to expand in the United States, questions about how and when immigrants can successfully organize to promote their local interests will become increasingly urgent. Jupiter and Immokalee are instructive case studies as they demonstrate the complex ways in which immigrant communities negotiate both the opportunities and obstacles for collective action. Drawing both on a sense of community rooted in common ties and on modern strategies of protest and alliances with student groups, the immigrants of Jupiter and Immokalee have achieved substantial, if qualified, success in their attempts to become part of the American dream. In the words of Leon Fink, the struggles of these new immigrant workers, located at the bottom rung of U.S. society, "will likely tell us as much about our own dreams as about theirs."[45]

APPENDIX: DATA, SAMPLE, AND METHODS

In Jupiter, census tract data from the 2000 census demonstrated a relatively contained geographic area in which an estimated 90 percent of the Hispanic population resides. This information corresponded with descriptions of high residential concentrations of immigrants by local Guatemalan leaders during our qualitative interviews. The target area for our sample contained a total of twenty-seven streets and two large apartment complexes. Approximately eight hundred addresses were calculated on these streets using a commercial address/phone-number software product.

Because of the uncertainty of the number of eligible respondents and an anticipated high refusal rate, we chose to visit each address on these streets instead of a selected sample of residences in Jupiter. In total, 771 residences were visited. We found 216 (28 percent) residences with Guatemalan or Mexican residents, 298 (39 percent) ineligible residences, and 257 (33 percent) with no residents at home. We completed surveys at 155 (72 percent) of the eligible residences, while 19 (9 percent) respondents refused and 42 (19 percent) were incomplete or asked that we return at a later date.

In Immokalee, census data indicated 108 census blocks with high concentrations of Hispanic/Latino residents (73 percent and above). We eliminated those blocks with less than 20 residents and were left with 86 blocks with 12,803 residents. We randomly selected 14 census blocks with a total of 3,037 residents. Because of the anticipated high refusal rate, we chose to visit each address in these blocks instead of a selected sample of residences. In total, we completed surveys at 148 residences. As in Jupiter, interviewers were instructed to interview only persons born in Mexico or Guatemala and to interview only one member of each household willing to participate in the survey.

The Jupiter sample was 66.5 percent Guatemalan and 33.5 percent Mexican,while the Immokalee sample was only 12.2 percent Guatemalan and 87.8 percent Mexican. The Immokalee sample was 64 percent male and 36 percent female. In Jupiter, the sample was 70 percent male and 30 percent female.

NOTES

1. Leon Fink, *The Maya of Morganton: Work and Community in the Nuevo New South* (Chapel Hill: University of North Carolina Press, 2003), 3–4.
2. According to Portes and Rumbaut, "reactive ethnicity is the product of confrontation with an adverse native mainstream and the rise of defensive identities and solidarities to counter it." Alejandro Portes and Rubén Rumbaut, *Legacies: The Story of the Immigrant Second Generation* (Berkeley: University of California Press, 2001), 284. In contrast, linear ethnicity represents a continuation of past cultural orientations and practices "rather than an emergent reaction to the present," according to Alejandro Portes, "Conclusion: Towards a New World: The Origins and Effect of Transnational Activities," *Ethnic and Racial Studies* 22 (1999): 463–478.
3. See also Eric Popkin, "Guatemalan Mayan Migration to Los Angeles: Constructing Transnational Linkages in the Context of the Settlement Process," *Ethnic and Racial Studies* 22 (1999): 267–289.
4. Portes, "Conclusion," 465.
5. See the appendix for a discussion of the survey data and methodology.
6. Ibid.
7. A key finding across the samples was the high number of individuals who reported that they had no friends in their current location (36.1 percent in Immokalee and 25.3 percent in Jupiter).
8. The survey only asked respondents for their perceptions of discrimination against themselves not against their group. A few scholars point to the importance of considering perceptions of both group-level and individual-level discrimination. For example, see Deborah Schildkraut, "Identity, Perceptions of Discrimination, and Political Engagement: The Causes and Consequences of Reactive Ethnicity among Latinos," paper presented at the 2004 Annual Meeting of the American Political Science Association, Chicago, Illinois.
9. See Dwayne Robinson, "Anti-Immigrant Protest Targets Day-Labor Site," *Palm Beach Post*, March 2, 2008, 3C.
10. The mean score for such participation was also significantly higher in Jupiter (means test is One-Way ANOVA).
11. Significance test is Kendall's tau b (correlation coefficient = .240 with a .000 significance).
12. Alejandro Portes, "Conclusion"; Peggy Levitt, *The Transnational Villagers* (Berkeley: University of California Press, 2001); Sarah J. Mahler, "Theoretical and Empirical Contributions toward a Research Agenda for Transnationalism," in *Transnationalism*

from Below: Comparative Urban and Community Research, ed. M. P. Smith and Luis Guarnizo, 64–100 (New Brunswick, NJ, and London: Transaction Publishers, 1998).

13. Portes, "Conclusion"; Popkin, "Guatemalan Mayan Migration."

14. Maria Herrera, "Guatemalans' Needs Heard," *South Florida Sun Sentinel*, February 17, 2007, 1B.

15. Letter to the bishop drafted by board members of Corn-Maya.

16. For an explanation of bonding and bridging social capital, see Robert Putnam, *Bowling Alone* (New York: Simon and Schuster, 2000), 22–23.

17. Luis Eduardo Guarnizo and Michael P. Smith, "The Locations of Transnationalism," in *Transnationalism from Below*, ed. Smith and Guarnizo, 11.

18. Goldring defines migrant-led transnationalism as "migrant-initiated practices and institutions that foster transnational social spaces." Luin Goldring, "The Mexican State and Transmigrant Organizations: Negotiating the Boundaries of Membership and Participation," *Latin American Research Review* 37 (2002): 57.

19. Guarnizo and Smith distinguish between the transnational practices of immigrants ("transnationalism from below") and the transnational engagements of sending country elites ("transnationalism from above"). Guarnizo and Smith, "The Locations of Transnationalism."

20. Peggy Levitt, "You Know, Abraham Was Really the First Immigrant: Religion and Transnational Migration," *International Immigration Review* 37 (2003): 847–873.

21. Chamácuaro is located in the municipal district of Acámbaro. The town has a population of approximately fifty-five hundred inhabitants. Residents have been migrating to the United States since the early 1900s, and significant communities can be found in Illinois, northern California, and Georgia.

22. Portes and Rumbaut, *Legacies*.

23. Most of the Otomí migrants are hñahñu speakers from the small rural community of Santa Teresa Davoxtha in Hidalgo.

24. This is an example of "bonding social capital" that is inward oriented and reinforces ethnic identity. Putnam, *Bowling Alone*.

25. Brian Payne, "Taking Back the Reins of Identity Formation: The Evolution of a Grassroots Organization in a South Florida Migrant Farm Working Community" (MA thesis, University of Florida, 2000).

26. Craig Jenkins, "The Transformation of a Constituency into a Social Movement Revisited: Farmworker Organizing in California," in *Waves of Protest*, ed. Jo Freeman and Victoria Johnson (Lanham, MD: Rowan and Littlefield Publishers, 1999), 295.

27. According to Johnston, Laraña, and Gusfield, the concept of public identity "captures the influences that the external public [has] on the way social movement adherents think about themselves." Hank Johnston, Enrique Laraña, and Joseph Gusfield, "Identities, Grievances, and New Social Movements," in *New Social Movements: From Ideology to Identity*, ed. Enrique Laraña, Hank Johnston, and Joseph Gusfield (Philadelphia, PA: Temple University Press, 1994), 18.

28. According to Snow and Benford, "master frames" are large-scale interpretive frames that are generally associated with the emergence of a cycle of protest. David Snow and Robert Benford, "Master Frames and Cycles of Protest," in *Frontiers of Social Movement Theory*, ed. Aldon D. Morris and Carol McClurg Mueller, 133–155 (New Haven, CT: Yale University Press, 1992).

29. McAdam, Tarrow, and Tilly define "scale shift" as "a change in the number and level of coordinated contentious actions leading to broader contention involving a wider range of actors and bridging their claims and identities." Doug McAdam, Sidney

Tarrow, and Charles Tilly, *Dynamics of Contention* (New York, NY: Cambridge University Press, 2001), 331.

30. The Student Farmworker Alliance (SFA) was founded in February 2000 to support the March for Dignity, Dialogue and a Fair Wage led by the Coalition of Immokalee Workers. The SFA has chapters on university campuses in Florida, Michigan, and California, and has ties to student organizations at three hundred colleges and universities.

31. The proponents of the resolution were the Center for Reflection, Education, and Action (CREA), Trillium Asset Management, the United Church of Christ Board for Pension Asset Management, United Church Foundation, Christian Brothers Investment Services, and the Needmor Fund.

32. Eric Schlosser, "A Side Order of Human Rights," *New York Times*, April 6, 2005; http://www.nytimes.com/2005/04/06/opinion/06schlosser.html (accessed April 7, 2005).

33. Coalition of Immokalee Workers, "Victory at Taco Bell," http://www.ciw-online.org/agreementanalysis.html (accessed May 12, 2006).

34. Guarnizo and Smith, "The Locations of Transnationalism."

35. Portes, "Conclusion."

36. Popkin, "Guatemalan Mayan Migration."

37. At the time of this of this writing, the Coalition was engaged in another campaign targeting fast-food giant Burger King.

38. Sidney Tarrow, *The New Transnational Activism* (New York, NY: Cambridge University Press, 2005), 76.

39. Portes and Rumbaut, *Legacies*, 285.

40. Portes, "Conclusion," 471.

41. Ibid., 472.

42. Tarrow, *The New Transnational Activism*, 139.

43. It should be noted, however, that the El Sol Center now has a Worker's Council that plays a major role in deciding policy for the day-labor portion of the center. Thus, the "bridging" social capital that was critical to the opening of the center has also provided an opportunity for individual transmigrants from Mexico and Guatemala to now organize themselves as "workers."

44. Putnam, *Bowling Alone*; and Richard Wood, *Faith in Action* (Chicago: University of Chicago Press, 2002).

45. Fink, *The Maya of Morgantown*, 200.

6

卐卐卐卐卐卐卐卐卐卐卐卐卐卐卐卐卐卐卐卐卐卐卐卐卐卐

Immigrant Regime of Production

The State, Political Mobilization, and Religious and Business Networks among Brazilians in South Florida

JOSÉ CLAÚDIO SOUZA ALVES

In this chapter, I use the concept of immigrant regime of production to understand the political economy of Brazilian immigration to the United States. In particular, drawing from research among Brazilians in South Florida, I explore how the interaction between, on the one hand, the demands and needs of the Brazilian and American state apparatuses and, on the other, the "micro-physics" of immigrant networks facilitates the formation of an abundant, malleable, and cheap transnational labor force. After defining what I mean by an immigrant regime of production, I discuss the convergence of interests reflected in immigration policies in Brazil and the United States. I then characterize the dynamics of religious and business networks among immigrants, taking care to analyze their operation within the framework of these converging political interests. I am also interested in assessing the role that these networks may play in the political organization and mobilization of Brazilian immigrants. I focus on these two networks because they represent the most visible markers of presence for Brazilians in Pompano Beach and Deerfield Beach, the two cities outside of Miami-Dade County in which they have concentrated. I argue that while business and religious networks allow a certain degree of political mobilization around local issues, like easy access to driver's licenses for immigrants, as well as national matters, like immigration reform, they ultimately do not challenge the transnational capitalist logic that compels Brazilians to migrate to the United States and to become incorporated into the American economy in a subordinate position. Moreover, often these two networks intersect to facilitate the extraction of surplus value from the Brazilian population in South Florida.

This chapter, thus, complements Manuel Vásquez's discussion on interpersonal immigrant networks in chapter 2 by focusing on larger, more institutionalized networks and their interactions with the state and the global economy.

Immigrant Regime of Production

In order to examine the interactions between religious and business networks, on the one hand, and the state and global economy, on the other, I depart from Karl Marx's holistic conception of mode of production. As he writes in "The German Ideology," "mode of production must not be considered simply as being the reproduction of the physical existence of the individuals. Rather it is a definite form of activity of these individuals, a definite form of expressing their life, a definite mode of life on their part. As individuals express their life, so they are. What they are, therefore, coincides with their production, both with what they produce and with how they produce."[1]

In other words, a mode of production is not simply defined by ownership of the means of production, but by the social and cultural arrangements that enable production. Following Michel Foucault, I see these sociocultural arrangements as organized in regimes of practice, "systems of ordered procedures for the production, regulation, distribution, circulation, and operation" of power.[2] Regimes of production function like crisscrossing and flexible yet hierarchical clusters of networks that allow domination and resistance, that is, the "action of men upon men."[3] At stake is the ability to harness the energies and capabilities of the body—in this case, the bodies of immigrants. For Brazilian immigrants in Broward County, intertwining religious and business networks provide the infra-structure of a regime of production that exploits them while simultaneously allowing them to navigate the challenges of a new destination.

My second point of departure is the fact this local immigrant regime of production is embedded within a new global regime of capitalist accumulation.[4] This regime is characterized by the rapid and mostly unregulated movement of capital and goods and a controlled flow of labor.[5] As the United States positions itself as the hegemonic power in a polycentric world system, it has come to rely increasingly on the cheap labor of immigrants to be competitive vis-à-vis emerging economic centers like India and China, which have much lower labor costs. Latin American immigrants come to work in the service, construction, and agricultural sectors, all of which buttress the accelerated expansion of knowledge-based, technology-intensive sectors of the economy that give the United States the competitive edge over growing economies in Asia.[6]

For its part, in the effort to insert itself in the global economy, Brazil has implemented neo-liberal policies that have generated considerable social dislocation, including migration to swelling and unruly urban centers like Rio de Janeiro and São Paulo. There rural migrants demand basic services that the state cannot satisfy. As a result, migration to the United States becomes one of the strategies to deal with this growing social unrest.

Both the United States and the Brazilian states, then, benefit from the process of migration. According to Michael Burawoy and Theda Skocpol, in

order to make possible production and the extraction of surplus within capitalist economies, the state must regulate the relations of production, especially
mediating through various legal and coercive means the conflicts and contradictions that emerge in these relations.[7] It is in this context that we must understand the militarization of the U.S.-Mexico border, the increasing criminalization
of immigrants in the United States, and the failure to pass a comprehensive
immigration reform. By maintaining the status quo, that is, not allowing a path
to citizenship for the 10 to 12 million undocumented immigrants in the country,
while, at the same time, policing work places and living quarters with great
vigor, the United States is limiting the possibility of immigrants to mobilize in a
politically significant way. In effect, the current policy amounts to production
and surplus extraction without enfranchisement. Immigrants fulfill the United
States' labor demand in the context of increasingly precarious and vulnerable
social conditions. This is where local immigrant networks become essential, not
only helping immigrants to create places to be but also benefiting the state by
taking on the cost of the reproduction of a cheap labor force. In fact, it is plausible to see the transnational livelihoods that immigrants establish as crucial in
the maintenance of a "reserve army of labor."[8]

Our field research revealed that religious congregations are one of the most
visible, institutionalized clusters of networks among Brazilian immigrants in
South Florida. As we shall see, these networks do, indeed, facilitate the formation of collective identity and solidarity among Brazilian immigrants, giving
them a measure of empowerment at the local level. However, participation in
these networks very seldom translates into more explicit and organized sources
of contestation, through which immigrants can challenge the logic of surplus
extraction without representation, without political power. Moreover, some
religious networks are even directly connected to the immigrant regime of production, closely interacting with business networks, the other visible cluster of
institutions among Brazilian immigrants in Broward County. This interaction
many times ends up reproducing dynamics of exploitation and domination.

Before I move to characterize religious and business networks among
Brazilians in Pompano Beach and Deerfield Beach and how these networks are
part of the immigrant regime of production, I need to say a few words about
political mobilization in Brazil. For part of the failure to contest the power asymmetries in the immigrant regime of production has to do with the political landscape in Brazil.

Collective Organization among Brazilian Immigrants

Debates around the emergence of new social movements in Brazil in the 1980s,
after the military dictatorship, showed that it was reductive to try to fit various

types of social and political organization along an evolutionary line, placing in the inferior stages associational forms based on kinship, locality, or interpersonal relations, with low levels of institutionalization and representation in the formal democratic system. This outmoded teleological approach also placed in a higher evolutionary stage heavily institutionalized forms of organization, with fixed bureaucratic norms and functions and high corporate representation. In other words, traditional ways of understanding political participation assumed that political parties and unions represented a more mature and effective way of organizing and mobilizing.

Despite their pioneering contributions, the first analyses among Brazilian immigrants in the United States, such as those of Maxine Margolis, Teresa Sales, and Ana Cristina Martes,[9] adopt this traditional focus on the most evolved forms of social organization. These studies demonstrate in rich detail the limits and contradictions in the ways in which Brazilians build collective identity abroad. However, by assuming that there is an organizational goal in terms of mature and effective collective life, which Brazilians have not met, these studies end up not identifying the real associational forms that already exist on the ground as well as the sociopolitical possibilities these forms open up. Therefore, I echo Vásquez's critique of the concept of community in chapter 2. A balanced assessment of the possibilities for solidarity and social action among Brazilian immigrants must grasp the existing dimensions of their movements and sociability. It does not help to specify a time and place to find a real social movement among Brazilian immigrants, a movement based on idealized models considered more advanced, and then regret not finding it in actual historical conditions.

Given that immigration from Brazil begins to gather steam toward the mid-1980s and that a large percentage of immigrants are in the range of thirty to forty years old, we safely can conclude that they experienced their key socialization period during the military dictatorship, which started in 1964. During this period, not only unions and political parties were severely repressed, but through the Institutional Act 5 (AI-5), promulgated in 1968, state apparatuses arbitrarily arrested, tortured, and even killed citizens in the name of national security. It is not surprising, thus, that for the generation that began to migrate to the United States, sociability and organizational experiences took place through safer and more intimate relations with relatives, neighbors, and friends and in churches. Of course, we cannot forget the patrimonial and populist relations, which exploit, to some extent, these intense interpersonal relations. In any case, interpersonal relations are a key ingredient of the sociocultural fabric that Brazilian immigrants bring with them to the United States.

These experiences of sociability in Brazil are reconstructed and reinterpreted abroad to make sense of the immigrant condition. This explains the heavy reliance among Brazilian immigrants on relations based on kinship and friendship, which, as Vásquez demonstrates, create some protective spaces of meaning and belonging in the face of spatiotemporal challenges posed by the process of migration. This reliance on past experiences, however, is mediated by social relations that the neo-liberal mode of capitalist production privileges, namely, self-interested individualism and competitiveness. If Brazilian immigrants are to succeed in securing a piece of the American dream, they must deploy their resources, including cultural ones, to maximize their personal material gains and social mobility. Often this means that Brazilian immigrants turn to their interpersonal relations to extract surplus and, in the process, reproduce a flexible immigrant labor force through self-exploitation. So, it is not uncommon for Brazilians to sustain potentially exploitative relations with relatives and friends. I am referring here to practices such as the "selling of houses" [*venda de casas*], that is, giving a compatriot a house to clean in exchange for a fee, or subcontracting landscaping jobs at reduced salaries. Practices of this kind demonstrate that, in a given regime of production, affective immigrant networks built on kinship, friendship, *paisanaje,* and church affiliation can interact with economic interests and activities with important consequences for immigrants and the nation-states linked by the migration process.

In the rest of this chapter, I will characterize two of the most important institutionalized networks among Brazilians in Pompano Beach and Deerfield Beach, taking care to show how their interaction contributes to the operation of the immigrant regime of production.

Religious Networks

Brazilian religious networks have a variegated morphology, ranging from complex, polynucleated webs, as in the case of evangelical Protestants, to a multiplicity of dyadic ties that are centralized around the figure of a single spiritual leader, as we found for a nascent Candomblé center. Catholicism represents a mixed model, containing highly centralized and hierarchical arrangements, but also relatively autonomous, horizontal religious movements that engage specific sectors of the Brazilian populations such as youth, women, and couples.

The Evangelical Protestant Network

The most visible and established religious network among Brazilians in Broward County is that constituted by the roughly forty evangelical Protestant churches in the area. Within this network of networks, congregations generally average forty to fifty members, a size that allows for intimate interpersonal relations and worship. Each congregation has its own organizational and ritual logic as well as its own theological inflections. However, they always demand of members a high level of participation in diverse activities such as services, outreach ministries, Sunday school, prayer groups, and band practice. There is also quite a bit of circulation among congregations, not just of members who break from one church and become affiliated with another, but also in terms of participation in events that have significance for the entire Brazilian evangelical "community," including visits by well-known preachers or Gospel musical groups from Brazil. In fact, one important dimension of the evangelical "social field" is its strong transnational character. Along with itinerant evangelists, who not only travel from Brazil to the United States but also actively missionize in Europe, Asia, and Africa, there are sustained flows of books and pamphlets that address theological and moral issues and bear witness to the conversions taking place at various locations in the network. Many churches in Pompano Beach and Deerfield Beach participate in this thriving transcontinental spiritual market, hiring professionals to record services or sermons on CDs or DVDs that are then sold by the thousands in both Brazil and the United States. The following quote from one pastor in Pompano Beach reflects the transnational enmeshment of local Brazilian evangelical churches in Broward County: "It was a challenge [desafio] accepting the invitation by a producer in Brazil to record those DVDs. I accepted, and I made one of Brazil's best recordings, rethinking the prophecies. Some recordings are longer than seventy-five minutes, so that I made a total of almost fourteen hours of taped programs. We had financial difficulties, because we couldn't find a partner in Brazil to speed up the process there. So we ended up producing a lot of the stuff here in the United States. For Brazil, we will just try to go with CDs, since DVDs are too expensive for the situation there."

In addition to the transnational flows, there are intra-national connections crisscrossing localities in the United States with sizable Brazilian populations. In particular, older, more established churches in the Boston metropolitan region send pastors to seed churches in Florida and to offer continuous support, advice, and spiritual renewal. This is the case of with the Assemblies of God's Ministério de Boston, one of the most visible Brazilian evangelical churches in Broward County. I will have more to say about this church later on.

Since they operate as a horizontal network of loosely connected small networks, following a model that has been termed "negotiated transnational religious organizations,"[10] Brazilian evangelicals have been able, on the one hand, to respond effectively to the ever-changing needs of the local population through a variety of pastoral and ecclesial styles, which compete vigorously with each other. On the other hand, evangelical pastors in the Broward region have been able to articulate a flexible interdenominational association, which has become active on topics of great concern to Brazilian immigrants, such as the ongoing debates on immigration reform and the possibility of legalization of undocumented workers. As we shall see, this collective form of organization, while promising, has had limited success because it is embedded within the regime of immigrant production described above.

One of the main protagonists in the evangelical pastors' association is the Baptist church, which has about fifteen hundred members. At a cost of close to three million dollars, they have built a large structure, which functions not only as a temple but as a gym, allowing them to have soccer tournaments in the morning and services in the evening. The head pastor of this congregation maintains a close connection with the Brazilian Baptist Church, especially with the Junta de Missões Mundiais, based in Rio de Janeiro, which supports 640 missionaries and their families in several countries.

As part of its outreach to the community, the Brazilian Baptist Church has provided a space for the Brazilian Consulate in Miami to hold weekly sessions. The church has also invited the local sheriff, health experts, and lawyers to discuss the situation of Brazilians in the region. Finally, between 2003 and 2004, the church played a major role in the attempt to gather one million signatures from throughout the United States asking for amnesty for undocumented immigrants. According to the head pastor of the Brazilian Baptist Church, this initiative emerged out of meeting between evangelical pastors and President George W. Bush: "Bush's declaration was very, very good, because he tried to create a propitious national climate. This petition drive helped him put a stop to anti-immigrant ideas. After that, the draconian bill proposed by the Congress was relaxed a bit. The treatment [of immigrants] in the courts on the whole question of driver's licenses eased up. . . . Now at least there is some tolerance. . . . [People] don't call Immigration, don't call the police. And this happened after Bush responded [to the petition]."

Obviously, in the current climate of strong anti-immigrant feeling, the Baptist pastor's reading of the impact of the signature drive is overly optimistic. Nevertheless, the church's involvement in the initiative shows that, despite the widespread perception that evangelical Protestants are apolitical, certain sectors of the evangelical networks are capable of mobilizing Brazilian immigrants, even if only for short-term collective action. The Baptist pastor has also engaged the Catholic network. After co-celebrating with the local Catholic parish priest the funeral of a Brazilian girl whose family had connections with the two networks, the Baptist pastor was invited to a national meeting of Catholic pastoral agents. There he spoke to about one hundred priests and two bishops about potential points of agreement on matters of faith and religious practice. In return, the Baptist pastor invited the parish priest to attend the inauguration of the new church-gym complex. This kind of ecumenical exchange once again challenges the stereotype that evangelicals are inherently sectarian and that this sectarianism contributes to divisions within the immigrant population, divisions that may hinder collective mobilization.

The Assemblies of God—Boston Ministry, now called World Revival Church (WRC-AD), the second most preponderant evangelical sub-network among Brazilians in the region, offers a stark contrast to the Baptist Church. The WRC-AD was founded at the end of the 1980s in the Boston area. It began with twelve individuals who met in a shoe store in Union Square in the city of Somerville.

Today, the WRC-AD is at the crossroads of two large networks. First, there is the Portuguese-language district of the Assemblies of God, which in 2004 had 486 pastors; many of them (such as the head pastor of the church in Pompano Beach) trained with their Euro-American colleagues. According to its founders, the WRC-AD has now more than eleven thousand members just in the United States, making it the largest Portuguese-speaking evangelical ministry outside of Brazil. The WRC-AD network has fifty churches throughout the United States, including twenty-six in Massachusetts and seven in Florida. In addition, there are twenty-nine churches outside the United States, of which eight are in Japan and six are in Brazil. This brings us to the second transnational network in which the WRC-AD participates: it is linked to the convention of the Assemblies of God in Paraná, Brazil. In Brazil, the WRC-AD also owns a TV channel (CNT) and an FM radio station, allowing for religious services to be transmitted sometimes simultaneously in the United States and Brazil. There are also services on line, which, like the TV programs transmitted through CNT, often include prayers, expressions of support, and advice, as well as blessings for those traveling to the United States or returning to Brazil. Clearly, the WRC-AD operates bifocally, attempting to minister to Brazilian Pentecostals at all points in a transnational social field.

Theologically, in recent years, the church has witnessed a revival movement (*avivamento*). Services now very frequently involve intense social effervescence, with members shaking uncontrollably and falling to the ground touched by the Holy Spirit, widespread glossolalia, prophetic utterances, and even cases of divine healing. Here, the WRC-AD simply follows the strong trend toward charismaticism among Latino churches. As we saw in the introduction, a recent study by the Pew Public Forum and the Pew Hispanic Center found that 57 percent of Latino Protestants identify themselves as charismatic or Pentecostal.[11] Following this trend, the WRC-AD has increasingly come to see itself as a "spiritual hospital," which seeks to treat physical, psychological, and social diseases like alcoholism, drug abuse, the breakdown of the family, and domestic violence against women and children. The church sees these diseases as manifestations of the hardships and isolation that Brazilian immigrants often experience.

The focus on personal and moral renewal, however, has not meant that the WRC-AD has not participated in struggles for the rights of Brazilian immigrants. Particularly in Boston, as part of the cultural-civic council created by the consulate, the church has often raised its voice against exploitative labor conditions faced by Brazilians. In Pompano Beach, the WRC-AD also participated in the drive to collect one million signatures supporting amnesty for undocumented immigrants.

As the examples of the Baptist Church and the WRC-AD show, evangelical networks among Brazilians in Broward County evince vitality, flexibility, and the capacity to operate at several scales, from the personal to the transnational. There is no question that these networks generate social capital, which can be mobilized to support causes beneficial to all Brazilian immigrants. However, building on the crucial distinction that Philip Williams, Manuel Vásquez, and Timothy Steigenga made in the introduction, this social capital has not translated into established political capital, into representative organizations that can contest power at the local, state, or national levels.

The Catholic Network

In Deerfield Beach and Pompano Beach, this network is nucleated around the Nossa Senhora Aparecida Catholic Church, situated at the border between these two cities. This church brings together approximately three thousand members, although the number of individuals who participate more intensely in pastoral groups, marriage counseling encounters, retreats, and vigils is much smaller. The church originated in 1996 as part of an initiative called the Brazilian Catholic Mission of South Florida, which was put together through the efforts of priests of the Scalabrini Order, an auxiliary bishop in Miami, and a lay group that wanted to worship in Portuguese. Prior to this initiative, Portuguese-speakers generally attended mass in Spanish or English. In the end, the mission brought together five Brazilian communities in the region: in addition to Nossa Senhora, there are churches in Kendall, Miami Beach, Hollywood, and Flamingo Road. In 2000, the congregation at Nossa Senhora was able to secure the building in which it is now housed.

Beyond the link to the diocese of Miami, Nossa Senhora is also connected with the National Conference of Catholic Bishops through its outreach to immigrants and ethnic groups, more specifically, through the Brazilian Apostolate, a group of priests, nuns, and lay people who work with various Brazilian populations across the United States. The Brazilian Apostolate is divided according to regions, each loosely organized by an informal rotation of duties among the various members. South Florida falls in the eastern region, with approximately seventy representatives who meet annually to exchange experiences and information.

Thus, in contrast to the evangelical networks, the Catholic network among Brazilians in Broward County is much more centralized and hierarchical, seeking to connect organically parishes, missions, dioceses, and national apostolates. Whereas evangelical networks operate through horizontal integration, flexibly connecting small, autonomous groups, the Catholic Church functions through vertical integration, privileging the role of pastoral agents in the production and transmission of knowledge, decision-making, planning, and executing.[12]

Despite this centralization and hierarchization, however, there are movements within the church that provide a measure of flexibility. Arguably, the most visible of these movements is the Catholic Charismatic Renewal (CCR), which offers what R. Andrew Chesnut calls a "virgophilic" version of "pneumacentrism," a focus on the gifts of the Holy Spirit, which respects and reinforces the Catholic clerical structure and stress on the Virgin Mary.[13] The CCR structures time and space around, on the one hand, the frequent weekly meetings of its participants to pray, sing, and study the Bible. On the other hand, just like the evangelical Protestant network, it depends on the national and transnational flow of speakers, leaders, books, CDs, and DVDs. However, in contrast to the evangelical Protestant network, the CCR in South Florida does not receive resources directly from the North, for example, from parishes with a strong Brazilian presence in Boston. Rather, the flow is more centralized, mediated through the Brazilian Apostolate, which coordinates the movement in and out of pastoral agents. Again, this difference has to do with the divergent morphologies adopted by Protestant and Catholic networks. Whereas the former thrives on multiple horizontal exchanges among mobile units, the later, due to its size and scope, allows for the proliferation of groups within a relatively unified and centralized structure.

For example, as a counterpoint to the stress that the CCR places on the personal and emotive dimensions of Catholicism, there is within the Catholic community in Pompano a *grupo social,* a lay outreach initiative that seeks to help immigrants, mostly through immediate assistance in the form of food and clothing for those recently arrived. They also gather to discuss labor problems which Brazilians in the area confront. The transnational dimension in the grupo social has to do with the fact that this pastoral initiative mirrors approaches that developed in Brazil during the 1970s and 1980s, such as base Christian communities and liberation theology, both of which attempt to challenge social and economic injustices that fly in the face of Catholic social teaching. This approach, particularly in its preferential option for the poor, also animates the work of the Scalabrini priests who have served the Brazilian Mission of South Florida. They have brought a commitment to immigrants that is global in scope.

Perhaps it is the internal pluralism and tension within the Catholic network, together with the liberationist themes, that limit the interaction between religious and business webs, which, as we shall see, is very intense among evangelical Protestants. To be sure, more established Brazilian Catholics hire recently arrived immigrants or those who do not speak English to do housecleaning jobs, often paying them low salaries and demanding long hours. However, this practice is constantly criticized by pastoral agents who would like all Brazilian immigrants to develop a sense of collective solidarity. In contrast, when neo-Pentecostals sacralize the quest for prosperity, they may be undermining the moral resources to condemn the practice of exploitation among immigrants.

The Spiritist Network

In comparison with the evangelical Protestant and Catholic networks, the Spiritist network is much smaller, gathering three centers with a total of seventy to eighty members. Because the centers depend on the contributions of their members to cover all expenses, these centers are located at the periphery of the city of Pompano Beach, where cheaper space to rent is more available. The network is essentially built around families and friends that share a common worldview, particularly, the idea that the spirits of the dead interact with the living through the work of mediums and that these consultations can help resolve everyday problems. The network is then loosely organized. Although each center has a president and group of trained mediums who are in charge of teaching the doctrine and conducting the sessions, all these groups stress the principle of charity, the necessity to treat each other with respect and to assist each other in order to achieve higher levels of enlightenment.

While Brazilian Spiritists, as a whole, do not have any concrete initiatives to address the needs of immigrants, the principle of charity, together with the call to avoid engaging in practices that may produce bad Karma, encourages members to act individually to assist other Brazilians, often helping them find work and a place to live. Moreover, a good number of Brazilian Spiritists in Broward County have incomes and levels of education above the average for the Brazilian immigrant population, mirroring the pattern observed in Brazil. This fact dovetails with the stress on charity, enabling the centers to engage in a certain redistribution of resources.

Economic success among Brazilian Spiritists in South Florida has a different meaning than it does for evangelical Protestants. Spiritists do share with Protestants the focus on the individual and his or her spiritual well-being or renewal. For both Spiritists and Protestants, each person is responsible for his or her actions and fate. According to a Spiritist leader we interviewed, "We do things because we want things to grow, so that our professional community can grow. And by doing this we bring more people in, because we shine, as it were. We demonstrate to our bosses that we can do things well, so that he can be happy. But it is not just his happiness that matters. We treat all our clients well, and our bosses will hear about it. So, we receive praise and prizes among all employees for our good work. It is the effort, a thing that I learned from Spiritism, the responsibility."

However, we heard Spiritist leaders critiquing the attachment to material things as an impediment to spiritual evolution. In their educational talks to the group, these leaders explicitly construed the United States as a "materialist country" that needs to hear and understand the Spiritist doctrine in order to move to the next level. Brazilian Spiritists, then, see their presence in the United States as part of a new phase in the spread of their religion. In this sense, this network is informed by a missionary thrust that is in many ways similar to that found among evangelical Protestants.

The three Spiritist centers in Broward County also sustain transnational and intra-national connections. Like evangelical Protestants, they often bring speakers who have achieved fame in the Brazilian Spiritist field. To sponsor these visits, the local centers may join forces with other centers in the Miami region. The linkages, however, extend beyond Florida: Spiritist centers throughout the United States exchange information and contacts through the Internet.

In particular, as Brazilian members move from one city to another, the centers have a system of referrals that helps new arrivals find sister groups.

The Network of African-Based Religions

Our fieldwork found two nodes of an incipient, precarious network of African-based religions. The first is a father of the saint (*pai de santo*), a Candomblé priest who attempted unsuccessfully to establish a religious center (*terreiro*) where he could perform spiritual consultations and train initiates. The second was an Umbanda initiate, who, upon his arrival to Broward County, found other initiates and began to hold rituals in his own house.

Born and initiated in northeastern Brazil, the Candomblé priest migrated to New York in 1978. As his practice grew in Queens, he was able to establish centers in Aracajú, Salvador, Interlagos (in São Paulo), and Lagos (Nigeria). Religiously, then, this pai de santo moves both transnationally, between Brazil and the United States, and diasporically, circulating in what Paul Gilroy has called the Black Atlantic.[14] This priest said, "I live my life from (Inter)Lagos to Lagos. That is my world." In 2002, seeking to "retire" to Florida, he attempted to open a terreiro in Pompano Beach but a year later returned to New York, where he continues to give consultations, interestingly, not to Brazilians, but to Spanish-speaking Latinos such as Colombians, Mexicans, and Ecuadorians as well as to Euro-Americans, especially Jews.

Our research team had the opportunity to visit his terreiro in Queens, New York. We were surprised by the eclecticism of his practices and the iconography. Depending on the matter at hand, he works with a diversity of tools, including divination with seashells (*jogo de búzios*), palm reading, tarot cards, astrology, and the Cabala. The images in the center include not only the African *orixás* (the ancestor spirits) but also Brazilian and Latin American spirits, like Caboclos (Native Americans), Pretos Velhos (the old slaves), Exús (the rogues and prostitutes), Maria Lionza (the Venezuelan female spirit of the forest), and other spirits of the Orient, like Buddha, Krishna, and Confucius.

We can see this creative blending of symbols and practices as one of the ways in which the pai de santo has negotiated his transnational and diasporic livelihood and has adapted to the religiously pluralistic and multi-ethnic environment of New York. The creative mélange may also explain the relative absence of Brazilians among his clientele. Despite the fact that there is considerable religious mixing in Brazil, Brazilians might prefer "purer" versions of Candomblé as a way to re-affirm their identity abroad. Similar strategies of purification and return to origins have been observed among practitioners of Cuban Santería.[15]

The precariousness of this Candomblé network may be partially explained by the type of bonds that sustain it. In this case, since the pai de santo does not have any would-be initiates training under him, his "community" is formed by all the clients who seek his help and advice. Each of these clients has a personal, confidential relationship with the pai de santo that may be fleeting, built around a particular problem that once solved does not require further interaction, or more permanent, on the basis of ongoing consultations. In either case, the network is centralized, dependent on the charisma, credibility, and trust emanating from the pai de santo. In turn, the authority and credibility of the pai de santo is predicated not only on his success in treating his clients, who then spread the word about his sacred power, but also on his participation in the transnational and diasporic realms, which link his practices to Africa and Brazil. Thus, his mobility is part of the charisma he has at his disposal. However, this mobility also limits the possibility of creating new nodes in the network, such as the center he attempted to open in Pompano Beach, since these emerging nodes need his presence more than the established terreiros.

The second network of African-based religion is anchored by a couple, an American who grew up Brazil and his Brazilian wife. While she came from a family that practiced Umbanda, he was not a follower. However, after getting married, she initiated him into the religion. Following his initiation they moved to New York in 1991, where they only stayed for two years because she could not stand the cold. They then returned to Brazil, but in 2001 they once again decided to move to the United States, this time to Florida. Once in South Florida, he began to attend a terreiro in Miami, organized by Venezuelans but led by a Brazilian pai de santo. However, he did not agree with some of the ritual practices of this group and decided to search for people interested in creating an alternative religious community in Broward County.

Although he used the Internet to establish contacts, it was his advertisement in a local Brazilian newspaper that finally succeeded in attracting some people. Today, he leads a group of about ten, which meets every two weeks at the couple's house. There they have set up a *congar* (altar) with the images of the saints as well as the *assentamentos* (the sacred objects where the orixás and spirits reside). They use CDs of Umbanda ritual music, since they do not have an *atabaque* (sacred drum). Participants at the sessions include not only several Brazilians but also a Venezuelan, a Cuban, an Uruguayan, and an American. Thus, in contrast to the Catholic and Protestant networks, this network is characterized by ethnic, linguistic, and cultural diversity. This diversity dovetails with Umbanda practices and cosmologies, which strongly stress syncretism, flexibility, and adaptability. Doctrinal and ritual pluralism and diversity in composition may be critical for the survival of this network in the dispersed context of South Florida.

Another important particularity of this network that is worth highlighting is the transformation of domestic spaces into sacred spaces, linking religious practice with participants' intimate lives. This dynamic, once again, resonates with the worldview of Umbanda, which is normally organized in tightly knit houses where a spiritual family dwells under the tutelage of a head orixá and a *pai* or *mãe de santo.* However, the anchoring of the network in private spaces might have more to do with the obstacles imposed by the urban and exurban context, which limit the public use of loud drums, alcoholic beverages, and cigars.

One of the Brazilians in the Umbanda group is currently in the process of completing his initiation at a terreiro in Rio de Janeiro, once again demonstrating that, even in incipient religious networks among Brazilians in Broward County, there is transnationalism. In fact, despite having lived in the United States for a long time, this initiate considers himself more Brazilian than American, attributing this fact to his religious trajectory and goals—his spirituality and authority in South Florida derive from his personal and familial experiences in Brazil.

Having characterized the key religious networks among Brazilians in Broward County, I will now turn to the other cluster of networks that has attained a relative degree of visibility, density, and institutionalization. We will see that these business and labor networks often interact with religious networks to give rise to a regime of immigrant production.

Work and Business Networks and Their Connections with Religious Networks

Brazilians in Pompano Beach and Deerfield Beach are involved in multiple business enterprises and occupations, including cleaning services (in hotels, office buildings, and condominiums), landscaping, construction (concentrating on drywalling and roofing), transportation (especially of other Brazilians), food services (either as cooks or as servers in or owners of restaurants), car sales and rentals, retail (particularly selling foodstuff, clothing, books, music, and other articles that are constantly brought from Brazil), translation, and paralegal counseling.

Despite the diversity of occupations, there are clear hierarchies of salaries based on personal ability and expertise and also dependent on time of arrival, on competence in English, and, more importantly, on relations of trust and reciprocity with clients and established brokers who provide valuable referrals. As with other immigrants, such as Italians and Irish in the Northeast at the turn of the twentieth century or Cubans in Miami, family—understood here as extended family, which includes uncles, aunts, cousins, godparents, and godchildren—and friendship are central in the articulation of Brazilian business and labor networks. The practice of recommending relatives or friends as *pessoas de confianza* (trustworthy individuals) is, indeed, generalized. For example, there is a booming business of "selling" houses to clean, where a person who has built a busy schedule of cleaning jobs through a long-term cultivation of clients transfers some of her or his jobs to friends or relatives, often recently arrived, for an amount. Or the more established person who has built trust with a client might subcontract a friend or relative to do the job. In this case, the subcontracted worker will receive a lower wage because he or she is new at the job. We found several small housecleaning agencies in which a more established Brazilian had three or four other immigrants working for her. While she can charge up to eighty dollars for each house, she only pays fifteen dollars per house to those who actually do the cleaning. A similar situation takes place in other areas of personal services such as babysitting. We found cases where Brazilians who started by taking care of the children of American families eventually became independent and set up their own child-care businesses. These new Brazilian entrepreneurs then hire other Brazilians to take care of their children while they run their business, paying their compatriots in a week what they earned in a day of work with an American family.

We see the infrastructure sustaining what I have called the "immigrant regime of production," a conflictive pattern of labor organization that runs on trust, intimacy, and reciprocity, all elements which are highly concentrated in familial and friendship networks as well as in religious organizations. Despite the conflictive and often exploitative character of this regime of production, it allows Brazilian immigrants to survive and even thrive through the tactical use of their own resources. Among Brazilians in Broward County, familial, friendship, and religious networks have often provided the initial capital, human resources (in terms of leadership and labor force), know-how, locales, and captive markets for the formation of business networks.

As we saw above, evangelical churches very often operate as business networks by virtue of their emphasis on material success as a sign of salvation and on the individual as autonomous and self-driven by an ethic of hard work and entrepreneurship. Books, CDs, DVDs, gospel singers, itinerant preachers, self-improvement courses, and outreach ministries are often part of a transnational market that strengthens local congregations. This is evident in the following statement given by a Brazilian evangelical pastor:

You see, . . . this community got together to construct this building, which cost three million dollars, without a single penny from the outside, from Americans, from anyone. [This building] is totally Brazilian, with our help and cooperation. . . . It has the first soccer school within a church. [But how can we] have services on Sunday . . . and the soccer school functioning [on the same day]? It is because we discovered that the best way to attract children [so] they can think about God is to give thirty minutes to God and one hour to soccer. Do you understand? We know that things will compensate each other. So, we have our soccer school functioning full steam, [with] two full-time teachers [*profession-ais*], meeting three times a week. In that way, children are enthusiastic [*vibram*] about coming to church. We have 250 kids here in this church and sixty teachers in our children's department [*departamento infantil*].

In particular, the figure of the influential evangelical pastor who is simultaneously a successful entrepreneur serves as a paradigmatic example of the strategic link between religion and economics:

> Robert, . . . he is director of marketing, and that's the reason why the work [the construction] was well done. He did a survey and discovered how many millions of dollars come in each month, the money that evangelicals make, each evangelical family. He calculated the salary of all evangelicals here in South Florida. He got a rough estimate from the money that each church collects. Each member gives at least 10 percent of his salary, which is the tithe, although in our church only 60 percent [of the members] tithe. So, he multiplied these figures for all churches and calculated the salary of evangelicals. And then he used [that number] as a guide, showing all the evangelical businesses that exist in the region. His idea—and there I don't agree with him—is that brothers [i.e., evangelicals] should buy from other brothers.

Notice the ambivalence of the evangelical Protestant leader in response to the proposal of explicitly linking religion, production, and consumption. This might explain why, among Brazilian immigrants in Broward County, evangelical networks do not constitute a niche or a segmented market. Yet, these networks are definitely a crucial ingredient in the ethnic economic landscape. Particularly, for recently arrived immigrants in new destinations, without pre-established immigrant networks that can facilitate settlement, access to the labor market is very often made possible by information and business contacts flowing through the religious networks. These networks offer a degree of trust and authority unmatched by other informal connections. One immigrant said, "I was already attending the church of Pastor Olavo, but I went to his house [to talk to him about my situation]. And [then] in the church it was announced that I had just recently arrived and that I was looking for work and a place to live. Then, a church deacon found a room for me and a job painting. Within a day, everything was set up [esquematizado]. I had a church, a place to stay, and a job."

While religious networks may facilitate entry into the job market, they often do so in a position of vulnerability, in which the fact that the newly arrived immigrant does not speak English and does not know how to get around or how to negotiate the rules and regulations of the host society becomes the justification for low salaries and unsafe work conditions. The low salaries provide the surplus that drives the immigrant business networks, making it possible for them to expand and continue hiring the newly arrived. Obviously, this arrangement is fraught with tension. And it is here that religion plays a key mediating role: the pastor's moral and spiritual authority, which is often expressed in his material success and that of his congregation, serves as a counterweight to the immigrant worker's awareness of the low salaries.

This is not to say that religious networks are particularly exploitative. We collected testimonies of newly arrived Brazilian immigrants who faced far lower salaries, longer hours, and worse working conditions in labor networks not having anything to do with religion. In fact, in many cases the jobs secured through church contacts were a good alternative to extremely exploitative labor arrangements. Still, I would like to highlight here that religious networks among the Brazilian immigrants we studied provide an important moral and spiritual infrastructure for the immigrant regime of production.

The Catholic network is also part of this infrastructure, enabling the extraction of surplus among immigrants. However, at least in comparison to evangelical networks, this process is more restrained by Catholic social doctrine, which, even in its more conservative version, as in the thought of John Paul II and Benedict XVI, is consistently critical of capitalist exploitation of the worker. In the words of a Brazilian Catholic leader in Pompano Beach,

> There are always people who benefit from one's ignorance and try to take advantage. This has always taken place and will always take place. Here we have even slave labor among Brazilians. There are people who take passports away, . . . people who have to submit to work, earning two or three dollars per hour, [people] who threaten: "Ah! I'm going to hand you over to immigration and . . . you have no passport." It is for that reason that I have been moved to do the work I do [with social outreach], to do for the people that are just arriving what I wish someone had done for me. Here when people arrive they are very vulnerable; they can fall pray to people of bad faith [*pessoas de má fé*] who use your precarious state. Thus, I felt the desire to get involved in this work for the church, which is not my work. It is work for the community, a work for the church, to support the church.

The Brazilian Spiritist networks we encountered in Broward County also have a more ambivalent relation with business networks. On the one hand, their humanism, their emphasis on human development and education, predisposes Spiritists to be critical of outright economic exploitation. This critical attitude is further strengthened by the Spiritist value of charity. However, the Spiritists also believe that success and well-being are predicated on individual merit. The Spiritist ambivalence to the link between religion and business is well expressed by the following statement from a Spiritist leader:

> No, it's not individualism. If you observe people, life, and religion, if you analyze everything, you will see that you will not be able to change anybody, that you cannot live somebody else's life for him. That is not individualism; that is [assuming] one's own responsibility. [One day] my boss called me to his office and told me: "Look, there is no other way about it. I will not find

another person like you to work on the [assembly] line. You are a good guy
[um cara certo] and I'm going to give you a raise and I will let you work as
much as you want, in other words, overtime, 50 percent more than you
normally earn." [My boss] knows that I like money, that I like to work. So, he
puts me to work six days a week, when everyone else only works four or five
[days]. I work six and sometimes even seven days, if it were for him. So it is
good for my professional development. And I will not change it. I already
have a profession; I'm a cook and I like what I do. It is an Americanized
thing, in an assembly line because it is a busy restaurant and you have to
produce. But it is a gratifying business and people around you perceive the
love that you put into things, the food comes out differently.

In the Candomblé network, in turn, legitimacy ultimately rests on the
authority and authenticity of the pai de santo, despite the fact that the network
is built according to the logic of a clientele which often exchanges money for
advice, healing, and other spiritual goods. In this setting, authority and authenticity may be adversely affected if the interactions are primarily defined by
financial gain. In the small circles that follow African-based religions abroad,
word gets around quickly whether one is a legitimate religious leader or a char-
latan. The potential for gossip, thus, limits the kind of business involvement
that the pai de santo can undertake. Moreover, the notion of fate, which is
closely associated with serving one's spirit, does not encourage the same pursuit of this-worldly success as the individualism advanced by evangelical
Protestantism, particularly in its neo-Pentecostal version. Here the pai de santo
that we interviewed offers a good illustration:

PAI DE SANTO: I do not look for people. I do not deceive [iludo] anyone. If someone wants to come [to my house], he just comes and believes.

INTERVIEWER: So they know about you from other people?

PAI DE SANTO: Yes, they know. . . . I have a radio program and a TV program. At
the moment I don't have anything. Programs like those are too
expensive. But I have time in Globo, also in Spanish. I left everything behind [when I went to Florida]. I'm well known here in
New York. You see that I have my program and you come [to my
house] if you want to. I'm not going to deceive and tell them,
"Do this and do that." I don't ask things like that.

INTERVIEWER: Yes, I saw your phrase: "Fate exists but you need to orient it,"
something like that.

PAI DE SANTO: Guide it.

A similar attitude is evident in the Umbanda center we studied. In the
words of the terreiro's founder, "In the seven months [that we have been open]

people come and go. Some come and then disappear. I believe that if they disappear it's because they won't come back. I leave that to them. I am happy with the results in the lives of the others [who stayed]. Their lives are improving just like mine, and without the financial side. I tell everyone in our group [that] I'm a mechanic. Everybody knows that. I'm not capable of charging for the services that I give them. If I were someone else, I would maybe charge. It is my sustenance [*sustento*]. I cannot put a price [on my services] for my friends or relatives."

We see here how for the African-based religious networks among Brazilians in Pompano Beach and Deerfield Beach the interplay with business networks and with an economic ethos of accumulation is rather tenuous. In fact, these networks seem to be at one end of the spectrum—the other being neo-Pentecostal churches, which overtly link religious affiliation and practice with a process of credentialing newly arrived immigrants, giving them the contacts and moral sanction to enter a hierarchical job market. This spectrum shows the diverse, complex, and contradictory ways in which religion is involved in the immigrant regime of production among Brazilians in South Florida.

Conclusion

In this chapter I offered the concept of immigrant regime of production as a tool to examine the role of transnational migration in the present stage of globalization, which is characterized by the geo-political hegemony of the United States and the economic dominance of neo-liberalism. Today, in the context of a "total war against terrorism," a regime of immigration has taken shape which, on the one hand, requires immigrants to sustain the growing service and construction sectors as engines for internal development in the United States. On the other hand, this regime marks immigrants as undocumented, effectively rendering them as "non-subjects," shadowy or even criminal figures with no political or social rights. In the case of Brazilians, this invisibility is reinforced by a Brazilian state which, while benefiting from the remittances sent by immigrants and using immigration as an escape valve to release the pressure produced by the social dislocation of its own neo-liberal policies, fails to have a coherent and comprehensive policy to re-enfranchise its citizens abroad. The Brazilian state basically benefits from the fruits of migration without any financial or political cost. Left to their own devices, immigrants assume the cost of their own reproduction as a labor force, drawing from their own social networks to create places to be. Further, by accepting low wages and precarious work conditions, immigrants are producing a capital surplus that is contributing to the growth of the U.S. economy.

Following Marx's holistic definition of mode of production and Foucault's notion of regimes of knowledge and practice, this chapter also focused on the cultural dimensions of immigrant livelihoods in South Florida, highlighting the role of religious networks in organization, mobilization, and reproduction of a cheap reserve labor army. In particular, in new destinations such as Broward County, religious networks offer a variety of protective spaces and strategies to enter the labor market that makes it possible for immigrants to survive the increasingly hostile terrain and, in the process, to produce surplus value for the economic system. Very often, religious networks offer the contacts, credentials, and the initial capital accumulation to set in motion the immigrant regime of production. In that sense, religious networks are not mere reflections of economic processes or just ideologies that hide deeper social realities. Rather, they actively contribute to the emergence and operation of structures of production, providing a whole social and moral infrastructure, the local and transnational capillaries upon which economic and political hegemony is based.

My argument, therefore, complements that made by Nina Glick Schiller, who has recently shed light on the role that fundamentalist Christian transnational networks play in the transmission of U.S. imperialism; according to her, the language of spiritual warfare and territorial conquest for Jesus in these networks contributes to the construction of an image of the entire world as a U.S. domain.[16] My argument is that some transnational religious networks among Brazilian immigrants may be contributing not only to the spread of a neo-imperialist ideology, but also to the incorporation of these immigrants into a new global form of capitalist accumulation.

I showed, however, that religious organizations among Brazilians in Broward County do not simply buttress the extraction of surplus from a vulnerable labor force. Congregations sometimes can confront the panoptical policies of the state—the intensifying push to criminalize, apprehend, and deport undocumented immigrants—by mobilizing immigrants to challenge all the exclusionary implications of the term "illegal." Nevertheless, because religious organizations need to attract immigrants to guarantee their own survival, they must offer day-to-day services that facilitate insertion in the immigrant regime of production. As a result, there are limits to what religious networks can do in terms of political mobilization and empowerment.

NOTES

I wish to thank Manuel A. Vásquez for his helpful comments and editorial work as well as for translating this chapter.

1. Karl Marx, "The German Ideology: Part I," in *The Marx-Engels Reader*, ed. Robert C. Tucker (New York: W. W. Norton & Company, 1978), 150.

2. Michel Foucault, *Power/ Knowledge: Selected Interviews and Other Writings, 1972–1977* (New York: Pantheon Books, 1980), 133.

3. Michel Foucault, "The Subject and Power," in *Michel Foucault: Beyond Structuralism and Hermeneutics,* by Hubert L. Dreyfus and Paul Rabinow (Chicago: University of Chicago Press, 1983), 218.

4. See David Harvey, *The Condition of Postmodernity: An Inquiry into the Origins of Cultural Change* (Cambridge, MA: Blackwell, 1989).

5. Ronen Shamir, "Without Borders? Notes on Globalization as a Mobility Regime," *Sociological Theory* 23, no. 2 (2005): 197–217.

6. Saskia Sassen, *Globalization and Its Discontents: Essays on the New Mobility of People and Money* (New York: New Press, 1998).

7. Michael Burawoy and Theda Skocpol, eds., *Marxist Inquiries: Studies of Labor, Class, and States* (Chicago: University of Chicago Press, 1982).

8. See Rouse, "Thinking through Transnationalism: Notes on the Cultural Politics of Class Relations in the Contemporary United States," *Public Culture* 7, no. 2 (1995): 353–420. For a discussion of the concept of reserve labor army, see T. Bottomore et al., eds., *A Dictionary of Marxist Thought* (Cambridge, MA: Harvard University Press, 1983).

9. Maxine Margolis, *Little Brazil: An Ethnography of Brazilian Immigrants in New York City* (Princeton: Princeton University Press, 1994); Teresa Sales, *Brasileiros longe de casa* (São Paulo: Editora Cortês, 1999); Ana Cristina Martes, *Brasileiros nos Estados Unidos: Um estudo sobre imigrantes em Massachusetts* (São Paulo: Paz e Terra, 2000).

10. Peggy Levitt, "Redefining the Boundaries of Belonging: The Institutional Character of Transnational Religious Life," *Sociology of Religion* 65 (2004): 1–18.

11. The Pew Forum on Religion and Public Life and the Pew Hispanic Center, *Changing Faiths: Latinos and the Transformation of American Religion* (Washington, DC: Pew Research Center, 2007).

12. Philip Berryman, "Churches as Winners and Losers in the Network Society," *Journal of Interamerican Studies and World Affairs* 41, no. 4 (1999): 21–34; Manuel A. Vásquez, "Toward a New Agenda for the Study of Religion in the Americas," *Journal of Interamerican Studies and World Affairs* 41, no. 4 (1999): 1–20.

13. R. Andrew Chesnut, *Competitive Spirits: Latin America's New Religious Economy* (Oxford: Oxford University Press, 2003).

14. Paul Gilroy, *The Black Atlantic: Modernity and Double-Consciousness* (Cambridge, MA: Harvard University Press, 1993).

15. Ana Celia Perera Pintado, "Religion and Cuban Identity in a Transnational Context," *Latin American Perspectives* 32, no. 1 (2005): 147–173.

16. Nina Glick Schiller, "Transnational Social Fields and Imperialism: Bringing a Theory of Power to Transnational Studies," *Anthropological Theory* 5, no. 4 (2005): 449.

PART THREE

Identities and Lived Religion

7

Lived Religion and a Sense of Home

The Ambiguities of Transnational Identity
among Jacaltecos in Jupiter

TIMOTHY J. STEIGENGA, SILVIA IRENE PALMA,
AND CAROL GIRÓN SOLÓRZANO

One of the initial goals of this project was to understand the impact that various forms of religious transnationalism have on the formation or continuation of collective identities among immigrants in South Florida. In turn, we hoped to assess how such identities might foster and/or hinder civic participation among immigrants in the public sphere. Based on four years of research among Mayan immigrants in the community of Jupiter, Florida, this chapter argues that certain elements of lived religion among the Jacaltec Maya of Jupiter symbolically and practically recreate conceptions of "home," thereby providing a sense of aggregate identity that has facilitated collective action. Some of the contextual factors acting as catalysts for this effect include a common sending community, ethnic and linguistic homogeneity, and the dominance of a single religious tradition. These factors, combined with low levels of social/cultural acceptance of immigrants in Jupiter, foster a sense of collective identity that has led to local-level political organizing and collective action.[1]

But the story does not end there. In many cases, comfortable and safe recreations of home are more imagined than real. Nostalgia, family difficulties, and shifting transnational identities intrude and can shatter shared conceptions of a re-created home. When contextual factors are not favorable, divisions and other barriers to collective identity formation limit the possibility for collective action and expose differences within immigrant conceptions of home. Furthermore, the very factors that provide a sense of collective identity at the level of village, church, and ethnic group are likely to lead to divisions that inhibit collective action at an expanded level of identity (Mayan, Hispanic, or immigrant). Ethnically based political mobilization may also carry a heavy price in terms of acceptance within the host community and inter-ethnic conflict.

In order to put this argument in context, we begin with a brief discussion of terminology and the transnational religious institutions and practices apparent in the Jupiter case. In particular, we focus on the transnational and identity linkages illustrated in the initial celebration of the Fiesta Maya in Jupiter in 2002 and the ensuing examples of collective action among Jupiter's immigrant population. We then turn to some of the specific impediments to broad community collaboration that are apparent in the case of Jupiter and may be inherent in social movements based in the formation of a shared identity politics characterized by reactive ethnicity. We conclude with some final theoretical reflections on religion and transnational migration.

Transnationalism and Lived Religion

It should come as no surprise that "transnationalism" is a contested term. Scholars in the fields of cultural studies, religious studies, migration studies, political science, sociology, and anthropology use the term to mean very different things in different contexts. As discussed in chapter 1, in the broadest terms, transnationalism refers to activities, organizations, ideas, identities, and social and economic relations that frequently cross or even transcend national boundaries.[2] As is the case in many academic fields, this broad definition creates a multidimensional levels-of-analysis problem for the study of transnationalism. Luis Guarnizo and Michael P. Smith distinguish between "transnationalism from above," as the processes of globalization anchored in multinational governmental and nongovernmental organizations, and "transnationalism from below," with a focus on the lived realities of migrants and their cross-border communities.[3] Within the definition of transnationalism from below, Alejandro Portes adds quantitative and chronological dimensions, arguing that the volume of individuals and activities crossing borders must be both significant and sustained in order to be called transnational.[4] Exactly how high the volume must be or for how long remains an issue of some debate.[5]

Moving beyond the study of individual transmigrants, Peggy Levitt focuses on the need to understand the social context of transnationalism.[6] The social groups, identities, beliefs, rituals, practices, and power relationships in both sending and receiving communities (as well as locations in transit) are also critical to our understanding of the process and effects of transnationalism. Here lies the critical nexus between the study of transnationalism and the study of lived religion, for it is precisely the social groups, identities, beliefs, rituals, practices, celebrations, meanings, and power relationships among people that make up the substance of the study of lived religion. According to this perspective, the Pentecostal pastor proselytizing among day-laborers on Center Street in Jupiter and the families of those laborers back home in Jacaltenango are as much a part of the "transnational community" as the transmigrants themselves. For each of these actors, lived religion encompasses their embodied practices as they navigate the multiple locations and relations that constitute the fabric of their daily lives. In other words, lived religion takes place both inside and outside the formal process of "belonging" to a religious group.[7] It is within this final level of analysis that this study is located, exploring the religious elements of transnationalism from below in the community that stretches between Jacaltenango, Guatemala, and Jupiter, Florida.

Much of the literature on transnational migration is concerned with proving that there is something fundamentally new about transnationalism. While there are key differences, we approach the question of religious transnationalism from the perspective that many of the social processes embedded in the "new immigration" are similar to those involved with previous waves of immigration. While the speed, quantity, and even the quality of transnational connections have certainly changed, the effects of these connections in terms of identity formation, empowerment, and collective action hold both similarities and differences with previous waves of migration.

In the case of Jupiter, this chapter seeks to demonstrate that recreated images of home have been both facilitated by and reinforced through a particular form of lived religion. Through planning, organizing, and celebrating a fiesta tied to their community of origin, Jacaltec Mayan immigrants in Jupiter have maintained and reinforced common ties of identity that facilitate cooperative public action beyond the festival. This process demonstrates clear parallels with the experience of previous migrant groups, such as those described in Robert Orsi's study of turn-of-the-century Italians in Harlem.[8] There are clear differences as well, however, as the very religious forces and ethnic and regional identities that foster collective mobilization in Jupiter also lead to differences among the larger Mayan immigrant population and continue to serve as impediments to Pan-Mayan or Pan-Hispanic activism.

Religious, Civic, and Transnational Organizations

In our initial mapping of religious institutions in Jupiter, we found evidence of what Peggy Levitt calls extended, negotiated, and re-created transnational religious organizations.[9] The Catholic Church generally falls within the first category. St. Peter's Catholic Church, located closest to the majority of the immigrant population in Jupiter, had no Spanish Mass and no mission to the immigrant population at the inception of our study. Repeated attempts by the leaders of the Mayan community to make inroads into the church were rebuffed. However, following the celebration of the first fiesta, Mayan leaders pressed the local bishop to address this problem. Beginning in 2003, St. Peter's started a Hispanic ministry, which has grown significantly since that time. One of the priests, a nun, and several congregation members of St. Peter's have become strong advocates on behalf of Jupiter's immigrant community, speaking up on their behalf in front of the town council and working with local nonprofits to organize to support the El Sol Neighborhood Resource Center.

South of Jupiter, the St. Ignatius Loyola Church in Palm Beach Gardens used to serve close to two hundred Guatemalans, divided between the Jacaltecos and

other Mayan groups. There was little mixing between the Anglo and Mayan congregations served in the church, with Spanish Mass held separately and few
opportunities for mingling. Some members of the St. Ignatius Church remain
very active through the Tepeyac Mission in projects in Jacaltenango, supporting
schools, fiestas, and a nutritional center. Tepeyac is an organization that is independent from the Jupiter parish, with its own independent board.

While there are some clear and growing transnational connections
between the institutional Catholic Church and the Mayan community in Palm
Beach County, the majority of transnational religious organizing seems to fall
into Peggy Levitt's final two categories of negotiated and re-created transnational religion.[10] Many of the more successful evangelical churches appear to
have been initiated by "religious entrepreneurs" who found both a survival
strategy and a source of authority through church founding. The Evangelical
Church of Kanjobal in Lake Worth, the Templo de Adoración Familiar, and
Cristo Rompe las Cadenas (an extremely charismatic evangelical group with a
radio program) were all founded by early religious entrepreneurs in Palm Beach
County. In a unique transnational twist, one pastor who left the Templo de
Adoración Familiar is now working to spread the influence of the Guatemalan
neo-Pentecostal Iglesia Elim in Palm Beach County through the use of the
Internet.

A relatively large number of Mayan immigrants also gravitate toward North
American evangelical and Pentecostal churches. The Baptist church on Center
Street in Jupiter has a significant immigrant membership, and a number of
Guatemalans attend the Assembly of God church as well as the local Mormon
church.

The primary civic organizations that operate in Jupiter and the surrounding
areas include Corn-Maya, Inc., the Maya Jacaltec Association, and, more recently,
a group that was mobilized to support the creation of a resource/labor center to
serve the immigrant community (formerly known as the Friends of the Jupiter
Neighborhood Resource Center, and now called the Friends of El Sol, the new
name of the resource center). Corn-Maya is a 501 (c) (3), nonprofit, non-sectarian
organization that was formed by Mesoamerican refugees and advocates in South
Florida in the early 1980s. The organization was formed initially to represent and
assist the thousands of refugees, mostly Mayan indigenous people, who were flee-
ing civil wars in Central America. Since that time, Corn-Maya's activities have
included immigration services, referrals, interpreting services, emergency services, and the sponsorship of community forums for immigrant education on different aspects of rights and responsibilities in U.S. society. Corn-Maya has also
sponsored a number of cultural events, including Guatemalan festivals, concerts,
and dances. In 2002, the organization became revitalized through the process of
planning for the first Fiesta Maya in Abacoa (a new planned community that
houses the Florida Atlantic University campus). The members of the Maya

Jacaltec Association (a non-incorporated group of Jacaltec Maya immigrants) asked permission from the original founders of Corn-Maya to reinstate the non-profit for operation in Jupiter. Corn-Maya opened a small office in Jupiter in 2003 to coordinate services to the immigrant community. Corn-Maya also provided the initial impetus as a lobbying force to convince local authorities to make available a location for the resource center. In collaboration with the Friends of El Sol and with the support of funding from Catholic Charities, Corn-Maya helped to found the El Sol Resource Center, which opened its doors in September 2006.

The Friends of El Sol is a wide-ranging advocacy group made up of members of St. Peter's, members of the Jupiter Democratic Club, representatives of Corn-Maya, students from Florida Atlantic University's Wilkes Honors College, and residents from the Charter Neighborhoods, where Jupiter's immigrant community primarily resides. Since 2004, this group met monthly to lobby the town in support of a neighborhood resource center (including a day-labor center) to serve the immigrant community. The group's support was critical in convincing the Jupiter Town Council to vote in support of using town property to house the resource center.

Together, these civic and religious organizations made up of and in support of Jupiter's immigrant community have been extremely effective in advocating for Jupiter's immigrants. On its own, the immigrant-run organization Corn-Maya was unable to make significant inroads with local politicians. As increasing numbers of Anglo and Hispanic residents began showing up at town council meetings to show their support for the center, however, town authorities began to take the prospect more seriously. As discussed in chapter 5, in the end, successful lobbying on behalf of the center required a particular combination of immigrant mobilization, institutional support (from the university and the Catholic Church), a group of motivated and concerned community residents, and a single town council member who became a major advocate for the center after he attended a meeting of Corn-Maya and the Friends of El Sol group held at his church (St. Peter's).

Lived Religion and Conceptions of Home

According to anthropologist Allan Burns, "a well-documented aspect of Maya cultural identity in Guatemala is the connection that people have to the communities where they were born. The coincidence of language, the town or community, and culture has been described as the basis for Guatemalan Maya identity."[11] In his study of the Maya in Indiantown, Florida, Burns recounts the story of one recent Mayan immigrant who directly addressed the question of home. According to this woman, Indiantown lacked a sense of providing a home during her early years in residence. For her, the fact that there were no "graves of the dead" in Indiantown precluded that sense of home. But, as Burns explains, "within 5 years there were graves of Maya who had died in the United States, so Indiantown joined the home villages in Guatemala as a place where Mayan identity is defined."[12]

If the study of transnationalism and lived religion is partly about re-created spaces and cultural reproduction, it is critical that we explore immigrant images and re-creations of home. This is hardly a novel idea or one that applies exclusively to the Mayan community. In his rich study of lived religion among Italian immigrants in East Harlem, *The Madonna of 115th Street*, Robert Orsi discusses some of the fundamental ambivalences that characterize the process of migration. He concludes, "The inner history of immigration is also a story of complex needs: for success, stability, participation and autonomy, faithfulness to tradition and openness to the new ways, the need to recreate the familiar while in the midst of change."[13] This is as true among Mayan immigrants in Jupiter today as it was among the Italian immigrants in Harlem at the turn of the century. Just as the southern Italians who came to New York sought to reproduce a sense of home through celebrating their devotion to la Madonna del Carmine through the celebration of the *festa*, Jupiter's Jacaltec Mayan immigrants proudly march the streets of Jupiter's newest development to honor their Virgin of Candelaria during their fiesta. For the Maya in Jupiter, these images of home entail physical, cultural, ideological, familial, religious, national, and local elements that combine to create a sense of belonging and identity in the face of a confusing and sometimes hostile environment. The fiesta, marimba, soccer tournaments, collections for return of the dead, and other transnational and religious elements combine to form a re-created sense of home in an otherwise foreign landscape.

It is worth noting that most of these elements of lived religion are public, rather than private practices. As in the case of Immokalee (see chapter 8), our respondents noted that their engagement in private religious practices (such as offering promises, candles, or prayers to saints) was much less frequent in the context of Jupiter than it had been in their hometowns.[14] Unstable and crowded living arrangements, lack of access to transportation to purchase religious icons and elements, and other impediments likely play some role in the fact that fewer migrants engage in these religious practices in Jupiter than they do in their hometowns. To a large degree, the lack of private outlet for the practice of lived religion is precisely what makes the celebration of the fiesta such a critical component of shared religious and cultural practice in Jupiter. With all of its planning, celebration, tensions, and ambiguities, the fiesta provides important insights into the role of transnationalism and lived religion in immigrant life in Jupiter.

From Fiesta Candelaria to Fiesta Maya

Planning for the initial celebration of the fiesta began in 2001 and evolved from plans for a much less ambitious cultural exchange program involving the Mayan community and university students. University representatives, members of the Mayan community, and university students met with the executive director of the Abacoa Partnership for Community to discuss the possibility of a cultural exchange event for the Mayan community, the Abacoa community, and the university. As talks progressed, the possibility of including marimba music in the presentation was discussed. As dates for the event were debated, we found that the best date for all parties was the first weekend of February, which would coincide with the celebration of La Fiesta de la Virgen de Candelaria for the Mayan community in Jacaltenango. Ultimately, all parties decided to schedule a series of activities around the fiesta (soccer games between Mayan teams and students, traditional Guatemalan food, and a talk about the situation of Mayan immigrants in the Jupiter community).

These initial conversations soon grew into a series of organizational meetings and plans for the festival. After many meetings and hours of planning, the Coalición Jacalteca de Jupiter formed a set of commissions, each responsible for different elements of the festival. The coalition met weekly in the months leading up to the festival to prepare for the Mass, procession, food, publicity, and other aspects of the celebration. Students and faculty from the university attended some of these organizational meetings and also participated in planning for the festival.

As planning for the festival moved forward, however, some further countervailing tendencies within the process of "community building" became evident. The religious nature of the festival was questioned by some participants, while questions of inclusion or exclusion of the wider immigrant community were debated. One potential conflict that arose during the planning stages of the festival centered around divisions in the community between the primarily Catholic and traditional Jacaltec coalition and a group of Mayan evangelicals associated with a North American pastor at a local evangelical church. While initially enthusiastic about the project, the pastor began to express skepticism when he learned more about the religious nature of the festival. As the pastor explained, "I started out enthusiastic about the fiesta, but I guess I was also a little naïve. . . . [A]s soon as I began to mention this to our people I got a surprise. This fiesta is only embraced in the Christian community by those who are Catholic or pagan. It is not participated in at all by other Christians in the evangelical groups. Though the majority in most Spanish-speaking countries are from Catholic background, this is not true in Guatemala, where the majority is evangelical."

As these religious and cultural dividing lines emerged, organizers of the festival were also warned by university officials about using university premises for religious events. After hours of discussion on the merits of inclusiveness, cultural identity, and religious significance, the Maya Jacaltec Association eventually came to the decision to remove religious references from publicity for the festival and to restrict religious activities to off-campus locations during the morning of the fiesta. The festival was renamed and advertised as the Fiesta Maya. We will return to this issue in the discussion below.

As outlined in chapter 5, the fiesta celebrated in Jupiter includes the final playoffs of the soccer tournament, traditional Guatemalan food, a procession and performance of the Dance of the Deer, and traditional marimba music and Jacaltec dance. With each year, the festival has grown in size (drawing nearly two thousand participants in 2008) and has expanded to include participating music and dance groups from other Latin American countries. Organizing for the initial fiesta sparked the rebirth of Corn-Maya and kicked off the process that would include a sister city agreement between Jacaltenango and Jupiter, visits from Guatemalan dignitaries (President Oscar Berger, Vice President Eduardo Stein, Minister of Foreign Affairs Jorge Briz, and Nobel Peace Prize winner Rigoberta Menchu), and culminate in a major campaign to support and fund the creation of a neighborhood resource center. In order to understand the movement from organizing a fiesta to organizing collective action in the interest of the immigrant community, it is necessary to explore the transnational connections as well as immigrant perceptions of the meaning of the fiesta.

The Fiesta as Transnational Landscape and Social Field

One of the clearest transnational connections in the Fiesta Maya relates to publicity and coverage of the event during the first year. No less than five video cameras were wielded by Guatemalan participants to document the procession, Mass, soccer game, and multiple interviews. Throughout the day, Guatemalan Mayans could be heard in front of the camera sending salutations to their friends and families in Jacaltenango. At least two of the cameramen flew to Guatemala to show their work during the celebration in Jacaltenango. During the nights of celebration before and after the fiesta, videos of previous celebrations in Jacaltenango were shown on a television set up in the backyard of a Jacaltec Mayan Association leader's home.

Another connection took place via the radio airwaves. One individual who was unable to attend ceremonies in either Jupiter or Guatemala received a live report of the Jupiter celebration from a local leader via cell phone. During the celebration in Jacaltenango, this individual called a local radio station in Guatemala and passed along news of the Jupiter fiesta.

The traditional marimba played for the procession also illustrates the transnational nature of this cultural and religious festival. In the months leading to the first festival, a traditional marimba was located, but it was in a serious state of disrepair. A local Mayan carpenter was able to make the major repairs, but the essential replacements were not available in Florida. Arrangements were made to ship the *tela* (vibrating reeds made from pig intestines) from

Guatemala in the final weeks prior to the festival. During the preparations for a subsequent celebration of the festival, project researchers found themselves negotiating with Guatemalan customs officials over export taxes and shipping on a new marimba after they found a fully constructed marimba waiting for them at the airport upon their departure for fieldwork in Florida. After considerable negotiations, they were able to deconstruct the marimba and carry it in various pieces of luggage, arriving just in time for the fiesta in Jupiter.

Some of the transnational connections related to the fiesta are institutionalized through the San Isidro Association, a group that works and organizes both in Palm Beach County and in Jacaltenango. The association is made up primarily of traditional Catholics who collect funds for social services and church-related organizations and fiestas in Jacaltenango. Some of them travel to Jacaltenango each year for the fiesta. Other connections are institutionalized through the leadership the Guatemalan-Maya Center, Inc., located in Lake Worth. The Guatemalan-Maya Center provided support and traditional attire for the procession and dance at the first fiesta. Each year, replacement *trajes* are frantically shipped from Jacaltenango to Guatemala City, where unsuspecting friends and family with plans to travel to Jupiter are deluged with requests to bring extra pieces of baggage containing the trajes, replacement parts, or other items related to the fiesta.

A final transnational religious connection is personified in the priest from Jacaltenango who said Mass during the first year's fiesta. The priest, who was forced into exile during the violence of Guatemala's civil war, is revered as a community leader in Jacaltenango and is widely respected among the Mayan immigrant population. He performed services to bless the traditional costumes for the *baile de venado* the night prior to the festival, said Mass the morning of the fiesta, and then flew to Guatemala to attend the final nights of the fiesta in Jacaltenango.

The nights of celebration preceding and following the public celebration of the Fiesta Maya also provide evidence of the creation of what Peggy Levitt has called "transnational religious space as an alternative landscape."[15] The night prior to the second year's festival, project researchers were invited to a community member's house for the blessing of the procession marimba and other materials. The entire backyard was covered with tarp, under which a central altar was erected with the image of the Virgin surrounded by candles and the costumes for the Dance of the Deer. *Churrasco* and tortillas were served to the sounds of a perpetually rotating set of marimba players. As the night progressed, coolers of beer appeared, more and more people arrived, and eventually the crowd formed a circle to begin the dancing. At that moment, we made our first visit to the transnational religious landscape of Jacaltenango, Guatemala. We returned to visit this remarkable alternative landscape each night for the rest of the week-long celebration.

Identity, Solidarity, Action, and Home

As illustrated in the festival and surrounding activities, religiously and culturally re-created images of home may assist transmigrants in the process of maintaining a sense of identity and solidarity in the face of the many difficulties
encountered in daily life. Our interviews with members of Jupiter's Jacaltec
community provide evidence for this process. As one young member of the
Jacaltec community explained, "the unity among Guatemalans is essential. We
unite with the purpose of showing this country who we are so that they pay
attention to us ... and so we can get our papers." A community leader in
Indiantown added the following: "The success of the Guatemalans is that they
help each other, in contrast to the Mexicans who don't have support. In the
larger cities there is less solidarity." Reflecting on the first year's fiesta during an
ensuing meeting of the Jacaltec coalition, one of the local leaders put it this way:
"This was the first time that we were able to show the people our culture, the
Dance of the Deer, the marimba. That was important. But what was even more
critical was that we were able to celebrate our most important event of the year
in such a place [Abacoa], . . . a place for rich people."

As noted in chapter 5, the roots of this solidarity and sense of accomplishment are to be found in shared images of home, shared practices, shared language, and a shared sending community. Funds collected to return *los muertos*,
soccer leagues organized around hometown groups, assistance paying loans to
coyotes, informal labor networks, and membership in hometown associations
such as the Maya Jacaltec Association all link to form a web of formal and informal networks of personal and institutional support. Given impetus by the fiesta,
these connections were translated into pathways toward political organizing
and institution building through Corn-Maya and the campaign for a resource
center in Jupiter.

Ambiguities within Immigrant Conceptions
of Home and Collective Identity

In light of the successful campaign for a resource center in Jupiter, it would be
tempting to conclude that mobilization based in transnationalism and re-created images of home represents a uniquely positive strategy for newly arrived
immigrant groups to pursue their collective interest. While this may be the case,
it is critical that we also explore the ambiguities, nostalgia, and contradictions
inherent in the process of transnational migration and community building.

In the years following the first fiesta, we have conducted focus groups and
individual interviews with the participants. The following description of one
such focus group exchange captures a sentiment repeated in multiple interviews. The interviewer prompted the group of seven men by asking what their

home was like when they left it. Her description, a summary report of their ensuing conversation, provides us with clues to some of the ambiguities within re-created images of home:

> In remembering Guatemala they recall the poverty, but also the freedom, the marimba music, the festivals, traditions (cacao drink), *semana santa*, processions, and most of all the Fiesta de la Candelaria. They talk about the flowers used in this festival; purple flowers that grow high in the trees and require the most agile young men to collect them. They also recall the food (*tamales*). Everyone participated in this festival. They are happy that they can do it in Abacoa because they feel like it's a rich place and it took a lot to get there. Still, they feel that the procession here is just a summary of the real thing. At home no one works on this day; it is solemn and at the same time joyous. Everyone drinks during the fiesta, even the women drink. This is a stress release for them; they don't have to worry, and it is seven days of true freedom. Mostly here in Florida during the fiesta they miss the landscape of their homes, the mountains and the rivers.[16]

As Allan Burns has demonstrated, transnational migrants often maintain multiple identities that cross national boundaries and traditional "ways of being Mayan."[17] In relation to images of home, Nadje Al-Ali and Khalid Koser add the insight that "conceptions of home are not static but dynamic processes, involving the acts of imaging, creating, unmaking, changing, losing and moving homes."[18] In other words, the relatively simple notions of home and collective identity we have utilized up to this point require further elaboration. Clearly, there is more to immigrant images of home than comforting thoughts of solidarity. There are also immeasurably strong feelings of nostalgia, stresses related to families separated by long distances and borders, and pressures to assimilate and shift identities to fit the alien context of Jupiter.

While there are multiple individuals in the Jupiter community who illustrate the more complex aspects of the strategic and changing nature of identity among the Maya in exile, we will focus here on a single case, Juan Gonzales. Juan maintains multiple identities and a life that spans the miles between Jupiter and Jacaltenango. In Guatemala, Juan initially held a job in road construction, traveling the country to work on multiple government and private projects. He made his first visit to the Jupiter area in 1993, but returned to Guatemala to finish a project building bridges. In the mid-1990s he returned to Jupiter, only to leave again for work in Guatemala, this time with a government-sponsored nonprofit organization. With the election of Alfonso Portillo in 2000 the program for which Juan worked was cut, and he made the trek to Jupiter a final time. His wife and children remained in Jacaltenango. Since Juan's daughter was *la reina* of the festival in Jacaltenango in 2001, he was able to obtain a special visa for a visit from his wife and daughter for the festival in Jupiter in 2002. This was the first time Juan had seen his wife and daughter in two years. Shortly afterward, Juan returned to Jacaltenango to reunite with his family.

Juan was a community leader here in Jupiter. His house served as a meeting place for Corn-Maya and was the central location for pre- and post-fiesta nights of celebration. In Jupiter, Juan worked in landscaping and restaurant work. Any funds above and beyond his expenses he weekly remitted to his family in Jacaltenango. Juan was, in the words of Allen Burns, able to live "with ambiguity and seemingly opposite values and ideals."[19] His house served as the center of the traditional Catholic celebration of the fiesta. The image of the Virgin and the lighted candles took center stage in his living room for the duration of the first year's celebration. Yet Juan also attended services at an evangelical church in Jupiter. When he first arrived in the early 1990s, Juan frequently attended Mormon services. Prior to leaving Guatemala, Juan played in a musical group that performed for services in both traditional and charismatic Catholic churches.

For Juan, these seemingly contradictory activities and values are part of a survival strategy or situational identity that makes perfect sense given the context and opportunities available. While in Jupiter, he was metaphorically with his family in Jacaltenango each and every day in the form of letters, phones calls, and financial contributions. He crossed borders based upon changing economic opportunities and changing political contexts. He was more than willing to utilize whatever religious or social connection appeared most expedient to survival in a changing and potentially hostile environment.

Juan's story suggests that immigrant conceptions of home and identity are not as straightforward as it might at first seem. As he navigated the multiple elements of his identity, Juan was faced with emotional difficulties and personal trials. During one of the nights of celebration preceding the fiesta, Juan stood with a group of older Jacaltec men reminiscing about the physical geography of Jacaltenango. As the night wore on, the group's conversation took on a distinct note of sadness as they discussed the particular type of flowers (mentioned above and necessary for the procession in the fiesta) that grow only on the mountain outside of town. By the end of the night, when the talk turned to family members (both living and dead), most of the group was in tears. Similar scenes have subsequently unfolded during many nights of gathering for the annual fiesta.

Juan's story provides only one illustration of the problems with accepting universally positive or simplistic notions of home and identity. When prompted to talk about their home and what they miss about it, most Mayan respondents in Jupiter referred to the unity, warmth, and caring of family life at home. Most expressed the desire to be reunited with family in a single location. On the other hand, some of the young Jacaltecos we interviewed were content to be away from home. As far as they were concerned, Jupiter provided the best of both worlds: they could live and work among other Jacaltecos without having to take on certain responsibilities or follow certain norms that would be enforced had they remained in Jacaltenango (as outlined in chapter 3). For the most part, however, these stories were the exception.

Almost inevitably, interviews focused on home and family quickly turned toward many of the interpersonal, economic, and family problems associated with carrying on relationships over distance. Stories of infidelity, illegitimacy, and changes in values were common. The Mayan men and women living in Jupiter are painfully aware that just as they seek to re-create some of their most positive images of home here, their very presence in this location is fundamentally changing their homes in Jacaltenango.

As remittances flow from Jupiter to Jacaltenango, the economic and social impact is not lost on the immigrants who send them. Most of those we interviewed were well aware that their remittances and construction of their newer block houses have driven up property values to the point that families who do not send migrants to the United States can no longer afford housing in Jacaltenango. Consumption of higher-cost imports has also increased among remittance recipients in Jacaltenango. One respondent explained that the kids back home now demand that their fathers send them Nike shoes—they refuse to wear the shoes made in Guatemala now that their fathers are making money in the United States. "People no longer want to work the land," one of our older respondents lamented, adding that they had become consumers, interested only in what people are doing in the cities and in the United States. He also mourned the damage done to the environment in Jacaltenango. He said that the land which was once so beautiful and could easily provide people with what they needed to eat had been sucked dry and destroyed by overuse and exploitation.[20]

Possibly even more distressing to the Jacaltecos in Jupiter are the social changes that they have begun to notice going on back home, changes that they willingly attribute to their own migration and remittance sending. Respondents reported discipline problems with children whose homes lack male authority figures, spouses who misuse remittances, and increases in alcohol abuse among women and children. There have been many cases where marriages have broken up and families have been divided because of the distance and time. As one respondent put it, "Some say that if we are doing well economically then we are doing well ... but if my wife is sleeping with another man then what do I have?"[21]

Three important insights arise from these interviews. First, images of home and the identities constructed around them are fragile and ambiguous. Just as home is re-created and celebrated through the festival and surrounding activities taking place in Jupiter, it is simultaneously under assault in Jacaltenango. From the need for transmigrants to assume different identities across contexts to the social and economic effects of remittances, Jupiter's Mayan immigrants find their most cherished memories of home and their aspirations for the future increasingly in peril.

Second, the migrants are fully aware of this tragedy. Because transnational connections are so strong, Jupiter's Jacaltecos remain painfully aware of events and activities at home. Frequent phone conversations, e-mails, videos, and the human grapevine pass information back and forth on a regular basis. What quickly becomes clear is that the decision to come to Jupiter is made in spite of these known risks. Here we see another parallel with Robert Orsi's analysis of Italian immigrants in Harlem. In describing the *festa* among Italians, Orsi writes that it is "not about individuality but about selves united in social worlds, not about transcendence but about religion's place in everyday life, not about autonomy but about the ways that people come to be within the forms of their culture, not about empowerment but about living within the coordinates of the possible."[22] While this statement characterizes many of the similarities between the experiences of Italians in New York and Mayans in Jupiter, it is the final line that is most fitting. The fiesta in Jupiter is about many things, but it is mostly about the everyday struggle of "living within the coordinates of the possible." Jupiter's immigrants are keenly aware of the trade-offs necessary to achieve the possible. They play out their lives within the tension between home and away, past and future, dreams and realities.

Sometimes during the nights of the fiesta, as the younger men drink and listen to the marimba music, they cry out with high-pitched screams and yells. The yelling appears almost involuntary. The sound invokes something between deep sorrow, frustration, and release. One young man described the yelling as a celebration of what is not. They yell for the women who are not here with them, for the families they cannot start or reunite with, for the steady work they cannot find, for the legal status that is out of their reach, and for their homes, which hold little promise for them should they return to them.

And this leads to a key difference between the experience of turn-of-the-century Italian immigrants and Mayan immigrants in Jupiter today. A fundamental difference is that most Jacaltecos come with the (frequently thwarted) intention of returning to their homes at some point.[23] For most, the hope is that four or five years of work in the United States will provide the financial assets necessary for them to return to life in their hometown. This is rarely possible. Some return only to come back again a few years later. Others stay but hold onto the dream of returning some time in the future. As one of the elder statesmen of the Jacaltec community explained, "In Guatemala when I was young I was very happy with my land, my little garden, my tomatoes. . . . I didn't have any psychological problems. Now I do. . . . I wish I could go back to Guatemala. I am a U.S. citizen, but I wish I could go back there so I could live the life that I wanted. So that my self [soul, being] could go back to what it used to be."[24]

Further Ambiguities: Religious and Ethnic Divisions

As with images of home, some of the religious and social institutions and processes surrounding the fiesta also hold ambiguities and contradictions. Clear religious cleavages exist in the transnational social field that has emerged between the Guatemalan Mayan immigrant community and the small Guatemalan town of Jacaltenango. These divisions cut across families and social groups. As noted earlier, divisions between evangelicals and Catholics nearly undermined the process of planning for the first fiesta. To this day, some of the evangelical churches discourage their members from attending the fiesta, though many of them find their way into the audience to view the procession and the Dance of the Deer.

Among the evangelicals we interviewed we also found significantly fewer connections to home villages and less interest in returning to Guatemala than we did among Catholics. While evangelicals also send remittances, their adoption of a new home in their churches in Jupiter, along with the notion that some of the traditional elements of their previous lives are now forbidden, leaves less room for the formation of a transnational Jacaltec identity than among Catholics. One evangelical young man explained, "I've managed to get a house and I've helped my brothers go to school. I have four brothers. I'm not married. But it is hard to find a good woman, because they're liberal and materialistic. My relationship with my worldly family in Guatemala is by telephone. From time to time I send them money." Another evangelical lay-pastor echoed this sentiment by stating that he sees himself as part of a new community of brothers and sisters in the church. Where they come from is less important than who they are now. His church is small, but it has members from El Salvador, Honduras, Guatemala, Venezuela, and Cuba.

Interviews we conducted with evangelicals in Guatemala also illustrate some of these differences, but from a very different perspective. An evangelical shopkeeper we spoke to in Panajachel was virulent in his critique of those who migrate: "Once they go away they become in love with the lifestyle, and they forget about their family and their church here. Immigration destroys our families and undermines our churches and our values."

The charismatic/non-charismatic split is also a powerful social dividing line. In Jacaltenango, the Catholic Church split into two congregations along the charismatic divide long ago. In Jupiter, this division continues and serves as a major impediment to cooperative collective action among the Mayan immigrants. While both charismatic and non-charismatic Catholics are active in community programs, philosophical, theological, and practical differences keep them from working together on a regular basis. Any event involving alcohol or some forms of marimba music is likely to be avoided by the charismatics. According to one Catholic lay leader, "some of them [charismatics] run the risk of being fundamentalist. They are against the Mayan *cosmovisión*. For example, they say that the marimba is the devil's rib. But they are also devoted to community work."

Other divisions that undermine solidarity relate to national, language, and ethnic differences. During the planning for the third year's fiesta, a group of Mayan dancers from Totonicapán were invited to perform during the festivities. After much discussion among the members of Corn-Maya, it was decided that the invitation should be withdrawn because people back in Jacaltenango who viewed videos of the event would be upset by the intrusion of seeing another town's queen in their fiesta. Despite the previous year's decision that the event was to be open to various groups, the Jacaltec leaders were more concerned with their own particular connections with home than with building a sense of community with other groups.[25] The very factors that facilitated unity and collective action among the Jacaltecos produced the opposite effect when applied to the larger Mayan community, the Hispanic community, and the immigrant community in general.

Conclusions

This study is located within the literature that focuses on transnationalism from below and the transnational community that is formed through social groups, rituals, practices, beliefs, and institutions that span borders. We argue that re-created images of home help Jacaltec immigrants in Jupiter to foster their sense of collective identity. The images of home are evident in the celebration of the fiesta, in the organization of soccer tournaments with teams from the corresponding *aldeas* in Jacaltenango, and in the practice of collecting funds to return the bodies of the dead to be buried in Jacaltenango. A transnational community has been created and reinforced by secular and religious institutions, practices, ideas, and individuals who frequently pass between the borders of Guatemala, Mexico, and Florida. This sense of collective identity has translated into public action, much of it directed toward resolving the common difficulties faced by the immigrant community. Since its rebirth through planning for the fiesta, Corn-Maya has worked to build bridges with the community, address questions of workers' rights, help individuals obtain language skills and immigration papers, and ameliorate some of the effects of loneliness and nostalgia through community organizing and social events.

The fiesta is particularly revealing, because the connections between religious, cultural, and social mobilization are clearly illustrated in the results of the process of planning and organizing the fiesta. As is often the case, religious and cultural institutions provide resources, motivations, and ideological legitimacy for community organization and collective action. In this case, a previously defunct social and political organization (Corn-Maya) was revived and reactivated through the process of planning and implementing the fiesta. Activities which began with a primarily cultural and religious motivation were transformed through dialogue and action into a springboard for community organizing and civic engagement.

On a cautionary note, we do not wish to assign unambiguously positive connotations to images of home or to mobilization through reactive ethnicity. As Juan's story suggests, identity is far from static and must be negotiated across borders and experiences for individual immigrants, a process fraught with emotional and physical hardship. Furthermore, recollections of home are often tinged with sadness, loss, pain, escape, and, in some cases, regret. Re-creations of home for transnational immigrants can bring forth all of the social, psychological, and physical images associated with home, including very negative images linked either to the horrific conflict in Guatemala or to other dramatic personal experiences. Jacaltec immigrants live with the tension of knowing that their presence in one place creates an absence in another and that the very support they send to their families in the form of remittances undermines some of their most deeply held community values.

We should also note that mobilization based on religious or cultural identity can create divisions within the transnational community as well as build connections. Our interviews with evangelicals suggest that they are less likely to retain strong connections with their families in the sending communities than are Catholics. However, the evangelicals we spoke to are more likely to attend churches that are made up of a multiplicity of ethnic and national groups. In other words, evangelicals may be more likely than their Catholic counterparts to join and participate in larger groups and assume identities as Hispanics or simply as evangelicals.

Finally, the very transnational religious and cultural factors that draw the Jacaltec community together may also serve to keep it apart from the larger Mayan and Hispanic communities in general. As Patricia Fortuny and Philip Williams point out in the case of Immokalee, transnational religious, cultural, and hometown connections are weak, but the pan-ethnic Coalition of Immokalee Workers is relatively strong. In Jupiter, by contrast, Corn-Maya is very active, but attempts to forge Pan-Mayan links remain in the incipient stages. The ethnic and cultural divisions that have emerged during the planning for the fiesta are not atypical of the relationships between the different Mayan immigrant groups in Palm Beach County.[26]

What generalizations and hypotheses emerge from this study? First, collective identity bolstered by ethnic, linguistic, and religious homogeneity and transnational connections can lead to successful collective action in immigrant communities. In the face of a foreign and relatively hostile environment such as Jupiter, this may lead to successful mobilization based in ethnic identity.

Second, the concept of lived religion and the practice of studying it can assist social scientists in understanding the way that collective identity is reinforced through re-creations of home in immigrant communities. At the same time, by examining lived religion in detail, we gain a window into the fundamental ambiguities within immigrant conceptions of home. Immigrant identities are flexible and fragile. To "live within the coordinates of the possible" for Jupiter's immigrants means living away from their loved ones while simultaneously witnessing the deleterious effects of their absence and the decidedly mixed impact of their social and economic remittances.

Third, the patterned differences in transnationalism and attitudes toward migration between Catholics and evangelicals merit further study. While these findings are only preliminary, it may be the case that evangelicals are less likely to migrate than Catholics. Furthermore, immigrants who join evangelical churches after migrating may be less likely to maintain their transnational connections or mobilize along ethnic lines. In other words, these evangelical immigrants may be more likely to form identities less linked to their ethnicity and also may be less likely to return to their communities of origin.

Finally, religious and ethnically based mobilization among immigrant groups is a double-edged sword. The very glue that holds Jupiter's Jacaltec community together serves as an impediment to Pan-Mayan, Pan-Hispanic, or even pan-immigrant organization. Among the many individuals we have interviewed in Jupiter, we have frequently heard the statement, *"Los jacaltecos son bien organizados"* (the Jacaltecos are well-organized). The significance of this statement, however, varies with the individual making it. While the members of Corn-Maya make this assertion with pride, many of the other Guatemalan and Mexican immigrants we have interviewed do so with a mixture of grudging respect and even resentment.

NOTES

1. See chapter 5 for a more complete description of the role of reactive ethnicity in this collective mobilization. Also see Alejandro Portes and Rubén Rumbaut, *Legacies: The Story of the Immigrant Second Generation* (Berkeley: University of California Press, 2001), 284.

2. See Peggy Levitt, *The Transnational Villagers* (Berkeley: University of California Press, 2001); Alejandro Portes, Luis Guarnizo, and Patricia Landolt, "Introduction: Pitfalls and Promise of an Emergent Research Field," *Ethnic and Racial Studies* 22 (1999): 217–238; Anna L. Peterson, Manuel A. Vásquez, and Philip J. Williams, eds., *Christianity, Social Change, and Globalization in the Americas* (New Brunswick, NJ, and London: Rutgers University Press, 2001).

3. Lius Guarnizo and Michael P. Smith, "The Locations of Transnationalism," in *Transnationalism from Below*, ed. Michael P. Smith and Luis Guarnizo, 3–31 (New Brunswick, NJ: Transaction Publishers, 1998).

4. Portes, Guarnizo, and Landolt, "Introduction."

5. See Nadje Al-Ali and Khalid Koser, eds., *New Approaches to Migration? Transnational Communities and the Transformation of Home* (London and New York: Routledge University Press, 2002).

6. Peggy Levitt, "Between God, Ethnicity, and Country: An Approach to the Study of Transnational Religion," paper delivered at the Center for Migration and Development, Princeton University, 2001.

7. See David Hall, ed., *Lived Religion in America: Toward a History of Practice* (Princeton: Princeton University Press, 1997); Robert Orsi, ed., *Gods of the City: Religion and the American Urban Landscape* (Bloomington: Indiana University Press, 1999); Karen McCarthy Brown, "Staying Grounded in a High-Rise Building: Ecological Dissonance and Ritual Accommodation in Haitian Vodou," in *Gods of the City*, ed. Robert Orsi, 79–102 (Bloomington: Indiana University Press, 1999). Indeed, our survey results showed that more than 50 percent of our respondents reported that they never participate in religious organizations.

8. Robert Orsi, *The Madonna of 115th Street: Faith and Community in Italian Harlem, 1880–1950* (New Haven: Yale University Press, 1985).

9. Levitt, "Between God, Ethnicity, and Country."

10. Also see Allan Burns, *Maya in Exile: Guatemalans in Florida* (Philadelphia: Temple University Press, 1993).

11. Ibid., 129.

12. Ibid., 130.

13. Orsi, *The Madonna of 115th Street*, 162.

14. The figures in Jupiter are even more striking than in Immokalee. In Jupiter, we found that only 16.2 percent of our respondents reported offering candles or food to saints, while 37.7 percent reported doing so at home. For making promises to saints, only 17.5 percent reported doing so in Jupiter, while 35.1 percent reported that they had done so at home.

15. Levitt, "Between God, Ethnicity, and Country."

16. Focus group conducted by Anya Canache for research on her honors thesis, "The Maya in Jupiter, Florida: Remittances and Immigrant Perceptions of Change in the Home Community" (Honors thesis, Harriet L. Wilkes Honors College of Florida Atlantic University, May 2003).

17. Allan Burns, "Identities in Diaspora: Mayan Culture and Community Today," in *Identities on the Move: Transnational Processes in North America and the Caribbean Basin*, ed. Liliana Goldin, 135–150 (Albany: SUNY Press, 1999).

18. Al-Ali and Koser, *New Approaches to Migration*, 6.

19. Burns, "Identities in Diaspora," 145.

20. See Canache, "The Maya in Jupiter, Florida," 55.

21. Ibid.

22. Orsi, *The Madonna of 115th Street*, xviii.

23. This is not to imply that significant numbers of Italian immigrants did not return home, for many of them were part of the transient labor pool of the early 1900s, sometimes referred to as the "birds of passage." The difference for the Mayan community is that the intention to return is nearly universal but frequently thwarted. See Reed Ueda, *Postwar Immigrant America: A Social History* (Boston and New York: Bedord/St. Martin's, 1994), 13.

24. See Canache, "The Maya in Jupiter, Florida," 55.

25. In the process leading up to the most recent fiesta (2008), a separate group of Jacaltecos broke away from Corn-Maya and attempted (unsuccessfully) to organize a competing fiesta after complaining that the leadership of Corn-Maya was not sufficiently attendant to their own cultural and religious suggestions for the celebration.

26. There has been some significant recent headway in this respect with the creation of the Guatemalan Coalition in 2007 through the work of immigration attorney and Guatemalan honorary consul Aileen Josephs.

8

Looking for Lived Religion
in Immokalee

PHILIP J. WILLIAMS AND PATRICIA FORTUNY LORET DE MOLA

Our research in Immokalee, Florida, was based on the assumption that religion would be highly salient for Mexican and Guatemalan immigrants. As discussed in chapter 1, the notion of the saliency of religion among immigrants is well established in the literature on religion and immigration in traditional gateway cities. Contrary to secularization theories that anticipated the privatization and marginalization of religion in modern societies, Stephen Warner argues that immigrants' "religious identities often (but not always) mean more to them away from home, in their diaspora, than they did before."[1] Similarly, Raymond Williams, in his study of Indian and Pakistani immigrants in traditional gateway cities in the United States, argues that "immigrants are religious—by all counts more religious than they were before they left home—because religion is one of the important identity markers in helping them preserve individual self-awareness and cohesion in a group."[2]

Recent work on religion and immigration in traditional gateways has tended to concentrate on congregational life.[3] This approach emphasizes "what new ethnic and immigrant groups [are] *doing together religiously* in the United States, and what manner of religious institutions they [are] developing *of, by, and for themselves*."[4] During our preliminary research in Immokalee, we learned that congregations can provide limited "spaces of sociability," which function as intimate spaces where immigrants can find voice and fellowship and develop civic skills.[5] Nevertheless, unlike the case of immigrants in traditional gateways, our preliminary research found that, given their "mobile livelihoods,"[6] most immigrants in Immokalee are not spiritually connected to religious congregations. On the contrary, it is the more established immigrants that are most active in congregational life; however, they represent a minority of the immigrant population in Immokalee.

Recent debates in anthropology have questioned the notions of locality upon which congregational studies are based. In the context of globalization characterized by transnational flows of capital, goods, people, ideas, and culture, the "natural" connection between culture and locality can no longer be assumed.[7] Instead, as Anthony Giddens argues, global modernity facilitates the "disembedding" of social relations from local contexts of face-to-face interactions and restructures them "across indefinite spans of time-space."[8] Paralleling these debates, in religious studies there has been a move to study religion beyond localized congregations.[9] These new approaches focus on lived religion, "what people *do* with religious practice, what they make with it of themselves and their worlds."[10]

Our research in Immokalee sought to build on these developments in anthropology and religious studies, assuming that religious life was just as likely to take place at home, in the workplace, or in the streets as in religious congregations. Moreover, following Robert Orsi, we viewed religion as "a network of relationships between heaven and earth," with all its ambiguities and ambivalence, avoiding the "notion of religious practices as *either* good *or* bad."[11] At the same time, we were careful not to ignore congregational life altogether. As Orsi warns, "it would be unfortunate if the turn to lived religion meant simply changing the valence of the familiar dualities while preserving them, just substituting religious practices in the streets and workplaces for what goes on in churches."[12]

We found that religion, while important, may be less salient for Mexican and Guatemalan immigrants in Immokalee than in their communities of origin. To make some sense of these findings, we begin with a discussion of the congregational life of immigrants, focusing particularly on two churches—one Catholic and one Pentecostal. The next two sections examine lived religion, including prayer, popular devotions, and public religious practice. We conclude with some reflections on the implications of the research for the broader literature on religion and immigration.

Congregational Life: "Here We Come to Work"

In Immokalee, immigrants can choose from a diverse array of churches to live their religion communally.[13] Here we will focus on the two most important congregations in Immokalee. The Catholic church, Our Lady of Guadalupe, is the largest Christian organization in Immokalee. It was founded in 1957 by a group of priests from the Scalabrini Order.[14] With the arrival of Father Richard Sanders in 1981, the church began to offer Masses in several languages (Spanish, Haitian Creole, and Kanjobal, in addition to English). During Sanders's time as priest (1981–1985), the parish established the Guadalupe Center, offering a number of social services. Of all the churches in town today, the Catholic church offers the most complete range of social services to the immigrant community. It runs a soup kitchen every day and Catholic Charities provides clothing and showers for the needy. Most importantly, the Guadalupe Center provides legal services and advice for immigrants. Since 1981, when Father Sanders was in charge, the Catholic church has supported the rights of farmworkers. The current parish priest, Father Ettore Rubin (from Italy), is very supportive of the Coalition of Immokalee Workers and has even obtained financial help from the Diocese of Venice for its members. In this sense, the Catholic church is embedded in a broad network of Catholic and community organizations that provides important resources for its social service delivery to the immigrant population in Immokalee.

A significant sector of more established immigrants attends the Catholic church. However, only a small minority of Catholics commit themselves to church activities beyond taking part in the sacraments (Mass, baptism, and other rites). The Catholic church does not provide many opportunities for immigrants to build "spaces of sociability." The time spent together is limited to the Sunday Mass. Although Guatemalan and Haitian Catholics also attend the church, the organization of religious services in English, Spanish, and Haitian Creole tends to reinforce the segregation of groups along ethnic lines. According to María, a lay leader at Our Lady of Guadalupe, the church has been unsuccessful in organizing a social hour after Mass: "We tried to offer coffee, a refreshment, *pan dulce* after the seven-thirty Mass, like on Mother's Day or Father's Day . . . but they just grab what there is and leave; they don't stay around to socialize. . . . Many people that come are single; families come but they are here to work not to make friends. They work; they have their group where they work . . . [and] they come here and pray but not to socialize with other people."

After the Catholic church, the Bethel Assembly of God Church (Iglesia Betel) has the next largest immigrant congregation in Immokalee. The church was founded in 1979 and now enjoys modern facilities with a congregation of approximately three hundred members. The steady growth of the congregation has prompted the church to offer two services on Sunday. The majority of members are Mexican immigrants and Mexican Americans, with a small number of Guatemalans. The pastor, Josué Rincón, came to the United States from Matamoros, Mexico, in 1975 and has lived in Immokalee since 1977. After two years working *en la labor*, Rincón found work in a local school and then as a car salesman. Rincón was raised by an evangelical family back in Mexico, but when he arrived in Immokalee there were few evangelical churches that ministered to migrant farmworkers. The church's founding families began worshiping in their homes, before renting a church in town to hold services. Rincón studied at a Bible institute in Fort Meyers and in 1986 abandoned his work *en el mundo* to dedicate himself full time to the ministry. Since then, his charismatic preaching style and appealing personal biography have facilitated the church's efforts to win over new converts.

As in the Catholic church, the most active members of the congregation tend to be more established immigrants, although many recently arrived migrant farmworkers attend services. The church is particularly effective in attracting younger couples and has a very active youth outreach program. In an effort to build a sense of community beyond the Sunday services and to propagate church doctrine, church leaders organize prayer groups that meet in different members' homes during the week. Once a group reaches a membership of thirty, a new group can be spun off in a constant effort to cultivate new members and leadership for the church.

Pastor Rincón is politically conservative and speaks openly in church of his fervent support for President George Bush and his policies. He often employs an apocalyptic discourse and biblical literalism to denounce homosexuality and abortion and to preach against drinking, smoking, and other pleasures *del mundo*. According to Rincón, alcoholism and drug addiction are the result of sin rather than social diseases. The asceticism required of church members can produce a transformation of household consumption patterns. When men convert, the resources normally spent on drinking, smoking, gambling, visiting prostitutes, and extramarital affairs are redirected into the household, thereby increasing household economic capital.[15]

Although churches in Immokalee do provide some limited "spaces of sociability" for building ties between church members, they also tend to reinforce rather than bridge ethnic, regional, and social differences. Moreover, the social capital[16] generated in these spaces resembles "bonding" social capital that is inward oriented and tends to reinforce group identity.[17] This is particularly the case with the Bethel church, where established immigrants have achieved not only "spiritual well-being" but also a level of social and economic success. Most of the members of the youth group study at the local high school, several women hold good jobs in local businesses, and a few members have their own small businesses in the area. The church plays a fundamental role in reproducing social networks that facilitate members' ability to find work in Immokalee or the surrounding area. Moreover, the church's theological and political conservatism and its social control over the lives of church members can have a beneficial impact in a context of extreme poverty, domestic violence, crime, and job insecurity.[18]

Although both churches generate social capital, different groups of immigrants access it differently. According to our survey (N = 148), 71 percent of respondents said that they "never" or "almost never" participate in a religious organization. Not surprisingly, it is the more established immigrants that participate most actively in congregational life and tend to benefit most from their access to the social networks created within the churches. Migrant farmworkers, on the other hand, attend Sunday services infrequently, as it is the only day that they can rest and take care of their household chores. Back home, church attendance is often a family affair; however, in Immokalee, the overwhelming majority of migrant farmworkers are young, single males. Lucas Benitez, a leader of the Coalition of Immokalee Workers, described the situation facing many migrant farmworkers:

When you're in your country, you have your family there, your children. If you're not married, you at least have a girlfriend or something; it's another form of relationships. In contrast, when you come here you find yourself in a situation of desperation: first, you live in a house with ten or eight people that you don't know; then you start feeling nostalgic; and instead of saying, "Let's go to the movies" or "Let's go with our friend to church" or something like that, more than likely you go to the store and buy some beer. And a little later you're drunk and the problems begin, because "I don't know anyone"; one of your roommates gets upset because of what you're doing, listening to music or something, and then the problems start.

When asked whether he attended church, Pánfilo's response was typical: "Here we come to work." Many immigrants make a clear separation between their religious participation in Immokalee and in their communities of origin. For example, here are the responses of some immigrants:

I have no time to think about religion. Back home I go to the Catholic church when I'm there, and our patron saint is St. John the Baptist and we organize a fiesta and everything. But here we don't have time to go. I arrive home late from work. It's important to go [to church]; maybe one day I'll be able to go. (Farmworker from Pacula, Hidalgo, Mexico)

If I'm free and if I have time, because my day off I try to spend with my children, because since I work and I don't have time for my kids. But when I can I go to the [Catholic] church but now I don't go regularly. It's like one doesn't have much religion now because one's work doesn't allow it. (Farmworker from Miahuatlán, Oaxaca, Mexico)

I'm Catholic but I don't attend church much. Here's it's just work, work, work. I only have time to pray, for my family, my mother and my brothers and sisters in Mexico. (Farmworker from Guanajuato, Mexico)

In Mexico I was Catholic. But I came here and now I'm not of any religion because I don't have time for it. Here it's pure work, pure work. Here I don't go to any church. But, yes, I read the bible; I read religious books. (Farmworker from Tamaulipas, Mexico)

I'll tell you, here I've lost much of my emotional sentiment because you close yourself off in your work; everyone works; everyone is in this situation. When I was in Mexico I went to church; when I felt bad or sad I entered a church, even if I was alone, and I left feeling very at ease, at peace and with another emotional state. Here I've gone very few times to church, but the times I've gone it's as if entering any other place. I don't feel the same vibration. I don't feel faith. So I hardly ever go to church. (Farmworker from Distrito Federal, Mexico)

For migrant farmworkers in Immokalee, churches provide few opportunities for creating "alternative places of belonging," where they can form meaningful relationships with the locales they inhabit and transform "space" into "place."[19]

Compared to other immigrants, migrant farmworkers are the dispossessed, *los de abajo* (the underdogs), *los jodidos* (the screwed). Often separated from their families, they suffer most directly and dramatically the consequences of a hostile, alien environment. Subjected to these "multiple marginalities,"[20] they are especially disadvantaged: first, because of their undocumented status; second, because of their limited social capital; and third, because their social networks are either non-existent, incipient, or with individuals in the same economic situation as themselves.[21] With average annual earnings of approximately seventy-five hundred dollars, migrant farmworkers have few possibilities to accumulate the kind of economic, social, or symbolic capital available to more established immigrants.

Our findings contrast with other studies of religion that demonstrate the role of congregations in providing "spaces of sociability." According to Nancy Ammerman, religious organizations (or congregations) are places of belonging, "where relationships of trust are formed, where a sense of identity is nurtured."[22] Moreover, while other voluntary organizations can serve as places of belonging, "belonging to a religious community has a moral weight not always granted to other memberships."[23] Similarly, Sidney Verba, Kay Schlozman, and Henry Brady argue that religious organizations are more effective than other voluntary organizations in facilitating the development of civic skills, and that those who develop civic skills in "an environment removed from politics" are likely to become politically competent.[24] Finally, studies by Lois Lorentzen and Marie Marquardt demonstrate how congregations provide contexts for the development of civic skills and leadership, especially among women migrants.[25]

Our research in Immokalee challenges these findings. The religious organizations that we studied tend to reinforce ethnic, regional, and social divisions between immigrants. They facilitate bonding social capital among more established immigrants that is inward oriented, but tend to neglect bridging social capital.[26] This is especially the case with the Pentecostal church. The Catholic church, on the other hand, is more effective at building bridges between it and other organizations and between its members and other groups but, like the Pentecostal church, is not very successful in generating bridging capital within the church.[27] Churches, while an important source of social capital, appear to be ill-equipped to deal with the heterogeneity and high degree of mobility of Immokalee's immigrant population. Additionally, most churches in Immokalee appear to be lacking the kind of leadership needed to establish relations with other churches and community organizations, relations that could in turn facilitate "links among communities that frequently coexist in relative isolation from one another."[28]

Evidence of Lived Religion

Despite immigrants' lower levels of participation in congregational life in Immokalee than in their communities of origin, we found plenty of evidence to

TABLE 8.1

Frequency of Prayer among Immigrants in Immokalee

How often do you pray?	%
Regularly	69.4
When having a problem	15.6
Almost never	9.5
Never	5.4

suggest that immigrants continue to draw on their religious beliefs and practices to navigate the challenges of everyday life in the workplace, at home, and in the streets. For example, almost 70 percent of respondents in our survey claimed to pray regularly (see table 8.1). The results from our survey mirror those of a recent survey conducted by the Pew Forum on Religion and Public Life and the Pew Hispanic Center.[29] According to that survey, 69 percent of Hispanics who belong to a particular religion pray on a daily basis. Several of the immigrants that we interviewed emphasized the importance of prayer in facing the sometimes dangerous work conditions to which they are exposed. Daniel, a Seventh-Day Adventist from Chiapas, Mexico, related the importance of prayer at his workplace: "Yes, my boss taught us to say a prayer before going to work, after returning from work, because when one gets up one should entrust oneself to God. He guides us along our path so there are no misfortunes." Similarly, Salvador, a farmworker from Oaxaca, relates: "Yes, sometimes I get up and entrust myself to God so that everything goes well at work, that a tree won't fall on me, that I won't get run over on the highway. These things I have to say to God so that he helps me to be able to survive here and that there are no disasters. . . . [I]n the fields many bad things can come to pass."

Many instances of lived religion take place in semi-public spaces that can serve both individual and communal religious practices. For example, home altars often function as private spaces for individual or family devotions but also bring together groups of *devotos* (devotees to saints) on special occasions to venerate saints. Otomí immigrants from Hidalgo, as discussed in chapter 4, celebrate baptisms and the Fiesta de Santa Teresa in these intermediate spaces, rather than in the streets or at church. Similarly, in an effort to build a sense of community beyond the Sunday services, lay leaders from the Bethel church organize prayer groups that meet in different members' homes during the week. Members' homes become semi-public spaces where *los hermanos* can gather to pray, sing, and study the Bible.

Despite the lower level of participation in congregational life in Immokalee, previous connections to churches in the communities of origin appear to shape everyday religious practice in Immokalee. Such is the case of Marcelino, a migrant farmworker from an indigenous community in Tlatlauquitepec, Puebla. Marcelino is forty-five years old, married, and has eight children. Unable to support his family back in Puebla, he journeyed alone to the United States five years ago. He was recruited on the border to work in Immokalee, where he had no contacts or family. In addition to working in the tomato harvest in Immokalee, he has worked in the Carolinas, Kentucky, Virginia, and Maryland. Since arriving five years ago, Marcelino has returned home once to visit his family.

Although Marcelino grew up Catholic he identifies more closely with a Pentecostal church back home. The influence of Pentecostalism is evident when he speaks of religious idols: "Here in Exodus 20 it says that one should not bow before idols made by man, because they can't speak or listen. So I learned to respect them but not to worship them." In Immokalee he never attends church and claims that God does not recognize any particular religion: "I know that there's only one God and there's only one God but without any religion." Although he says he has no time to attend church in Immokalee, he sometimes finds a spare moment to read the Bible and to pray to God: "Well, yes, I sometimes pray. I don't have a particular place, rather . . . when I'm sleeping and I ask God to support me, to take care of my family because I'm far away from my family. I ask Him to take care of us and I always put myself in God's hands." Marcelino maintains a direct relationship with God, unmediated by religious institutions. Moreover, when he needs help with a personal problem, he seeks advice from the Coalition of Immokalee Workers as opposed to religious organizations in town.

Tránsito, from Altamirano, Guerrero, provides another example of religious practice unmediated by institutions. She is a forty-six-year-old single immigrant who arrived in Immokalee in 1972. When she was sixteen she left home and went north to help her mother and twelve siblings. Over the years Tránsito has worked in the fields, sending money back to her family in Altamirano. Years after arriving, she helped some of her brothers to emigrate from Mexico. Today Tránsito works on and off in a storehouse packing tomatoes and oranges. Despite spending the better part of her life working *en la labor*, she has been unable to accumulate sufficient capital or property to ensure even a minimal level of economic security.

Having lived in Immokalee over thirty years, Tránsito knows the different churches and the social services they provide. In fact, the day we met her she had just picked up some free clothing from the Catholic Charities office. As we walked with her, some members of the Baptist church greeted her. During our conversation, she mentioned that she had also visited the Bethel church. Nevertheless, she is not a regular member of any of these religious organizations. She sees organized religion as overly demanding and coercive and has not found personal or spiritual satisfaction in any church.

Tránsito's relationship with religious congregations goes beyond receiving social services and has played an important role during difficult phases of her life in Immokalee. Like Marcelino, Tránsito attended a Pentecostal church back in Mexico before emigrating. This was despite the fact that the rest of her family remained practicing Catholics. As a legacy of her childhood participation in a Pentecostal church, she learned how to relate to God without intermediaries. During our conversation, Tránsito recounted two important dialogues she sustained with God during serious emotional crises. In the first one, she asked: "God, do you exist or not? Why do you allow people like me to suffer so much? If I have worked all my life to support my mother and my family, isn't it my turn to enjoy myself?" For several months Tránsito stopped believing in God, even attempting suicide. At that point she tried again to communicate with God. In her words, "I put myself in his hands. I asked him to give me light. I asked him to give me peace, and then I started to cry a lot, to sob for a long time. Afterwards, I felt a great sense of peace in my soul again." Thus, despite an apparently instrumental relationship with religion, Tránsito's ongoing dialogue with God has provided her with an important source of spiritual and emotional support during trying times.

These examples of "believing without belonging"[30] illustrate unique relationships with the sacred outside the realm of religious congregations and underscore the limited reach of churches among diverse and mobile populations. Marcelino and Tránsito found a solution to their spiritual needs without joining churches. Moreover, in Marcelino's case, he has established an important link to a civic organization (the Coalition of Immokalee Workers) in town and has developed labor networks throughout the Atlantic coast. On the other hand, Tránsito, who has no family in town, has not developed strong ties to religious or civic organizations. Despite having worked in the United States for thirty years, Tránsito's isolation from the usual sources of social capital has prevented her from accumulating wealth or achieving a modicum of economic security.

Popular Devotions and Public Religious Practice

We found plenty of evidence that immigrants "worship particular saints or deities, or engage in informal, popular religious practices that affirm their continued attachments to a particular sending-country group or place."[31] Some immigrants entrust themselves to favored saints or virgins during their border crossings. María, a farmworker from Oaxaca, is a devotee of the Virgin of Juquila, a widely venerated virgin in the state of Oaxaca. When crossing the border into the United States, she prayed to the Virgin of Juquila, she said, "to help me, to stay with me in these difficult times, with no water, nothing to eat. We walked day and night through the cold, soaking rain, our clothes wet, hardly able to walk." Rodolfo, an immigrant from Cortazar, Guanajuato, was brought up to

TABLE 8.2

Religious Practices of Immigrants in Immokalee

	Immokalee			Mexico/Guatemala		
	% yes			% yes		
	Catholic	Protestant	All	Catholic	Protestant	All
Made promises to a saint	34.0	0	24.3	51.0	4.5	38.5
Offered candles/ food to a saint	32.0	9.1	25.2	47.0	18.2	36.5
Cured miraculously	22.2	31.8	21.1	33.0	18.2	27.7
Participated in Mayan ceremony	8.0	9.1	6.8	8.2	13.6	8.2
Spoken in tongues	8.0	27.3	10.8	7.0	22.7	11.5
Been possessed	4.0	27.3	3.2	7.1	22.7	8.2
Practiced witchcraft	2.0	0	1.4	1.0	0	2.0
Religious conversion	6.0	27.3	10.8	8.0	13.6	11.5

venerate the popular Saint Padre Nieves.[32] Much like a patron saint, his image is prominently displayed in homes throughout this region of Mexico. Rodolfo entrusted himself to Padre Nieves before crossing the border and recently asked his mother to send him an image of Padre Nieves to display in his room in Immokalee: "I asked her to send me an image of Padre Nieves, who the pope made a saint. In Cortazar, Guanajuato, there's a cross where they killed him. I believe during that month they go on horseback to where they killed him. The priest at the church there also goes on horseback. My rancho is just before you get to Cortazar. The majority of people in my rancho have an image of Padre Nieves in their homes and stickers in their cars. Locally, Padre Nieves is almost as important as the Virgin."

Despite the continued importance of popular devotions, we discovered that many immigrants were less likely to engage in these practices in Immokalee than in their communities of origin (see table 8.2). This was especially true of popular Catholic devotions that appear to be practiced less frequently in Immokalee than in immigrants' communities of origin. Whereas as 38.5 percent of all respondents reported to have made promises to saints in their communities of origin, only 24.3 percent did in Immokalee. Similarly, 36.5 percent reported making offerings of food or candles to saints in Mexico/Guatemala but only 25.2 percent reported making such offerings in Immokalee.[33] For Catholics, the contrast is even more striking. Whereas 51 percent of Catholics reported making promises to a saint in their communities of origin, only 34 percent reported doing so in Immokalee. Likewise, 47 percent of Catholics reported making offerings of food or candles to saints in Mexico/Guatemala, compared to 32 percent in Immokalee.

There also appears to be significant differences between Catholics and Protestants. Whereas Protestants reported a lower frequency of popular devotions in Immokalee compared to Mexico/Guatemala,[34] they reported significant increases in the frequency of having been cured miraculously, speaking in tongues, having been possessed, and of religious conversion in Immokalee compared to their communities of origin. However, given the small number of Protestant respondents in the sample (N = 22), it is premature to draw too many conclusions from the data. When the Immokalee sample is combined with the sample from Jupiter, increasing the total number of Protestant respondents (N = 48), the differences between Catholics and Protestants are less significant. As with the Immokalee sample, the combined sample shows a decrease in popular devotions among Protestants, but no change in the frequency of having been cured miraculously, a slight decrease in the frequency of having spoken in tongues (20.8 percent in Guatemala/Mexico compared to 16.7 percent in Immokalee/Jupiter), a slight increase in the frequency of having been possessed (12.5 percent compared to 14.6 percent in Immokalee/Jupiter), and a significant increase in religious conversion (16.7 percent compared to 25.0 percent in Immokalee/Jupiter). This limited sample of Protestant respondents suggests that the most significant difference between Catholics and Protestants is in the changing frequency of experiencing religious conversion. Catholics appear to be less likely to experience religious conversion in the United States than in their home country, whereas Protestants are more likely to have conversion experiences in the United States.

How do we explain these puzzling findings? As in the case of church attendance, it may be the case that some immigrants, especially Catholics, make a clear separation between their religious practice at home and in Immokalee. Also, given that the majority of migrant farmworkers are young, single males, they may not have been very well socialized into traditional religious practices back home. Even more significant may be the relationship between religion and space. As Orsi writes with regards to urban landscapes, "The spaces of the cities, their different topographies and demographics, are fundamental to the kinds of religious phenomena that emerge in them."[35] Despite the apparent portability of religion, transnational migrants sometimes face significant spatial obstacles to living and practicing their religion. Among recent and marginalized immigrants, deterritorialization takes the shape of dislocation and "ecological dissonance," leading to what Karen McCarthy Brown has termed a "cosmo-logistical problem," the problem of practicing religions that are tied to places when one is no longer in that place and when travel to that place can be difficult.[36] The cosmo-logistical problem is heightened when sacred and public spaces are absent in the communities of settlement. In Mexico and Guatemala, the sacred is an integral part of the landscape and the religious calendar is closely linked to the agricultural cycle. Ancestral spirits inhabit hilltops and mountains throughout the countryside. Religious shrines dot the landscape, many of them intimately tied to natural features such as trees, streams, or caves. In sharp contrast, the rural landscape of southwest Florida with its endless extensions of orange groves and tomato fields is bereft of any recognizable sacred ecology.

In Immokalee, Mexican and Guatemalan immigrants have to contend with the cultural and psychological implications of the very different spatial arrangements they encounter. Although less threatening than many large cities, Immokalee presents immigrants with few public spaces for social interaction. There are no town squares and few parks for recreation. Not surprisingly, 82 percent of respondents to our survey stated that they felt most comfortable "at home,"—only 6 percent chose public places. When asked what he did in his spare time, a farmworker from Guatemala responded: "Nothing. Take advantage of the day to rest, wash clothes. There's nowhere to go for entertainment. Also it's not safe to be walking around on the streets because immigration might pick us up. Generally, I don't go out. Only if there's a real need, otherwise no. Even if it's really hot, it's better to put up with the heat inside than to risk having problems." The complete absence of public transportation, combined with the immigrants' undocumented status, sharply circumscribes their circulation within and outside the town. On a typical weekday, farmworkers leave home early to walk to a designated pick-up place where old school buses take them to the fields. In the afternoon, they stop at a nearby store to buy food or beer on their way home. Some evenings they venture out to a money transfer agency or a public telephone along Main Street to make a call home. Those few immigrants who have time to *pasear* on the weekends are more likely to pay for a ride to Wal-Mart or the flea market *la pulga* (both of which are some twenty-five miles away) than to visit a public place in Immokalee.

According to Michel de Certeau, the very act of walking can represent a clandestine "tactic" by groups or individuals to reappropriate space.[37] It is a "spatial acting-out" of place, creating public space rather than being subjected to it. While it may be true that immigrants have carved out their own spaces where they feel comfortable to speak Spanish or to drink beer in store parking lots, Immokalee resembles a segmented "space of enclosure," where farmworkers are isolated and subjected to constant supervision and surveillance by contractors and crew leaders.[38] Labor contractors maintain their power over farmworkers through their ability to withhold services such as housing, job contracts, transportation, and wages, or to report them to immigration authorities. Moreover, labor contractors ensure that power is internalized through reciprocity—through the social debt placed upon the worker to remain loyal to a "benevolent" boss. Caught in these "nets of discipline," immigrants' ability to resist the spatialization of social control is much more limited than what de Certeau would suggest.

These new spatial configurations are also evident in more private spheres such as living arrangements. Despite claiming to feel most comfortable at home, migrant farmworkers are often crammed into dilapidated trailers with eight to ten strangers. A farmworker from Chihuahua, Mexico, described having to share a room with six other farmworkers: "The living conditions are very cramped because we have to wait in line for the bathroom, wait in line to cook, wait in line to wash clothes. So I believe we're too many people for one room; the conditions are deplorable, because in one small room we're squeezing in too many people, dirty clothes, dirty socks. The conditions are not hygienic."

Unlike the case of Brazilians in Broward County (chapter 2), for whom home is a powerful organizing trope, for Guatemalan and Mexican migrant farmworkers in Immokalee, home does not represent a domesticated space protecting them from the hostile world outside. It is often a space of alienation and sometimes conflict. Moreover, in their cramped living quarters, immigrants do not have their own personal spaces to construct home altars, hang religious images, or light candles to their preferred saints. This can present important obstacles to religious practice and undermine efforts to sacralize home. For example, in describing his living arrangements, a farmworker from San Pedro Xoconutla, Guatemala, related the following: "There [Guatemala] at home all the family gets together and puts our candlestick in the corner. We express what we feel, from the heart. It's to ask [the spirits] to protect us, to guide us with good ideas and on a good path. I do this back home. But here I can't because I live with a heap of people and can't do anything. I bought my candlestick a little while ago and they kept putting it out and making fun of me. Because of this I stopped using it here. In my heart I hope the spirits will forgive me. I'm not giving it up because I want to, but because they won't allow me."

Peggy Levitt refers to religion as "the ultimate border crosser."[39] Accordingly, "God needs no passport because faith traditions give their followers symbols, rituals, and stories they use to create alternative sacred landscapes, marked by holy sites, shrines, and places of worship."[40] However, the mobile livelihoods of farmworkers raise questions about the limits on the portability of religion. The experience of María, a farmworker from Oaxaca, is illustrative: "I don't have any religious images because I rent; I move from one place to another; I don't have any furniture. I'm living in the living room of this woman because where we live they're all men. Now it's difficult because I don't have any way to move and because of this I don't carry anything, but where I am now, as it's the woman's trailer, she has images of the Virgin of Guadalupe."

These examples highlight the serious spatial constraints limiting even the private devotions of migrant farmworkers, who sometimes have no place to hang their religious images and are often forced to share private living spaces with strangers. Public expressions of popular devotions, such as *fiestas patronales*, face even more difficult spatial obstacles. Unlike Guatemalans in Jupiter, immigrants in Immokalee find few opportunities to re-create images of home via popular religious practice. Just over a third (34.2 percent) of those surveyed reported having attended a religious procession or fiesta. The Catholic church in Immokalee organizes a public procession in honor of the Virgin of Guadalupe on December 12, but, according to informants, the procession is not very well attended (often times the procession falls on a weekday when most immigrants are working) and is a poor imitation of the celebrations organized throughout Mexico. The Catholic church also organizes a *viacrucis* (stations of the cross) during Holy Week. However, according to one farmworker, the viacrucis in Immokalee hardly compares with the procession in his hometown in Mexico: "During Holy Week we follow the entire journey that Jesus made . . . [and] we reproduce everything that happened to Jesus along the way. It's something very different; here it's nothing; it's all work."

Uncertain access to public space is often a constraint on public religious practices. In the case of Holy Week, in 2004 the parish priest, Father Ettore Rubin, proposed to organize the Good Friday procession on church grounds. His reasoning was the danger posed to participants from passing cars and the bureaucratic obstacles, including soliciting permission from county officials and the local police. Some of the more established immigrants, who make up the active lay leadership in the church, successfully lobbied Rubin to allow the procession to take place on the streets nearby the church. Although the procession began with only two hundred participants, more and more people joined in. By the time they arrived back at the church there were over two thousand in the procession. According to Father Rubin, this was the first time in his four years of ministry that the streets around the church had been converted into a sacred space.[41]

The temporary appropriation of the streets during the viacrucis contrasts with Latin America, where religion is regularly "performed" in the public spaces of streets and town squares. With the exception of Holy Week and the Virgin of Guadalupe celebration, we found few examples of public religious practice in Immokalee. Unlike Guatemalans in Jupiter, Mexican immigrants in Immokalee prefer to celebrate their fiestas patronales in their homes or to return to Mexico for the celebration. As described in chapter 4, immigrants from Chamácuaro, Guanajuato, return each year in May for the Fiesta de Santa Cruz.[42] They are joined in Chamácuaro by immigrants from all over the United States. As demonstrated by a number of studies of Mexican migration,[43] fiestas patronales constitute one of the most important mechanisms through which Mexican immigrants reaffirm their sense of belonging to their places of origin.

The case of Chamácuaro and the example of the Otomís, discussed in chapter 4, resemble emerging transnational communities in that solidaristic ties "reach beyond narrow kinship systems" and encompass shared meanings and beliefs expressed in the form of collective identity.[44] Emerging transnational communities can provide immigrants without access to social capital via religious organizations an alternative space through which to develop and deploy social and other forms of capital. Immigrants' monetary contributions to the Fiesta de Santa Cruz in Chamácuaro or to community projects in their village in Hidalgo "can be deployed as status claims (and perhaps increased power), and translated into status through appropriate valorization" by their *paisanos* in Immokalee and in Mexico.[45] However, given the increasingly restrictive border control policies, it is primarily immigrants *con papeles* who are able to participate in transnational activities that require travel back to Mexico.

The absence of fiestas patronales in Immokalee may also have to do with the low levels of social capital and the ethnic/regional heterogeneity of immigrants. As discussed in chapter 5, compared to Guatemalans in Jupiter, who enjoy higher levels of social capital and ethnic/cultural homogeneity, immigrants in Immokalee face less discrimination and social exclusion in their everyday lives. Not surprisingly, in Immokalee we witnessed little of the reactive ethnicity that has emerged in Jupiter in response to the sometimes hostile reception on the part of the local community.[46] Reactive ethnicity, in turn, provides the basis for greater collective solidarity and mobilization in defense of ethnic group interests. These are often expressed through popular religious practices—like the Fiesta Maya in Jupiter—that stake "a claim to living in a particular kind of nation."[47]

Conclusion

"Immokalee *es un desmadre*" (Immokalee is a mess, screwed up). This was how an immigrant whom we spoke to during the final day of the fiesta in Chamácuaro, Mexico, described Immokalee, where he had spent three years off and on working in *la labor*. Comparing Immokalee to Windsor, California, where he works in a *winería*, he noted the absence of public spaces to *pasear* with his family during his days off in Immokalee. For many migrant farmworkers, who are passing through Immokalee on their way to another destination, Immokalee resembles the "non-places" described by French anthropologist Marc Augé.[48] These "non-places" are bleak locales of contemporary modernity, "transit points and temporary abodes ... proliferating under ... inhuman conditions" and distinct from "anthropological places" that provide cultural identity and memory, which bind inhabitants to the history of locale.[49] Unlike immigrants in traditional gateway cities, most immigrants do not come to Immokalee to make a home, to put down roots, to give meaning to the temporary locales that they inhabit. For the five to six months they are in Immokalee, they come to work, to earn *dólares* to send back home, and to one day return and reunite with their family.

However, Augé may go too far in accentuating the alienating nature of non-place. Even in his example of airport terminals (the ultimate non-places), for the permanent denizens (the baggage handlers, check-in clerks, security personnel, and janitors) the terminal "is clearly a 'real' place—their workplace."[50] Similarly, for the established immigrants who live and work in Immokalee in a permanent fashion, as pointed out in chapter 4, it as a very "real" place "with all the anthropological richness, . . . the subtleties of daily interpersonal contact, the friendships, rivalries and so on" that apply to any "anthropological" place.[51]

According to Manuel Castells, in the face of intense social dislocation and atomization, "people anchor themselves in places, and recall their historic memory."[52] This is because "when the world becomes too large to be controlled, social actors aim at shrinking it back to their size and reach."[53] Setha Low refers to this counter social force as "vernacularization": "the process by which the global is made local through the attribution of meaning."[54] Whereas other scholars have emphasized the importance of religion in processes of vernacularization, our research in Immokalee shows that many immigrants do not draw on religion "to make their own space and find their own place."[55] Although churches do provide some limited social spaces to develop social networks that can be used to accumulate social capital, they tend to reinforce the disparities between established immigrants and migrant workers. Consequently, most immigrants do not look to churches in "the search for secure moorings in a shifting world."[56] Similarly, we found significant structural and spatial obstacles that inhibit immigrants from living and practicing their religion as they do in their communities of origin. Public religious practices, like fiestas patronales, that are so important to building a sense of place, are largely absent in Immokalee. Instead, much of the lived religion we found is practiced in intermediate, semi-public spaces, as in the examples of home altars and Pentecostal prayer groups.

Although we do not presume to generalize from this single case, our findings do present us with a cautionary tale. Within the social sciences, for those of us who study the poor, there is a "propensity to romance the politically successful actors among the dispossessed" and to ignore "those who are not successful, not interested, or not aware."[57] Similarly, in studies of transnational migrants there is a tendency to assume transnationalism exists and less concern with explaining when it doesn't. And in religious studies, the temptation is to focus on good religion only, thereby defining off the table the less savory dimensions of religion. Our findings challenge scholars of religion and migration to take seriously the religious practice and imagination of the poorest and most marginalized immigrants. Recalling the words of Edward R. Murrow, our study reminds us of the importance of not ignoring "the forgotten people," the "migrant workers in the sweatshops of the soil."[58] They may not have built havens, let alone heavens, but they nonetheless deserve a place in our stories of new immigrant religions in the United States.

NOTES

We are grateful to Robert Orsi and Alejandro Frigerio for their comments on an earlier version of this chapter.

1. Stephen Warner, "Immigration and Religious Communities in the United States," in *Gatherings in Diaspora: Religious Communities and the New Immigration*, ed. Stephen Warner and Judith Wittner (Philadelphia: Temple University Press, 1998), 3.

2. Raymond Williams, *Religions of Immigrants from India and Pakistan: New Threads in the American Tapestry* (Cambridge: Cambridge University Press, 1988), 11. Similarly, Thomas Tweed's study of Cuban migrants in Miami found that they "turned to religion to make sense of themselves as a displaced people" and that religion, "both in churches and homes, took on increased significance for many Cubans in Miami." Thomas Tweed, *Our Lady of the Exile: Diasporic Religion at a Cuban Catholic Shrine in Miami* (New York: Oxford University Press, 1997), 29.

3. See Warner and Wittner, *Gatherings in Diaspora*; and Helen Rose Ebaugh and Janet Salzman Chafetz, *Religion and the New Immigrants: Continuities and Adaptations* (Walnut Creek, CA: AltaMira Press, 2000). In their recent study of religion and new immigrants in Washington, D.C., Foley and Hoge reject the term "congregation" in favor of "local worship communities." They argue that the use of the term "congregation" implies a congregational template characteristic of American Protestant churches that "obscures important differences" between worship communities. Michael Foley and Dean Hoge, *Religion and the New Immigrants: How Faith Communities Form Our Newest Citizens* (New York: Oxford University Press, 2007), 218–219.

4. Warner, "Immigration," 9.

5. See Nancy Ammerman, *Congregation and Community* (New Brunswick, NJ: Rutgers University Press, 1997); and Sidney Verba, Kay Lehman Schlozman, and Henry E. Brady, *Voice and Equality: Civic Voluntarism in American Politics* (Cambridge, MA: Harvard University Press, 1995).

6. The term "mobile livelihoods" underlines the fact that "livelihood practices quite commonly engage people in extensive movements at local, regional, national and transnational levels." Karen Olwig, "Transnational' Socio-Cultural Systems and Ethnographic Research: Views from an Extended Field Site," *International Immigration Review* 37 (2003): 795.

7. See Arjun Appadurai, *Modernity at Large: Cultural Dimensions of Globalization* (Minneapolis: University of Minnesota Press, 1996); and James Clifford, *Routes: Travel and Translation in the Late Twentieth Century* (Cambridge: Harvard University Press, 1997).

8. Anthony Giddens, *The Consequences of Modernity* (Stanford: Stanford University Press, 1990), 21. This transformation of the place-culture relationship is often referred to as deterritorialization: "the weakening attachments to place, to territorially defined communities and cultures ranging from the household, the urban neighborhood, and the town or city, to the metropolis, the region, and the most powerful of contemporary territorial communities of identity, the modern nation-state." Edward Soja, *Postmetropolis: Critical Studies of Cities and Regions* (Oxford: Blackwell, 2000), 151–152.

9. See Karen McCarthy Brown, "Staying Grounded in a High-Rise Building: Ecological Dissonance and Ritual Accommodation in Haitian Vodou," in *Gods of the City: Religion and the American Urban Landscape*, ed. Robert Orsi, 79–102 (Bloomington: Indiana University Press, 1999); David Hall, ed., *Lived Religion in America: Toward a History of Practice* (Princeton: Princeton University Press, 1997); Robert Orsi, "Introduction: Crossing the City Line," in *Gods of the City*, ed. Orsi; and Manuel Vásquez and Marie

Marquardt, *Globalizing the Sacred: Religion across the Americas* (New Brunswick, NJ: Rutgers University Press, 2003).

10. Robert Orsi "Everyday Miracles: The Study of Lived Religion," in *Lived Religion in America*, ed. David Hall (Princeton: Princeton University Press, 1997), 7.

11. Robert Orsi, *Between Heaven and Earth: The Religious Worlds People Make and the Scholars Who Study Them* (Princeton: Princeton University Press, 2005), 2.

12. Orsi, "Everyday Miracles," 9.

13. We identified forty churches in town.

14. The Scalabrini Order was founded in Italy in the early 1900s with the objective of accompanying Italian Catholics that emigrated to the Americas. Since its founding, the Scalabrini Order has dedicated its efforts to ministering and evangelizing to immigrants around the world.

15. Several scholars of Pentecostalism in Latin American have observed this phenomenon. For example, see Elizabeth Brusco, *The Reformation of Machismo: Evangelical Conversion and Gender in Colombia* (Austin: University of Texas Press, 1995); John Burdick, *Looking for God in Brazil: The Progressive Catholic Church in Urban Brazil's Religious Arena* (Berkeley: University of California Press, 1993); and Andrew Chesnut, *Born Again in Brazil: The Pentecostal Boom and the Pathogens of Poverty* (New Brunswick, NJ: Rutgers University Press, 1997).

16. Bourdieu and Waqcuant define social capital as "the sum of resources, actual or virtual, that accrue to an individual or a group by virtue of possessing a durable network of more or less institutionalized relationships of mutual acquaintance and recognition." Pierre Bourdieu and Loic Wacquant, *An Invitation to Reflexive Sociology* (Chicago: University of Chicago Press, 1992), 119.

17. Robert Putnam, *Bowling Alone* (New York: Simon and Schuster, 2000).

18. The other side of coercion and social control is protection, stability, and a strong sense of belonging for those who find refuge from life's afflictions within the protective walls of the church.

19. Peggy Levitt, "You Know, Abraham Was Really the First Immigrant: Religion and Transnational Migration," *International Immigration Review* 37 (2003): 863.

20. The term refers to the "stresses and ambiguities," generated by social, economic, and cultural factors at the group, family, and individual levels, that lead to multiple forms of exclusion. James Vigil, *Barrio Gangs: Street Life and Identity in Southern California* (Austin: University of Texas Press, 1988), 11.

21. As Menjívar's study of Salvadoran immigrants in San Francisco demonstrates, "social capital cannot be generated automatically when immigrants do not have access to desirable resources, because reciprocal obligations are undermined under these conditions." Cecilia Menjívar, *Fragmented Ties: Salvadoran Immigrant Networks in America* (Berkeley: University of California Press, 2000), 234.

22. Ammerman, *Congregation*, 363.

23. Ibid.

24. Verba, Schlozman, and Brady, *Voice and Equality*, 310.

25. Lois Lorentzen, "El milagro está en casa: Gender and Private/Public Empowerment in a Migrant Pentecostal Church," *Latin American Perspectives* 32, no. 1 (2005): 57–71; Marie Marquardt, "From Shame to Confidence: Gender, Religious Conversion, and Civic Engagement of Mexicans in the U.S. South," *Latin American Perspectives* 32, no. 1 (2005): 27–56.

26. According to Putnam, bridging social capital is outward looking and encompasses people "across diverse social cleavages." Putnam, *Bowling Alone*, 22.

27. In their study of religion and new immigrants in Washington, D.C., Foley and Hoge also found "that worship communities vary both in the civic skills cultivated and in the degree to which these might transfer to actual participation in the political system." Whereas Protestant evangelical churches "rarely encouraged their members to exercise these skills outside the worship community, Catholic parishes "promoted widespread participation among parishioners, volunteering outside the community, and civic activism." Foley and Hoge, *Religion and the New Immigrants*, 233.

28. Richard Wood, *Faith in Action* (Chicago: University of Chicago Press, 2002), 144.

29. See the Pew Forum on Religion and Public Life and the Pew Hispanic Center, *Changing Faiths: Latinos and the Transformation of American Religion* (Washington, DC: Pew Research Center, 2007).

30. This is the subtitle of Grace Davie's book on religion in Britain during the postwar period. Grace Davie, *Religion in Britain since 1945: Believing without Belonging* (Oxford: Blackwell, 1994). According to Davie, increasing numbers of postwar Britons no longer look to organized religion to satisfy their spiritual needs. Wade Clark Roof and Robert Wuthnow have documented similar trends in the United States. Roof refers to this phenomenon as a "quest culture" and Wuthnow argues that American culture has experienced a move from a "spirituality of dwelling" to a "spirituality of seeking." Wade Clark Roof, *Spiritual Marketplace* (Princeton: Princeton University Press, 1999); and Robert Wuthnow, *After Heaven* (Berkeley: University of California Press, 1999).

31. Levitt, "You Know, Abraham," 851.

32. Elias del Socorro Nieves was a Augustinian priest in the Cortazar region of Guanajuato. He was executed by Mexican troops during the Cristero Rebellion and beatified by Pope John Paul II in 1997.

33. There was no significant difference between men and women.

34. This may suggest that Protestant churches in Immokalee are more successful in eliminating popular devotions associated with folk Catholicism than churches in Guatemala and Mexico.

35. Orsi, "Introduction: Crossing the City Line," 43.

36. Brown, "Staying Grounded in a High-Rise Building," 79–102.

37. Michel de Certeau, *The Practice of Everyday Life* (Berkeley: University of California Press, 1984)

38. Michel Foucault, *Discipline and Punishment: The Birth of the Prison* (New York: Vintage Books, 1991).

39. Peggy Levitt, *God Needs No Passport: Immigrants and the Changing American Religious Landscape* (New York: New Press, 2007), 12.

40. Ibid., 12–13.

41. Father Rubin's reaction to the Holy Week procession underlines the importance of religious leadership (of lack thereof in this case), not just structural factors. We thank Alex Stepick for this insight.

42. Chamácuaro is located in the municipal district of Acámbaro. The town has a population of approximately fifty-five hundred inhabitants. Residents have been migrating to the United States since the early 1900s, and significant communities can be found in Illinois, northern California, and Georgia.

43. See Jorge Durand, *Mas allá de la línea. Patrones migratorios entre México y Estados Unidos* (México, DF: Conaculta, 1994); Víctor Espinosa, "El día del emigrante y el retorno del purgatorio: Iglesia, migración a los Estados Unidos y cambio sociocultural en un pueblo de los Altos de Jalisco," *Estudios Sociológicos* 50 (1999): 375–418; and Mónica Gendreau and Gilberto Giménez, "La migración internacional desde una perspectiva

sociocultural: Estudio en comunidades tradicionales del centro de México," *Migraciones Internacionales* I (2002): 147–178.

44. Thomas Faist, "Transnationalization in International Migration: Implications for the Study of Citizenship and Culture," *Ethnic and Racial Studies* 23, no. 2 (2000): 196.

45. Luin Goldring, "The Power of Status in Transnational Social Fields," in *Transnationalism from Below*, ed. Michael P. Smith and Luis Eduardo Guarnizo (New Brunswick, NJ: Transaction Publishers, 1998), 175. See Brettell for a similar discussion of how Portuguese immigrants in France convert their economic success abroad into social prestige back home. Caroline Brettel, *Anthropology and Migration: Essays on Transnationalism, Ethnicity, and Identity* (Walnut Creek, CA: AltaMira Press, 2003).

46. According to Portes and Rumbaut, "reactive ethnicity is the product of confrontation with an adverse native mainstream and the rise of defensive identities and solidarities to counter it." Alejandro Portes and Ruben Rumbaut, *Legacies: The Story of the Immigrant Second Generation* (Berkeley: University of California Press, 2001), 284.

47. Orsi, "Introduction: Crossing the City Line," 42.

48. Marc Augé, *Non-Places: Introduction to the Anthropology of Supermodernity* (London: Verso, 1995).

49. Ibid., 78.

50. John Tomlinson, *Globalization and Culture* (Chicago: University of Chicago Press, 1999), 112.

51. Ibid.

52. Manuel Castells, *The Power of Identity* (Oxford: Blackwell, 1997), 66.

53. Ibid.

54. Setha Low, *On the Plaza: The Politics of Public Space and Culture* (Austin: University of Texas Press, 2000), 244.

55. Thomas Tweed, *Our Lady of the Exile: Diasporic Religion at a Cuban Catholic Shrine in Miami* (New York: Oxford University Press, 1997), 136.

56. David Harvey, *The Condition of Postmodernity* (Oxford: Basil Blackwell, 1989), 302.

57. Matthew Gutmann, *The Romance of Democracy: Compliant Defiance in Contemporary Mexico* (Berkeley: University of California Press, 2002), xxiii.

58. Edward R Murrow, *Harvest of Shame* (New York: Ambrose Video, CBS Broadcast International, 1960).

9

꙳꙳꙳꙳꙳꙳꙳꙳꙳꙳꙳꙳꙳꙳꙳꙳꙳꙳꙳꙳꙳꙳꙳꙳꙳꙳꙳

Brazilian and Mexican Women

Interacting with God in Florida

PATRICIA FORTUNY LORET DE MOLA, LÚCIA RIBEIRO,
AND MIRIAN SOLÍS LIZAMA

This chapter analyzes the relationship between lived religion, gender, and migration in South Florida. Few studies examine this tripartite relationship,[1] as analyses of female migration normally emphasize social processes related to labor markets.[2] Even those studies that explore changes in gender roles, conceptions of femininity and masculinity, and family life that result from the process of migration tend to privilege the economic variable and ignore religion altogether. For example, Pierrette Hondagneu-Sotelo and Ernestine Avila offer a very nuanced analysis of "transnational motherhood," showing how the meaning of motherhood changes for Latinas who have left their children behind, in their countries of origin, to work as nannies for American children. According to them, "transnational mothers seek to mesh caregiving and guidance with breadwinning. While breadwinning may require long-term and long-distance separations from their children, they attempt to sustain family connections by showing emotional ties through letters, phone calls, and money sent home."[3] Hondagneu-Sotelo and Avila, however, do not examine the role of religion in the attempts by transnational mothers to deal with the alienation and anxiety of family separation and to maintain emotional, moral, and spiritual connections with the children in their sending countries.

Building on and going beyond previous studies, we highlight the cultural dimensions of gender that contribute to the creation of social differences among people. Because we see male-female distinctions as human constructs, which are produced and reproduced through ideologies and cultural practices, we argue that it is crucial to understand the multiple roles that religion plays in the formation of fluid and contested gender identities, relationships, and ideologies.[4] After all, despite increasing secularization, religion continues to be one of the most significant frames of reference for Mexican and Brazilian women. Our objective is to analyze how gender and the power relations that exist among immigrants are expressed through religious practice in a specific migratory context.

As discussed in chapter I, we adopt Robert Orsi's concept of "lived religion" that focuses on the formation of the self in "an ongoing, dynamic relationship with the realities of everyday life."[5] In this manner, we avoid reproducing the patriarchal view of religion, which assumes that power, authority, and legitimacy are located exclusively at the apex of religious structures. Rather, power and resistance flow through them, from top to bottom and vice versa. Stressing only the patriarchal dimension of religion denies women's agency within the religious sphere. As Orsi emphasizes, "theological practice cannot be gridded in any simple way along the axis of 'elite' and 'popular.' " Rather, religion "is shaped and experienced in the interplay among venues of everyday experience."[6]

The narratives we collected among immigrant women constantly reveal relations of subordination, resistance, and negotiation with men in family settings, in churches, and beyond. Men are present in women's narratives as social actors that women respond to and interact with through opposition or subordination, according to the circumstances. Immigrants exercise power in the religious, social, and economic domains. As many studies show,[7] immigrant women often take advantage of the American multicultural environment—with its new and different opportunities—to develop an increased awareness of gender and a capacity to resist systemic inequality. As Patricia Pessar writes, "Many scholars have examined the impact that immigrant women's regular wage work has on gendered relations. A review of this literature points to the fact that despite gender inequalities in the labor market and workplace, immigrant women employed in the United States *generally gain greater personal autonomy and independence, whereas men lose ground*" (emphasis added).[8]

This presents a contradiction: immigrant women are perceived, and perceive themselves, to occupy a situation of social, cultural, economic, and political disadvantage and a subordinate position simply because they are women. In the United States, however, women discover socioeconomic opportunities not available in their homelands. Pessar argues that "a gendered perspective . . . encourages an examination of the ways in which migration *simultaneously reinforces and challenges patriarchy in its multiple forms*" (emphasis added).[9]

For our purpose of comparing and contrasting immigrant women's experiences, we chose two immigrant groups in Florida: Brazilians in Deerfield Beach and Pompano Beach and Mexicans in Immokalee. The first important difference between these groups of women is income: most Brazilian women earn between $1,000 and $2,000 per month, while only 36 percent of Mexican immigrant women in Immokalee earn $1,000 to $1,400 monthly. This disparity reflects the fact that 60 percent of Mexican immigrants (men and women) work in agriculture, while the majority of Brazilians work in the service sector. Some 70 percent of Mexican women work in the fields or packing plants. The other 30 percent (fourteen in our sample) are in domestic service, the service sector, or are unemployed. Of the Brazilian women surveyed, 68.0 percent work in low-skilled service sector jobs like housecleaning and domestic service, 20.0 percent have secretarial positions or are merchants or saleswomen, while a small minority (7.6 percent) attained a higher technical level, and 1.1 percent went to a university and aspire to professional positions. Estimates indicate that the number of Brazilian men and women immigrants is about equal, while we found that only 36 percent of Mexican immigrants in Immokalee are women.

Immokalee presents a number of employment opportunities for Mexican immigrant women. Though they often earn less than men, by holding jobs they acquire greater freedom and autonomy from family and spouse. With their earnings, women are free to go out and spend their time and money as they please and can save money to invest in modest businesses to increase their capital. Similarly, for Brazilian immigrant women employment means more economic and social autonomy, though most suffer downward social mobility because their occupational and educational qualifications exceed the requirements of their jobs. Although immigration tends to have a negative impact on Brazilian women's social mobility, it is generally positive for the mostly rural, low-skilled Mexican immigrant women.

Given this context, we will examine how religion shapes and is shaped by (1) participation in organizations, (2) everyday individual practices inside and outside institutions, (3) practices in intermediate spaces, and (4) religious faith as a source of personal empowerment. In the first section we discuss the extent to which immigrants' socialization in their countries of origin predisposes them to certain kinds of religious behavior in their new destinations, and the relationship between their socialization and cultural constructions of gender. The second section examines the dialectical relation between the migratory condition and lived religion, given that people's social circumstances influence and are influenced by the religious sphere. The third section reveals how lived religion infuses private spaces with sacred landscapes, showing that lived religion does not necessarily require sacred objects or spaces to flourish. In the final section, we analyze how lived religion, though derived from religious institutions, is often practiced in "in-between" social spaces where sacred power flows and is appropriated by spiritual leaders. This is a novel approach that avoids dualist conceptualizations of private/public space by focusing on intermediate domains that often exist in religious institutions but have been rarely studied from a gender theoretical perspective.

Relocating Lived Religion from Place of Origin to New Destinations

Religious diversity has increased markedly in Mexico over the past thirty years: the percentage of the population that does not profess Roman Catholicism rose from 3.8 percent in 1970 to 12.0 percent in 2000,[10] while the percentage of Catholics fell from 96.1 percent to 88.0 percent. These indices vary widely in different regions. For example, in 2000, some states in western Mexico (Guanajuato, Jalisco, Michoacán, Zacatecas, Durango, San Luis Potosí) had a Catholic population of 94.0 percent, 6 percentage points above the national average, with indices of evangelicals and Protestants of only 4.4 percent[11] against a national mean of 7.6 percent. However, a survey from Immokalee in 2004 suggests that immigrants from western Mexican states are 88.5 percent Catholic and 11.1 percent evangelical/Protestant. In contrast, census data from southeastern Mexico (Chiapas, Oaxaca, Veracruz) show Catholic and Protestant populations of 77.1 percent and 14.0 percent, respectively. In Immokalee, our survey of immigrants from those Mexican states found that 66.6 percent were Catholic and 33.3 percent were Protestant.

A bastion of Catholicism and resistance to evangelical conversion, western Mexico has a migratory tradition that stretches back over one hundred years. The Fiesta de la Santa Cruz in Chamácuaro, Guanajuato (see chapter 4), illustrates the strength of traditional Catholicism. Women's behavior during the fiesta reflects subordination and the reproduction of "feminine" roles. Though they are clearly more devout than men, on the main festival day (May 3) women must first do their domestic chores, even if—as sometimes happens—they miss the rituals. In this context, religious doctrine leads them to accept their inferior position—cultural baggage they take with them when they migrate. In women's desire to see themselves as autonomous actors, we detect the influence of religious norms on their daily lives. As Florencia, a sixty-four-year-old Catholic from Cristero Territory[12] and a first-generation immigrant who arrived in Immokalee in the 1970s, observes:

> My grandmother was abused and humiliated. . . . [S]he cried and implored God. She inculcated that faith in us, devotion to the Virgin, to God. I followed my grandmother the most, to Rosary every day. I taught my brothers and sisters the good manners and ways I learned from my mother and grandmother, who taught me to always turn to God, fear God, and love God. I worked in the fields; we suffered a lot because my father, rest in peace, liked to drink. We suffered from domestic violence; my mother would end up bathed in blood and when I defended her he'd hit me too. All my life I worked picking tomatoes, oranges, peppers. . . . When I picked oranges my husband took my check. I worked more than him but he had no compassion [emphasis added].

In Florida's agricultural fields, women like Florencia work alongside men, but this labor status has no apparent effect on gender relations. Women must still fulfill their double duty at home and are under constant male domination. The traditional, conservative Catholicism they bring with them from Mexico provides the ideological foundation on which the "resignation" of many women rests. Nevertheless, analyses of gender must go beyond simply documenting women's submission and demonstrate, as Elizabeth Juárez Cerdi suggests, their capacity to resist and contravene social and religious norms.[13]

Though Florencia was dominated by her father and then her husband, she achieved some economic independence that allowed her to leave her spouse and his abuse. Upon arriving in Immokalee, she picked tomatoes, eventually becoming a *pintera*,[14] and accumulated some capital. She opened a fruit stand in a flea market that continues to be very profitable. A few years ago, she bought a lot where she lives comfortably in her own house. Her son studied architecture at the University of Houston in Texas, and she still works at the market every weekend. To explain the social and economic progress such women achieve, we must examine individual agency and the structural conditions of global capitalism in immigrant destinations, which differ from those in their places of origin and contribute to attaining female autonomy. In the United States, women like Florencia do not renounce their conservative Catholicism, but reinterpret their inherited religion and abandon certain attitudes (resignation) that form part of female codes of conduct. They may also adopt new forms of behavior.

In Brazil, as in Mexico, the religious field is becoming increasingly diverse. First, the relative number of Catholics is declining: the 2000 census shows 73.7 percent Catholics, 10.0 percent less than in 1991. Second, evangelicals have increased to 15.5 percent, over two-thirds of them Pentecostals. Third, more people declare "no religious affiliation"; though a small minority (7.3 percent), this sector shows the highest relative rate of growth since 1991.[15]

As in Mexico, change in Brazil varies among regions. In Minas Gerais (origin of 28.3 percent of the immigrant women we interviewed), the proportion of Catholics is 78.8 percent, while evangelicals represent 14.2 percent. In Río de Janeiro, home to 23.9 percent of the women surveyed, the gap narrows: 56.8 percent Catholic versus 21.0 percent evangelical. In São Paulo (13.0 percent of immigrants), 70.6 percent are Catholic and 17.2 percent are evangelical. Finally, in Goiás (7.6 percent of immigrants) 66.4 percent are Catholic and 20.8 percent are evangelical. In contrast to the predominance of Catholicism in Brazil, among Brazilian immigrants evangelicalism seems to prevail and this is reflected in the type of Brazilian churches we found in Florida.[16] Of thirty-nine religious organizations, Brazilian Catholics congregate in a single church: Nossa Senhora Aparecida. As described by José Claúdio Souza Alves in chapter 6, the great majority of the other religious congregations are evangelical Protestant, either Pentecostal or neo-Pentecostal.[17] This distribution reflects a growing Protestantization and Pentecostalization of Brazilian Christianity.[18] This tendency may be accelerated by the processes of migration. Perhaps the loss of everyday support networks in the process of migration, together with the large size and impersonal nature of the Catholic parish, encourages Brazilians abroad to search for small, highly affective groups—the hallmark of Pentecostalism and charismatic Catholicism—in which they can reconstruct their intimacy. Manuel Vásquez documented this quest for protective interpersonal networks in chapter 2, but more research needs to be done to understand the prevalence of Protestantism among Brazilian immigrants.

Angela provides a good example of how Brazilian women draw from religion to negotiate the processes of immigration. She is married with two children. To avoid a family separation, in 2000 she migrated with her businessman husband and children to the United States. However, she felt unhappy with her subordinate role and redefined her new situation in the following terms: "I'll put myself in God's hands. *I won't live in the U.S. because it's my husband's plan*; I'll only stay if I feel it's His plan" (emphasis added). Angela transferred the power that her husband exercised over her to God and felt she had a "mission" to fulfill. Her loss of social status and her role as a subordinate wife were accentuated because she had to give up her profession (psychologist) and devote herself to home and family, but she made use of her psychology background to do volunteer work with Brazilian immigrants: "When I arrived, M. took us right to the church, saying, 'There's a prayer group today, so you can see what it's like.' The priest knew we'd worked with couples' groups in Brazil and wanted to organize a meeting, so two months later we organized the first meeting [there]. Being a psychologist helped a lot. I knew that many people needed help, and *I had time to spare and knew what to do, so I went.* People looked for me and we'd meet in the priest's little office in the church" (emphasis added).

Despite her recent arrival, Angela soon joined a prayer group, helped organize the Encontro de Casais com Cristo (Marriage Encounter with Christ) movement, and taught catechism; but what really marked her experience was her discovery of the charismatic movement outside Brazil: "I think Jesus wants me to do more. . . . It's a call to devote myself more to the church, to community service, *even if it means giving up my profession. I came here to work for God.* Now they called me to work as a pastor. I'm very happy in the group and really committed. The group's real strong and God's presence is unique; you can't just be a spectator there. They introduced me to a Jesus not imprisoned on a cross, but who literally acts in your life because you feel that he talks to you" (emphasis added).

This opportunity provided Angela with a space of empowerment, not just in the movement, but in the wider Catholic community. She perceives her intense involvement in Catholic groups as a "sacred mission"[19] that gives meaning and transcendence to her new life as an immigrant. The loss of social status she suffered is no longer a negative attribute because it is legitimized by the mission Christ conferred upon her. Though unable to practice as a psychologist, her profession constitutes a form of social and cultural capital that, combined with her experience in group work, brings her added social prestige as a charismatic leader.

As the cases of Florencia and Angela show, immigrant women carry religious beliefs and practices with them, reinvent them in their new destinations, and live according to their precepts. This reinvention of their religiosity, however, rests on various sociocultural and economic factors linked to their personal biographies. As Florencia recounted, religion can strengthen and empower women to face adversity; but, as Angela explained, it is sometimes a balm that softens the impact of migration by giving women a "sacred mission." Nevertheless, there is a difference of degree in the religious conduct of Mexican and Brazilian women. Florencia's religious socialization in Mexico and her rural, peasant origins did not include experience with formal Catholic groups and limited her participation in groups in Florida because of her lack of free time. For Florencia, the years she spent in agricultural work were her only option for survival, though it meant that participating in a religious group was a luxury. Angela, in contrast, was able to participate in religious groups in Brazil and Florida. Being from a professional social class, her sociocultural resources bestowed certain advantages in Florida, such as free time and her husband's financial support. These social, cultural, and economic factors interact in the migrant context to predispose and/or condition women to behave in certain ways with respect to religion.

Dialectics of Migration and Lived Religion

Lived religion is not practiced in isolation but is embodied in social contexts.[20] Thus, the migratory condition is a central factor in understanding the religious behavior of Brazilians and Mexicans in Florida. Conversely, belief affects immigrants' behavior in a dialectical relationship.

In the previous chapter, Philip Williams and Patricia Fortuny Loret de Mola identified structural and spatial obstacles in receiving communities that can limit or condition lived religion. As a result, immigrants—especially recently arrived Catholic migrants—are less likely to practice popular devotions in Immokalee than in their communities of origin. However, as Paul Freston observes, there is no mechanical relationship between religious experience and migratory status.[21] For immigrants, religious experience may intensify as a form of cultural defense or, on the contrary, be diminished by the influence of the more secular context or built environment that impedes its realization, as in the case of Immokalee.

As was discussed in chapter 8, migratory status in Immokalee affects people's religious behavior. Established immigrants, who arrived ten or more years ago, enjoy greater social and economic stability and participate more actively in churches, while recently arrived migrants (five years or less) participate little or not at all in churches. Religion seems to fulfill different functions for established and recent immigrants. Participation in officially sanctioned religious practices may permeate the lives of the former, as they have the time, social networks, and socioeconomic stability that allow them to devote themselves to religious activities. Amalia, an established immigrant from Tamaulipas, Mexico, arrived in Immokalee with her husband, Fernando, in 1978. She discussed her active participation in the Catholic Church: "When I was a girl back home, I'd run to Rosary every afternoon and, as soon as I finished my chores, I'd go to church. [Here] I rose as high as Eucharistic minister, but had to pass through several stages, because this doesn't happen overnight. . . . [M]y husband also studied for the ministry. I've participated in prayer groups, with charismatic nuns and in *cursillos de cristiandad*. My husband, Fernando, belongs to Knights of Columbus. . . . [T]hey hold weekly meetings at the church."

Amalia's words reflect a more equitable relationship with her husband than Florencia's narrative of frequent confrontations and violence. Fernando, Amalia's partner, is not an oppressive, abusive spouse. Together they strive to become committed Catholics and to improve their socioeconomic status. While Amalia worked in the fields, then in nurseries, a local company hired Fernando as a tractor operator. With their combined incomes, they are paying off a mobile home that they furnished with Amalia's savings, though she recently retired. In 2003, they celebrated their younger daughter's *quiceañera* with a lavish party that cost them a substantial amount of money but reaffirmed and widened their local social networks, displayed their socioeconomic achievements, and reinforced their status as good Catholics, respected citizens, and successful immigrants.

Instead of becoming more involved in the Catholic church like Amalia, recently arrived migrant farmworkers generally limit their participation to attending Sunday Mass or may simply avoid churches altogether. For many, this is unavoidable as their working conditions leave no time for religion and they lack the resources (social and economic capital) to celebrate rites of passage like baptisms, weddings, and *quinceañeras*. This is the case of Magdalena, a young mother from Miahuatlán, Oaxaca, who arrived in Immokalee in 2000 and immediately found work picking tomatoes: "I go to Mass on Saturdays, sometimes every other Saturday, because sometimes I get home late from work, need to give my son a bath, and there's no time. At home I went to Mass every Sunday, but work's hard here and women may work even more than men. . . . [My husband] wastes his time drinking, gambling . . . . *but I have the same right*. What I earn is for me, to make sure my son and I do okay" (emphasis added).

Recent immigrants like Magdalena must work to survive and satisfy their daily needs before turning their attention to God. Though interested in religion, their material conditions oblige them to accept wage work that provides them with the minimal resources needed to attain relative independence from men. As Pessar has observed, even though women's wage work does not always lead to men's greater contribution to household sustenance—as in Magdalena's case—men are no longer able to dominate women who have access to social and economic resources beyond the domestic sphere.[22]

Among Brazilian women there is no clear distinction between established and recent immigrants. Brazilian migration to South Florida is a much newer phenomenon,[23] so differences in religious involvement are not as clear as in the case of Mexican immigrants. However, other factors may predispose immigrants toward, or away from, religion. Among the first are the search for support and references that are so important for them. Religion provides resources that reassure immigrants and help them adapt to the confusion and alienation caused by their uprooting.[24] Our interviews revealed that many Brazilian immigrant women in Florida intensify their religious activities, finding support and solidarity among their fellow women. Also, when discussing their migratory condition, their religious beliefs often replace other life references: "When you're a migrant in a country that's not yours, [you] feel that *God's* [presence] *gets stronger.* You need a support base when you're outside your country. Life here is different, the culture's different, everything's different, and you need a point of reference" (emphasis added).

Religious conversion often releases intense emotions, as we found among some Brazilians with little religious experience in their homeland, who, once alone in a foreign country, sought new frames of reference. Teresa noted: "When you reach the Miami airport, you're obliged to meet Jesus. It's like *you're more sensitive* because *you're exposed . . . . fragile.* They took me to see Jesus and I became devoted to Him right away. That was one of the most important things that happened to me [there]; it changed my view. Before, my only priority was me; now I'm still number one (because I'm God's child) but my priorities changed. Once I found Jesus *I decided to make the place I live the best place in the world*" (emphasis added). Teresa believes that her "encounter with Jesus" gives meaning to the uncertain and confusing conditions of migration. To explain the many sacrifices made to survive in a foreign country, she adopts a theodicy that makes sense of new, adverse circumstances under the protection of a closer, more visible God who provides the emotional stability that immigrants may lose.

Examples from Brazil and Mexico show that the relationship between the migratory condition and religious behavior is unpredictable. In places like Immokalee, working and living conditions often impede religious practice, especially for newly arrived women who are obliged to work in agriculture. Though they arrived later, Brazilian immigrant women have better jobs and a higher standard of living than Mexicans. These social advantages create conditions that favor—but do not determine—increased religious participation in the receiving community. Although the religious practices of established Mexican immigrants like Amalia are similar to those of Brazilian women, the reasons are different. First, Brazilians enjoy greater economic, social, and political stability than established Mexican immigrants do; and, second, religion allows Brazilian immigrants to legitimize their new material conditions, while the church provides a support base amidst the uncertainty of a foreign land. Churches serve as intermediaries between society and Brazilian believers, facilitating a smoother adaptation to the country of settlement. In contrast, established Mexican immigrants like Amalia turn to religion for other reasons, not necessarily related to their migrant condition, which they have largely overcome. As Marie Marquardt suggests, they join churches because they find opportunities for personal development and to broaden their social networks and elevate their social status.[25] This, in turn, allows immigrant women to exercise power and attain authority and autonomy in private and public domains, like the progressive Catholics that Anna Peterson studied in El Salvador: "For many [women], the church mediates between private life at home and the larger, public realm of work and community participation."[26]

Lived Religion Everywhere in Everyday Life

Religious practice cannot be reduced to official rituals held in institutional spaces; it is present in people's daily lives (lived experience)[27] and permeates both intimate, private domains and public spheres shared by believers.

Angela, the Brazilian immigrant discussed earlier and in chapter 2, illustrates the presence and meaning of the sacred in daily life. Upon placing herself in God's hands she felt supported and received signs that confirmed her decision to migrate, though she did so to accompany her spouse: "Before entering the house where we were going to live, I prayed Our Father and Ave María, asking Mary to bless and protect us. When I went in it was empty except for two images of the Virgin and a cross that said, 'My home and I will always serve the Lord.' 'Hadn't I asked Him for a sign?' He said, 'I chose this house for you. You came because I need you; you came to serve me.' One image is in the same place (the kid's bathroom), the other in the garage with the cross; I left them that way. 'Hadn't I asked for a sign? *That's why I say I came for God*'" (emphasis added). Her trust in God helps Angela face life's challenges and even the forces of nature. As a hurricane neared, she prayed for God's protection and seemed to hear a voice that said, "No wind will touch your window." The hurricane veered away and missed her home. She said, "If you really live something . . . not just attend Mass, but really internalize it as integral to your life, . . . you live your [whole] life differently."

Angela expresses the importance of closeness to God, not just paying lip service to a doctrine but in her total existence, suggesting that religiosity is central to an immigrant's fate. Like Angela, Florencia is close to her Catholic faith and church, attending Mass every weekend and collaborating when asked to do so. Her faith and devotion often emerge in everyday conversation and actions: "What's important is to put everything in God's hands." Florencia's devotion epitomizes religion-in-action linked to daily life. At home, for example, she has various altars with images of the Virgin[28] and she often supports Catholic organizations in Florida and, in return, receives numerous gifts that nurture her spirituality. In December 2004, she went to Europe with her son and grandson, visited St. Peter's Basilica, and attended Pope John Paul II's dawn Mass. Clearly moved, she said, "I saw the pope close up. . . . He looked right at me and gave me his blessing."

These believers' life experiences demonstrate that religion-in-action "cannot be separated from other practices of everyday life."[29] Angela finds in her religious practice a satisfactory explanation for her new role as a Brazilian immigrant in a hostile place. Her renewed, re-legitimized faith has been key to adapting to Florida, where she often sees "signs" from God. Florencia's faith is so pervasive that it filters into her "spaces of recreation," like her religious tourism in Europe, where her personal devotion became public when shared with thousands of other believers at the Vatican.

Lived Religion Outside of Institutions

The cases of Tránsito[30] (Mexican) and Antonia (Brazilian), who "believe without belonging,"[31] reveal other ways of relating to the sacred. Their lack of commitment and participation in churches is due to their dissatisfaction with dogma and practice. This process—religious de-institutionalization—has been studied in Brazil, Mexico, Spain, and elsewhere in the guise of greater adherence to religious forms that do not require membership in an organized church but that modify beliefs and practices to re-create or reinvent their own symbolic universe.[32] Regina Novaes writes that there are more "religious people without religion," meaning individuals who seek "symbols and beliefs in diverse spaces and spiritual traditions to weave their personal religious synthesis."[33]

Tránsito, introduced in chapter 8, is from rural Mexico. Though born a Catholic, she attended a small Pentecostal church for a time. Now a forty-six-year-old single woman, she arrived to Immokalee in 1972, leaving home at the age of sixteen to help support her mother and twelve siblings. She always worked in agriculture and sent money home, but has never been able to accumulate her own savings. Today, she works part-time at a warehouse packing tomatoes and oranges, but her time in Immokalee has not been rewarded: despite thirty years of hard agricultural labor, she has neither the economic stability nor the legal status needed to enjoy a better quality of life. Though she knows the area's churches (Catholic, Baptist, Pentecostal) and their social services, she is not a member of any. She says, "Being in a church is the same as having a job" (Estar en una iglesia es como tener un trabajo). For her, organized religion is too demanding and coercive. She finds no personal or spiritual satisfaction in church but maintains a personal relationship with God by praying alone.

Like Tránsito, Antonia is an independent believer. In Brazil, she lived with her parents in stable economic conditions. She started to work at seventeen, studied psychology, and began a professional career in a psychiatric hospital, but in 2001, the poor pay spurred her to emigrate to the United States in search of independence. *"My reason wasn't to save money.* The problem was . . . I was twenty-nine and fed up with my parents supporting me. I didn't want to live at home anymore; I wanted to be on my own" (emphasis added). Upon arriving in Florida she worked hard in restaurants and cleaning houses. Although she still works sixty-five to seventy hours a week as a waitress in a Brazilian diner, she has achieved the autonomy she desired: "Here, I have my own house, my car, pay my bills, my insurance, do what I want, go out with whoever I want."

The diner where Antonia works serves more Brazilian evangelicals than Catholics, but she prefers not to talk about religion with the former to avoid their attempts to convert her: "You [feign interest] and don't talk about religions. *I don't like any religion here.* To me, 'believers' [evangelicals] are false and hypocritical. . . . [T]hey say, 'Jesus gave me a car.' Well, I'm sorry, but if you don't work then Jesus ain't givin' nobody nothing. *I believe strongly in God, . . . in Jesus. But I think it's work that pays. God helps those who help themselves.*[34] People say, 'Hi brother. Christ's peace. God's peace,' then sit down and start in: 'Remember X . . .' They talk badly about people. Is that religion? My view is different. . . . [T]he question of religion here is really complicated. I don't like the church" (emphasis added).

Antonia's family is Catholic and she always attended Catholic schools, but today she considers herself a Baiana Catholic with a syncretic religiosity.[35] "I go to the [Catholic church] once a year, or when I feel like it, but I don't want commitments. I like a *macumba* [an African-based religion] . . . playing *búzios* [36] . . . lots of things. . . . [I]f it catches my eye, I'm into it."

Though re-created in the present, Tránsito's and Antonia's religious preferences derive from their countries' religious cultures and the socialization they received when young. Their life stories illustrate their social class differences and the factors and motivations that lead them to approach the sacred independently. While Antonia went north looking for the personal growth she could not find in Brazil, Tránsito left home for reasons of survival, her own and that of her family. Tránsito's instrumental relationship with churches reflects her precarious social position, while Antonia requires no material support from churches because her income gives her relative economic and social autonomy. Both are critical of churches: Tránsito accepts material benefits from them, but rejects them as places of worship; Antonia disapproves of evangelical behavior and reaffirms her faith through secular work rather than through God's "goodwill." For distinct reasons, both refuse to belong to a religious organization, but each maintains her faith in her own way.

Lived Religion in "In-Between" Spaces

The tension between institutional affiliation and practices and lived religion is not always sharp. Churches create social spaces to reproduce and/or propagate their religious beliefs and doctrine. These include the cells [37] of some Pentecostal churches and Catholic prayer groups like Encontro de Casais com Cristo (Marriage Encounter with Christ), where believers meet in homes or other places outside of church. They are examples of "in-between" or intermediate spaces, where believers exercise authority and power, precisely because they operate outside institutional limits, though with the support or authorization of a religious organization.

Through their religious commitments and activities, immigrant women gather knowledge and information that they turn into human and social capital and may use to obtain positions of authority, recognition, or respect both within and outside of their religious communities. María, a Pentecostal convert from northern Mexico, illustrates the positions of authority that believers can achieve through intermediate spaces. She belongs to the Bethel Assemblies of God Church and preaches at many of its cells. She is admired as a fluid, eloquent preacher, well-versed in the Bible, and able to relate scripture to people's everyday lives and to exercise control and authority over her listeners.[38] To exercise this power, she must create an effect and reaction in the audience: "those who exercise power depend on the actions of others who recognize that power . . . [and] a common form of recognition is subordination."[39] We observed subordination among María's listeners as she preached the Scriptures. Cell members praised the importance of her work as a spiritual leader blessed with authority and charisma, even though she was a woman.

According to Magdalena Villarreal, subordination "does not mean that those who give in become powerless, but that [power] is fluid and constantly negotiated" through the nature of relationships.[40] María obeys the wishes of others (church authorities), but her actions show how church members can become empowered. Irma, another member of the Bethel church, from Guerrero, Mexico, is training to be a preacher. Her experience illustrates the interplay of power relationships in intermediate religious spaces: "I haven't preached yet, but I want to. The Lord says we must *prepare* ourselves through books to learn to speak, because everything done for the Lord must be done well, not just any old thing. . . . I mean, you're speaking the *Word of a King, not idle chatter*. To preach, you have to enter the church or cells and earn merit. . . . [T]hen they'll make you a leader" (emphasis added).

Irma is anxious to become a leader like María, a desire that has led her to extend her religious practice from temple to home. She founded a cell at her home, where María preaches, and this serves a dual purpose: allowing her to participate in God's work and helping her prepare her knowledge of the scriptures "to do God's will" and thank Him for all He has given her. "*I feel good about what I've done* and I thank God because I know everything comes from Him. People get ahead in life but don't remember Him. He made things tough for me here but allowed me to stay, and I've been very happy since I reconciled with God, because I've received many good things" (emphasis added).

Among these "good things" is economic progress. She and her husband came to the United States in 1978, still young, and lived in Dallas for several years before moving to Florida. At first they worked in agriculture, but to increase their income Irma suggested they organize *tandas*:[41] "In Orlando ... *I said* we should organize tandas, but he said there's no time, ... no money. I started with my family, eleven people. We organized tandas for about three years. That's how we started getting money, first to buy clothes for my kids. Through tandas we saved fifteen thousand dollars, and *I told* him I wanted to open a restaurant. He said, 'You need lots of money for that business,' so *I said* we had to do something because we weren't going to work in the fields all our lives. 'What about opening a *paletería?*' "[42] (emphasis added).

The shop they opened in Immokalee in 2002 has been so successful that they earned enough money to obtain a home loan.[43] Irma is key to their businesses: "Nobody can hold me back.... I manage everything, ... permits, the house, loans, subcontracting." This Pentecostal believer demonstrates not only exceptional personal agency, but a strong religious motivation that has helped her to develop and grow in both material and spiritual dimensions.

Among Brazilians, Marilia's life history echoes María's and Irma's, while offering an important counterpoint. Marilia comes from a poor family, although her studies to become a nun give her important symbolic capital. She worked as a nun for some years before leaving Brazil for the United States in the early 1980s, where she cared for her ailing father. She met a Brazilian man, became pregnant, and decided to marry and stay in Florida, a decision that changed her life: from nun to wife and mother, confronted with the challenges and hardships of daily life in a new destination. "Back home, the rhythm of life was very different ... intense pastoral work, academic studies and I felt really fulfilled. *It was a radical change, because here you have to accept your situation as a migrant and work to survive*" (emphasis added). Because religion was such a fundamental part of her life before migrating, she looked for a religious space after arriving in Florida but found no Brazilian Catholic churches. So, with her family she helped to organize the first meetings of Brazilian Catholics in the area: "Lay couples that had been in movements in Brazil took the initiative. Each week they'd go to one family's home, pray, and socialize, until priests organized the community. Here the church is more conservative, the CEBs (Ecclesial Base Communities), evangelization groups that held Bible study and awareness sessions in homes, began in the '80s down there [in Brazil] but didn't start here 'til the '90s."

Today, Marilia only occasionally attends meetings of the evangelization groups, as she and her husband joined the Encontro de Casais com Cristo movement, another Catholic organization from Brazil: "The idea is to do something more autonomous. There [in Brazil] it was an elite movement that later became popularized. Here it's adapted to the context of migrants' realities. *The Church was the path that helped us adapt better to American society*. With the groups we reflect on what living the faith [means] here. *Why are you here? This is a question we ask ourselves through the eyes of faith. We believe there must be a greater "why," beyond work and social and financial stability"* (emphasis added).

Given her academic training and experience as a nun, Marilia illustrates better than Angela the importance that women place on becoming carriers of a sacred mission that gives them a dimension of power and authority despite their marginal position. She constructs a theodicy that responds to her new material conditions. Like the other Brazilian immigrant women we interviewed, Marilia needed to transform her migrant condition into a kind of vocation or calling from God (something not characteristic of Mexicans). Here, the spiritual factor replaces economic and social motives in explaining migration. These examples also demonstrate that interaction with the sacred provides believers with desired benefits according to their socioeconomic circumstances. Though Marilia left the convent, her desire to continue her religious practice led her to form an evangelization group and become active in the Catholic Church. Through her membership in Encontro de Casais, she preserves her religiosity and finds guidance as she seeks answers to her dilemma of being an immigrant and a woman. Like Irma, she improved her well-being by cleaning houses before becoming a nurse's assistant with better wages and working conditions. Now, she and her husband have their own house and a comfortable economic situation.

In contrast to Marilia's life history, Irma's contains no evidence of an urgent search for self-fulfillment to legitimize migration. She accepts the hardships implicit in living in a foreign country as her fate and never pauses to ask why she left Mexico because in the United States her socioeconomic status has improved markedly. She sees positive changes between what she once was and what she has accomplished. Her relation to the sacred (including her interest in preaching) reflects different motives than Marilia has. Though she wants to increase her prestige/status in her religious community, the benefits of her greater knowledge of the Scriptures will not serve to legitimize her new social position in Florida since she did not experience downward social mobility as did Marilia. The devotion of these two women leaves no doubt that they consider themselves good believers; but here we wish to emphasize the reasons that they themselves give to explain their religious behavior in the migratory context.

The intermediate spaces that churches offer these immigrant women constitute privileged sites of authority and power where women can achieve their personal goals.[44] These spaces are at the same time institutionally accredited domains, yet distant from centers of religious power. In churches, the priest or minister has knowledge and authority over the congregation, but in Pentecostal cells or Catholic evangelization groups it is María, Irma, and Marilia who possess such knowledge and authority. Intermediate spaces function as excellent sites for distributing sacred power, as the distance from churches and the privacy of homes allow people to compete for institutional leadership in such groups.

Moreover, because these women's religious authority, charisma, and knowledge are legitimized by institutions, they can aspire to higher positions as believers.

Conclusions

In migratory contexts, there are multiple ways of interacting with God and converting religion into a means of emancipation. Analyses of gender and religion have largely ignored rural Mexico's traditional (popular) Catholicism, viewing it exclusively as a mechanism of oppression. However, the narratives presented here show that traditional Catholicism, the Charismatic Movement, and Pentecostalism (also considered conservative) can all serve as "liberating raw material" for immigrant women if social conditions allow it. The cases analyzed in this chapter demonstrate that immigrant believers can attain greater self-esteem and autonomy, while not necessarily eradicating the conditions of female subordination.[45] In particular, we showed how what we call in-between religious spaces can help women link private and public spheres, offering the possibility for empowerment through their simultaneous association with institutional religious networks and their relative autonomy.

Throughout this chapter we have highlighted the important socioeconomic differences between Brazilian and Mexican immigrants. Brazilians arrived in Florida with more human and social capital than Mexicans and were able to secure higher-paying jobs in the service sector, while the latter more often worked in agriculture. This is explained largely by the socioeconomic background of immigrant women, their migration trajectories, and the type of socialization they received before emigrating. The Brazilian immigrants we interviewed are from middle-class backgrounds. Most attended high school or university and enjoy social positions in Florida markedly higher than those of the Mexican women. Some Brazilian women are housewives, economically dependent on their husbands, with free time to study or participate in religious activities. Their discourse expresses a theodicy that legitimizes, explains, and justifies migration and their new social position in the receiving community, where they have lost social status due to the kinds of low-prestige jobs and lifestyles they were forced to accept as immigrants. For these women, "evil" materializes when they arrive in a foreign country that treats them as second-class citizens; so to explain their new living conditions they turn to God's goodness and their sacred mission to transform this evil from a form of punishment into a personal commitment with the sacred.

Narratives of Mexican immigrant women, in contrast, contain no theodicy to legitimize migration, nor the social implications that accompany it. These women reconstruct theodicies—or forms of divine justification—to comprehend the hardships of daily life in a manner that is more extensive but less precise than that of Brazilian women. The Mexican women we interviewed were from rural, lower social classes. They do not see migration and its consequences as evil; to the contrary, they see their material conditions improving despite the double discrimination they suffer as women and as a national minority. Thus, they re-elaborate a theodicy that helps them overcome the vicissitudes of life in a foreign country where they are seen as second- or even third-class citizens.

This comparison between Brazilian and Mexican immigrant women shows the fruitfulness of taking the variable of religion seriously in the study of gender and migration, while not ignoring the economic factors which condition the available religious options and call for different forms of religious legitimation. Religion, however, does not simply reflect the dynamics of labor markets and class differences. Its relations with the economics of migration are often unpredictable. Moreover, in contributing to the re-articulation of gender roles and family relations during the process of migration, religion also plays active roles that must be researched further.

NOTES

1. See Lois Lorentzen, "El milagro está en casa: Gender and Private/Public Empowerment in a Migrant Pentecostal Church," *Latin American Perspectives* 32, no. 1 (2005): 57–71; Marie Marquardt Friedmann, "From Shame to Confidence: Gender, Religious Conversion, and Civic Engagement of Mexicans in the U.S. South," *Latin American Perspectives* 32, no. 1 (2005): 27–56; and Patricia Fortuny Loret de Mola, "Religión y figura femenina: Entre la norma y la práctica," *La Ventana* 14 (2001): 126–158.

2. Dalia Bassols and Cristina Oehmichen, eds., *Migración y relaciones de género en México* (Mexico: GIMTRAP-UNAM/IIA, 2000); Patricia Pessar and Sarah Mahler, "Gender and Transnational Migration," paper presented at the conference Transnational Migration: Comparative Perspectives, Princeton University, June 30–I July 1, 2001; Patricia R. Pessar, "Engendering Migration Studies: The Case of New Immigrants in the United States," in *Gender and U.S. Immigration: Contemporary Trends*, ed. Pierrette Hondagneu-Sotelo, 20–42 (Berkeley: University of California Press, 2003); Ofelia Woo, "Las mujeres mexicanas indocumentadas en la migración internacional y la movilidad transfronteriza," in *Mujeres, migración y maquila en la frontera norte*, ed. Soledad González et al., 65–87 (Mexico: COLEF-COLMEX, 1995). The religious dimension is ignored even in recent publications on gender issues from varying perspectives, such as in Hondagneu-Sotelo's edited volume, *Gender and U.S. Immigration.*

3. Pierrette Hondagneu-Sotelo and Ernestine Avila, "I'm Here, but I'm There," in *Gender and U.S. Immigration*, ed. Hondagneu-Sotelo, 333.

4. Pessar and Mahler, "Gender and Transnational Migration," 2.

5. Robert Orsi, "Everyday Miracles: The Study of Lived Religion," in *Lived Religion in America*, ed. David Hall (Princeton, NJ: Princeton University Press, 1997), 7.

6. Orsi, "Everyday Miracles," 9.

7. Pessar, "Engendering Migration Studies"; Víctor Espinosa, *El dilema del retorno: Migración, género y pertenencia en un contexto transnacional* (Mexico: El Colegio de Michoacán/El Colegio de Jalisco, 1998); Woo, "Las mujeres mexicanas indocumentadas"; María Eugenia D'aubeterre, *El pago de la novia* (Mexico: El Colegio de Michoacán/Benemérita Universidad Autónoma de Puebla, 2000).

8. Pessar, "Engendering Migration Studies," 27.

9. Ibid., 20.

10. Of this 12.0 percent, 3.52 percent are people who declared "no religion" in the census.

11. This includes evangelicals and "non-biblical" evangelicals. According to the 2000 National Census, the former includes members of historical Protestant and Pentecostal churches; the latter, Seventh-Day Adventists, Mormons, and Jehovah's Witnesses.

12. The Cristero rebellion took place in the Bajío region of Mexico (1926–29), when broad sectors of the Catholic population confronted an anti-clerical, post-revolutionary Mexican state.

13. Elizabeth Juárez Cerdi, *Modelando a las Evas: Mujeres de virtud y rebeldía* (Zamora, Michoacán: El Colegio de Michoacán, 2006).

14. The term *pintero* indicates people who pick "colored" tomatoes, those that have begun to turn red and that buyers do not purchase. Once Florencia learned this work, she began to operate as an independent *pintera*, which allowed her to accumulate some capital that she later multiplied through new businesses.

15. Antonio Flavio Pierucci, "Bye, bye, Brazil—O declínio das religiões tradicionais no Censo 2000," *Revista Estudos Avançados* 52 (September/December 2004): 17–28; César Romero Jacobi et al., *Atlas da filiação religiosa e indicadoes sociais no Brasil* (Rio de Janeiro/S. Paulo: PUC Rio/Loyola/CNBB, 2003).

16. Comparisons of these data are risky: the Brazilian census reflects peoples' self-classification of religion, while in Florida we ascertained the number of churches and estimated the number of immigrants that frequent them.

17. "Evangelicals" include historical Protestants, Pentecostals, and neo-Pentecostals.

18. Paul Freston, "Becoming Brazuca: Brazilian Immigration to the US," unpublished paper, Harvard University, David Rockefeller Center for Latin American Studies, 2005.

19. Otto Maduro explains that when Latino migrants join churches (especially evangelical ones), they cease to be "undocumented," "suspicious" or "without rights" and become people chosen and protected by God to fulfill a "sacred mission." We use the notion of a sacred mission in a broader sense that includes transforming oneself. Otto Maduro, "Notas sobre pentecostalismo y poder entre inmigrantes latinoamericanos en la ciudad de Newark," paper presented at the thirteenth Congress on Religious Alternatives in Latin America, Porto Alegre, Brazil, September 27–30, 2005, 4.

20. The anthropological study of religion speaks of systems of religious meanings but also links those meanings to social processes. See Clifford Geertz, *La interpretación de las culturas* (Barcelona: Editorial Gedisa, 1995).

21. Freston, "Becoming Brazuca."

22. Pessar, "Engendering Migration Studies," 27.

23. See chapter 2 in this volume.

24. Cecília Menjívar, "Latino Immigrants and Their Perceptions of Religious Institutions: Cubans, Salvadorans, and Guatemalans in Phoenix, Arizona," *Migraciones Internacionales* 1 (July/December 2001): 4.

25. Marquardt Friedmann, "From Shame to Confidence," 30.

26. Anna Peterson, "The Only Way I Can Walk: Women, Christianity, and Everyday Life in El Salvador," in *Christianity, Social Change, and Globalization in the Americas*, ed. Anna L. Peterson, Manuel A. Vásquez, and Philip J. Williams (New Brunswick, NJ: Rutgers University Press, 2001), 28.

27. A phrase from existentialism and the source of the neologism "lived religion." Orsi, "Everyday Miracles," 7.

28. The symbol of the Virgin of Guadalupe is highly polysemic and can be associated with religious, nationalist, gendered, and/or secular meanings.

29. Robert Orsi, *The Madonna of 115th Street: Faith and Community in Italian Harlem, 1880–1950*, 2nd ed. (New Haven, CT: Yale University Press, 2002), xxi.

30. See additional references to Tránsito in chapter 8.

31. This is the subtitle of Grace Davie's book on religion in Britain during the postwar period. Grace Davie, *Religion in Britain since 1945: Believing without Belonging* (Oxford: Blackwell, 1994).

32. See Faustino Teixeira and Renata Menezes, "Introdução," in *As religiões no Brasil: Continuidades e rupturas*, ed. Faustino Teixeira and Renata Menezes, 7–16 (Brazil: Ed. Vozes, Petrópolis, 2006); Patricia Fortuny Loret de Mola, ed., *Creyentes y creencias en Guadalajara* (Mexico: CIESAS/INAH/El Colegio de Jalisco, 1999); Rafael Díaz Salazar, "La religión vacía: Un análisis de la transición religiosa en Occidente," in *Formas modernas de religión*, ed. Rafael Díaz Salazar, Salvador Giner, and Fernando Velasco, 71–114 (Madrid: Alianza Universidad, 1994); Roland Campiche, "De la pertenencia a la identificación religiosa: El paradigma de la individualización de la religión hoy en día," *Religiones Latinoamericanas* 1 (January–June 1991): 73–85; Danièle Hervieu-Lèger, "Religion and Modernity in the French Context: For a New Approach to Secularization," *Sociological Analysis* 51 (1990): 15–25; José María Mardones, *Postmodernidad y neoconservadurismo* (Estella, Navarra: Editorial Verbo Divino, 1991).

33. Regina Novaes, "Pentecostalismo, política, mídia e favela," in *Religião e cultura popular*, ed. Victor Valla, 41–74 (Rio de Janeiro: DP&A, 2001).

34. An old Portuguese proverb: "Deus ajuda a quem cedo madruga."

35. The Baiano Catholics from Bahía, Brazil, are known for their broad syncretism.

36. Rituals linked to Afro-Brazilian religions.

37. "Cells" are weekly gatherings of sympathizers and potential members to propagate the faith, formed outside the church and led by families.

38. In her study of Mexican immigrants in metro Atlanta, Marquardt found that "religious conversion encouraged women in particular to become 'popular subjects': confident, articulate and capable persons with the habits and dispositions necessary for leadership in their religious organization." Marquardt Friedmann, "From Shame to Confidence," 28.

39. Magdalena Villarreal, "La reinvención de las mujeres y el poder en los procesos de desarrollo rural planeado," *La Ventana* II (Universidad de Guadalajara, 2000): 6.

40. Ibid., 6.

41. In Mexico, *tandas* (*mutualistas*) are a form of popular rotating savings: people give a monthly payment for a certain time and each month one participant receives the entire amount, allowing people who do not qualify for bank loans to accumulate an incipient capital.

42. A *paletería* is a shop that sells popsicles and ice cream.

43. Today, the shop is a restaurant that serves Mexican food. Open every day, it has become very popular. Irma's husband manages the restaurant, and she takes care of related businesses.

44. Robert Smith, in his study of Mexican immigrants in New York, found that a women's prayer group created "a space for female authority and power" and gave its members public roles in a male-dominated immigrant organization. Robert Smith, *Mexican New York* (Berkeley: University of California Press, 2006), 118.

45. Working with neo-Pentecostal women in Brazil, Machado discovered that their social place has changed and that some topics from the feminist agenda are being incorporated, though recognizing that male-female relations are still asymmetrical. Maria das Dores C. Machado, "Neopentecostalismo: Relações de poder entre os gêneros," *Caminhos* I (July-December 2003): 67–82.

10

۞ ۞

A Place to Be

New and Old Geographies of Latin American Migration in Florida and Beyond

TIMOTHY J. STEIGENGA, MANUEL A. VÁSQUEZ, AND PHILIP J. WILLIAMS

The key concepts that frame the chapters in this volume, transnationalism, collective mobilization, and lived religion, represent both empirical subjects of investigation and critical analytical tools for understanding and interpreting the dynamics of immigrant life in new destinations. The preceding chapters provide ample empirical evidence and measures of transnationalism, mobilization, and lived religion in each of the cases we have studied. While the experience of Brazilians, Guatemalans, and Mexicans in South Florida cannot be generalized to all Latin American immigrants, it does highlight some of the central processes and trends that characterize Latino immigration to new destinations in the United States.

Transnationalism in New Destinations

The case studies presented in this volume suggest that transnationalism plays an influential role in new destinations of Latino immigration. The preceding chapters demonstrate that transnational practices and forms of organization can assist immigrants in the construction of individual and collective identities as they negotiate the process of settlement—as they find a place to be.

As Manuel Vásquez argues in chapter 2, the concept of community, as it has been traditionally utilized, may be ill-suited for understanding the complex web of border-spanning connections that characterize such immigrant lives. At first glance, there is very little to suggest the existence of a Brazilian "community" in the areas we studied. But beneath the surface and "ideology of disunity" among Brazilian immigrants,[1] we uncovered a rich tapestry of interpersonal networks that connect individuals, families, and worshippers across and within borders. In the face of structural constraints (economic, spatial, legal, and otherwise) Brazilians form such networks as part of their "ways of being" even if the networks do not yet add up to a visible Brazilian "community" which could propagate more institutionalized "ways of belonging."[2]

The case of Brazilians in Broward County shows that in new destinations where immigrants have to reconstitute the fabric of sociability almost from scratch in the face of an increasingly inhospitable environment, it may be more fruitful for scholars to focus on the myriad of emerging and shifting personal networks than on a reified concept of community. This focus can give us a more nuanced understanding of the gradual and precarious formation of collective identity and mobilization. Our survey results document the "multiple embeddedness" of Brazilian immigrants, at least at the level of information, finances, and personal relations. Thus, the Brazilian case demonstrates the centrality of "core transnationalism"—transnational "activities that form an integral part of an individual's habitual life [and] are undertaken on a regular basis,"[3] even when an institutionalized "transnational community" does not formally exist.[4] Put in another way, many Brazilians in Broward County live transnational lives, making cultural bifocality an essential ingredient in their day-to-day interactions. Nevertheless, they have not become "transnational villagers," with visible, full-fledged organizations, such as hometown associations, linking particular locations across national borders.[5]

As in the Brazilian case, the Guatemalan Mayan immigrants of Jupiter have constructed an intricate web of transnational family and personal networks. But unlike the Brazilians, the levels and forms of transnationalism we found among the Jupiter Maya were significantly expanded. A fully developed transnational social field with networks that carry material as well as symbolic and moral goods has developed and become institutionalized between Jacaltenango and Jupiter. While the Brazilians in Deerfield Beach and Pompano Beach come from various locations throughout Brazil, many of the Guatemalans in Jupiter are bound by ethnic, geographic, language, and religious ties that facilitate the building of a more visible transnational community. Comparison of these two cases, thus, shows us that the intensity and extensity of transnationalism in new destinations is affected by the cultural and social capitals that immigrants bring to the process of settlement. In the absence of networks established by previous immigrants that can be redeployed transnationally, new arrivals have to rely more heavily on the sense of belonging and the multiple identities they had in the country of origin.

In the face of a foreign and frequently hostile environment, Mayan immigrants in Jupiter turn to their primary sources of physical and emotional support: family, community, and church. In the process, they consciously and unconsciously adopt a survival strategy that entails the construction of deep and increasingly institutionalized transnational linkages at all of the levels outlined in chapter I. The most striking finding from the Jupiter case is the profound ambiguity and elusiveness that characterizes the construction and maintenance of this transnational social field.

As outlined in chapters 3 and 7, the transnational lives of Jupiter's most recent Mayan immigrants combine re-created images of their homes in the past, the struggle to survive in the difficult conditions of the present, and an effort to imagine a future that entails a return to home, filled with hope and aspirations but simultaneously conditioned by uncertainty and fear. The psychological stress associated with this form of multiple embeddedness has thus far received scant attention in the literature on transnationalism.[6] Two factors outlined in chapter 3 merit significantly more attention in work on transnational migration. First, the meaning and implications of transnational fields are mediated by gender, stage of life, and location within the immigration process. For example, Jacaltec women in Jupiter are faced with pressures to reproduce gender roles from the home village while simultaneously adapting to the difficulties of living in a society with different expectations. Since there are relatively few women (females represent less than one-third of Jupiter's total immigrant population) and they have little access to transportation, women frequently face these challenges in relative social isolation.

In terms of life cycle and immigration wave, we found key differences between previous waves of immigrants (refugees and asylum seekers) and more recent economic refugees, whose economic and social remittances help them to maintain a material and symbolic presence with their families in their communities of origin. Because the more recent immigrants are more likely to be undocumented, they face significant obstacles to both their integration into existing institutions in the receiving community (bridging social capital through participation in religious, work-related, or civic institutions) and their ability to deepen transnational ties (as physical, legal, and financial impediments limit their mobility).

Second, the distance and separation generated by migration inflicts a heavy burden on family relations for transmigrants. Moving to the United States removes individuals from social enforcement of norms through communal and family authorities, a void that is filled, at least for some, by churches and other civic organizations. Furthermore, transnational gossip, primarily in the form of frequent phone conversations (but also through videos and e-mail) puts constant pressure on transmigrants and their family members at home. As one young man recently explained, "My wife already knows what happens here before I even talk to her. I called her yesterday and she already knew that Francisco was leaving tomorrow. It is supposed to be a secret but it looks like everybody already knows. Honestly, the same thing happens in the other direction. My wife calls me and tells me about events in Jacal that are already old news here—but I pretend not to know about them."[7] Transnational gossip serves as a form of social control that has a direct impact on all members of the transnational community. The lives of women who remain in Jacaltenango are circumscribed by fears of reports of bad behavior that might reach their husbands in Jupiter. Meanwhile, in

Jupiter, the slightest rumor of impropriety by a family member or acquaintance back in Guatemala can pass like wildfire throughout the community. As is often the case with gossip, events are quickly distorted in the retelling.[8]

From the Jupiter case, we learn to treat the multiple levels and forms of transnationalism as a double-edged sword. While the transnational Fiesta Maya allows Mayan immigrants to celebrate their culture and reaffirm their identity in a new an alien context, the aforementioned elements of transnational gossip and expectations add immense pressures to their daily lives. The ambiguities, nostalgia, and contradictions of maintaining lives in multiple locations are palpable. Furthermore, the immigrants themselves are painfully aware of the ways in which their physical presence in one location fundamentally alters the other through the changes wrought by ever-growing economic and social remittances. Forced to operate within the "coordinates of the possible," Jupiter's Mayan immigrants, like other waves of immigrants before them, establish and maintain their transnational families because that is the option that is available to them.[9]

The case of Mexicans in Immokalee also adds key insights to our understanding of transnationalism in new and old destinations. In contrast with Jupiter, low levels of social capital, significant cultural/ethnic heterogeneity, and extreme economic deprivation present significant obstacles to constituting and reproducing transnational ties. Although our survey research and qualitative interviews provide plenty of evidence of "migrant-led transnationalism"[10]—such as sending remittances, videos, and letters and maintaining kinship networks across borders—more institutionalized forms of transnationalism (hometown associations and collective community projects) are largely absent in the Immokalee case.

In that sense, the Mexican case has striking parallels with that of Brazilians in Pompano Beach and Deerfield Beach. This is despite the fact that Brazilians are located in an urban and exurban space, while Immokalee is a rural setting, and that Brazilians have on the average a higher socioeconomic status and higher levels of formal education than Mexican immigrants. Nevertheless, both groups face spatiotemporal constraints that limit their capacity to engage in transnational practices. In spite of the fact that there is a long history of Mexican immigration to Immokalee, the harsh labor and housing conditions and the constant internal movement following the harvest seasons have made it very difficult for Mexicans to build institutionalized forms of transnationalism, in effect, putting them in the same situation as newer arrivals like Brazilians, who have not had the time to establish formalized links. What these two cases suggest is that there is a need to study systematically more than just the various types of transnationalism, or how widespread or durable this phenomenon is across different immigrant generations, as Peggy Levitt, Alejandro Portes, and associates have done. We also need to study the economic, spatial, physical, temporal, social, and other factors that constrain the practice of transnationalism, particularly in new destinations where immigrant networks are incipient.

An exception in the Mexican case is an ethnically cohesive group of indigenous Otomí immigrants who have constructed a "transnational moral community"[11] with institutionalized positions of responsibility, networks of mutual aid in employment, a common language, and the frequent celebration of rituals and fiestas. Despite their relatively recent arrival, the Otomíes have parlayed this transnational social capital into economic resources, allowing them to escape the bottom-rung jobs of the agricultural industry in Immokalee.

For the more established immigrants, such as the Chamacuarenses from Guanajuato, the form and level of transnationalism follows a more well-worn path. The Chamacuarenses primarily express their transnational ties through participation in and support of their *fiesta patronal*. Their connections are institutionalized primarily through their relationship with the Catholic Church; however, the unstructured nature of immigrant participation and organization of the fiesta resembles the kind of decentralized, flexible transnational religious ties that Levitt refers to as "negotiated transnational religious organization."[12] With more than thirty years of immigration between Chamácuaro and Immokalee, these immigrants have gained greater social status and diversified their social networks over time. They have adapted to (rather than assimilated into) the environment of Immokalee.

Finally, it appears that the absence of established immigrant pathways that facilitate settlement and integration encourages Otomíes in Immokalee and Jacaltecos in Jupiter to develop transnational networks that link them with their communities of origin. In other words, cultivating transnational relations can be part of a survival strategy for immigrants in new destinations. In contrast, for more established immigrants like Chamacuarenses, participation in transnational fiestas is largely unrelated to questions of survival in the community of settlement. These findings suggest that the emergence of transnational communities has less to do with the time of arrival of immigrants than with the context of reception and the group's level of social and cultural capital as manifested in ethnic solidarity.

Transnationalism and Collective Mobilization

The different forms of transnationalism and solidarity among the Guatemalan and Mexican immigrants provide an excellent transition to our next set of questions about collective mobilization. What are the implications of the various models of transnationalism we uncovered for collective action among immigrant groups, and how do they interact with the contexts of new destinations in South Florida?

The cases of Immokalee and Jupiter present us with clear contrasts in terms of social capital, reactive ethnicity, and transnationalism. As we demonstrated in chapter 5, Jupiter's immigrants experience the social and economic conditions necessary to produce reactive ethnicity at significantly higher rates than immigrants in Immokalee. They also have more institutionalized networks, greater economic stability, and more established transnational ties. Over time, this bonding social capital was transformed into bridging social capital, bringing multiple groups together to focus on the creation of an immigrant resource center for the town. Thus, defensive identities were translated into project identities with the help of local churches and the university.[13] These institutions provided the networks, skills, spaces, leadership, and resources to translate the existing social capital into political capital at the local level.

With the exception of the small group of Otomíes, levels of social capital and institutionalized transnationalism in Immokalee were significantly lower than in Jupiter. With a majority Latino population, Immokalee is a less fertile ground for the growth of defensive identities or reactive ethnicity. Interestingly, class-based rather than identity-based organizing has been more effective in the context of Immokalee. Even so, the mobile livelihoods of migrant farmworkers present serious obstacles to the Coalition of Immokalee Workers' organizing efforts. Consequently, the Coalition has attempted to amplify and extend its struggle to new constituencies beyond Immokalee. What began as a farmworker organization focused on local issues has evolved into a broader national movement. Although the Coalition has developed transnational linkages with social movements in Latin America and elsewhere, unlike the case of Jacaltecos in Jupiter, transnationalism has not been a key element in its mobilization efforts. Early on, support from the Catholic Church was critical in providing organizational resources and networks for the Coalition. As in the case of Jupiter, the Coalition has relied on the support of external actors, including churches, students, and labor organizations, to transform its struggle from localized actions into a nationwide boycott of the fast-food giants Taco Bell and McDonald's.

In each context, there are potential dangers, pitfalls, and drawbacks to the form of mobilization initiated. In Jupiter, ethnic cleavages, counter mobilizations, and some degree of downward assimilation represent serious risks for incipient immigrant social movements. In Immokalee, the Coalition's success in projecting its struggle on the national stage is conditioned by a growing sense that the organization is out of touch with local issues. Such concerns may have been behind the Coalition's recent decision to play a highly visible role in organizing the march in Fort Meyers, Florida, as part of the massive immigrant rights mobilizations of April and May 2006.

The case of Brazilians in Broward County highlights some of the formidable structural obstacles facing immigrants in building on interpersonal networks to create their own organizations. In chapter 6 we saw how under an "immigrant regime of production" Brazilians come to populate the "secondary sector proletariat and the reserve army"[14] of the U.S. economy. Given their undocumented status, precarious work conditions, and lack of access to public spaces, many immigrants seek protection and invisibility in religious and business networks.[15] Religious networks provide an important source of information, job referrals, as well as spiritual and emotional support for immigrants. As in the case of Jupiter, the creation and evolution of these networks has relied on transnational linkages with religious organizations in Brazil and the United States. In the absence of other Brazilian community organizations, some leaders in the Catholic and Baptist churches have assumed more visible roles in advocating on behalf of immigrants both in the United States and in Brazil. Whether these networks remain latent and submerged or become activated for future mobilization is an open question. In contrast to Mexican and Guatemalan immigrants in Jupiter and Immokalee, it appears that most Brazilians have opted for a strategy of "hunkering down," as evidenced in their general distrust of neighbors and withdrawal from collective life.[16] However, the organizational success of Brazilian immigrants in traditional gateway cities such as Boston and New York points to the possibilities for future mobilization.

As discussed in chapter 1, the gap between empowerment and power can be a long-term process, often necessitating the establishment of bonds of solidarity and trust before achieving more community-oriented activism.[17] It may be that after an initial period of hunkering down in a new destination, the bonding social capital generated within religious and labor networks will evolve into bridging social capital that enables Brazilians to build the connective structures necessary for collective organization.

What role does religion play in immigrant collective action and mobilization? Both in the United States and in Latin America, much has been written about the role of religion in "framing" ideological or motivational resources to social movements.[18] Our research suggests that immigrant activists frequently frame their identity through certain religious resources, beliefs, practices, rituals, and cultures that make them more prone to be engaged and mobilized for collective action.[19] Beyond framing, the common factors we found that link religion and immigrant mobilization are community building, resource mobilization, and a role for religious institutions and leaders as interlocutors. These are familiar themes for social movement theory that echo earlier findings from studies of the role of religion in the civil rights movement in the United States.[20] In numerous social movement studies, religious organizations have been found to provide the networks, skills, discretionary resources (time and effort of members), free spaces (from the physical or ideological control of other powerful actors), and collective identity (shared sense of community) necessary to begin and maintain social movements.[21] As discussed in chapter 5, in Jupiter, an interfaith alliance of religious congregations generated an expansive discourse of tolerance and social justice that paved the way for the approval of a new employment and resource center. In Immokalee, the Coalition of Immokalee

Workers drew from religious traditions of social activism in framing its successful boycott against the corporate giants Taco Bell and McDonald's. Moreover,
the Coalition forged a network of support groups including many religious
organizations and people of faith across the country.

In Deerfield Beach and Pompano Beach, local church leaders have been the
most visible voices in advocating on behalf of Brazilian immigrants. Still, in
many cases, this advocacy is not framed in overtly "political" terms, emphasizing social justice and the need to transform the structures that exclude immigrants. Particularly, Brazilian evangelical Protestant churches in Broward County
are wary of openly challenging the current Republican administration, with
which they share a conservative social agenda. Their advocacy, then, is often
couched as a plea not to punish the like-minded Christians that make up their
congregations. For many of these Protestant congregations, religious identity
trumps immigrant identity, although sometimes the argument is made in evangelical circles that immigrants are bringing a type of Christianity that can
morally regenerate this country.[22] Thus, to provide amnesty to immigrants is to
advance the conservative Christian agenda in America. Whether this kind of
advocacy will translate into political influence and power is an open question.

Lived Religion, Identity, and Gender

The authors in this volume adopted the lived-religion approach to be able to
explore religious narratives and practices that were not directly connected with
visible congregations, since one of the likely characteristics of new destinations
is the relative absence of institutionalized religion. However, our study did not
simply substitute "religious practices in the streets and workplaces for what
goes on in churches"[23] in new destinations. We paid attention to the connections between congregations and lived religion as well as the in-between or
intermediate spaces. Particularly in the early stages of community formation,
when there are few support networks available, we found that congregations
often serve as quasi social service agencies, providing diverse forms of material
and moral support, ranging from English classes to legal assistance with immigration matters to meeting space for labor unions and other civic organizations
working on behalf of immigrants. By sponsoring activities like festivals, soccer
leagues, and family picnics, they also offer entertainment and catharsis in the
face of heavy work schedules and a hostile environment. Finally, by using the
native language—be it Spanish or Portuguese—and by preserving and re-enacting
the cultural and religious traditions of the societies of origin, congregations can
help immigrants carve out new spaces of livelihood, often transposing the landscapes of the homeland onto the new places of settlement.

Congregations can also provide "spaces of sociability" where church members can develop important civic skills and competences that can potentially be

translated into more community-oriented initiatives.[24] Our case studies found that congregations are especially important locations for immigrant women to gain human and social capital. For example, in chapter 9 we saw how Brazilian and Mexican immigrant women found opportunities to develop leadership skills through evangelical prayer groups and the Catholic marriage encounter movement. Nevertheless, our study also reveals that while some churches in new destinations have fulfilled a civic role, generally it has been somewhat limited. For example, in the Brazilian case, while some local church leaders have become more vocal in advocating on behalf of Brazilian immigrants, the civic skills developed in congregations have yet to generate the kind of leadership and organizations that have emerged in more traditional gateway cities. And in Jupiter and Immokalee it tends to be more established immigrants that have benefited most from their participation in churches and emerged as leaders in the community.

Whether churches will come to play a more civic-minded role depends to a large extent on the theologies and pastoral approaches they develop. In all three cases, we found that the religious field in new immigrant destinations is a highly contested terrain populated by a range of theological and pastoral currents. For example, in Catholic churches we found a growing Charismatic Renewal Movement operating alongside traditional popular Catholicism and liberationist approaches. Moreover, the Catholic Church shares the stage with evangelical churches espousing a gospel of health and wealth, Spiritist centers focusing on individual intellectual and moral development, and Afro-Brazilian religions that emphasize spiritual purification and growth. While the growth of more emotive, personalistic pastoral and theological currents may seem to undermine the civic and community-oriented potential of religious organizations, this is not necessarily the case. As we saw in chapter 9, traditional Catholicism, the Charismatic Renewal Movement, and Pentecostalism can all serve as "liberating raw material" for immigrant women, while not necessarily eradicating the conditions of female subordination. We found that immigrant women in these faith traditions were able to attain greater personal autonomy and independence.

Despite the importance of congregational life, our case studies in new destinations confirmed that congregations reach only a small minority of Latin American immigrants. Compared to more established immigrants, we found that recent immigrants are less likely to be members or frequent participants in congregational life. In part this is because the most recent immigrants lack the financial capital to pay for or participate in fiestas, the social capital to be invited, and the leisure time to spend in the first place. Many simply choose to practice their lived religion in the spaces between religious organizations, rather than through them—or to worship in intermediate spaces of prayer groups, where women, in particular, have access to equal treatment and can exercise their own religious authority and power, self esteem, and autonomy.

The importance of these intermediate spaces in dealing with the dislocations produced by migration and settlement in new destinations is evident in all three of our cases. Our survey data clearly shows that the overwhelming majority of immigrants feel most comfortable at home—even when sharing a trailer with eight to ten strangers. So, it should not be surprising that these spaces are the preferred locations for prayer groups and communal celebrations of popular devotions. While some of these intermediate spaces are "authorized" and supported by religious officials, sometimes they emerge at the margins of churches and can often be overlooked by congregational studies.

We found numerous examples of "believing without belonging,"[25] where immigrants "mix and match elements from different faiths rather than observe strict boundaries between traditions."[26] In the most extreme case, the great majority of Mexican and Guatemalan farmworkers in Immokalee find it nearly impossible to be involved in local congregational life due to the extremely heavy work schedules, their precarious legal status, and the need to move across the country following the various growing seasons. To the extent that migrant farmworkers in Immokalee practice their religion, they do so extra-institutionally, drawing from the rituals, narratives, and symbols of traditional popular Catholicism in an attempt to deal creatively with concrete existential predicaments. To capture these grassroots, embodied, everyday, and pragmatic dimensions of immigrant religion, we found the concept of lived religion particularly helpful.

The lived-religion approach proved especially fruitful in exploring how Mayan immigrants in Jupiter re-created images of home, drawing from religious resources ranging from embodied memories to material culture like marimbas, costumes, masks, and the icons of patron saints and of the Virgin Mary. The construction of home among Jacaltecos certainly passes through institutional Catholicism, as demonstrated by the fact that the fiesta begins with a solemn Mass. Nevertheless, home is religiously performed in the "secular" urban spaces of Jupiter, where Mayas literally transpose Jacaltenango through their procession and ritual dances. For a day, they sacralize streets to which, in everyday life, they only have access through their labor in construction or landscaping. These practices of carving extra-congregational religious and cultural spaces of being are precisely what we wanted to capture with the lived-religion approach. We believe that these practices gain great importance in new destinations, where immigrants are more likely to face isolation and outright hostility.

The Fiesta Maya in Jupiter can be understood as "the sacred theater of a community," through which different Maya groups in the town come together to enact and celebrate their collective identity. Robert Orsi uses this metaphor of sacred theater to characterize the feast of the Virgin of Mount Carmel among Italian immigrants in Harlem at the turn of the twentieth century. In this feast, "the streets became a stage and the people revealed themselves to themselves.

The immigrants' deepest values, their understandings of the truly human, their perceptions of the nature of reality were acted out; the hidden structures of power and authority were revealed."[27] In the case of the Maya in Jupiter, the fiesta tells us about their deep yearning and struggles to create a place to be, a place to be recognized as a community of human beings not just a faceless mass of "illegals." Indeed, the process of constructing images of home through the fiesta, music, soccer leagues, procession, and religious images and practices has helped the Jacaltecos to maintain a sense of identity and solidarity that translated over time into collective action. The process of organizing, mobilizing, and carrying out the fiesta sparked the formation of institutional linkages with the university, local churches, and nonprofits. Thus, the momentum generated through a public manifestation of lived religion (the fiesta) provided both the sense of efficacy and the set of networks and institutional linkages necessary for the Mayan community to launch what would ultimately become a successful campaign to create the El Sol Community Resource Center in Jupiter.

At the same time, by taking seriously the lived-religion school's emphasis on the lived reality of in-between spaces (between institutional religion, ritual, and everyday life), we were struck by the underlying ambiguities and tensions that characterize the lives of Jupiter's transnational migrants. Once again the fiesta provides an instructive example. The very sense of community and home that Jacaltecos savor in the fiesta cut precisely the other direction for the group of migrants from Totonicapán who were ultimately excluded from formal participation on stage. Despite attempts to imbue the fiesta with an ecumenical ethic, obvious tensions between religious groups also came to the fore. Thus, the very public nature of the fiesta exposed religious, ethnic, and cultural dividing lines that otherwise may remain hidden from view. The very ties that promote social capital and bond one group of migrants in solidarity may serve as a barrier to collaboration with the larger Mayan or immigrant community in general.

While we welcome the renewed interest in religion among immigration scholars, our case studies point to the clear structural and spatial obstacles to practicing religion or participating in congregational life and also raise important questions about the portability of religion. Our survey evidence from Immokalee and Jupiter demonstrates that popular religious practices, especially traditional Catholic devotions, are practiced with less frequency in the United States as compared to immigrants' communities of origin. In the case of Immokalee, many immigrants do not have their own personal spaces to construct home altars, hang religious images, or light candles to their preferred saints. Similarly, we found that the lack of access to public spaces inhibited immigrants from organizing *fiestas patronales* that are so important to building a sense of place. Even in Jupiter, where Guatemalan immigrants have succeeded in organizing the Fiesta Maya on an annual basis, their temporary appropriation of the streets to honor the Virgin of Candelaria is fleeting at best.

The focus on new destinations, thus, not only demonstrates the creativity of immigrants in sustaining religious lives linked to but extending beyond congregations, but also shows the fragility of religious experiences and practices in precarious existential contexts. Here the experience of Mexicans and Guatemalans parallels those of older immigrant waves, such as Irish Catholics, who, particularly following the potato famine in the late 1840s, came to American cities with meager resources to reconstitute their religious life. For them, as for Guatemalans and Mexicans, a combination of religious institutions, such as schools and fraternities, and popular devotions proved crucial in forging a viable defensive identity.[28] However, the Irish could rely on the centralizing structure of the parish, which in the mid-1800s was undergoing transcontinental renewal as part of a process of Romanization. In contrast, as the New Paradigm in the sociology of religion rightly posits (see chapter 1), Mexicans and Guatemalans today face highly pluralistic religious markets with no hegemonic institutional morphology. Rather, this market is populated by shifting symbols, practices, and forms of organization that circulate and cross-fertilize often instantaneously through global, transnational, and diasporic networks.[29]

In contrast to Guatemalan and Mexican immigrants, Brazilian immigrants, though they arrived in South Florida later, enjoy certain social advantages—higher educational and social status—that tend to favor increased religious participation in the receiving community. Although we cannot draw comparative findings from the Brazilian survey data, our qualitative interviews revealed that many Brazilian immigrants, especially women, intensify their religious activities in the United States. Religious participation provides them an important source of support, solidarity, and self-improvement in the face of a hostile world.

Nevertheless, as Vásquez's chapter shows, even Brazilians struggle to extend their religious practices beyond the safe and intimate spaces of home. Robert Orsi has documented the centrality of home in religious life for earlier immigrant groups. Facing "a poor, densely populated, and physically deteriorating place, troubled by crime and juvenile delinquency," Italian immigrants in East Harlem carved "a place that people came to love, a place where . . . [they] created a community life."[30] They did so by relying on the "domus," a complex world of reciprocal duties and exchanges anchored on the family and home. Brazilians, too, transpose memories, desires, moral maps, and emotional attachments associated with home into the decentered spaces of Broward County, building and extending personal networks that often operate transnationally. However, in contrast to Italians in East Harlem in the late 1880s, Brazilians today cannot as readily tap into the extended family ties that were at the heart of the domus in southern Italy at the turn of the twentieth century. Rapid urbanization and globalization have drastically transformed traditional notions of family and home in Brazil. And when Brazilians come to Pompano Beach and Deerfield Beach, they face geographical dispersion, not the heavily populated tenements that Italian immigrants in New York encountered. In the absence of a physically circumscribed neighborhood, of public spaces not subject to the logic of the automobile, the building of sociability is a more daunting task.

By comparing Mexicans in Immokalee, Guatemalans in Jupiter, and Brazilians in Broward County with Irish and Italian Catholics in New York, we want to underline the fact that in order to understand the specificities of new destinations we need to compare them with "old" migrations. The "newness" of nontraditional destinations can only be assessed through an analysis of historical continuities and ruptures.[31] Such a comparative analysis suggests that, in exploring new destinations, we must not assume that religion will always play a prominent role in the lives of immigrants. While we need to look beyond visible congregational expressions in order to capture the creative ways in which religion is lived existentially amid strange and hostile territories, we also must avoid focusing exclusively on the positive contributions religion can make to the migration process.

In taking seriously the complexity and ambiguity of religion, we can see that it can sometimes empower immigrants, but not always.[32] As José Cláudio Souza Alves discusses in chapter 6, religious networks can facilitate the formation of collective identity and solidarity among Brazilian immigrants, but these networks often serve as the moral and spiritual infrastructure for an immigrant mode of production that extracts surplus from undocumented immigrants. Souza Alves's claim resonates with the experiences of other recent immigrants groups. For instance, Kenneth Guest has observed a similar ambivalent role for religious organizations among Chinese immigrants from Fujian Province (Fuzhounese) in New York City. "Fuzhounese religious communities are central sites for constructing and reconstructing networks of ethnic solidarity and accessing financial and social capital as immigrants make their way along an often precarious journey. At the same time, this isolated ethnic enclave [the Chinatown in which immigrants settle with the help of religious communities] is a trap for many Fuzhounese who, marginalized by language, culture, and class from both the mainstream U.S. economy and the Chinatown elites, have no way to escape."[33]

The practice of exploiting the newly arrived using immigrant networks built on trust (such as kinship-based and religious organizations) is, of course, not new. Chinese immigrants after the California gold rush of 1849 relied heavily on familial networks to borrow the money necessary to travel to the United States, often having to pay it back at a very high interest rate.[34] Similar dynamics of inter-ethnic exploitation and competition have been documented by Sarah Mahler and Cecilia Menjívar among Salvadoran immigrants.[35] What is different for new destinations today is the heightened vulnerability of immigrants, particularly those who are undocumented, due to the new capitalist regime of production. More specifically, the transportation and communication technologies associated with this regime have allowed the formation of a vast and lucrative transnational economy of smuggling that is light years beyond the activities of your average local *coyote*.[36] In fact, localized smuggling activities that operate through networks of relatives, friends, and members of the same religious or ethnic group are increasingly colonized by sophisticated and impersonal human trafficking syndicates, further disempowering immigrants. While we did not find any cases of religious organizations being involved in this economy, Souza Alves's work on the interaction between religious and business networks among Brazilians points to the need to examine more carefully the explicit and indirect links between religion and economics in new destinations.

In sum, religious congregations provide vital "spaces of sociability" for some immigrants but not for most. Instead, intermediate spaces between private and public spheres appear to be at least as significant for religious practice. Public expressions of popular religion, such as *fiestas patronales*, take place in some new destinations but often face important spatial obstacles in others. Moreover, while religion may be "the ultimate border crosser,"[37] the portability of religion should not be simply assumed given the mobile livelihoods of some immigrants. And finally, although transnational fiestas like the Fiesta Maya provide immigrants with the opportunity to reaffirm their ethnic identity and strengthen transnational connections, they also celebrate "what is not"—the family members who are absent, the legal status that is out of reach, the improbability of returning home. In this sense, religion is as much about opening wounds as it is about healing.[38]

Looking Ahead

When we began research, we initially envisioned a study divided into two phases: the first one would map out the configuration of Latino communities in Florida, characterizing their religious beliefs, practices, and institutions. The second phase would trace the transnational civic, cultural, and religious networks that these communities maintain with their countries of origin. During the course of the research we discovered that changes in the post-9/11 (September 11, 2001) immigration climate, together with the fact that these communities are either too nascent or too economically and socially vulnerable, have made it difficult for them to build sustained and intensive transnational ties. We found that most immigrants prefer to remain invisible or to "hunker down" in ethnic enclaves rather than engage in organized collective action. In fact, the key challenge facing the Latino immigrants we studied has shifted toward securing their survival in the United States in what has become an increasingly hostile environment. This was exemplified by the conflict around the creation of a labor center in Jupiter. As religious leaders and nonprofits worked with town staff to regularize the employment of day-laborers through the creation of an employment and resource center, anti-immigrant groups (including the Federation for American Immigration Reform, FAIR) came in to mobilize opposition among the Euro-American population. In the process, all kinds of derogatory stereotypes about Latinos, and immigrants in general, came to the fore, fueling misunderstandings and tensions.

In response to these types of conflicts, it makes sense that future research in non-conventional sites of migration should shift the focus from transnationalism per se to the "politics of encounter," the inter-ethnic, inter-racial, and inter-faith tensions and relations between immigrants and natives and among immigrant groups settling in the same spaces. This is not to suggest that we abandon a transnational framework that is attentive to the multiple relations that Latino immigrants maintain with their societies of origin. In fact, our study demonstrates that the level of transnationalism is strongly conditioned by the context of reception of particular immigrant groups. Conversely, as the Guatemalan case highlights, for immigrants in new destinations, transnational networks and social remittances might be the go-to resources to build meaningful places to be in the face of precarious and hostile local conditions in the United States. However, in addition to focusing on the local and translocal world views and practices of immigrants, we need to pay increasing attention to the perceptions, attitudes, and behaviors that the broader communities of reception express vis-à-vis Latino immigrants. In particular, we need to explore how Euro-Americans and African Americans see Latino immigrants and how Latino immigrants respond to these perceptions with their own forms of self-identification and strategic representations of the native "others." Moreover, we need to know what, if anything, religion contributes to these processes of identity construction.

Our study showed that religious narratives and institutions are central to these processes of identity formation among Latinos and that religion can be both part of the problem and part of the solution. Thus, looking ahead, it is important to continue the focus on lived religion but concentrate more on the roles religion and culture play in generating, mediating, and resolving inter-group conflicts. Given the highly polarized debates about immigration at the national and local levels, we need to look for models of religious and civic organization that have been successful in bridging divisions and fostering communication and even multiracial cross-cultural alliances. This effort takes on even greater importance in the face of a deteriorating economy, especially in the hard-hit housing, construction, and service sectors, which provide significant employment opportunities to Latin American immigrants.

In the post-9/11 climate, the economic recession is likely to fuel even more immigrant scapegoating and inter-ethnic strife. Moreover, with the continued failure of the federal government to pass rational, comprehensive, balanced, and humane immigration reform, local conflicts are likely to intensify, particularly in states like Georgia, North Carolina, Arkansas, Oklahoma, and Nebraska, which have only recently experienced substantial immigration from Latin America. Indeed, many cities and towns in these states have sought to deal unilaterally with the problem of undocumented immigration by passing a host of draconian ordinances that limit the number of tenants that can live in a housing unit, deny driver's licenses to those who do not have the proper documentation, or penalize employers who hire unauthorized workers.[39] The net effect of these ordinances has been to generate great anxiety among already precarious immigrant "communities," forcing them further into the shadows and encouraging reliance on submerged transnational networks to support the arduous process of settlement. This appeal to transnationalism, in turn, further inflames the nativist sentiments of U.S.-born local populations.

Despite this ominous scenario, the success of El Sol Resource Center in Jupiter, Florida, shows that along with conflict come promising initiatives that point to the emergence of what Putnam calls a more "capacious sense of 'we,' a reconstruction of diversity that does not bleach out ethnic specificities, but creates overarching identities that ensure that those specificities do not trigger the allergic, 'hunker down' reaction."[40] A focus on new destinations can bring these models into the national debate, thus helping to counteract the vociferous exclusionary and nativist rhetoric that is at odds with the increasing diversity of American society and its deeper engagement with globalization.

NOTES

1. Maxine Margolis, *Little Brazil: An Ethnography of Brazilian Immigrants in New York City* (Princeton: Princeton University Press, 1994).

2. Peggy Levitt and Nina Glick Schiller, "Conceptualizing Simultaneity: A Transnational Social Field Perspective on Society," *International Migration Review* 38 (2004): 1010–1011.

3. Peggy Levitt and Mary C. Waters, introduction to *The Changing Face of Home: The Transnational Lives of the Second Generation*, ed. Peggy Levitt and Mary C. Waters (New York: Russell Sage Foundation, 2002), 11.

4. Thomas Faist, "Transnationalization in International Migration: Implications for the Study of Citizenship and Culture," *Ethnic and Racial Studies* 23, no. 2 (2000): 89–222.

5. Peggy Levitt, *The Transnational Villagers* (Berkeley: University of California Press, 2001). This lack of transnational community in the case of Brazilians might be a function of the newness of the settlement. The great diversity of Brazilian migration to the county, especially in terms of region of origin and class, and the spatial dispersion in Broward County are also contributing factors.

6. For an example of the limited psychological literature addressing these questions see Celia J. Falicof, "Working with Transnational Immigrants: Expanding Meanings of Family, Community, and Culture," *Family Process* 46, no. 2 (June 2007): 157–171.

7. When migrants make plans to return home, they frequently do so secretly to avoid becoming the victims of robbery in Guatemala. As the number of deported and returning migrants has soared over the past two years, the returnees have become targets of organized crime not only in the capital but also in the outlying areas of Huehuetenango.

8. For an excellent example of this process see Sarah Mahler, "Transnational Relationships: The Struggle to Communicate across Borders," *Identities* 7, no. 4 (2001): 583–619.

9. Robert Orsi, *The Madonna of 115th Street: Faith and Community in Italian Harlem, 1880–1950* (New Haven: Yale University Press, 1985), xviii.

10. Luin Goldring defines migrant-led transnationalism as "migrant-initiated practices and institutions that foster transnational social spaces." Luin Goldring, "The Mexican State and Transmigrant Organizations: Negotiating the Boundaries of Membership and Participation," *Latin American Research Review* 37 (2002): 57.

11. See Alejandro Portes and Alex Stepick, *City on the Edge: The Transformation of Miami* (Berkeley: University of California Press, 1993).

12. Peggy Levitt, "You Know, Abraham Was Really the First Immigrant: Religion and Transnational Migration," *International Immigration Review* 37 (2003): 847–873.

13. Manuel Castells, *The Power of Identity* (Oxford: Blackwell, 1997).

14. Roger Rouse, "Thinking through Transnationalism: Notes on the Cultural Politics of Class Relations in Contemporary United States," *Public Culture* 7 (1995): 370.

15. Religious and business networks have played prominent roles in other immigrant communities as well. Similarly, these networks can produce highly exploitative relations between immigrants. For a discussion of this phenomenon among Salvadoran immigrants in Long Island, see Sarah Mahler, *American Dreaming: Immigrant Life at the Margins* (Princeton, NJ: Princeton University Press, 1995).

16. Robert Putnam, "E Pluribus Unum: Diversity and Community in the Twenty-first Century," *Scandinavian Political Studies* 30 (2007): 137–174.

17. Daniel Levine and David Stoll, "Bridging the Gap between Empowerment and Power in Latin America," in *Transnational Religion and Fading States*, ed. Susanne Rudolph and James Piscatori, 63–103 (Boulder: Westview Press, 1997).

18. Doug McAdam, *Political Process and the Development of Black Insurgency, 1930–1970* (Chicago: University of Chicago Press, 1982). Also see Charles Tilly, *From Mobilization to Revolution* (Reading, MA: Addison-Wesley, 1978).

19. See David A. Snow, "Frame Alignment Processes, Micromobilization, and Movement Participation," *American Sociological Review* 51 (August 1986): 464–481; and David A. Snow and Robert D. Benford, "Ideology, Frame Resonance, and Participant Mobilization," in *International Social Movements Research* (Greenwich: JAI Press, 1988), I:197–217.

20. McAdam, *Political Process*. For a review of some of this literature, also see Mayer N. Zald, "Theological Crucibles: Social Movements in and of Religion," *Review of Religious Research* 23 (1982): 4.

21. On resource mobilization see John D. McCarthy and Mayer N. Zald, "Resource Mobilization and Social Movements: A Partial Theory," *American Journal of Sociology* 82 (May 1977): 1212–1239; Anthony Oberschall, *Social Conflict and Social Movements* (New York: Prentice Hall, 1973).

22. Charlie Savage, "Hispanic Evangelical Offering GOP a Bridge to the Future," *Boston Globe*, March 6, 2006, A3. We found the same views expressed by Pentecostals in Jupiter. At the very least, these findings suggest the need for further research on the question of whether evangelical Protestant immigrants are less transnational and more "assimilated" than other immigrants.

23. Robert Orsi, "Everyday Miracles: The Study of Lived Religion," in *Lived Religion in America*, ed. David Hall (Princeton: Princeton University Press, 1997), 9.

24. See Nancy Ammerman, *Congregation and Community* (New Brunswick, NJ: Rutgers University Press 1997); and Sidney Verba, Kay Lehman Schlozman, and Henry E. Brady,

Voice and Equality: Civic Voluntarism in American Politics (Cambridge, MA: Harvard University, 1995).

25. This is the subtitle of Grace Davie's book on religion in Britain during the postwar period. Grace Davie, *Religion in Britain since 1945: Believing without Belonging* (Oxford: Blackwell, 1994).

26. Peggy Levitt, *God Needs No Passport: Immigrants and the Changing American Religious Landscape* (New York: New Press, 2007), 168.

27. Orsi, *The Madonna of 115th Street, xxii–xxiii.*

28. Jay Dolan, *The Immigrant Church: New York's Irish and German Catholics, 1815–1865* (Notre Dame: University of Notre Dame Press, 1983).

29. Manuel A. Vásquez, "Studying Mobile Religions: A Networks Approach," *Method and Theory in the Study of Religion* 20, no. 2 (2008): 151–184.

30. Orsi, *The Madonna of 115th Street,* 48.

31. Manuel A. Vásquez, Chad Seales, and Marie Friedmann Marquardt, "New Latino Destinations," in *Latinos/as in the United States: Changing the Face of America*, ed. Havidán Rodríguez, Rogelio Sáenz, and Cecilia Menjívar, 19–35 (New York: Springer, 2007).

32. As Robert Orsi reminds us, scholars of lived religion would do well to take seriously the religious practice and imagination of the poorest and most marginalized immigrants. At the same time, in our propensity to relate stories of successful immigrant adaptation, we must be careful not to romanticize the empowerment of poor immigrants by vesting them with the agency formerly sought in the working class or, more recently, the subaltern subject. Robert Orsi, "How Do We Study the Lived Religion of Men and Women Who Don't Have the Walls to Hang Their Religious Images On?" (paper presented at the Conference on Latinos in Florida: Lived Religion, Space, and Power, Antigua, Guatemala, December 9–11, 2005).

33. Kenneth J. Guest, "Religion and Transnational Migration in the New Chinatown," in *Immigrant Faiths: Transforming Religious Life in America*, ed. Karen I. Leonard et al. (Walnut Creek, CA: AltaMira Press, 2005), 145.

34. Roger Daniels, *Coming to America: A History of Immigration and Ethnicity in American Life* (New York: Perennial, 2002), 241.

35. Mahler, *American Dreaming*; Cecilia Menjívar, *Fragmented Ties: Salvadoran Immigrant Networks in America* (Berkeley: University of California Press, 2000).

36. See David Kyle and Rey Koslowski, eds., *Global Human Smuggling: Comparative Perspectives* (Baltimore: Johns Hopkins University Press, 2001).

37. Levitt, *God Needs No Passport*, 12.

38. Orsi, "How Do We Study."

39. Ordinances directly targeting undocumented immigrants have surfaced in places as diverse as Avon Park, Florida; Hazleton, Pennsylvania; Arcadia, Wisconsin; Farmingville, New York; and Riverside, New Jersey. See David Fried, "Local Illegal Immigration Laws Draw a Diverse Group of Cities, *NC Times*, September 2, 2006, http://www.nctimes.com/articles/2006/09/03/news/top_stories/21_40_499_2_06.txt (accessed March 12, 2008).

40. Putnam, "E Pluribus Unum," 164.

CONTRIBUTORS

PATRICIA FORTUNY LORET DE MOLA is a researcher in the Center of Research and Advanced Sciences in Social Anthropology (CIESAS)–Peninsular in Mérida, Mexico. She received her PhD in social anthropology from the University College London in 1995. Since the 1980s, she has studied religious minorities such as evangelicals, Mormons, and Jehovah's Witnesses in Mexico. She has published a book on religious change, *Creyentes y Creencias en Guadalajara* (2000), and has done research among Mexican immigrants in the United States who belong to an important Mexican Pentecostal church. She has published numerous articles on diverse topics related to religion in Mexico and, most recently, among Mexican immigrants in the United States.

CAROL GIRÓN SOLÓRZANO received her Licenciatura in International Relations from the Universidad de San Carlos de Guatemala and is currently completing a master's in human rights at the Universidad Rafael Landívar de Guatemala. Previously, she was a researcher for the Migration Program of FLACSO Guatemala (2000–2004). Currently, she is a founding member and researcher for the Instituto Centroamericano de Estudios Sociales y Desarrollo (INCEDES), which initiated its activities in 2005.

SILVIA IRENE PALMA studied clinical psychology at the Universidad Rafael Landívar de Guatemala (1979–1985) and completed a master's in social psychology at the UNAM–México (1989–1992) and a master's in social development at the Universidad del Valle de Guatemala (2000–2001). She is currently pursuing a PhD in sociology at the Universidad Pontifícia de Salamanca/Programa Guatemala. She was coordinator of the Migration Program for FLACSO Guatemala (1999–2005). Since February 2005, she is the executive director of the Instituto Centroamericano de Estudios Sociales y Desarrollo (INCEDES). She has numerous publications related to the issue of international migration in Guatemala, Mexico, and the United States.

LÚCIA RIBEIRO received her master's in sociology (FLACSO-Chile, 1970) and pursued doctoral studies in sociology (Mexico City, Mexico, 1977). She worked as a researcher, in the areas of sexuality, reproduction, and religion in different organizations in Rio de Janeiro. Since 2000, she is a member of the staff of ISER/ASSESSORIA (Rio de Janeiro). She is the author of several books, including *Entre o desejo e o mistério: Novos caminhos da sexualidade* (1992), *Entre (in)certezas e contradições: Práticas reprodutivas entre mulheres das Comunidades Eclesiais de Base da Igreja Católica* (1997), and *Sexualidade e reprodução: O que os padres dizem e o que deixam de dizer* (2001). She recently coauthored, with Leonardo Boff, *Masculino/Feminino: Experiências vividas* (2007).

MIRIAN SOLÍS LIZAMA is a master's student in regional development at the Colegio de la Frontera Norte. She received her Licenciatura in anthropological sciences with a specialization in social anthropology from the Universidad Autónoma de Yucatán. She has participated in a number of research projects focused on international migration, including Yucatecos en el Norte, funded by CONACyT; the Proyecto Tunkás, supported by the Ford Foundation; and Latino Immigrants in South Florida: Lived Religion, Space, and Power, coordinated by the University of Florida.

JOSÉ CLAÚDIO SOUZA ALVES is a professor of sociology and dean of Extension Programs for the Universidade Federal Rural do Rio de Janeiro. He received his PhD in sociology from the Universidade de São Paulo. He is the author of *Dos Barões ao Extermínio: Uma História da Violência na Baixada Fluminense*.

TIMOTHY J. STEIGENGA is an associate professor of political science at the Wilkes Honors College of Florida Atlantic University. He received his PhD from the University of North Carolina in Chapel Hill. He is the author or editor of four books and numerous other publications on religion, politics, and immigration, including *Conversion of a Continent: Contemporary Religious Change in Latin America* (2007), *Resurgent Voices in Latin America: Indigenous Peoples, Political Mobilization, and Religious Change* (2004), and *The Politics of the Spirit: The Political Implications of Pentecostalized Religion in Costa Rica and Guatemala* (2001). In 2006, he was honored to serve for six months in Guatemala as a Fulbright Visiting Scholar.

MANUEL A. VÁSQUEZ is an associate professor of religion and co-director of the Latin American Immigrants in the New South Project at the University of Florida. He is author of *The Brazilian Popular Church and the Crisis of Modernity* (1998) and coauthor of *Globalizing the Sacred: Religion across the Americas* (2003). He has also coedited *Christianity, Social Change, and Globalization in the Americas* (2001) and *Immigrant Faiths: Transforming Religious Life in America* (2005).

PHILIP J. WILLIAMS is a professor of political science and co-director of the Latin American Immigrants in the New South Project at the University of

Florida. He is author of *The Catholic Church and Politics in Nicaragua and Costa Rica* (1989) and coauthor of *Militarization and Demilitarization in El Salvador's Transition to Democracy* (1997). He has also coedited *Christianity, Social Change, and Globalization in the Americas* (2001) and published numerous articles in journals such as *Comparative Politics, Journal of Church and State, Journal of Latin American Studies, Journal for the Scientific Study of Religion*, and *Latino Studies*.

INDEX

Italicized page numbers refer to tables.

Abacoa (Jupiter, Fla.), 75, 113–115, 154, 157, 160–161
African Americans, 21, 41, 109, 223
African-based religions, 139–141, 145–146, 201, 208n36, 217
agricultural economy, 3–5, 21, 213–214, 218; and collective mobilization, 117–120, 123; and concept of family in Jupiter, 65; and gender, 191, 193–194, 196–198, 200, 203, 205, 207n14; in Immokalee vs. Jupiter, 104–105, 109; and lived religion in Immokalee, 172–178, 180–184; and solidarities in Immokalee, 83, 86–87, 92–94, 96n3, 97n11, 99n32
Al-Ali, Nadje, 161
alcohol use. *See* drinking; substance abuse
aldeas, 20, 166
Ammerman, Nancy, 175
amnesty, 134–135, 216
Anglo-Americans, 20, 108–109, 123, 154–155. *See also* Euro-Americans
anomie, 11, 27n82, 54–55n31, 82
anti-immigrant climate, 2, 10, 17, 51, 109, 121, 124, 134, 222–223. *See also* hostile environments
Appadurai, Arjun, 9, 25n47, 81, 96n7
Assemblies of God, 116, 133–135, 154, 172–173, 176–177, 187n18, 202
assimilation, 27n84, 87, 97n17, 122, 124, 161, 213–214, 225n22
associational life, 11, 37–38, 41–43, 109–110, 131
asylum seekers. *See* refugees/asylum seekers
Augé, Marc, 184–185
autonomy, personal, 58, 64, 77, 142, 164; and gender, 191–194, 199, 201, 205, 207n14, 217
Avila, Ernestine, 190

Baiano Catholics, 201, 208n35
baptisms, 91–92, 94–95, 172, 176, 197
Baptist Church, 47, 52, 133–135, 154, 177, 200, 215
Basch, Linda, 5, 38–39
base communities, 137, 203. *See also* Ecclesial Base Communities (CEBs)

"believing without belonging," 178, 188n30, 200, 208n31, 218, 226n25
Benedict XVI, Pope, 144
Benford, Robert, 126n28
Benitez, Lucas, 119, 173
Berger, Oscar, 74, 79n24, 114, 158
Berkowitz, S. D., 35
Bethel Assembly of God Church (Immokalee, Fla.), 172–173, 176–177, 187n18, 202
bifocality, 5, 39, 135, 210
bonding social capital, 214–215; and collective mobilization, 116, 119, 124, 126n24; and concept of family in Jupiter, 76; and lived religion in Immokalee, 173, 175; and Otomí immigrants in Immokalee, 13, 81, 92, 119
Booth, John, 14
Bourdieu, Pierre, 12, 49, 187n16
Bourne, Randolph, 4
Bowling Alone (Putnam), 13
boycotts, 118–120, 124, 127nn30,31, 214, 216
Brady, Henry, 175
Brazilian Apostolate, 136–137
Brazilian Baptist Church, 52, 134
Brazilian Catholic Mission of South Florida, 136
Brazilian Conference of Catholic Bishops (CNBB), 52
Brazilian immigrants, 1, 4, 11, 18–22, 209–210, 212, 214–217, 220–222, 224n5; and gender, 190–192, 194–196, 198–201, 203–206, 207n16, 208nn35,45; and immigrant regime of production, 128–147; and interpersonal networks, 33–52, 53n6, 54n21
Brazilian Mission of South Florida, 137
bridging social capital, 13, 211, 214–215; and collective mobilization, 116, 118, 124, 127n43; and concept of family in Jupiter, 58, 76; and lived religion in Immokalee, 175, 187n26
Briz, Jorge, 79n24, 114, 158
Broward County (Fla.), 21, 33–52, 53nn6,7, 128–147, 182, 210, 214, 216, 220–221, 224n5
Brown, Karen McCarthy, 180
brujo (traditional healer), 83–84, 95
Burawoy, Michael, 129
Burns, Allan, 155–156, 161–162

Since the beginning of the eighteenth century the philosophy of art has been engaged in the project of finding out what the fine arts might have in common, and thus how they might be defined. Peter Kivy's purpose in this very accessible and lucid book is to trace the history of that enterprise and then to argue that the definitional project has been unsuccessful, with absolute music as the continual stumbling block. He offers what he believes is a fruitful change of strategy: instead of undertaking an obsessive quest for sameness, let us explore the differences among the arts. He presents five case studies of such differences, three from literature, two from music.

With its combination of historical and analytic approaches this book will appeal to a wide range of readers in philosophy, literary studies, and music, as well as to nonacademic readers with an interest in the arts. Its vivid style requires no technical knowledge of music on the part of the reader.

Philosophies of Arts

Philosophies of Arts
An Essay in Differences

PETER KIVY

CAMBRIDGE
UNIVERSITY PRESS

PUBLISHED BY THE PRESS SYNDICATE OF THE UNIVERSITY OF CAMBRIDGE
The Pitt Building, Trumpington Street, Cambridge CB2 1RP, United Kingdom

CAMBRIDGE UNIVERSITY PRESS
The Edinburgh Building, Cambridge CB2 2RU, United Kingdom
40 West 20th Street, New York, NY 10011-4211, USA
10 Stamford Road, Oakleigh, Melbourne 3166, Australia

First published 1997

Printed in the United States of America

Typeset in Palatino

Library of Congress Cataloging-in-Publication Data
Kivy, Peter.
Philosophies of arts : an essay in differences / Peter Kivy.
p.   cm.
Includes bibliographical references.
ISBN 0-521-59178-3 (hardback). – ISBN 0-521-59829-X (paperback)
1. Arts – Philosophy.   2. Aesthetics, Modern.   3. Arts – Philosophy –
History.   I. Title.
BH39.K575   1997
700'.1 – dc21
96-37698
CIP

*A catalog record for this book is available from
the British Library.*

ISBN 0-521-59178-3 hardback
ISBN 0-521-59829-X paperback

For Frank Sibley,
who showed me the way

Now from hence may be seen, how these Arts *agree*, and how they *differ*.

James Harris (1744)

Contents

Preface

In the fall of 1992 I was privileged to deliver the Presidential Address to the American Society for Aesthetics on the occasion of its fiftieth anniversary. The event called, I thought, for some stock taking and perhaps something in the way of a suggestion, at least, of one direction the philosophy of art might take in the coming years. For I thought we were at a point where an alternative to the single-minded pursuit of art's "definition" was open, and beckoning.

I saw my task in that lecture as twofold: to try to show how we had come to the place we were at in Anglo-American aesthetics, which might well be called the period of Danto, without exaggerating that philosopher's importance to the discipline; and to try to mark out, by precept and example, another direction that some of us, at least, might take: the direction of "differences."

In the speaker's allotted fifty-minute hour I could present only a historical sketch and two minute "case studies" in "differences." But the project continued to possess me. The result is the present monograph: an attempt to trace in more detail the theoretical pathway that has led from the origination of the task of defining the work of art, in the eighteenth century, to the present state of affairs in which that task still seems to dominate discussion and, so it seems to me, to discourage philosophers from the equally interesting task of studying the arts in their particularity.

The organization of the volume is fairly straightforward. In the first two chapters I give an account of how I see the history of aesthetic theory from Hutcheson to Danto, in its attempt to define the "modern system of the arts," with absolute music as the litmus test of success or failure. Chapters 3 through 7 provide case studies in literature and music as an antidote to the obsessive search for what is common to the arts: they provide, that is, "differences," the "philosophies of arts," as opposed to the philosophy of art, that my title is supposed to suggest.

In no way am I urging, on philosophical grounds or any other, that the traditional task of defining the work of art is either impossible or exhausted as a philosophical enterprise. Nor am I recommending that it be given up for any other reason. What I am recommending, or gently suggesting, perhaps, is that at least some of us give it a rest and try to study the arts, *as philosophers,* in their differences rather than in their sameness: that alongside the philosophy of art we have philosophies of arts. Many of my colleagues in the profession may not be by nature or learning so inclined. Those who are I hope will join me in a task that is not so much new as new to these times. It is a task that deserves to be revived to the enrichment and diversification of the discipline.

I am indebted to a number of people who were immeasurably helpful to me in producing the final manuscript of this book. Stephen Davies and Richard Eldridge read the entire manuscript, and provided valuable and searching criticism. Professor Eldridge motivated me to include a whole new chapter on truth in fiction, which I had been working on as a lecture and an article. And I also tried to respond to his worries over my avoiding any discussion of the value component in the concept of poetry. I tried to answer a number of objections Professor Davies made with regard to my treatment of Jerrold Levinson on musical profundity, the theory of musical value sketched in the final chapter, and various other points.

But some of Eldridge's and Davies' comments and criticism I had to let alone, not because they were off the mark, but, to the contrary, because they raised such broad issues that they could not be treated in short responses. Rather, such issues will have to be addressed at length as the discussion develops (or I hope develops) after the publication of my book. In any event,

Messrs. Davies and Eldridge are responsible for numerous improvements in my text and, of course, for none of its remaining faults.

My colleague and friend Laurent Stern was kind enough to accede to my request to read, on very short notice, the new chapter (Chapter 5) on truth in fiction. I am most grateful for his help in that regard and absolve him from complicity in its remaining weaknesses.

I would also like to thank Terrence Moore of Cambridge University Press, who has, for the past few years, been a constant source of encouragement to me in my work. He has eased my manuscript through the intricate maze that leads from a gleam in the author's eye to a real book one can hold in one's hand. I greatly appreciate his help and support.

This book is dedicated to the late Frank Sibley. Alas, he died before he could know that I had done so. It is a pitifully inadequate tribute in comparison with the contribution he made to the profession, and to my work.

Chapter 1

How We Got Here, and Why

§1 The most widely and persistently pursued problem in aesthetics, or the philosophy of art, is the problem of stating what it is to be a "work of art," what it is to be "art." It is sometimes called the problem of *defining* "art."

This problem was bequeathed to philosophy by eighteenth-century philosophers and critical theorists. It is the result of certain crucial changes in our attitude toward what we now call "the fine arts" that occurred in the age of the Enlightenment. These changes are dealt with and explained in what might be called the "standard account" of the matter. It is an account generally accepted by philosophers of art and intellectual historians, including myself. I have not come to quarrel with the standard account. But I do have a quarrel with the major outcome of things, as the standard account understands them. I have a quarrel with the task that was bequeathed us, of stating what it is to be "art." But before I can quarrel I must first present the standard account – at least my version of it.

§2 Certain things transpired in the eighteenth century to alter, in very important ways, how we think about and experience works of the fine arts, some of them philosophical or in some other way theoretical, others "institutional" (for want of a better word). There is no particular order in which they ought to be listed, for they are not a chronological series of causes and effects. Rather, they must be thought of as an interrelated, reciprocal system of causes and effects, all operating simultaneously. The following are the philosophical, theoretical, and institutional

1

"happenings" I have in mind, listed in an almost completely arbitrary order:

1. The coming into being of the branch of philosophy known as "aesthetics"
2. The forming of what Paul O. Kristeller has denominated "the modern system of the arts"[1]
3. The evolution, in various forms, of what has come to be called, after Kant, the "aesthetic attitude," or the "attitude of aesthetic disinterestedness"[2]
4. The establishment of the fine arts museum, the concert hall, and the institution of the public concert
5. The rise of instrumental music into an equality with vocal music, both as an occupation for composers and as a focal point for audience interest

§3 When I took my first courses in philosophy, I was told in more than one of them that there were five branches of the discipline: logic, metaphysics, epistemology, ethics, and aesthetics. The division seemed to me etched in marble. But as most philosophers, and all philosophers of art, know, such a division of labor would have been unthinkable before the middle journey of the eighteenth century. In particular, there was nothing that was, or that could have been called, the autonomous philosophical discipline of aesthetics (or philosophy of art).

This is not to say, of course, that what we call the philosophy of art, or aesthetics, was not practiced until 1746. As is well known, Plato and Aristotle spoke eloquently, and with a philosophical voice, of poetry and painting and something we translate as "music." They raised clearly philosophical questions about these activities and obviously thought they were in some sense related to one another.

But even so cautious a statement about what Plato and Aristotle were doing as this one must be tempered with more than a grain of salt. For Plato, it is clear from the *Ion,* thought that poetry was radically different from both painting and sculpture, in an absolutely crucial way, since the whole point of the dialogue between Socrates and the rhapsode is that epic and lyric poetry, like divination, come from the god, not from "art," and two of the "arts" that can be mastered, and hence do not come from the god, are painting and sculpture, along with such other "arts" as generalship, navigation, and driving a chariot. Thus "there is an art of painting as a whole," but "all the good epic poets utter all those fine poems not from art but as inspired and possessed, and the good lyric poets likewise. . . ."[3] So even in acknowledging that Plato discussed some of the things philosophically that we call the fine arts, it is a mistake to think he was engaging in *the* philosophy of art as we think of it. He simply did not have the subject matter, namely our "modern system of the arts," to mark out the discipline and, indeed, did not even apparently think of our "arts" of poetry, painting, and sculpture as the same in all crucial respects, witness the separation of the former from the two latter vis-à-vis the sources of creation.

The same caution must be exercised in our reading of what Plato and Aristotle said about "music," since it is unclear what they were really talking about – certainly not "absolute music" in the nineteenth-century sense. And, indeed, the same caution must be expressed in regard to what philosophers (or any one else) said about music in the High Renaissance, where we do know what the music sounded like. For it was the "science" rather than (in our sense) the "art" of music that was the subject.[4]

Again, it would be a mistake to think that philosophical questions concerning the arts were not discussed in the Middle Ages and Renaissance. It is clear that Medieval "aesthetics" was not solely expressed in theological terms, as is sometimes thought, but "naturalistically" as well;[5] and although the Renaissance did not yet possess either the modern system or the discipline of "aesthetics" to go with it, it was the cauldron in which they both were brewing.[6] In both periods people were philosophizing about beauty and the "arts."

Without the modern system there could not be *the* philosophy of art – only philosophizing about things that were later to be seen as of a piece. Before they were seen as of a piece, however, there was nothing for *the* philosophy of art to be about, that is to say, *the* philosophy of all of *the* arts.

I am not, of course, saying that the arts of music, painting, literature, and the rest did not exist before the eighteenth century. What did not exist was the belief that they formed a separate class: that they belonged with each other. And it was that belief that made the discipline of aesthetics possible: that gave it its subject matter, *the* arts, all of them, and the task of saying why they were *they*.

§4   The evolution of what Kristeller called "the Modern System of the Arts" was "officially" completed just before midcentury. In Kristeller's words, "The decisive step towards a system of the fine arts was taken by the Abbé Batteux in his famous and influential treatise, *Les beaux arts réduit à un même principe* (1746)."[7] In Batteux's work, the system is fully in place and named: *les beaux arts*. Equally significant, Batteux gives, in his title, not only the system and its name but the philosophical project they imply: finding the *même principe*. The quest for the real definition of the fine arts was now in full swing and, except for a brief and by no means universally observed Wittgensteinian interlude, continues to the present moment.

Indeed, although Batteux dots the "i," a number of earlier writers were already engaged in the modern philosophical discipline of aesthetics. In England, Joseph Addison's "Pleasures of the Imagination" (1712) and Francis Hutcheson's *Inquiry Concerning Beauty, Order, Harmony, Design* (1725); in France, the Abbé DuBos's *Réflexions critiques sur la pöesie et sur la peinture* (1719); in Germany, Alexander Baumgarten's *Meditationes philosophicae de nonnullis ad poema partinentibus* (1735) – all can be seen as pioneering treatises in the new "science" of aesthetics: the first full-length works devoted solely to the subject, with Baumgarten giving us the name in something like its modern sense.

Thus by midcentury the discipline of aesthetics was a going concern, with its primary goal of a "definition" of the fine arts already set and, for most, seen as *achieved*, in the Platonic and Aristotelian theory of mimesis: the *même principe* of Batteux and various others.

That representation was the principle on which the first modern definitions of art were based is not surprising. It was a principle venerable with age and with the authority of classical antiquity – in particular, Plato and Aristotle. And the art world had no apparent counterexamples, except for pure instrumental music, which was at midcentury still a minor art, if an art at all, in the eyes of philosophers, literary theorists, and the general public.

Thus the confluence of the modern system of the arts and the autonomous discipline of aesthetics as a recognized department of philosophy laid upon philosophers the task of giving a real definition of art and produced the first modern examples of such a definition in a plethora of mimetic accounts.

Given the classical texts and the apparent nature of the case, it did not seem difficult to encompass all of the literary and dramatic arts as well as all of the visual arts under the umbrella of mimesis or representation. Of what Kristeller characterizes as "all the five major arts of painting, sculpture, architecture, music and poetry,"[8] only music and architecture would have been problematic. Architecture is, of course, a very special case, being both a fine and a useful art. But certainly there were attempts to make it out to be representational, at least in two ways: first, in the rather straightforward claim that its gross, manifest features were indeed representational, columns as trees and that sort of thing; second, in the far more sophisticated Pythagorean claim of Renaissance theorists that architectural proportions represent harmonic proportions of the universe, as was also claimed for the proportions of the division of the musical octave.[9] In any case, it is my impression that architecture was not at the center of the enterprise, and I will have nothing more to say about it.[10] It is the other problematic, music, that, I think, plays the pivotal role, and I will have a good deal to say about that.

§5 Why music? Noel Carroll has argued that what has motivated and driven new "definitions" of art in the twentieth century has been "the theoretical task of coming to terms with virtually continuous revolutions in artistic practice. . . ." The "task has been to provide the theoretical means for establishing

5

that the mutations issued from avant-garde practice belong to the family of art." In other words, "one might say that a great deal of modern philosophy of art is an attempt to come to a philosophical understanding of the productions of the avant-garde."[11]

That the twentieth century has, as Carroll puts it, produced "virtually continuous revolutions in artistic practice" makes the motivating force of the avant-garde on the task of defining the work of art palpably obvious during the period. But if Carroll is right, it suggests that we might look more closely at the eighteenth-century attempts to define the fine arts – the first such attempts in the modern era – to see if perhaps the same is true there.

Given that artistic revolutions can be slow as well as rapid, it does not seem inappropriate to interpret the rise of absolute music in the second half of the eighteenth century as an artistic revolution of impressive magnitude and, further, to see the new instrumental idiom as *the* avant-garde art of the age of Enlightenment. I have argued elsewhere that the obvious, prima facie difficulties in construing absolute music as a representational art made it the crucial case for any attempt to understand the nature of the fine arts in terms of mimesis, which was, at the time, the only game in town.[12] The *même principe* was representation of nature; and if absolute music could not be perceived as that, either the project must fail or absolute music, which was rapidly becoming at least the equal of vocal music in the eyes of composers, would have to be read out of the "modern system of the arts."

We can now see more clearly, with the help of Carroll's observations concerning the prominent role of the avant-garde in motivating definitions of art, why absolute music was a crux for the Enlightenment theorists. It is not as if pure instrumental music had been invented in eighteenth-century Mannheim and Vienna. Music for instruments alone had been performed at least since the Middle Ages. The point is that during a certain period in the history of art music, namely, the second half of the eighteenth century and the first years of the nineteenth, the writing of music for instruments alone rapidly moved from sideshow to center ring, from the relatively peripheral interest of the composer to at least equality with vocal music. Before this time the composer made his living in the service of the church, patron, and opera house. And the overwhelming majority of his works, even in the case of as devoted a composer of absolute music as Bach, were vocal. But in the period from the time of Bach's death to the flowering of Haydn, Mozart, and the early Beethoven, the tide was reversed, to the point that for Haydn the opposite was the case (although Haydn valued his vocal works above his instrumental ones). It is for musicologists to suggest which sociological and economic influences came to bear on this trend. It is for us to scrutinize its effect on the philosophical task of defining the fine arts.

Because there has always been instrumental music in the West, there has always been a potential threat to a mimetic theory of the arts that included music *tout court* in the system. But during the early period of theorizing, from DuBos (say) to Batteux, the relative unimportance of instrumental music made it impotent as a challenge to the representational theory of art. It could simply be ignored as a peripheral case, indeed ignored without mention or explanation.

What could not be ignored was vocal music, which is probably what most philosophers in the period meant by "music" anyway. But vocal music did not present the difficulties to theory that instrumental music was to do when it emerged fully fledged. Indeed, the groundwork for the acceptance of vocal music into the modern system had already been laid by the end of the sixteenth century.[13] How so?

The story is something like this. Vocal polyphony before the Council of Trent (pre-Tridentine polyphony) had evolved into an extremely complex musical fabric that might well be described as a "setting" for the text very much in the jeweler's sense of the word. The text, like a jewel, was placed in a structure so elaborate and alluring in its own right as to overpower it aesthetically: a great compliment to the text, indeed, to consider it a gem worthy of such a luxuriant setting but not a compliment to its *meaning*, which, as the clerics complained, was rendered completely unintelligible by the music. As is

well known, the abolition of polyphony was actually considered as a way of foregrounding the text. Polyphony prevailed,
although in a different form. One might say that in the works
of Palestrina it was curtailed. However, that is a needlessly
negative and largely uninformative way of putting it. What really happened was that one aesthetic of text setting began giving way to another: the "jeweler's" way to the way of
representation. For what, I suggest, Palestrina was attempting
to do in his "curtailed" counterpoint was to represent in music human linguistic expression, on the hypothesis that since
human linguistic expression can make a text intelligible, so too
can the musical "representation" of it. Whether or not this is
the way Palestrina and his contemporaries put it to themselves, it is a viable and rewarding way to read his (and their)
works.

In any event, the representational aesthetic of text setting soon
emerged in a quite explicit and theory-driven form, in the invention of the *stile rappresentativo* and in the opera, both her-
alded by theories and admonitions to the effect that the musical
representation of passionate human speech is or ought to be at
least one of the composer's major goals. Pietro de' Bardi described this new aesthetic of composition as "imitating familiar
speech by using few sounds. . . ."[14] While Giulio Caccini, one of
the first composers of *stile rappresentativo* and opera, said that
". . . I have endeavored in those my late compositions to bring
in a kind of music by which men might, as it were, talk in harmony. . . ."[15] If Palestrina had this cat in the bag, it certainly was
out now.

Thus more than one hundred years before Batteux et al. enunciated the "modern system" and brought it under the *même principe,* the groundwork for vocal music's induction into the fine
arts club had already been laid. By the end of the sixteenth century, vocal music was consciously and explicitly, as well as in-
tuitively and implicitly, being practiced as a representational
project: the representation, broadly speaking, of human expression. It was ripe for the plucking, and at least as early as
DuBos it was plucked.

We now understand something about the role of music in the

formation of the modern system and the mimetic theory that tied its members together in the first half of the eighteenth century. Neither vocal nor instrumental music posed a problem: the former because it was easily seen, and had been since the end of the sixteenth century, as representational of human expression; the latter because, compared with vocal music, it was simply inconsequential, at the center of neither the composer's nor his audience's concerns. Indeed, one gets the idea that in educated circles a "gentleman" who played a musical instrument was, far from being admired for it, considered something of an eccentric. It was his "hobby horse" or his addiction. Thus instrumental music was not one of the "liberal arts," but a kind of curiosity, and it could safely be ignored by the modern system or, if noticed at all, given fairly perfunctory treatment (as in DuBos).

But all of this changed as absolute music started coming to the fore. I want to be careful here about stating my hypothesis. I am certainly not saying that composers before this period were not deeply interested in pure instrumental music, did not lavish the whole arsenal of their compositional skills on it when the occasion arose, or that it did not sometimes form a substantial part of their output. The instrumental music of Bach alone would belie all of those claims (as would the instrumental music, earlier, of Frescobaldi and Giovanni Gabrieli). But even in a case like Bach's, vocal music was the center of professional life, the major source of income, and the spiritual core of the creative life. It was this that changed in the second half of the eighteenth century, when it became possible to make instrumental music one's profession, the spiritual core of one's creative life. For some major composers, instrumental music thus became at the same time the cutting edge, the "experimental" art of the century, the avant-garde among all the other arts. And in becoming all of these things, it became at the same time the major challenge to the representational theory of the modern system, the only apparent and important counterexample, the "Fountain" of its time. We must look at the attempt to meet this challenge now if we are to understand how we got from there to here.

9

§6 In the second half of the eighteenth century, two options were open to philosophers for dealing with the growth of absolute music: to reject its bid to become one of the fine arts or to find a way of making it, broadly speaking, a "representational" art. Both options were explored with a fair degree of uncertainty reigning among all concerned, most notoriously Kant, who for profound reasons could never quite make up his mind. The obvious third option, a theory of art other than some form of representationalism, was not yet in the offing, even in Kant's third *Critique* (at least as I read that ever-problematical text). And when alternatives to mimesis began to appear, again I would suggest it was the avant-garde art of absolute music that provided the major initiative.

To give some brief idea of the struggle with absolute music in the latter half of the eighteenth century, one can do no better than to adduce the example of Kant. The question for Kant was not so simple as whether music was representational. And it might be useful to weigh what he had to say in this regard against his Scottish contemporary, Thomas Reid, with whom he has been compared, in recent years, in more than one respect.

For Reid, there is no hesitation in construing music as one of the fine arts on the basis of melody alone, with mimesis the connecting thread. "To me it seems," he writes, "that every strain in melody that is agreeable, is an imitation of the human voice in the expression of some sentiment or passion, or an imitation of some other object in nature; and that music, as well as poetry, is an imitative art."[16] Nor is there any doubt that instrumental as well as vocal music is intended, for at the very outset of the discussion Reid refers to both.[17]

The notion that even melodies played on instruments are representations of human vocal expression was old hat by Reid's time; Francis Hutcheson, whose work in aesthetics Reid knew well and referred to explicitly, had already expressed such sentiments, not new in 1725.[18] What is perhaps more original is Reid's attempt to construe "harmony" as a representation of human speech as well. Hutcheson had left harmony to the innate sense of "original" beauty (in his terminology), as opposed to the "relative" beauty of imitation: "Under *original beauty* we may include *harmony,* or *beauty of sound,* if that expression be allowed, because harmony is not usually conceived as an imitation of anything else."[19] But Reid is bound and determined to make harmony as well a representational feature of music, and he tries to do so, furthermore, without appeal to any neo-Pythagorean notion of musical harmony as a reflection of the *harmonia mundi.*

As might be expected, the analogy drawn between harmony, which is to say, the simultaneous production of many sounds, and human linguistic behavior is not between sound and soliloquy but between sound and conversation. Reid begins: "As far as I can judge by my ear, when two or more persons, of a good voice and ear, converse together in amity and friendship, the tones of their different voices are concordant, but become discordant when they give vent to angry passions; so that, without hearing what is said, one may know by tones of the different voices, whether they quarrel or converse amiably."[20] The same contrast between harmony and discord in conversation is reflected, Reid continues, in what, though vaguely and naively described, we would call "functional harmony":

> When discord arises occasionally in conversation, but soon terminates in perfect amity, we receive more pleasure than from perfect unanimity. In like manner, in the harmony of music, discordant sounds are occasionally introduced, but it is always in order to give a relish to the most perfect concord that follows.[21]

Reid, like most philosophers of his age, was a self-proclaimed musical naif. Had it been otherwise, he might also have seen the possibility of extending his conversational analogy, along with the notion of conflict resolution, to the important larger musical forms of his day: the large-scale sonata movement, for one. In any case, Reid concludes on a tentative rather than confident note: "Whether these analogies, between the harmony of a piece of music, and harmony in the intercourse of minds, be merely fanciful, or have any real foundation in fact, I submit to those who have a nicer ear, and have applied it to observations of this kind."[22]

11

§7   If Reid showed some diffidence in applying the *même principe* to music, he showed no lack of confidence in construing music as a fine art, on the basis at least of melodic representation; and melody, after all, was agreed on all hands to be the "soul of music," its most essential element. With Kant, however, the question of music was never conclusively resolved. And it was Kant, not Thomas Reid, whose influence in this regard pervaded philosophical thought in the first half of the nineteenth century.[23] Saying that in the third *Critique* absolute music did not come to be seen, decisively, as one of the fine arts is tantamount to saying that for *philosophy*, for *aesthetics*, it did not – that is how important *that work* is to the philosophy of art, as the culmination of eighteenth-century aesthetic thought and the continuation of same in the first half of the century to come.

The question, for Kant, was not nearly as straightforward as it may appear from his rather confident statement in the *Anthropology* (1798) that "it is only because music serves as an instrument for poetry that it is *fine* (not merely pleasant) art."[24] For if this statement is to be credited, Kant *had* made up his mind to exclude absolute music from the modern system, and had done so merely on the basis of its lack of representational content. A poetic text could supply such content in the case of vocal music, and vocal music alone, then, was to be designated fine rather than agreeable art. But in the third *Critique* Kant is far from so simple a statement and has pushed the question of absolute music beyond merely the question of "representation" or "content" – indeed, to the question of "form."

Kant, let me hasten to add, is no "formalist," if by that is meant someone who thinks, as Clive Bell and Roger Fry seemed to have thought at certain points in their careers, that form is the only artistically relevant feature of artworks. The whole difficult doctrine of the "aesthetic ideas" in the third *Critique* demonstrates this beyond doubt. But he did think that the question of whether music – absolute music – is a fine art crucially involved form in two very distinct ways. And in regard to both, at least when they are put together, the answer is far from decisive for absolute music.

What is most familiar in the literature on the third *Critique* with regard to music is the question, in §14, as to whether single musical tones can be beautiful or, at best, merely agreeable. We might call this the first stage of Kant's argument, and it turns on whether individual musical tones are perceived as having form. For it is only through the conscious perception of form that the free play of the cognitive faculties, and hence pleasure in the beautiful, can arise.

The notorious passage in which Kant expresses his view on this matter is rendered as follows by Kant's early English translator, J. H. Bernard (1892): "If we assume with Euler that colors are isochronous vibrations (*pulsus*) of the ether, as sounds are of the air in a state of disturbance, and – what is more important – that the mind not only perceives by sense the effect of these in exciting the organ, but also perceives by reflection the regular play of impressions (and thus the form of the combination of different representations) – which I very much doubt – then colors and tone cannot be reckoned as mere sensations, but as the formal determination of the unity of a manifold of sensations, and thus as beauties."[25] The next English translator to attempt the third *Critique*, James Creed Meredith (1911), gives a very similar reading of this passage, except that the crucial phrase Bernard has as "which I very much doubt" is given by Meredith the opposite sense: "which I still, in no way doubt."[26] He is followed in this by the third *Critique*'s most recent English translator, Werner S. Pluhar, who renders it "and which, after all, I do not doubt at all."[27]

To doubt or not to doubt is the question, and it arises simply because of textual variation. The first and second editions of the *Critique of Judgment* have it Bernard's way, "gar sehr zweifle," the third edition Meredith's and Pluhar's, "gar nicht zweifle."[28] Is the third edition's version a correction or a misprint? The smart money, these days, seems to be on the former, and I will adopt that assumption, because for one thing, as Theodore E. Uehling has pointed out, it accords better with what Kant has to say later on.[29] So we may take it that Kant has decided, in the first stage of his argument about absolute music, that individual musical tones, since they have consciously perceivable form, as regular perturbations of a physical medium, can be beautiful. As yet, however, he has said nothing of their being *fine art.* That is to come.

A second stage of the argument can be discerned in §51, where Kant again frames the question of whether Euler's vibrations can be taken in as objects of perception present to consciousness or whether we merely register their effect. The details of Kant's argument need not detain us here. What does interest us is Kant's conclusion with regard to music. Of the two alternatives, Kant concludes:

> The difference which the one opinion or the other occasions in the estimate of the basis of music would, however, only give rise to this much change in the definition, that either it is to be interpreted, as we have done, as the *beautiful* play of sensations (through hearing), or else as one of *agreeable* sensations. According to the former interpretation, alone, would music be represented out and out as a *fine* art, whereas according to the latter it would be represented as (in part at least) an *agreeable* art."[30]

Uehling has called attention to the significance in this passage of the phrase "as we have done," which implies that Kant has already, presumably in §14, treated music as the beautiful play of sensations, and thus implies as well that he has opted there, as here, for the view that Euler's vibrations are present to sensible representation.[31]

Of interest too is the phrase "in part at least," which suggests that, for Kant, the question of whether music (or anything else) is a fine art may not always have a categorical yes or no answer: that, in other words, something can be artlike or, rather, art in one respect but not in another. I shall return to this thought in a moment.

In any event, it appears that in §51 Kant has plumped for music as a fine art on the basis of his decision that individual tones have a perceivable form as Euler's vibrations. This brings us to the third stage of the argument.

It would be curious indeed if Kant, or anyone else in the eighteenth century, should let the question of whether music is a fine art turn merely on whether it has perceivable *form.* For the *même principe* that holds the fine arts together is representation, and Kant, for all his emphasis on form, has not rejected it. So although it may seem as if, in §51 Kant has let form do the whole job for him, that impression is quite dispelled in §53 and §54, as we now shall see.

What, then, is the "representational content" of music for Kant? He begins with a platitude of his time: the "representation" of the emotions through musical "representation" of passionate human speech. But to it Kant adds the distinctively Kantian notion of the "aesthetic ideas."[32] The complete thought is this:

> Its [music's] charm, which admits of such universal communication, appears to rest on the following facts. Every expression in language has an associated tone suited to its sense. This tone indicates, more or less, a mode in which the speaker is affected, and in turn evokes it in the hearer also, in whom conversely it then also excites the idea which in language is expressed with such a tone. Further, just as modulation is, as it were, a universal language of sensations intelligible to every man, so the art of tone wields the full force of this language wholly on its own account, namely, as a language of the affections, and in this way, according to the law of association, universally communicates the aesthetic ideas that are naturally combined therewith. But, further, inasmuch as those aesthetic ideas are not concepts or determinate thoughts, the form of the arrangement of these sensations (harmony and melody), taking the place of the form of a language, only serves the purpose of giving an expression to the aesthetic idea of an integral whole of an unutterable wealth of thought that fills the measure of a certain theme forming the dominant *affection* in the piece.[33]

It will not be necessary for present purposes to explicate fully the difficult notion of the aesthetic ideas. Suffice it to say that it is through the evocation of the aesthetic ideas that "representational content" becomes integrated into works of the fine arts in the way appropriate to them *qua* fine arts. They do not constitute a statable content – they are "unutterable." A statable

15

content is what gives birth to them – but must not be confused with the aesthetic ideas that are the true, "unutterable" content of the fine arts as fine arts. It is the aesthetic ideas that for Kant satisfy the demands of the *même principe*.

But something else is necessary for the aesthetic ideas to constitute, on the "representation" side, a work as a work of fine art. The evocation of the aesthetic ideas is a necessary but not sufficient condition. In addition, the aesthetic ideas must provoke the free play of the cognitive faculties of imagination and understanding. And this, we learn in §54, the aesthetic ideas in music cannot do; in absolute music they ultimately have their payoff not in the free play of the cognitive faculties but merely in a physical feeling of bodily well-being. "In music the course of this play is from bodily sensations to aesthetic ideas (which are the Objects for the affections), and then from these back again, but with gathered strength to the body."[34] And the conclusion to be drawn from this failure of the aesthetic ideas in absolute music to engage the free play of the cognitive faculties is that, like "jest," music "deserves to be ranked rather as an agreeable than a fine art."[35]

We now have an apparent contradiction: in §51 Kant says that music is a fine art because sounds exhibit perceived form as Euler's vibrations, but in §54 he says that music is not a fine art but an agreeable art because its aesthetic ideas engage only the body and not the imagination and understanding in free play. But the proper response to this apparent contradiction, I suggest, is to recognize, as Kant seems to license us to do in §51, that the answer to "Is it fine art?" is not necessarily a categorical yes or no but quite possibly " 'Yes' in part, 'No' in part." The answer that Kant gives is that absolute music is artlike in one respect and not artlike in another. It is a fine art in respect of form but not in respect of representational content. And hence it is not fully a fine art. Furthermore, in seeing this we now understand his statement in the *Anthropology* that it is the addition of poetry that makes music a fine rather than an agreeable art. For the aesthetic ideas in poetry, unlike those in absolute music, can engage the imagination and the understanding in free play. This is the Kantian way of saying that poetry makes music fully a fine art, and not just a fine art in respect of form, by giving it the representational content it lacks without a text.

Kant, then, was not so much indecisive in his view of absolute music as decisive in placing absolute music in an indecisive position: half fine art, half not; fine art in respect of form, agreeable art in respect of content; fine art–like but not fully fine art – not, in short, categorically one of the fine arts. And so large does the figure of Kant and the third *Critique* loom, retrospectively, over eighteenth-century philosophy of art, prophetically over that of the nineteenth, that from the philosopher's standpoint if Kant did not conclusively make absolute music a fine art, that must be taken as the judgment of his century as well. The making of the modern system of the arts was left philosophically unaccomplished, the failure of absolute music to be understood philosophically as a full-fledged member evidence of failure.

Nor was the problem of absolute music completely resolved in the work of the two greatest aestheticians of the nineteenth century, Schopenhauer and Hegel. For in this regard Schopenhauer played Reid to Hegel's Kant, and the philosophical vote on absolute music is again one for, one against. To this standoff we now must turn our attention.

§8 It has been said that music is *the* Romantic art. It was said by the Romantics. It cannot be a mistake (I am tempted to say *therefore*) to see music, in the first half of the nineteenth century, as maintaining its place as the avant-garde art form: the art form that challenged and motivated the continued attempt to give art its real definition.

Nowhere is this motivating force of music more apparent than in Schopenhauer's philosophy of art, where it occupies the highest rank among the arts. For Schopenhauer there was certainly no hesitation at all in classifying music as a fine art, and absolute music is unequivocally what he meant, first and foremost. That he played Reid to Hegel's Kant in this respect is reinforced by the fact that Schopenhauer's theory of the fine arts still retains the character of a representational theory, although the object of representation has changed from a psychological or behavioral to a metaphysical one.

There is little need to delve deeply into the intricacies of Schopenhauer's metaphysics. For present purposes we need only remind ourselves that for Schopenhauer "the object of art, the depiction of which is the aim of the artist, and the knowledge of which must consequently precede his work as its germ and source is an *Idea* in Plato's sense, and absolutely nothing else . . ."[36] and that the Platonic ideas are an expression of the ultimate reality, the Kantian thing in itself, which Schopenhauer characterizes as a metaphysical "will." Finally, it is the peculiar nature of music, alone among the fine arts, to represent the will, not indirectly by representing the Platonic ideas, as the other arts do, but by being a direct copy of the will itself:

> Thus music is as immediate objectivication and copy of the whole *will* as the world itself is, indeed as the Ideas are, the multiplied phenomenon of which constitutes the world of individual things. Therefore music is by no means like the other arts, namely a copy of the ideas, but a *copy of the will itself,* the objectivity of which are the Ideas."[37]

It should not go unnoticed that even though Schopenhauer puts absolute music squarely among the fine arts, and gives it pride of place in its direct relation to the will, this can also be seen as evidence of the difficulty absolute music still presented. For one cannot help feeling that it is just because absolute music is so difficult to construe representationally that Schopenhauer gives it as object of representation the very thing that we cannot directly experience at all, thus putting the success or failure of music to represent it beyond our powers to determine.

But furthermore Schopenhauer is very clear about its being absolute music with which he is concerned. For when he is through talking about music *sans phrase* and goes on to discuss music with text, he warns of the danger of the music following the text too closely and becoming its slave, thus losing its unique identity as music, the direct copy of the will. The words

> should never forsake that subordinate position in order to make themselves the chief thing, and the music a mere means of expressing the song. . . . Everywhere music expresses only

the quintessence of life and of its events, never these themselves, and therefore their differences do not always influence
it. . . . Therefore, if music tries to stick too closely to the words,
and to mould itself according to the events, it is endeavouring
to speak a language not its own.[38]

If Schopenhauer, then, fully enfranchised absolute music as a
fine art, independent of text, on fairly recognizable "representational" grounds, Hegel was still waffling on the question at
about the same time.[39] And to see how up in the air the question
still was, from the philosophical point of view, it is to Hegel's
Lectures on the Fine Arts that we now must turn.

§9 What is so infuriating about Hegel's remarks on music is
not merely their lack of clarity. As well, it is impossible to tell
what specific musical works he has in mind when he says what
he does about "music." He makes only one reference to a specific composer as a composer of absolute music, and none at all
to a particular work of absolute music. And as we shall see, this
makes any interpretation of what he believes about absolute music, *as we know it*, pure guesswork. In a word, we don't know
what Hegel was talking about, even if *he* did.

A certain irony emerges, I think, when one compares what
Schopenhauer did to advance absolute music's claim to the
status of fine art with what Hegel did. For although Schopenhauer was firm in his conviction that absolute music merited
such a status, and Hegel, as we shall see, equivocated, Schopenhauer supported his conviction with what can only be described
as the moribund theory of musical representation, while Hegel
was perhaps the first philosopher of the first rank to avoid "representation" talk altogether in this regard and construe music
purely in terms of "expression": *ausdrücken* and *Ausdruck* are
the verb and noun, respectively, that Hegel consistently used to
explicate the relation between music and its "content." And to
the extent that expression theory was the wave of the future in
the first quarter of the nineteenth century and representation
theory was, increasingly, an outmoded vestige of the past, and,
furthermore, to the extent that expression theory was to do for

music what representation theory never could – convince a philosophical community that absolute music deserved its place in the Pantheon – Hegel's waffling did more for the future status of music as a fine art than Schopenhauer's conviction.

For Hegel, then, music was expression: the expression of the inner life. The theory is three-termed: the composer "expresses," the music is his "expression," and the listener is "expressed to" to the extent that she is deeply moved by the musical experience. It is a self-expression theory in that the composer must be deeply moved by what he expressed in his music in order for the music to be a successful expression and, therefore, for the listener to be expressed to, which is to say, deeply moved by what is heard.

When "music" satisfies the threefold criterion of expression, it is fine art. The question before us is, Over what real objects does the term "music" range when they succeed in satisfying this criterion, and over what real objects when they do not? In particular, does absolute music satisfy the criterion in respect of *expressive content?* For that is the crucial point over which Hegel anguishes and which it is so difficult for us to get clear about in anguishing over his text.

Perhaps the most suggestive statement that Hegel makes with regard to the status of absolute music as a fine art is the following:

> [A]mongst all the arts music has the maximum possibility of freeing itself from any actual text as well as from the expression of any specific subject-matter, with a view to finding satisfaction solely in a self-enclosed series of the conjunctions, changes, oppositions, and modulations falling within the purely musical sphere of sounds. But in that event music remains empty and meaningless, and because the one chief thing in all art, namely spiritual content and expression, is missing from it, it is not yet strictly to be called art. Only if music becomes a spiritually adequate expression in the sensuous medium of sounds and their varied counterpoint does music rise to being a genuine art, no matter whether this content has its more detailed significance independently ex-

pressed in a libretto or must be sensed more vaguely from the notes and their harmonic relations and melodic animation.[40]

We learn three important things from this passage: that absolute music without spiritual content is not fine art; that music can gain spiritual content, and thus possess the status of fine art, by being married to a text; and that at best some absolute music can have spiritual content, though "more vaguely" than texted music, and thus can possess the status of fine art. But what we do not learn is what specific examples are, and what are not, fine art. The reason we must know this is that if what we take to be paradigmatic instances of art music fail to be that for Hegel, then we would be loath to say that Hegel had succeeded, philosophically, in enfranchising absolute music, as we understand it, as a fine art.

One passage that does indeed strongly suggest Hegel's failure to enfranchise fully what we take to be art music is the following critical comment on the absolute music of his own day. "Especially in recent times," Hegel writes, "music has torn itself free from a content already clear on its own account and retreated in this way into its own medium; but for this reason it has lost its power over the whole inner life, all the more so as the pleasure it can give relates to only one side of the art, namely bare interest in the purely musical element in the composition and its skillfulness, a side of music which is for connoisseurs only and scarcely appeals to the general human interest in art."[41] The text leaves no doubt that the music under discussion fails to be fine art, in failing to appeal "to the general human interest in art." But whose music is this? One possible answer, all too obvious, is suggested by the recent translator, T. M. Knox, in a footnote to the passage: "Is this an allusion to, for instance, Schubert and Beethoven?"[42] That conclusion is hard to escape, and damaging enough, since if Beethoven's instrumental music fails on Hegel's account to qualify as fine art, we can reasonably question whether in Hegel absolute music itself has qualified.

Furthermore, "recent times," *neurer Zeit,* is far from precise in its extension. "Modern times" is another possible translation.[43] Would that include the instrumental music of Haydn and Mozart? Hegel does, in fact, give high praise to the symphonies of Mozart. Indeed, it is the only reference of a specific kind to absolute music in the whole section on music in Part 3 of the *Lectures*. Unfortunately, it is of no help whatever in answering our question, since Mozart is being praised only for his masterful orchestration, his use of instruments, which is the topic under discussion in that place.[44]

So we are left with the likely conclusion that Hegel did not think the instrumental music of Beethoven and Schubert qualified as fine art, and at least the possibility that he thought the late Haydn and Mozart may have failed to qualify as well. That Hegel's doubts about absolute music were wide-ranging rather than confined to the "contemporary" music of Beethoven and Schubert (which is denigrating enough to the status of absolute music as a fine art) is given support by a passage at the beginning of his discussion of poetry, which follows directly after the section on music. In his transition from music to poetry, Hegel tells us,

> music must, on account of its one-sidedness, call on the help of the more exact meaning of words and, in order to become more firmly conjoined with the detail and characteristic expression of the subject-matter, it demands a text which alone gives fuller content to the subjective life's outpouring in the notes. By means of this expression of ideas and feelings the abstract inwardness of music emerges into a clearer and firmer unfolding of them.[45]

It is indeed quite hard to square this passage with the position Hegel seems to start out with. For whereas in the beginning Hegel holds out the possibility of music as a fine art with or without a text to fix its content, here he says that music must – "so muss sich die Musik"[46] – seek the support of a text to gain its content and, one must assume, its status as a fine art. Knox, early on, takes this, rather than the more liberal view, to be Hegel's doctrine and sees in it the seeds of Hegel's failure to talk intelligibly about music without text:

He seems to think music ought to have a meaning but that this can only be detected when it is associated with words in opera and songs. This is perhaps why he may be at sea when he comes to deal with instrumental music.[47]

Without undertaking the imposing task of producing a complete, systematic account of Hegel on the fine arts, I can do little here but enumerate the positions Hegel might be taking, on first reflection, with regard to absolute music. On Knox's interpretation, he would seem to be denying that music without text can be fine art at all. On the most liberal interpretation, he must at least be denying that the instrumental works of two of the greatest practitioners of that art – one, indeed, arguably the greatest – have the status of fine art. And somewhere between would be the view that, according to Hegel, the whole body of "modern" instrumental music, back to and including the late instrumental masterpieces of Haydn and Mozart, fails to be inducted into the modern system, which would mean either that Hegel thought some music of the future might gain that status or, perhaps, that Hegel was more comfortable with baroque and preclassical instrumental style. (The latter, as a matter of fact, is not altogether without textual support: some of Hegel's descriptions of how absolute music might gain intelligible emotive content sound like descriptions of music where there is, in each movement, one *dominant affection* rather than the contrasting affections of "contemporary" sonata form.)

But even on the most liberal construction, we are driven to the conclusion that Hegel did not, any more than Kant, make a single-minded, philosophically persuasive case for absolute music as one of the fine arts: as an undisputed member of the modern system. The only thing that is certain and decisive is that Hegel thought music with a text qualified. In Hegel, absolute music, and therefore the modern system itself, still hung in the balance.

§10 From the rise of the instrumental idiom in the last thirty or so years of the eighteenth century, through Hegel as well as Kant, absolute music precipitated an extended crisis for the project of "defining" art. But absolute music did, of course, finally make it into the modern system, partly, as I have suggested, because of the "expression" theory that Hegel, among others, developed. Other causal factors, or perhaps symptoms (it is difficult to tell which), also played a role: in particular, the development of program music and the tone poem, and the increasing willingness of nineteenth-century writers to put literary or pictorial interpretations on such monuments of absolute music as the piano sonatas, string quartets, and symphonies of Beethoven, which became fair game for poets and poetizers and others of that ilk. It was, so to speak, a case of life imitating art or, in this instance, art imitating its philosophy.

With music firmly settled in the modern system, the next crisis, at least as I read the history of aesthetics, came from another quarter: the visual arts, with music this time providing the anchor rather than the tide. I refer to impressionism, postimpressionism, and the rise of formalism in the writings of Clive Bell and Roger Fry.

If we return to Noel Carroll's claim that it is the problematic works of the avant-garde that drive aesthetic theory to formulate new definitions of art, and ask ourselves whether this holds good for the rise of formalism, the answer is a resounding affirmative and the artworks precipitating the crisis are not far to seek. For beginning with impressionism, and accelerating with the postimpressionists, it was increasingly difficult to reconcile what was seen in these paintings with the accepted principles of realistic representation or competent draftsmanship. If rendering *la belle natur* was to be the standard of success, then Manet and Monet, Cézanne and Van Gogh, Seurat and Gauguin could not pass muster. Combine with this the fact that the camera, a "gadget," could now put the representation of nature within the grasp of anyone, child or adult, and you can easily surmise the motive behind Roger Fry's remark that "if imitation is the sole purpose of the graphic arts, it is surprising that the works of such arts are even looked upon as more than curiosities, or ingenious toys, are even taken seriously by grown-up people."[48]

The turn to form, "significant form," as Clive Bell famously put it,[49] as the sole defining property of the representational and contentful arts seems even more bizarre (to the present writer at any rate) than the turn to representation and content, previously, as the means of establishing absolute music in the modern system. For as Bell himself observed, the ability to maintain "formal" concentration at a concert is a hostage to fortune; and when concentration lapses, there is nothing more natural or easy than to slide into revery. "Tired or perplexed, I let slip my sense of form . . . and I begin weaving into the harmonies, that I cannot grasp, the ideas of life."[50]

Now leaving out Bell's obviously normative assumption that attention to pure form is the favored stance before absolute music, the having of "ideas of life" in response to it a "slide" or a "slip" from genuine aesthetic concentration, what his scenario of musical listening does remind us of is how easy it is for anyone, even a dyed-in-the-wool musical formalist, to have pictorial or narrative images occasioned by absolute music, or, in opposite terms, how difficult it is to keep this from happening, if one so desires. It's "natural," if one wants to put it that way, to respond to music with images; and that makes it all the easier, all the more plausible, to those so inclined to appeal to such images as the representational "content" of absolute music in order to capture it for representation and (by consequence) the modern system.

But the reverse procedure has just the reverse character. Indeed, it is far harder, nigh on to impossible, *not* to see even abstract visual designs "as" representational (cf. "seeing figures in clouds").[51] And reading a novel merely as a formal structure seems just about like the Zen problem of *not* thinking of crocodiles. You may say that I am caricaturing formalism. To the contrary, at least in its first gush of enthusiasm, when it was still *formalism,* that is exactly what Bell and Fry were asking us to do. Bell says, "The representative element in a work of art may or may not be harmful; always it is irrelevant."[52] But if at best representation is irrelevant, at worst irrelevant and harmful, what else are we being asked to do than frame it out: experience the work without it. That, indeed, is just what the musical model is meant to illustrate. For in ab-

25

solute music, when our concentration is unimpaired, pure form is what we are perceiving:

> [W]hen I am feeling bright and clear and intent . . . I get from music that pure aesthetic emotion that I get from visual art. . . . [A]t moments I do appreciate music as pure musical form, as sounds combined according to the laws of a mysterious necessity, as pure art with a tremendous significance of its own and no relation whatever to the significance of life; and in those moments I lose myself in that infinitely sublime state of mind to which pure visual form transports me.[53]

Roger Fry, in *Transformations*, presented unequivocally the formalist creed for literature, as well as for the visual arts.[54] And if you find it difficult to imagine experiencing Rembrandt as pure form, abstracted from all representational content, how much more difficult will you find the exercise when its object is *Pilgrim's Progress*. Yet that is precisely what Fry demands of you: "[T]he appearance of an esthetic structure is deliberately chosen as a bate to lure the reader for an ulterior, non-esthetic end, but it surely is a common experience that a reader can fully relish the bait without so much of a scratch from Bunyan's hook."[55] Nor is Fry loath to generalize the point in claiming that "the purpose of literature is the creation of structures which have for us the feeling of reality, and that these structures are self-contained, self-sufficing, and not to be valued by their reference to what lies outside."[56]

Bell says, "To appreciate a work of [visual] art we need bring with us nothing but a sense of form and colour and a knowledge of three-dimensional space."[57] I assume Fry must endorse its equivalent for the literary arts. That anyone could actually believe this about literature – believe, that is, that its content is irrelevant to its artistic merit or significance or to our aesthetic experience – may be hard for us now to credit. But if any doubt remains that this is what Bell and Fry were saying, even in light of the above quotations, the following reminiscence of Bell's, written at a time when he apparently had withdrawn some distance from his early extravagances, will convince even the most ardent skeptic. Bell recalls some gibberish Roger once wrote – for the benefit of intimate friends only – gibberish which did possess recognisable similarity of sound with [Milton's] *Ode on the Nativity* but did not possess what he firmly believed it to possess, i.e. all, or almost all, the merits of the original. The gibberish was, of course, deliberate gibberish – a collection of sounds so far as possible without meaning. It was highly ingenious, and I am bound to reckon the theory behind it pretty, seeing that it was much the same as one I had myself propounded years earlier as an explanation of visual art.[58]

It hardly seems necessary, considering what has gone before, to say anything further about what Roger Fry's exercise in gibberish was supposed to show or how obvious its utter failure to show it – obvious, in the event, even to Bell, from whence came its inspiration.

§11   I do not know of any case in the philosophical literature – at least in the literature of aesthetics – more prone than that of formalism, as a real definition of art, to the charge that, whatever its technical difficulties, vicious circles, and the like might be, it so violates our common sense as to constitute an obvious reductio ad absurdum of itself on that basis alone. And one way of putting the matter is to say that the formalists came a cropper by choosing exactly the wrong model – perversely wrong – for the visual and literary arts, namely, absolute music.

Absolute music, as we have seen, eventually achieved the status of fine art. After it had, through, I suggested, the Romantic "expression" theories of art, the willingness of so many nineteenth-century writers to give literary and pictorial interpretations of the absolute music canon and the rise of "literary" instrumental forms, it was still in no condition to provide a model for formalist aesthetics. Far from it, the "contentful" arts were the model for *it*.

But by midcentury, a profound change was being wrought in musical aesthetics, with which the name of Eduard Hanslick is closely associated. In 1854 Hanslick published his widely read monograph, *Vom Musikalisch-Schönen*, which went through no less than ten editions during the author's lifetime. It was Hanslick who first put before the world (in a readable, nontechnical prose) a palpably formalist account of absolute music. "The content of music is tonally moving forms," Hanslick happily put it.

> What kind of beauty is the beauty of a musical composition?
> It is a specifically musical kind of beauty. By this we understand a beauty that is self-contained and in no need of content from outside itself, that consists simply and solely of forms and their artistic combination.[59]

Hanslick's example was followed in England by Edmund Gurney, whose compendius *The Power of Sound* (1880) presented a systematic and detailed version of formalism in music based on what Gurney called "ideal motion," initially described by him as "the *oneness of form and motion* which constitutes the great peculiarity of melody and the faculty by which we appreciate it."[60] The resemblance of Gurney's "ideal motion" to Hanslick's "tonally moving forms" and to Bell's "significant form" is, I think, no illusion. In any case, by the time Bell came to write *Art* in 1916, music had, besides Hanslick and Gurney, numerous formalist interpreters, including the young Heinrich Schenker. And although the notion that music is a purely formal art was by no means universally subscribed to, absolute music had become, in many circles, *the* paradigm of aesthetic formalism: ready and waiting to serve as Bell's exemplar and so to partially verify Walter Pater's familiar and prophetic declaration that it is to music that all other arts aspire, just the reverse of a long history in which music aspired to the other arts.

But just as the contentful arts are the wrong model for absolute music, so absolute music is the wrong model for the contentful arts. And it seems to me at this point in the history of aesthetics that one might well have begun to doubt seriously whether a single theory, a single real definition, could lasso both the contentful arts and absolute music together in the same modern system. Furthermore, one might well have begun to suspect that if literature or painting was an inappropriate model for absolute music, and absolute music was an inappropriate model for painting and literature, there are as well other poor models deeply imbedded in the tradition, so old and undisputed as to be unnoticed. But there they may be, unperceived obstacles to our understanding of "the" arts.

Indeed, "wrong models" is the theme of this monograph. And Chapters 3 through 7 present case studies in the individual arts, meant to reveal the wrong models and, it is to be hoped, supply the right ones. But before we get to that, and to appreciate more fully the predicament we are in, we must first take cognizance of not just how we got here, but where, in fact, we presently are. I turn to that question now.

Chapter 2

Where We Are

§1   As I said at the close of the preceding chapter, one might well have begun to suspect, with the rather obvious failure of formalism to deal with the "representational" arts of painting and fiction, and with a long history of failures of representation and expression theory to deal with absolute music, that perhaps there was something deeply flawed in the whole enterprise of defining art itself. I said it, of course, with the benefit of nearly a century's worth of hindsight and am under no illusion that I would have been any more capable, then, of either diagnosing the disease or prescribing a cure. A lot of philosophy had to come and go before alternatives to the *traditional* "task of defining a work of art" could be seriously contemplated.[1]

The prevailing theory of art, from Croce to Collingwood, from Ducasse to Dewey, was expression theory, in a streamlined, twentieth-century model. Formalism was in the background, expression theory pretty much in center ring. There were, of course, alternatives: "aesthetic attitude" theory, to name one; but expression theory, for the most part, had a stranglehold on the philosophy of art.

This stranglehold and the lure of aesthetic attitude theory were both terminated not so much by technical objections to the theories themselves, which certainly were abroad, but rather, finally by the realization, from two separate quarters, that the enterprise itself, the task of defining a work of art, for which expression theory and aesthetic attitude theory were merely the current options, was suspect: seriously flawed in some philosophically deep way.

Two paths have been followed, in recent years, away from the traditional task of defining art. The first has led to a denial of the whole project. This is the path of the Wittgensteinians, who claim that the term "art" has a different "logic," different logical criteria of application from the "common property" criteria always assumed by the traditional task.

Another, and in my view more difficult, path has been taken by, most notably, Arthur Danto. Here the traditional task is not repudiated; rather, the concept of the *kind* of property we are looking for when we undertake the traditional task is profoundly changed.

One might well ask why I think the latter path more difficult (and, I should add, more fruitful and exciting). Isn't altering the task more radical than "merely" altering the property? I think not. It is far easier to throw out the baby with the bathwater than to perceive that you were mistaken about which was which. And it is a far more drastic perturbation of our conceptual scheme to take the baby for the bathwater than to start with an empty tub.

Be that as it may, it is important for understanding where we are in the traditional task, and where we might go, to canvass both alternatives. I begin with the earlier: the Wittgensteinian transformation.

§2   We derive the notion of what a "real definition" is supposed to do, of course, from Plato. And although the underlying ontology of the quest has been held to be different by different practitioners of the art, the generally stated goal has always been to find the "common property" with which "it" is, without which "it" isn't. For if there is no such property, then when we call all of the "its" by the same name, "we gibber," as Bell put it for the visual arts.[2]

The *locus classicus* for demurring from this traditional task of real definition is the discussion of "games" in Ludwig Wittgenstein's *Philosophical Investigations* (1953), the first, most familiar application of this discussion to the traditional task of defining "art" that of Morris Weitz.

That the common-property quest in defining art was compromised well before the entrance of the *Philosophical Investigations* on the philosophical scene is graphically illustrated by the opening pages of an article the American philosopher De Witt Parker published in 1939. Parker began: "The assumption underlying every philosophy of art is the existence of some common nature present in all the arts, despite their differences in form and content; something the same in painting and sculpture; in music and architecture."[3] He continued:

> The philosophy of art [which seeks some common nature in the arts] has however many things against it. The very possibility of a definition of art may be challenged on at least two grounds. In the first place it may be claimed that there is no significant nature common to all arts which could serve as a basis for a definition.[4]

If I were to read these sentences today to anyone in the philosophy of art who was unfamiliar with Parker or his essay, he or she would be convinced I was reading from Weitz or one of his followers. Clearly, the real definition of art, through the common-property route, was suspect long before Wittgensteinian aesthetics made its appearance in Anglo-American philosophy. But Parker's prescience ends here. For the alternative he offers for finding the common property of artworks is not some drastic Wittgensteinian change in the "logic" of concepts but merely the substitution of a three-property definition for a one-property one. The notion of a real definition is still very much in place, in terms of a common, albeit complex, "property."[5] As Weitz himself observed, "[I]nstead of inveighing against the attempt at definition of art itself, Parker insists that what is needed is a complex definition rather than a simple one."[6]

Weitz's own proposal, first put forward in his widely read essay, "The Role of Theory in Aesthetics" (1956), was that the real definition of art be given up as a hopeless, useless, and misdirected endeavor: hopeless because there is no common property, simple or complex; useless because we do not need such a common property to talk about works of art intelligibly or to give "meaning" to the general term "art"; misdirected because the project completely misconstrues the "logic" of the term. "Knowing what art is is not apprehending some manifest or latent essence but being able to recognize, describe, and explain those things we call 'art' in virtue of these similarities."[7]

Art then, on Weitz's view, is an "open" concept (following Wittgenstein's discussion of games in *Philosophical Investigations* 66 and 67).

> A concept is open if its conditions of application are emendable and corrigible; i.e., if a situation or case can be imagined or secured which would call for some sort of *decision* on our part to extend the use of the concept to cover this, or to close the concept and invent a new one to deal with the new case and its new property. If necessary and sufficient conditions for the application of a concept can be stated, the concept is a closed one.[8]

But the concept of "art" cannot be closed. For "the very expansive, adventurous character of art, its ever-present changes and novel creations, make it logically impossible to ensure any set of defining properties."[9] And so:

> "Art" itself is an open concept. New conditions (cases) have constantly arisen and will undoubtedly arise; new art forms, new movements will emerge, which will demand decisions on the part of those interested, usually professional critics, as to whether the concept should be extended or not.[10]

As became apparent in the years following the publication of his essay, Weitz failed to distinguish between two theses, an epistemic one and an ontological one. Weitz himself came to acknowledge this in later writings. For it might well be that we tell whether something is a work of art by noting family resemblances (the epistemic claim) even though, in fact, what makes it a work of art is some (unknown) property common to all artworks (the ontological claim). The analogy here is with natural kinds like "water," where we tell that something is water, in ordinary circumstances, by its resemblance to other samples of the stuff we have experienced in the past and have been doing so since time out of mind, even though (as we now know) all samples of water *do* in fact have a common "property" that makes them all water, namely, their molecular structure (i.e.,

H_2O). Similarly, it might well be that all works of art have a common (unknown) defining property (the ontological claim) even though we perforce tell which are and which are not works of art by noticing "strands of similarities."

Finally, there is what one might call a "meaning" question here, not always fully disentangled from the ontological and epistemic claims. For in saying that we do not need a common property to talk intelligibly about art, Weitz is answering Plato's claim, present so prominently in Bell but implicit in others as well, that it is through *reference* to a common property that the word "art" at least in part gets its meaning; that common-property reference is a necessary condition on the word "art" having meaning at all.

I shall put aside the meaning question altogether, although it is by no means a trivial one. My interest is in the ontological and epistemic claims: in particular, in what would follow for the future course of aesthetic inquiry if the Wittgensteinian account were true, either in its epistemic or in its ontological form or in both forms together. In his 1956 article Weitz argued that the end of aesthetic theory making has been to come to a real definition of "art." For Weitz the end of the quest for a real definition is ipso facto the end of theorizing. What then is left for us to do? Weitz says:

> The primary task of aesthetics is not to seek a theory but to elucidate the concept of art. Specifically, it is to describe the conditions under which we employ the concept correctly. Definition, reconstruction, patterns of analysis are out of place here since they distort and add nothing to our understanding of art.[11]

Suppose, now, you believe that the Wittgensteinian epistemic claim is correct but the ontological claim is false – in other words, you believe that we do generally tell whether something is a work of art by the method of family resemblance and the rest. If you believe this, then, presumably, there is no need for you to give up "theorizing" about art if that is your inclination. Since the Wittgensteinian claim is, for you, an epistemic, not an ontological, one, you can leave it to the "aesthetic epistemologists" to explicate and go on pretty much with business as usual, looking for that elusive common property.

If, on the other hand, you are a down-and-out ontological Wittgensteinian who believes that family resemblances are all there is out there, either epistemically or ontologically, you will of course, have to eschew "theorizing," at least as Weitz understands it, and stick to the task, as Weitz describes it, of elucidating the concept of art.

But at least as I understand matters, what you would be doing in elucidating the concept of art, once the Wittgensteinian "logic" itself was elucidated, which in the main it has been, at least for present purposes (or else you wouldn't be at the stage you are, of accepting it), would be examining problematic cases and trying to determine whether or how they might be works of art. And you would do so by noting family resemblances to paradigm cases. In other words, you would look for similarities and differences, tote them up, and either declare them in or declare them out and, in the process, sometimes alter the "concept" of art by so doing. You would be right back in the "sameness" business. The search for sameness might not be as obsessive for the Wittgensteinian as it must be for the traditional theorist. Nonetheless, it would have to be firmly in place, or else the problematic cases, the works of the avant-garde that were putting pressure on the concept, cluster concept thought it be, would be too frequently put down as nonart or borderline cases, and that would be simply to give up the game. The Wittgensteinian's central concept is, after all, family *resemblance.* It is resemblance that makes the thing work.

My advice to the Wittgensteinian, then, would be the same as to the traditional theorist: give resemblance (and your project) a rest. My theme is *differences.* But I still have a way to go before I can be more specific.

§3 The Wittgensteinian move in the philosophy of art was never a popular one, and at the present time it is not a going concern. The traditional task of defining the work of art is back in fashion, with a vengeance, if indeed it ever really was absent.

Many developments in the philosophy of language have taken

place since 1953; and the Wittgensteinian model, in general, does not seem so attractive an alternative to a supposedly bankrupt tradition, although analysis by necessary and sufficient condition is not in high repute these days either. The fact is that there are alternatives to cluster concepts or business as usual, à la Plato. But I must leave these questions to those who know better than I how to deal with them.

There is a simpler, less philosophically expansive reason why I reject the Wittgensteinian model for art. It is simply that the only argument for its being a proper model is a bad argument. Here it is, in Weitz's words: "[W]hat I am arguing, then, is that the very expansive, adventurous character of art, its ever-present changes and novel creations, make it logically impossible to ensure any set of defining properties." Any traditional definition "forecloses on the very conditions of creativity in the arts."[12] It is no exaggeration to say that Weitz places almost the full weight of his argument that "art" *must* be an open concept on the claim that this and only this is consistent with the "creativity" of art, that a traditional definition "forecloses" on artistic "creativity."

But it is not at all clear just what the cash value of "creativity" is in Weitz's original claim. Even if (say) representation were a necessary condition for an art, it could hardly foreclose on "originality" or "creativity," since both (and I assume they are not synonymous) can be exhibited within the constraints of representation and, as far as I can tell, can continue to be exhibited in infinitum: there are infinite changes to be rung on the theme of "representation."

What Weitz has in mind for "creativity" and "originality" must be something other than this. What it is becomes more apparent in his writing after the essay of 1956; and that his argument is exactly the same except for the absence of the word "creativity" is, as I shall argue, highly significant. Here is Weitz's argument as restated in *The Opening Mind* (1977): "For my argument against theories of art was (and is) that they attempt to state definitive criteria for a concept whose use has depended on and continues to depend, not on its having such a set, but rather on its being able, for its correct use, to accommodate new criteria that are derived, or derivable, from new art forms whose features demand emendation, rejection, or expansion of extant criteria."[13]

This is the same argument, exactly, that we had in "The Role of Theory in Aesthetics," except for the palpable absence of the word "creativity," notably present in the earlier argument. Why the absence? I think it is because Weitz has simply made the term synonymous with the terms of his own (Wittgensteinian) logical model, redefined it in a way that does indeed make it impossible for there to be creativity in art unless "art" is understood in the Wittgensteinian manner.

Here is what has happened. Creativity, at least of a certain kind, call it "radical creativity," has simply come to mean by definition, in Weitz's account, adding new criteria to the cluster concept of art or deleting established criteria. Radical creativity is what we see happening in artistic revolutions, where something startling, even outrageously new, is achieved in the art world, where the thing produced is so different from previous things we recognized as artworks as to lead us to doubt whether the thing could be an artwork at all. And in the passage just quoted this has become, by stipulation, the process of Wittgensteinian criterion making and criterion breaking. So of course it now turns out that the only logical model that can accommodate radical creativity in the arts is the Wittgensteinian model, because radical creativity has been implicitly defined in terms of the model. Furthermore, this was already the case in Weitz's earlier statement, where the term "creativity" was still in place.

Now we have already seen that nonradical creativity is perfectly compatible with real definitions of art. There is no limit to novelty within (say) representational painting or, to take another example, tonal music. Weitz's argument must be taken to be, then, that the open-concept model has to be the correct one for the concept of "art" because it is the only model consistent with radical creativity in the arts. But now we see directly that there is no argument. Weitz has not shown that the open-concept model alone can accommodate radical creativity. He has made it the only possible model by defining radical creativity in terms of that model. And since, as Weitz himself asserts, the creativity "argument" is the one on which he bases his Wittgensteinian analysis of "art," the only reason for accepting the analysis has gone down the tubes. That radical creativity can be accommodated only by the Wittgensteinian model is in need of an argument, which Weitz never gives.

Can radical creativity be accommodated by the tradition-al, common-property necessary-and-sufficient-condition model? Weitz has not, as I have just argued, given us any reason to think it cannot. And, as a matter of fact, the most powerful anal-ysis of radical creativity in our time, that of Arthur Danto, is based on that very model. We cannot know where we are in the philosophy of art, or where we might go, without taking the measure of Danto's work in the field.

§4   The "crisis" in aesthetics reflected by the Wittgensteinian move is precipitated by the acute awareness that the tradition-al task of defining the work of art by common property, neces-sary and sufficient conditions, genus and difference has so far been a failure, and a failure that began with Plato – with, in other words, the beginning of philosophy itself, as we under-stand and practice it. Weitz sees in this failure the persistent application of the wrong logical model to the concept of art. But there are those, beginning with Maurice Mandelbaum and, later, George Dickie, who diagnose the failure rather as the persistent search for the wrong kind of "common property." Among these I place Danto – but not, as others do, among the defenders of the so-called institutional theory of art, at least nar-rowly construed.

Danto's most systematic exposition of his view can be found in *The Transfiguration of the Commonplace* (1981). In that work he offers the seemingly old-fashioned, indeed antique, proposal that the common property of all works of art, their genus in the Aristotelian scheme of definition, is *representationality*. All art-works are representations.

To see how Danto's proposal represents a new beginning as well as a return to a tradition – "neorepresentationalism" might be the appropriate name for it – we must briefly examine Danto's favorite example: a pair of visually indistinguishable objects, one an artwork, the other just a real thing; or its augmented version, a trio of visually indistinguishable objects, one an artwork, the second a different artwork, the third just a real thing.

So much has been written in recent years about this aspect of Danto's aesthetic theory that it scarcely seems necessary for me to add my voice to the chorus. Suffice it to say that because such objects as urinals, bicycle wheels, snow shovels, Brillo boxes, beds, and blank canvases have been exhibited, and apparently accepted, as works of art, it becomes a pressing philosophical problem to explain how these artworks are distinguished from their counterparts outside the museum and in their workaday worlds and, in addition, how two visually identical objects, two blue canvases, for example, might be two different works of art with two distinctive subjects (or no subjects at all).

Danto's now-famous response to this philosophical puzzle was to claim that identifiable features can indeed be found to distinguish artworks from their real-world counterparts and art-works from their perceptually identical artwork twins, but features "the eye cannot decry – an atmosphere of artistic theory, a knowledge of the history of art: an artworld."[14] It was this claim that separated Danto at once from Wittgensteinian anties-sentialism on the one hand and traditional essentialism on the other, while still enabling him to produce an essentialist defi-nition of art.

Specifically, Danto maintained in *The Transfiguration of the Commonplace* that works of art are distinguished from the real things with which they might now be confused, in the present state of things, in that "the former are about something (or the question of what they are about may legitimately arise)."[15] And, by consequence, perceptually indistinguishable artworks can be told apart by what, in particular, they are about.

However, "aboutness" can be only the genus of "artwork," not its full essence, for clearly things other than artworks belong to it. So to the genus must be appended its difference. "The thesis is that works of art, in categorical contrast with mere rep-resentations, use the means of representation in a way that is not exhaustively specified when one has exhaustively specified what is being represented."[16] To put the point another way, a work of art, in contrast to a mere representation, not only possesses a content but *"expresses* something about that content."[17]

The genus of artworks – what might be called the "aboutness" criterion – has, it is apparent, been quite circumspectly formulated to ward off counterexamples. Not all visual works of art, let alone works of absolute music, are about anything. It is always open to the artist or critic to correctly claim that a work of art possesses no content whatever, yet remains a work of art for all that. But all the aboutness criterion requires is that it *make sense* to ask what the work of art is about, not that it actually be about something, as it wouldn't, for example, to ask what a bicycle or a fish is about. So the aboutness criterion can exclude the bicycle or the fish while embracing the contentless canvas.

The problem of the aboutness criterion concerns, it hardly needs pointing out, the parenthetical escape clause: *"or* the question of what they are about *may legitimately arise."* What legitimizes the question of aboutness? How do we determine, if not merely by intuition, that it can be legitimately asked of a blank canvas in a museum of contemporary art but not of a bicycle in a department store or a fish in a net? And can it be legitimately asked of a piano sonata or a string quartet?

If we are going to decide the question merely by intuition – decide, perhaps, how the question "What is it about?" sounds to the ordinary language ear in any given case – then many, like myself, will find it as odd to ask what most pieces of absolute music mean as to ask what any piece of decoration or pure design means or, for that matter, what a bicycle or a fish means. It might be replied that absolute music is art, that is, "fine art," and neither decorative art nor a bicycle or fish is *that.* Now thus baldly put, the response seems clearly question-begging. For it is just the status of absolute music as a fine art that is being tested by asking whether the question of aboutness can be legitimately raised with regard to it, and one can't very well invoke its status as a fine art to prove that very thing.

There is, however, a less obviously question-begging way of responding to the question of whether aboutness can at least sensibly be asked of absolute music. Absolute music, after all, has at least a history since the eighteenth century of being classed by some (though not all) with the fine arts. So that should make it at least a possible candidate for aboutness or content of some kind. Bicycles and fish have no such history, and so no even prima facie case to be made for their being about anything. Easel painting has a long history of aboutness, in other words, of representation. So when one sees a blank canvas exhibited in an art gallery as (ostensibly) a work of art, it seems altogether plausible to ask, no doubt perplexedly, "What is it about?" even though the answer might well be, "It isn't about anything." Now absolute music has no such history of (undisputed) representation. But because it has, since the late eighteenth century, been customarily classified, at least in some circles, with the representational fine arts, absolute music has gained, so to say, a representational history "by association." Although it has no such history as absolute music, it does as a "generally accepted candidate for fine art membership." The answer to the question "What is it about?" may, in the case of absolute music, *always* be, "It isn't about anything." Nonetheless, the question is legitimate because of the association of absolute music with the representational arts since the Enlightenment. Bicycles and fish have no such association and hence lack even prima facie candidacy for aboutness. To ask what they are about is to ask an obviously illegitimate, not to say absurd, question.

But this response will impress only someone who is not initially skeptical about the very process by which absolute music is supposed to have been gathered into the fold of the fine arts. As we have seen, however, that process was far from decisive and did not run its course until one hundred years after Kristeller's "Modern System of the Arts" is assumed to have been in place. Thus the historical tradition of absolute music as a fine art is both recent and tentative. It can well be questioned, therefore, whether absolute music is a fine art at all, on the basis of the very tradition being appealed to by those who might claim that the "traditional" association of absolute music with the fine arts legitimates the raising of the aboutness question in regard to it. It is just not clear whether the question "What is it about?" can legitimately be asked of absolute music, and so it is at least arguable that absolute music does not even satisfy the most minimal condition, on Danto's view, for something's being art.

There may yet, however, be ways to bring absolute music within the ambit of Danto's theory: kinds of "aboutness" for absolute music beyond the minimal criterion. Here are three candidates: (a) Absolute music may be "about emotions." (b) Absolute music may be "about fictional worlds" of some kind that it generates (the way a novel is). (c) Absolute music may be "about itself." None of these alternatives will work. But each deserves a run for the money.

§5 The first alternative, call it the theory of "emotive about-ness," is at least mentioned in passing by Danto himself:

> Music is not generally regarded as an imitative art, though both Aristotle and Plato regarded it that way, and there have been those who supposed that if it did not merely express the emotions, it in some way mimed them. But from the perspec-tive of the concept of medium, the intermediary substance and avenue of transmission from subject to spectator, music shares crucial features with painting and sculpture and drama.[18]

It is not clear whether Danto is suggesting here that he might endorse some version of "emotive aboutness" for absolute mu-sic or is merely calling our attention to its existence.[19] Is the fact that Plato, Aristotle, and others have found such a view attrac-tive being used, if not as an argument from authority, or a vox populi, at least as a hint that the view is not altogether implau-sible?

In any case, Danto lets the matter drop and (as a substitute?) goes on to argue that music shares other "crucial features with painting and sculpture and drama." There is no need for us to canvass these other shared features. *They* cannot bring absolute music into Danto's account, for aboutness is the necessary (though not sufficient) condition. What these (purported) fea-tures can show, which no one doubts, is that music is at least like the fine arts in certain nontrivial ways.

But whether or not Danto has entertained an "emotive about-ness" theory for absolute music, we certainly can do it for him. First, what, briefly, would such a theory look like?

A very large number of those who theorize about such matters (including myself), as well as (I venture to say) all lay listeners to music, believe that, in some sense or other, music possesses expressive properties: that is to say, it is sometimes sad, sometimes joyful, sometimes angry, and so on. Accounts of what is meant by music's being sad or joyful or angry or whatever differ widely. But at least some suggest or imply that if a piece of music is (say) sad in one section, then sadness is its "content" there; in that place, the music might be said to be "about sadness." Indeed, one might even want to say that we can specify more fully what is conveyed about the sadness. Jerrold Levinson, for example, writes: "Granted, musical works typically lack a representational content. . . . However, musical works have other sorts of content, in particular *expressive* content."[20] Furthermore, this expressive content may be articulated beyond the bare statement that such and such a passage is melancholy or joyful or whatever. Thus, on Levinson's view, some passages in Brahms's Sonata for Violin and Piano in D Minor "express violent passion, and thus . . . express passion as violent."[21]

Now once we have gotten to the point of saying that passages in a work of absolute music have expressive "content," that that expressive content is violent passion, and that the passages express the passion *as* violent, we have quite enough, one would think, to satisfy Danto's aboutness requirement. And as a great deal of Western art music since the sixteenth century has such recognizable expressive features where an emotion is expressed as so-and-so, we have a firm historical tradition in place that validates the question "What is it about?" for *any* passage of music in the tradition, even though the answer in many cases will be "It's not about anything," since a great deal of music is not expressive of any particular emotion at all. Danto, then, seems to have his desired conclusion in Levinson's analysis.[22]

But does he? The crucial question is whether agreeing that sadness, joy, and so forth – what I like to call the "garden-variety emotions" – are properly "perceived in" music commits one to anything like Levinson's conclusion. Specifically, does it commit one to ascribing any semantic or representational property to music? Does it commit one to musical aboutness? It is common to characterize a musical passage as "calm" or "turbulent" or "vigorous." Surely it makes no sense to claim that that, ipso facto, commits one to saying that the music represents those things, or is about them, or that those things are its "content" in a semantic sense of the word. They are merely its "content" in that they are "in" the music, as the colors are "in" the painting: they are part of its "musical content." Why should it not be the same with "sad," "joyful," "angry," or any of the other garden-variety emotions as ascribed to music?

Clearly, one compelling motive behind the move from "sad" to "about sadness" might be prior commitment to Danto's analysis of art. If one were convinced that Danto (or a Danto-like theory) were right, one would have a big stake in having it the case that absolute music, a potential counterexample, is *about* the garden-variety emotions when expressive of them. But one cannot, after all, take up that view merely on systematic grounds. It would be a nice outcome for Danto's position if music's being expressive of the garden-variety emotions, which it often is, meant ipso facto that it were also about them. It remains, however, to be proved that that is the case. That calm music is not, ipso fact, about calmness, or turbulent music about turbulence, makes that abundantly clear.

But, it may be objected, if we are not attributing at least minimal semantic content to absolute music by ascribing the ordinary emotions to it, what are we doing? My view is that we are ascribing perceptual qualities to the music, perhaps emergent or supervenient ones, just as we are apparently doing when we call it calm or turbulent. I have spelled out some of the details and consequences of that elsewhere, and will not discuss them here.

§6 That absolute music could be about fictional worlds might seem a bizarre thing to claim at this point in the history of aesthetics, and more appropriate to late Romanticism than to the present state of aesthetic and musical analysis. Nevertheless, such a claim has recently been made by a philosopher of extraordinarily keen insight and intelligence, far from a wild ecstatic. And if he is right, then a conclusion about absolute music compatible with Danto's analysis of the visual arts will have been made in a completely unexpected way.

In an intriguing article called "Listening with Imagination: Is Music Representational?" Kendall Walton adduces numerous examples of what he describes as absolute music generating at least fragmentary "fictional worlds."[23] The general purpose of his article is to bring absolute music into the ambit of his own theory of representation as "make-believe."[24] That purpose is not directly relevant to my concerns here, although I shall come back to it briefly in a moment. Nor is it necessary for us to canvass all of Walton's ingenious examples and their ramifications. What I shall do is examine one of his illustrations of musical fiction, which will give us enough of an idea of what he is about to see how, if Walton is right, absolute music can be secured for Danto. In the event, I will argue that the case has not been satisfactorily made.

Consider the opening eight bars (piano solo) of the Adagio of Mozart's Piano Concerto in A, K. 488. Walton writes:

> The upper voice is *late* in coming to the A in bar 8. There are precedents for this tardiness earlier in the passage. The upper voice was late in getting to the A (and F#) at the beginning of bar 3; in bar 4 it participates in a suspension; in bar 6 it is late getting to the C#. In the first two cases the bass waits "patiently" for the soprano to arrive. But in the second phrase, the bass can't wait. It is locked into a (near) sequence, which allows no delay. In bar 6, as in bar 8, the bass has moved on, changing the harmony, by the time the soprano arrives.[25]

Walton sees in this description of the music the implication of a musical fiction – a kind of "story" in the opening of Mozart's Adagio. The musical story may not have characters with names and personalities, events with fully fleshed-out fictional details. "But why shouldn't it count as fictional anyway, as representing instances of lateness, fortuitousness, etc.?" He goes on:

It would be inadequate to think of the music as merely indicating or expressing the *property* of lateness; it portrays a particular (fictitious) instance of something's being late on a
particular occasion. Listeners imagine something's being late
on a particular occasion; they do not merely contemplate the
quality of lateness.[26]

The lateness of Mozart's theme is, of course, but one among
many, indeed a multitude of, such "fictions" in absolute music.
So the ultimate conclusion to be drawn from this example, and
ones like it, which Walton is not reluctant to draw, is that the
works of so-called pure instrumental music are fictional to their
very core:

It looks as though they may have worlds teeming with life,
just under the surface at least – like swamp water seen
through a microscope. If we follow through on our purist in-
clinations to reject stories or images or meanings attached to
music as unmusical, if not childish or silly, we must begin to
wonder how much of what we love about music will be left.[27]

Walton, a trained musician, is well aware of the dangerous
implications of what he is saying for the understanding of the
music he and we most cherish for its "purity." "Our experiences
of music seem shot through with imaginings," he writes, "yet
I, at least, continue to resist the idea that Bach's *Brandenburg
Concerti* and Brahms's symphonies have fictional worlds, as
Crime and Punishment and *Hamlet* do."[28] A good deal of Walton's
article is devoted to how he can save our experience of the "purity" of absolute music while still seeing it as a veritable zoo of
"fictions." I shall have something more to say about the "content" of music when I discuss, later on, my own views on absolute music, which are at the very heart of the thesis of this
book – the thesis of "differences." But our present task is to see
if the initial premise of "fictions" in absolute music, in Walton's
sense of that term, is initially plausible, convincing enough to
save absolute music for Danto's account of art.

I begin by extracting from Walton's account what I take to be
an implicit argument something to this effect: (a) Listening suc-

cessfully to music requires listening to it with "imagination" – "imaginatively." (b) Listening to music "imaginatively," with "imagination," implies imparting fictions to it, hearing fictions in it. (c) Therefore, music contains fictions, is fictional, at least in some minimal sense of those words.

I think this argument is totally wrongheaded because although the first premise is certainly true, the second is just as certainly false. And whether or not Walton ever intended that his article express such an argument, it is an argument worth refuting, for the process of refuting it will be a convenient way of revealing what in his "fictional" way of listening to music is troubling and implausible.

I believe the argument in question gains its footing on the confusion between or the ignoring of two different roles the imagination can be seen to play in our lives or, perhaps, the failure to recognize two different faculties we possess that have both been called "imagination." This bipartite division of the faculty of imagination (if "faculty" is the right term for it) has been recognized at least since Kant's first *Critique*, if not before. I shall call these two parts or functions or "imaginations" "fictional imagination" and "constructive imagination."

The fictional imagination is familiar enough and seems to have been what seventeenth- and early-eighteenth-century thinkers had exclusively in mind, as, for example, in Francis Bacon (1605): "[T]he Imagination, which beeing not tyed to the Lawes of Matter, may at pleasure ioyne what Nature hath seured, and seuer that which Nature hath Ioyned, and so make vnlawfull Matches and diuorses of things. . . ."[29] In this sense of "imagination," it is axiomatic that to listen to music "with imagination" is to listen to music "fictionally" – to impute fictions to music or hear fictions in it.

But surely it is not that kind of imagination that is necessary for musical listening; rather it is the kind of imagination we have become familiar with from the *Critique of Pure Reason* – the kind that synthesizes raw data into our perceptual/conceptual world. It is perfectly true that listening "without imagination" would impoverish our musical understanding. Indeed, that is a gross understatement: more accurately, it would make listening to *music* impossible; it would not be music that we heard.

Let me try to clarify this point with a simple illustration that, by degrees, can be worked up to any complexity one wishes, including Walton's musical fictions. Without the functioning of what I called the "constructive imagination," a listener would not hear melodies but merely individual tones occurring seriatim. Hearing individual tones melodically, as "joined together," when, after all, they are not is an "imaginative" task.[30] But this hardly makes melodies "fictions": it is not fictionally true that the individual tones of "Là ci darem la Mano" are a melody; it is literally true.

But just as one hears individual tones as connected, as a melody, with the operation of the constructive imagination, one hears a melody as having a certain character as well with the constructive imagination's cooperation. One hears a calm melody or an agitated melody and so on. And again, it is not fictionally true that the melody is calm or agitated; it is literally true.

We can now return to Walton's example of the delayed melody and see directly that it is no more fictionally true that it is delayed than that it is a melody or that it is tranquil. Nothing is represented as delayed: the melody *is* (nonfictionally) delayed, although it requires imaginative listening to hear the delay, just as it does to hear the melody; it requires, in other words, the constructive imagination.

Now to this it might be replied that, after all, it does no harm to talk about the melody as fictionally delayed, and such talk has the advantage of bringing absolute music into the ambit of Danto's theory of aboutness or Walton's own theory of make-believe. But for someone like myself, who has no such prior theoretical commitments, neither consideration carries any weight. Furthermore, it is not a harmless *façon de parler* at all. Rather, it leads to conceptual troubles of its own.

Music does sometimes "represent"; it does sometimes generate (or help to generate) fictions; and we want, indeed *have*, a way of talking about this. A melody that delays reaching a musical goal, like the one Walton talks about, can be used, for just that reason, to represent fictionally a character's delay in an opera (say) or a programmatic symphony. The melody of "Là ci darem la mano," we want to say, "represents" Don Giovanni's expression of feigned love to Zerlina by its melodic sweetness, seductiveness, and beauty. The melody is the medium, not the message; the fact, not the fiction. We want to say that a few dabs of yellow represent a flower, make it fictionally true perhaps that the flower is there, in front of the apple. What we do not want to say is that the *yellow dabs* are represented. *They* are what is doing the representing. What we do not want to say is that the melody is fictionally delayed; its literal, musical delay is what is making it fictionally true that some character in an opera or a programmatic symphony is fictionally delaying.

Perhaps someone can find another intelligible way of talking about these things. But the way we now talk about them, as above, seems all right to me: it is natural, conforms to the way we talk with regard, for example, to representational painting, and is firmly in place. That being the case, I have no reason to change my way of talking about such things, and see awkwardness or even unintelligibility lurking in the prospect. To conclude, I find no help for a Danto-like theory of musical aboutness from Walton's direction. His notion of how absolute music might generate fictional worlds, and what these worlds might be like, avoids many of the pitfalls of the familiar Romantic effusions, with their overly detailed, largely irresponsible "readings" of the musical literature. However, it fails to convince me of either its plausibility or its utility as an account of what we appreciate and enjoy in music. (More about the latter is to come.) Only the third alternative remains: that music may be internally representational, that, in other words, it may refer to and be "about" *itself.*

§7   A number of years ago, before Danto's full account appeared in *The Transfiguration of the Commonplace* and existed only in some sketches in the periodical literature, Richard Kuhns quite presciently saw a possible direction a Danto-like theory of absolute music might take. This is not to say that that was the stated purpose of Kuhns's brief article. Rather, Kuhns aimed at

refuting Roger Scruton's claim that music cannot be representational,[31] by showing that Danto's theory (in the form it then
was in) allowed a kind of musical representation in its own
terms. Nevertheless, the result of Kuhns's exercise, if he is correct, is to establish a way in which music can fulfill Danto's
aboutness criterion.

Kuhns enumerates three ways in which music might be seen
to be self-referential and hence about itself:

> Music quotes music. Bach quotes Vivaldi. Bach quotes
> Bach. . . .
>
> Tones in music represent other tones. A modulation from
> major to minor refers as it moves, and establishes referring
> relationships as it sounds. . . . Tones both sound and refer as
> they sound. . . . This mode of representation is one of music's
> most powerful representational capacities.
>
> Music is built on repetitions, repeats, themes and variations,
> modulations, twelve-tone rows – all of these means are rep-
> resentational because each heard phrase or section leads the
> listener to hear other phrases and sections.[32]

Of course, all of the phenomena Kuhns cites are genuine phenomena of musical listening and appreciation. The question is,
Should they be interpreted *semantically* – that is to say, in terms
of "reference" and "representation"? Again one might argue
"from above." Having already accepted Danto's analysis of art,
a semantic interpretation of the phenomena is a theoretical de-
sideratum or imperative. But viewed in the absence of such a
theoretical commitment, what are we to say? We do surely experience these musical features. Is our experience semantical or
representational? With that question in mind, let us go through
them one by one.

In absolute music, musical "quotations" (that many of us put
them in scare quotes is indicative of our skepticism) are of two
general kinds. First is the kind where someone else's theme is
taken by a composer for his own composition; for example,
someone else's theme is used as the subject for a fugue or as the
theme in a theme and variations. Second is the kind where a
composer at some point weaves another composer's theme into

his composition, as in the twenty-second of the Diabelli Variations, Op. 120, where Beethoven introduces a theme from *Don Giovanni*, Leporello's "Notte e giorno faticar," just as if it were a "natural" part of its structure. (It is the latter kind that we are most prone, I think, to call "quotation.")

Of course, to call such things "quotations" in the first place is to beg the question in favor of a semantic interpretation of them. We usually mean to assert propositions thereby when we "quote" other authors' words in our own writings. And because of that, the term "quotation" is frequently put in scare quotes when used to refer to these musical cases, obviously evidence of many people's reluctance to give the term its literal, semantic sense in the musical cases.

If musical "quotations" are really *quotations*, then their use must be, at least in some of the standard cases, to *assert* things. But what do they assert? What did Beethoven (or his work) assert when he incorporated Mozart's theme in the twenty-second of the Diabelli Variations? What did he (or his work) assert when he used Diabelli's waltz for his variations in the first place? The desperate will say that he (or it) asserted: "It is possible to get from Diabelli's theme to Leporello's aria with musical coherence," or "It is possible to get all of these variations out of Diabelli's waltz." Is that what we want to say? Is that how wide we want to make the concepts of quotation, assertion, and the rest? On such a construal, a pot would make an "assertion": "It is possible to be a pot of this shape, of this material, of this size, etc." Therein madness (and semiology?) lies. There is more to quoting, on my view, than absolute music has to give, which is why music only "quotes." (That is not music's shortcoming, but its nature; not its curse, but its blessing.)

Kuhns's other two examples rely heavily on the idea of intraopus reference: that is to say, features of a work "referring" to other features of it, either predictively, where a passage "refers" to another that is to come, or retrospectively, where a passage "refers" to or "recollects" a passage that has gone before. In the former instance, one might want to say that the "referring" passage leads you to expect what is to come, in the latter to remember what has taken place; and in both cases, the "referring" passage "suggests" to you, brings to mind, what you have heard or will hear but are not now hearing.

The question again is whether there is enough of the right stuff here to compel us to construe these musical phenomena as even vaguely or remotely "semantic." It is *not* enough simply because a passage "suggests," raises in your mind, another passage that was, or is to come to describe the passage as "referring," the relationships as, even broadly speaking, "semantic," even though that suggestion was intended by the composer and reliably occurs in the qualified listener. Plenty of artifacts, after all, are designed with the intention of parts suggesting other parts without our wanting to impute semantic properties to them. And nature abounds with cases of "suggestion" as well. (Clouds are a "sign" of rain, and unless one is a Bishop Berkeley, one hardly wants to remove the scare quotes.) Such intention to suggest, and success in suggesting, may indeed be necessary conditions for meaning, but they are certainly not sufficient.[33]

To be sure, music is a complicated artifact involving in its creation, its study, and its performance many complex symbol systems, musical notation being the most obvious and complex among them. But I speak here only of absolute music as a heard and aurally appreciated object of aesthetic attention. And Kuhns, I think, has provided no convincing argument that that "object" of aesthetic attention and appreciation exhibits semantic, referential, or representational features of the kinds he discusses. I see no promise in this direction of musical self-reference for the gathering up of absolute music into Danto's theory of art. And although I cannot claim to have canvassed all other possibilities to that end, I am at least persuaded that so far the prospects are bleak. So until I am confronted with more favorable prospects, I will consider the case against an "aboutness" account of absolute music closed.

§8 I have been arguing that the history of aesthetic theory, from its modern beginnings in the eighteenth century to its present, flourishing state, has been almost a single-purpose quest for the "common property," with absolute music as the perennial *experimentum crucis* (except in formalism, where it is the paradigm case). And as things presently stand, that quest remains the major activity of philosophers of art, with no settled-on solution in hand.

This is not to say that differences in the arts have not, historically, been recognized as an object of philosophical concern. In the eighteenth century, how the arts differ, and what their rank order of value is, was a central question for the young discipline of aesthetics. This question persisted well into the nineteenth century. In general, the eighteenth-century answer was that the arts differ in medium, the nineteenth-century answer (Schopenhauer, for example) that they differ in kind of object of representation. And it is perhaps in the work of Hegel and Schopenhauer that the quest for differences produced its most interesting philosophical results.

However that may be, the overriding concern was, and continues to be, the search for sameness; and that search has blinded the philosophical community to a bevy of questions of more than trivial importance, involving the arts not in their sameness but in their particularity. Furthermore, the near hegemony of representation, or, to use Danto's more inclusive concept, "aboutness," as the defining theoretical concept has determined the way we perceive, misperceive, or fail to perceive the individual arts in various pernicious ways.

I am not for a moment suggesting that the search for definition, for sameness, is either fruitless or necessarily doomed to failure. Nor am I even suggesting that as a philosophical enterprise it be held in abeyance until the times are more propitious. It will always, in the nature of the case, have a firm hold on the philosophical consciousness of many, if not most. To recommend that it be abandoned, even temporarily, would be to no useful purpose whatever.

Rather, what I am urging, by both precept and example, is that the project of philosophically scrutinizing the individual arts – both "high" and "low" – and their distinctive differences be taken off the back burner and put up front. There is no reason we cannot keep two kettles boiling at once. Such is my precept.

My example, which follows, consists of "case studies" in the

pursuit of differences in the arts. With the long historical narrative of how we got to the present point in aesthetics behind
us, we now turn to artistic differences, at least some of them, as
I presently perceive them. It is the first step in a project that
others besides myself have already undertaken and that, I hope,
more will be enticed to explore.

Chapter 3

Reading and Representation

§1 Most philosophers of art would agree, I thank, that if anything is an established fact in their discipline, it is that literature is largely, and in an important way, a "representational" art. There are, indeed, some isolated dissenters from this orthodoxy. A vigorous and insightful argument against the representational status of poetry was indeed run by Edmund Burke in Part 5 of his highly influential *Philosophical Enquiry into the Origin of Our Ideas of the Sublime and Beautiful,* where he concluded "that poetry, taken in its most general sense, cannot with strict propriety be called an art of imitation."[1] But it seems to have gotten lost in the flap over the sublime. Clive Bell and Roger Fry, as well as other formalist critics, have made a brave attempt to discredit this generally accepted "fact." And there is a school of literary theory today that, by implication, denies it, since according to its members, texts are about texts, not about "the world out there," whereas believers in literature as representation surely believe that what literature represents is precisely "the world out there" (and, of course, the bodies and minds that inhabit it). On the whole, however, the "fact" of literature as a representational art remains intact.

Furthermore, if literature being representational in essence is an almost universally accepted fact among philosophers of art, it is also one of the most venerable, having been established, most would say, in the earliest "philosophy of art" we possess: Plato's, as laid out in *Republic* 3 and 10.

This old and established "fact" I wish to question seriously. For although Plato certainly believed that certain kinds of what we would consider literature, and certain parts thereof, are representational, he did not, as readers of the *Republic* well know, believe that "literature" *tout court* is mimetic (for which read "representational"). I suspect that a general tendency, throughout the history of thought on the subject, to ignore this important aspect of Plato's doctrine has helped lead to the general complaisance with regard to the received opinion that *all* literature is quintessentially a representational art.

But before we get to Plato and the historical roots of our problem, we must deal with two preliminary matters. First, we must have some idea of how we are construing the troublesome concept of "representation." Second, I must give at least an initially plausible reason for challenging such a well-entrenched view as that literature, the oldest, most established of the arts in the modern system, is paradigmatically a representational art. So (for some perverse reason) second things first.

§2   If any art is paradigmatically representational it surely must be the art of painting (with the exception of pure decoration) as it has been practiced from antiquity to the twentieth century. And surely the first (but by no means the only) genre that would come to the contemporary mind at the mention of "literature" would be the novel, which has an unbroken tradition going back at least to the eighteenth century. So deeply is the former art "representational" and the latter "literature" that I can make the following two claims about each, respectively, with great confidence. No philosophy of painting worthy of the name could be considered successful if it could not give an account of how representation functions as an integral artistic part of what we call "representational" paintings. And no philosophy of literature worthy of the name could be considered successful if it could not give an account of how we experience and appreciate novels. I do not argue for these claims. I simply assume them. If you cannot share these assumptions, follow me no further.

To continue: if an argument is to be made for "literature," *tout court*, as a representational art, then the argument must certainly be made for the special case of the novel. There may be peripheral cases of literature – nonsense verse, for example –

that we would allow to elude the net of representationality without seriously compromising the representation theory of literature. But if such a central case as that of the novel should elude the net, we would justly consider the claim that literature is essentially representational thereby refuted outright. This is not to say, of course, that we could not continue to maintain, quite correctly, that some genres of literature, or some aspects of some genres, are indeed representational. Nonetheless, we would surely have to give up the familiar and comfortable notion that the representationality of "literature" is an old and established "fact." The case of the novel would mock such a notion.

But that is just what I want to claim: that novels cannot be construed as representational works of art at all, at least not in the sense of "representation" traditionally taken for granted.

Take the typical case of representation in the arts. I gaze at a Cézanne landscape and see a mountain. Well, a pedantic German professor is supposed to have corrected his young pupils in a similar situation: "No, you do not see a mountain; you see a picture." But we all know what we are talking about, at least for present purposes. We see a picture. We see a mountain. We see oil paint. We see a mountain "in" the picture, we "see in," to use Richard Wollheim's way of putting such things. All of these "seeings" and more make up our experience of the representation. And at this point we need be no more precise than that.

But it seems clear, to begin with, that we do not see things represented in novels. Indeed, novels are not perceptual objects at all. Of course we see pages and words and so forth. No one, however, thinks that *that* is seeing novels in an aesthetic or artistic sense. And we hardly "see in" novels their characters and settings, the way we see the mountain in Cézanne's painting or in any other analogous way.

It might be responded that we see in the imagination, in the mind's eye, what we read when enjoying a novel; and although that is not literally "seeing," it is close enough to save the notion that the art of the novel is representational. On this view, my reading a novel produces in my imagination, in my mind's eye, a kind of mental cinema, and my experience of the novel lies in the "perception" of that inner narrative motion picture. A novel, then, is a movie of the mind.

I believe that many people who are not in the business of making theories but read novels for whatever rewards and satisfaction that activity affords have something like the "cinema" idea of the thing in the backs of their minds. Furthermore, such an idea was widely held in the eighteenth century, minus, of course, the cinema analogy, when the modern system of the arts was in the process of being established and mimesis was the cement that was to bind the arts together. This picture was fully supported, it is important to note, by the then-reigning (though not completely unchallenged) account of language: John Locke's, as laid out, most fully, in Book 3 of the *Essay Concerning Human Understanding*.

According to the well-known Lockean view of language, words (with perhaps the exception of syncategorimatic terms) refer to "ideas" in the writer's or speaker's mind. When these words are uttered or written, they have the effect, if communication is successful, of arousing tokens of the types of those self-same ideas in the auditor or reader, respectively. Communication consists in the successful "transference" of ideas from writer or speaker to reader or auditor. And understanding a spoken or written message just is having tokens of the types of the speaker's or reader's ideas so aroused.

There are, I think, at least two good reasons for rejecting the cinematic account of novel reading. The first and more informal reason is that, judging from my own experience, it is quite out of step with the way I – and presumably others like me – read novels and, when you think about it, is quite repugnant to common sense. Second, to the extent that it relies on the Lockean model of language and communication, or something like it, it relies on a discredited model – not a real option for us at this time.

If I read, or hear recited, the immortal "Jack and Jill," I really do think that I sometimes visualize in my mind's eye a little girl in a dirndl and a little boy in lederhosen (don't ask me why), going up that hill to their tragic denouement. But, by contrast, when I read *Howards End,* at adult speed, it hardly does, or can, raise such images in my mind's eye as a running commentary, so to speak, on the text. This is not to say that no images at all are aroused. And I suspect that different parts of a novel will be arousal-effective for different readers, for all sorts of personal reasons, although some parts, perhaps because of their importance in the narrative, the vividness of the writing, or impressiveness of the event, are likely to be arousal-effective for everyone. I doubt, for example, that any competent reader fails to carry away from *Crime and Punishment* an image etched in memory of the murder scene.

Thus, in denying that the cinematic model is a plausible one for the experience of adult novel reading, I am certainly not denying that mature readers sometimes visualize in their imaginations, while reading, certain scenes or characters or whatever. What I am denying is that the arousal of such images can possibly be the whole ball of wax, or even a large part thereof. Vast stretches of novels are not *visualized* but *comprehended.* And that leads me to my second objection to the cinematic model of novel reading. For it is the main thrust of the Lockean account of language, as I understand it, that to comprehend just is to "visualize." And if it is the Lockean account that allowed various eighteenth-century writers to maintain the cinematic model of read literature as a way of saving literature for the representational theory of art, that salvage operation fails because the Lockean account fails.

That the Lockean account of language will not pass muster need hardly be belabored, I would think, at this point in time. It can come as no surprise to any of us that language comprehension cannot be a matter of images of dogs or donkeys popping into the reader's or listener's head as these words are read or heard. Surely that may happen, but that it must would make reading, speaking, and comprehension, at least as we know them, impossible. The meanings of words do not accrue by virtue of their reference to "images" or Lockean "ideas," and to so claim is, among other things, to fall afoul of Wittgenstein's private language argument. When we comprehend words and sentences, whether in a treatise on metaphysics or a three-volume novel, we do not do so by having a running commentary of images present before the imagination.

Perhaps at this point the defender of the cinematic model will make the following suggestion. You grant that *sometimes* words cause images to pop into our heads, and that to *that* extent at least some vestige of Locke's linguistic model remains intact. We need not say that even where images are raised, the meanings of words lie in their reference to those images. All we need do is recognize that in certain circumstances words have that power of arousal. In what circumstances? Precisely in *literary* circumstances, of course. For it is precisely the nature of literary language to evoke images. Naturally, reading the *Critique of Pure Reason* or a mathematical treatise will not give rise to images in the mind's eye, because such books are written in prosaic or technical, in a word nonliterary, language. But it is just the genius of an E. M. Forster or a Jane Austen to maximize the image-provoking powers of language that we recognize as "literary."

I am willing to go a certain distance with this response. I think it is true that certain kinds of literary language, or, better, certain literary uses of language, are notable for their image-arousing powers. Furthermore, in certain literary genres – lyric poetry, for one – such language predominates and "imagining" is a major part of the exercise. When, for example, I read Goethe's *Das Veilchen* or listen to Mozart's setting of the poem, I do indeed have a rather vivid image – can hardly help having one – of the violet and the girl who mindlessly tramples it underfoot; and I am sure that is an important part of the artistic experience the poet intended.

But when the work is a three-volume novel or a long narrative poem, something very different is going on through protracted segments: certainly comprehension, but without visualization. And these protracted segments, both descriptive and narrative, are, I want to claim, not representational – neither as a picture is representational, nor even as an image-arousing part of a description or narrative might be. To a large extent, then, literary works such as novels and narrative poems are not representational arts.

Of course, there is a quite genuine, uncontroversial sense in which many literary narratives – one might even want to argue *all* – are "representational," the sense in which, for example, the "letter novels" of the eighteenth century consist in representations of letters through which the story is told. One might call this "textual representation," because a text is being represented by another text.

Letter novels are by no means the only examples of textual representation. Novels that present themselves to the reader as diaries, journals, and ship's logs are examples of textual representation. And even where the manner of textual representation is not made explicit, one might, if one had reason to do so, argue that textual representation of some kind or other is always "implied," as is, some have argued, a fictional narrator. The opening of *Moby Dick*, for example, is an unlikely candidate. "Call me Ishmael" sounds, without textual evidence to the contrary, like the opening of a conversation rather than a diary or other non-literary text. But even if that is how we construe it, we are not, after all, literally listening to a speaker. We are reading a text. And someone, it might be argued, had to have written this text – not, of course, Herman Melville; rather, some implied fictional writer. And so, it might be argued further, when the fictional writer is not made explicit, as in *Pamela* or *Gulliver's Travels*, we are to imagine one and, along with the imagined writer, an imagined text that the book in our hands represents. Perhaps we imagine Ishmael telling his story to one listener, while another, overhearing it, writes it down, like a court recorder; or perhaps the listener himself writes it down (as it is being told or afterward?).

But however far you want to carry this idea, and however doubtful carrying it this far, to imagined scribes and implied texts, may be, it is uncontroversial that some novels and other forms of literary narrative are textual representations. Nonetheless, this does not make even those uncontroversially textual representations counterexamples to the argument I am running here against the notion of literary representation. For it is the representation of the world by the literary work, whether that work consists in a textual representation or not, that is being denied. And a letter novel, no less than a fictional work that does not in any obvious way function through textual representation, is claimed to "represent" the world by those who think of read fiction in representational terms. It is *Pamela*'s "representation" of Pamela's world, not *Pamela*'s representation of Pamela's letters, that is here being denied. *Pamela* is not a "picture" of the world, even in the sense of a running series of mental images in the reader's mind.

Here, however, we reach a crucial juncture. It is now high time to state, at least approximately, how the concept of representation is to be taken. For it is bound to be pointed out by the defender of literature as a representational art that the way pictures represent hardly exhausts the resources of the concept. In particular, philosophers of mind talk about consciousness representing the world to us, and even talk about the "language of thought," without meaning to suggest that consciousness and thinking must be a matter of mental pictures. It seems sufficient reason to attribute representation to conscious thought that it possesses semantic content. And since literature certainly possesses *that*, it is "representational" in what has now become a perfectly canonical sense of the word. This riposte requires some careful attention, which brings us to the first (and so far evaded) question: How are we to construe the troublesome and difficult concept of "representation"?

§3   That the term "representation" is currently used in the way just described by philosophers of mind is not to be taken lightly or dismissed out of hand. Indeed, I do not intend to dismiss it at all.

As I understand this use, a system is representational if it possess not only syntax but semantic properties as well: a content. Using "representation" in this way properly distinguishes literature from, for example, absolute music (at least as many people, including myself, construe it). I have no desire to legislate this use of the representational concept out of existence, and couldn't if I wanted to. It is a valuable use and, as far as I can see, a canonical one.

But recognizing and applying this semantic, "content" sense of "representation" does not cut through the present thicket. We have not, at a stroke, made a case for literature in general or the novel in particular as a "representational" art. We have simply changed the subject. To put it another way, we have not solved a territorial dispute one way or the other, but simply redrawn boundaries.

The traditional question of whether something or other is a representational art is not, as I construe it, the same as the question of whether something or other has content. It is not as if the latter is an irrelevant or unimportant question. It *is* an important artistic fact that novels and plays have semantic content and string quartets do not. This matters greatly in how we appreciate these kinds of works. And there is nothing wrong with – indeed, there is much that is right about – framing such a distinction as between the representational and the nonrepresentational, as long as we know exactly what we are talking about. For before this use of the representational–nonrepresentational distinction, people were saying something very different when they said, for example, that literature is representational and absolute music is not. And what they were saying is simply not captured by the idea that the one possesses content and the other not.

What were they saying? It is not easy to answer that question exactly. But this much is apparent. The experience of (say) enjoying, artistically, a Cézanne still life or a seventeenth-century Dutch landscape painting has something intrinsically to do with the root meaning of "representation," that is to say, *representation* (as has been often enough observed). Something is *presented* to us that we experience *as*, in some "phenomenological" way, the thing represented. And it is in phenomenologically experiencing this that we gain some large part of our artistic enjoyment of these artworks.

I am well aware that this is an extremely vague way of putting things. But for present purposes there is no need to make them more precise. All I require from the reader, to get on with my agenda, is the admission that the subjective experience of content in a text is, from the artistic, aesthetic point of view, very different from the subjective experience of phenomenological presentation in a *re*-presentation.

63

"Representation" is a term currently in use for two very different kinds of things: the semantic properties of consciousness, or text, and the "phenomenological" properties of "presentation" in various of the visual arts (and elsewhere). It is in its latter use that I say we are mistaken in seeing the novel as a representational art. And it is no use to say the novel clearly is representational as that word is currently employed by philosophers of mind. For the way they use it does not capture what the term was meant to capture in its other, "phenomenological" use. It is the latter use, and what it picks out, that I am denying to the novel.

Perhaps it might be objected here that if "representation" in its semantic use and "representation" in its "phenomenological" use do not capture something common to both, there is no proper explanation of why the term has come to be used semantically. Well, there is no need to get stuck on this. Of course, there is something (perhaps more than one thing) that these uses have in common. They both pick out *content*, intentional objects *of* "representation." With both landscape paintings and novels we can verbalize what is "in" them, what they are about. This we cannot do for most string quartets, which are "just music." But even though in the case of artworks such as novels and landscapes, we can identify a content and thus call them semantically "representational," this does not make the former representational in the way the concept has been used since Plato. And it is in this traditional, vaguely "phenomenological" use that I am denying that the novel and some other literary genres are "representational."

§4 I suggested, at the outset of this chapter, that the subsuming of literature, *tout court*, under the umbrella of "the representational arts" has been thought by many to have taken place as early as *Republic* 3 and 10. That seems to be a part of aesthetic folk wisdom. In fact, it is false in an interesting way.

To be sure, Plato did construe literature, *as he knew it*, as a representational, which is to say *mimetic*, art. But literature as he knew it, let me suggest, was basically a performing art: its aesthetic or artistic payoff was not for a reader but for a spectator/auditor.

It is obvious, of course, in the case of tragic and comic drama that Plato has performance in mind. But I think it is important to remember that this is true also of epic poetry, Homer in particular, as well as other poetical genres. Thus, when Plato addresses those who experience poetry, that of Homer in particular, but apparently "the poets" in general, he describes them as "spectators" who "behold" the poets' "performances."[2]

What these "performances" of epic poetry were like we can only conjecture. We do know, from Plato's *Ion*, that the rhapsodes not only recited poetry to a "musical" accompaniment but also commented on it as well (as "critics" or "interpreters" perhaps?). And we know also, from *Republic* 3, that these "performers" were not only reciters and commentators but frequently "acted" and even provided vocal "sound effects." Thus Plato describes (with outspoken disapproval) the performer who

> will be inclined to omit nothing in his narration, and to think nothing too low for him, so that he will attempt, seriously and in the presence of many hearers, to imitate everything without exception, . . . claps of thunder and the noise of wind and hail, and of wheels and pulleys, and the sounds of trumpets and flutes and pipes and all manner of instruments; nay even the barking of dogs, the bleating of sheep, and the notes of birds; and his style will either consist wholly of the imitation of sounds and forms, or will comprise but a small modicum of narration.[3]

Such "performances" were "representational" with a vengeance.

Of course the Greek playwrights, like modern ones, intended their plays to be experienced as performances, as "representations" in the phenomenological sense. But apparently this was true, if Plato is to be credited as a chronicler of his times, of epic poets as well. So that even after the Homeric corpus ceased to be an oral tradition (where clearly performance was the only payoff) and became solidified into the texts we read, it continued to be a performance art, at least during Plato's lifetime.

Thus it is not Plato's account of "literature" I am opposing when I argue against the notion that literature is a representational art. I think Plato was correct in characterizing literature *as he knew it* as mimetic. And I, of course, am characterizing literature as I know it, and as it has been known since modern times, as nonrepresentational. The difference is that Plato's literature was a spectator art and literature in modern times is significantly a reader's art. (It is no accident, then, that the novel is a modern phenomenon – being the most reader-oriented of all literary forms.)

However, it is surely an overstatement to claim that literature as I know it, literature across the board, is a nonrepresentational art, just as it is an overstatement to characterize Plato as claiming that literature as he knew it, literature across the board, is a representational art. The reason it is an overstatement for me is obvious. Drama is a literary art form and is clearly representational: its aesthetic payoff is meant to be in a performance, where characters, actions, speaking, and setting are represented before our eyes and ears. The reason it is an overstatement to describe Plato's account of literature as representational, *sans phrase,* is far more interesting for what is to come and merits a separate hearing.

§5 In Plato's description of the mimetic performer, quoted in the preceding section, he ends by saying that "his style will either consist wholly of the imitation of sounds and forms, or will comprise a modicum of narration." Those familiar with this part of the *Republic* will recognize here an allusion to the well-known distinction, which Plato has made shortly before, among three "branches" of poetry:

> [O]ne branch of poetry and legend-writing consists wholly of imitation, that is, as you say, tragedy and comedy; another branch employs the simple recital of the poet in his own person, and is chiefly to be found, I imagine, in dithyrambic poetry; while a third employs both recital and imitation, as is seen in the construction of epic poems, and in many other instances, if I make you understand me.[4]

66

Plato's point here, easy to let slip away in the great to-do over the immorality of representation, is that *pure* narration, where we have only "the simple recital of the poet in his own person," where, in other words, the poet does not speak in the voices of his characters, but *tells* us what they said and did, we do not have representation at all. And this is invariant with whether or not the narration is recited; for a recited narrative of events and speeches is no more a phenomenological representation of them than is a read one. It says, rather than shows, how things went and what was uttered.

This is no minor concession to nonrepresentation in literature. The *Iliad*, for example, is a mixed mode (remember that we are talking about a performance, not a reading to oneself): it contains both "imitation" and "the simple recital of the poet in his own person," which is to say, narration and depiction. But when one considers how much of the *Iliad* is "the simple recital of the poet in his own person," it becomes evident that, far from thinking that literature *tout court* was mimetic, Plato thought that a large segment of it was not.

Furthermore, because Plato was working with a concept of literature, *all* literature (as he knew it), as a performing art, his theory, at least stated in this coarse-grained way, is not by any means unreasonable. For Greek drama, a performing art, it is obviously true – or as obviously true as for Shakespeare's or Ibsen's or Arthur Miller's drama. And since epic poems like the *Iliad* and *Odyssey* were not for Plato's contemporaries something to read, but something to see and hear, a play, as it were, a one-man show, they were also representational in much the same sense as the tragedies and comedies, except where it was "the simple recital of the poet in his own person."

§6   I do not think I am alone in seeing that Plato's is not a representational theory of literature but a representational theory of a part of literature. And certainly I cannot be alone in seeing that, for Plato and his contemporaries, literature was a performing art, not a reading art, its devotees spectators and auditors at a "representation," whether it was Euripides, with actors and a chorus, or Homer, with a "one-man band." I have, however, never read anything that gave the latter kind of performance its due, that recognized the significance of poetic recitation in understanding what Plato said when he said that literature was a mimetic art.

Where, then, does the notion of read literature as a representational art have its origin, if not (and it does not) in *Republic* 3 and 10? One can conjecture that the corner is turned, if not fully negotiated, in Aristotle's *Poetics*.

Paul Thom, in his book on the performing arts, calls attention to the place in *Poetics* 1450b where Aristotle says of the parts of a tragedy: "Spectacle is something enthralling, but is very artless and least particular to the art of poetic composition. The potential tragedy exists even without a performance and actors. . . ."[5] Of this passage Thom writes, in part, that Aristotle "thinks . . . staging is a dispensable accessory to tragedy: for if the tragedy is the poem, then staging is indeed incidental to it. The tragic effect is possible without staging: that is, the reader of the poem can be moved to pity and fear."[6]

Aristotle himself says nothing about *reading* tragedies in the passage Thom quotes. But if he is talking here about experiencing such works as the plays of Aeschylus, Sophocles, and Euripides without the "spectacle," the most obvious construction one can put on this passage is the one Thom does put on it: that Aristotle is envisaging the reading of such works.

There is, however, a problem in construing what Aristotle says in 1450b as a denial that spectacle is an essential part of tragic plays. Indeed, there would seem to be a blatant contradiction between such a denial and the famous definition of tragedy in 1449b, which says: "Tragedy is a representation of a serious, complete action which has magnitude, in embellished speech, with each of its elements [used] separately in the [various] parts [of the play]; [represented] by people acting and not by narration; accomplishing by means of pity and terror the catharsis of such emotions."[7] For if it is part of the definition of a tragic play that it is represented by people acting and not by narration, and if that is taken to mean people acting on the stage, not merely in the text, then "spectacle" must be an essential part of the tragic play, since people acting on the stage are a part of the spectacle and also a part of the definition of the tragic play.

However, there is no contradiction here. For note carefully what Aristotle says in 1550b: "[T]he potential for tragedy exists even without a performance and actors . . . ," which I take to mean not that you can have the tragedy of *Antigone* in its complete form without a full performance, but that you can have tragedy in genres other than tragic plays; that, in other words, the class of tragedy is larger than the class of tragic plays. Not only does this interpretation avoid any contradiction between 1449b and 1450b; it avoids attributing to Aristotle the counterintuitive notion that the art of Aeschylus, Sophocles, and Euripides is not, essentially, a performing art.

What genre, then, was Aristotle referring to that has the potential for tragedy without performance? It seems likely to me that he was thinking of epic poetry, and in particular Homer, which comports well with *Republic* 10, where Plato refers to Homer as the chief among the tragedians.[8] Furthermore, if it is epic poetry that Aristotle is saying can be tragic "even without a performance and actors," then he is merely denying that "spectacle" – that is, a full dramatic production – is necessary for the appreciation of epic poetry, for epic poetry to have its tragic effect, and not that performance of the kind Plato describes, performance by the rhapsode, is unnecessary. So Aristotle is not saying anything new; in particular, he is not saying that epic poetry requires no performance at all and is, essentially, a reading art.

But although the passage under discussion does not yield the result of either tragic drama or tragic epic as a reading art, Aristotle does, in fact, make mention of "reading" in two places at the end of the *Poetics* (as we have it) where he compares tragic drama to epic poetry. He writes that "tragedy can produce its own [effect] even without movement, as epic does. For it is obvious from reading it what sort [of tragedy] it is." And again: tragedy "has vividness in reading as well as in performance."[9] It is not of minor significance, as we shall shortly see, that one translator renders the first of these passages in a slightly different way, to wit: "[T]ragedy fulfills its function even without acting, just as much as epic, and its quality can be gauged by *reading aloud*."[10]

The first of these passages asserts that a tragic play need not be acted, as the second translator makes clear. Furthermore, the second translator makes "reading" out to be "reading aloud," which may well mean, then, being "read to" by the rhapsode; and in that case it would seem that Aristotle means by "reading" a tragic play simply experiencing the kind of one-person performance characteristic of epic poetry. And the second passage is ambiguous between being read to and reading to oneself; so there may be nothing new here beyond the assertion that tragic plays do not need the entire spectacle of a theatrical performance, but can be recited or performed by a rhapsode, like epic poetry, and still have the tragic effect. But "performance" it remains.

However, even if Aristotle really had in mind reading a tragic play to oneself, the second translation of the first passage calls our attention to the fact that when the ancients read "to themselves," they read *aloud*. Silent reading was a much later accomplishment.[11] So even where Aristotle speaks of a tragedy or epic being "read" rather than acted, he is talking about a minimal "performance": you are reading aloud to yourself. We are still not concerned with the modern experience of curling up with a good book.

In sum, then, we may say that Aristotle at most pushed literature in the direction of a reading art, as well as a representational one, by perhaps leaving his text open to that interpretation, in the following respect. He may have been suggesting that the tragic effect of plays can be experienced in reading the plays to oneself (which does not contradict his "definition" of tragic drama as including "spectacle," since what he is saying is that one can experience "catharsis" without spectacle, not that one is experiencing thereby tragic drama *as defined*). In Aristotle's world this "reading" meant reading aloud to oneself, in which case the reading remained a minimal performance: you performing the play to yourself. But as silent reading became the rule, there would be a strong inclination to understand Aristotle as referring to silent reading when he referred to reading *simpliciter.*

Out of this arises a possible source of a representational theory of literature *tout court,* including literature as a read art, not just a performed one, as in *Republic* 3 and 10. The argument can be summed up in the following statements. (a) The *Poetics* presents a quintessentially representational theory of tragedy, until the modern era one of the prominent, if not the most prominent, of the literary genres. (b) Aristotle's theory of representation is extended to the reading as well as the performing arts, although reading aloud, still a minimal performance, is what he is talking about. (c) In the period in which modern aesthetics was incubating, namely, the High Renaissance and seventeenth century, far and away the most influential aesthetic text was the *Poetics.* By the High Renaissance no one thought of epic poetry as an oral, performing art, and that Plato had so thought of it was either ignored or forgotten in the midst of the Aristotelian hegemony. This, I suggest, is how literature, *all* literature, read and performed, became thought of as a representational art and how Plato came to be seen as the source of the doctrine.

But this is a book about differences. And one difference that I mean to explore is that between read literature and the representational art of performed literature. Aristotle, if my reading of the history of aesthetics is to be credited, helped us, perhaps unintentionally, to take the wrong turn when he defined the tragic drama as mimetic and then denied that the tragic, for its cathartic effect, required spectacle. For that suggested, to a different age, that read tragedy, *silently read tragedy,* hence read literature, *silently read literature,* was a representational art.

The attraction of a theory that could encompass both performed and read literature under a single principle need hardly be dilated upon now, considering what has gone before in the preceding chapters. And in a period when reading was not widespread, the attractions of such a theory for literature far outweighed its perceived defects. But it will hardly pass muster in an age in which the most widely cultivated and consumed literary genre is the novel, the paradigm of reading art. It is high time for an alternative to be offered.

71

§7 What is literature, then? It is, in part, a representational art. Drama has its aesthetic payoff in production, where characters, speeches, actions, and scenes are "represented." Drama is a major part of literature, and it is representational.

But what is the novel? If it is in part representational, it is so only where distinct mental images are evoked in some "canonical" way (not, that is, as idiosyncratic images); and that would be "representation," at best, in a rather attenuated sense of the word. Attenuated though it is, I will grant that to representationalism.

What of the rest, though? What is the nature of that large part of the novel, as a read experience, that cannot for reasons given at the outset of this chapter be construed as representational even in the sense of image-evoking? I will not even attempt an answer to that question. For the novel is not one thing, and to track down all of the things it is would require an entire book, not merely a chapter in one. What I shall do, rather, is to try to say what, in part, one of the things in the novel is. That is a modest enough undertaking. But perhaps one of the precepts to be gleaned from this book is that modest undertakings, rather than grand designs, are the order of the day.

What I would like to talk about, oddly enough, are *descriptions:* those places where time is taken in the course of a narrative to introduce and describe to the reader some person, place, or object. I say "oddly enough" because it might be thought that descriptions in novels are just the parts that evoke images of the persons, scenes, or things described and, therefore, just the parts one should call "representational" in the attenuated sense. But I am of a different mind. And if I can convince you that descriptions, which seem a bad case for a nonrepresentational theory, are indeed not to be understood as "representational," even in the attenuated sense, I will have done a lot for my cause.

§8 Let me begin with a restricted generalization, full of exceptions. A very large proportion of the novels written since (and including) the eighteenth century take the form of a narrative stream, broken intermittently by pauses for fairly elaborate descriptions of persons, places, or things of later importance to the narration (notable departures from this scheme being the letter novels of the eighteenth century and self-conscious efforts to break narrative structure, as in such cases as Stern, Joyce, Faulkner, and Virginia Woolf). "Islands in the stream" is, I suppose, a good metaphorical first approximation, although frequently the stream will *begin* with an island, which is to say that frequently a novel will open with an elaborate description of a major character or important setting. (I will offer an aesthetically more enlightening model later on.)

Let us look at an example:

> When Flem Snopes came to clerk in her father's store, Eula Varner was not quite thirteen. She was the last of the sixteen children, the baby, though she had overtaken and passed her mother in height in her tenth year. Now, though not quite thirteen years old, she was already bigger than most grown women and even her breasts were no longer the little, hard, fiercely-pointed cones of puberty or even maidenhood. On the contrary, her entire appearance suggested some symbology out of the old Dionyon times – honey in sunlight and bursting grapes, the writhen bleeding of the crushed fecundated vine beneath the hard rapacious trampling goat-hoof. She seemed to be not a living integer of her contemporary scene, but rather to exist in a teeming vacuum in which her days followed one another as though behind sound-proof glass, where she seemed to listen in sullen bemusement, with a weary wisdom heired of all mammalian maturity, to the enlarging of her own organs.[12]

The most obvious point to be made about this description (from William Faulkner's *The Hamlet*) is that it hardly evokes an "image" of Eula at all. The prose is convoluted and rich. There are numerous allusions of a fairly intellectual kind. The passage is a veritable feast for the aesthetic taste in the beauties of language: indeed, we would not be far wrong in describing it as a kind of prose poem.

What, then, are the functions of this description, if not image evocation? We have flagged one already: it provides sheer, unadulterated aesthetic enjoyment of the American language at its highest literary level. But of course that cannot be the whole of it. For the description is part of a narrative, and functions within that narrative *qua* description. And if it does not evoke an image of Eula, what function *qua* description does it perform? Clearly, I think, it shares a function with artistic visual representations: it conveys information. What it does not share with them is the capacity to give one a phenomenological re-presentation. We learn from this description that Eula is a prematurely voluptuous young woman, dripping with sexuality. And this information is vital for the narrative that follows. An image of Eula, however, we do not have. That is not the point of this description, nor within its capability to provide.

Let me begin to fill out this account of literary description by first dealing with the following objection. Granted, the defender of the image model might say, the description of Eula does not, by itself, arouse a mental picture of her. But it does give us the material out of which *we* construct mental images through the mutual interaction of our imaginations, personal experiences, and fantasies. We know from Faulkner's description that Eula is a voluptuous, prematurely sexual girl. The rest we fill in, in a mental image based on young girls we have seen and known, and perhaps on our own sexual fantasies.

I imagine some of this kind of thing does go on in people's reading experiences. How much must vary with the individual. But if you believe, as I do, that reading a novel is an experience that should be under the control of the author to some large degree, then you cannot allow "free fantasy" to take charge. A writer on the subject of our emotional reaction to fiction has said, "It should seem quite extraordinary that so many philosophers should seek to make our responses to Anna's suicide or Desdemona's fate more intelligible by relating these masterpieces to our own banal fantasies."[13] A fortiori it can make little sense to say that what Faulkner's description "represents" – what it is meant to evoke – is my or your banal fantasy of over-ripe adolescence. The blurb on the back cover of my copy of *The Hamlet* says, "The Snopes family . . . is one of William Faulkner's most notable fictional creations. . . ." Just so: Eula is the creation of Faulkner's extraordinary, fecund literary imagination, not my my feeble, paltry one.[14]

But at this juncture I can imagine another objection taking form. It is to the effect that I have carefully chosen, in Faulkner's description of Eula, a favorable case for what I am arguing: a case where the language is "intellectual" rather than cast in visual terms, so, naturally, not a case of image evocation. It will be objected that I have stacked the deck.

There is some truth in this allegation. I chose this case carefully, with an eye to supporting my position – but the ease with which I found the appropriate one suggests in itself how many such there are. I pursued this strategy to claim a quick victory. What I think I have established is that there are obviously many descriptions of the kind Faulkner gives of Eula that are neither intended to (I assume) nor capable of evoking a *controlled* mental image. Information vital to the narrative is provided in plenty, and artistic satisfaction in the beauty, richness, and structure of the language no less so. But even in the attenuated sense in which the linguistic evocation of images might be "representational," Faulkner's description of Eula, and others like it, are not examples of a representational art.

But what about descriptions that are more straightforwardly visual than conceptual? Those are the ones that seem to favor the representationalist's objections and to be recalcitrant to my own position. To the contrary, I want to argue that even straightforward visual descriptions – "He was tall, dark, and handsome," and the like – are not, in many of the interesting cases, image-evoking at all, but serve the same basic functions as the conceptual ones, of conveying information and affording aesthetic satisfaction. To make this case requires filling out more fully my own conception of the role of descriptions in narrative.

§9   "Winnie Verloc was a young woman with a full bust, in a tight bodice, and with broad hips. Her hair was very tidy. Steady-eyed like her husband, she preserved an air of unfathomable indifference behind the rampart of the counter." "Winnie's mother was a stout, wheezy woman, with a large brown face. She wore a black wig under a white cap. Her swollen legs rendered her inactive."[15]

Here are two brief, pithy descriptions (from Joseph Conrad's *The Secret Agent*) as straightforward and visually oriented as one could wish. Yet I ask the reader to say in all candor that she formed a mental picture of Winnie Verloc and her mother by attending to these lines by a master of English prose. For starters, the "pictures" are woefully underdetermined. Winnie Verloc has a full bust, broad hips, and tidy hair. But what color is her hair? And what does "tidy" hair look like, anyway? How tall is Winnie? What does she look like? All we have are hips, a bust, and tidy hair. These are body parts, not the appearance of a human being. Nor are we better off with Winnie's mother. She has a brown face and swollen legs. What's in between? How can I form a mental picture of a face when all I know is that it is brown? (I don't even know what shade of brown.)

Furthermore, descriptions come, so to speak, in the heat of battle, particularly "quick sketches" like these. If I am an adult reader, reading a page-turner at adult speed, a description can no more paint a picture than can a fleeting glimpse from the window of a train fix an image of the passing scene. This is not to say that reading at speed is the only way of reading. Certainly the reader, particularly the serious reader with a serious novel, may pause at a particularly arresting passage to savor, analyze, and, in the process reread. If the passage in question is a description and if the description is, upon such scrutiny, capable of evoking a mental picture, then so be it. I will not argue that point. *My* point is that there is a very common, indeed a paradigmatic, way of reading novels, in which the reader is engrossed in the narrative and reads accordingly, eager, if not breathless (depending on the novel), for the events to unfold. Descriptions go by, like the rest of the story, at a fair clip. In such a reading there is no time for images to form, even if the descriptions are not underdetermined. This I know from common sense and from my own experience, and I presume neither is eccentric.

If, then, it is not in evoking mental images that the purpose of a description lies, what is its purpose within a literary narrative? I have suggested two: to convey information relevant to the narrative and to provide, like the rest of the narrative, aesthetic appreciation in the linguistic medium. (I take it that enjoyment of the narrative is also a form of aesthetic appreciation.) But to say this much is not to say nearly enough. For what we want to know is not merely how literary descriptions resemble the rest of the narrative but how they differ: what makes them special. A former answer might have been: they are peculiarly "representational" in the sense of peculiarly suited to evoking mental pictures. Having rejected that answer, it is incumbent upon me to come up with another. That is the next task.

§10 I characterized literary descriptions earlier as islands in the stream of the narrative. We can begin to fill out this rather banal metaphor by remarking that it suggests the stationary versus the mobile: pauses in the narrative train of fictional events – not, it should be emphasized, pauses in the activity of reading.

Furthermore, descriptions present themselves as "set pieces" (at least that is the way they present themselves to me). They thrust out of the narrative to be appreciated as a separate literary genre, as it were, within the genre of the modern novelistic narrative. Two analogies suggest themselves: Shakespearean monologue and operatic aria. The latter is the one I shall explore.

What is known as "number" opera is made up of separate movements or "numbers," arias, duets, ensembles, choruses, and so forth, separated by a connecting tissue of "recitative." In its most paradigmatic form, in the eighteenth century, the recitative is for the most part "secco," a rapid parlando accompanied solely by a keyboard instrument. The secco recitative has essentially no musical interest in itself, but serves merely to advance the plot through a minimal musical conversation and monologue.[16] At certain crucial points in the drama, this narrative train is halted and a character "steps forward" to sing an aria. The arias are "concerted" pieces. The simple keyboard accompaniment gives way to a full-blown orchestral one; and each such "number" is a complete, self-contained musical composition that can be (and frequently is) lifted from the larger work of which it is a part and performed separately in a concert or recital.

In listening to an aria as part of a number opera (and I speak now from my own experience), one is listening to an utterance (usually of a heightened emotional kind) in a musical drama. But one is also listening to a musical composition, in a particular style, of a particular genre: the "rage" aria, the "patter song," da capo aria, cabaletta, cavatina, in Mozartian style, Handelian style, and so on. For opera is, among other things (as Edward Dent described it), a concert in costume.[17] And just as in all other examples of high art, we appreciate operatic arias under those descriptions whether or not we can call them by name or describe them in the accepted terms, or merely know them, half-consciously, "by acquaintance."

Let me suggest, now, that full-blown, extended literary descriptions are very much like the kinds of operatic arias I have been discussing in the way we experience and enjoy them aesthetically. Like operatic arias, many of them have a self-contained form. They represent a pause in the narrative flow out of which they thrust themselves. They are "set pieces" – "concerted" pieces, as it were – and like operatic arias are frequently "virtuosic," displaying, as in Faulkner's description of Eula, the writer's "musical" gifts. They fall into types; they have styles (compare Faulkner's descriptions with Fielding's). They are genres within genres.

In one respect, however, the relation of descriptions to their narrative frames differs in an important way from that of operatic arias to theirs. Whereas in the latter case the artistic value of the narrative structure, that is, the secco recitative, is usually nil, the artistic value of literary narrative is certainly equal to that of literary description. But this difference, marked though it is, does not affect the present argument in any way.

Furthermore, the development of operatic aria and recitative into the nineteenth century expands the description–aria analogy in an interesting way. Secco recitative disappeared in the Romantic era, in favor of a more continuous musical fabric in which, if the distinction between concerted number and recitative is maintained (as it tends not to be in Wagnerian music drama), there is nevertheless not a sharp discontinuity between them, the one flowing into the other, and there is even a "dialogue" between the two (something that Handel had already tried in his opera seria). Variations on the same theme of separation versus continuity are apparent in literary descriptions as well. For against the "standard" cases of pause in the narrative stream for descriptive set pieces there is also the interpenetration of the one with the other in a continuous narrative fabric.

What I have in mind is beautifully illustrated by the following passage (from George Eliot's *Scenes of Clerical Life*):

> Look at him as he winds through the little churchyard! The silver light that falls aslant on church and tomb, enables you to see his slim black figure, made all the slimmer by tight pantalouns, as it flits past the pale gravestones. He walks with a quick step, and is now rapping with sharp decision at the vicarage door. It is opened without delay by the nurse, cook, housemaid, all at once – that is to say, by the robust maid-of-all-work, Nanny; and as Mr. Barton hangs up his hat in the passage, you see that a narrow face of no particular complexion – even the small-pox that has attacked it seems to have been of a marginal, indefinite kind – with features of no particular shape, and an eye of no particular expression, is surmounted by a slope of baldness gently rising from brow to crown. You judge him, rightly, to be about forty. The house is quiet, for it is half-past ten, and the children have long been gone to bed. He opens the sitting-room door, but instead of seeing his wife, as he expected, stitching with the nimblest of fingers by the light of one candle, he finds her dispensing with the light of a candle altogether. She is softly pacing up and down by the red firelight, holding in her arms little Walter, the year-old baby, who looks over her shoulder with large wide-open eyes, while the patient mother pats his back with her soft hand, and glances with a sigh at the heap of large and small stockings lying unmended on the table.[18]

If we want to call this long passage by its appropriate name, I think it would be "A Description of Amos Barton"; "Description of a Character" is the genre. The main function of the paragraph (which I have quoted in full) is to convey information about Barton: he is slim, narrow-faced, pockmarked, bald, of no particular complexion or expression, about forty years old, walks briskly, acts with decision. But instead of laying that out in the standard set piece, Eliot presents us with a nonstandard layout in which fragments of character description are interspersed with narrative fragments, as well as with fragments of mise-en-scène. She thus gets across the description without impeding the narrative flow – indeed, gets it across in the very midst of the action (simple though that action may be).

Thus I suggest that part of our aesthetic appreciation of this passage lies in apprehending it as a different "solution" to the "description problem": as in the genre "Description of a Character," but in nonstandard form. Nor need we do this in a self-conscious way; for we can be perfectly well aware that we are enjoying this in the way I have described without being able to put it in just these terms. Furthermore, it is apparent not only that Eliot herself was well aware of doing what I have described, namely, giving a nonstandard character description, but that she purposely underlined this intention, thus forcing the reader to experience the passage in the very way I have described. For the fragmented, nonstandard description of Amos Barton segues, in the end, into the introduction of Mrs. Barton; and the very next paragraph turns out to be an absolutely standard, set-piece description of her, beginning in the most straightforward manner: "She was a lovely woman – Mrs. Amos Barton; a large, fair, gentle Madonna, with thick, close, chestnut curls beside her well-rounded cheeks, and with large, tender, short-sighted eyes," and continuing in kind.[19]

To summarize this part of the argument, I am claiming that character descriptions in novels, short stories, and other novelistic works are not examples of representational art, even in the attenuated sense of evoking "mental pictures," but do share both the capacity and the sometime function of representation, namely, to convey information. *Narratively,* that is their function. But what marks them out, aesthetically, from the general flow of the narrative – which also, after all, conveys information in the form of the "story" – is that character descriptions present themselves as a kind of separate, self-contained form-within-a-form and are appreciated as such. They are set pieces, "concerted numbers" in operatic lingo, that interrupt the narrative flow much as operatic arias interrupt the conversational flow of recitative. And the same argument, I would urge, can be made for descriptions of scenes and objects, although the orientation of the novel and related genres is so much toward people that character descriptions quite naturally have pride of place, high visibility, a more clearly discernible form and tradition.

So I have argued that just where one might expect read literature to be a representational art, if it is one at all – in the descriptions of characters in visual terms, how they look, how they behave – literature is not representational at all. The Horatian dictum of "Ut pictura poesis erit" is then a dangerously false analogy, and we should look elsewhere than pictorial or "phenomenological" representation for a proper aesthetic understanding of it.

"But what of the narrative train itself?" an objector might respond. "Surely it is goring the wrong ox to argue that description is not representational. The far more important question is whether or not pure narrative is, and that question you have not undertaken at all."

Well, of course, the main objections to why character descriptions are not representational in even the attenuated sense of image-evoking apply, pari passu, to read narrative. And the information-conveying function that character descriptions share with pictorial representations they share with narrative as well. What remains to be done for the narrative train, which I have done in small part for character description, is to provide a positive account of its aesthetic appeal. Many literary critics and theorists have undertaken bits and pieces of this task. But this is not the place for me to add my voice. For my main purpose is now complete, which was to at least cast serious doubt on the age-old and seemingly impregnable thesis that literature – *read* literature – is a representational art.

§11 Perhaps, though, it will be objected in the end by readers who have come with me all this way that I am just beating a dead horse. For I did say early on that the cinematic, mental-image concept of read literature flourished in the eighteenth century and received a devastating critique – indeed, what should have been its death blow – in Burke's *Sublime and Beautiful*. But such skeptical readers can assure themselves that the death of this horse has been greatly exaggerated by picking up almost any modern edition of a classic novel and reading the editor's introduction or afterword to the contemporary reader.

Here, for example, is Geoffrey Tillotson's characterization of the genius of Dickens in his afterword to a recent paperback edition of *Bleak House:* "With words he makes us see and hear his fifty men and women with the clarity of a talking film." There then follows a quotation of Dickens's description of a dog, on which Tillotson's comment is: "Do we not feel we know that dog – we can see him!"[20]

No: this horse is very much alive and kicking, and I have felt justified in going out to get him. Whether I have succeeded the future will determine. What remains is to show how what has transpired here fits into the general theme of this book.

§12 My theme is artistic differences. What I argued in the first chapters is that the general thrust of aesthetic theory, from the first formulation of the discipline itself in the age of Enlightenment, through the most recent contemporary examples, is toward unification: finding the commonalty that makes the modern system of the arts a system. We have been eager to find sameness, at the expense of difference.

I am not proposing total abandonment, or even a temporary moratorium, to the makers of theory, as some Wittgensteinians have done. What I am proposing is that there is another way to engage in philosophy of art, for those who may share my tastes and skills, and that is to pursue not the samenesses but the differences. Such an undertaking will have two beneficial results. It will tell us more about the individual arts. But, further, it will test our theories and keep them honest by, I believe, discovering to us old and unexamined assumptions about commonalties among the arts, which, on closer scrutiny, will turn out to be false.

Such, I believe, has been the result of my first "case study" in differences. No assumption has seemed so venerably secure as that literature is a representational art. Yet if my arguments here are good, a very large part of literature, including the modern novel, is not representational. And this certainly demands recognition by the makers of theories.

In my next "case study," I will continue my examination of literature, this time from the side of formalism (of a certain kind). Just as pictorial representation, so I have argued, is not a proper model for read literature, neither is formalism, even in the moderate form in which I am now going to discuss it. To think so would be going from Scylla to Charybdis. Another firmly entrenched assumption, although not nearly as antique as the representationality of literature, will in the process fall away.

Chapter 4

On the Unity of Form and Content

§1 In the preceding chapter I suggested that the earliest conclusion in aesthetics, still generally accepted, may be that literature is a representational art, like painting, sculpture, and (for both Plato and Aristotle) music. I argued, furthermore, that that conclusion is, for *read* literature, seriously mistaken. The point was that in the overarching quest for unity, for sameness, in the arts, a fairly obvious disanalogy between read literature and the visual arts has been continually overlooked, or plastered over with a patchwork of philosophical cosmetics. In the age of Plato and Aristotle, when literature, which is to say, poetry, was entirely a performed art, the representational theory of literature made a good deal of sense. But with the advent of such reading arts as the novel and short story, the notion that literature, *all* literature, is representational becomes quite untenable. Only the obstinate quest for sameness has kept us from acknowledging the fact; and the first fruits of the quest for differences form at least the beginnings of a new approach to read literature that is more faithful to its peculiar genius.

My second plea for differences is again directed at the art of literature. But this time the literary shibboleth in my sights is not an ancient one; it is, rather, of fairly recent coinage, though no less obstinate and pervasive among "literary types" for its youth. It is the thesis that literary form and literary content are inseparable; or, put another way, that they are indistinguishable, the one from the other. Its main proponent and, I think, the source of the doctrine in its twentieth-century form is A. C. Bradley. In his formulation, Bradley spoke of it as a defining characteristic, not of literature in general but of poetry in particular. Yet, for a reason that will soon become apparent, I think it is inherent in Bradley's formulation of the doctrine, and certainly the case with others who have subscribed to it, that it must apply to the whole art of literature, as opposed to the nonliterary uses of language. And I shall so construe it here in this wider application.

Why, though, it may be asked, should a critique aimed at the doctrine of form–content inseparability be appropriate to the theme of my study: differences in the arts? For, after all, the unity of form and content in poetry is meant, is it not, to *distinguish* poetry from other things. Well, that is very true. But the things it was *not* meant to distinguish poetry from were the other fine arts. Quite the opposite: that is very clear in Bradley's highly influential statement of the doctrine, where he writes: "Poetry in this matter is not, as good critics of painting often affirm, different from the other arts; in all of them the content is one thing with the form."[1] And again: "And this identity of content and form, you will say, is no accident; it is of the essence of poetry in so far as it is poetry, and of all art in so far as it is art."[2]

We can now see straightaway why it would be queer to ascribe to Bradley the view that the inseparability of form and content applies to poetry but not to other forms of literature. For Bradley explicitly says that it applies to all of the arts. So if it applies to poetry and not to the novel (say), then Bradley would be committed to the absurd position that the novel is not art. I take it, therefore, that Bradley did not intend to distinguish poetry from prose artworks with the thesis of form–content identity, but meant to apply the thesis to all of the fine arts and, at least in part, to distinguish them from other modes of expression thereby.

So I see Bradley's claim that, in poetry, form and content are indissoluble as being deeply motivated by the same quest for commonality in the arts as the claim that read literature (and music, for that matter) is representational. From now on, therefore, I will take the thesis of the indissolubility of form and content to be a thesis about the fine arts *tout court:* it is the thesis that at least one thing all of the arts have in common, and separates them from other modes of expression, is the total fusion of form with content. I shall argue that this thesis, at least as far as I understand it, and am able to make it intelligible to myself, is false. It is false with respect to literature and the visual arts because form can frequently be distinguished from content in them. It is false with respect to absolute music because absolute music has no content at all, and hence it makes no sense to claim that *its* content is indissoluble from its form.

But before I go on to criticize the thesis of form–content identity, we must have some notion of where it came from and what precisely its philosophical attractions are. For if it is a thesis without attractions, there is little point in bothering with it, much less taking the trouble to refute it.

§2 The *fons et origo* for all twentieth-century versions of the form–content identity thesis is, I imagine, A. C. Bradley's lecture "Poetry for Poetry's Sake," in the *Oxford Lectures on Poetry* (1909). That statement of the view will provide both my basic understanding of the doctrine and the main target of my criticism. But, as we shall see, it is not likely to yield a single understanding of the claim that form and content are inseparable. Rather, a number of claims seems to fall under that description, not necessarily either equivalent or implied by one another. However, one claim stands out from the rest, both by precept and by example. I shall call it the "no-paraphrase" claim and use it as my first stab at understanding the form–content unity thesis, mainly because it has, I believe, an easily identifiable origin in modern philosophy.

I shall say a great deal here about poetry, because that is what Bradley does. But the reader must bear in mind that the doctrine in question is meant by him to apply to all of the fine arts. The "no-paraphrase" claim, then, with regard to poetry is that any attempt to state the content of a poem in any words other than those of the poem itself will not accurately paraphrase its content. So if we think of the words of the poem as its form, and what the poem says as its content, it turns out that they cannot be prised apart. The content can be stated only by those words, just that form, and just that form, hence, just is that content. If that were not the case – if the words, the form, were one thing and what the words said another – then, according to Bradley and his followers, what the poem says could be said in other words, its content could be put in another form. However, such is not the case. The poem cannot be paraphrased. Therefore, its content and form, what it says and how it says it, are one and inseparable. In short, in Bradley's words, "What that meaning is *I* cannot say: Virgil has said it."[3]

What could the attraction of such a doctrine be? It is, after all, on the face of it, pretty implausible. Isn't it the case that one of the very things literary critics are supposed to do, and what Bradley did, with no little distinction, is to help us understand what poems are saying by paraphrasing them for us in what is sometimes a very sophisticated critical language?

One way, I think, that we can help make clear to ourselves what the attraction of the claim might be that, in poetry, form and content are one, is to place it in historical perspective. And to do so I shall indulge in some slightly a priori history, which, I hope, is not too far from the facts.

I shall begin by asking what sense the classical world, either Greek or Roman, would have made of Bradley's claim. I think the answer is that it would have found the claim very puzzling indeed and rejected it out of hand. We can see why by recalling one very prominent role poetry played in the intellectual lives of the Greeks and Romans.

Recall that among the more famous and impressive poetic performances of the ancient world were not merely such narrative epics as the *Iliad, Odyssey,* and *Aeneid,* but Lucretius's *De rerum natura* and Parmenides' *Way of Truth* (lost to us, of course, except for some puzzling fragments). We can gather immediately, from the existence of these latter, didactic works, that for the Greeks and Romans it was as natural to convey philosophical and "scientific" results at the cutting edge in poetry as it is natural for us to convey the former in learned journals and the latter in mathematics.

We know, too, that narrative poems, though "fiction," were not treated in the classical world merely as "literary entertainment" (whatever that might really mean). They were themselves taken to be the sources of both practical and theoretical knowledge, their authors seers and wise men. Indeed, that epistemic claim was one of the objects of Plato's devastating critique of poetry in the *Republic* and elsewhere. In the event, in a way, Plato's critique prevailed. (More of that later.)

Thus it was natural for the Greeks and Romans to think of poetry as having a content with a vengeance. The content was not some out-of-the-way, esoteric, scare-quotes "content," but the rich, deep, full-blooded content of science, cosmology, and philosophy as they were then known and practiced.

How odd it would have seemed, then, to Lucretius, to instance the most obvious case in point, to read that somehow the content of his great poem was some ineffable thing, somehow inseparable from his mode of expressing it. On the contrary, Lucretius saw his poem as one of the ways of transmitting a cosmology, a science and a moral doctrine that certainly could be expressed nonpoetically and, in part, had been so expressed by his great Greek predecessors.

I am assuming here, I should add, that Lucretius's poem is not merely a compilation of other men's work – it is that, partly, of course – but a contribution to the atomists' "research" agenda, original both in its bold systematization of previous discoveries and in its contribution, I am conjecturing, of new thoughts and observations. The reader who cannot follow me in this assumption may substitute Parmenides' *Way of Truth* or the fragmentary poem of Empedocles' as an instance. I choose Lucretius's poem because my readers will be more or less familiar with it and because, in fact, Lucretius had a clear concept of what he was doing, shared by his contemporaries, that was generalizable to at least a large part of the poetic enterprise and might justly be termed the "sugar-coated-pill" theory.

As Lucretius would have it, poetic expression is the honey that makes palatable the medicine of content, be it philosophical, moral, or "scientific." On this view, the content of a poem is no more inseparable from its form, or mode of expression, than is the medicine inseparable from the honey. In this regard, I cannot resist quoting the great poet himself:

[B]ut as with children, when physicians try to administer rank wormwood, they first touch the rim about the cups with the sweet yellow fluid of honey, that unthinking childhood be deluded as far as the lips, and meanwhile may drink up the bitter juice of wormwood, and though beguiled be not betrayed, but rather by such means be restored and regain health, so now do I: since this doctrine commonly seems harsh to those who have not used it, and the people shrink back from it, I have chosen to set forth my doctrine to you in sweet-speaking Pierian song, and as it were to touch it with the Muses' delicious honey, if by chance in such a way I might engage your mind in my verses, while you are learning to see in what shape is framed the whole nature of things.[4]

Now I do not say that this is a good theory of poetry. But nor, by the way, am I convinced that it is a terrible or silly, or absolutely false theory, of at least *some* kinds of poetry. All I am saying right now is that this theory, and theories like it, which countenanced, indeed insisted upon, the precept that form or mode of expression in a poem is one thing, content, or what is expressed, another, were abroad in the ancient world, and indeed beyond it. For such a theory, it is no more plausible that what a poem says can be said only by that poem than that what a philosophical treatise says can be said only by that treatise.

When, then, and why did the notion that the content of a poem is ineffable in any other vehicle but the poem itself come to seem plausible? What need motivated the collapsing of poetic form into poetic content?

I have neither the time nor the expertise to trace the history of poetic theory from Plato to Bradley. But I venture the conjecture that by the time the eighteenth century rolled around, poetry as the source and conveyor of scientific, philosophical, or any other categorizable kind of human knowledge was a dead issue. The scientific revolution, the growth of specialization and professionalism in all forms of knowledge, practical as well as theoretical and humanistic, put an end to the epistemic claims of the ancient poets that Plato so deplored. It would have seemed almost as absurd in the Enlightenment to assert that the poem was a vehicle for the expression of scientific or philosophical knowledge at the cutting edge as it seemed sensible and commonplace in the ages of Parmenides, Plato, and Lucretius. Poetry, it would seem, had lost pretensions to knowledge, and Plato at last was vindicated.

§3   Perhaps a good place to begin to take the measure of the collapse of poetry as a purveyor of knowledge at the cutting edge in the Enlightenment is Pope's famous phrase: "what oft was thought, but ne'er so well expressed."[5] In a way, it might seem much like Lucretius's sugar-coated pill in early modern dress. But there is an obvious and crucial difference. For Pope, the poet is no longer a "seer," a discoverer of truths, but the purveyor of other people's truths. This is not the sugar-coated-pill theory of Lucretius. It is the old-wine-in-new-bottles theory. The distinction between form and content remains in place; and the form and content may both be splendid things. There is, however, no kudos for the poet as far as the content is concerned. The poet has merely selected it; it is the discovery of others.

Thus Pope's epigram does not save the poet's epistemic status. In order for that to be done we must secure for the poet a kind of knowledge that only he can command. What kind of knowledge can that be?

Well one thing the poet is in sole command of is poetic form or expression. If he were not in command of that, he would not be a poet. But if the form or expression *were* the content, then the poet would be in sole command of that content.

Put another way, if the content of the poem is ineffable, if, that is, only the poem can say what it says, then what the poem says, which only it can say, is an expression of content that only the poet can have "discovered." The poet is the world's greatest expert, the world's only expert, on the kind of knowledge his poem expresses, because it is the *only* example of that kind: it is sui generis content.

What I am suggesting, then, is that what makes the thesis of form–content identity in poetry attractive is its seeming power to regain for poetry its ancient epistemic status, lost in the wake of the scientific revolution and the specialization of the "knowing game." If the content of the poem could be paraphrased, then that paraphrase would inevitably fall into one of the categories of human knowledge populated by resident authorities who perforce would outrank the poet in expertise. (That, after all, is the substance of Plato's argument against the poets.) The poet would be thereby reduced to Pope's purveyor of platitudes. The ineffability thesis assures the poet his expertise. The poem just *is* its subject matter, and there can be no expert on the poem, no creator of that poem, no discoverer of that subject matter other than the poet. He cannot be outranked.

If I am right that it is this desire to rescue the poet's epistemic status by making him sovereign over a special, unpoachable knowledge reserve that drives the ineffability thesis, it should come, I think, as no surprise that the first powerful statement of that thesis comes in the final flowering of the Enlightenment, with the modern system of science and scholarship more or less in place. It comes, I suggest, in Kant's *Critique of Judgment,* also, significantly, the cradle of modern formalism (with Kant perhaps the unwilling father). So at least I shall now argue.

§4   In §49 of the third *Critique,* Kant introduces the both obscure and fascinating notion of the "aesthetic ideas," which we discussed briefly in the first chapter in regard to music. They are, Kant says, a counterpart of the "rational ideas" of the first *Critique,* in that both are concepts "to which no intuition (presentation of the imagination) can be adequate."[6]

In §49 Kant speaks primarily of the role of the aesthetic ideas in poetry, although he makes it clear that they function in painting and sculpture too.[7] And, as we have already seen, they figure as well in music, although they fail there in their ultimate aesthetic payoff of engaging the free play of the cognitive faculties.

It is the power to arouse the aesthetic ideas that imparts to works of the fine arts what Kant calls "spirit" (*Geist*).[8] And it is the sole privilege of *genius* to be able to make works of art in which this power resides.[9]

It is clear from the outset, even before Kant ascribes the ability to impart the aesthetic ideas to genius, that the possession of spirit, which is the ability to arouse the aesthetic ideas, is an important artistic value. Kant writes:

> Of certain products that are expected to reveal themselves at least to be fine art, we say that they have no *spirit*, even though we find nothing to censure in them as far as taste is concerned. A poem may be quite nice and elegant and yet have no spirit.[10]

It is worth noting that Kant says something can be "in part" a work of art without possessing spirit, which is to say, the power of arousing aesthetic ideas. This leads us to believe that spirit is not merely a value of artworks, but a necessary condition for being *entirely* art as well. As we shall see later on, there is a similar waffling in Bradley between the thesis that the unity of form and content is a necessary condition for being good poetry and the thesis that it is a necessary condition for being poetry at all. Kant, I think, is clearer about what he is claiming, as we have already seen in Chapter 1, that being fine art is a matter of degree or, to put it another way, that something can be fine art in one respect and not in another. In any case, I will not bother here about whether spirit is for Kant a defining property of poetry *qua* fine art or merely a good-making property. My sole interest is the nature of the aesthetic ideas themselves in Kant's scheme, which, I am claiming, is the first clear statement of what was later to become the form–content identity thesis. So I return now to the aesthetic ideas.

Kant's most detailed example – indeed, the only detailed example – of the workings of the aesthetic ideas is a poem by Frederick the Great. And when we recall that the imparting of the power to arouse aesthetic ideas is the province of genius alone, the choice of that example seems puzzling, to say the least. Did Kant really think Frederick the Great a poetic genius?

Part of the problem here may be that Kant is not yet quite comfortable with the modern sense of "genius," meaning an extraordinary creative gift, which, I believe, he himself gave its first philosophically deep formulation. For a good part of the eighteenth century the word "genius" referred to a faculty of mind that perfectly ordinary people could have in varying degrees: the faculty of generating ideas, mediocre or more than that, depending upon how much "genius" one possessed. According to this meaning of the term, anyone capable of producing a poem at all must have some degree of "genius," including the Great King.

But although this consideration may somewhat ease our puzzlement over Kant's choice of an example, it cannot entirely dispel it. For Kant does make it clear, in introducing and developing the concept of genius, that he is indeed formulating something like the modern notion of genius as the highest form of artistic creativity: Homer and Wieland are his examples. So we cannot entirely let Kant off the hook here in choosing a poem by Frederick the Great as an illustration of the power of genius to generate aesthetic ideas. There it is, and there is no getting around it. So after smiting our brows sufficiently, we can get on with the business at hand.

Kant says that "by an aesthetic idea I mean a presentation of the imagination which prompts much thought, but to which no determinate thought whatsoever, i.e. no [determinate] *concept*, can be adequate, so that no language can express it completely and allow us to grasp it."[11] And here is how Kant characterizes the working of the aesthetic ideas specifically in Frederick's poem: "The king is here animating his rational idea of a cosmopolitan attitude, even at the end of life, by means of an attribute which the imagination (in remembering all the pleasures of a completed beautiful summer day, which a serene evening calls to mind) conjoins with that presentation, and which arouses a multitude of sensations and supplementary presentations for which no expression can be found."[12]

We might characterize Kant as saying something to the effect that there are two levels of "content" in the king's poem: a statable, manifest content and an ineffable "sub-text," which is constituted by the huge range of "aesthetic ideas" the poem arouses in the reader. And it is the aesthetic ideas that constitute the true aesthetic content of the poem.

What might drive one to such a position? I suggest it is the following, in part mistaken chain of reasoning. The poem surely has a "content": it is not, in Kant's terminology, a "free beauty," like wallpaper or flowers. But this content cannot be the easily stated, manifest content of the poem, which would be nothing specially poetic and more properly the province of a scientific, philosophical, or practical discipline. And *any* statable content underlying the manifest content would suffer the same fate: for example, the statable allegory beneath the manifest content of an allegorical poem. So the true, poetic content of the poem must, by nature, be completely ineffable. This is Kant's doctrine, as expressed in the thesis of the aesthetic ideas; and it is the source, I suggest, in modern philosophy, both of the problem of how artworks can possess a content all their own, possible for them alone, immune to the inroads of the special sciences and practical disciplines, and of the first attempt at a powerful solution.

Furthermore, although Kant is certainly not a formalist with regard to the fine arts in general, nor with regard to the thesis of content ineffability, the constant companion of form–content identification, he forges a strong link between his own brand of formalism and his own concept of poetic content, and so sets a kind of precedent that later leads from the idea of a link between formalism and ineffability to the idea of their coalescence.

§5 The link that I speak of – between formalism in the Analytic of the Beautiful, and Kant's account of the content of art, in particular the aesthetic ideas, in the Deduction of Pure Aesthetic Judgments – is forged through the concept of the cognitive faculties' free play. That is to say, the free play of the cognitive faculties is the common source of our pleasure in the beauty of form, free beauty, as outlined in the Analytic of the Beautiful, and our pleasure in the true content of art, the aesthetic ideas, as outlined in the Deduction.

There is, to be sure, a subtle change in Kant's way of describing the "free play" from the Analytic to the Deduction. In the former place, we have such familiar descriptions as "the cognitive powers brought into play by this presentation are in free play" or "a free play of the presentational powers directed to cognition in general"[13] and so forth. By contrast, in the latter we get clearly similar but nevertheless interestingly distinctive char-acterizations. Here is one: "Hence it [the aesthetic idea] is a pres-entation that makes us add to a concept the thoughts of much that is ineffable, but the feeling of which quickens our cognitive powers and connects language, which would otherwise be mere letters, with spirit." And here another: "But the understanding employs this material not so much objectively, for cognition, as subjectively, namely, to quicken the cognitive powers, though indirectly this does serve cognition too."[14]

If I am right that, both in the Analytic of the Beautiful and in the Deduction, Kant is laying the satisfaction of free beauty and the aesthetic ideas to the same source, namely, the same state of the cognitive faculties, usually denominated their "free play," there is nevertheless a distinctive though subtle contrast in em-phasis. If I am not mistaken, the formulations in the Analytic of the Beautiful suggest a kind of pure, hedonistic satisfaction in the mere act of perceiving, those in the Deduction a satisfaction that is somehow spiritually uplifting and mind-expanding. This mind-enhancing propensity of the aesthetic ideas is made even more apparent in §53, Comparison of the Aesthetic Value of the Fine Arts, where Kant writes of poetry, which, among "all the arts . . . holds the first rank": "It expands the mind; for it sets the imagination free, and offers us, from among the unlimited variety of possible forms that harmonize with a given concept, though within the concept's limits, that form which links the exhibition of the concept with a wealth of thought to which no linguistic expression is completely adequate, and so poetry rises aesthetically to ideas."[15]

Now this distinction, between a kind of pure, perceptual plea-sure on the one hand and a quickening, mind-enhancing satis-faction on the other, is just what one might expect, given the contrasting objects of the two experiences. Both free beauty and the aesthetic ideas are alike in that they pleasure us without a concept: without a concept, *sans phrase,* in the former case, with-out a *definite, framable* concept in the latter. But the pleasure of free beauty is a pleasure in form, the pleasure of the aesthetic ideas a pleasure in "content," ineffable as that content might be. And it seems altogether appropriate that the pleasure in content

should have a profound effect on our cognitive powers where
the pleasure in form should not. At least so it seems to me.

But notwithstanding this altogether plausible difference in effect, given the Kantian aesthetic, between the perception of free
beauty and the cognition of the aesthetic ideas, it is the sameness
of effect that is crucial, I want to argue, in the evolution of the
form–content identity thesis. Whether one reads Kant, mistakenly, as a formalist in regard to the fine arts, as some have done,
or, correctly, as a formalist in regard to free beauty but certainly
not in regard to the fine arts, Kant has forged a link between
content in the fine arts and formal beauty by subsuming them
both under the play of the cognitive faculties. And it is this link
that I see as the first stage in the process that culminates in
Bradley's conflation of form with content in the *Oxford Lectures
on Poetry*.

Kant himself should by no means be implicated in the conflation of form with content. He maintained, it seems to me, a clear
distinction between them. What he did do, I suggest, was, perhaps for the first time, address the problem of their relation and
resolve it to his own satisfaction, if not to ours, in a way that
led others to complete the process of conflating the two – a result
completely unintended by Kant, I am certain, and, as I shall
argue shortly, completely wrongheaded as a solution to the
problem it is supposed to address.[16]

Many, I have no doubt, will be skeptical about my belief that
Kant's aesthetic ideas are to be seen as the first (or any) historical
step in the aesthetic conflation of form with content that was
completed by Bradley. But two further steps, as I see it, inter-
vene between Kant and Bradley in this regard. And these steps,
I think, are obvious enough to be beyond controversy. I want to
turn to an examination of them now.

§6 As so often has been the case in our previous reflections,
we find again that music plays a decisive role in the historical
proceedings. For it well may be that the notion of conflating
form with content finds its first, or at least its first influential
statement in Hanslick's musical formalism. And after Hanslick,

music exercises its influence once again, in Walter Pater's well-known and, as it turns out, decisive discussion of form and content in his essay "The School of Giorgione."

Hanslick was not so much a systematic philosopher as a maker of philosophically pregnant phrases, the most well known of them being "The content of music is tonally moving forms."[17] I emphasize that Hanslick was a phrase maker rather than a philosopher so that the conflation of musical form with musical content expressed in his famous epigram not be made too much of – in particular, that it not be taken as ascribing to music some esoteric meaning that can be expressed only in terms of its form. This is not a new and subtle account of how music expresses ideas. It is not an account of musical content at all. Hanslick's *bon mot* is, on the contrary, a catchy way of saying, not that music has a content peculiar in that it is inseparable from its form, but that *music has no content at all.*

However, now that I have cautioned the reader not to make too much of Hanslick's intriguing phrase as an early formulation of the form–content identity thesis, I had better caution against making too little of it either: that is, we should not make too little of its *historical* significance, just because his contemporaries and later readers *did* make too much of its philosophical importance vis-à-vis the *content* side of the equation. It is Hanslick's phrase, transmogrified into a metaphysical insight concerning the mysterious fusion of a real artistic form with a *real artistic content,* that, I think, provided the impetus for the doctrine of form–content fusion in poetry (and the other arts).

But the most proximate step to Bradley's doctrine is undoubtedly Walter Pater, whom Bradley mentions by name and whose "authority" he invokes in the *Oxford Lectures.*[18] There is, as far as I know, no evidence of a direct link between Hanslick and Pater. However, that music plays the leading part in Pater's attempt to integrate form with content (without, I should emphasize, totally obliterating the distinction) suggests the evident power of Hanslick's phrase and of his musical formalism, either direct or indirect as the case may be, over Victorian aesthetics. (Pater, after all, read German.)

§7   Pater was also no philosopher; and, like Hanslick, his greatest contribution to the form–content identity thesis (and to the philosophy of art) was a phrase – indeed, one that is far more familiar than any Hanslick ever coined. Pater famously said in "The School of Giorgione" (1877), "*All art constantly aspires towards the condition of music.*"[19] In fact, he liked the phrase so much that he said it four more times in the same essay.[20]

Pater is not the well-known and admired thinker that he is because of his philosophical views on art or any theory of criticism. So there is no point in trying to extract a sophisticated view from "The School of Giorgione." What we *can* get are some "tendencies."

Pater begins the essay by suggesting that it is differences in the arts, rather than what they have in common, that are most important to him. "Each art . . . having its own peculiar and untranslatable sensuous charm, has its own special mode of reaching the imagination, its own special responsibilities to its material." Thinking otherwise Pater calls "the mistake of much popular criticism."[21]

But as things develop, it becomes clear that Pater is only yet another seeker after the common demominator. Indeed, his famous motto is an expression of that very thing: that which all the arts share.

What, then, is the "condition" of music toward which all of the other arts strive? Pater leaves no doubt that it is the very identification of form and content that Hanslick had enunciated before him. And when we see Pater's celebrated phrase in its context, this becomes quite unmistakable:

> *All art constantly aspires towards the condition of music.* For while in all other kinds of art it is possible to distinguish the matter from the form, and the understanding can always make this distinction, yet it is the constant effort of art to obliterate it.[22]

Pater suggests at one point that in "the ideal examples of poetry and painting . . . form and matter, in their union or identity, present one single effect to the 'imaginative reason'. . . ." But it would seem to be his basic idea that the other arts may approach the condition of music – its form–content identity – while never truly attaining it, because their very essence is otherwise:

> It is the art of music which most completely realises this artistic ideal, this perfect identification of matter and form. . . . Therefore, although each [other than music] has its incommunicable element, its untranslatable order of impressions, . . . yet the arts may be represented as continually struggling after the law or principle of music, to a condition which music alone completely realises.[23]

One might venture to say, then, that Pater's theory, if we may so call it, aspires to the condition of formalism. But Pater is far too sensible to let its aspirations be fully realized. He no doubt perceived that formalism, among other things, was not consistent with his own practical criticism. It remained for Bradley, a far more "philosophical" critic, and a Hegelian one at that, at least as an interpreter of Shakespeare, to close the gap entirely between music and the other arts, although insisting that his was not thereby "a doctrine of form for form's sake."[24]

§8   I think it not too wide of the mark to characterize Bradley as wanting his cake and eating it too, for he wants all of the advantages of formalism without having to pay the price of a doctrine that, as he says, "empties poetry of its meaning. . . ."[25] But it is terribly hard, as we shall see, to determine what sort of thing, on Bradley's view, that "meaning" is that is left to him.

Before we can get to the main point of interest for us in Bradley's lecture, namely, the form–content identity thesis, some extraneous matters, at least from a contemporary perspective, must be cleared up.

To begin with, it appears that one of Bradley's major goals in "Poetry for Poetry's Sake," perhaps even the whole purpose of the thing, is to adjudicate between "the two contentions that the poetic value lies wholly or mainly in the substance, and that it lies wholly or mainly in the form."[26] We are likely, I think, to find this disjunction somewhat nonsensical and to give it short shrift: as to "wholly," a resounding "no" to either disjunct, and as to "mainly," an obvious "it all depends on the poem." Brad-

ley, however, took it very seriously indeed, and the whole theoretical apparatus of the lecture is martialed to reach our same
conclusion. The alternatives

> imply that there are in a poem two parts, factors, or compo-
> nents, a substance and a form. . . . But really in a poem, apart
> from defects, there are no such factors or components; and
> therefore it is strictly nonsense to ask in which of them the
> value lies.[27]

This aspect of Bradley's lecture I think we can safely ignore.
What is important is the theoretical apparatus itself, not the specific question that seems to have motivated it.

Second, Bradley has left it very unclear whether he is saying
that the fusion of form with content is the defining property of
poetry, whether it is the defining property of *good* poetry,
whether the goodness of poetry varies in degree with the degree
of fusion, or whether the degree to which something is poetic
varies with the degree to which it has fusion of form with content. Most generally Bradley seems to be hung up between giving a definition of what it is to be a poem and an analysis of
what it is to be a good poem.

In response to my reading of Bradley, here, as failing to distinguish clearly between the question of whether something is
a poem and whether it is a good poem, it might be replied that
this is no confusion at all, because the word "poem" is an *evaluative* word, the concept of poetry an *evaluative* concept. But
this response is, I think, itself a confusion, a failure to distinguish
among (at least?) three value issues. It will be useful to clear
this matter up before proceeding.

The word "poem," like the word "art" and many other such
words, is, indeed, both descriptive and evaluative. And it is evaluative in at least two ways, which I can best explain through
examples.

If I ask you whether the speech you heard last night was a
good speech, and you reply, "Good? It was *poetry!*" you are
using "poetry" in what might be called the "rhetorically evaluative way." You do not mean that the speech was really a
poem, but that it was a very good speech. You are playing on

the fact that we tend to think of poetry as the highest form of linguistic expression and using the sentence "It was *poetry*" rhetorically, to say that the speech was a very good one.

But there is a second way in which the words "poem" and "poetry" are evaluative. For *because* we think poetry is the highest form of linguistic expression, when we judge something (literally) to be a poem we are putting it in a more prestigious class of linguistic things than if we withheld that judgment from it, just as we do when we promote a soldier from major to general or give him the Legion of Honor.

Now the rhetorical use of "poem" and "poetry" to evaluate is, it seems to me, completely irrelevant to the confusion between the questions of whether something is a poem and whether it is a good poem. In their rhetorically evaluative use, the words "poem" and "poetry" are employed not to evaluate poems, but to evaluate other things. That's just the point of the rhetorical use.

It must be, then, the other way in which "poem" and "poetry" are evaluative – the bestowal of rank or prestige – that people have in mind when they aver that there is no distinction, and hence can't be any confusion, between the "factual" question of whether something is a poem and the evaluative question of whether a poem is a good one. For the so-called factual question isn't a nonevaluative question at all, since deciding that something is a poem is to bestow honor, prestige, value upon it, as when one promotes a soldier to higher rank.

However, it by no means follows that because "poem" and "poetry" are evaluative terms in the sense of bestowing rank, there is no distinction between the question of whether something is a poem and whether it is a good poem. To elevate something to the rank of "poem" is to place *some* value on it, to be sure. But that hardly renders meaningless the question of whether it is a good poem, except in the trivial sense that every poem has whatever minimum worth something must have to be elevated to that status at all. Surely, though, it would be pedantic in the extreme to point out that the answer to the question "Is it a good poem?" must always be yes, because every poem has that minimal good, hence is, in that respect, a "good" poem. The minimal is assumed, and the question is about something beyond that. Moreover there is the question of *comparative* goodness, which is not affected at all by the evaluative use of "poem" and "poetry" now under discussion. Some poems are better than other poems, regardless of the fact that "poem" and "poetry" are evaluative as well as descriptive words, and every poem has (some) value.

Thus the current notion, among some, that art words are evaluative by no means erases the fact that a clear distinction has to be made between the decision as to whether something is a poem or a symphony or an artwork, for that matter, and the other decision as to whether it is a good poem or good symphony or good artwork. And with regard to poems, it is that distinction that Bradley, so I believe, has failed to make clear to himself or to us.

Bradley himself must have been more than dimly aware of this ambiguity in his project, for he addressed it specifically in a note he later appended to the lecture. But even here the ambiguity never seems to get totally sorted out. So I shall simply assume that he is offering a definition of poetry, and generally of art, the closest he comes to saying as much being, "[T]his identity of content and form . . . is of the essence of poetry in so far as it is poetry, and of all art in so far as it is art."[28]

Contemporary analytic philosophy of art is comfortable with the notion that to define art is one project, to say what makes a work of art good or bad quite another. Bradley was not. Nor was Collingwood much indebted, I think, to this lecture of Bradley's, but very clear about what he was doing in conflating the definition question with the question of value, and in possession of a carefully worked out conceptual scheme to cover our contemporary intuitions, which want to keep those things distinct. Writing from a contemporary perspective, however, I have no compunction about seeing the question of defining poetry (or art) as a question apart from the question of poetic (or artistic) value. And thus shall I construe Bradley's thesis.

§9 With these preliminary matters disposed of, we can get down to our real business of determining what exactly the cash value *is* of the thesis that, in poetry, form and content are one, and evaluating that thesis as we go along.

The claim most central to Bradley's thesis, reiterated throughout his lecture, is that we can verify the form–content identity of any poem by simply trying and perforce failing to reexpress the content of that poem in different words. "Hence in true poetry," Bradley writes, "it is, in strictness, impossible to express the meaning in any but its own words, or to change the words without changing the meaning."[29]

This is not to say that we cannot state in our own words what a poem is "about," in some reasonable sense of the word. We can state what Bradley calls a poem's "subject." For example, "The subject of *Paradise Lost* would be the story of the Fall as that story exists in the general imagination of a Bible-reading public." But "the subject, in this sense (and I intend to use the word in no other), is not as such inside the poem, but outside it."[30] However, the identity thesis does not apply to the subject of the poem; that isn't even part of the poem: it is "outside it." It applies, rather, to something else called the "substance" or "content":

> Those figures, scenes, events, that form part of the subject called the Fall of Man, are not the substance of *Paradise Lost;* but in *Paradise Lost* there are figures, scenes, and events resembling them in some degree. These, with much more of the same kind, may be described as its substance, and they may be contrasted with the measured language of the poem, which will be called its form.

Unlike the subject, "substance is within the poem, and its opposite, form, is also within the poem.[31]

It is substance, or content, then, not subject, that the identity thesis is about. It is *this* that is inseparable from form in virtue of being unsayable in any form of language other than that of the poem itself. "A translation of such poetry is not really the old meaning in a fresh dress; it is a new product, something like the poem, if one chooses to say so, more like it in the aspect of meaning than in the aspect of form."[32]

§10   We have now reached the first vantage point from which we can look back and take stock. How plausible is the thesis that we cannot successfully say in words other than those of the poem what the poem is expressing?

In order to answer this question, we need to know what the criterion or criteria would be for a successful reexpression of a poem's content. How would we know whether it was possible unless we could evaluate our attempts and know when we had failed?

When we frame the question this way, two suspicions immediately creep in. One is that Bradley has made the criterion of success so stringent that we are bound to fail in the task of reexpression. The other is that this criterion might not just be unreasonably, excessively stringent but amount to a conventionalist sulk: making the nontranslatability thesis true by stipulative definition.

Of the latter possibility, we have evidence in such statements as "Meaning they have, but *what* meaning can be said in no language but their own . . .";[33] and "[I]f we insist on asking for the meaning of such a poem, we can only be answered 'It means itself' ";[34] and, finally, and I think most conclusively, "[I]t is, in strictness, impossible to express the meaning in any but its own words. . . ."[35] But if the failure of paraphrase is ensured merely by changing the words in any way, then, by definition, paraphrase is doomed to failure, because it just is the process of reexpressing one sequence of words with a different sequence of words. On this criterion of success for paraphrase, no linguistic expression, poetic or otherwise, would be susceptible of paraphrase.

But if we are generous and willing to acquit Bradley of the charge of conventionalist sulk, what can we substitute as a criterion of success in paraphrase? We get a good idea of what that might be in another way Bradley has of putting his argument for the impossibility of poetic paraphrase. "When poetry answers to its idea and is purely or almost purely poetic, we find the identity of form and content; and the degree of purity attained may be tested by the degree in which we feel it hopeless to convey the effect of a poem or passage in any form but its own."[36] The eye falls here naturally on the word "effect," which seems to be doing duty for "content" or "substance" or "meaning." For where it sounds profoundly wrong to claim that you can't ever convey the *meaning* of a poem through a paraphrase, it surely sounds altogether plausible to claim that you can't ever convey its *effect*. The *experience* of reading *Paradise Lost* cannot be got by doing anything but reading *Paradise Lost* – a fortiori, certainly not by reading a paraphrase or interpretation of the meaning of *Paradise Lost*. So if the criterion of success in reexpression of the content of *Paradise Lost* is reproduction of the poem's total effect on the reader, it is an unreasonable, certainly an overstringent criterion. It would, indeed, like the conventionalist sulk, rule out all paraphrase whatever, even from prose to prose. A teacher would not be able to paraphrase her textbook.

But even to call this criterion of success in paraphrase too demanding is to pay it a compliment it does not merit. It is in fact nonsensical, because it demands of paraphrase something that never was the object of the exercise in the first place. A lamb is being hanged for a sheep. No one who sets out to say in prose the content of what a poem says in poetic form intends as the goal of the task to provide an alternative way of experiencing the poem. And to fault the interpreter for failing to do what is not the point of interpretation in the first place is plain nonsense.

It is not difficult to see how Bradley has gotten into this peculiar, untenable position. For he tends to describe paraphrase of meaning as "translation," as, for example, in a passage quoted before, where he says, "A translation of such poetry is not really the old meaning in a fresh dress. . . ."[37] But if *translation* is your goal, then your goal *is* generally taken to be the production of the poem's whole effect in different words: words of another natural language, of course. And we all agree that that is an unattainable goal. *Tradutor, traditor* always to some palpable degree. No one really thinks that you can ever devise an English translation of the *Iliad* that will give the Greekless reader the same poetic experience as reading the poem in the original, although we may think that Lattimore came closer to it (for us) than Pope.

But once we see that literary or poetic "translation" is entirely the wrong model for content paraphrase, the claim that poetic content cannot be rendered in prose paraphrase loses any hold it might have had on us. It is plainly false. It may even be false in its most extreme form, short of truth by stipulation. I see no reason why, in principle if not in practice, it is not possible to give a *complete* paraphrase of poetic meaning, leaving nothing of the content out. But in any event, no one who claims the content of a poem can be stated in words other than those of the poem is (or need be) claiming that full content can be captured, that perfect paraphrase is possible. And surely the modest claim that we can say in plain words more or less what the content of a poem is seems an unobjectionable one. Where it seems to fail is when we either place upon paraphrase the completely inappropriate criterion of success of translation or simply make its denial true by stipulation.

Thus it appears to me that Bradley's most often repeated reason for maintaining the form–content identity thesis for poetry, namely the supposed impossibility of content paraphrase, is utterly groundless. It is not clear to me from repeated readings of "Poetry for Poetry's Sake" whether failure of paraphrase is supposed to be the way we recognize that there is form–content identity in a poem, whether it is the reason we should believe that the form–content identity thesis is true, or whether it is simply a statement of what the cash value is of the form–content identity thesis. But in any event, once it goes by the boards, there is little else in Bradley's lecture to offer in defense of the thesis. There are, however, a few further considerations to be taken stock of, and I will get to them now.

§11 Perhaps the most eye-catching claim in "Poetry for Poetry's Sake," after the nontranslatability thesis, is to the effect that both the experience we have in reading a poem and the manner in which poems are created are incompatible with the separability of form from content. Of the reading experience, Bradley writes: "In these words [in *Hamlet*], . . . the action and characters (more of them than you can conceive apart) are focussed; but your experience is not a combination of them, as ideas, on the one side, with certain sounds on the other; it is an experience of something in which the two are indissolubly fused."[38] And of the creative act:

> Pure poetry is not the decoration of a preconceived and clearly defined matter: it springs from the creative impulse of a vague imaginative mass pressing for development and definition. If the poet already knew exactly what he meant to say, why should he write the poem? The poem would in fact already be written. For only its completion can reveal, even to him, exactly what he wanted.[39]

Even a casual acquaintance with Collingwood's philosophy of art will allow one to recognize, in Bradley's description of the poem's genesis, a remarkably close approximation to the concept of expression as it appears in the latter's *Principles of Art* – far too close for coincidence. And it carries with it the same defect (among others) in the later, more sophisticated formulation.

Taken as an account of how *all* poems (or works of art) come into being, it is plainly false. It may indeed be the case – I certainly believe it is so – that sometimes a poem has its beginning as vague, inchoate impression, some "I know not what" that gradually becomes clear to the poet as the work progresses, and reaches full, self-conscious clarity only in the completed utterance. It is a possible scenario and, I feel certain, an actual one on many occasions (which specific occasions it being impossible to tell).

But why should we believe that this "clarification-in-process" scenario is the exclusive one? I find it quite plausible to believe, to instance two cases in point, that Lucretius, on the contrary, had a well-formed idea of what he wanted to say in his great poem and that Shakespeare did too, at least some of the time. It seems likely that, given the length of these works, some parts were preconceived and some came into being in the the very way Bradley (later Collingwood) described. That, however, just goes to show that, as one would naturally suspect if untainted by "expression theory," the bringing into being of poems and other works of art, as well as their various parts, is a mixed bag:

different artists, different artworks, different parts, different methods and processes. Why not? The idea of a single thing called "the creative process" seems to me a damaging myth.

If, however, we accept this more moderate claim, that sometimes poems or parts of poems do, and sometimes do not, come into being the way Bradley makes out, the claim loses its power to discriminate between poems and other forms of linguistic utterance. For there seems no reason not to believe that essays, philosophical treatises, nonfiction works of all kinds, including scientific books and papers, show the same character as poems in respect of sometimes following the Bradley–Collingwood scenario of creation and sometimes not.

§12 Moving now from the creation of poems to the experience of them, I think we will see the same problem attaching to Bradley's account. Bradley says that when reading a poem, at least as one should, one does not experience form and content, words on the one side and meanings on the other, as separate entities but the two as one: "[I]t is an experience of something in which the two are indissolubly fused." But here, as in the preceding case, it is clear that if we understand the claim as a universal generalization, it is plainly false, the addition of "should" notwithstanding. And if we understand it as the more moderate claim that sometimes the form and content of a poem are experienced as "indissolubly fused," sometimes (quite properly) not, it becomes harmlessly true, harmlessly in that it completely fails to distinguish the experience of poetry from the experience of any other text or utterance.

Now Bradley is well aware that we do not, in reading poetry, always experience the fusion of form with content. We can analytically separate "them." But when we do, we cannot be said to really have "them" separate; for, by hypothesis, they cannot be separated, and therefore what we end up with is not parts of the poem: the so-called content that you get in "analytic" reading is "no part of it [the poem], but a product of it in your reflective imagination, a faint analogue of some aspect of it taken in detachment from the whole."[40]

What we have here, I suggest, in metaphysical dress, is simply the normative claim that the *proper* way of reading a poem is the way that is in conformity with Bradley's fusion claim. Dressing it up in talk about what is "in" and what is "out" of the poem is a pretty thin disguise and is strangely at odds with Bradley's "definition" of a poem, which is frankly mentalistic and another clear prefiguration of Collingwood. On Bradley's account, "an actual poem is the succession of experiences – sounds, images, thoughts, emotions – through which we pass when we are reading *as poetically as we can.*"[41] A poem is, in other words, an "imaginative experience."[42]

I say that Bradley's sense of what is "in" and what "out" of the poem is at odds with his frankly mentalistic definition of "the poem" because the in–out dichotomy is always stated by Bradley as if it were between what is "in" the poem and what is "out" of the poem *because* "in your head." But since the whole existence of the poem, on Bradley's account, is "in your head," an "imaginative experience," a distinction between what is "in" the poem and what is not, based on what is "in" the poem as opposed to what is "in your head," obviously won't wash. It is *all* "in your head." So the question becomes what part of the experience "in your head" when you read the text is "the poem" and what part is not but in your head. Well, when we read "as poetically as we can," our experience "in the head" is "in the poem"; and reading "as poetically as we can" means reading in a manner in which form and content are fused, not in the analytic manner in which they are not.

But now see where we have arrived. The experience of reading a poem is supposed, on Bradley's view, to be incompatible with the thesis that form and content can be prised apart; and that is because, when we are *properly* experiencing a poem, experiencing it "as poetically as we can," we always experience form and content as fused. How do we know when we are properly experiencing a poem, experiencing it "as poetically as we can"? Why, when we are experiencing form and content as fused. And why should we think that is the only proper way of experiencing the poem, the way that is "as poetically as we can"? Because, in a word, the form–content identity thesis is true – which is to say, we have moved in a perfect logical circle.

Now I take it that we can experience poetry as a fused form and content, and we can experience it with form and content prised apart. Furthermore, I take it that both ways are valuable, proper ways of experiencing it. I also am of the opinion that every such experience is a bit of both and that our attention is divided in all sorts of other ways as well. What I have in mind here is splendidly captured in the following description by Donald Francis Tovey of how we listen to Bach's *Art of Fugue:*

> Psychologists tell us that it is impossible to attend to more than two things at once. From this it must follow that we cannot attend to all four parts of these fugues at once, and that it must be still more impossible to attend to all the details of augmentation, diminution, stretto, inversion, double, triple and quadruple counterpoint through which Bach develops his subject and countersubjects. But it ought never to be supposed that any such attention is required of the listener. Nothing prevents the listener from *hearing* all these things at once and *attending* to one thing at a time. It is even doubtful whether he need often, or ever, attend to two. If the complexity is artistic it will make a single harmonious impression all the time, and the attention will move with enjoyment from point to point according as it is wisely directed.[43]

What Tovey has given us here is plain, simple wisdom about how we experience and enjoy a complex work of art (or a game of baseball, for that matter). And if we think of the content and form of a poem, the meaning and the medium, as two-voice counterpoint, Tovey's description will suit a poem as well as a fugue. Sometimes we concentrate on the "subject," sometimes the "counterpoint," and sometimes they "fuse" in our attention. The notion that the mode of attention in which form and content, medium and message fuse is some special, favored way of attending is just not in touch with reality. It is redolent with the aroma of "aesthetic attitude" theories and has aught to do with how real people experience poetry (or any of the other fine arts).

It seems reasonable to conclude, then, that the *moderate* thesis of form–content fusion is true for the experience of reading poetry. Sometimes we experience the medium and the message as one rather than two objects of attention; sometimes we are not aware of the medium and the message but only the medium-and-message, undifferentiated. But sometimes, too, our attention flits rapidly back and forth from one to the other or concentrates for a while on one rather than the other.

The moderate thesis, however, will not do the job for Bradley of distinguishing between poetry and other forms of linguistic expression. For it is true of all kinds of written texts, as well as speech, that sometimes we are aware of a fused meaning-and-form and sometimes our attention divides them and wanders from one to the other. What is even more damaging to Bradley's viewpoint, it seems to me, is that one will be far more likely to experience form–content fusion in the nonpoetic and nonliterary cases than in poetic and prose literature. When I read textbooks or newspapers, I am concerned only with the message, not the medium. The medium is "transparent" to me. Of course, I must *experience* the medium to get the message. But just because I do not pay particular attention to it, it is perfectly fused with its meaning. It is quite different with poetry, and literary language in general, just because the medium is thick, interesting, and so, far more frequently, the object of my attention: attention-getting, in fact. So it appears that, far from the experience of form–content fusion being exclusive to poetry, it is linguistically ubiquitous and more prevalent in nonpoetic forms to boot. The form–content identity thesis for poetry again comes to nought.

§13   I have expended a good deal of effort tracing the evolution of the form–content identity thesis from Kant to Bradley and trying to refute it in Bradley's lecture "Poetry for Poetry's Sake," its most well-known and vigorously defended exposition. It is now time for us to be reminded of why I thought this was an important thing to do and to determine what conclusions we can reasonably draw from the development and ultimate failure (at least as I see it) of the doctrine that in poetry, and in the other arts, there is no viable distinction between form and content.

Two forces, I suggested early on, were behind the development in the modern era of this notion. One force was the attempt to find, for poetry, some unique knowledge claim that the special sciences, practices, and disciplines could not preempt. This is quite explicit in Bradley's lecture. The "heresy," as Bradley calls it, of paraphrasing a poem, putting its content in our words, is tantamount to "putting our own thoughts or fancies into the place of the poet's creation." But that is a mistake, for then: "What he meant by *Hamlet,* or *Abt Vogler,* we say, is this or that which we knew already; and so we lose what he had to tell us."[44] Thus, for Bradley, to paraphrase is, of necessity, to attribute to the poem knowledge we must have already got from another source, and the poem, therefore, is prevented from giving us the new and special knowledge that it alone possesses. That, at least as I read Bradley, is the implication.

Equally apparent, if not more out front in Bradley's lecture, as we saw early on, is the intention of binding poetry together with the other fine arts through the thesis of form–content identity. It is an important enough point to bear quoting from Bradley to that effect yet again. (The reiterations are numerous.) "Just as there is in music not sound on one side and a meaning on the other, but expressive sound, and if you ask what is the meaning you can only answer by pointing to the sounds, just as in painting there is not a meaning *plus* paint, but a meaning *in* paint, or significant paint, and no man can really express the meaning in any other way than in paint and in *this* paint; so in a poem the true content and the true form neither exist nor can be imagined apart."[45]

Reminded, now, of these two motivating forces behind the form–content identity thesis, and assured of their visible presence in Bradley's highly influential lecture, we should now be able to weave the identity thesis – its history, its raison d'être, its (in my view) demise – into the thematic structure of the general argument. Let us concentrate first on the identity thesis as an effort to bind together the fine arts.

In the opening two chapters I traced the high points (as I saw them) in the history of aesthetics that represented, in my view, the persistent, single-minded attempt to find some defining similarity among the fine arts. The basic strategy was to make out all of the arts to be representational, or at least "contentful," with absolute music always the problematic case: the *experimentum crucis*.

Formalism is an island in this historical stream of representation and content theories, a brief interlude in which absolute music becomes the paradigm and everything else an anomaly. And the form–content identity thesis shares that characteristic with formalism, all the while its major practitioner, Bradley, insisting that the thesis is not to be identified with formalism because the formalist "goes too far. . . ."[46] Thus it is not music as pure form that the form–content identity theorist takes as his paradigm but music as the paradigmatic art in which form and content are fused, inseparable, identical.

In Hanslick, who, as we have seen, coined the famous phrase "The content of music is tonally moving forms,"[47] the identification of form with content is, I have argued, simply a rhetorical way of *denying* that music has a "content" at all, as that word is customarily used with reference to the arts. It is therefore only a stimulus to the real form–content identity thesis, not an early version of the thing itself. To get from Hanslick to Bradley, the notion of musical "content" must be given real substance, or formalism it remains. And it is clear what that substance must be. It is the ineffable, the "I know not what"; and so it presents itself in Bradley's thesis that the content of poetry cannot be paraphrased, is unutterable except by the poem itself.

For those, like myself, who see the resort to ineffable content as a council of despair, the attempt to knit the fine arts together under its banner will hold little attraction. It is another attempt at discovering that essential sameness in the arts, with the added liability of having the worst of both worlds. Instead of, as in the case of content theories, ascribing to music something the other arts have but it does not or, as in the case of formalism, ascribing to the other arts something that music has but they do not, the form–content identity thesis ascribes to *all* of the arts something that *none* of them has: "ineffable content."

A great deal more, doubtless, needs to be said about the ineffable business in regard to music, but for now I shall leave it alone, resting in the conclusion that one motive behind the form–content identity thesis, our old friend the quest for defining sameness in the arts, failed in its purpose. It seems to me that it is vital to maintain the very distinction between music and the "contentful" arts that the identity thesis is designed to rub out. Music is the art in which form (broadly speaking) and content cannot be distinguished, the art in which the form is the "content." That is something extremely important that distinguishes music from most examples of visual and literary art, where form, or medium, and content, or subject, can be and, in experience, frequently are distinguished. It is only in recognizing this "difference" that we can come to understand the arts as we have them.

But this cannot be our last word on the form–content identity thesis. For we will recall that the quest for sameness is not the only motivating force behind it. There is still to be dealt with the other: the attempt to carve out for poetry and the other arts a class of knowledge claims all their own. Is this a sensible thing to attempt? Does the form–content identity thesis address, if unsuccessfully, a real problem in our experience of the arts? To these matters I want to turn next.

§14 If a molecular biologist were to submit her results to *Nature* in poetic form, it would be thought utterly absurd, hardly less so if John Rawls had submitted the manuscript of his *Theory of Justice* to Harvard University Press in rhymed couplets. Yet Lucretius presented his "results," at the cutting edge of atomic theory and moral philosophy, in a longish poem that has come to be thought of as one of the masterworks of Western literature. That Lucretius was able to do this and we are not implies, needless to say, a profound change in the practice of science and philosophy, as well as a profound change in the role of poetry, at least in some of its aspects, in our lives.

From this profound change, however, it seems to be a mistake to conclude that poetry must be "defended" by showing that it imparts some special knowledge, unique to itself and expressible, in each individual case, only by the poem that is supposed to contain that particular body of knowledge (whatever it might be). The practice of poetry is not a way of knowing some particular kind of thing but, in one of its offices, one of the various ways we may have of expressing all kinds of things we know or believe, wish or hope, fear or value. And the reason poetry is not a viable way to express scientific results today but was in the times of Parmenides and Lucretius is not that poetry has changed but that science has.

Two things Bradley says are directly relevant here, one quite wrong, the other profoundly right. He says there is something wrong, you may recall, with the conclusion that a poem might express "this or that which we know already. . . ."[48] What is so strangely mistaken about this idea is that it overlooks one of our deepest and most persistent needs: the need, so obvious already in childhood, of being told the same things over and again. Truth saying is the office of poetry as well as of newspapers and scientific periodicals. But perhaps what separates poetry from these others (and many more organs of expression) is that it needn't necessarily be reporting the news for the first time; literary art forms need not give us the scoop, although there is no reason to believe they do not do it some of the time, and properly so. The Greeks were right, pace Plato: poets sometimes are seers. But Pope was right too: they sometimes pronounce "what oft was thought, but ne'er so well expressed."

The role of poetry and the other literary arts in our lives is not a simple one. And it cannot be my place here to tease out the strands. But thinking of literature, either poetry or prose fiction, as a source of some special kind of human knowledge, as Bradley and others have done, is, in my view, profoundly mistaken and often seems to border on a kind of "aesthetic mysticism" that is not just unhelpful to the philosophical understanding. Poetry and fiction are not special conduits to the font of wisdom. They are ways some wise folks (and some not so wise) have tried to express some of the things they have found out or others have found out (and some things that nobody has found out, because they are not the case). There is no one kind of knowledge, effable or ineffable, that is the particular province of poets. And this leads us to the point in this regard on which Bradley is profoundly right.

Bradley insisted that there is no special *subject* of art in general or of poetry in particular. (Bear in mind here his distinction between "subject" and "content.") He writes, "[I]t is surely true that we cannot determine beforehand what subjects are fit for Art, or name any subject on which a good poem may not possibly be written."[49] It was *content*, of course, not *subject*, that Bradley said was unique to the poem and its own special knowledge. But of both content and subject, *we* may want to say that there are no a priori limits on what might be poetically expressed. There may, of course, be practical limits on what might usefully be expressed, and so it may well be a foolish exercise to report results in quantum theory in blank verse. But that poetic expression of the quantum-mechanical "vision" might be both appropriate and moving is not thereby denied.

The quest for a special poetic knowledge, which motivates the form–content identity thesis, is, I have been arguing, a fruitless, misdirected one. The practice of poetry is not a method or methods of gaining some special, esoteric form of knowledge, but a method or methods of expressing knowledge (and other things too) that people have (or think they have) acquired in all of the various ways people do acquire such things, from scientific investigation to philosophical discussion, from common sense to ecstatic vision, from moral argument to religious conversion. To the extent, then, that the form–content identity thesis is a quest for special knowledge, unique to poetry (and art), it fails to connect with any valid intuition about or genuine problem in the philosophy of art. The question remaining is whether it connects with *any* valid intuition or problem at all. I think that it does, but comes to a mistaken conclusion.

§15   Throughout this chapter I have referred to two motivating forces behind the form–content identity thesis. They are the quest for the common essence of the arts, the quest for sameness that is the *bête noire* of my book, and the quest for a special poetic (or art-specific) kind of knowledge. To these I must now add a third. It appears to me that we have a deep intuition that in the arts there is an especially intimate relation between form and content not exhibited in other modes of expression. To a degree, that is a valid intuition, and the form–content identity thesis is a response to it – the wrong response, as it turns out. For it construes the intimate relation of form to content as identity: an intimate relation indeed. But the real trick is to avoid that extreme conclusion, to show the special intimacy of form and content in the arts while maintaining the distinction between them. This the identity thesis fails (quite intentionally) to do.

There is currently abroad a philosophically deep way of approaching our intuition about the intimacy of the form–content relation, in Arthur Danto's second condition on something's being a work of art. On Danto's view, it will be recalled, the first condition for arthood is "aboutness." Works of art are essentially about something, or at least the question of what a true work of art is about can be sensibly raised, even if the answer is "nothing." But the aboutness criterion cannot be all there is to it, for modes of expression other than artworks are "about." So to the genus must be appended a difference. In Danto's words (quoted also in Chapter 2): "The thesis is that works of art, in categorical contrast with mere representations, use the means of representation in a way that is not exhaustively specified when one has exhaustively specified what is being represented."[50]

What Danto is saying, I take it, is that when one exhaustively specifies what the content of a work of art is, what, in other words, has been represented *by* the medium of representation, one has not exhaustively specified the relation of medium to subject, form to content, whereas, say, in a philosophical or scientific treatise one has exhaustively specified the relation between medium and content, form and representation when one has exhaustively paraphrased the content. The relation between form and content simply is, in the nonart case, that *this* form has expressed *this* content.

What is extra in the artistic form–content relation is that one must also specify the way in which the form, the medium, is employed. And that way is what makes the relation more intimate. For the *way* in which the artist employs the medium is, in effect, part of the content, because it expresses something in the artist's point of view about the content.

My point is that Danto's way of seeing the relation of medium to representation in art, as opposed to nonart, is also a way of explaining the intuition, which the form–content identity thesis was also (in part) contrived to explain, that the relation of form to content in art is particularly, uniquely intimate. Furthermore, Danto manages to do the business without obliterating the distinction between form and content, medium and object of representation. And that is crucial to the success of the enterprise.

I was somewhat cagey in my statement of the intuition that, in art, form and content are intimately connected in a special way alien to other forms of expression. I framed it in terms of degree. For I think there are other cases besides that of the fine arts where the mode of expression sometimes performs the function Danto is talking about. (Philosophical works like Spinoza's *Ethics*, the *Tractatus*, as well as the later writings of Wittgenstein come to mind, where the special or even startling modes of expression seem to "comment" implicitly on the content in ways akin to the cases of the fine arts Danto adduces. I intentionally omit mention of Plato's dialogues, as these might be construed as works of the fine arts themselves.) But I think it would be carping to place too much emphasis on these instances, which can be construed as the exception rather than the rule (unless one has a "theory" about this, which some people do). It remains the case that it is especially in the arts where we feel a particular, intimate relation between form and content. The form–content identity thesis responded to this valid intuition in, it seems to me, a disastrous way, by obliterating the distinction altogether. Danto, I suggest, gives us a way of supporting our intuition that manages also to preserve it. And whether or not one can buy into Danto's solution, any other successful competitor will have to preserve it as well.

§16   I have argued in the present chapter that the notion of a form–content fusion, in the literary arts in particular, is symptomatic of a desire to reveal in them some special kind of knowledge that only they can possess and impart: a kind of knowledge immune to the inroads of the specialized scientific, academic, and philosophical disciplines, which claim exclusive domain over the "knowledge game." My own belief is that literature has been, and continues to be, a conduit for knowledge not unique to itself, but common to the specialized disciplines as well, at least within the limits of its demesne. But this is a highly controversial belief, and stands in need of defense and amplification. That will be my project in the following chapter.

I hasten to add that any thorough defense and development of a "truth-in-literature" thesis of any kind would require not a chapter but a volume. So my goal in what follows must be more modest than that. It is to defend a moderate thesis about, principally, *fictional* literature, to the effect that, sometimes at least, one of the functions of a literary work, *qua* literary work, is to present hypotheses of a philosophical, religious, moral, or "social" kind (or what have you) for readers' consideration as to truth or falsity. This defense will be conducted against the background of a thorough and closely reasoned argument in contradiction of such theses, published recently. As usual, my theme will be differences, although in the present instance I vary it slightly. For whereas in one place I shall indeed argue at length that an implicit musical model of fictional literature, taken for granted in our thinking about the question of literary truth, is quite misplaced and wrongheaded, I shall argue in another place that a musical model for the role of the literary critic, a crucial point in the argument, is both helpful and valid. So, now, on to that task.

Chapter 5

The Laboratory of Fictional Truth

§1   The publication of Peter Lamarque and Stein Olsen's book, *Truth, Fiction and Literature,* was an event of the first magnitude in contemporary philosophy of art. I intend to defend here, in the face of some trenchant criticism by Lamarque and Olsen in that book, a version of what they call there the Propositional Theory of Literary Truth – henceforth, the Propositional Theory for short. I underscore that I will defend a *version* of this theory because I will not defend it in as strong a form as stated by Lamarque and Olsen. And I underscore that I will defend it against *some* criticism by Lamarque and Olsen because I cannot, in a single chapter in a single book, hope to defend it against all. But if at least a modest version of the Propositional Theory cannot be salvaged from Lamarque and Olsen's powerful attempt at demolition, my own literary experience will be very difficult for me to comprehend. Indeed, part of my "worldview," if I may risk being too grandiose, is going to totter. So what I am attempting here is of no small importance to me. And if, as I think, there are others who share my literary experience and the worldview in which it inheres, it will be at least of some interest to them as well.

§2   Proponents of the Propositional Theory, as Lamarque and Olsen characterize them,

> admit the reasonableness of the view that literature at the "literal level" is for the most part fictive, i.e. that characteristically its content is fictional and its mode of presentation is not that of fact-stating. But they claim that at a different level literary

works do, perhaps must, imply or suggest general propositions about human life which have to be assessed as true or
false, and that these propositions are what make literature valuable.[1]

More specifically, the Propositional Theory is founded, as
Lamarque and Olsen present it, on the distinction between two
different kinds of proposition a fictional literary work might express:

> Propositions which describe or mention particular situations
> and events, characters and places in a literary work may be
> labelled *subject descriptions.* Propositions which express gen-
> eralizations or judgements based on or referring to these de-
> scribed situations, events, characters and places may be
> labelled *thematic statements.*[2]

Furthermore, thematic statements – with which the Propositional Theory is principally concerned – "may be of two types,
explicit and *implicit.* Explicit thematic statements occur in the
literary work itself," whereas implicit statements are "extracted
from the work by the reader in interpretation."[3]

With these distinctions in hand, we are ready for a more precise statement of the Propositional Theory. In the words of Lem-
arque and Olsen, "A Propositional Theory of Literary Truth
could then be formulated as follows: *the literary work contains
or implies general thematic statements about the world which the
reader as part of an appreciation of the work has to assess as true or
false.*"[4] I intend to defend a somewhat weaker form of this theory
against some criticism by Lamarque and Olsen. But before I state
their criticism, or my defense, I must make my modifications.

First, I am not saying that all works of fiction contain general
thematic statements; only some of them do. (And from now on
I will use the terms "fiction" and "fictional," "literature" and
"literary" in the general sense of "fiction that is literature," as
contrasted with literature that is not fiction and fiction that is
not literature.)

Second, I am not saying that every general thematic statement

121

is or ought to be the subject of truth-value assessment, as part of the reader's literary appreciation. Whether it is or is not, ought or ought not to be depends on the work in which it is expressed as well as the role it may play in the work.

Third, I am not saying that the truth of a general thematic statement is ever necessary for a work's being evaluated positively or ever sufficient for a work's being evaluated positively. The truth of general thematic statements is just one literary value among many, their falsity just one literary disvalue among many. In any case, it is reader-relative plausibility rather than truth that is at issue, as we shall see.

With these amendments on the table, I can now state the version of the Propositional Theory that I want to defend: *Some fictional works contain or imply general thematic statements about the world that the reader, as part of an appreciation of the work, has to assess as true or false.*

I am basically interested, in this regard, in two closely related claims Lamarque and Olsen make, meant to cast doubt on the Propositional Theory. They are that critics do not, as part of their ordinary business, try to determine the truth or falsity of general thematic statements and that the determination of the truth or falsity of such claims is not part of literary appreciation. And the reason I say that they are closely related is that they imply one another, the way Lamarque and Olsen put matters. That is to say, if true–false determinations are not part of critical practice, then they cannot be part of literary appreciation, since critical practice deals with all aspects of literary appreciation; and going in the other direction of implication, if true–false determinations are not part of literary appreciation, then they will not be part of critical practice, since, again, critical practice deals with all aspects of literary appreciation. This reciprocal implication can be understood in the following succinct statement by Lamarque and Olsen. "Debate about the truth or falsity of the propositions implied by a literary work is absent from literary criticism since it does not enter into *the appreciation of the work as a literary work.*"[5]

I want to look, first, at the claim that literary critics do not as a rule engage in determinations of the truth or falsity of general

thematic statements in or implied by literature. I will then turn
to the wider, related question of literary appreciation.

§3 Briefly, the criticism argument can be stated as follows. According to the Propositional Theory, part of the appreciation of
a literary work may consist in the reader's assessing the truth-
value of general thematic propositions expressed therein. But if
that is so, then we could rightfully expect that such assessment
should also occur in the work of the literary critic, under the
assumption that anything relevant to literary appreciation is also
the critic's job to discuss. But critics typically engage in no discussion of the truth or falsity of general thematic statements,
only the interpretive task of bringing them out. So the Propositional Theory is incompatible with the practice of literary criticism, and hence must be false. In the words of Lamarque and
Olsen, "The issues of literary criticism concern aspects of literary
works, and among these issues will be their handling of certain
types of themes and concepts, but there is no accepted place for
debate about the truth or falsity of general statements about
human life or the human condition."[6] Nor is this absence a trivial matter. On the contrary, it is of the essence. "The lack of
debate in literary criticism and critical discourse in general about
the truth of such general propositions must therefore be understood as a feature of the literary practice itself."[7]

I confess that when I first read these observations, I was rather
knocked back on my heels and felt, intuitive believer that I was
in the Propositional Theory, awakened from my dogmatic slum-
ber. For it seemed to me then, and still seems to me now, that
Lamarque and Olsen are right about most literary criticism:
there is, most of the time, no true–false evaluation in it of the
general thematic statements. And it seemed to me then, too, that
this fact – and fact it seems to be – was completely incompatible
with my deeply held belief in the Propositional Theory.

Subsequent reflection, however, has convinced me that there
is no incompatibility between the Propositional Theory and the
uncontested fact that critics do not usually engage in verifying
or disconfirming practices vis-à-vis the propositions fictional

works might be thought to express. The problem is to choose the right model for the relation between critic, reader, and work.

Our problem is this. If the Propositional Theory is true, there must be some significant place in the literary experience for the confirmation and disconfirmation of general thematic statements. The most obvious place to look is critical practice. But when we look, we do not find any such proceedings. So the Propositional Theory seems to be in deep trouble.

But what about the general readership for fiction? Why not look there for the true–false evaluation we fail to find in the practices of literary critics? Perhaps it is just not the critic's job but the reader's.

Lamarque and Olsen do indeed give the reader a passing glance, but come up empty-handed: "There is no debate about truth in literary criticism, so the argument might run, because every mature reader is in possession of such reasons as would lead to broad agreement with other readers on the acceptance or rejection of the explicit and implicit thematic statements of a literary work."[8]

Notice that the possibility Lamarque and Olsen canvass is not there being no true–false evaluation among critics because it takes place among readers. Rather, it is that there is no true–false evaluation among critics because readers have already agreed on truth–value themselves. Thus in neither case does literary appreciation provide space for true–false evaluation. The latter alternative is no better than the former, as Lamarque and Olsen quickly conclude; and with that conclusion I concur.

I wish to propose an alternative designed to provide a place in literary appreciation for considerations of truth and falsity of the general thematic statements. My model is drawn from music, and it is the triadic relation of work to performer to listener.

Let us say that the job of the musical performer is to make musical works available for the listener's appreciation, which seems uncontroversial. Furthermore, let us say that, analogously, it is *one* of the jobs of the literary critic to make works of fiction *more* available for the reader's appreciation.

There is, of course, a big difference between the two cases. For very few of us can make a work of music available to ourselves for appreciation. Some of us can appreciate a piano sonata by playing it to ourselves. And a very small number of us can appreciate music merely by reading scores. But by far the vast majority of us require the performer to, so to speak, be the middle man between us and the work.

But all of us who are literate can make fictional works available to ourselves, by reading them. Nevertheless, the critic can make things that we do not notice available to us by revealing them through interpretation. And among those things are the explicit and implied general thematic statements. So we may say that as the pianist makes available to us a Beethoven sonata for our appreciation, so the literary critic makes available to us for our appreciation those great thematic statements that she perceives and we do not.

Now if one thinks, as I do, that part of the reader's literary appreciation consists in confirming and disconfirming for himself the general thematic statements he perceives in the fictional works he reads, sometimes unaided, sometimes through the writings of literary critics, one will see why it is quite compatible with the Propositional Theory that such confirmation and disconfirmation should be absent from the writings of literary critics. For confirmation and disconfirmation are part of *appreciation*, and appreciation is the job, if I may so put it, of the reader, not the critic *qua* critic. The critic's job, *qua* critic, is, among other things, to make available to the reader whatever hypotheses the fictional work may, directly or indirectly, propose. It is the reader's job to appreciate them, in part, by confirming or disconfirming them for himself. The job of the critic, like the job of the performer, is to make the work available for appreciation. And since confirmation and disconfirmation are part of appreciation, it is no business of hers to mess about with it – and she does not.

None of this, I should add, implies that readers must be – and, as Lamarque and Olsen quite rightly observe, they are not – in agreement with one another about the truth or falsity of the general thematic statements. Different readers may come to different conclusions about them. And most of these statements, at least in literary works of depth and value, will be such that the same reader may never decide one way or the other during a lifetime of thought about them. The reason for that and further elucidation of the reader's role in the verification or disconfirmation process will occupy me for the next few pages.

§4 The community of readers, in their consideration of the truth-values of the general thematic statements, constitute the "laboratory of fictional truth" to which the title of this chapter refers. What goes on in this laboratory?

To help answer this question I would like to introduce a distinction made by William James in one of his most well known and widely read essays, "The Will to Believe." James distinguished there between what he called "live" and "dead" hypotheses. "A live hypothesis," he said, "is one which appeals as a real possibility to him to whom it is proposed."[9] Contrariwise, a dead hypothesis is one that makes no such appeal, but is an impossibility to the person who considers it. Thus, as James concluded, "deadness and liveness in an hypothesis are not intrinsic properties but relations to the individual thinker."[10] What is a dead hypothesis to one person then, may be a live one to – indeed, taken for true by – another.

Fictional works present us, in the general thematic statements, explicit or implicit, hypotheses dead to some, live to others, and frequently concerning the profoundest religious, metaphysical, moral, and social questions. Works of fiction may or may not also provide reasons for believing such propositions. But what I am most interested in here are the reader's own efforts in the laboratory of fictional truth to confirm or disconfirm such hypotheses himself.

A reader may have one of three attitudes toward a general thematic statement. If it is a dead hypothesis for him, his attitude will be disbelief, and if it is a live one, his attitude *could* be belief or it could be merely inclination to believe combined with inclination not to believe, the reader being still agnostic with regard to it. It is the third kind of case that will initiate, one would think, the most active attempt on the reader's part to confirm or disconfirm. For where the question is already decided for him, he will obviously have less motivation to put his belief to the test. It is therefore those cases where the hypothesis is live and the reader agnostic with regard to it that I will talk about in what follows. But I do not think that the other cases are unimportant. To begin with, there seems to be a deep and abiding human need to hear again what is already believed, and literature seems to serve this need in a way peculiar to itself, which merits further investigation. That there is something of ritual in this I think is obvious. But that is a topic for another time.

So I am suggesting that one of the things fiction sometimes does is to propose to the reader live hypotheses, in the form of general thematic statements, which the reader, as part of the literary experience, attempts to confirm or disconfirm, either in thought or in action. The action part of the process, I should add, is a can of worms, and I am not going to open it here. I shall confine myself to talking about the confirmation–disconfirmation process in mentalistic terms. Or, less pompously put, I shall discuss the obvious and, it seems to me, uncontentious claim that intelligent readers of the canon often have proposed to them live hypotheses of a religious, metaphysical, or moral content that they continue to think about and try, thereby, to evaluate during and after the reading process. Certainly Lamarque and Olsen believe this takes place. What they do not believe, and what I do believe, is that this process of critical thinking about the truth or falsity of the general thematic statements is, broadly speaking, part of *literary appreciation*.

In the next section I shall argue for the *literary* claims of the confirmation–disconfirmation process. And I think I can segue smoothly into that discussion by suggesting here that academics in general, philosophers in particular, tend to vastly underestimate the importance of the higher forms of fictional literature for the general nonacademic, nonspecialist readership of these works, as a source of what can, in a generous sense, be thought of as "philosophy." Whether or not it is an indictment of philosophy, few people outside of the Academy read Plato or Hume or Quine. What they know of the great questions of philosophy they know from novels and plays and, in our century, the movies.

Nor is this true of the modern world alone. It is even more true of antiquity, where, indeed, the epistemic claims of literature would scarcely have needed to be argued for and against which Plato launched so stout a criticism, Aristotle so stout a defense. If one is seriously interested in literature as an institution, and Lamarque and Olsen certainly are, one ignores at one's peril how deeply implicated fictional literature is and has been in the process by which an intelligent and educated public obtains what knowledge it does of the "big questions," and what motivation it is given to thinking these questions through to whatever conclusions the individual reader may draw. A world without the Greek playwrights, without Shakespeare and Cervantes, Dostoyevski and Tolstoy, Austen and Goethe would be a world in which a vast number of people remained ignorant of philosophical speculation and bereft of the means to acquire it. It is, to me, a hard saying that the philosophical and moral education fictional literature imparts to so many, and the verification processes it sets in motion, both of which they get in fictional works and nowhere else, can't be part of what they certainly would call their literary appreciation.

Now these considerations in themselves prove nothing. The general readership for literature may simply be misdescribing its epistemic experience of literary works by calling it a part of "literary appreciation," and if so, it is the task of philosophy to correct it. Nevertheless, the institution of literature, as it has existed since Parmenides and the Homeric epics, is at least prima facie evidence in favor of the idea that part of literary appreciation is, and has been since time out of mind, thinking about general thematic statements to the end of confirming or disconfirming them.

I doubt that the individual reader always or even often reaches firm conclusions with regard to the general thematic statements – because of the nature of the general thematic statements themselves, at least as they occur in serious works of fiction. For the hypotheses themselves, when they are live, usually state the most perennially contested themes, of which Kant's Antinomies might serve as examples. Thus a reader may never decide, in the process of deliberation that a profound work of fiction stimulates in him, between freedom and determinism, Voltaire or a benevolent theodicy, deism or atheism, the role of men and women in a well-ordered society, and so on. Or he may find himself on one side of the question after an encounter with *Candide,* another after an encounter with Milton. In other words, the laboratory of fictional truth, unlike the laboratory of natural science, does not necessarily aim at, or achieve, consensus. But this should not disqualify it as essentially a truth-seeking institution, for it shares this character with philosophy. And unless one has some philosophical position on philosophical truth itself, one uses philosophy as a model of truth seeking that fiction must stand favorable comparison with if it has pretensions to the truth game itself.

I have, then, been arguing that the institution of fiction, since antiquity, has contained a strong epistemic part in the form of the reader's propensity for thinking about, and attempting to confirm or disconfirm thereby, the live hypotheses that may be proposed to him in the general thematic statements, either explicit or implied. Furthermore, I have been arguing that this provides at least prima facie evidence for the truth of the Propositional Theory, in a modest version. But prima facie evidence it remains – certainly far from conclusive. I shall now say a little more on its behalf, although I hasten to add that even when I have finished, I will be far from convincing you, or indeed myself, that even my modest Propositional Theory is beyond doubt.

§5   I want now to talk about my own idea of why we should consider truth-value determination of the kind outlined just now to be part of literary appreciation, over and above the fact that it seems to play such a conspicuous role in the institution of literary fiction, on the reader's side, and has done since antiquity. I take my departure from some remarks by Lamarque and Olsen to the contrary. But I want to emphasize that the speculations directly following are not directed toward any specific argument of theirs, but rather to what I imagine to be a difficulty that many will have with my proposal and that might be at least vaguely suggested by what they say.

As I noted previously, Lamarque and Olsen do not deny that

readers are frequently stimulated by the general thematic statements of fiction to ruminate over their truth or falsity. What they
deny is that this is any part of literary appreciation:

> This question is not a question whether the general proposi-
> tions used to organize events, characters, and situations of a
> work into a significant and meaningful pattern have any ap-
> plication in contexts outside literature. Clearly they do and
> may have been so used. The question is whether assessment
> of their truth enters into the reader's appreciation of a literary
> work as a literary work.[11]

Their answer to the question, of course, is no. As they say of the
critic, with regard to what they take to be one of the central
themes of George Eliot's *Middlemarch* but which applies, pari
passu, to the ordinary reader:

> A debate about the substance of this thematic statement will
> be a debate about the possibility of free will and this is central
> in philosophy. The critic is free to join this debate, of course,
> but when he does he has moved on from literary appreciation
> of *Middlemarch*.[12]

There is something about the way this point is put that will
be very compelling, on first reflection, to many readers, because,
I think, of an implicit assumption about what appreciation of a
work of art, in general, is like. The assumption has as its basis
what I would describe, to return to musical analogies once
again, as a *musical* model of how these things go. And that
model, I suggest, is the wrong one for the literary work of art.
Here, yet again, is a *difference*.

Suppose I were to give the following scenario of a musical
"experience." I listen to the first movement of Beethoven's Fifth
Symphony with great concentration and with a pleasure intense
enough to border on rapture. So vividly has the thematic unity
of the first movement, in particular, impressed itself on my consciousness that I become convinced that Beethoven meant to
convey a hypothesis concerning it. And the hypothesis that
keeps presenting itself to me is that all humanity is unified as
the notes of Beethoven's music, in familial bonds of harmony

stronger than the dissensions and differences that separate us. To coin a phrase, Beethoven is telling us that all men are brothers, and in mulling over this proposition, in the days and weeks following my audition of the work, I come to the conclusion that this hypothesis is true. What a fine thing, I keep thinking, for a composer to be able to accomplish with his music.[13] And how much richer my appreciation of the music is because this is a part of that appreciation.

There are two reasons why a skeptical chap like myself would be highly suspicious of such a notion of musical "appreciation." The first is well known, and I will not dwell on it here. It remains, at best, highly controversial whether absolute music can possibly express such semantical content as exemplified by theses like the one about "unity" that I have just sketched. Or, to put the point more broadly, it seems impossible to me that absolute music can express what I have been calling, following Lamarque and Olsen, general thematic statements of the kind we find in works of literary fiction. There are plenty of reasons for this skepticism, but as I and others have presented them many times before, I will refrain from any further discussion of that kind here.

Rather, I am particularly interested in another objection to the picture sketched above, of the musical experience, based on what I shall call the "afterlife" of purported artistic appreciations. Musical works, unlike at least read works of fiction, novels or epic poems (say), have a self-contained appreciation time, so to speak. By that I mean that it would be common for a reader of a novel to put it down from time to time, sometimes for an extended period, and then pick it up again, with no experienced break in fictional time. I have always found this phenomenon quite remarkable. Somehow, one can leave the heroine poised on the precipice for an hour or two, or even a weekend or a week, and return with no feeling of narrative or aesthetic discontinuity. Nor need this be a less than optimal way to experience fictional works. Indeed, it is normal, as one can assure oneself by recalling that the great "three-volume novels" of the nineteenth century, those of Dickens and the rest, were published in installments in the literary periodicals of the day.

But how absurd to think one could properly appreciate a symphony, let alone a movement or section thereof, in bits and pieces. Could I listen to Beethoven's Fifth Symphony to the end of the first movement, go away for the weekend, and come back for the other three and be thought to have experienced the work properly? Yet such gaps occur in my experience of novels all the time. (Who can read *War and Peace* in a single sitting?) What this strongly suggests is that the relation of fictional time to real time is very different from the relation of musical time to real time, in that fictional time tolerates large gaps in real time and musical time does not.

Now the "gappy" experience of read fictional literature, as opposed to the continuous experience of music, suggests that real time and fictional time have a more "sloppy" relationship, if I may so put it, than the rather strict relationship between real and musical time; and this leads to the discovery of another temporal disanalogy, also describable as sloppy versus strict.

Those who savor good wine will be familiar with the notion that the appreciation includes an aftertaste; and the quality of the aftertaste matters to the quality of the wine experience. What I want to suggest is that the appreciation of fiction by the normal reader has a long, somewhat indeterminate aftertaste, which I will designate its "afterlife," whereas the appreciation of music, at least for most musically untrained listeners, ends with the end of the music: it has little if any afterlife at all, except perhaps for the accomplished musician.

The fictional experience, then, both is gappy with regard to real time and has a somewhat indeterminate outer boundary. The appreciation has a considerable afterlife. The musical experience, on the contrary, neither is gappy with regard to real time, nor has an afterlife to speak of, for most listeners. It is continuous and ends with the coda.

Now suppose there is ingrained in one, without one's really having thought about it, a preconceived notion of artistic appreciation that has *musical* appreciation as its model, in respect of the gappiness and afterlife phenomena, as, I suspect, there is in many people. If there is, then one will feel an intuitive pull toward the view that verifying the general thematic statements cannot be part of literary appreciation. For, after all, such a verification process – which is to say, mulling things over and reaching at least tentative, temporary conclusions – is just not something expected to go on, or at least not very extensively, *during* the reading experience but, mainly, in the gaps and the afterlife. And if one thinks in terms of the musical model, then one will think that the appreciation of fiction has no gaps or afterlife or, put another way, that the gaps and the afterlife of reading are not part of literary appreciation. It doesn't much matter which way you put it; I prefer the former.

I believe, however, that the musical model of artistic appreciation casts a false light on the literary experience. It assumes artistic appreciation to be, *tout court,* a neat, self-contained kind of thing, whereas the literary experience, as I have suggested, is a gappy, sloppy sort of thing.

That the literary experience is gappy, I think, will be agreed on without argument. We all know that we can put down a work of fiction and take it up again without loss of narrative continuity. But that it is sloppy as well as gappy, that it has an afterlife, and that part of that afterlife, as well as part of the gaps, consists in verifying or disconfirming the general thematic statements will certainly require more than an appeal to intuition or common experience. There is no quarrel, I presume, about whether we go on thinking about what we have read in a literary work, intentionally and, perhaps, for an extended period of time, when we have finished (say) a novel by Tolstoy or Jane Austen or other of our serious novelists, even those of lesser rank. The question before us is whether the gaps or afterlife or any part thereof can be considered literary appreciation. Am I still enjoying *Pride and Prejudice* as a literary work when I am savoring the aftertaste and mulling over serious issues it has raised?

To try to answer this question let us forget, for a moment, the crucial case of thesis verification and just consider the very general phenomenon, with contents unspecified, of thinking about, remembering, reimagining what we have experienced in the gaps or after completing a good novel. Should this be considered part of our literary appreciation of that novel or not?

I doubt that I can give, in so limited a space, a completely satisfactory answer to this question. But consider the following thought experiment. Imagine going to a concert, listening with pleasure to a Beethoven symphony, and then going about your business, the experience all but forgotten in the press of affairs. Next imagine finishing *Pride and Prejudice*, having read it with pleasure, and going about your business, the experience all but forgotten in the press of affairs, as in the case of the Beethoven symphony.

Let me suggest to you that the experience of the Beethoven, although not what I would call an optimal one, is nevertheless a full, complete one. It is the way serious music is appreciated by people who love music but do not have good musical memories, do not think about or study it. Let me suggest, further, that the experience of *Pride and Prejudice*, without the afterlife, is not merely less than an optimal literary experience but less than a literary experience altogether: less than a *full* literary experience of *that work*. What I have described is a full literary experience of a time waster: a whodunit or one of the lesser genres of sci-fi – literature intended to be read and forgotten, intended not to provoke thought, not to have an afterlife. By my lights, though, to experience *Pride and Prejudice* and its ilk without the afterlife is to have less than a full experience, not merely less than an optimal one.

This is not to say that every thought sequence, no matter how wide, long, diffuse, or irrelevant, a novel sets in train is part of the literary experience of the work. And to draw boundaries of relevance is obviously a nontrivial matter, not to be taken up here. All that must be agreed upon for present purposes is that *some* significant afterlife, suitably circumscribed, is a bona fide part of literary experience. That, I think, I have shown is neither initially implausible nor without some fairly strong intuitive appeal, if one simply imagines what the literary experience of serious works would be without it.

But I asked you to put aside, for the moment, the question of hypothesis verification and consider only the general idea of the literary afterlife. That moment is over, and we must confront the question of whether, given that at least some part of the literary afterlife can be construed as literary appreciation, hypothesis verification can be construed as part of that part, that is to say, as part of literary appreciation. For someone might well accept the more general claim but balk at the specific one. What can I say to such a person?

Perhaps another thought experiment will help. Presumably no one wishes to deny that part of literary appreciation consists in understanding the general thematic statements and their relations to the literary work that expresses them. And if I am right in my argument so far, at least some of that appreciation, perhaps a very large part of it, takes place during the afterlife of the work, as well as during the gaps. So now I ask you to imagine appreciating these general thematic statements, but without any consideration of truth-value at all. Can you do that? And if you can, would your experience still constitute full literary appreciation of the general thematic statements? I suspect not.

The logical positivists claimed, notoriously, that an unverifiable hypothesis was a meaningless one, and that meaning was spelled out *in* real or envisioned verification procedures. This is a discredited claim, and I am certainly not asserting it. But there is, I do want to claim, a grain of truth in the positivists' verification principle, and it is this. In many cases we really do not fully grasp a hypothesis, fully grasp its import, anyway, what it means to us without at least mulling over the question of whether or not it is true, which is to say, without trying to "argue" mentally for its truth or falsity, to mentally image possible means of verification. Indeed, apart from reaching a conclusion about a hypothesis, how could we determine whether, in James's terms, it was a "live" or "dead" hypothesis for us without at least some consideration of its truth or falsity? If it is a dead one, then it is dead because we are convinced of its falsity, and we ordinarily have at least some grounds for that belief; and if it is a living one, we must have at least some reason to believe that it might be true, or at least no conclusive reason to believe it is false.

Thus I suggest that fully understanding the general thematic statements and fully appreciating them as part of the literary experience require an evaluation of their possible truth or falsity.

Indeed, I think that Lamarque and Olsen all but admit something like this in the last chapter of their book, where they raise the question of the value of literary fiction. I would like to conclude with a consideration of what they have to say in this regard.

§6 Lamarque and Olsen, in their discussion of literary value, locate it largely in the presence of what they call the "perennial themes":

> One central, characteristic purpose defined by the literary practice and served by the literary work is to develop, in depth, through subject and form, a theme which is in some sense central to human concern and which can therefore be recognized as of more or less universal interest. Appreciation and consequent evaluation of the individual literary work is a matter of eliciting and supporting the identification and development of a "perennial theme."[14]

Perennial themes present, not surprisingly, just those deep questions of philosophy – religious, moral, metaphysical – that are perennially contested. And the example Lamarque and Olsen choose to illustrate their position will equally suit our purposes. It is the theme of free will and determinism, its literary setting Arnold Bennett's novel *Anna of the Five Towns*. Of the theme and its setting, Lamarque and Olsen say:

> *Anna of the Five Towns* organizes a described universe in such a way that the reader who applies concepts like "freedom of the will," "determinism," "victim of external forces beyond human control" in the appreciating of that work will come to see how, in that universe, human beings are controlled by external forces. There is no similar order in the real world that will make these concepts meaningful in this way. Daily life does not offer the sort of visible connections that artistic narrative defines. These connections emerge in the artistic presentation of the subject.[15]

Contrast this big, "perennial" theme of *Anna of the Five Towns* with what we find in trivial works of art, television soap operas, and the like, and we will have a fairly clear picture of what Lamarque and Olsen are after, which is, as I see it, thinking about themes without thinking about truth. As Lamarque and Olsen put the contrast:

> There may be a coherent vision in such [inconsequential] works, with clear choices, but very little for the mind to grapple with. . . . It makes no demands on either the intellectual, emotional, or moral nature that are not also made in daily life with its simple choices and short term goals. For literature like philosophy challenges the reader to make his own construction, to invest time and effort in reaching a deeper insight into the great themes, though this insight is "literary."[16]

The question we must now pose is whether the position Lamarque and Olsen have taken here can be made intelligible without the intrusion of truth and falsity into the equation, whether, that is to say, the notion of "perennial themes" as a (or the) source of literary value can possibly be sustained while at the same time considerations of truth and falsity, as part of the reader's literary appreciation, are denied. I think the answer must be no.

Consider, now, the perennial theme of freedom and determinism that Lamarque and Olsen perceive in Bennett's *Anna of the Five Towns*. In the novel, in the world of that work, determinism is true: "in that universe," as Lamarque and Olsen put it, "human beings are controlled by external forces." What makes the theme of *Anna of the Five Towns* a perennial one is that determinism is a live option for many of us but also that freedom of the will is as well. If only one or the other were a live hypothesis, then of course the theme of freedom and determinism would not be a perennial one; it would have been decided one way or the other. It is *perennial* because we can't decide, and so it constantly or with regularity engages and perplexes us.

But how could we appreciate the theme of *Anna of the Five Towns* as a perennial one without, at the same time, taking part in some kind of at least mental verification process? To experience a theme as perennial, it seems clear enough, we must know whether its opposing hypotheses are live hypotheses; and to know if the hypotheses are live we must have some reason or reasons for believing each; and to arrive at some reason or reasons for believing each we must go through a process of verification.

Two things that Lamarque and Olsen say, therefore, must strike one as extremely puzzling, given their, so to speak, antiepistemic stance with regard to the perennial themes. They say of the determinism in *Anna of the Five Towns* that "[t]here is no similar order in the real world that will make these concepts meaningful in this way." Well, of course, the narrative exaggerates the determinism. But if the real world did not offer us "similar order," that is, order at least suggesting that determinism might be true, then determinism would scarcely be a live hypothesis for us, and hence not a perennial theme. We all know the examples that suggest determinism, as we do the ones that suggest the opposite thesis. So I will say no more about it.

Another puzzling thing that Lamarque and Olsen say, this time about the perennial theme versus its opposite, is that the latter "provides little for the mind to grapple with and develop." But what is it that the mind is meant to "grapple with and develop"? Well, with what the hypotheses of the theme mean and, I would think, what their significance is for us if they were true (or false). Nor can this grappling with and development have any real interest for us unless the hypotheses we mean to grapple with and develop are live ones. It is hard to imagine being engaged in deep thought about the hypothesis that the universe rests on a giant tortoise or that the enslaving, buying, and selling of human beings might really be a good thing after all. These are dead issues for us. The perennial themes are perennial because they are live, live because we think they might be true.

What makes the theme of determinism in *Anna of the Five Towns* a theme to grapple with and develop? Surely not that it is an "interesting" hypothesis (whatever that would mean in the absence of any consideration of possible truth). No one, I trust, grapples any longer with the geocentric worldview, even though it might be in some sense an "interesting" view. Presumably, those themes are perennially interesting to us that present live hypotheses. These are the ones worthy of grappling with and developing. But to grapple with and develop them without raising questions of truth and falsity – without any attempt at verification – seems impossible, and if possible, an empty, profitless exercise.

§7   In this chapter and the two before, I looked at three problems in the philosophy of literature: the problems of literary representation, the form–content relation, and literary truth. In each case I argued that traditional solutions had been proposed by analogizing literature to other arts. In the first case the paradigm was the visual arts, in the second and third absolute music. In each case I argued that the proffered analogy was, if not preposterous, then at least singularly unenlightening. For the analogies are infelicitous; and a stubborn devotion to them over a long period of time has obscured crucial ways in which literature (in the first instance) differs from visual representation and (in the second) from absolute music.

In my final two chapters, I shall turn to the art that, it appears to me, has suffered more from false analogies to the other arts than any of the other arts have suffered from analogy to it: that is, the art of absolute music. If there is any place in the philosophy of art where differences have been obscured, and deserve to be acknowledged, it is here. Music, of all the arts, is the most philosophically unexplored and most philosophically misunderstood where it has been explored at all. That this is due, in large measure, to the persistent practice of basing our understanding of absolute music on literary or painterly models is not an exaggeration. It will be the purpose of the final two chapters to try to undo some of this mischief. Alas, to undo it all is as impossible as bailing dry a leaking boat.

Chapter 6

The Quest for Musical Profundity

§1 The theme of this chapter is the misapplication of a literary model to absolute music, with predictably dire results. I begin on something of a tangent. But if the reader is patient, all, I promise, will be made plain.

I concluded my book *Music Alone* (1990) with a chapter called "The Profundity of Music." In that chapter I reached a somewhat skeptical conclusion about whether absolute music could be "profound," properly so called, although I did explore a way in which I thought it might be. Much to my surprise, this chapter provoked a good deal of discussion, partly because, at least as far as I know, the subject had not been broached before.

I suppose I should not have been surprised. For I was, after all, denying that music was capable of doing (or, rather, *being*) something important, or at least was casting some serious doubt in that direction. And long experience has taught me that whenever someone denies to music any power at all, or any important property, such denial tends to be seen as treachery or barbarism or some kind of musical insensitivity only to be expected from philosophical analysis or formalism, both of which I suppose my work exemplifies. Had I denied that music can predict the future or remove warts, I am certain there would have been at least two responses in the literature to the effect that I had missed some sense in which music can predict the future or remove warts, although of course, one must not be quite so rigid or pedantic about what it means to "predict" or "remove" or what exactly the "future" or a "wart" might be.

Needless to say, that's not the whole of it. The substantive issue, for our purposes, of musical profundity, and any skepticism that might be evinced toward it, is our old familiar theme of the unity of the arts. This can immediately be inferred from the opening statement of one of the first of those who have taken issue with me on the subject of musical profundity. Here is how David A. White begins his essay called "Toward a Theory of Profundity in Music":

> Is music meaningful? Current reflection tends to be domi-nated by the view that it is a mistake to look for meaning in music, since music is not the sort of ordered activity to have meaning in any of the usual senses of that (itself vexed) term. But it is worth noting that philosophers, in perhaps un-guarded moments, still talk about music as if it were mean-ingful. And one particularly enticing kind of discourse concerns those musical works described as "profound."[1]

There is an argument lurking somewhere in the vicinity here that goes (informally) something like this. In order to be pro-found, a work of music must be meaningful, because it must be profound *about* something. We have at least some evidence that some works of music are profound, because philosophers in their "unguarded" moments – and, I might add, plenty of mu-sical analysts in their guarded moments as well – talk about individual works of absolute music as being profound. So "cur-rent reflection," my own reflection included, must be mistaken in denying "meaning" to music – at least to "profound" music.

Skepticism about profundity in music, then, turns out to be the result of skepticism about the meaningfulness, in some ro-bust linguistic sense of that term, of absolute music. And if we don't have such musical meaning, then the project of construing music as a fine art through the analogy to literature must break down. And as an analogy to representation in the visual arts seems, these days, a fairly unpromising alternative, the project of bringing absolute music into the circle of the fine arts itself breaks down, if the analogy does.

Now, although it does seem to follow that if absolute music cannot have meaning, cannot have a subject matter about which it speaks, it cannot be profound, it certainly does not follow that if absolute music cannot be profound, it cannot be meaningful, cannot have a subject matter. It may be that music can have meaning, yet fail to be profound because it is unable to have profound meaning: unable to have a profound subject or be able to say anything profound about it. Furthermore, perhaps it really does not follow that because it cannot have meaning, it cannot be profound. Perhaps there is another way that something can be profound besides by having profound meaning – without, indeed, having any meaning at all.

As for the project of allying music with the literary arts, the musical project of "sameness," neither of the above possibilities is helpful, the latter quite obviously so. For since the latter alternative is profundity without meaning, proving the possibility of profundity fails to prove the possibility of meaning; and it is *meaning* that is the thing required for the sameness project in music to go through.

It is, perhaps, somewhat less obvious why the former alternative, musical meaning without musical profundity, or with the profundity completely unrelated to the meaning, is a fruitless conclusion for the sameness project. But not much reflection is required to show that it is so.

If music is to be a fine art in virtue of an analogy to literature, that analogy must be a good fit in the crucial respects. As we shall see shortly, literature is profound, in large part, in virtue of its having profound meaning – which is to say, profound subject matter about which it profoundly speaks. If music is profound in some other way, a way that has nothing to do with meaning, even if it has meaning, then, I submit, the analogy to literature would be so significantly defective as to be worthless for the purpose to which it is being put, namely, the legitimization of music as a fine art.

The question of musical profundity, then, lies at the heart of the question of musical meaning. And the question of musical meaning lies at the heart of the question of whether music can be brought into the circle of the fine arts by means of an analogy to literature.

In this chapter I shall try to answer some criticism of my views of musical profundity as laid out in *Music Alone*, and criticize some suggestions that have been made about how musical profundity might be possible. The general theme, as before, is that the quest for sameness in the arts has led us down the garden path, the garden path being the literary model of absolute music. There are many, perhaps more direct ways I could have made my point. I have chosen to do so by way of the musical profundity question mainly because it is a fresh question and therefore preferable to one of the more familiar alternatives. My first task, before I can get to the debate over my view, is to acquaint the reader with it.

§2   I shall begin the way I should have begun when I first broached the subject of musical profundity in *Music Alone,* with a very simple distinction between what I call the adjectival and the adverbial senses of the word "profound." Had I made this distinction then, I think it would have saved us a good deal of confusion now.

The *Critique of Pure Reason* is both a profound work and a profoundly influential one. What it means for a work to be profound we shall get to shortly. But what it means for the *Critique of Pure Reason* (or any other work) to be profoundly influential is easily said: it means, roughly, that it is not merely influential, or even very influential, but perhaps very very influential. Whether it may mean anything more than that we shall discuss later. For the time being, the rough gloss will do: to be *profoundly* anything is to be very very that thing.

Furthermore, we cannot infer from a work's being profoundly *anything* that it is a *profound* work. In other words, to be profoundly something is not, ipso facto, to be profound. The *Critique of Pure Reason* is a profound work and a profoundly influential one; but Norman Vincent Peale's *The Power of Positive Thinking,* although profoundly influential, at least in its own day, is, far from being a profound work, a profoundly silly one.

So much, then, for the distinction between the adjectival and the adverbial senses of "profound," except to add, emphatically, that it was solely the *adjectival* sense of "profound" that I was concerned with in *Music Alone.* And to point out that a work can be profoundly sad or profoundly unified or profoundly anything else, in answer to my guarded skepticism with regard to the possible profundity of absolute music, is just an *ignoratio;* it completely misses my point. And although I don't claim that any one of my commentators has blatantly made this blunder, I think that two of them are at least subtly committed to the (fallacious) move from profoundly to profound, or to the substitution of the first for the second, neither of which is an answer to either skepticism about musical profundity or the very tentative suggestion I made about how perhaps music might be "profound" in a full-blooded sense, appearances to the contrary notwithstanding.

With these preliminaries taken care of, I can now briefly present the view of musical profundity I put forth in *Music Alone* and then get to a more leisurely examination of the criticism and alternatives it has elicited.

§3 I began with Kant's first *Critique* as an example of a profound work, so I will stick with it. What makes this work "profound"? First, it raises, or is about, profound issues. But that, of course, is not enough. Many recent shallow books raise the profound question of the mind–body problem. Second, the first *Critique* gives searching, original, thorough, thought-provoking responses to the profound issues it addresses: it says profound things about its subject matter. We can sum this up by saying that the treatment the *Critique of Pure Reason* gives of its profound subject matter is *adequate* to that subject matter.

Moving on, now, to works of art, it seems clear that at least literary works can be, and sometimes are, profound. (I will say nothing about painting or other visual arts here.) For some literary works do indeed treat a profound subject matter in a manner adequate to its profundity. So literary works can obviously fulfill both conditions for being profound.

But what it means to *adequately* treat a profound subject matter must undergo some alteration when we move from works of philosophy, science, history, or anything else of that kind to literary works, which is to say, works of art. We must add, not surprisingly, an "aesthetic" dimension. For as I claimed in *Music Alone,* and see no reason to demur from now, a profound work of literature (or any other kind of artwork) must not only possess a profound subject matter and say things profound about it (not necessarily or frequently in a direct manner), but must also be aesthetically or artistically exemplary: of a very high quality. A work of literature may be profound in content, but if it is not a great or exemplary work of art, it is not profound *qua* literature, *qua* art. In other words, for a novel (say) to treat a profound subject matter *adequately*, it must not only say profound things about it, but say them supremely well in an aesthetic or artistic way.

I feel certain this is true – that aesthetic or artistic excellence is part of art profundity. I feel certain that one would never call a mediocre work of art "profound," even if it said profound things about a profound subject matter, except with qualifications like "Looked at as a *philosophical* work (or whatever) it is profound; but it is not a profound novel." The problem is that I do not know exactly why this is so. One might venture a Danto-like hypothesis to the effect that, since, in a work of art, *how* the work of art is "about" is part of *what* it is "about," or something of the kind, the aesthetic or artistic greatness of the work is part of what makes its subject profound. But however that may be, it does appear to me just to be so, that no one calls a work of literature profound literature, no matter how profound its subject matter or how profound the things said about it, unless the work is of supremely high artistic or aesthetic value. So I will leave it at that.

To summarize, then, for a work of art to be profound – and literature is the obvious example here – it must (1) have a profound subject matter and (2) treat this profound subject matter in a way adequate to its profundity – which is to say, (a) say profound things about this subject matter and (b) do it at a very high level of artistic or aesthetic excellence. This is my analysis of what I have called here the "adjectival" sense of "profound." It is the only sense I was or am now interested in, and the only sense according to which I was and am now denying that absolute music can, in any *obvious* way, be "profound."

This denial that music can in any obvious way be "profound" in the adjectival sense I shall refer to as the negative aspect of my position on musical profundity. It arises from my reluctance to allow that absolute music can have any subject matter or could say anything about it if it had. For if it cannot have or say anything about any subject matter whatever, then, a fortiori, it cannot have a profound subject matter or could not say anything profound about it if it could have any. Absolute music fails to fulfill both criteria of profundity in the adjectival sense and hence cannot, in that sense, be profound.

But in *Music Alone* I also made a positive suggestion about how music might in something like its adjectival sense be "profound." My idea was that although absolute music cannot be about, or be profound about, extramusical matters, it might nevertheless sometimes be about and be profound about *itself:* that, in other words, music might at times be profound about music. This positive aspect of my position I hope to develop further in another place. My purpose here, however, is to go on to discuss two responses to the negative aspect of my view, those of Aaron Ridley and Jerrold Levinson.

§4 I think that Ridley knows quite well the adverbial sense of "profound" and its inadequacy as a solution to the problem of profundity in music. Nevertheless, I do not think he succeeds in getting beyond it to what I would consider a satisfactory account of how absolute music might be profound in the adjectival sense. But to show this will require some careful work.

Ridley begins with my contention that in order to be profound a musical work must be about something profound and treat that something in a way adequate to its profundity, "[w]hich, of course," he quite rightly observes, makes music, "which isn't much good at being about things, an outsider from the start."[2] Furthermore, he claims that both the profundity condition and the adequacy condition are invalid: that, in other words, something can be profound without being about anything profound and profound without being adequate to its profound subject matter.

Ridley's counterexample to both of my conditions is *belief.* Thus "...Natasha believes profoundly in a religion," Ridley suggests by way of example and adds, as particularly worthy of emphasis, "It is clearly her belief which is being described as profound."[3] Suppose her belief is in a profound religion. We need know nothing about the "adequacy" of her belief to maintain that her belief is "profound." Perhaps her belief is not "adequate" to the profound religious subject matter. It is a profound belief for all of that. So much, then, for my adequacy condition.

But, of course, Natasha's religion might be utterly silly, shallow, a singularly unprofound one:

> Would this mean that her belief could not, after all, be profound? Of course it wouldn't. . . . [B]ecause profundity is a quality of the *belief* – and not, as Kivy would have it, a quality of the subject matter which the belief somehow inherits by being adequate *to* it – the apparent triviality of what the belief is about is irrelevant to the assumption of profundity to the belief itself.[4]

A belief, then, can be profound, even though its content is not. So much, then, for my profundity of subject matter condition.

I think it ought to be pretty clear by now, from previous considerations, what has gone wrong here with the first stage of Ridley's argument. He waffles between adjectival and adverbial descriptions of belief in a way that obscures the implausibility of what he is saying. Everything Ridley says about *profoundly held* belief, about believing *profoundly*, is true; but everything he says about *profound* beliefs, if there were such, which there aren't, is false.

Let me first get rid of the notion of profound belief, in the adjectival sense of "profound." In the sense in which the *Critique of Pure Reason* is a profound work and *The Power of Positive Thinking* a shallow one, there is no such thing as a profound belief. One belief cannot be profound. A *set* of beliefs might be profound. The *Critique of Pure Reason* is a set of beliefs that Kant wrote down. And although Socrates never wrote down his beliefs, I think we can safely say that a substantial set of them must have been a profound set of beliefs.

A single belief cannot be profound, then, nor can it be adequate or inadequate to its subject matter. If Thomas Aquinas and Mrs. Grundy both believe in God, there is absolutely no sense I can make of the claim, about that one belief, that Thomas's is more adequate to the profound subject matter than Mrs. Grundy's. What *is* more adequate is the set of his beliefs in and about God.

Belief, then, turns out to be a palpable red herring. In the adjectival sense, no belief can be profound, because, although a belief may be about something profound, it makes no sense to talk about its adequacy vis-à-vis its profound subject. And as I understand the English language, "profound belief" does not mean "belief about something profound." The only sense in which *a* belief can be profound is the adverbial sense: a belief can be very very strongly held, in other words, profoundly held. But as I am not concerned with the adverbial sense of "profound," that is irrelevant to my argument.

However, if we apply what Ridley says about belief to things that can be or fail to be profound in the adjectival sense, we see that it is flat out wrong about those things. A philosophical work, for example, that is about a trivial subject matter cannot be a profound philosophical work; and a philosophical work about a profound subject matter that is not adequate to that subject matter cannot be a profound philosophical work. If I should write a book about the mind–body problem that consists of all sorts of bad arguments and silly theories, then my work is, clearly, not profound, even though it is about a profound question, because I have not treated that question adequately: my book is not adequate to its profound subject matter. And if I should write a philosophical work on the subject of bottle caps, my work cannot be profound, no matter how adequately I treat my subject, because my subject is trivial, not profound.[5]

Thus it is only by equivocating between the adverbial and the adjectival senses of "profound" that Ridley can make belief seem to be a counterexample to my claim that a philosophical work, or work of art, must be, in order to be profound, both about something profound and adequate to its profundity. It appears to me, then, that in his quest for musical profundity Ridley is off to a very shaky start.

§5 Matters do not improve in the second stage of Ridley's argument, in which he aims to show that not only needn't a thing be about something profound to be profound, the way a belief is said to be by Ridley, but that "a thing needn't be about *anything at all* in order to be profound."[6] This of course, is not very hard to show since, again, it is the adverbial sense of "profound" that is clearly intended. The example now is Natasha's gullibility. She is very very gullible, profoundly gullible in fact. But gullibility is a disposition, and dispositions aren't *about*. So Ridley has his conclusion, with which I heartily concur. That is not at issue.

What is at issue – and it becomes crucial in the latter stages of Ridley's argument – is the analysis he proposes of what it means to be profoundly gullible:

> Now imagine that Natasha is capable of being persuaded of just about anything; that most of her actions are determined by beliefs far less critically acquired than they might have been; that she is continually surprised to learn that what she has just taken for gospel is pure baloney; that her whole life is structured, at every level, by her tendency willingly to believe whatever she is told. Clearly, and (I take it) uncontroversially, Natasha is profoundly gullible. . . . This opens the door to any mental item, trait of character, habitual attitude, or propensity, which is capable of structuring significant aspects, or simply significant quantities, of a person's life. Thus one might be profoundly cheerful, profoundly mean, profoundly suspicious, profoundly courageous, and so on. And in each case it can be true of one's cheerfulness, meanness, courage, etc., that it is *profound*. This accords well with common usage, and is also quite unmysterious.[7]

Now a great deal that Ridley says here is quite uncontentious. Of course one can be profoundly gullible, profoundly mean, profoundly suspicious, and the rest; and if one is profoundly any of those things, another way of saying it is that one's gullibility is profound, one's meanness is profound, one's courage is profound. All of this does accord well with common usage.

However, there is one very crucial respect in which what Ridley seems to be saying is neither uncontentious nor in accord with common usage – indeed is, I think, completely wrong. As far as I can make out, there is no requirement whatever, nor does it accord with common usage, that for someone to be profoundly gullible, "her whole life," as Ridley puts it, must be "structured, at every level," by her gullibility; nor with regard to any of the other dispositions he mentions does this appear to be the case.

It may indeed be the case that if someone structures her life around gullibility, she will be rightly judged profoundly gullible. But it is just affirming the consequent to go from being profoundly gullible to having a life structured by gullibility. It accords well with common usage to call someone profoundly gullible when she is very very gullible. And I submit that one need know nothing about the "structure" of a person's inner or outer life to pronounce the judgment "profoundly gullible" with full justification. A person may perfectly well lead a completely haphazard, unstructured life of gullibility and be justly adjudged profoundly gullible, nor would the revelation of the lack of structure around the gullibility require withdrawal of the judgment. It does not offend common usage to assert profound gullibility while denying a "structure" of gullibility. One can, of course, just stipulate that one will call someone profoundly x only when one is very very x *and* the structure is in place. But stipulation doesn't settle an argument.

I belabor this point beyond, perhaps, apparent cause, because Ridley makes a lot of mileage out of it later on. It is the way he tries to work his passage from the adverbial sense of "profound" to a workable theory of musical profundity. But it won't do. This step is an unwarranted one. Profoundly x just means very very x, and there's an end on't.

Furthermore, that this gratuitous addition of structure to the adverbial sense of "profound" is a mistake and unable to help us with the question of musical profundity can immediately be seen in the first use Ridley tries to make of it at the end of this second stage of his argument. Of my positive account of musical profundity, Ridley writes:

He suggests that certain contrapuntal music might be called profound because it is in some sense about (and adequately

about) the possibilities inherent in music, which are themselves profound. . . . But how much simpler to say that the
music is *profoundly contrapuntal* – that every aspect of the music is informed, controlled, and given shape by the counterpoint that lies at its heart! It seems to me that this is a vastly
more natural way of speaking.[8]

I have no quarrel with the phrase "profoundly contrapuntal,"
needless to say, nor with the notion, hardly controversial, that
some music is "profoundly contrapuntal." The problem is that
profoundly contrapuntal music was not, is not, my problem. My
problem is *contrapuntally profound* music, which is quite another
thing. My problem is, as I have said so many times before, the
adjectival sense of "profound": the sense not in which the *Critique of Pure Reason* is profoundly philosophical but the sense in
which it is philosophically profound. For a work can be profoundly philosophical, to appropriate Ridley's words, in being
"informed, controlled, and given shape by" philosophy without
being a profound philosophical work at all.

And as for music, *all* of the art music of the Renaissance was
profoundly contrapuntal: that was, after all, the golden age of
polyphony. But only *some* of the works of the masters were contrapuntally profound: profound musical works in a contrapuntal
way. The *Kleinmeisters* wrote yards and yards of profoundly contrapuntal music. Only the likes of a Josquin, however, could
achieve contrapuntal profundity.

Nor, by the way, do I think that profoundly contrapuntal music need be "informed, controlled, and given shape by the counterpoint," any more than a profoundly silly person's life need
be "informed, controlled, and given shape by" his silliness. All
that is required is heaps and heaps of counterpoint, however
haphazard it may be. And the reason I suspect that someone
might think it odd to call such stuff *profoundly* contrapuntal is
that he or she is mixing up the profoundly contrapuntal with
the contrapuntally profound, which, of course, cannot be haphazard, cannot lack the inner structural logic that *profound* counterpoint requires.

However, the last point is beside the point. Even if we give

Ridley his analysis of what it means to be profoundly contrapuntal, he cannot reach an interesting conclusion about the question of musical profundity. For that question, with regard to counterpoint, is how music can be contrapuntally profound, not how it can be profoundly contrapuntal. The latter is no more difficult to understand than how music can be profoundly boring.

§6 In the third stage of his argument Ridley finally faces the music in earnest and endeavors to apply to it what has gone before. His interest is confined to "music which is profound in virtue of its *expressive* properties."[9] It is here that his principal chicken comes home to roost.

The strategy, given what has gone before, will be to say that a musical composition is profound when it is profoundly some expressive property: cheerfulness, to take Ridley's example. But, as we have seen, Ridley will not say that a musical work is profoundly cheerful, or whatever, just because it is very very cheerful. For "there is a difference between being profoundly cheerful and being merely regularly or relentlessly cheerful."[10] And given Ridley's previously expressed views on being profoundly gullible, namely, that one's life must be structured around the disposition if it is to be profoundly instantiated, the nature of the "difference" will not be surprising. So, of the "defiance" that Ridley supposes Beethoven's Fifth Symphony to be *profoundly* expressive of, "The quality of defiance . . . appears to structure the expressive content of the symphony as a whole. . . ."[11]

I have already registered my objection to this move. There is no reason in the world to believe that being structured around a property is a necessary condition for its being profoundly instantiated. The way I understand the English language, to be profoundly x is just to be very very x; and to be very very x, as far as I can tell, hardly requires being "structured" around x. Indeed, things without any "structure" at all can be profoundly x. When you are very thirsty, a drink of water is *profoundly* satisfying.

But suppose we give Ridley his premise about structure. What have we got? Well, if Ridley is saying that it is a degree – that is to say, the degree to which something is x is high enough for it to be profoundly x only if that thing is structured around x – then being profoundly x still means being x to some certain very high degree. And we are still stuck with the adverbial sense of "profound," which is irrelevant to the question of musical profundity that I originally raised.

I think at this point in his argument Ridley must be beginning to realize this himself. For the next step is in the direction, not surprising from my point of view, of *content*, of "aboutness," which is the only way to get to the adjectival sense of "profound."

Back to Natasha. "Now suppose it is *Natasha* who is profoundly defiant, in a way analogous to that in which Beethoven's Fifth is defiant.... [A]lthough her defiance is not *about* anything in particular, it certainly does suppose an attitude *towards* things in general."[12] In contemporary philosophical lingo, Natasha's defiance, by being a conscious mental state, takes an "intentional object." But how can that be true of absolute music? Ridley replies:

> I am not suggesting, of course, that music literally *has* an outlook of some kind.... But I am suggesting that, in experiencing certain pieces of music intently, and responsively, and so coming to grasp their profoundly expressive qualities, we at the same time gain an intimation of the outlook on the world implicit *in* those qualities: so that, for example, in grasping the profoundly defiant character of Beethoven's Fifth Symphony we gain an intimation of what it would be to have a defiant outlook on the world, of what it would be to view the world as threatening but outfaceable.[13]

Well, we do not quite have "content" here, but we are getting close. Music can be expressive of qualities that imply attitudes or, indeed, that, like defiance, are attitudes. Ridley is saying that when these qualities are profoundly instantiated in absolute music, they can somehow get us to know what it would be like to have the attitudes they imply or are toward the world. That is how I understand him, although I am not quite sure whether he means that the music enables us to feel what it would be like or know what it would be like. Let us call this "quasi-content." And in regard to it, let us consider two questions. Can absolute music possess quasi-content? And, if it could, would that give us any reasonable grounds for calling at least some works of absolute music "profound"?

That Ridley is in immediate trouble with regard to the first question should be readily apparent from the quotation he adduces to illustrate what he has in mind. It is from Michael Tanner, a philosopher whose opinion certainly carries weight, deservedly so in such matters. Of this quotation Ridley says, "The responses described in this passage reflect rather fully, I believe, the kind of engagement with music which I have suggested is central to understanding the expressive qualities of certain musical works as *profound*."[14] There is no need to discuss the content of the passage from Tanner. It suffices to say that it talks about Tanner's experiences of Bach's *St. Matthew Passion* and Wagner's *Tristan und Isolde!* They are works with texts, and with regard to texted works all bets are off. There is no need to ascribe quasi-content to Bach's passion music or Wagner's music dramas. They have real content, in the full-blooded sense of the concept, and profound content into the bargain. Who would demur from that? Certainly not I. But how can the "responses" of Tanner to these kinds of texted works "reflect rather fully" a response to a work of absolute music like Beethoven's Fifth Symphony, which does not have a text? Quoting Tanner on Bach's *Passion* or Wagner's great music drama is just an empty rhetorical gesture. Ridley might just as well have quoted A. C. Bradley on Shakespearean tragedy. Of course, these works can be profound. They have profound subject matter to which they are adequate (although the role of *music* in the affair is no easy task to explicate).

Ridley's problem is to convince such skeptics as me that *absolute music* can possess even such quasi-content as he ascribes to Beethoven's Fifth Symphony. He has an uphill fight.

That one of the things Beethoven's Fifth Symphony could be expressive of is defiance let us grant; and let us grant too that the Fifth is *profoundly* defiant. I think I know how this might be established – by pointing to various musical figures, melodies, harmonies, and structural features that contribute to the expressive quality I am claiming to perceive in the work.

What I do not see is the next step – how it might be established that the defiance Beethoven's Fifth is expressive of conveys to us "an intimation of what it would be to have a defiant outlook on the world, what it would be to view the world as threatening but outfaceable." I do know how I would establish that *King Lear* tells us what it would be to be defiant, to outface a threatening world. I would quote his defiant speeches and describe his defiant behavior: that, I would say, is what it is like to be defiant and to outface a threatening world; it is in those speeches and actions.

What should I point to in Beethoven's Fifth Symphony to convince you that it tells what it is like to outface a defiant world? There are no speeches. There are no actions. What *is* it like to be defiant and outface a threatening world *according to Beethoven's Fifth Symphony?* It is just avoiding the issue to say that it gives only "intimations." Even "intimations" must have a content, must be discussable. Lear evinces a certain *kind* of defiance. We might compare it to the defiance of Faust or, in "real life," Patrick Henry or Giordano Bruno. Which of these is the defiance of the Fifth more like? Does the question even make sense?

We are up against the same old problem that has been with us since Hanslick dug in his heels against just the sort of argument Ridley is trying to run. It is always easy to make a claim about what some piece of absolute music is "saying." The difficult part is making it good. What we can point to in Beethoven's Fifth Symphony is what makes it expressive of defiance. What we cannot point to is anything more about that defiance, even in the limited sense of what I called "quasi-content."

But let us grant Ridley his quasi-content: let us grant that Beethoven's Fifth Symphony gives us "intimations" of what it might be like to be defiant. How can *this* work our passage from the Fifth's being "profoundly defiant" to its being "profound" in any sense other than "profoundly defiant"? Certainly it cannot make the Fifth "profound" in the adjectival sense. *Love Story* and *Anna Karenina* are both profoundly sad; and certainly if Beethoven's Fifth can give us an "intimation" of what it would be like to be defiant, *Love Story*, soap opera though it is, certainly has the power, a fortiori, to give us an "intimation" of what it would be like to have whatever attitudes profound sadness entails. But *Anna Karenina* is profoundly sad, and profound in part because of its profound sadness, just because it can give us more than an "intimation" of what the attitudes involved in this sadness are like. It speaks *profoundly* about these attitudes, as *Lear* and *Faust* speak profoundly about defiance. And that Beethoven's Fifth Symphony cannot do. It cannot speak at all.

Once more, then, I conclude that Ridley cannot get beyond the adverbial sense of profundity to any sense relevant to my concerns. And at this point in the argument Ridley himself has obviously come to the same conclusion. For in the final stage of his argument he explicitly describes his position as so far dealing merely with the adverbial sense of "profound" and attempts to ameliorate the situation, not, in my view, successfully.

§7   What Ridley sees his view lacking, as so far developed, and rightly so, is a *normative* element. For, after all, in the adverbial sense of "profound," a work can profoundly instantiate the worst as well as the best properties: a work can be profoundly ugly as well as profoundly beautiful, profoundly silly as well as profoundly sensible. As Ridley states the objection:

> Surely, it will be objected, the account given here simply *ignores* what is most interesting about profundity, musical or otherwise. It simply ignores the kind of metaphysical or moral content characteristic of the profound – the kind of content which Peter Kivy attempts to capture. . . . Indeed, the present essay gives only an adverbial account of profundity. . . . Thus the essential link with *evaluation* is severed. When we call something profound, after all, we are surely – among other things – meaning to commend it.[15]

The problem, obviously, is that Ridley wants to go from "X is profoundly φ" to "X is profound"; but if "φ" is "silly" or "shallow" or some other negative quality, it seems hardly plausible to go from "His novel is profoundly silly" or "profoundly shallow" or whatever to "His novel is profound." There are a number of steps in this last stage of Ridley's argument, and we will have to go through them carefully. There is, I think, something wrong with each. Let us begin with a return to Natasha.

How can one connect a trivial property profoundly instantiated with *value?* In my original account of musical profundity, I suggested that what it would be for some subject matter or content to be profound was "something of abiding interest and importance to human beings" that was at the same time "not just of great concern but *worthy* of great concern, in some suitably strong sense of 'worthy'...."[16] That was half of my value component in glossing the adjectival sense of "profound" (the other half being the aesthetic and adequacy conditions). Ridley is apparently trying to use that kind of value component to put a normative component into the adverbial sense. For he writes of Natasha's gullibility, not, one would think, a very profound subject, although profoundly exemplified in her: "It still seems to me appropriate to call Natasha's gullibility profound...," and adds: "If you're *interested* in Natasha, then her profoundly gullible quality will strike you, without doubt, as worthy of regard (of reflection, of contemplation), because it will strike you as *valuable* in your efforts to *understand* her."[17]

Now this strategy cannot possibly bestow a value component, at least of the kind I was explicating in *Music Alone*, on such profoundly exemplified properties as Natasha's gullibility. No doubt, Natasha's psychiatrist might find her gullibility of deep and abiding interest, and it is indeed worthy of his interest, since she is in his care. But my conditions spoke of abiding interest and importance to human beings, obviously not every human being in the world, but at least a broad spectrum of human beings in my cultural neck of the woods. Thus it cuts no ice with me that for *any* profoundly instantiated property there is at least one person who finds it, for some personal reason or other, of deep and abiding interest, and rightly so, given who that particular person is. However, this is beside the point. What we are interested in is the profundity of *music*. So let us see what this strategy can do for musical works that profoundly instantiate "negative" properties.

Ridley quotes the philosopher Ernst Bloch to the effect that Richard Strauss's *Elektra* is profoundly "hollow": the " 'brilliant hollowness' that disturbs Bloch would almost certainly count as a profound quality of *Elektra*."[18] Now one can't think of a quality any more incompatible with a novel's or play's or philosophical treatise's being profound than its being hollow, empty of significant content. Being "hollow," I should say, is just about the opposite (along with "shallow") of having profound subject matter. *Elektra*, being an opera, hence having a text, mise-en-scène, and the rest, is not a very felicitous example. But, in any case, if the *music* of *Elektra* is not only hollow but profoundly hollow, it seems equally damning of *its* profundity, except in the adverbial sense, where its being profound simply means that it is profoundly hollow. How can we get from the profound hollowness of *Elektra* to the normative component of profundity in the adjectival sense?

The case of *Elektra*'s profound hollowness is analogous, Ridley wants to argue, to the case of Natasha's profound gullibility:

> And similarly with the Strauss example: If I'm genuinely interested in *Elektra*, and really want to understand it, or what's off-putting about it, I may well be glad to recognize (with Bloch's help) just how profoundly hollow it is. . . . But my recognition of *Elektra*'s hollowness as profound is conditional upon my desire to understand *Elektra*, and the value which that recognition has for me lies in the understanding of *Elektra* which it yields.[19]

But, as in the case of Natasha's gullibility, this example hardly gives the normative element of profundity that I was seeking in *Music Alone*. Understanding *Elektra* may have *value* for someone; and understanding the profound hollowness of the music might be instrumental in achieving that understanding – and hence have *instrumental value*. But that seems completely beside the point. What we want is value that accrues specially to profundity. And Ridley has given us nothing of the kind. All sorts of features of music, profoundly instantiated or not, have instrumental value in helping us to understand the music that possesses them. Furthermore, and more important, Ridley gives us no way of determining what is worth taking an interest in and what is not, which, it seems to me, must be part of any understanding of profundity in the adjectival sense. Anyone might take an interest in any profoundly instantiated property, no matter how worthless the property or how worthless the work that possessed it, and perceiving that property would then have value to that person, in the instrumental way of helping her understand that worthless work through that worthless but profoundly instantiated property. Is there anything here resembling what we think of as valuable about the profound? I think not.

Of course, Strauss's *Elektra* is not a worthless work, but a very important work in the development of modernism in our musical world, whether you think it is hollow or hallowed. And if it is hollow (which I do not believe), that hollowness is surely worthy of our interest, study, and understanding. If that is so, however, then the value conditions are satisfied not for the profundity of *Elektra*; rather for the profundity of a person's *understanding* of *Elektra*: the set of beliefs, written down or not, with the hollowness of *Elektra* as its profound subject matter. Perhaps Bloch's essay, from which Ridley quotes, is such a profound set of beliefs. But that scarcely makes *Elektra* a profound work – only a profound subject matter for a profound work. We are no closer, I conclude, to a suitable value component for the adverbial sense of "profound."

At this point Ridley makes a distinction between what he calls "work profundity" and "world profundity." The defiance of Beethoven's Fifth Symphony is an example of work profundity: "defiance plays a structuring role within the work, and is interesting and valuable for that, at least for anyone with a desire to understand Beethoven's Fifth Symphony." And the attitude implied in this defiance is an example of world profundity: "an attitude for which the world falls under the description 'threatening but outfaceable'. . . ."[20]

With this distinction in hand Ridley now tells us what the "world profundity" is that Beethoven's mighty Fifth Symphony imparts, through the attitude of defiance that it is expressive of: "The attitude contains one possible answer to the metaphysical question, What is the world really like? (Answer: threatening.)

And one possible answer to the moral question, How ought one to regard such a world? (Answer: as something to be out-faced.)"[21]

Now if my Uncle Harry put his arm around my shoulder and, with great earnestness, imparted the intelligence that the world is threatening and one should try to outface it, I would think him a Polonius for enunciating such a platitude. Yet Ridley would have us believe that this banality is the profound content of one of the most profound of musical utterances (if profound musical utterances there be), what E. M. Forster called "the most sublime noise that has ever penetrated the ear of man." I cannot credit it. If *this* is what the mighty Fifth tells us, then, indeed, *parturient montes, nascetur ridiculus mus.*

Indeed, Ridley, throughout his discussion, does not talk about any of the things that I would adduce to support the belief that Beethoven's Fifth Symphony is musically profound. He has not talked about the incredible thematic economy and concentration with which the master has constructed the sonata movement, the wonderful fugatto passages of the scherzo's trio, the miraculous harmonic bridge between the scherzo and the finale. In a word, he hasn't talked about the *music*. If there is profundity in Beethoven's Fifth Symphony, *there* is where to look for it. If not there, then the game is lost.

§8 Let me conclude this discussion of Ridley's quest for musical profundity by suggesting the difference, in this regard, between what my program was and is and what I perceive his to be (whether on not he so perceives it).

I began my account of musical profundity in *Music Alone* with the intuition that, like some exemplary works of literature or philosophy, some exemplary works of absolute music are not merely great works of art, but profound ones. I had a vague idea of what it might mean for a novel or play or a treatise in philosophy to be profound, and also a vague suspicion that there might be some problem applying this sense of profundity to absolute music, as I understand it. So I tried to state as clearly as I could what I thought people were saying about works of philosophy, literature, and the like when they called these works "profound"; and I then tried to see whether the works of absolute music that I and my friends in the musical world tended to call profound really could be in the sense I had made clear, at least to myself. Though I was skeptical that absolute music could be profound in what I have been calling the adjectival sense, in the end I made a positive suggestion about how, after all, it might be so. My program was, then, to take what I perceived to be an accepted, bona fide, presystematic sense of the word "profound," the adjectival, and see if works of absolute music we generally call "profound" really satisfied the conditions of this sense.

I perceive Ridley to be doing something quite different. He does, indeed, start with an accepted, presystematic, altogether *echt* sense of the word "profound," as I have done, namely, the adverbial sense: the sense in which something can be profoundly this or profoundly that. But he knows that just being (say) profoundly sad or profoundly defiant, in the sense of being very very sad or very very defiant, which is the sense I understand in these adverbial expressions, cannot make a musical work the kind that would generally be described as "profound." So he piles on to this adverbial sense various other conditions, the structuring condition being the most prominent, until he arrives at what he calls "work profundity," and "world profundity," hoping thereby that these beefed-up senses of "profound" will gather up those works that musical people, by and large, are inclined to call "profound."

My problem with this strategy is that these two senses of "profound," what Ridley calls "work profundity" and "world profundity," are made-up senses. I do not believe anyone uses "profound" in Ridley's sense of the word. It is a constructed sense of "profound": the word has become a term of art.

We could, of course, stipulate that from now on only works of absolute music that are "profound" in Ridley's constructed sense of "profound" are to be called "profound." I don't know why we should do that, but we could. But in any case, Ridley's project, as I see it, is irrelevant to mine. I have tried to apply what I take to be a presystematic sense of "profound," which I have called the adjectival sense, and asked some hard questions

about whether absolute music can ever be profound *in that sense.*
Ridley has done something else. Perhaps it is as worthwhile as
what I have tried to do. But it does not answer my question,
nor does it invalidate my answer. Ridley and I are doing profoundly different things: which is to say, very very different
things.

§9 The second of my critics, Jerrold Levinson, sees quite clearly
what my project is and pursues that very project himself, as far
as I can see. He is, in other words, looking for adjectival profundity in music, as I was, and where we differ is in where we
see that profundity to lie. Levinson, I guess, thinks that I am
more skeptical than I should be about some very straightforward things that absolute music can be profound about, and is
skeptical about the rather less than straightforward way that I
think music might just possibly be profound. And I, in my turn,
am very skeptical about those straightforward ways Levinson
thinks absolute music can be profound.

My skepticism was fueled by very strong reservations concerning whether absolute music can be "about" anything:
whether it can have a subject matter or say anything about a
subject matter it might, per impossible, have. For if absolute
music cannot be about anything, cannot have a subject matter,
then, a fortiori, it cannot have a profound subject matter or say
anything profound about it.

Levinson's optimism concerning the possibility of profound
absolute music is born of his skepticism about my skepticism
about the possibility of absolute music's having a subject matter
or the capacity to "say things" about absolute music.

The first step in the direction of a notion as to how music
might be profound is to show how music can have a subject
matter. For, obviously, unless music can have a subject matter,
be "about" something, it cannot say anything about it; and saying something profound about a subject matter is, at least on
my view, a necessary condition for profundity in the adjectival
sense. I assume that Levinson thinks likewise, because the first
step in his article "Musical Profundity Misplaced" is to make
out a case for musical "aboutness."

He begins: "The profundity of music, it is often said, has something to do with its emotional or, perhaps more broadly, human content."[22] Naturally enough, given the long tradition of connecting music with expressive properties, Levinson straightaway gloms on to "emotional content" and tries to make an argument for the view that music can be about the emotions it displays:

> If musical works have expressive properties, if composers generally intend them to have such, if listeners generally expect them to have such, and if it is widely acknowledged that a considerable (though not the greatest) part of the interest in music resides there, I don't see why we should be barred from saying that one of the things music as a whole is *about*, i.e. is concerned with, is emotional expression. . . . In addition, if we consider that when music is expressive of emotional states, listeners who grasp that are often led to reflect, if obscurely, on such states – possibly through inhabiting them temporarily in imagination – and that this result must often be envisaged by the creators and and transmitters of music, then it is hard to see what can be wrong in allowing that some music is about emotional states and their expression – when it is often an express point of the music to bring such to the consciousness of listeners.[23]

The argument in this densely packed passage proceeds in two stages. Here is how I see the argument of the first stage, in the form of four propositions:

(1) Musical works have expressive properties.
(2) Composers generally intend that their works have the expressive properties they do.
(3) A considerable part of the interest of a musical work resides in its expressive properties.
(4) One of the things music as a whole is about is [therefore?] expression.

I am assuming that proposition (4) is meant to be the conclusion of an argument, of which propositions (1)–(3) are the premises, although it is not altogether clear what the argument exactly is. I take the phrase "I don't see why we should be barred from saying . . ." to mean to suggest not that propositions (1)–(3) imply (4), but that they are meant to imply the possibility of (4). That is to say, I take Levinson to be saying that (1)–(3) are stating necessary but not sufficient conditions for (4); if they are false, (4) could not possibly be true, but if they are true, (4) could still be false.

I think it is clear that (4) does not follow from (1)–(3). I take it, then, that Levinson is making the weaker claim: (1)–(3) state necessary conditions for (4), and they do in fact obtain. Hence (4) could be true. I shall argue that (2) and (3) are false, or at least not obviously true, and hence in need of independent support.

Is it true that composers *generally* intend that their works have the expressive properties they do? The answer is negative. But a statement that might be mistaken for it is true. The expressive properties of musical works are generally the direct result of the intentional acts of composers. An example will help.

Bach intended the first fugue in Book 1 of the *Well-Tempered Clavier* to be in C, to be a stretto fugue, and to have many other musical qualities. The piece is also noble and joyful in expressive character. But I do not think Bach intended it to be noble and joyful at all. These came with the territory, so to speak. They are the unintended result of Bach's other, intentional choices. I say this because, as I hear this fugue, the expressive properties play no significant role in the musical happenings. And for this reason alone it seems absurd to say the fugue is "about" joy or nobility. To be sure, the expressive properties are neither accidental nor unintentional in the sense of not anticipated by Bach; they may or may not have been anticipated – that all depends merely on whether or not Bach was ever aware of what expressive properties his other choices were imparting to his work. But they were not intentionally put there to perform a musical function in that piece. Thus it is false to say, as proposition (2) does, that expressive properties were *generally* intended, generally put in works with malice aforethought. In many cases they were not and are of little or no musical significance.

It is just as obviously false, then, to assert, as proposition (3) does, that a considerable part of the interest of absolute music resides in its expressive properties. A very large amount of the stuff has expressive properties of little if any real interest whatever. And even where expressive properties do play an important role in the musical proceedings, it is doubtful that the music is usefully seen as being organized around them or written principally for the purpose of displaying them. Indeed, it is, I believe, the rare case rather than the general case of which one can truthfully assert, "A considerable (though not the greatest) part of the interest in such music resides there [in the expressive properties]." The claim is contentious at best, and false, in my opinion.

One thing that certainly is true in this regard is that during a certain period in the history of music, roughly, the Romantic period, certain musical compositions of the absolute kind do display expressive properties so prominently as to make them at least one aspect of such works demanding top billing and our careful attention. Nor do I wish to deny that some of these works, perhaps many of them, have expressive properties as part of their structural "plan." After all, it is no accident that Brahms's First Symphony progresses as part of its musical plan not only from C minor to C major, but from the "tragic" to the "triumphal," from the dark emotions to the light.

But it begs an important question to go from the fact, which I do not deny, indeed assert, that many works of music have expressive properties as part of their structure to the conclusion that these properties, therefore, make up some emotive, semantical content. My own view is that, like other "phenomenological" properties of musical works, "turbulence" or "tranquillity" or the like, they are part of absolute music's "syntactic" fabric and require no further musical explanation than that.

As for composers' claims that they have "meant" this or that or the other in their music, claims that no doubt increased in number and conviction in the nineteenth century, they must be evaluated not merely by the sincerity or vehemence of their expression but by a reasonable estimate of the enterprise itself. If a composer claims that he did something in his music that mature philosophical reflection (or plain common sense) concludes *cannot* be done, we quite rightly follow reason in the matter and dismiss the expressed intention as irrelevant to musical appreciation.

In the present instance, it may perhaps be true that a composer intended to "say" profound things about emotions in his music. That he could not, hence did not, settles the matter.

But does such a failed intention not suggest, if it is an important one in the compositional process, a failed composition? And if it *were* true, of which I by no means am convinced, that most of the great works of absolute music of the Romantic era were written with the end in view of saying profound things, or even just plain ordinary things, about the emotions, would it not imply the intolerable result that most of that repertoire, which comprises some of the most valued absolute music we possess, is an artistic failure? Or, to put the thing more modestly, if some purportedly great works of absolute music were composed with one of the dominant ends in view being the making of statements about the emotions, which I am inclined to believe is true, wouldn't it follow, on the view I am arguing for, that at least these works are artistic failures, because one of the dominant intentions behind their creation must be, on my view, a failed intention? And isn't that also an intolerable conclusion?

I see no reason to think that the failed intention to say things about the emotions should render what we take to be the great instrumental works of the nineteenth century artistic failures. Many artists have failed in their intentions because they have had crazy ideas about the world, or about what art can accomplish. Of course, if enough of an artist's intentions fail, then his works will be failures. But if enough of the crucial intentions succeed, then the fact that some intentions fail, no matter how deeply felt they may be or how important to the artist, does not spell artistic disaster for the works.

In the case in question, no matter how widespread the failed intentions of work-meaning may have been among the great Romantic composers, one intention of supreme importance, which one must presume almost all of them had, was to compose musical works that were *musically* coherent, well constructed, and as full as possible of inherently interesting musical invention: harmonic, melodic, contrapuntal, formal, orchestral, and so forth. In other words, it is likely that almost every great composer of the nineteenth century intended, when he wrote symphonies or string quartets or sonatas or any other forms of "pure" instrumental music, to produce perfectly wrought musical compositions, capable of being appreciated as such, no matter what other intentions he may have had. And where they failed, because of programmatic or other "semantic" intentions, as some think Liszt, Berlioz, Richard Strauss, and others sometimes did, to write compositions completely satisfying musically, those compositional failures, whatever their other artistic virtues, have put such compositions lower in our estimation.

What I am saying is that the pure musical parameters, when masterfully handled by the "great ones" – by Schumann, Mendelssohn, Brahms, Tchaikovsky, Mahler – are enough to overcome any failed intention to "say" things in their instrumental compositions. That intention – the intention, quite simply, to make perfectly wrought musical structures – when it succeeds, is enough to ensure musical success, whatever crackbrained or plausible intentions, impossible or possible, may fail. In instrumental music, the pure musical parameters are always trump. And that is why, I surmise, a person such as myself, who does not perceive meaning, pictures, or narratives in the great works of absolute music the nineteenth century produced, can still derive such a rich and deep aesthetic satisfaction from them.

The second stage of Levinson's argument goes on in this way:

(5) Where music is expressive of emotional states, listeners are frequently led, when they recognize these emotional states, to reflect, if obscurely, on them.

(6) Perhaps listeners perform this reflection on these emotional states by temporarily "inhabiting" them in imagination.

(7) This effect on listeners must frequently be envisaged by the creators and transmitters of music.

(8) Therefore, there seems to be nothing wrong [does that mean it is *right?*] in saying that such music as described by (5) and (6) is "about" the emotions it is expressive of.

This second stage seems much more to me like a straightforward argument than the first, and I will so treat it. Proposition
(5), I think, is flat out false, but I cannot prove that, nor can
Levinson prove its truth. For it is an empirical claim that could
be confirmed or disconfirmed only by the boring and laborious
process of polling listeners. For myself, I cannot but think it
beyond belief that very many listeners to absolute music are led
in any systematic way – indeed, in any way whatever – to think
about emotions. Almost *anything*, I suppose, can provoke someone to think about almost anything. It seems a slender thread
on which to hang a theory of musical "content."

Proposition (6) immediately raises a question about its central
concept, "inhabiting" an emotion. What does it mean for someone to "inhabit" an emotion in imagination? I suppose the most
likely candidate is imagining that one is feeling the emotion. But
that in itself raises questions. Nor do I see what I might find out
about an emotion by imagining I am feeling it, beyond what I
already know. To make proposition (6) intelligible, let alone believable, a great deal more of explaining would have to be done.
And it would be pointless, in any event, to undertake that task
until we had determined that proposition (5) was true, since it
is obviously pointless to try to figure out how something occurs
if it doesn't occur.

Propositions (5) and (7) are related in much the same way as
(1) and (2). For even if (5) were true, which I doubt, (7) does not
follow from it for the same reason (2) does not follow from (1).
I think it would be an extremely rare case indeed in which a
composer, in the compositional process, planned his music in
such a way as to make his listeners think about emotions, to
make them reach conclusions about them, and so forth. That just
is not what composers do when they compose instrumental music or what their teachers have taught them to do. If someone
thinks it is, it is incumbent on that person to provide us with
the evidence. Until I have seen such evidence, I remain highly
skeptical. And I would require evidence, by the way, beyond
the occasional, vague remark of a Haydn or a Beethoven that he
meant to educate humanity or reveal truths. Such talk is cheap,
and usually ends where it begins, whereas the musical listener

– which is to say the listener who is musical – goes elsewhere for an emotional or moral education.

Proposition (8) I take to be the conclusion of an argument of which propositions (5) and (7) are the premises. But it is, it seems to me, a completely unwarranted one. Even if it were true that listeners are frequently led to think about the emotions they hear in music, and even if it were true that composers frequently envisaged this, it would emphatically not make music "about" these emotions, any more than coffee mugs are "about" coffee, even though the perception of them causes people to think about coffee, which makers of coffee mugs well know.

"Aboutness," I take it, is more than the result merely of a contingent connection between what we perceive and what that perception causes us to think, however regular the connection might be. "Aboutness" is a semantic concept; and the causal connection between perceiving music's expressive properties and, frequently afterward, "obscurely" thinking about them is hardly enough to make absolute music a "language," even in the most distant, scare-quote way.

It seems to me, then, that Levinson has failed to make out a plausible case for musical "aboutness." And without "aboutness" the case for musical profundity must also fail. But perhaps some might think this a logical quibble or my concept of "aboutness" overly stringent and restrictive. So let us grant, for the sake of the argument, that Levinson has established the possibility of musical aboutness and ask ourselves whether, even then, a case can be made for musical profundity based on this kind of "aboutness." For profundity does not just require being able to say *something* about *something;* it requires being able to say something *profound.* I do not believe, even given the concept of musical aboutness as a gift, that Levinson can make his case for musical profundity.

§10   As we have just seen, Levinson's case for musical aboutness is based on the expressive aspect of music. Not surprisingly, therefore, one of the ways Levinson thinks music can be profound is by being profound about our emotions or about our emotive life. In addition, it can be profound, Levinson says, about what he calls "modes of growth and development" and can be what might be called "metaphysically" profound as well:

> So, finally, what might it plausibly mean to say that a piece of instrumental music was profound . . . ? The following, it seems, are still worth considering: 1) it explores the emotional or psychic realm in a more insightful or eye-opening way than most music; 2) it epitomizes or alludes to more interesting or complex extra-musical modes of growth and development than most music, and gives us a vicarious experience of such modes; 3) it strikes us as touching, in some fashion or other, on the most fundamental and pressing aspects of human existence – e.g. death, fate, the inexorability of time, the space between aspiration and attainment.[24]

The problem is, as Levinson well knows, that these are empty claims and can be made convincing only by providing real, full-blooded examples of music expressing profound thoughts about profound subject matter. In the absence of such examples, why should we believe the claims? As Levinson himself observes of them, "Of course these are just suggestions, brief promissory notes which only a more extensive analysis could redeem."[25]

But these promissory notes have been out a long time. Why have they not yet been paid? May I suggest it is because the account is bankrupt?

Let us run through Levinson's three possibilities for musical profundity briefly. Levinson offers no example in the essay on musical profundity of what music might "say" about the emotions, but he does in another of his essays, called "Truth in Music." Levinson makes the following suggestion there: "A work that expresses emotions ϕ and θ in successive passages suggests that in the experience of a single individual θ could *naturally* succeed ϕ."[26] Thus, on Levinson's view, the mournful first subject of Mozart's G-minor Symphony (K. 550) with the happy second subject is stating that in the experience of a single individual happiness could *naturally* follow unhappiness. It scarcely needs pointing out that whatever this assertion is, it is scarcely profound. And if the whole G-minor Symphony is a series of such assertions, their sum can scarcely make a profound utterance or a profound work.

Now I do not suggest that Levinson offers this kind of thing as an example of how absolute music can be profound about the emotions. But it *is* the kind of thing he offers as an example of how music can be truthful about the emotions, can, indeed, be "about" the emotions in the first place. And this seems to be all he has to offer to date on that regard. In the absence of any other more promising example of how music can say things about the emotions, this is what we have to work with, and it will never, in its paucity of propositional potential, add up to profundity. Levinson's first promissory note seems to have bounced.

What are we to make of the second claim, that profound music "epitomizes or alludes to more interesting or complex extramusical modes of growth and development than most music . . ."? Of course, we would like to know just what work "epitomizes" and "alludes" are doing in this sentence. And although Levinson does not tell us directly what he means, he does refer us, in a note, to an essay by the late Monroe Beardsley for further elucidation. I think we can get a good idea of what Levinson might have in mind by looking there.

In an essay called "Understanding Music," Beardsley discusses the perennial question of whether music can have extramusical "content" in any sense related to that in which linguistic utterances have "extralinguistic" content. In other words, can music *mean* in anything like the linguistic sense?

After rejecting, quite rightly, some of the more flamboyant claims made on behalf of musical "meaning," Beardsley turns to Nelson Goodman's theory of "exemplification" for a more plausible, if less ambitious account of musical reference. On Goodman's account, artworks refer to the properties they "exemplify." His now-familiar example of this relation is the tailor's swatch of cloth, which exemplifies – is a sample of – its color (say) or its texture (but not its shape or weight) and, insofar as it exemplifies one of these properties, at the same time refers to it.

Not every property of an artwork is one that it exemplifies

and (hence) refers to. How can one distinguish the exemplified properties of (say) a piano sonata from the others? According to Beardsley, "[T]he properties of the sonata that are exemplified by the sonata are just those properties which are *worthy of note* in the context of concert-giving and concert going (and record-ing, too): that is, they are those properties whose presence or absence, or degree of presence, have a direct bearing on the sonata's capacity to interest us aesthetically."[27]

Now "development," "growth," and "change" are terms that we consistently find ourselves applying to absolute music. And the quality that all of these terms seem to be picking out would be an exemplified quality, if any were. So, Beardsley con-cludes, "the idea that music exemplifies – indeed, exploits and glories in – aspects of change that are among the most funda-mental and pervasive characteristics of living seems to me to be true."[28]

Given, then, that Levinson himself has directed us to Beards-ley's essay for further elucidation, given too that Levinson's "epitomize" and "allude" are pretty good synonyms for Good-man's and Beardsley's "exemplify," one can fairly conclude, I would think, that Levinson is running here a Goodman–Beards-ley analysis of what it might mean for a piece of music to epitomize or allude to extramusical modes of growth and de-velopment. Such a piece of music would exemplify extramusical growth and development, and (hence) refer to them. Profound music, on this analysis is, then, music that exemplifies and (hence) refers to more interesting extramusical modes of growth and development than does less profound or trivial music.

My first problem with this analysis concerns the step from exemplifying growth or development to either exemplifying or referring to *extramusical* growth or development. There is no doubt, to take an obvious example, that the first movement of Beethoven's Fifth Symphony, and particularly its development, exemplifies, if any piece of music does, *musical* growth, *musical* development. But what licenses us to say that it refers to (or exemplifies) any other kind of growth or development besides the musical? There is no doubt that texts can fix such external reference. The wonderful resolution to D major in the last measures of *The Marriage of Figaro* seems unmistakably to exemplify musical "resolution," but the "resolution" of the plot, and the alienation of the various characters as well, nor is it too much to say that *our* alienations and (one hopes) resolutions are also alluded to. The text and dramatic situation make that clear. With Beethoven's Fifth Symphony, however, or any other work of absolute music, there is no such linguistic connection with an extramusical reality; and the assumption that an extramusical connection exists at all is just that: a completely unfounded *assumption*.

To be sure, the first movement of Beethoven's Fifth has perhaps caused some people to think about extramusical growth: perhaps the growth of embryos or of human beings or of the cosmos since the Big Bang, or who knows what. And it may indeed regularly cause people to think of examples of "growth" and "development" (although I know of no evidence that it does, except among philosophers). But it will seldom lead anyone to have profound thoughts about these things, because few of us, obviously, are capable of having profound thoughts about "growth" or "development" or anything else. If, however, the first movement of Beethoven's Fifth Symphony should stimulate profound thoughts about growth and development in some "genius" listener, it would be the thoughts, not the notes, that were profound. I don't see how Beethoven or his symphony could claim the credit. (All sorts of unprofound things have occasioned profound thoughts in those capable of them.)

Suppose, though, that we grant extramusical exemplification and reference as a gift. Where are we then? Hardly closer, I think, to musical profundity.

Even if Levinson can show that Beethoven's Fifth Symphony exemplifies and refers to profound subject matter, whether it be growth, or development or anything else, he has not shown that the *work* is profound. For as I pointed out earlier, it takes more than a profound subject matter to make a profound work. Even I can make reference to the human condition. (I just did.) What I cannot do is say anything profound about it, nor (for a different reason) can Beethoven's Fifth Symphony, for all of its musical magnificence. Even if it could achieve reference to the profound, as long as it is bereft of profound things to say about it, it is bereft of profundity.

I move on, now, to Levinson's final "promissory note." Music, he says, "strikes us as touching, in some fashion or other, on the most fundamental and primary aspects of human existence – e.g. death, fate, the inexorability of time, the space between aspiration and attainment."

Those are a veritable gaggle of metaphysical profundities that Levinson tells us music is "touching, in some fashion or other." But the promissory notes get harder and harder for us to imagine ever being made good. What, to begin with, is the "fashion" in which music is supposed to "touch" these profound questions? If it is the Goodmanian combination of exemplification cum reference, then what we have just said about these two will suffice. If there is some other analysis of how absolute music can be understood as "touching" these profundities, then we are owed it; and I have no doubt that in due course Levinson will try to pay this debt. But until then, the account seems in the red.

Furthermore, Levinson's rather too easy assumption that absolute music strikes "us" as touching all of these metaphysical profundities seems to me far from plausible. Perhaps it strikes a few of "us" that way, a few philosophers with theoretical axes to grind. I doubt if it so strikes the general public of music lovers or the general population of musicians and musically trained amateurs.

§11 Experience has taught me that proposals for how music might be about one thing or another are limited only by the ingenuity of philosophers in thinking them up. And since the ingenuity of philosophers is limitless, so are the proposals. It would be a life's work to keep up.

Indeed, the Goodman–Beardsley theory of exemplification gives us a machinery for generating "aboutness" in regard to *any* quality a piece of music can be said to exemplify, which amounts to *any* quality a piece of music can possess *qua* music. Is it a minuet? Then it exemplifie "minuetness," and hence is about minuets (or about dances?). Does it resolve to the tonic?

Then it exemplifies resolution and hence is "about" it. Is it turbulent music? Then. . . . And so on in infinitum. But however philosophical ingenuity may produce candidates for aboutness in music, it is a hollow logical victory, simply a parlor trick, unless it can be shown that that aboutness is something we should care about, something that makes the music interesting or valuable to us. It sometimes does matter, musically, that a piece of music is turbulent in such and such a place or resolves to the tonic at another. But what is *added*, what makes it matter more, if we then say, "So it must be *about* turbulence, so it must be *about* resolution"?

The obvious answer is: in order for aboutness to matter in music, the music must say something interesting or useful or in some other way valuable *about* what it *is* about. Naked aboutness is nothing at all.

In the case of produndity, of course, in order for aboutness to achieve it, what the music is about must be profound *and* something profound must be asserted about this musical content. It is very hard to see how this second condition can be fulfilled.

Indeed, it is very difficult to see how much of anything either interesting or valuable – forget about profound – can be said by music about what it is about, even if the minimal, Goodman–Beardsley aboutness is achieved. Of course I cannot prove it is impossible. But let me try to underscore the difficulty with an example.

In "Truth in Music," Jerrold Levinson tries to show, with considerable philosophical ingenuity, that Beethoven's Sonata for Violin and Piano in C minor, Op. 30, No. 2 asserts, in one of its very crucial musical places, a false proposition. This work, one would be forced to conclude, is significantly false.

Now if we find a philosophical or scientific work seriously false, it is a heavy judgment against it. Yet with regard to the "falsity" Levinson thinks he has revealed in this much-admired work of Beethoven's, he is forced to conclude that "none of this prevents the C minor Violin Sonata from being overall probably the finest of Beethoven's efforts in that medium."[29] One wonders, then, what the cash value of this kind of truth and falsity is if it should leave the works it inhabits of just about the same musical value, whatever the truth-value? "Who cares?" one is tempted to ask. And Levinson, who has far more invested in musical truth and falsity than I, seems almost to feel the same way. For of the kinds of falsity he has identified in musical works Levinson remarks: "I want ... to caution readers who sense a threat to some favored piece of music that I do not mean to imply that if a piece of music admits of ... falsity it is *necessarily*, or even *probably*, a bad piece of music."[30] Isn't Levinson himself essentially saying "Who cares?"

Of course, Levinson is not out to establish, in the essay under discussion now, either that the truths music can express can be profound or even, as we have just seen, that they can be of any great importance at all to the music at any level below profundity. And this, I suggest, is because one cannot get much beyond bare reference, if one can even get there, for absolute music. One can perhaps get the music to be "about." But to make it say anything interesting, let alone profound about anything, seems beyond the ingenuity of philosophy, at present, to achieve. Of course, one can never prove the negative, so I will be forced to leave it at that.

But let me reemphasize that an account of how music "touches" profound questions must be rich enough not merely to attain bare reference but to attain some recognizable profundity of comment on what is referred to. Without that, there is only the relation to profundity that even the mediocre of us can attain in our work. A cat can look at a king, and reference to the profound is what most of us can attain. It is going beyond that to speaking profoundly about the profound that achieves work profundity. And it is that further step that absolute music can never take, even if, as I doubt, it can take the preliminary step of exemplification of and reference to extramusical profundity. This does not make absolute music less worthy than philosophy or poetry or science or tragedy. It does make it *different*. And difference is my theme.

§12   It is time now to extract what moral we can from the quest for musical profundity, and the failures of the quest that I have just chronicled. The quest for profundity in music comes out of a genuine and general feeling – intuition, if you want to beg the question – that certain works of absolute music are limitless in their "musical substance," whatever that might be. They are the works one feels one can explore forever, the works that always bear rehearing, the works one takes on summer vacation, when baggage space is limited and the nights empty. I suppose that those who think this way will have some "odd" cases of their own. But I cannot imagine anyone's list not having Bach's *Well-Tempered Clavier, Musical Offering, The Art of Fugue,* and the major organ works; the thirty-two piano sonatas of Beethoven, along with the late quartets and the major symphonies; and select instrumental works of Haydn, Mozart, Schubert, and Brahms. Those, at least, are the core, the canon; and there is not much to be gained, for present purposes, by arguing over the details.

But if there is bona fide musical profundity, what is its foundation? And if there is not, if it is just a "feeling" and nothing more that we have about the "profundity" (so called) of the works above-mentioned, where does that leave absolute music in the pantheon of the arts, in the hierarchy of human values?

The question of musical profundity, then, is really a special case of the question, Why does instrumental music matter? Why should it be mentioned in the same breath as great (or even good) literature and painting?

Some eighteenth-century thinkers, including Kant, as we have seen, had a ready answer: "It doesn't. It shouldn't." It is wallpaper for the ears and should be accorded equal treatment with the stuff on your walls. For such thinkers, Muzak would have been the expected destiny of absolute music, not its ultimate degradation.

For Western literature, "profundity," I guess, is the ultimate value. If absolute music is also to have that ultimate value, it must, so I suspect its defenders think, be capable of profundity too – and profundity about the same kinds of things. The question of musical profundity is the question of music's ultimate worth.

But profundity is the top of a scale. And the question of musical profundity is, as I see it, not so much whether its best examples can ever really reach the top of the scale as whether it is on the scale at all: whether, that is, absolute music has to any degree whatever that substance that the scale quantifies and measures. But if it does not possess that substance at all – namely, *extramusical subject matter* – what can its value possibly be to us? Why should we, as we seem to do, take it so seriously? It is the quest for "sameness" in yet another guise.

In the following chapter I will not, then, as might have been expected, try to argue for musical profundity in a way more successful than those ways I have found wanting. I will leave that alone for now.

What I do want to tackle is the question that lies at the heart of the flap over musical profundity: the more general question, which I am frequently asked, usually in an aggressive manner given my so-called formalist proclivities, What really matters to us, in absolute music, if formalism is true? (Nothing: therefore formalism is false.) Again, the quest for sameness – the compulsion to see music as another example of literary or painterly values – drives the argument.

Can we have musical value *and* musical "difference"? To this crucial question I now turn my attention. But let me caution the (perhaps) overly expectent reader that I will not – cannot – in what follows give a complete account of musical value (whatever such an account would look like). What I will do, in keeping with the theme of my book, is to show how *one* value of music accrues to *one* musical *difference*. I should add, however, that it is a very crucial difference, and hence a very crucial value.

Chapter 7

The Liberation of Music

Zip. I was reading Schopenhauer last night.
Zip. And I think that Schopenhauer was right.
Lorenz Hart

§1 Whatever the value of the literary arts in human life, and however this value is connected with the pleasure we take in them, few would deny that both the value and the pleasure are deeply beholden to what we are used to calling its "content." Literature is language, and it speaks to us as language does, of many and various things. Aristotle thought at least some of it more philosophical than history. And except for an occasional flirtation with "formalism," philosophers of art and literary theorists have, from Plato and Aristotle onward, seen literature as a way some people – people we admire very much – have of telling us how things are with us, them, and our world. They – the philosophers and theorists, that is – do indeed differ greatly on the "what" and the "how" of literary "speech," and some in our own day have even doubted that literature does or can have direct reference to us and our world, but only to the world of the text itself. Yet however the thing is done, however reference is achieved, few would deny that the value of and our pleasure in literature have a great deal, though not of course wholly, to do with what it "says," one way or another, about one thing and another.

Of the arts of visual representation, something like the same sort of thing can be said – but neither so strongly nor so unequivocally, nor, I think, with quite the same philosophical clout. Whether the visual arts of representation "say," in any full-blooded sense of that word, can be seriously doubted. None except formalists, however, would deny that what the visual arts of representation mean in our lives, the value we place on them, as well as the pleasure we take in them, has intimately to do not only with their formal and sensual elements, but with their representational subject matter: *what* it is they represent. Indeed, as concerned as we are with the physical, painterly, or sculptural medium of the visual arts of representation, it makes little sense to suggest that it can be valued or enjoyed in vacuo. It is a medium of representation, and we can neither value nor enjoy it, *qua* medium, apart from what it represents, *qua* medium. We cannot have the *how* without the *what*, which is to say, we cannot enjoy how the painterly or sculptural medium represents what it does without cognizing what it represents. This seems obvious and hardly in need of argument.

The difficult case is absolute music. If so much of what we enjoy and value in the arts of literature and visual representation is involved with content, with subject matter, where does that leave the apparently contentless, subjectless art of instrumental composition? Schopenhauer was so impressed with considerations of this kind that he was willing to argue from them to the conclusion that, appearances to the contrary notwithstanding, absolute music (*in*correctly so called) must be a representational and, indeed, linguistic art after all.

I shall play with three themes from Schopenhauer in what follows, and the second of them has now been alluded to, namely, the theme of music as an art of hidden, hermeneutical representation. This theme, as will become apparent, I repudiate. But this discordant theme is introduced by a simple first theme that, unadorned, I fully endorse. Of the art of absolute music, Schopenhauer states, with boldness, "It stands quite apart from all the others."[1]

Had Schopenhauer developed this theme as boldly as he stated it, he would, I believe, have gotten far closer to the truth than he did. But after recognizing a radical difference between music and the other fine arts, he then cashed out that difference not in any radical way, rather in the event, merely as a difference in the *what* and *how* of music's reaffirmed representationality. For Schopenhauer, the nonmusical arts are representational not of our familiar world of space, time, cause, and human intention, but of the Platonic ideas that lie behind. Music is distinguished in being representational *not* of these Platonic ideas but of what Schopenhauer conceives of as the underlying metaphysical reality of the whole shebang: the striving noumenal will. The argument is straightforward. Accept the representationality of the other fine arts and the similarity of our experience of music to our experience of them; accept how deeply our experience of the nonmusical arts is imbued with their content – accept all of this and you are compelled to accept the representationality of music in some form or other. "That in some sense music must be related to the world as the depiction to the thing depicted, as the copy to the original, we can infer from the analogy with the remaining arts, to all of which this character is peculiar; from their effect on us, it can be inferred that that of music is on the whole of the same nature, only stronger, more rapid, more necessary and infallible."[2]

I shall return to Schopenhauer's murky and cumbersome metaphysics later on, when we encounter the third, and main, Schopenhauerian theme. For now, let me just say that, shorn of its metaphysics, Schopenhauer's view characterizes absolute music as having a hidden content, not apparent on its artistic surface, but in need of hermeneutical revelation. Stated this way, metaphysics aside, Schopenhauer's view is now widely held among musical scholars and analyists. This requires some brief explanation.

§2 Archibald, as I shall call him, is looking at a picture of a man sitting at a table, writing. At the man's feet lies what Archibald takes to be a pet animal of the four-legged variety; and the man seems to Archibald to have a peculiar ring around his head, which Archibald presumes is a funny kind of hat. Let me add that Archibald, except for his name, is your average ten-year-old.

Archibald, I want to say, is taking in what might be called the manifest representational content of the picture. Anyone who could not see at least this much in the representation – who could not see the man, the table, the ring around the man's head, the four-legged creature, the act of writing – we could fairly call illiterate with regard to visual representation.

But you and I would see something beyond what Archibald sees. We would see Saint Jerome with his halo and his lion. We would see the seated figure as a saint because we have imbibed enough elementary iconography and background information to know that the ring is a halo, that Saint Jerome's "familiar" is a lion, and so forth. We have some superficial acquaintance with the inner, nonmanifest content of the picture. Archibald does not.

Let me caution that I am launching no profound philosophical argument here meant to explicate, with logical rigor, the boundary between manifest and hermeneutical content in the visual arts of representation or in literature. All I mean to do is illustrate, with this intentionally crude example, that we commonly recognize such a distinction and are in some kind of vague agreement, if not about where hermeneutical content begins, then at least where total illiteracy begins. If Archibald cannot even see the saint as a human being or the lion as an animal with four legs, we are likely to say that he is not seeing the picture as a *picture*, whatever his visual experience may be.

I press this point because when we are told, either by Schopenhauer or by his late-twentieth-century reincarnations, that absolute music has a hidden, nonmanifest content that the commentator in question will now reveal, the claim is made against the familiar background of a practice in which the commentator upon a literary work, or a work of the visual arts, digs beneath the manifest content of the work to reveal the hermeneutical content underlying it. But we must not be lulled by this familiar background into missing a rather startling incongruity between the cases. For in the case of absolute music there is no manifest content. And that is a nontrivial fact. In the familiar case, the manifest content is medium for the hidden content, whereas in the case of absolute music, there is no manifest content to serve the purpose.

There is a familiar plausibility to the notion that one can appreciate a representational work at a certain "level," as Archibald does, without perceiving the levels beneath. Archibald can enjoy how well the representation of a man and his pet is brought off without yet perceiving it as a representation of Saint Jerome and his lion. Think, though, of the position I am in, or that Hanslick or Schenker is in, before the musical hermeneutist reveals to us what something we thought was absolute music represents, something we have been enjoying all of our lives under the impression that it represents nothing. Archibald is a connoisseur, a mavin compared with us. We are perceiving no representational content at all in a work that is supposed to derive a major portion – perhaps the whole – of its aesthetic payoff from its representationality. A ten-year-old is closer to appreciating rightly the picture of Saint Jerome than Hanslick, Schenker, and I are of appreciating Beethoven's Fifth Symphony rightly (or at all?). Perhaps you are prepared to dismiss my musical experiences as of no account. But what about Hanslick's and Schenker's?

I say that this is a nontrivial stumbling block for any account of absolute music on representational grounds. It is so, let me remind you, because the argument from Schopenhauer is founded on the premise that our appreciation of the obviously contentful arts – literature, painting, sculpture – is largely appreciation of content represented or presented. From this premise, and the further one that our "experience" of music seems like our "experience" of those other, contentful arts, it is supposed to follow that absolute music must, despite appearances, be contentful as well. So if it now seems as if absolute music, unlike the contentful arts, can be richly appreciated without experiencing its content at all, the argument begins to look very doubtful indeed. For absolute music is strikingly dissimilar to the other, contentful arts in this respect. To be able to richly appreciate a contentful work of art in complete ignorance of its content seems bizarre in the extreme.

This deep chasm separating absolute music from the arts of content and representation has for a long time seemed to me conclusive against any account of absolute music as some kind of occult representation or narrative. But I want, for the sake of argument, to put such considerations aside and take a look at two actual cases of musical analysis in the hermeneutical vein.

In the preceding chapter we encountered suggestions from philosophers as to where one might look for representational, even propositional, content in absolute music. But philosophers tend, in Levinson's words, to only issue "promissory notes." Musical analysts and scholars, on the other hand, are in the business of cash transactions. So I want to see if they can really deliver the goods, in terms of believable musical analysis of a representational or contentful kind. Can the musical hermeneuticists really convince us that absolute music has the content they say it has? And can we convince ourselves that that content, even if music has it, constitutes a plausible account of what we value and enjoy in absolute music? My answers to both questions will be negative. And I hope to go on from there to give, if only in bare outline, an account of my own.

§3   I dare say that no more central or obvious cases of absolute music could be adduced than Bach's *Art of Fugue* or Haydn's late symphonies. If these are not absolute music, one hardly knows what else might answer to that description. And yet I am about to examine the claims of two professional practitioners of the discipline of musical analysis, each claiming, for one of the above-mentioned, remarkable content of, I suppose one might say, a, "philosophical" kind. I begin, chronologically, with Bach's *Art of Fugue.*

The eternal symbol of the musical art at its most abstract, its most absolute, is surely Bach's musical homage to the fugue and its near relations. If it has been praised, it has been praised for that, if criticized, criticized for that: praised for its perfection of sonic form, criticized for its lack of "human values" (under the odd assumption that musical structure in its highest form is not one of them).

But the temper of the times made it inevitable, I guess, that even such a bastion of music at its most absolute should finally be assaulted by the musical content crowd. It would seem to be far easier to show that *The Art of Fugue* is a dark saying and encoded pronouncement in defense of its human value than to take on the difficult and so far neglected task of showing the human value in a musical structure altogether without content, hidden or otherwise. And so we have from Hans Eggebrecht, most sober and scholarly of German musicologists, an analysis of Bach's unfinished contrapuntal last testament, purporting to show "that Bach relied upon a specific extramusical idea to control the invention and development of the musical materials in *The Art of Fugue*." although Eggebrecht raises our suspicions concerning this rather extraordinary claim with two fairly damaging disclaimers, to wit, that his views "cannot be proved" and that what he is presenting is "a personal subjective theory."[3] What these odd expressions of self-doubt amount to – particularly the strange specter of a theory that is "personal" and "subjective" – is not clear. But the kind of "extramusical" analysis Eggebrecht offers is suspicious enough without his disclaimers, because it seeks "an aesthetic meaning concealed within the work's musical substance,"[4] a view of how music might mean or represent that, in our preliminary discussion of Schopenhauer, we have already found dubious indeed.

Every commentator on *The Art of Fugue,* hermeneutist or not, will agree that the musical climax of the work begins at the place in the great unfinished fugue were Bach introduces as the third theme his own name spelled out in notes: B-flat, A, C, H (which is to say, B-natural, in German notation). The whole subject also includes the notes C-sharp and D (an important musical fact that I shall return to presently).

Example 1

We can identify this as the beginning of the musical climax, independently of knowing that the third theme spells "Bach," because we can show that the three subjects so far introduced can be combined with the main theme of the work. Thus it appears that Bach intended the final fugue, which breaks off shortly after the introduction of the Bach theme, to be a quadruple fugue in which the third theme was his own name and the fourth the ground theme of the work, as yet not heard in the unfinished fugue. Needless to say, it can hardly be a coincidence that the ground theme can be combined with the others simultaneously. So it seems to follow both that the final fugue of the work was to be a quadruple fugue – triple fugues being the most ambitious theretofore – and that the final climactic stroke would be the combining of the three themes, already introduced, with the main theme, not yet heard in the piece. On this all students of *The Art of Fugue* now agree.

For most folks, I would think, that the third subject of the fugue spells out Bach's name in German musical notation is an amusing conceit that, once known, plays no future part in the appreciation of Bach's massive musical architectonic. That the master died, apparently, shortly after introducing this theme lends that musical event a poignancy no lover of Bach can escape. But for most of us the thing ends there. Not so, however, for Professor Eggebrecht.

"Until now," Eggebrecht observes, "it has been generally accepted that the B–A–C–H motto was simply the composer's way of autographing *The Art of Fugue*."[5] But Eggebrecht's understanding of this seemingly innocent play is quite different, and heavy with significance. To begin with: "It is quite possible that Bach did not so much engrave his name in the closing fugue to denote authorship, but rather to say: 'I desire to reach, and am in the process of reaching, toward the *Tonic* – I am identified with it.' "[6] As evidence for this puzzling interpretation Eggebrecht offers the following: "An examination of the musical materials indeed confirms that the tonic note (d) is the central reference pitch of every movement. In fact, d is both the starting pitch and goal pitch of the overall musical structure in the work as a whole. Therefore, the addition of a *double discant clausula* to the pitches B–A–C–H in the third subject of the closing fugue is very significant."[7]

For those not initiated into this musicological jargon, a double discant clausula is, simply, two cadences (*clausulae*), one right after the other for emphasis, in the highest voice, that is, the *discant*.

Example 2[8]

Thus Eggebrecht's argument seems to be that the *double* cadence on the tonic is meant to call our attention emphatically to the tonic, and to the resolution to it, while the fact that the theme in which the double cadence is embodied spells out the composer's name tells us that the composer is saying, "I desire to reach, and am in the process of reaching the *Tonic* – I am identified with it."

There is something rather breathtaking in the combination of audacity and insouciance with which Professor Eggebrecht travels, in the course of four sentences, from two simple musical events to this astonishing assertion. Suppose Bach had really intended to say what Engelbrecht thinks he said in his music. *Could* he have said it?

Of course not. In order to say this one must employ a linguistic artifact in an appropriate rule- and convention-governed way. Music simply is not such an artifact. So if Bach did intend this, it is a necessarily failed intention. And it is tempting to let the discussion end with this, it seems to me conclusive refutation.

But it might be well, instead, to go on. For even though it is impossible to say such things in music as Eggebrecht claims Bach says in *The Art of Fugue* – and these claims get more ambitious as his book proceeds – it would be a nontrivial fact that Bach even intended to say them, failed though that intention must perforce be from the start. As will become apparent, I am not convinced that the evidence adduced proves anything of the kind.

§4 It makes little sense, it should be apparent, for Bach, or anyone else, to have the intention of delivering the message that he desires to reach the tonic, that he identifies with it. If that escapes being nonsense, it is hard to imagine how. And before long Eggebrecht amplifies this message into one heavy with religious and metaphysical significance:

> Because Bach connected the pitches B–A–C–H to this emphatic cadential process, I cannot believe that he only intended to say: "I composed this." Rather, appending the double discant clausula to the B–A–C–H motto seems to say, "I am identified with the *Tonic* and it is my desire to reach it." Interpreted more broadly, this statement could read: "Like you I am human, I am in need of salvation; I am certain in the hope of salvation, and have been saved by grace."[9]

It bears repeating that, whatever Bach's intention, his music cannot say what Eggebrecht construes. If it cannot say, "I seek the tonic," it cannot, a fortiori, say, "I seek salvation." But what evidence is there that he even intended it?

I think we can cut to the core of the problem with the simple observation that the double discant clausula could be used, not to say anything, but to *represent* any number of things. In particular, it could be used to represent the seeking and achieving of any goal you like: salvation, to be sure, but, as well, victory over your enemies, getting home after a long journey, solving a problem, living happily ever after, and so on.

I say it *could* be used to represent any of those things. But how do we claim to know which of them it does represent? And, prior to that, how do we claim to know that it represents anything at all?

I think we know that the wonderful resolution and cadence to D major in the last scene of *The Marriage of Figaro* represents the resolving of the conflicts and the unraveling of the plot entanglements because the text and mise-en-scène make it apparent. And we know Bach interlarded his vocal works with many such examples of "tone painting," which are easily recognized through the texts they accompany. But *The Art of Fugue* has no text. So how do we claim to know what, if anything, of the many things the double discant clausula could represent it does represent? Why, in particular, assume it represents *religious* things?

The most, indeed the only, obvious connection between *The Art of Fugue* and religion is the fact that when the unfinished work was first published, by Bach's son Carl Phillip Emanuel, he appended to it as a coda what is reputed to be his father's last completed work, the chorale prelude, *Vor deinen Thron tret ich hiermit,* supposedly dictated by the blind composer to his son-in-law Altnikol. And Eggebrecht remarks somewhat disingenuously, after introducing his religious interpretation of *The Art of Fugue,* "Indeed, there is an unmistakable similarity between the conviction established in this interpretation and the hymn text of Bach's last chorale setting. . . ."[10]

I say that the drawing of this connection is somewhat disingenuous because Eggebrecht well knows – indeed devotes an entire chapter to – the history of how the chorale prelude became attached to *The Art of Fugue;* and he well knows, in particular, that it was no part of J. S. Bach's intention that it should conclude his monument to the fugue. Thus he writes, "Although I will use the traditional association of this chorale with *The Art of Fugue* in order to help clarify my interpretation, it should be remembered that the chorale does not really belong to the work at all."[11]

It is hard to think of a better reason to consider Bach's last chorale prelude irrelevant to the interpretation of *The Art of Fugue* than Eggebrecht's own admission that "it does not really belong to the work at all." But it is instructive to consider the case further.

Suppose Bach had really concluded *The Art of Fugue* with the chorale prelude? If he had, if the chorale prelude really were a part of the work, then we would have license, by virtue of its associated text, to give *The Art of Fugue* a religious interpretation, perhaps even the one Eggebrecht puts on it. This consideration is instructive because it gives us a clue to Eggebrecht's whole strategy – a not uncommon one in music analysis these days. If the chorale had been part of the work, the work would have had a religious text; and if it had a religious text, there would be no difficulty in putting a religious interpretation on various of the musical parameters, seeing them, in effect, as "tone painting." Thus, I suggest, Eggebrecht's strategy throughout his analysis is to try to discover "hidden texts" in *The Art of Fugue.* Let us pursue this thought further.

§5 Eggebrecht's problem is this. Toward the end of what appears to be the intended climax of the concluding, and hence climactic, moment of *The Art of Fugue,* Bach introduces as the third subject of a quadruple fugue his own name spelled out in notes. Were that to be the only place where the Bach theme occurs, we would be hard put to see the whole *Art of Fugue* as somehow "about" Bach, let alone about his religious salvation. So if one is convinced that there is deep religious significance in this appearance of the Bach theme and that, in consequence, this significance is the ruling extramusical principle of the work, one had better find that Bach theme all over the place. For if it is merely a lone occurrence, it would have only the kind of casual interest that accrues to such musical tricks. And, indeed, Eggebrecht sees as many Bach themes in *The Art of Fugue* as Senator McCarthy saw communists in the State Department. And his methods of detection are pretty much as disreputable.

Eggebrecht has two methods for detecting – or, I would have to say, manufacturing – Bach themes. One I call "tune-tinkering," the other Eggebrecht calls "alpha-numeric symbolism." They are, in my view, equally fallacious. Let us take a look at tune-tinkering first.

The tones B–A–C–H, in that order, spelling out the composer's name, appear in only one place in *The Art of Fugue,* where the third theme of the projected quadruple fugue is introduced, although had Bach completed the fugue, they would have continued to appear until the close. However, the tones B–A–C–H, along with the associated tones, C-sharp and D, occur with great frequency throughout the entire work, although not in the order that spells out "Bach." "In this study," Eggebrecht tells us, "we shall call this group of six variously ordered pitches the B–A–C–H sphere."[12] And because these pitches as a group – the B–A–C–H sphere – are a ubiquitous presence in the work, "the presence of these elements," says Eggebrecht, "also support [*sic*] our view that the B–A–C–H–C#–D theme is a symbol which unlocks the hidden meaning of this work."[13]

Those familiar with Rudolph Reti's book, *The Thematic Process in Music*,[14] will be well acquainted with the method by which Eggebrecht "locates" the appearance of the B–A–C–H theme in *The Art of Fugue*. Roughly, it works this way. Remove any notes you wish, without independent justification of why you are removing just those notes, until you have left only the notes that constitute the theme you are looking for. Eggebrecht has, indeed, refined this method even beyond Reti's by disregarding not only the notes that don't belong to the theme but the order in which those notes appear that do, which is tantamount to arguing that the use of the word "dogged" in a poem has deep religious significance, since, by leaving off the last three letters and reversing the order of the first three, you get the word "god."

The method of Reti and his ilk has been so thoroughly discredited by myself[15] and others that its reappearance yet again, in the work of an established musical scholar, gives one pause to wonder whether rational persuasion in matters musical is ever possible. But, yet again, the method, if that is not paying it too high a compliment, of finding a theme by tinkering with the notes until you get it is a self-fulfilling one. It cannot fail to find what it is seeking because the only rule for tinkering is, "Tinker until you get what you have already decided *must* be there."

What is especially egregious about Eggebrecht's hunt for the B–A–C–H theme is that, as any first-year theory student can tell you, the notes of what Eggebrecht calls the "B–A–C–H sphere," B–A–C–H–C#–D, constitute the ascending and descending upper tetrachord of the natural D-minor scale. *Of course* this group of notes appears with great frequency in a work every movement of which is in D minor: it is part of the very grammar of D minor. And to discover its ubiquitousness is about as surprising as discovering that *every* sentence in *Paradise Lost* has a verb. Thus the presence of the B–A–C–H sphere does not require, for its explanation, any symbolic interpretation at all, but is accounted for completely by the musical syntax. It cannot, therefore, be adduced as evidence for a symbolic interpretation.

§6 If possible, Eggebrecht's other method for finding B–A–C–H themes in *The Art of Fugue* is even more outrageous than the one just canvassed. It is, in a word, "numerology." We are now in the world of Nostradamus and Revelation. I will adduce one example.

First, affix a number to each letter of the alphabet, "A" being 1, "B" being 2, and so on, with the pair "I" and "J" being assigned the number 9, and the pair "U" and "V" the number 20. "By this method," Eggebrecht now points out,

> the surname "Bach" is represented by the number fourteen. That is, "Bach" can be numerically represented by the sum of the numbers which represent the letters B, A, C, and H (2 + 1 + 3 + 8 = 14). Correspondingly, the name "J. S. Bach" can be represented by the number forty-one (9 + 18 + 14 = 41), and the full name, "Johann Sebastian Bach," by the number one hundred fifty-eight.[16]

Having conveyed this intelligence, Eggebrecht then observes, "At this point, it is imperative that we distance ourselves from the grotesque speculation about alpha-numeric symbolism which runs rampant in many treatises on Bach."[17] It sounds like very good advice. But as far as I can see Eggebrecht goes right on to ignore it. Here follows a typical application of alpha-numeric analysis, as Eggebrecht employs it.

The second subject of the unfinished quadruple fugue has, Eggebrecht has determined, exactly forty-one pitches, thus, by alpha-numeric symbolism, spelling out the name "J. S. Bach." It is, I suppose, a nice question in numerology whether one counts pitches or counts note characters. For if you count note characters, the second subject, because of two ties over the bar, has forty-three of those. Perhaps it seems more reasonable to you to count pitches instead of note characters. But you can be assured that if it were necessary to count note characters rather than pitches to get forty-one, that is what Eggebrecht would have counted. And it is just this kind of freedom to choose that makes numerology, like tune-tinkering, a method that cannot fail to produce the results desired.

But now suppose that the composer really has "signed" his

name, albeit cryptically, in the second theme as well as une-quivocally in the third. What can we really make of that? Here is what Eggebrecht makes of it:

> Though this relationship is pure conjecture, I wish to stress again that my interpretation does not regard any symbolic reference to "Bach" in *The Art of Fugue* simply to mean: "I have composed this." Instead, the forty-one pitches contained in the restless second subject might well express the thought: "I, J. S. Bach, am the one who is running toward the goal, though I am yet living an imperfect human existence. . . ." Be-cause of a possible connection between the alpha numeric symbol (forty-one) and the restless motion of the second sub-ject, I shall consider the second subject of the closing fugue to be a musical representation of Bach's goal-directed but human existence.[18]

It is instructive to follow the course of the argument, in this passage, for it is a pattern familiar to anyone who has ever delved into the pages of what might be called crypto-history, of which books meant to prove darkly concealed conspiracies are a prime example. The inferences always go from *possible* to *actual*, the reverse of the order of Aristotle's well-known and in-contestable precept. Were it the other way round, pigs would indeed have wings. But in the books I am describing what is shown to be possible in Chapter 1 somehow, on the strength of that, has become true in Chapter 2, and what is possible in 2 true in 3, and so on. Likewise, in the passage just quoted, we begin with a "conjecture," which becomes, erelong, a "possible connection" and ends up a baldly asserted truth: "I shall con-sider the second subject of the closing fugue to be a musical representation of Bach's goal-directed but human existence."

But possible does not make true. Eggebrecht has not here or anywhere else provided a shred of evidence to show that Bach intended the second subject of the final fugue to represent what Eggebrecht considers it to represent, namely, Bach's goal-directed human existence. That is simply woven from whole cloth out of mere possibility; and to accept possibility for truth is simply to indulge in fantasy, however it might masquerade as rational argument. Of course Bach could have used such a running figure to represent running toward a goal. He probably did so more than once in the cantatas. But the fallacy of going from the tone painting in the cantatas to representation in Bach's instrumental music has been well known since Pirro and Schweitzer and, as a general fallacy of going from texted music to absolute music, since Deryck Cooke's *The Language of Music*. I see no reason to refute the inference yet again.

It is my conclusion, then, that Eggebrecht has failed to reveal any extramusical content in Bach's *Art of Fugue* or any intention on Bach's part to express such content, aside from "spelling" his name in notes in the finale. It nevertheless remains an interesting question as to what significance it would have if the content Eggebrecht ascribes to Bach's work, or content like it, really were contained therein. For, after all, one might object that even though Eggebrecht has provided bad arguments – indeed, no arguments at all – for believing such content is there, it may be there for all of that; the conclusion of a bad argument may nevertheless be true.

I shall return to this point later. But first I would like to have before us one more example of the musical hermeneuticist's trade, just to assure the reader that Eggebrecht's venture is not, in our times, by any means an isolated one. For this purpose I shall leave behind the murky atmosphere of German religious mysticism for the healthy daylight of New World analysis. Unfortunately, as I will try to show, the hermeneutical venture fairs no better in this more salubrious intellectual climate.

§7 As I said earlier on, Haydn's last twelve symphonies, the London Symphonies, have an honored place among what many people would take to be the paradigmatic instances of absolute music. And they are far more familiar to the listening public than Bach's fugal essay, so problematic from the performance point of view. Whether it is more or less surprising that they too should gain the attention of the neo-Schopenhauerians I can't say. But gain it they have, in a book by David P. Schroeder called *Haydn and the Enlightenment: The Late Symphonies and Their Audience.*

It is Professor Schroeder's hypothesis that Haydn tried – and I guess Professor Schroeder thinks succeeded – in expressing, particularly in the late symphonies, certain moral precepts characteristic of the Enlightenment, but in particular of the work of Anthony Ashley Cooper, third earl of Shaftesbury. Thus a substantial part of the book is an attempt to convince, with the usual historical arguments, that Haydn was acquainted with the philosophy of Shaftesbury and to present that part of the philosophy he thinks Haydn was expressing in his music.

I am not concerned here with whether Schroeder has succeeded in demonstrating that Haydn was familiar with the philosophy of Shaftesbury, either directly, through his reading of the author's major work, the *Characteristics,* or indirectly, through what Leonard Meyer has happily called "intellectual scuttlebutt." The point, in my opinion, is contentious. What is far more interesting from the philosophical perspective is whether, even given the premise that Haydn was familiar with Shaftesbury's philosophy, we can establish either the intention to express it in his music or the successful carrying out of that intention. My own view is that we cannot.

§8   Let us take a fairly representative example of what Professor Schroeder is up to. Here is what he says about the conclusion of Haydn's Symphony No. 92:

> With the final appearance of the closing theme at bar 225, the two polar forces of the movement are heard, as in No. 83, simply standing side by side. The conclusion does not provide a resolution but instead presents a coexistence; like No. 83, there is a message here concerning tolerance.[19]

Tolerance, needless to say, is high on the list of Enlightenment virtues, and certainly part of Shaftesbury's philosophical agenda. So this is one example of how Haydn expresses Shaftesbury's thought in his music. He has sent us, by musical means, a "message concerning tolerance."

But here is a puzzlement. Schroeder fails to tell us what Haydn's message concerning tolerance *is.* Is Haydn recommending tolerance of Catholics but not atheists? That was a very

common form of "tolerance" among philosophers in the En-
lightment. Or, genius that he was, was he perhaps advanced in
his thinking in tolerating atheists as well? What about Jews? I
would like to think that Haydn's "message" was against anti-
Semitism as well, but I rather doubt that he managed to escape
that common and pernicious form of intolerance so prevelant
then, as now, in Austria.

Did Haydn believe in the kind of toleration that embraces
freedom of expression? If he did, would that include freedom
to blaspheme or freedom to speak against the sovereign?

Clearly the way to answer these questions is to look more
closely at Haydn's "expression" of tolerance, namely, the music.
With the hypothesis in hand that Haydn was delivering us a
message concerning tolerance in the first movement of Symphony No. 92, what we should do to determine that message
more precisely is to comb the work for further indications as to
whether Haydn was recommending tolerance for atheists and
Jews as well as Catholics and Protestants; whether he was advocating freedom of expression and, if so, whether he meant for
us to tolerate the public utterance of blasphemy and treason.
What was Haydn's message concerning tolerance? I know how
to determine Locke's: by looking closely at the texts. I have
Haydn's "text" before me. I shall look.

Now everyone knows I am speaking nonsense. No matter
how closely I study the score of Haydn's Symphony No. 92, I
can never find such a message about tolerance. And anyone who
claims to do so we know is making it up. I think Schroeder must
know this, which is why he never tells us what that message is.
Indeed, when he gets even the least bit more detailed, as he does
in his description of the message concerning tolerance in Symphony No. 83, which that of 92 is supposed to duplicate, we
begin to squirm uncomfortably. This is what he says:

> In the conclusion of the first movement of No. 83, Haydn can
> be seen to be demonstrating a very fundamental yet difficult
> truth: opposition is inevitable, and the highest form of unity
> is not the one which eliminates conflict. On the contrary, it is
> one in which opposing forces can coexist. The best minds of

196

Haydn's age aspired to tolerance, not dogmatism. It is precisely this message that can be heard in many of Haydn's late
symphonies.[20]

Here is a little more for us to get our teeth into. Haydn, in
Symphony No. 83, is demonstrating a fundamental truth,
namely, that opposition is inevitable and the highest form of
unity is not one that eliminates conflict, but rather one in which
opposing forces can coexist.

What will perhaps stand out most prominently here for members of the philosophical profession is the startling, I am tempted
to say mind-boggling, claim that Haydn, in his music, is presenting a *demonstration*, a *proof* of this moral truth. Indeed, our
author seems to be saying not only that Haydn has presented
an argument for this truth, but a successful one. What kind of
demonstration? What are its premises? Does Haydn think that
conflict is inevitable because of some constant, unalterable human nature? Does he try to prove that tolerance, in the face of
conflict, is better than repression on (say) consequentialist
grounds? Or is Haydn a deontologist in ethics? How can one
"argue" in music, even if one is a Haydn, which is to say, a
transcendent genius?

No wonder Schroeder is reluctant to tell us what Haydn's
message concerning tolerance is. The result of the attempt just
has to be nonsense.

§9 "Let's get real," as my students used to say in a now-
outmoded argot. In order for one to say anything about anything, one must first succeed in referring to it: reference is the
minimal necessary condition. And philosophers who bother
about music are in some disagreement about whether music can
even do that, that is, refer, let alone express propositions about
what is referred to as we have seen in the last chapter. Furthermore, even those who think that music can refer will not think
that it can refer to tolerance.

Musical reference is thought to occur, by those who counte-
nance it, where music is called expressive of the emotions. These
folks think that where a piece of music is expressive (say) of

197

sadness, it, ipso facto, refers to sadness. Others who agree that music can be expressive of emotions do not think that that implies reference to the emotions.

There is also disagreement about the variety of emotions music can be expressive of, some thinking that "sad" and "happy" pretty much exhaust the repertoire, others expanding it to more of the common emotions, such as anger, fear, and the like. But there is hardly a philosopher I know of who thinks music's power to be expressive goes beyond that, to the more "conceptual" emotions and attitudes such as "pride" and "envy," because music does not have the capacity to provide the conceptual materials such "conceptual" emotions require. And for it to be expressive of a concept such as "tolerance," or any other moral or philosophical notion, seems beyond credibility. Thus music does not fulfill even the minimal necessary condition for delivering a "message concerning tolerance," namely, the possession of power to *refer* to it.

But even if we grant that in the various places in Haydn's late symphonies singled out by Schroeder, reference to tolerance has successfully been made, this still leaves us light years away from the music's being able to convey any message about it, even one telling us whether Haydn was in favor of it. If I carry a sign around that has "TOLERANCE!" painted on it, how are you to know whether I am recommending or denouncing it? Such a sign might be carried by the Grand Inquisitor as well as by Thomas Jefferson, each with a different intent. So even if, per impossible, Haydn succeeded in referring to tolerance in his late symphonies, he could not *say* anything about it, even whether or not he endorsed it. So much, then, for Haydn the moralist.

§10 But look here, I can imagine Schroeder replying: we know Haydn's message concerning tolerance as follows. In the first part of my book I give an account of what Shaftesbury said about tolerance, and historical evidence that Haydn knew what Shaftesbury said. In the final part of my book I show where and how Haydn referred to tolerance in his music. A reasonable conclusion to reach, therefore, is that Haydn's message concerning tolerance in the late symphonies is identical to Shaftesbury's message concerning tolerance in the *Characteristics,* including, of course, the endorsement. If you want to know what Haydn said in his late symphonies about tolerance, read what Shaftesbury said in the *Characteristics.*

A few observations on this line of argument. To begin with, it would obviously be a very bad inference to go from the fact that Haydn referred to Shaftesbury's views concerning tolerance to the conclusion that he endorsed them. Such a line of argument would lead us from the fact that Kant referred to Hume's position on causality in the *Critique of Pure Reason* to the conclusion that Kant endorsed it, which is, of course, the opposite of the truth.

Second, it would be bizarre indeed to say that Shaftesbury's doctrine concerning tolerance is expressed in Haydn's late symphonies if all Haydn succeeded in doing was to refer to Shaftesbury's doctrine, albeit with approbation. Haydn would then essentially be saying, "For my views on tolerance, see Shaftesbury." The doctrine is expressed in Shaftesbury, not Haydn. All Haydn provides is a footnote, poor compliment to one of the greatest composers in the Pantheon.

To put this point another way, if a book on Shaftesbury successfully expresses Shaftesbury's views on tolerance, I could apprise myself of them either by reading Shaftesbury or by reading the book on him. Who would ever claim that one could listen to Haydn's late symphonies in lieu of reading Shaftesbury, as one could read a secondary source in lieu of reading him? The only way one could possibly hear Shaftesbury in Haydn would be by first reading Shaftesbury (or a gloss of him). And once one did that, it is hard to see what the point would be of listening to Haydn. I certainly might want a second or third opinion on Shaftesbury's doctrine and go to the secondary literature to get it. That I should get it from Haydn's music seems to me a suggestion too silly to consider further.

§11 Let me make an end to my discussion of these two musical hermeneuticists, Eggebrecht and Schroeder, by offering a general remark on their individual projects and on my own project, to which I have been trying to apply them.

Eggebrecht and Schroeder, each in his own way, has tried to find extramusical content in what one would have thought to be a paradigm of absolute music, which is to say, *contentless* music. In Eggebrecht's case, the content is religious and "metaphysical," in Schroeder's moral and "philosophical." Both, I have argued, have failed completely to demonstrate either that the content really is there or that the composers had any intention of putting it there.

But others unknown to me may have been, or perhaps will be, more successful than Eggebrecht and Schroeder in showing that music like *The Art of Fugue* or Haydn's London Symphonies has the kind of content Eggebrecht and Schroeder are talking about. So it is reasonable for me to ask whether, if *The Art of Fugue* or Haydn's London Symphonies had the content Eggebrecht and Schroeder, respectively, ascribe to this music, this would solve my problem, which is, it will be recalled, what in or about absolute music we enjoy and value.

To answer this question, let us remind ourselves what content Eggebrecht and Schroeder are ascribing to the works in question. According to Eggebrecht, Bach is saying in *The Art of Fugue*, "Like you, I am human; I am in need of salvation, and I have been saved by grace." And according to Schroeder, Haydn is saying in various places in his late symphonies, "Opposition is inevitable, and the highest form of unity is not the one which eliminates conflict. On the contrary, it is one in which opposing forces can coexist." Could the expression of these sentiments, or sentiments like them, be what we enjoy and value in absolute music?

How could they possibly be? They are, naked and unadorned by argument or elucidation, utter banalities. If this were the heart of their matter, and if their matter were what mattered, what we enjoyed and valued, then *The Art of Fugue* and Haydn's London Symphonies would provide the value of a sampler or welcome mat or a message from the Hallmark Co.

But surely "naked and unadorned by argument or elucidation" gives the game away. Of course, it might be objected, what any great work of art says can be trivialized by a thumbnail sketch of its content. The "intellectual" sister in Leonard Bernstein's *Wonderful Town* offers the following gloss of *Moby Dick:* "It's about this *whale."* Well, it *is* about this whale; that about sums it up. So if *Moby Dick* is valued and enjoyed, in some very large measure, for its content, then it joins the rank of the trivial, as must Shaftesbury's *Characteristics,* which is epitomized by Schroeder's representation of Haydn's message in the late symphonies, and the works of many great theologians, whose content is correctly described by Eggebrecht's spare account of Bach's message in *The Art of Fugue.* But fully elucidated and argued for, the content of all of these works, the musical ones included, lifts them to the level of masterpieces.

The emptiness of this reply, however, is not difficult to see. It is just the very possibility of elaboration of content that makes works of literature or philosophy so different from works of absolute music. Even if we could attribute the minimal content to *The Art of Fugue* and Haydn's late symphonies that Eggebrecht and Schroeder have, which I do not think we would do, that is all we could do without entering Disneyland, whereas the interpreter of *Moby Dick* or the *Characteristics* can dig into the text to fill out what such trivial descriptions as "It's about this *whale"* only hint at or abstract. There is no need for me to dilate upon the procedures by which the interpreter, closely examining the literary or philosophical text, puts flesh on the dry bones of such formulas as "It's about this *whale"* or "It's a treatise on toleration." Back and forth the interpreter goes, from interpretation to text, text to interpretation, until the full story emerges. It is just that commerce between interpretation and text that immediately breaks down, at least if you are sane, once the barest philosophical or literary or religious construction is put on a work of absolute music. And it is for just that reason that one reads through as elaborate an analysis as Eggebrecht's of *The Art of Fugue* or Schroeder's of Haydn's late symphonies, only to come away with empty banalities that cannot advance us one whit in our understanding of what we value or enjoy in these wonderful works. With regard to absolute music, content analysis is the light that fails.

§12   If musical representationalism is supposed to be an answer, then, to the question of why we should care about absolute music, it turns out, so I have been arguing, to be an utter
failure: a failure because of its initial implausibility and a failure
again, initial implausibility aside, for possessing a kind of musical content scarcely interesting enough to care about – scarcely
interesting enough to make us say, "Why, *that* is why I love *The
Art of Fugue* or Haydn's London Symphonies."

But this brings us again, face to face, with our original dilemma. If absolute music has no content, why on earth are so
many people so interested in it? Why, in a word, do they love
it so much?

When I am asked this question, my answer is always quite
simply: I do not value, enjoy, or love music *in spite of* the fact
that, unlike the literary arts and arts of visual representation, it
has no content. On the contrary, I value, enjoy, and love absolute
music just *because* it has no content. And that brings me to the
third, and major, of my themes from Schopenhauer, indeed, the
theme that has given this chapter its title.

Schopenhauer believed that our ordinary workaday lives, as
well as the lives of scientists and practical men, are dominated
by what he called the "fourfold root of the principle of sufficient
reason," which is to say, we are in a way driven to see, reason
about, deal with our world – the world of "appearance" – in
terms of cause and effect, motive and action, premise and conclusion, space and time. We are in thrall to a kind of Hobbesian
tyrant of a will forever impelling us to reason, seek, and possess,
only to find that our conclusions and possessions give us no
rest, but make another starting place for yet further reasoning,
seeking, and possessing, in a never-ending and restless quest for
peace and finality. That, for Schopenhauer, is the human condition, were it not for art.

It is through art, either in the external form of an object of
contemplation or in the inward form of an impulse to create
such an object, that we are lifted, if only temporarily, from our
servitude. As Schopenhauer puts his point in one of his most
eloquent passages:

When, however, an external cause or inward disposition raises us out of the endless stream of willing, and snatches knowledge from the thraldom of the will, the attention is now no longer directed to the motives of willing, but comprehends things free from their relation to the will. Thus it considers things without interest, without subjectivity, purely objectively; it is entirely given up to them in so far as they are merely representations, and not motives. Then all at once the peace, always sought but always escaping us on that first path of willing, comes to us of its own accord, and all is well with us. It is the painless state, prized by Epicurus as the highest good and as the state of the gods; for that moment we are delivered from the miserable pressure of the will. We celebrate the Sabbath of the penal survitude of willing; the wheel of Ixion stands still.[21]

The insight I would like to rescue from Schopenhauer's metaphysics is the notion of *liberation:* of music's liberating power. But liberation from what? And why music rather than, as Schopenhauer believes, the fine arts *tout court?* Let us tackle the second question first.

I do not ask you to accept Schopenhauer's metaphysical structure of the world. I certainly cannot accept it myself. In particular, I certainly cannot accept Schopenhauer's notion that the representational and contentful arts liberate us from our world of cause and effect, premise and conclusion, motive and action, space and time. On the contrary, far from retreating to a world of Platonic ideas, as Schopenhauer would have it, I am far more inclined to believe that the visual arts of representation and the contentful literary arts are, pace Aristotle, eminently particular, presenting our world in ways transformed, to be sure, but reveling in its haecceity. General or particular, however – and I am inclined to think that varies with artist and with style – the representational and contentful arts scarcely liberate us from the labor of thought about the world in just those terms Schopenhauer designates as the fourfold root of the principle of sufficient reason. And when it is the world of Shakespeare's *Lear* or Verdi's *Otello,* the labor of thought and the act of confrontation are so frought with difficulty that we will avoid such works, for all of their rich rewards, except on those occasions when we feel up to the task. We are not relieved of the problems of life by much of the arts of visual representation and literature. We are plunged into them more often than not. This is my first demur to Schopenhauer's theme of liberation.

§13 My second demur naturally has to do with Schopenhauer's characterization of music. In what I called his first theme, Schopenhauer recognized the striking disanalogy between music and the other fine arts. This, I think, was an insight – but a failed insight, in the event, because Schopenhauer cashed out this perceived disanalogy merely in terms of his idiosyncratic metaphysics of representation, simply giving absolute music a metaphysically "deeper" object of representation than he gave the contentful arts of literature, painting, and sculpture.

In what I call Schopenhauer's third and major theme, Schopenhauer, again insightfully, recognizes an element of liberation in the general vicinity of the fine arts. But, again, his insight falls short of the goal because he fails to realize what I take to be its peculiar relevance to absolute music alone. If one, then, puts the first and third themes together in their proper contrapuntal relation, one gets the result that, first, absolute music is strikingly dissimilar to the contentful arts, not, however, because it has a dissimilar content but because it has no content at all, in the sense of "content" at issue here. (Obviously it has *musical* content: themes, harmonies, counterpoint, etc.)

Second, one gets the result, so I shall argue presently, that the disanalogy lies in the liberating quality that absolute music alone of the fine arts possesses and the contentful arts, just because of their content, palpably lack. Or, to put it more precisely, it is neither a "lack" in music that it possesses no content, nor a "lack" in the contentful arts that they possess no power to liberate. On the contrary, it is a defining virtue of the contentful arts that they do *not* liberate us from our workaday world but engage us, albeit in ways characteristic of the fine arts. And it is a defining virtue of absolute music, so I shall argue, that it does not engage us in our workaday world but liberates us from it. That is my contention. Now I must try to convince you of its truth.

§14 To begin with the familiar, there is nothing very new or surprising about the idea that absolute music is a pure sonic structure or design. It was an idea familiar in the Enlightenment, and thought by those who entertained it then as quite damning of the whole enterprise of music without text. From Hanslick onward it was an idea explored to just the opposite end: to redeem absolute music from the representational and contentful arts as a thing worthy unto itself, and not an appendage to them of doubtful value. Our century has designated this view of absolute music, unhappily, musical "formalism." And I say "unhappily" because the designation suggests, quite mistakenly, that if one construes absolute music as pure, contentless sonic structure, one must think that only its musical *form* matters.

But that is not the nature of my musical formalism, which my friend and fellow tiller of the soil, Philip Alperson, has described as "enhanced formalism" – a view that accords value and pleasure not merely to musical "form," properly so called, but to all of the sensual and phenomenological properties that absolute music possesses, including, most importantly, its *expressive properties.* Nor does my musical formalism fail to recognize that the cognizing and enjoyment of musical structure is not some bloodless intellectual exercise but a deeply moving and exciting experience. It is, no doubt, far too late in the day to give up the "formalism" tag in favor of some more suitable label. For like many other labels of the kind, it has taken on a philosophical life beyond its original, literal meaning. And only confusion would result from giving it up now. Most philosophical practitioners know that "formalism" is not a doctrine, in any of the arts, that either promotes or allows interest only in "form" in its most restrictive sense. So I will continue to refer to my position now and in the future as musical formalism and require that you remember it is "enhanced formalism" that I mean by it.

Now if musical formalism is true, even in its "enhanced" version, which countenances expressive properties as part of musical structure, one can well ask why such a structure should be of interest and value to human beings. Why should we be interested in, not to put too fine a point on it, organized but meaningless noise?

I have suggested elsewhere that this question does not admit of any simple, single answer.[22] There is not one property of absolute music that makes it interesting or valuable to us: there are many. And only detailed study *of* music – the musical nuts and bolts – can reveal to us all of its many intriguing aspects.

But once these intriguing aspects are isolated and explained, there remains that gnawing question with which these remarks began, of why, in comparison with the contentful arts, absolute music should hold the fascination that it does for us; but not only that, why it should be held in such deep reverence that the figure of a Bach or a Beethoven can hold the same pride of place for many of us as that of a Shakespeare or a Michelangelo. How can that be? Our provisional answer is: we value and enjoy absolute music not in spite of its lack of content but *because* of it; its lack of content is a value to us, not a disvalue. That answer must now be fleshed out.

§15 Consider another familiar claim. Works of absolute music, like works of the contentful arts, create, so to speak, "worlds" for us to cognize and contemplate. These worlds are as varied and individual as the artists who have created them. They range from the complex world of the *Iliad* to the miniature, simple world of Goethe's poem about a trampled violet; from the violent, almost unbearably painful world of *King Lear* to the lighthearted, inconsequential world of a play by Kaufmann and Hart; from the vast world of the Sistine ceiling to the constricted world of Van Gogh's shoes; from the incredibly intricate and musically demanding world of the six-voice Ricercare in the *Musical Offering* to the transparent simplicity of *Eine kleine Nachtmusik*.

But what is crucial for our purposes is that worlds of absolute music, unlike the worlds of the contentful arts, are, as it were, "worlds apart," which is to say, they are worlds of musical sound that make no contact with – no reference to – the world in which we live and move and have our being. From that world they are apart.

This is not to say that it is altogether clear just what relation the world of a contentful work bears to *the* world or how that relation is logically constituted. The problem is particularly nasty when, like Tolstoy's *War and Peace,* the work intermingles the factual with the fictional, real names with made-up ones. In spite, however, of such genuine difficulties, and even attempts to jar the contentful arts loose from the "real" world altogether, the fact remains that those readers and gazers not in thrall to various of the postmodern theses that construe texts as solely about texts – which, I dare say, are most of us – the world of our lives is deeply implicated in the worlds of our novels and plays, statues and paintings. And only academics, whose professional world is constituted only by texts, are likely to think that texts are the only objects of artistic concern.

But just because the world of our lives is so deeply implicated in the world of our contentful artworks, we cannot have genuine, aesthetically rich encounters with such works without these works, intentionally and purposefully, setting in motion our intellectual and emotional engagement not only with the worlds of the works themselves but with our own world as well, which imbues even the most remote fantasy or the most escapist romp. And such intellectual and emotional engagement accrues to the worst as well as the best: the soap opera as well as the profoundest Shakespearean tragedy, the Norman Rockwell as well as the canvases of Cézanne.

But thinking about our world and its problems, and inevitably our problems in our world, is hard and painful work. And that is partly why some of the most profound literary works, and such paintings as Goya's *The Disasters of War* and Picasso's *Guernica,* elicit in us what psychologists used to call an "approach–avoidance conflict."

From Aristotle's *Poetics* to the most recent issue of the *Journal of Aesthetics and Art Criticism,* the paradox of this conflict, the paradox of aesthetic pain, its value, its nature, why we should seek it, has been the subject of the closest philosophical scrutiny. Yet whatever the result of such inquiry has been, or will be, the brute fact remains that our encounters, particularly with our profoundest, most valued, most serious examples of the contentful arts, are fraught with the deepest satisfactions but also with the deepest agony of thought about our deepest, most recalcitrant moral and metaphysical questions.

Of course, this is not to suggest that the pain of serious thought is some kind of irrelevant and undesirable side effect of serious contentful art. If that were so, there would be no paradox of aesthetic pain. The fact of the matter is that the agony of thought that *King Lear* or *Faust* elicits is not some unfortunate appendage to an otherwise satisfying experience, but an integral part of the experience itself: part of the very reason we value such works and derive the deep satisfaction we do from them. To contemplate the beautiful, the awesome, the finely wrought aesthetic world of *Lear* or *Faust* or *Bleak House* is to have a deeply satisfying experience. But you cannot have that experience without the other: the experience of gnawing, persistent, ultimately irresolvable thought about our world, with its moral agonies and metaphysical mysteries. It's part of the territory.

But it is freedom from just this agony of thought that absolute music provides. Absolute music gives us the world of the work without the world of the world.

This is by no means to suggest that music is a world without thought. As I have argued elsewhere, absolute music is not a thing of the nerve endings but a thing of the mind: a thing of *musical* thought.[23] What I am suggesting is that in the contentful arts our thought processes work both in the world of the work and in the world of the world, whereas in absolute music our thought processes, at least ideally, are at play in the world of the work alone. That, it appears to me, is music's blessing and *difference.*

How the mind works in our appreciation and enjoyment of music is a topic of great complexity that I cannot enter into here. I will say only that whether you are listening at the level of a lay music lover or at the level of a Mozart, or at any level between, what you are doing is perceiving that and how musical events are taking place, under whatever description you understand them, and in so doing you are enjoying those musical happenings. It is in this sense that I am insisting that absolute music is an object – an intentional object – of the mind, and the pleasure we take in it a pleasure of the mind, at whatever level of musical expertise we find ourselves.

Furthermore, as I have been arguing, what is so distinctive about this pleasure is its complete freedom from connection with our workaday world and its problems. It is both the blessing and the curse of the contentful arts that their worlds are, to borrow some familiar philosophical jargon, possible-world versions of our own and so must, as part of their nature, engage us in thought processes that bear with them a heavy burden. A passage in a long-forgotten novel of James Hilton's captures my thought: "Then she went to the piano and he took out his violin and they began to play Mozart. The music streamed into the room, enclosing a world in which they were free as air, shutting out hatreds and jealousies and despondencies, giving their eyes a look of union with something rare and distant."[24]

It is the blessing of absolute music that it frees our thought to wander in worlds that are completely self-sufficient: worlds where all is resolved, so to speak, with no loose ends, worlds that when they are grasped satisfactorily, give us that to think about which, for the duration of the experience, completely frees us from, so to speak, the failure of thought and gives us thought processes that, if the composer is up to it, can only succeed, can only resolve to a satisfactory conclusion.

It is of course true that the visual arts have produced examples of nonrepresentational objects, paintings, sculptures, "constructions" in our own century, and there is no reason to doubt that in such cases the same kind of liberating quality I have attributed to the experience of absolute music may well accrue to the experience of these artistic objects as well. But the fact remains – and it is a fact in need of explanation – that no artistic practice in the Western world has approached absolute music in significance as an art of this "liberating" kind. So although absolute music is not altogether unique in this regard, it is singular enough to require the special attention I, following Schopenhauer, have bestowed on it.

Furthermore, the power of liberation of which I speak may

not be limited to the fine arts at all. The experience of pure mathematics immediately comes to mind; and it may, for all I know, provide the same feeling of liberation in its experience as I have attributed to the experience of absolute music. This fact, if fact it is, does not trouble me in the least, as I see no reason why the experience of liberation should be exclusive to the fine arts. But let me just add that if the experience of pure mathematics does share this liberating quality with absolute music, that neither makes mathematics fine art nor makes music mathematics.

§16 I have spoken at length of the liberating *value* of music, as opposed to the contentful arts, and I underscore "value" to introduce some remarks concerning that philosophically troublesome concept. The quality of liberation is not *the* value of absolute music. There is no such thing as that. Absolute music has diverse values, which is to say, we enjoy many things about it. All of these things that have to do with its aesthetic structure and surface, when suitably described, we also enjoy in the other arts that possess them. A poem or a painting, as well as a sonata, may have unity and thematic structure, expressive and dynamic qualities, tension and release, and the rest. When we perceive these qualities we enjoy them, and when we enjoy them we value the works in which they inhere.

Of course, to the extent that a musical work has the aesthetic qualities we value and enjoy, to that extent it will fascinate and enthrall; and to the extent that it fascinates and enthralls, to that extent it will liberate. In other words, if you are busy perceiving and enjoying musical design and structure, you will not be worrying about the problem of evil or the comparative merits of sense over sensibility.

Thus the value of liberation is keyed to the other values of a musical work. But it must be observed that the liberation value of a work may well exceed its other values, in a way that might merit censure. If, for example, I were utterly enthralled at a certain stage of my musical life with the music of Leroy Anderson, you might well chide me for my lack of musical taste and sophistication, for not preferring Bach or Haydn, even though

Leroy Anderson is more liberating for me at this point than Bach or Haydn would be, since their musical virtues would go unperceived and unappreciated for the most part, and my mind, therefore, would not be as musically occupied when listening to their music.

To this, first of all, there might be the reply that if I were to cultivate the music of Bach and Haydn, there would be so much more to enthrall me than ever there could be in the music of Leroy Anderson that the "liberation sum" could be represented as correspondingly higher. Furthermore, unless I were a musical vegetable, the likelihood is that I would, in the course of time, find the music of Leroy Anderson to pall and seek musical satisfaction in more worthy examples. But even if it were the case that liberation is invariant with other musical values – that is, even if it were the case that Leroy Anderson, now and forever, provides as much of it for the person who enjoys Leroy Anderson, but not Bach and Haydn, as Bach and Haydn provide for their devotees – it does not obviate the fact that one value absolute music has, across the board, is liberation. Nor does it render us incapable, on other grounds, of placing more overall musical value on Bach and Haydn than on Leroy Anderson.

Thus it appears that the liberating quality of absolute music, as a value of absolute music *tout court*, is compatible with all of the usual grounds we have for valuing one piece of absolute music over another, unless we bring in values of "content" and "meaning" (in which case, of course, it will not be a value at all, being incompatible with those other "contentful" things). But it is those values that I am denying apply at all, so about them nothing more need be said.

I might add by the way that in making use of Schopenhauer's notion of artistic liberation in my account of absolute music, I am by no means buying into the well-known Schopenauerian pessimism, although anyone looking back over the twentieth century from our present vantage point might well think Schopenhauer a wide-eyed optimist in the light of what two world wars and the Holocaust have revealed to us about the human condition. The point is that I intend my appeal to the blessings of musical liberation to be consistent with a rather wide range of views with regard to the moral and physical state of human beings. Anyone, pessimist or optimist, who does not *sometimes* find the world a burden and the kind of release I am talking about something devoutly to be wished, is hard for me to imagine as a human being "completely formed." In any case, I don't think there could be too many such Pollyannas. I hope not, anyway; and this account of absolute music is not written for them. For them liberation is no value at all.

§17 So far I have been speaking in rather vague terms about the experience of liberation from this veil of tears that only absolute music, among the fine arts, can provide. And before I close I think it incumbent on me to say something more about what exactly this experience is like. To inaugurate the discussion let me return briefly to Schopenhauer.

In the quotation from *The World as Will and Idea* that I introduced earlier, there is an attempt to characterize the experience of freedom that, on Schopenhaur's view, all of the fine arts are supposed to convey and that, on my view, only absolute music among them can. Let me extract that characterization for examination, somewhat contrary to Schopenhauer's intentions, as a possible description of that experience of liberation that, as I am insisting, only absolute music, among the fine arts, is capable of providing.

Here, you will recall, is what Schopenhauer says: "Then all at once the peace, always sought but always escaping us on that first path of willing, comes to us of its own accord, and all is well with us. It is the painless state prized by Epicurus as the highest good and as the state of the gods; for that moment we are delivered from the miserable pressure of the will."

Few of us, I think, will be at all attracted by Epicurus's vision of the good life as being constituted wholly by the absence of pain, all else being sacrificed to that pallid, bloodless state. Most of us, I am sure, want the passion as well as the prose and are willing to pay the price of an acceptable level of pain.

Furthermore, as a characterization of the experience of musical liberation, Schopenhauer's Epicurean metaphor will strike any lover of the art of music as hopelessly inadequate in capturing either the quality or the intensity of it. Schopenhauer is ascribing to the experience a negative quality, an absence of something, whereas what we are experiencing, most of us would say, is a positive quality, the presence of something. But, you are bound to ask, how can liberation *from* something impart a *positive* quality to our experience? Is not the experience of liberation from, by very definition, the experience of an absence, a lack, a negativity?

Let me try to answer this question, and in the negative, by turning for assistance from Schopenhauer to another great philosopher, the Socrates of Plato's *Phaedo*. Socrates is discovered to us in that dialogue on the last day of his life, just having been released from his leg irons, upon awakening. I will let Plato set the scene:

> ... Socrates sat up on his couch and bent his leg and rubbed it with his hand, and while he was rubbing it he said, "What a strange thing, my friends, that seems to be which men call pleasure! How wonderfully it is related to that which seems to be its opposite, pain, in that they will not both come to a man at the same time, and yet if he pursues the one and captures it, he is generally obliged to take the other also, as if the two were joined together in one head. . . . Just so it seems that in my case, after the pain was in my leg on account of the fetter, pleasure appears to have come following after."[25]

One of the things Socrates is urging here, and the thing I want to call attention to, is that, in being released from pain, he is experiencing pleasure; or to put it more precisely, experiencing the cessation of pain is, ipso facto, to experience a positive pleasure: the cessation of pain just *is* a pleasure. My own experience, for what it is worth, has been the same, at least where severe pain is concerned. When I have been in severe pain and been released from it, the experience has seemed to me a pleasurable one: not merely the negative absence of pain, but the positive presence, therein, of pleasure – and, I should say, one of the most intense pleasures of which I am capable. Socrates' observation on this regard, I think, is dead right.

But now we can compare what Schopenhauer is talking about

with what Socrates is talking about to some useful purpose. Briefly put, Schopenhauer is describing, in his Epicurean figure, the *absence* of pain, a negative quality of *indifference,* and Socrates is describing the *cessation* of pain, a positive quality of *pleasure.* "Liberation" from pain is a description applicable to both conditions, signifying in the former case the *state* of being free of pain, in the latter the *process* of being freed from pain. I want to suggest that it is the latter, the process of being freed from pain, wherein the liberating power of absolute music lies, thus conforming to our experience of this liberation as involving a positive quality of pleasure rather than a negative quality merely of the absence of pain. But I must amplify this somewhat.

§18   There is, it appears to me, a very important difference between the absence of pain and the cessation of pain experientially. I can best bring this out with examples. Suppose someone has gone for a considerable period of time without having been in any real pain. She awakens one morning during this protracted period, as she has many times before, totally free of pain. As likely as not, she will not be aware that she is free of pain. Why should she be? It is just what the course of her life has been, fortunately for her, during this period. Her freedom from pain is the background against which her life has been played. What she *would* notice would be a change. If she were to awaken one morning with severe back pain, she would notice that.

Compare this case with that of someone suffering from a severe toothache. He is in agony. But his dentist anticipated this eventuality and prescribed a powerful narcotic just in case. Our toothache sufferer pops one of these pills, and in a few minutes his agony rapidly begins to subside. That experience, of the cessation of pain, is as deliciously pleasurable as the pain was excrutiatingly the opposite.

What seems to emerge from these two examples is that the positive pleasure of the cessation of pain, as opposed to the quiescent, negative state of the absence of pain, requires that the subject be conscious of and attending to the process of cessation or at least attending to the absence of pain with the memory of its former presence still vividly held before the mind. For when the memory fades and the attention falls away, the subject then lapses into the quiescent state of the mere absence of pain. That at any rate is how these matters appear to me.

But if this is right, then my position with regard to how pleasure accrues to music's power to liberate cannot be right unless, in listening to music, we *are* aware of this liberation, as the sufferer from a toothache is aware of the cessation of pain in experiencing the positive pleasure it brings. Is it plausible to think that this is so: that part of the experience of absolute music, at least some of the time, is the conscious, closely attended to realization that one is both involved in thought on the world of musical sound while, at the same time, liberated from the burden of thought on the world in which one lives, strives, and all too often suffers? Let me suggest to you, in concluding, that this is not an implausible conjecture.

No experience of absolute music can be, needless to say, a perfect one. But what is a perfect one? What is the ideal case? I used to think that it would be the case of total absorption, exemplified perhaps, if the story is true, by the eight-year-old Donald Francis Tovey becoming engrossed in the reading of a musical score – a string quartet, I think it was – and being discovered applauding when he had finished. His explanation of this odd behavior – the applauding, that is – was that his concentration had been such as to make him completely oblivious to anything but the music in his head, which came to seem to him an actually present performance and which, in this abstracted state, he instinctively reacted to by clapping (an intriguing instance of self-congratulation, as the "performance" was his own).

But whatever the value of such a trancelike state of musical concentration might have for the professional musician, it is not, I now tend to think, partly because of the points I am making now, the ideal case of musical concentration when the object of such concentration is the appreciation of absolute music as it should be for a musical audience. For when the awareness of the world from which the world of musical sound liberates you is completely lost, then the positive pleasure that that liberation can bring is lost to you too. And although that sense and plea-

sure of musical liberation is not the whole of what we value in
absolute music, it is certainly not the least of what we value
either, and it has a kind of overarching effect on all else that we
do value in the experience.

The view I have been presenting is, as I characterized it earlier, "enhanced formalism." It can also be described, and frequently is, in a derogatory way, these days, as the doctrine of
"musical autonomy." Its defenders are becoming few, and embattled, particularly in musicological circles. And in urging it on
you, I cannot do better than to quote one of its few remaining
defenders in the historians' camp, someone on whose side, in
musical matters, I am always happy to find myself. Thus Leo
Treitler writes in a recent article:

> Belief in the absolute autonomy of music and in the perma-
> nently closed-off character of the experience of music has
> given us some bad history, indeed, but that is not sufficient
> cause to abandon the belief that a provisional personal en-
> gagement with a musical utterance for the moment unrelated
> to anything else is not only a possible but a necessary condi-
> tion of eventual understanding of it in its most dense connec-
> tions.[26]

Surely no one can accuse Leo Treitler of being oblivious to the
social and historical context in which Western art music has
been made since its very beginnings. That he should also, even
with misgivings, be a defender of musical autonomy is all the
more to be taken seriously.

But as I described my musical formalism as "enhanced formalism," perhaps it might be appropriate for me to describe my
version of the autonomy of absolute music as "enhanced autonomy." And this for the following reason. If musical autonomy,
sans phrase, is the doctrine that takes Tovey's experience of the
string quartet as its ideal case, that is not my musical autonomy.
For me the experience of absolute music is not, to appropriate
Treitler's phrase, "permanently closed-off" from the world of
the world. At the risk of sounding paradoxical, I am suggesting
that absolute music is always connected to the world by its very
disconnection from it. And in that sense, enhanced by the con-

nection of its disconnection, my musical autonomy is "enhanced autonomy." For it is the autonomy that says that the genius of absolute music is to make you think of aught but itself and, in so doing, of its (and your) liberation from the world. This is not its tragedy. It is its difference, and its triumph.

Epilogue

This book has no thesis. It does have a theme. It may seem that this book has a thesis. One could easily read me as aligning myself with those, notably Wittgensteinians, who have argued that there is no common, definitional thread tying what we now call the "fine arts" together into a system. For in my first two, historical chapters, I tried to trace, to the present moment, the failed attempts to produce such a thread (or threads) in the form of a "definition" of "art." And I followed that historical exercise with five "case studies" purporting to show ways in which choosing the "wrong model" has led to binding pairs of arts together in ways alien to one of them.

But it would be a mistake, as I pointed out early on and want to reemphasize now, to read this book as arguing that the quest for a definition of art is unfruitful or impossible. What I am arguing for is that at least some of us in what is called "the philosophy of art" pursue another project: looking for differences among the arts rather than accidently finding them in flawed definitions. Indeed, the case can be made that in looking for differences, the search for sameness is forwarded rather than thwarted, under the assumption that a theory put under stress is, if it survives, a stronger theory than one that is never tested at all.

So I say that my book has a theme rather than a thesis. Its theme is the pursuit of differences among the arts. It is not a rival project to that of defining art but part of the same enterprise: the philosophical understanding of the fine arts in all of their particularity, as well as their commonality.

Where do we go from here? Where I would like to go, and in

the company of others rather than alone, is on to further studies of artistic differences. Where *all* others should go I cannot say. But I think that the pursuit of differences, if it should become the monolith that the pursuit of sameness has been since the Enlightenment, would have as evil an effect on the philosophy of art.

I think the Enlightenment, surprisingly, was more sensitive to differences than was either German Romanticism or twentieth-century analytic philosophy. And I would like here, as elsewhere, to renew the Enlightenment spirit. If, in this book, I have seemed to be extreme in my quest for differences and rejection of sameness, I have aimed at the extreme only to regain the mean. In that spirit, the spirit of the Enlightenment, my epigraph will serve not only as my beginning but as my end: "Now from hence may be seen, how these Arts *agree,* and how they *differ.*"

Notes

1. How We Got Here, and Why

1. Paul Oskar Kristeller, "The Modern System of the Arts," reprinted in *Essays on the History of Aesthetics,* ed. Peter Kivy (Rochester, N.Y.: University of Rochester Press, 1992).
2. See Jerome Stolnitz, "On the Origins of Aesthetic Disinterestedness," *Journal of Aesthetics and Art Criticism* 20 (1961): 131–44.
3. Plato, *Ion,* trans. W. R. M. Lamb (Cambridge, Mass.: Harvard University Press; London: William Heinemann, The Loeb Classical Library, 1962), pp. 417 (532E) and 421 (583E).
4. See Ann E. Moyer, *Musica Sacra: Musical Scholarship in the Italian Renaissance* (Ithaca, N.Y.: Cornell University Press, 1992).
5. See Umberto Eco, *Art and Beauty in the Middle Ages,* trans. Hugh Bredin (New Haven, Conn.: Yale University Press, 1986), chap. 1 and passim.
6. See David Summers, *The Judgment of Taste: Renaissance Naturalism and the Rise of Aesthetics* (Cambridge University Press, 1987).
7. Kristeller, "The Modern System of the Arts," p. 38.
8. Ibid., p. 4.
9. On the latter see Rudolf Wittkower, *Architectural Principles in the Age of Humanism* (London: Alec Tiranti, 1962). On the former, at least as in regard to classical Greek architecture, see the strange but stimulating book by Indra Kagis McEwin, *Socrates' Ancestor: An Essay on Architectural Beginnings* (Cambridge, Mass.: MIT Press, 1993).
10. It is much to be regretted that philosophers of art, in general, know little about the "philosophy of architecture" in the eighteenth century. I am certainly no exception, and so offer my estimate of the role of architecture in the early fine arts discussion with caution and only very tentative conviction.

11. Noel Carroll, "Historical Narrations and the Philosophy of Art," *Journal of Aesthetics and Art Criticism* 51 (1993): 314.
12. See Peter Kivy, "Is Music an Art?" in *The Fine Art of Repetition: Essays in the Philosophy of Music* (Cambridge University Press, 1993), pp. 360–73.
13. Ibid.
14. Pietro de' Bardi, Letter to G. B. Doni, in *Source Readings in Music History*, ed. Oliver Strunk (New York: Norton, 1950), p. 364.
15. Giulio Caccini, Foreword to *Le nuove musiche*, in *Source Readings in Music History*, ed. Strunk, p. 378.
16. Thomas Reid, *Essays on the Intellectual Powers of Man*, in *The Works of Thomas Reid*, ed. Sir William Hamilton (8th ed.; Edinburgh: James Thin, 1895), vol. 1, p. 504.
17. Ibid.
18. Francis Hutcheson, *Inquiry Concerning Beauty, Order, Harmony, Design*, ed. Peter Kivy (The Hague: Martinus Nijhoff, 1973), p. 81 (sec. 6).
19. Ibid., p. 46 (sec. 2).
20. Reid, *Essays on the Intellectual Powers*, p. 504.
21. Ibid.
22. Ibid.
23. This is not to say that Reid lacked influence in the nineteenth century. He seems to have influenced the French aestheticians, as James Manns has revealed in "The Scottish Influence on French Aesthetic Thought," reprinted in *Essays on the History of Aesthetics*, ed. Kivy, pp. 285–303. And his was, as is well known, the "textbook" philosophy of nineteenth-century American undergraduates. But he was not in the mainstream after his own time.
24. Immanuel Kant, *Anthropology from a Pragmatic Point of View*, trans. Mary J. Gregory (The Hague: Martinus Nijhoff, 1974), p. 114.
25. Immanuel Kant, *Critique of Judgement*, trans. J. H. Bernard (New York: Hafner, 1961), p. 60.
26. Immanuel Kant, *Critique of Aesthetic Judgement*, trans. James Creed Meredith (Oxford: Clarendon Press, 1911), p. 66.
27. Immanuel Kant, *Critique of Judgment*, trans. Werner S. Pluhar (Indianapolis: Hackett, 1987), p. 70.
28. See Pluhar's footnote to this passage, ibid., p. 70n, and Theodore E. Uehling, Jr., *The Notion of Form in Kant's "Critique of Aesthetic Judgment"* (The Hague: Mouton, 1971), pp. 22–6.
29. Uehling, *The Notion of Form*, pp. 24–5.
30. Kant, *Critique of Aesthetic Judgement*, trans. Meredith, p. 190.

31. Uehling, *The Notion of Form*, p. 25.
32. For a more thorough exposition of this point, see Peter Kivy, "Kant and the *Affektenlehre:* What He Said and What I Wish He Had Said," in *The Fine Art of Repetition*, pp. 250–64.
33. Kant, *Critique of Aesthetic Judgement*, trans. Meredith, p. 194.
34. Ibid., p. 199.
35. Ibid. Kant's thought here is expressed as follows: "In jest (which just as much as the former [i.e. music] deserves to be ranked rather as an agreeable than a fine art) the play sets out from thoughts which collectively, so far as seeking sensuous expression, engage the activity of the body."
36. Arthur Schopenhauer, *The World as Will and Representation*, trans. E. F. J. Payne (Indian Hills, Colo.: Falcon's Wing Press, 1958), vol. 1, p. 233 (book 3, §49).
37. Ibid., p. 257 (book 3, §52).
38. Ibid., pp. 261–2 (book 3, §52).
39. The first volume of Schopenhauer's *World as Will and Representation*, from which I have been quoting, was published in 1818. Hegel's *Lectures on the Fine Arts* was first published by G. H. Hotho in 1835. This book represents a compilation of Hegel's lecture notes and manuscripts of 1823, 1826, and 1828–9.
40. G. W. F. Hegel, *Aesthetics: Lectures on the Fine Arts*, trans. T. M. Knox (Oxford: Clarendon Press, 1975), vol. 2, pp. 901–2.
41. Ibid., p. 899.
42. Ibid., p. 899n.
43. For the German text, see G. W. F. Hegel, *Werke in zwanzig Bänden*, vol. 15, *Vorlesung über die Aesthetik, Dritter Teil* (Frankfurt am Main: Suhnkamp, 1970), p. 145.
44. Hegel, *Lectures on the Fine Arts*, vol. 2, p. 923.
45. Ibid., p. 960.
46. Hegel, *Werke*, vol. 15, pp. 223–4.
47. Hegel, *Lectures on the Fine Arts*, vol. 2, p. 892n.
48. Roger Fry, "An Essay in Aesthetics," in *Vision and Design* (New York: Meridian Books, 1960), p. 17.
49. Clive Bell, *Art* (New York: Capricorn Books, 1958), part 1, chap. 1, "The Aesthetic Hypothesis."
50. Ibid., p. 30.
51. On this see Peter Kivy, *Music Alone: Philosophical Reflections on the Purely Musical Experience* (Ithaca, N.Y.: Cornell University Press, 1990), chap. 1.
52. Bell, *Art*, p. 27.

53. Ibid., p. 30.
54. Fry called his view an expression theory and acknowledged Tolstoy as an influence. Bell too spoke, with as close to purple prose as he could get, of the "aesthetic emotion." But the emotion was, of course, defined in terms of the form that evoked it, leading, in Bell, to a notorious vicious circle in which the aesthetic emotion is distinguished from other emotions by the fact that it is caused by significant form, and significant form is distinguished from other forms by the fact that it is the form that arouses the aesthetic emotion. This is all quite well known. In any event, formalism it was, "aesthetic emotion" to the contrary notwithstanding.
55. Roger Fry, "Some Questions in Aesthetics," in *Transformations* (Garden City, N.Y.: Doubleday Anchor Books, 1956), p. 10.
56. Ibid., p. 11.
57. Bell, *Art*, p. 28.
58. Clive Bell, *Old Friends* (London: Cassell, 1988), p. 76.
59. Eduard Hanslick, *On the Musically Beautiful: A Contribution towards the Revision of the Aesthetics of Music*, trans. Geoffrey Payzant (Indianapolis: Hackett, 1986), pp. 28–9.
60. Edmund Gurney, *The Power of Sound* (London: Smith, Elder, 1980), pp. 164–5.

2. Where We Are

1. The phrase is Paul Ziff's, coined in "The Task of Defining a Work of Art," *Philosophical Review* 62 (1953): 58–78.
2. Bell, *Art*, p. 17.
3. De Witt H. Parker, "The Nature of Art," reprinted in Eliseo Vivas and Murray Krieger, *The Problems of Aesthetics: A Book of Readings* (New York: Holt, Rinehart & Winston, 1960), p. 90.
4. Ibid., p. 91. I have not quoted the passage stating the second of Parker's grounds for rejecting the search for a common property because it is not relevant here.
5. Actually, there is a far more impressive and prophetic anticipation of Wittgensteinian aesthetics in the essay "Of Beauty" (1810) by the Scottish philosopher Dugald Stewart. Stewart proposes there, not for "art" but for "beauty," a cluster analysis that has all the logical structure of Wittgenstein's "family resemblance" concept. I am not the first to notice this. See Dugald Stewart, *Works*, vol. 4, *Philosophical Essays* (Cambridge: Hilliard & Brown, 1829), part 2, essay first. See also Peter Kivy, *The Seventh Sense: A Study of Francis*

Hutcheson's Aesthetics and Its Place in Eighteenth-Century Britain (New York: Burt Franklin, 1976), pp. 203–6 and 258n.

6. Morris Weitz, "The Role of Theory in Aesthetics," reprinted in *Philosophy Looks at the Arts*, ed. Joseph Margolis (3d ed.; Philadelphia: Temple University Press, 1987), p. 146.
7. Ibid., p. 148.
8. Ibid.
9. Ibid., p. 149.
10. Ibid.
11. Ibid., p. 150.
12. Ibid., p. 149.
13. Morris Weitz, selections from *The Opening Mind*, in *Aesthetics: A Critical Anthology*, ed. George Dickie, Richard Sclafani, and Ronald Roblin (2d ed.; New York: St. Martin's Press, 1989), p. 158.
14. Arthur Danto, "The Artworld," in *Philosophy Looks at the Arts*, ed. Margolis, p. 162.
15. Arthur Danto, *The Transfiguration of the Commonplace: A Philosophy of Art* (Cambridge, Mass.: Harvard University Press, 1981), p. 82.
16. Ibid., pp. 147–8.
17. Ibid., p. 148.
18. Ibid., p. 152.
19. There is at least a hint in Danto's *Transfiguration of the Commonplace* (p. 152) that he might endorse some version of "emotive aboutness" for music, at least as I read him.
20. Jerrold Levinson, "Truth in Music," in *Music, Art and Metaphysics: Essays in Philosophical Aesthetics* (Ithaca, N.Y.: Cornell University Press, 1990), p. 280.
21. Ibid., p. 288.
22. I am not suggesting that it was Levinson's intention here to defend Danto, who as a matter of fact is not mentioned in Levinson's essay.
23. Kendall Walton, "Listening with Imagination: Is Music Representational?" *Journal of Aesthetics and Art Criticism* 52 (1994): 47–61. Some of the points I make here about Walton were made independently by Stephen Davies, "General Theories of Art versus Music," *British Journal of Aesthetics* 34 (1994): 315–25.
24. Walton's general theory is to be found in his *Mimesis as Make Believe: On the Foundations of the Representational Arts* (Cambridge, Mass.: Harvard University Press, 1990).
25. Walton, "Listening with Imagination," p. 51.
26. Ibid.
27. Ibid., p. 52.

28. Ibid.
29. Francis Bacon, *The Advancement of Learning* (1605), in *Critical Essays of the Seventeenth Century*, ed. J. E. Spingarn (Oxford: Oxford University Press, 1957), vol. 1, p. 5.
30. This point is made quite effectively in an article by Thomas Miller with direct reference to Kant. See his "On Listening to Music," *Journal of Aesthetics and Art Criticism* 52 (1994): 215–23. But the general idea is not new and was given a gestalt-psychological account in, for example, Victor Zuckerkandl, *Sound and Symbol: Music and the External World*, trans. Willard R. Trask (New York: Pantheon Books, 1956), and in other of his works.
31. Roger Scruton, "Representation in Music," reprinted in Scruton, *The Aesthetic Understanding* (London: Methuen, 1983), pp. 62–76.
32. Richard Kuhns, "Music as a Representational Art," *British Journal of Aesthetics* 18 (1978): 122.
33. The great complexity of this problem is pursued relentlessly by Paul Grice in his work on meaning. See his *Studies in the Way of Words* (Cambridge, Mass.: Harvard University Press, 1989).

3. Reading and Representation

1. Edmund Burke, *A Philosophical Enquiry into the Origin of Our Ideas of the Sublime and Beautiful*, ed. Adam Phillips (Oxford: Oxford University Press, 1990), p. 157.
2. Plato, *The Republic*, trans. John Llewelyn Davies and David James Vaughan (London: Macmillan Press, 1950), p. 340 (598–9).
3. Ibid., p. 90 (397).
4. Ibid., p. 87 (394).
5. Aristotle, *Poetics*, trans. Richard Janko (Indianapolis: Hackett, 1987), p. 10 (1450b).
6. Paul Thom, *For an Audience: A Philosophy of Performance* (Philadelphia: Temple University Press, 1993), p. 27.
7. Aristotle, *Poetics*, trans. Janko, p. 7 (1449b).
8. Plato, *Republic*, p. 340. "And now, I continued, we must proceed to consider the case of tragedy and its leader, Homer" (598).
9. Aristotle, *Poetics*, trans. Janko, p. 41 (1462b).
10. Aristotle, *The Poetics*, trans. W. Hamilton Fyfe (Cambridge, Mass.: Harvard University Press; London: William Heinemann, The Loeb Classical Library, 1953), p. 115 (1462b); emphasis mine.
11. My colleague Tim Maudlin tells me that he seems to recall the first

reference to silent reading to be in St. Augustine. How widespread
it was then, among those who could read at all, I do not know.

12. William Faulkner, *The Hamlet: A Novel of the Snopes Family* (New
York: Vintage Books, 1956), p. 95. Having just listed Faulkner as a
major exception to the narrative scheme I am dealing with here, I
suppose it is necessary to explain why my first example is from
Faulkner. The reason is, simply, that many of Faulkner's novels
exhibit that scheme. *The Hamlet* does, even though the narrative is
peculiarly in Faulkner's style, and more jagged and broken than
the typical cases of other authors.

13. R. M. J. Damman, "Emotion in Fiction," *British Journal of Aesthetics*
32 (1992): 19.

14. To keep the record straight, Eula is not a Snopes, but later becomes
one by marriage.

15. Joseph Conrad, *The Secret Agent* (Garden City, N.Y.: Doubleday
Anchor Books, 1953), pp. 18 and 19.

16. To say that secco recitative has no musical interest in itself is not
to say that it has no musical *function*. On this see, Peter Kivy, *Osmin's Rage: Philosophical Reflections on Opera, Drama and Text* (Princeton, N.J.: Princeton University Press, 1988), pp. 153–61.

17. Edward J. Dent, *Opera* (Harmondsworth: Penguin Books, 1949), p.
40.

18. George Eliot, *The Sad Fortunes of the Rev. Amos Barton: Scenes of
Clerical Life* (Harmondsworth: Penguin Books, 1973), pp. 53–4.

19. Ibid., p. 54.

20. Charles Dickens, *Bleak House*, ed. Geoffrey Tillotson (New York:
Signet Classic, 1980), p. 883.

4. On the Unity of Form and Content

1. A. C. Bradley, "Poetry for Poetry's Sake," in *The Problems of Aesthetics*, ed. Vivas and Krieger, p. 575.

2. Ibid., p. 569. Unfortunately, Bradley is not entirely consistent. In
the very last sentence of the note that he appended to the lecture
some years after it had been written, he says: "Poetry, whatever its
kind, would be pure as far as it preserved the unity of form and
content; mixed, so far as it failed to do so – in other words, failed
to be poetry and was partly *prosaic*" (ibid., p. 577; my emphasis).
This is a disasterous statement and I cannot but think that it was
a hasty afterthought rather than a well-considered pronouncement.
For if it is combined with Bradley's statements in regard to poetry,

painting, and music, it suggests that he thought poetry, painting, and music are arts, by virtue of exhibiting form–content identity, and no kind of prose whatever could be art, since the implication of the above quotation is that where poetry loses form–content unity, it becomes prose. In other words, prose does not possess, in any form, the necessary condition for being art, namely, form–content identity, since poetry, when it loses that, becomes "prosaic." This is an intolerable conclusion, and I can't believe Bradley could have subscribed to it. (Did he not think the great novels of the nineteenth century were art?)

3. Ibid., p. 573.
4. Lucretius, *De rerum natura*, trans. W. H. D. Rouse and M. F. Smith (Cambridge, Mass.: Harvard University Press; London: William Heinemann, The Loeb Classical Library, 1975), revised by Martin Ferguson Smith, pp. 78–9 (book 1, lines 936–50). Lucretius repeats these lines, almost verbatim, in book 4, lines 1–25.
5. See the *Essay on Criticism.*
6. Kant, *Critique of Judgment,* trans. Pluhar, p. 182.
7. Ibid.
8. Ibid., pp. 181–2.
9. Ibid., pp. 185–8.
10. Ibid., p. 181.
11. Ibid., p. 182.
12. Ibid., p. 184.
13. Ibid., p. 62.
14. Ibid., p. 185.
15. Ibid., p. 196.
16. Unintended, that is to say, under the assumption that Kant was no formalist with regard to art – an assumption I make and that others share.
17. Hanslick, *On the Musically Beautiful,* p. 29.
18. Bradley, "Poetry for Poetry's Sake," p. 572.
19. Walter Pater, "The School of Giorgione," in *The Renaissance: Studies in Art and Poetry,* ed. Donald L. Hill (Berkeley: University of California Press, 1980), p. 106.
20. Ibid., pp. 109, 111, 117, 118. Pater also talks of the various arts as, in individual cases, aspiring toward one another, and Hegel sometimes talks this way too. On the possible Hegelian sources, see the editor's note to "The School of Giorgione" (p. 389). But as the editor remarks, "This famous phrase is not a translation of Hegel, and Hegel never quite makes Pater's point."

21. Ibid., p. 102.
22. Ibid., p. 106.
23. Ibid., p. 109.
24. Bradley, "Poetry for Poetry's Sake," p. 564.
25. Ibid.
26. Ibid., p. 568.
27. Ibid.
28. Ibid., p. 569.
29. Ibid., p. 572.
30. Ibid., p. 565.
31. Ibid., p. 567.
32. Ibid., p. 572.
33. Ibid., p. 576.
34. Ibid., p. 575.
35. Ibid., p. 572.
36. Ibid., p. 574.
37. Ibid., p. 572.
38. Ibid., p. 571.
39. Ibid., p. 575.
40. Ibid., p. 571.
41. Ibid., p. 562; my emphasis.
42. Ibid.
43. Donald Francis Tovey, "A Listener's Guide to *Die Kunst der Fuge*," in *Essays in Musical Analysis: Chamber Music,* ed. Hubert J. Foss (Oxford: Oxford University Press, 1944), p. 76.
44. Bradley, "Poetry for Poetry's Sake," p. 575.
45. Ibid., p. 569.
46. Ibid., p. 667.
47. See note 17.
48. See note 44.
49. Bradley, "Poetry for Poetry's Sake," p. 566.
50. Danto, *The Transfiguration of the Commonplace*, pp. 147–8.

5. The Laboratory of Fictional Truth

1. Peter Lamarque and Stein Haugom Olsen, *Truth, Fiction, and Literature: A Philosophical Perspective* (Oxford: Clarendon Press, 1994), p. 321.
2. Ibid., p. 324.
3. Ibid.
4. Ibid., p. 325.

5. Ibid., p. 334.
6. Ibid., p. 332.
7. Ibid., p. 333.
8. Ibid., p. 332.
9. William James, "The Will to Believe," in *Essays in Pragmatism*, ed. Alburey Castell (New York: Hafner, 1951), p. 89.
10. Ibid.
11. Lamarque and Olsen, *Truth, Fiction, and Literature*, p. 331.
12. Ibid., p. 336.
13. Anyone who thinks I am setting up a straw man here need only consult any number of recent "interpretations" of the canon of absolute music to discover that my made-up interpretation of Beethoven's Fifth is subdued in comparison.
14. Lamarque and Olsen, *Truth, Fiction, and Literature*, p. 450.
15. Ibid., p. 454.
16. Ibid., p. 455.

6. The Quest for Musical Profundity

1. David A. White, "Toward a Theory of Profundity in Music," *Journal of Aesthetics and Art Criticism* 50 (1992): 23. I will have nothing further to say about Professor White's article because, alas, repeated readings of it have failed to reveal to me an intelligible position with which to grapple. Perhaps that is his fault, perhaps it is mine.
2. Aaron Ridley, "Profundity in Music," in *Arguing about Art: Contemporary Philosophical Debates*, ed. Alex Neil and Aaron Ridley (New York: McGraw-Hill, 1995), pp. 260–1.
3. Ibid, p. 261.
4. Ibid.
5. Of course, my book might be ostensibly about bottle caps but really about something profound. And if my book were adequate to that hidden subject matter, then it could be profound.
6. Ridley, "Profundity in Music," p. 263.
7. Ibid.
8. Ibid., p. 264.
9. Ibid.
10. Ibid.
11. Ibid., p. 265.
12. Ibid.
13. Ibid., p. 266.

14. Ibid., pp. 266–7.
15. Ibid., p. 267.
16. Kivy, *Music Alone,* pp. 203 and 214.
17. Ridley, "Profundity of Music," p. 268.
18. Ibid.
19. Ibid.
20. Ibid., p. 269.
21. Ibid.
22. Jerrold Levinson, "Musical Profundity Misplaced," *Journal of Aesthetics and Art Criticism* 50 (1992): 58.
23. Ibid.
24. Ibid., p. 59.
25. Ibid.
26. Jerrold Levinson, "Truth in Music," in *Music, Art and Metaphysics,* ed. Levinson, p. 298.
27. Monroe C. Beardsley, "Understanding Music," in *On Criticizing Music: Five Philosophical Perspectives,* ed. Kingsley Price (Baltimore: Johns Hopkins University Press, 1981), p. 67.
28. Ibid., p. 70.
29. Levinson, "Truth in Music," p. 303.
30. Ibid., p. 301.

7. The Liberation of Music

1. Schopenhauer, *The World as Will and Representation,* vol. 1, p. 256.
2. Ibid.
3. Hans Heinrich Eggebrecht, *J. S. Bach's "The Art of Fugue": The Work and Its Interpretation,* trans. Jeffrey L. Prater (Ames: Iowa State University Press, 1993), pp. xvii–xviii.
4. Ibid.
5. Ibid., p. 6.
7. Ibid.
8. Example from ibid., p. 7.
9. Ibid., p. 8.
10. Ibid.
11. Ibid., p. 30.
12. Ibid., p. 43.
13. Ibid.
14. Rudolph Reti, *The Thematic Process in Music* (London: Faber & Faber, 1961).
15. For my critique of Reti, see *Music Alone,* chap. 7.

16. Eggebrecht, *"Art of Fugue,"* p. 22.
17. Ibid.
18. Ibid., p. 23.
19. David P. Schroeder, *Haydn and the Enlightenment: The Late Symphonies and Their Audience* (Oxford: Clarendon Press, 1990), p. 163. "Toleration" would have been the more usual word in the eighteenth century, but "tolerance" had been used for the same concept as early as the sixteenth century.
20. Ibid., p. 88.
21. Schopenhauer, *The World as Will, and Representation*, vol. 1, p. 196.
22. See, in particular, Peter Kivy, "The Fine Art of Repetition," in *The Fine Art of Repetition*, pp. 327–59.
23. On this see my *Music Alone*, passim, but especially chap. 6.
24. James Hilton, *We Are Not Alone* (Boston: Little, Brown, 1937), p. 158.
25. Plato, *Euthyphro, Apology, Crito, Phaedo, Phaedrus*, trans. H. N. Fowler (Cambridge, Mass., Harvard University Press; London: William Heinemann, The Loeb Classical Library, 1966), pp. 209–11.
26. Leo Treitler, "Postmodern Signs in Musical Studies," *Journal of Musicology*, 13 (1995): 12.

Bibliography

Aristotle. *The Poetics.* Translated by W. Hamilton Fyfe. Cambridge, Mass.: Harvard University Press; London: William Heinemann, The Loeb Classical Library, 1953.

Poetics. Translated by Richard Janko. Indianapolis: Hackett, 1987.

Bell, Clive. *Art.* New York: Capricorn Books, 1958.

Old Friends. London: Cassell, 1988.

Burke, Edmund. *A Philosophical Enquiry into the Origin of Our Ideas of the Sublime and Beautiful.* Edited by Adam Phillips. Oxford: Oxford University Press, 1990.

Carroll, Noel. "Historical Narrations and the Philosophy of Art." *Journal of Aesthetics and Art Criticism* 51 (1993): 313–26.

Conrad, Joseph. *The Secret Agent.* Garden City, N.Y.: Doubleday Anchor Books, 1953.

Damman, R. M. J. "Emotion in Fiction." *British Journal of Aesthetics* 32 (1992): 13–20.

Danto, Arthur. *The Transfiguration of the Commonplace: A Philosophy of Art.* Cambridge, Mass.: Harvard University Press, 1981.

Davies, Stephen. "General Theories of Art versus Music." *British Journal of Aesthetics* 34 (1994): 315–25.

Dent, Edward. *Opera.* Harmondsworth: Penguin Books, 1949.

Dickens, Charles. *Bleak House.* Edited by Geoffrey Tillotson. New York: Signet Classic, 1980.

Dickie, George, Richard Sclafani, and Ronald Roblin, eds. *Aesthetics: A Critical Anthology.* 2d ed. New York: St. Martin's Press, 1989.

Eco, Umberto. *Art and Beauty in the Middle Ages.* Translated by Hugh Bredin. New Haven, Conn.: Yale University Press, 1986.

Eggebrecht, Hans Heinrich. *J. S. Bach's "The Art of Fugue": The Work and Its Interpretation.* Translated by Jeffrey L. Prater. Ames: Iowa State University Press, 1993.

Bibliography

Eliot, George. *The Sad Fortunes of the Rev. Amos Barton: Scenes from Clerical Life*. Harmondsworth: Penguin Books, 1973.

Faulkner, William. *The Hamlet: A Novel of the Snopes Family*. New York: Vintage Books, 1956.

Fry, Roger. *Transformations*. Garden City, N.Y.: Doubleday Anchor Books, 1956.

Vision and Design. New York: Meridian Books, 1960.

Grice, Paul. *Studies in the Way of Words*. Cambridge, Mass.: Harvard University Press, 1989.

Gurney, Edmund. *The Power of Sound*. London: Smith, Elder, 1980.

Hanslick, Eduard. *On the Musically Beautiful: A Contribution towards the Revision of the Aesthetics of Music*. Translated by Geoffrey Payzant. Indianapolis: Hackett, 1980.

Hegel, G. W. F. *Aesthetics: Lectures on the Fine Arts*. Translated by T. M. Knox. 2 vols. Oxford: Clarendon Press, 1975.

Werke in Zwanzig Bänden. 20 vols. Frankfurt am Main: Suhnkamp, 1970.

Hilton, James. *We Are Not Alone*. Boston: Little, Brown, 1937.

Hutcheson, Francis. *Inquiry Concerning Beauty, Order, Harmony, Design*. Edited by Peter Kivy. The Hague: Martinus Nijhoff, 1973.

James, William. *Essays in Pragmatism*. Edited by Alburey Castell. New York: Hafner, 1951.

Kant, Immanuel. *Anthropology from a Pragmatic Point of View*. Translated by Mary J. Gregory. The Hague: Martinus Nijhoff, 1974.

Critique of Aesthetic Judgement. Translated by James Creed Meredith. Oxford: Clarendon Press, 1911.

Critique of Judgement. Translated by J. H. Bernard. New York: Hafner, 1961.

Critique of Judgment. Translated by Werner S. Pluhar. Indianapolis: Hackett, 1987.

Kivy, Peter. *The Fine Art of Repetition: Essays in the Philosophy of Music*. Cambridge University Press, 1993.

Music Alone: Philosophical Reflections on the Purely Musical Experience. Ithaca, N.Y.: Cornell University Press, 1990.

Osmin's Rage: Philosophical Reflections on Opera, Drama and Text. Princeton, N.J.: Princeton University Press, 1988.

The Seventh Sense: A Study of Francis Hutcheson's Aesthetics and Its Place in Eighteenth-Century Britain. New York: Burt Franklin, 1976.

Kivy, Peter, ed. *Essays on the History of Aesthetics*. Rochester, N.Y.: University of Rochester Press, 1992.

Kuhns, Richard. "Music as a Representational Art." *British Journal of Aesthetics* 18 (1978): 120–5.

Lamarque, Peter, and Stein Haugom Olsen. *Truth, Fiction, and Literature: A Philosophical Perspective.* Oxford: Clarendon Press, 1994.

Levinson, Jerrold. *Music, Art and Metaphysics: Essays in Philosophical Aesthetics.* Ithaca, N.Y.: Cornell University Press, 1990.

    "Musical Profundity Misplaced." *Journal of Aesthetics and Art Criticism* 50 (1992): 58–60.

Lucretius. *De rerum natura.* Translated by W. H. D. Rouse and M. F. Smith. Cambridge, Mass.: Harvard University Press; London: William Heinemann, The Loeb Classical Library, 1975.

Margolis, Joseph, ed. *Philosophy Looks at the Arts.* 3d ed. Philadelphia: Temple University Press, 1987.

McEwin, Indra Kagis. *Socrates' Ancestor: An Essay on Architectural Beginnings.* Cambridge, Mass.: MIT Press, 1993.

Miller, Thomas. "On Listening to Music." *Journal of Aesthetics and Art Criticism* 52 (1994): 215–23.

Moyer, Ann E. *Musica Sacra: Musical Scholarship in the Italian Renaissance.* Ithaca, N.Y.: Cornell University Press, 1992.

Neil, Alex, and Aaron, Ridley, eds. *Arguing about Art: Contemporary Philosophical Debates.* New York: McGraw-Hill, 1995.

Pater, Walter. *The Renaissance: Studies in Art and Poetry.* Edited by Donald L. Hill. Berkeley: University of California Press, 1980.

Plato. *Ion.* Translated by W. R. M. Lamb. Cambridge, Mass.: Harvard University Press; London: William Heinemann, The Loeb Classical Library, 1962.

    Enthyphro, Apology, Crito, Phaido, Phaedrus. Translated by H. N. Fowler. Cambridge, Mass.: Harvard University Press; London, William Heinemann, The Loeb Classical Library, 1966.

    The Republic. Translated by John Llewelyn Davies and David James Vaughan. London: Macmillan Press, 1950.

Price, Kingsley, ed. *On Criticizing Music: Five Philosophical Perspectives.* Baltimore: Johns Hopkins University Press, 1981.

Reid, Thomas. *The Works of Thomas Reid.* Edited by Sir William Hamilton. 8th ed. 2 vols. Edinburgh: James Thin, 1895.

Reti, Rudolph. *The Thematic Process in Music.* London: Faber & Faber, 1961.

Schopenhauer, Arthur. *The World as Will and Representation.* Translated by E. F. J. Payne. 2 vols. Indian Hills, Colo.: Falcon's Wing Press, 1958.

Schroeder, David P. *Haydn and the Enlightenment: The Late Symphonies and Their Audience.* Oxford: Clarendon Press, 1990.

Scruton, Roger. *The Aesthetic Understanding.* London: Methuen, 1983.

Spingarn, J. E., ed. *Critical Essays of the Seventeenth Century.* 3 vols. Oxford: Oxford University Press, 1957.

Stewart, Dugald. *Works.* 7 vols. Cambridge: Hilliard & Brown, 1829.

Stolnitz, Jerome. "On the Origins of Aesthetic Disinterestedness." *Journal of Aesthetics and Art Criticism* 20 (1961): 131–44.

Strunk, Oliver, ed. *Source Readings in Music History.* New York: Norton, 1950.

Summers, David. *The Judgment of Taste: Renaissance Naturalism and the Rise of Aesthetics.* Cambridge University Press, 1987.

Thom, Paul. *For an Audience: A Philosophy of Performance.* Philadelphia: Temple University Press, 1993.

Tovey, Donald Francis. *Essays in Musical Analysis: Chamber Music.* Edited by Humbert J. Foss. Oxford: Oxford University Press, 1944.

Treitler, Leo. "Postmodern Signs in Musical Studies." *Journal of Musicology* 13 (1995): 3–17.

Uehling, Theodore E., Jr. *The Notion of Form in Kant's "Critique of Aesthetic Judgment."* The Hague: Mouton, 1971.

Vivas, Eliseo, and Murray Krieger, eds. *The Problems of Aesthetics: A Book of Readings.* New York: Holt, Rinehart, & Winston, 1960.

Walton, Kendall. "Listening with Imagination: Is Music Representational?" *Journal of Aesthetics and Art Criticism* 52 (1994): 47–62.

———. *Mimesis as Make Believe: On the Foundations of the Representational Arts.* Cambridge, Mass.: Harvard University Press, 1990.

White, David A. "Toward a Theory of Musical Profundity." *Journal of Aesthetics and Art Criticism* 50 (1992): 23–34.

Wittkower, Rudolf. *Architectural Principles in the Age of Humanism.* London: Alec Tiranti, 1962.

Ziff, Paul. "The Task of Defining a Work of Art." *Philosophical Review* 62 (1953): 58–78.

Zuckerkandl, Victor. *Sound and Symbol: Music and the External World.* Translated by Willard R. Trask. New York: Pantheon Books, 1956.

Index

aboutness: and art, 39–42; and music, 42–52, 169–75, 224n

absolute music, 6–7, 9–28, 40–52, 64, 86, 113–14, 131, 139–78; and representation, 180–202; and value, 180

Addison, Joseph, 4

Aeschylus, 68–9

aesthetic emotion, 223n

aesthetic ideas, in Kant, 12, 15–16, 91–6

aesthetics, 4–5

"afterlife" of aesthetic experience, 131–4

Alperson, Philip, 205

alpha-numeric symbolism, 190, 192–4

Altnikol, Johann Christoph, 189

analytic philosophy, 219

Anderson, Leroy, 210–11

architecture, 5, 220n

aria, 77–9, 81

Aristotle, 2–3, 5, 38, 42, 68–71, 84, 128, 179, 193, 203, 207, 225n

Augustine, Saint, 226n

Austen, Jane, 60, 128, 133

autonomy of music, 216–17

avant-garde, 5–6, 24, 35

Bach, J. S., 7, 9, 46, 110, 154, 164, 177, 184, 189, 200–2, 206, 210–11

Bacon, Francis, 47, 225n

Bardi, Pietro de', 8, 221n

Batteux, Charles, 4, 7–8

Baumgarten, Alexander, 4

Beardsley, Monroe, 171–5, 230n

Beethoven, Ludwig van, 7, 21–2, 51, 125, 130–2, 134, 152–6, 159–60, 168, 172–3, 175, 177, 183, 206

Bell, Clive, 12, 24–8, 31, 34, 55, 222n, 223n

Bennett, Arnold, 136–7

Berkeley, George, 52

Berlioz, Hector, 167

Bernard, J. H., 13, 221n

Bernstein, Leonard, 201

Bloch, Ernst, 158–9

Bradley, A. C., 84–7, 89, 92, 96–7, 99–100, 102–16, 154, 226n, 227n, 228n

Brahms, Johannes, 43, 46, 165, 177

Bruno, Giordano, 155

Bunyan, John, 26

Burke, Edmund, 55, 82, 225n

Caccini, Giulio, 8, 221n

Carroll, Noel, 5–6, 24, 221n

Castell, Alburey, 229n

Cervantes, Miguel de, 128

Cézanne Paul, 24, 57, 63, 207

cluster concepts, 35–6

Collingwood, R. G., 30, 102, 107, 109

Conrad, Joseph, 75–6, 226n

content: and literature, 201; and music, 154–6, 162–76

Index

modern system of the arts, x, 2–5, 8–9, 23–5, 28, 41, 82
Monet, Claude, 24
Moore, Terrence, xi
Moyer, Ann E., 220n
Mozart, Wolfgang Amadeus, 7, 22–3, 45–6, 51, 60, 170, 177, 208
music, 96–9, 139: aboutness of, 42–52, 169–75, 224n; absolute, 6–7, 9–28, 40–52, 64, 86, 113–14, 131, 139–78; and Alpha-numeric Symbolism, 190, 192–4; appreciation of, 130–4; aria, 77–9, 81; autonomy of, 216–17; content of, 154–56, 162–78; and enhanced autonomy, 216–17; and enhanced formalism, 205–17; expressiveness of, 19–21, 42–4, 152–6, 163–70, 197–8; and fiction, 44–7; and form, 12–15; and formalism, 205–17; and harmony, 10–11; and imagination, 47–9; liberation of, 204–5, 209–17; and literature, 142–3; meaning of, 141–3; opera, 8, 77–9, 81; performance of, 124–5; profundity of, x, 140–78; program, 24; quotation in, 51; recitative, 77–9, 81; and reference, 197–9; representation in, 6–9, 15–19, 25, 48–9, 180–202; *stile rappresentativo*, 8; and tolerance, 195–202; truth in, 175–6; and tune-tinkering, 190–1; value of, 178, 200–1, 206–17; vocal, 7–9

narration, 81
natural kinds, 33
Neil, Alex, 229n
novel, 56–64, 66, 76–82; description in, 73–82; and representation, 81–2

numerology, *see* alpha-numeric symbolism

Olsen, Stein Haugom, 120–39, 228n, 229n
open concepts, 33–8
opera, 8, 77–9, 81
originality, 36

pain, 213–15
painting, 56–7
Palestrina, Giovanni Pierluigi da, 8
paraphrase of poetry, 86–7, 103–6, 112–13
Parker, De Witt H., 32, 223n
Parmenides, 87–8, 90, 115, 128
Pater, Walter, 28, 97–9, 227n
Payne, E. F. J., 222n
perennial themes in literature, 136–9
Phillips, Adam, 225n
photography, 24
Picasso, Pablo, 207
pictorial representation, 57, 62–4
Plato, 2–3, 18, 31, 34, 38, 42, 55–6, 64–7, 69, 71, 84, 88–91, 115, 118, 127–8, 179, 213–14, 220n, 225n, 231n
pleasure, 213–15
Pluhar, Werner H., 13, 221n, 227n
poetry, 84–96, 99–116; evaluative sense of, 100–2; and knowledge, 114–16, 119; paraphrase of, 86–7, 103–6, 112–13; sugar-coated-pill-theory of, 88–90; and translation, 105–6; and truth, 114–16, 119
Pope, Alexander, 90, 105, 115
Prater, Jeffrey L., 230n
principle of sufficient reason, 202
Price, Kingsley, 230n
profundity, 143–6; of music, x, 140–78
program music, 24

240

Index

propositional theory of literary
  truth, 121

Quine, W. V. O., 127
quotation in music, 51

rational ideas, in Kant, 91
Rawls, John, 114
readers of fiction, 124–9
reading (silent), 225n, 226n
recitative, 77–9, 81
reference in music, 51–2, 197–9
Reid, Thomas, 10–12, 17, 221n
Rembrandt van Rijn, 26
representation, 10–12; and fiction,
  55–72; and music, 6–9, 15–19, 25,
  48–9, 180–202; and the novel, 81–
  2; pictorial, 57, 62–4; textual, 61–
  2
Reti, Rudolph, 191, 230n
Ridley, Aaron, 146–62, 119n, 230n
Roblin, Ronald, 224n
Rockwell, Norman, 207
Rouse, W. H. D., 227n

sameness, in art, 53
Schenker, Heinrich, 28, 183
Schopenhauer, Arthur, 17–20, 53,
  180–5, 202–4, 209, 211–14, 222n,
  230n, 231n
Schroeder, David P., 194–202, 231n
Schubert, Franz, 21–2, 177
Schumann, Robert, 167
Sclafani, Richard, 224n
Scruton, Roger, 50, 225n
seeing in, 57
Seurat, George, 24
Shaftesbury, third earl of, 195–6,
  198–202
Shakespeare, William, 67, 99, 107,
  128, 154, 203, 206–7
Sibley, Frank, xi
significant form, 24, 28

Smith, M. F., 227n
Socrates, 3, 147, 213–14
Sophocles, 68–9
Spingarn, J. E., 225n
Spinoza, Baruch, 118
spirit, in Kant, 91–2
Stern, Laurent, xi
Stern, Lawrence, 73
Stewart, Dugald, 223n
stile rappresentativo, 8
Strauss, Richard, 158–9, 167
Strunk, Oliver, 221n
Stolnitz, Jerome, 220n
Summers, David, 220n

Tanner, Michael, 154
Tchaikovsky, Peter Ilyich, 167
textual representation, 61–2
Thom, Paul, 68, 225n
Thomas Aquinas, Saint, 147
tolerance, 231n; and music, 195–
  202
toleration, 231n
Tolstoy, Leo, 128, 133, 207, 223n
Tovey, Donald Francis, 110, 215,
  228n
tragedy, 68–71
translation, 105–6
Trask, Willard, 225n
Treitler, Leo, 216, 231n
truth: and fiction, xi, 120–39; and
  music, 175–6
tune-tinkering, 190–1

Uehling, Theodore E., Jr., 13–14,
  221n, 222n

value: literary, 179–80; musical,
  178, 200–1, 206–17; and visual
  arts, 179–80
Van Gogh, Vincent, 24, 206
Vaughan, David James, 225n
Verdi, Giuseppi, 203

241